ANTITRUST ECONOMICS

Irwin Publications in Economics

ANTITRUST ECONOMICS

Roger D. Blair
Professor of Economics
University of Florida

David L. Kaserman
Associate Professor
University of Tennessee

1985

RICHARD D. IRWIN, INC.
Homewood, Illinois   60430

ISBN 0-256-02807-9

Library of Congress Catalog Card No. 84–82009

Printed in the United States of America

1 2 3 4 5 6 7 8 9 0 K 2 1 0 9 8 7 6 5

This book is dedicated to
Chau, Don, and Dave
and to
Lois, Laura, and David.

Preface

Monopoly and its effects on social welfare have elicited two broad types of public policy response: (1) antitrust laws that are supposed to promote competition and (2) direct regulation of government franchised monopolies. In principle, the former approach is employed when the underlying technological conditions will permit a competitive market. In contrast, direct regulation is used to deal with the monopoly problem when technological conditions are not consistent with a competitively structured market. This text deals with the law and the economics of the monopoly problem in the former situation—where competition is, in fact, a viable alternative.

In addressing this subject area, we have attempted to wed the analytical methods and models of industrial organization analysis to the myriad facets of antitrust policy. This approach is founded on two important attitudes that we share. First, we take the U.S. antitrust laws as the basic and most pervasive expression of our public policy regarding monopoly. And second, we view the careful consideration of public policy questions to be the most important and interesting purpose for studying industrial organization. Accordingly, this text organizes the industrial organization theory around a natural development of antitrust policy. In so doing, we develop all of the customary industrial organization topics, but we do so as a natural consequence of some facet of the public policy response to monopoly.

We feel that there are two major advantages to adopting this approach. First, by presenting the industrial organization analysis along with the relevant antitrust issues and case histories, they both become more interesting and accessible to the student. If the subject of industrial organization is, as many have argued, primarily applied microeconomics, then a presentation that ties the analysis directly to public policy applications should serve to vivify the otherwise dry theoretical models. And second, by focusing the text on this one area of public policy, we are able to devote the amount of space required to provide a reasonably thorough treatment of the topic of antitrust. As anyone who has taught the standard course in government and business knows, it is simply impossible to adequately cover the topics of antitrust and direct regulation in a single term. Thus, to the extent that we have been successful in implementing this approach, we feel that we should have solved two basic problems that have vexed teachers in this area for a long time: (1) motivating students to master the concepts and logic that underlie industrial organization theories and (2) having sufficient time in the course to address all of the pertinent antitrust issues.

The text is intended for use by advanced undergraduates or by graduate students in an industrial organization sequence. There is very little overt use of mathematics in the text, and that which is used could, in most cases, be circumvented if so desired. At the same time, however, it would be quite easy to incorporate mathematics in the theoretical models presented by supplementing the book with appropriate journal articles, most of which are cited as suggested readings at the end of each chapter. Graphical analysis is rather heavily relied upon to explain the logic of the various models. While a fairly large number of court cases are discussed, we have attempted to limit the amount of detail provided regarding the facts of each case to a level that is sufficient to understand the basic points involved and to stimulate interest without drowning the student in the endless minutiae that are contained in the actual case records.

The book is organized into four major parts. Part I provides the economic rationale for a public policy that is intended to promote competition. Here, we present the simple standard comparison of competitive versus monopoly equilibria. We then buttress this comparison with a survey of the ongoing debate concerning the appropriate theoretical and empirical measurement of the welfare loss due to monopoly pricing in order to convey the real complexities surrounding this issue. We then describe the public policy response to monopoly as revealed in our antitrust statutes, providing some historical perspective on the conditions leading to the passage of these laws. In addition, we include a chapter dealing with the increasingly important topic of private enforcement.

In Part II of the book, we address horizontal antitrust issues including monopoly, price fixing (both overt and tacit), other collusive agreements, horizontal mergers, and price discrimination. In each chapter, we develop the relevant microeconomic theories and industrial organization tools of analysis and follow that with a (sometimes critical) consideration of the legal treatment revealed in the case history. At relevant points, we also survey the empirical evidence pertaining to the specific issues.

Part III treats the economics and the law of vertical relationships. The first chapter of this part of the book surveys the existing economic theories of vertical integration to provide a framework for analysis. The remaining five chapters then address the specific practices that have raised increasingly important antitrust questions in recent years: vertical merger policy, vertical price fixing, territorial and customer restrictions, tying arrangements, and exclusive dealing and requirements contracts.

Finally, Part IV is devoted to conglomerate antitrust issues. The two chapters contained here deal with conglomerate merger policy and reciprocity.

In writing a textbook, authors usually acquire a multitude of debts. We are no different in this regard. Jean Adams of Iowa State University and Malcom Burns of the University of Kansas provided detailed comments on the manuscript. James Ferguson of the Federal Trade Commission gave us some much needed assistance in the early stages of the project. Our colleagues, Tom Cooper and Ginny Maurer at the University of Florida and John Mayo at the University of Tennessee, criticized numerous drafts in a most constructive fashion. None of these scholars can be blamed for any of the failings that remain since we did not always heed their advice. This book is now finished due to the efforts of our good friend Jody Imperi, who flogged us unmercifully and then worked like the devil to get the manuscript typed on time. We owe her a great deal.

Roger D. Blair
David L. Kaserman

Contents

PART I

Rationale and expression of public policy

In this section of the book, we investigate the rationale and expression of public policy with regard to industrial organization. We begin by examining the case for competition in our market economy. After reviewing the economic model of the competitive firm and industry, we turn to an analysis of social welfare. We shall see that competition is consistent with the maximization of social welfare. This, it turns out, provides the intellectual foundation for a procompetition policy in the United States.

The polar model of monopoly reveals the problems inherent in an absence of competition. We examine the social welfare losses associated with monopoly market structures. After investigating the theoretical and empirical literature, we turn to the question of innovation and market structure.

Given the case for competition and the case against monopoly, we have the rationale for public policy as embodied in the antitrust laws. Our third chapter is devoted to a discussion of the antitrust laws. We review briefly the legislative history of the various laws as well as their substantive provisions. The activities of the antitrust authorities, who enforce the statutes, are also reviewed. The final chapter of this section examines an interesting aspect of the antitrust statutes: the provision for private enforcement. Although there are several limitations, those who are injured by antitrust law violations can sue the violators for the injury suffered. As a consequence, the public enforcement of the antitrust laws is supplemented in an important way by private enforcement efforts.

1

The case for competition

In economics, the term *competition* refers to a market structure and the consequent behavior of buyers and sellers in that market. Popular usage of the word *competition* generally conjures up images of intense rivalry as between baseball teams, runners, or tennis players. In contrast, the economist's conception of competition does not rely upon strong personal rivalry. Rather, economic competition is highly impersonal in nature, and there is actually an absence of active rivalry. In fact, perfect competitors are often good friends and may be quite cooperative. For example, two automobile workers may be the best of friends while competing for jobs. Similarly, two farmers may be friendly neighbors while competing in the wheat market. The hallmark of economic competition is the absence of control over price by any economic agent.

Economists and others generally applaud the presence of competition and despair its absence. There are good reasons for this. In this chapter, we will examine the competitive firm and industry. In so doing, we will see why economists prefer competition. The next chapter will be devoted to monopoly and what is wrong with it.

1–1 CONDITIONS CONDUCIVE TO COMPETITION

The central characteristic of competitive markets is that all economic agents behave as price takers. In other words, neither the buyer of a good nor the seller of the good behave as if they can affect the price of the good being transacted. For example, if the market for pencils is competitive, then each buyer of pencils would be a price taker. The purchase of an additional box of pencils by a student will not alter the price that the student pays for pencils. This is competition on the buying side: The price per unit is unaffected by the quantity purchased. Correspondingly, in a competitive pencil market, the producers of pencils would also be price takers. Any particular producer would not feel that its production of an extra 100 boxes of pencils would influence the price.

In short, the inability of an individual buyer or seller to affect price is the critical characteristic of a competitive market. Now, let us consider briefly several conditions that are conducive to competition.

1. Homogeneous products. The first condition is that the market must be defined so that consumers have no preference for any particular firm's output. In other words, consumers must be indifferent as to the source of supply. Otherwise, the preferred producer could raise its price. This absence of consumer preference for one producer over another will occur if the product is homogeneous. For example, all granulated sugar is the same; thus consumers do not care which brand of sugar they buy. Similarly, firms that want sheet metal of a particular specification will be indifferent as to the source of supply because all producers will provide the same thing. This requirement precludes a seller from having whatever market power (i.e., control over price) would result from a consumer preference for its output.

2. Large number of buyers and sellers. The second condition involves the number of buyers and sellers. Typically, a consumer would feel like a price taker simply because his purchases of any single commodity are small relative to the total sales of that commodity. Similarly, if a firm accounts for a very small share of the total industry output, the manager is likely to feel that he cannot affect the price. An industry with a large number of similarly sized buyers and with a large number of similarly sized sellers accordingly is more likely to be competitive than an industry with few buyers and/or few sellers. Of course, if buyers got together to boycott a commodity or if sellers got together to fix prices, the market would not be competitive. In principle, boycotts can occur in industries with large numbers of buyers, and price fixing can occur in industries with large numbers of sellers. Neither occurrence is frequent, however, because the large numbers make collusion unmanageable.

3. Perfect information (knowledge). The third condition involves information in the market place: Information facilitates competition. Consumers who are aware of the price being offered by each firm in the industry never will pay a higher price than the lowest price offered, other things being equal, such as product quality. Consequently, firms offering higher prices will go out of business as they will not sell anything. If information is costly, however, consumers may be aware of the prices of only several firms. In this situation, a firm may raise its price without losing all of its customers. The consumer's lack of full information, therefore, would give each firm the ability to alter the price it charges and thereby give it market power. Where there is full information, a single price will prevail in the market, other things being equal.

4. Absence of serious barriers to entry and exit. All resources must be free to move into or out of any particular occupation. This does not mean that entry into an occupation or industry must be costless or even particularly easy, but it does mean that costs are not higher for outsiders than for established firms. For example, to enter the restaurant business one needs to have enough capital to obtain a building and the necessary equipment, which may cost thousands of dollars. Thus, entry may not be easy, but it is said to be free in the sense that there are no artificial barriers to surmount. Examples abound of industries where entry is not free: local cable TV service, banking, electric power generation, retail liquor sales, and radio broadcasting are just a few. In all of these examples, the government does not permit free entry.[1]

1–2 THE COMPETITIVE FIRM: PROFIT MAXIMIZATION

The objective of a competitive firm is to maximize profits. To see what this entails, we must define profit. For economists, profit (Π) is defined to be the difference between total sales revenue (TR) and the total costs of producing and distributing the product (TC):

$$\pi = TR - TC$$

In order to maximize profit, the firm must select the quantity of output that maximizes the difference between total revenue and total cost.

The revenue function

Because of its small size relative to the entire market, the competitive firm can produce as much or as little as it wishes without affecting the market price. This means that the demand curve facing the competitive firm is perfectly elastic at the market price. We can see this in Figure 1–1 where P is the market price and the firm's demand curve is the horizontal line labeled d. The most important consequence of a horizontal demand curve is that the firm can sell one unit of output for P, two units for P each, three units for P each, and so on. The market price does not change no matter what output is produced by the firm.

If a competitive firm increases output from Q to $Q + 1$, total revenue will rise from PQ to $P(Q + 1)$, which is an increase of P dollars. Thus, we see that the increase in total revenue from expanding output by one unit

---

[1] Perfect competition only requires free entry and exit in the long run since the short run is a period of time during which the number of firms in the industry is constant.

FIGURE 1-1

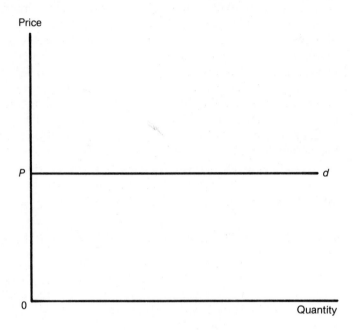

equals P, which is the competitive price. Now the change in total revenue that results from a one-unit change (increase or decrease) in output has a special name: marginal revenue. Thus, for the competitive firm, marginal revenue ($\Delta TR/\Delta Q$) equals the competitive price.

The cost functions

We shall suppose that the competitive firm faces the traditional U-shaped cost curves depicted in Figure 1–2. Total cost (TC) in the short run is composed of total variable costs (TVC) and total fixed costs (TFC):

$$TC = TVC + TFC$$

The various total cost curves are cumbersome to use, so we usually divide by quantity Q to obtain the corresponding average cost curves. Thus, we have

$$ATC = AVC + AFC$$

Because the vertical distance between average total cost and average variable cost is average fixed cost, we can omit the latter from our graph.

FIGURE 1–2

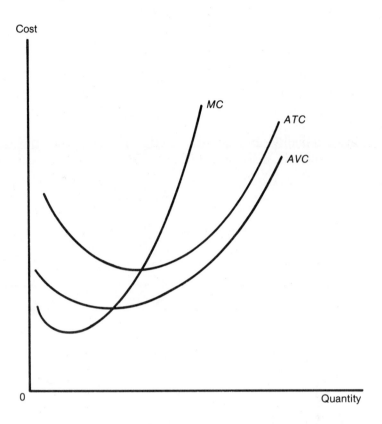

The U-shaped average total cost and average variable cost curves reflect the fact that in a given production facility, low levels of output and high levels of output are relatively inefficient. There is a middle ground where the production facility is used most efficiently.

Marginal cost (MC) is defined to be the change in total cost when output is changed by one unit ($\Delta TC/\Delta Q$). We see in Figure 1–2 that marginal cost falls initially and then increases. Notice that the marginal cost curve intersects the minimum points on the average total and average variable cost curves.

Profit maximization

By varying output, the manager of a competitive firm can alter total revenue and total cost and thereby profit. Output will be expanded and contracted until the firm finds the point where the effect on profit of a small change in output is zero:

$$\frac{\Delta \Pi}{\Delta Q} = \frac{\Delta TR}{\Delta Q} - \frac{\Delta TC}{\Delta Q} = 0$$

We have just seen that $\Delta TR/\Delta Q$ is marginal revenue and that $\Delta TC/\Delta Q$ is marginal cost. Thus, profit maximization requires that the manager select that output where marginal revenue equals marginal cost:

$$MR = MC$$

In a competitive industry, the marginal revenue equals the market price. Consequently, in a competitive industry, profit is maximized by producing where

$$P = MC$$

FIGURE 1–3

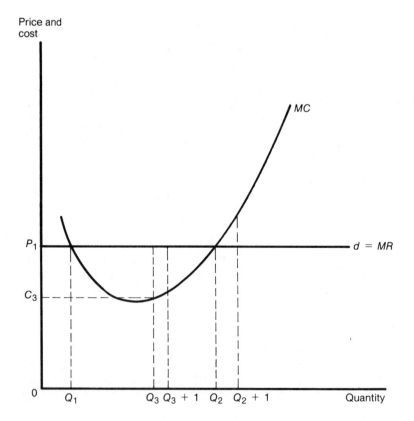

Let's try to see why this is true. In Figure 1–3, we have drawn both the firm's marginal cost curve and the firm's demand curve. Consider the situation at output Q_3. Profit is *not* maximized by producing Q_3 units of output because marginal revenue exceeds marginal cost. By producing one more unit, total revenue rises by P_1 while total cost rises by the marginal cost, which equals C_3. Profit increases when output expands from Q_3 to $Q_3 + 1$ because total revenue increases more than total cost increases. To be precise, the increase in profit from the production of one more unit equals $P_1 - C_3$. As long as price exceeds marginal cost, the manager is able to bring about additional increases in the firm's profit by expanding production. The manager therefore will expand production until price equals marginal cost. In Figure 1–3, Q_2 is the output level that maximizes profit. If the firm expands output beyond Q_2 to $Q_2 + 1$, profit will fall because marginal cost exceeds marginal revenue. In other words, as output expands by one unit, the increase in total cost is given by the height of the marginal cost curve. Since MC exceeds P at an output of $Q_2 + 1$, profit falls below the maximum.

1–3 A COMPETITIVE FIRM'S SUPPLY CURVE

The firm's supply response to different prices is represented by the firm's supply curve. The *supply curve* of the firm shows the maximum amount that the firm will produce per unit time at different prices, all other things being equal.

Derivation of the firm's supply curve

In Figure 1–4, we have drawn the average total cost, average variable cost, and marginal cost curves of the firm. Let us begin with a market price equal to P_1. At this price, profit is maximized by producing Q_1 units of output because price equals marginal cost at this output. Similarly, if the price falls to P_2, marginal cost is equal to price (or marginal revenue) at Q_2 units of output. In both instances, price exceeded average total cost so we could be confident that the firm's profits would be positive.

This is not the case, however, for price P_3. At a price of P_3, if the firm produced where marginal cost equaled price, average total cost would be greater than the price. When per unit cost exceeds per unit revenue, losses occur. Interestingly, the firm will still elect to produce Q_3 units of output and sell them at a price of P_3 because the firm's losses are minimized this way.

If the firm had decided to produce zero output, revenue obviously would have been zero. Cost, however, would have been equal to the total fixed costs, which are unavoidable. Thus, the firm's loss in that period would have been equal to the total fixed costs. These fixed costs

FIGURE 1-4

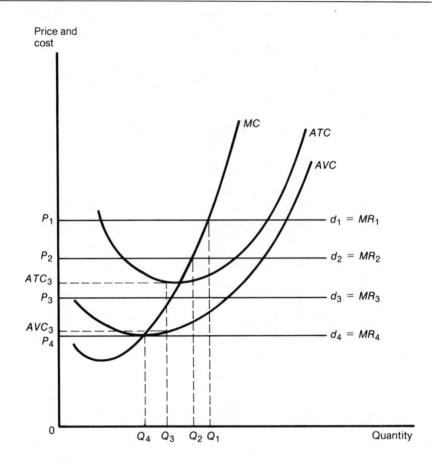

are measured in Figure 1-4 by the difference between average total cost (ATC) and average variable cost (AVC) at Q_3 times Q_3: $(ATC_3 - AVC_3)Q_3$. This is because the difference between average total cost and average variable cost equals average fixed cost.

If the firm elects to produce Q_3, where marginal cost is equal to P_3, then total revenue will be $P_3 \cdot Q_3$, and total cost will be equal to $ATC_3 \cdot Q_3$. The firm's loss will then be equal to $(ATC_3 - P_3)Q_3$, which is smaller than the loss at zero output: $(ATC_3 - AVC_3)Q_3$. Consequently, in the short run[2] the firm minimizes its loss by producing when the price

---

[2] For the *firm*, the short run is a period of time during which there is at least one input whose scale cannot be adjusted. For example, a steel producer may be able to readily adjust its labor input and its raw materials inputs, but not its physical plant. In this case, the plant is a fixed input. For the *industry*, the short run is a period of time during which neither entry nor exit can occur.

equals P_3. This is because the revenue that the firm receives from selling Q_3 units of output is greater than the variable cost involved in producing Q_3 units of output.

Consider price P_4. At this price, variable costs are just covered by the total revenue generated by selling Q_4 units of output at P_4. Thus, the firm's losses are equal to total fixed costs whether it produces Q_4 or zero. Thus, the firm is indifferent between producing Q_4 or zero.

For all prices below P_4, the price will fail to cover the per unit variable costs. As a result, total revenue will fail to cover all of the variable costs. Thus, the loss incurred by producing where marginal cost equals price will equal total fixed cost plus the portion of total variable costs that are not covered by the revenue. Consequently, losses will be minimized by producing no output at all.

All of these results can now be put together to construct the firm's short-run supply curve. For all prices below the minimum point on the average variable cost curve, the manager maximizes the firm's profit by producing no output and just closing the doors. For all prices above the minimum point on the average variable cost curve, he maximizes profit by producing where price equals marginal cost. Thus, the relationship between the price offered and the quantity that the firm supplies is given by the marginal cost curve above the average variable cost curve. In other words, the firm's supply curve is its marginal cost curve above its average variable cost curve.

1–4 COMPETITIVE INDUSTRY SUPPLY

The industry supply curve represents the collective supply response of all firms in the industry to different prices. As we shall see, its derivation depends upon whether input prices change when industry output rises or falls.

Industry supply with constant input prices

When a particular industry's use of inputs is small relative to the size of the input markets, the prices of the inputs employed in the industry are unaffected by changes in the industry output. For example, the manufacturers of coffee cups use inputs that are employed in many other industries. As a result, the demands that coffee cup producers make on the input markets are very small relative to the size of these markets. Thus, if the output of coffee cups were to rise by say, 20 percent, there would be an almost negligible increase in the total quantity demanded of these inputs. Consequently, the prices of the inputs used to produce coffee cups will be unaffected by fluctuations in coffee cup production.

If input prices do not respond to changes in industry output, we may simply add up the marginal cost curves of the various firms to obtain the

FIGURE 1–5

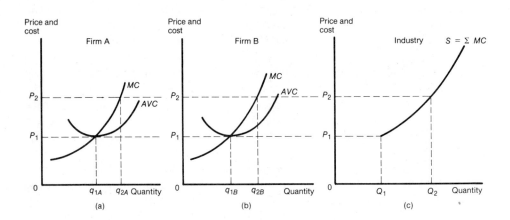

industry supply curve. A small example of this is shown in Figure 1–5, which depicts the supply curves associated with a two-firm industry. The industry supply curve in panel c is obtained by summing the relevant sections of the marginal cost curves of firms A and B. At the price P_1, firm A supplies q_{1A}, and firm B supplies q_{1B}. The quantity that is supplied by the industry at this price (Q_1) equals the sum of q_{1A} and q_{1B}. Similarly, q_{2A} plus q_{2B} equals Q_2. Of course, nothing would be forthcoming at any price below P_1 because that price fails to cover the average variable cost of either firm.

Industry supply curve under varying input prices

When the industry accounts for a substantial share of the total market for an input, a change in industry output may have an impact upon the price of the input. The most likely effect would be for an increase in the demand for the input to push up its price. All of the firm's cost curves have been constructed for given input prices. When input prices change, however, the cost curves will shift. In particular, if industry output expands, we should expect at least some input prices to rise, and as a result, the average and marginal cost curves for each firm will shift up. We can examine the effects of this in Figure 1–6.

Suppose that the firm in Figure 1–6 is supplying Q_1 units of output in response to a market determined price of P_1. If the price were to rise to P_2, the firm would attempt to expand its output to Q_2. At that output, marginal cost MC_1 would equal the new price P_2, and profits would be maximized. But if all of the firms in the industry respond to the rise in

FIGURE 1–6

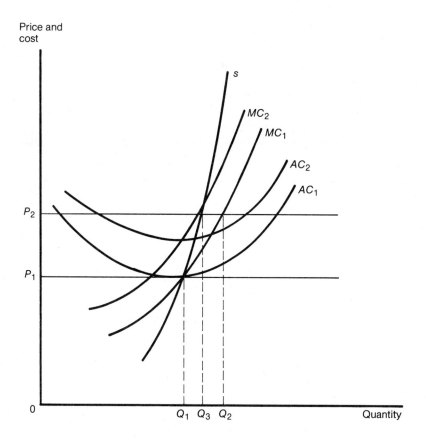

the output price by increasing production, the price of some inputs will rise, and consequently, the average and marginal cost curves will shift to, say, AC_2 and MC_2. Under these new input prices, the optimal output for this firm would be the somewhat smaller output Q_3 rather than Q_2.

In this way, we can construct a firm's supply curve that reflects the increases in input prices that occur as *industry* output rises. In Figure 1–6, we have labeled the firm's supply curve s. Note that the points (Q_1, P_1) and (Q_3, P_2) lie on the s curve. We can easily see that the firm's supply curve is much steeper than any of its marginal cost curves.

When input prices depend on industry output, the industry supply curve is the horizontal summation of the short-run firm supply curves s. Graphically, the summation technique is the same as that used in summing the marginal cost curves. Clearly, this industry supply curve is steeper than the corresponding industry supply curve associated with constant input prices.

1–5 LONG–RUN PROFIT MAXIMIZATION FOR THE COMPETITIVE FIRM

In the short run, the manager of a firm maximizes profit subject to the constraints imposed by having at least one input fixed. In the long run, however, all of the firm's inputs are variable.[3] Consequently, there may still be an incentive to alter the quantity of the fixed input in the long run even when the manager has maximized short-run profits. Unless all such incentives are absent, the firm will not have maximized long-run profits. Figure 1–7 illustrates these issues.

FIGURE 1–7

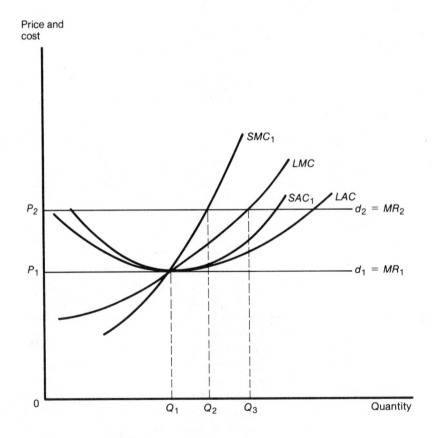

---

[3] For the industry, the long run is a period of time in which entry and exit are possible (i.e., the number of firms is variable).

Suppose that the manager was producing Q_1 units of output and selling them at the market-determined price of P_1. If price increases to P_2, the manager's immediate response will be to increase output to Q_2. At Q_2, the short-run marginal cost SMC_1 is equal to the new price of P_2. We can see, however, that the firm's short-run average cost SAC_1 exceeds the long-run average cost LAC at an output of Q_2.[4] Consequently, the firm will recognize that its current plant is being utilized too intensively. Thus, it will want to increase the size of its plant to reduce the per unit costs of the output. This incentive will exist until the plant size is adjusted so that the firm produces where long-run marginal cost (LMC)[5]

FIGURE 1–8

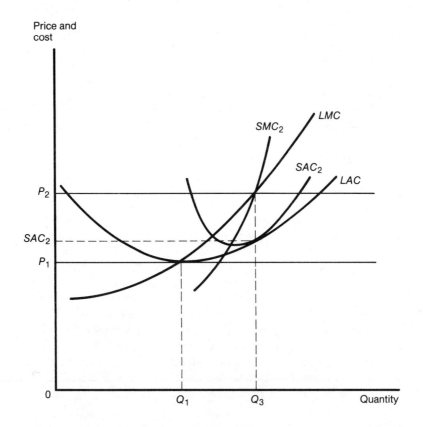

---

[4] The long-run average cost curve describes the per unit cost of producing any particular output when all inputs are variable. The relationship between the long-run and short-run average cost curves is described in some detail in Roger D. Blair and Lawrence W. Kenny, *Microeconomics for Managerial Decisions* (New York: McGraw-Hill, 1982).

[5] The long-run marginal cost shows the change in total cost that results from a change in output when the firm can adjust all of its inputs.

equals price P_2. At that point, the new short-run average cost will be tangent to the long-run average cost at output Q_3. This is shown in Figure 1–8 where we can also see that the new short-run marginal cost curve equals price P_2 at output Q_3.

In summary, the conditions that must be satisfied for long-run profit maximization are

$$P = LMC = SMC$$

and

$$SAC = LAC$$

If these equalities do not hold, the manager has failed to maximize the firm's profit.

A manager in a competitive industry maximizes profit in the long run by operating on the long-run marginal cost curve (LMC). But once again, some points on the marginal cost curve will prove to be unacceptable. For example, in the long run, the firm will choose not to operate when it is suffering economic losses. Accordingly, any point on the long-run marginal cost curve below the long-run average cost curve is unacceptable to the firm, for these points represent economic losses. Thus, the firm's long-run supply curve is that part of the long-run marginal cost curve that is above the long-run average cost curve.

1–6 COMPETITIVE INDUSTRY EQUILIBRIUM: LONG RUN

The situation depicted in Figure 1–8 is one of equilibrium for the firm but not necessarily for the industry. At an output of Q_3 and with a plant size denoted by SAC_2, the competitive firm is maximizing long-run profits. As a result, it has no incentive to alter anything: It is in equilibrium. But we should note that P_2 exceeds SAC_2 at an output of Q_3. Consequently, the firm is enjoying economic profits equal to $(P_2 - SAC_2)Q_3$. This represents a return that exceeds the next best alternative investment for the firm's assets. As a result, resources outside the industry will have an incentive to flow into this industry. The magnitude of this response is dependent upon the characteristics of potential firms. In the following analysis, we will assume first that there is an infinite number of potential entrants with identical cost curves. Subsequently, we will assume that some firms are more efficient than other firms, which is reflected in different cost curves.

Constant input prices with identical firms

In Figure 1–9, we consider the case where input prices remain constant to the industry and there are an infinite number of potential firms with identical cost curves. In panel *a*, industry supply and demand

FIGURE 1–9

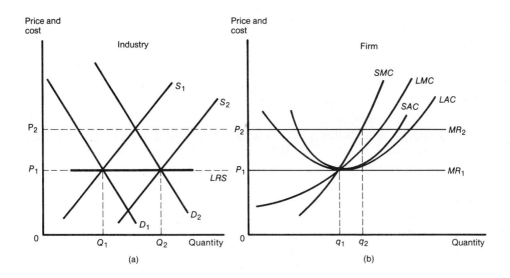

curves are depicted. In panel *b*, we examine a competitive firm's reactions.

Initially, the demand curve is D_1, and the short-run supply curve is S_1. Since we have assumed that input prices are constant, the industry short-run supply curve is the horizontal sum of the relevant sections of the short-run marginal cost curves of the n_1 firms that are producing in this industry. At the intersection of D_1 and S_1, Q_1 units of output are produced at a price of P_1. At this price, each firm elects to produce q_1 units of output, thereby earning a competitive return. Since no economic profit is made under this solution, firms have no incentive to enter or leave the industry.

Now, suppose that the demand curve shifts from D_1 to D_2. The immediate impact will be for price to increase from P_1 to P_2. In response to the price rise, our firm in panel *b* has increased its output from q_1 to q_2. Since P_2 exceeds the firm's short-run average costs, profits will be positive and equal to $(P_2 - SAC)q_2$. These profits, which are shown as the shaded area in Figure 1–9, will attract the entry of outsiders. As new firms enter the industry, the short-run industry supply curve will shift to the right because we are adding together more short-run marginal cost curves. As the supply shifts, the price will fall and the individual firm will move back along its short-run marginal cost curve. As long as the price exceeds P_1, however, the firms in the industry will enjoy economic profits and, consequently, still more firms will enter. The incentive for further entry disappears only when the short-run industry supply function shifts to S_2 and price has fallen back to P_1. Now, industry output will be Q_2, and the firm's output will be q_1, which is back where the firm began. The increase in the industry output of $Q_2 - Q_1$ is accomplished by having more firms in the industry; each firm's output is still q_1 in long-run equilibrium. Although many firms may have been lured into the industry by the prospect of economic profits, entry continues until only a competitive rate of return is earned.

The *long-run industry supply curve* is made up of long-run equilibrium positions. In long-run equilibrium, firms have no incentive to enter or leave the industry. Thus, we see that the points (Q_1, P_1) and (Q_2, P_1) are long-run equilibrium points and, therefore, lie on the long-run supply curve. In Figure 1–9, we have labeled the long-run supply curve *LRS*. When input prices are constant, the long-run supply function is horizontal.

In summary, we can see from panel *b* of Figure 1–9 that if an industry is made up of identical firms and is in long-run equilibrium, then

$$P = LMC = SMC = LAC = SAC$$

If any of the equalities does not hold, either the manager has failed to maximize profit or the industry is not in equilibrium.

Constant input prices with differences in firms

We will now consider the case where input prices remain constant and some firms are more efficient than other firms. Figure 1–10 shows the cost curves of three representative firms and the demand and supply curves of the industry. Firm A is a relatively efficient firm and enters the industry when the price equals P_0; this is called firm A's entry price. At

FIGURE 1–10

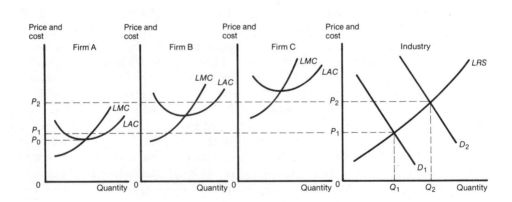

this price, firm A makes no economic profits. At higher prices, however, firm A makes positive economic profits, and other less efficient firms, which would have operated at a loss at lower prices, enter the industry. The entry of less efficient firms does *not* drive the price back to P_0 because these less efficient firms lose money at P_0. The long-run supply curve (*LRS*) reflects the entry decisions of all potential firms; it is the horizontal sum of all long-run marginal cost curves above the minimum points on the long-run average cost curves.

If the industry demand curve is D_1, then the price equals P_1, and all firms with entry prices at or below P_1 are producing. The more efficient firms in the industry are making positive economic profits while firms with an entry price of P_1 are making zero economic profits. The industry is in long-run equilibrium, despite the existence of economic profits in the industry, because no firm not already in the industry can enter the industry and make positive economic profits. Firms such as firm B and C would lose money at the price P_1.

If the industry demand curve shifts out to D_2, the price rises to P_2. This leads each firm in the industry to produce more and attracts less efficient firms, such as firm B, into the industry. The industry price (P_2) and quantity (Q_2) represent a long-run equilibrium because no firm can enter the industry and make an economic profit. Firms such as firm C would lose money if they tried to produce at the price P_2.

Varying input prices with identical firms

Let us return to the assumption that there are an infinite number of identical, potential firms and that input prices rise as the industry expands its output. In panel *a* of Figure 1–11, we depict industry supply and demand, while in panel *b* we depict a firm's long-run cost curves. The corresponding short-run cost curves have been deleted to reduce congestion in the diagram.

Initially, the demand curve is D_1, the industry short-run supply curve is S_1, and the number of firms in the industry is n_1. The industry short-run supply curve is the horizontal sum of the n_1 short-run firm supply curves. Now, S_1 is constructed so that the effects of changes in the output of these n_1 firms on input prices are already incorporated into S_1. We can see that S_1 and D_1 intersect at the price P_1 and quantity Q_1. When the industry is producing Q_1, each firm's cost curves are LAC_1 and LMC_1. Consequently, in this solution, each firm is making zero economic profits, and there is no incentive for firms to enter or exit the industry.

Suppose that demand shifts to D_2. The immediate response by the n_1 firms in the industry is to increase output to Q_2 and price to P_2. But at this new price, price exceeds average cost, and each firm consequently is earning economic profit. This brings new firms into the industry, and as

FIGURE 1–11

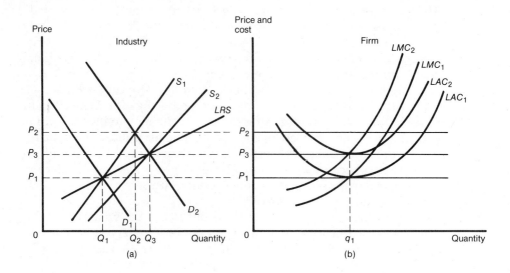

(a) (b)

industry output thereby increases, input prices rise. As a result, the firm's cost curves rise. Entry continues until each firm in the industry earns a competitive return. In Figure 1–11, this occurs when the short-run supply curve has shifted to S_2, and LMC_2 and LAC_2 are each firm's cost curves. Thus, the increase in demand from D_1 to D_2 results in an expansion of output from Q_1 to Q_3 and an increase in price to P_3. Price does not return to the previous level because the expansion in output caused at least some input prices to rise.

It is not possible to say what necessarily happens to the firm's output as a matter of pure theory. In Figure 1–11, we examined the special case where the minimum points on LAC_1 and LAC_2 occurred at the same output level. Under these circumstances, the firm's output remains the same, its costs rise, its total revenue rises, and its profits remain at the competitive level. This need not be the case in all circumstances. Clearly, if the long-run average cost curve shifts up and to the right, then the firm would produce a higher output.

The long-run supply curve is made up of long-run equilibrium points, such as (Q_1, P_1) and (Q_3, P_3), and is labeled LRS in panel a of Figure 1–11. It is positively sloped because input prices increase as industry output expands. Since the analysis of the effects of increasing cost on an industry comprised of firms of varying levels of efficiency is virtually identical to what was just discussed, we will not undertake that analysis.

1–7 SOCIAL OPTIMALITY OF COMPETITION

To this point, we have not indicated why economists prefer that industries be organized competitively. We shall see, however, that competition permits the optimal allocation of society's scarce resources. This is a desirable end because it allows us to get the greatest benefit out of our limited resources.

First, notice that competitive equilibrium involves price equal to marginal cost. When this condition holds, we can be sure that the appropriate quantity of output is being produced. The price that consumers are willing to pay for, say, a loaf of bread reflects the value that consumers place on that particular product. But a loaf of bread is simply the result of mixing together a huge number of inputs in the production of wheat and its subsequent distribution and further processing into a final product on the grocery store shelf. As a result, the price consumers are willing to pay for a loaf of bread reflects the value that they place on using all of those inputs in a particular way: namely, to make a loaf of bread.

The marginal cost measures the change in total cost incurred by the firm when it expands production by one unit of output. Given the production technology, these costs reflect the costs of the inputs used in producing an extra loaf of bread. As a result, the marginal cost that the firm incurs represents the cost to society of employing a vast array of inputs in the production of a loaf of bread. When price is equal to marginal cost, we see that the marginal value to consumers of society's resources used in producing a loaf of bread is just equal to the marginal cost of those resources. If output were expanded beyond the point where price equaled marginal cost, the incremental cost to society would exceed the value placed on those resources necessary to expand production of bread by one loaf. In contrast, if production fell short of that point so that price exceeded marginal cost, too few resources would be employed in the production of bread. The value to society of employing more resources in bread production would exceed the cost to society of doing that. Consequently, society would gain by expanding the production of bread. In competitive equilibrium, we have just the right amount of production because output is expanded to the point where price equals marginal cost.

Second, we notice that in competitive equilibrium there are no economic profits. This means that we have the correct number of firms in the industry. As long as profits are positive, there are too few firms, and the existence of those profits will attract outsiders. If profits are negative (i.e., losses), there are too many firms, and the losses will cause some firms to leave the industry. In competitive equilibrium, each firm is producing at the minimum point on its long-run average cost curve, and price equals average cost ($P = LAC = SAC$). This means that the total cost of producing society's output is minimized by having just the right number of firms producing as efficiently as possible.

1–8 A NONECONOMIC ARGUMENT FOR COMPETITION

The previous discussion should indicate that competition is not a desirable end in itself. Rather, it is a very useful means to a desirable end. In particular, competition is a way of organizing production and determining prices. Its economic role is to induce producers and resource owners to supply their goods and services cheaply and skillfully. In so doing, competition permits the maximization of consumer welfare. Most economists consider this to be the fundamental argument for competition.

There are some advocates of competition who simply prefer the structure of a competitive economy. When we speak of a competitive market, we think of a large number of small firms. There is something appealing to this in a democratic society where everyone is regarded as being equal. In a democracy, we should anticipate policies designed to restrict aggregations of financial power. This is a manifestation of the Jeffersonian view, which embodies an instinctive fear of all concentrations of private power.

In his early debates with Alexander Hamilton, Thomas Jefferson espoused a populist ideology. He argued that large aggregations of economic power posed a serious threat to political democracy. Accordingly, Jefferson advocated the wide dispersion of economic power. This position has been endorsed throughout our history, but our society has been somewhat reluctant to embrace this philosophy without reservation. In particular, we have been hesitant about the costs that such a policy could entail due to curtailed efficiency. In Chapter 3, we will see how public policy has been influenced by our Jeffersonian heritage.

QUESTIONS AND PROBLEMS

1. The price of a Big Mac at the local McDonald's restaurant does not change whether I order one, three, or five of them. Is the market for Big Mac sandwiches competitive on the buyer's side? Do you think that it is competitive on the seller's side? Explain.

2. "Rock singing is not a competitive industry, because the requirement of having talent is a serious entry barrier." True or false? Explain.

3. Start at the point where price equals marginal cost for the competitive firm. Show that deviations from that output result in lower profits.

4. Examine Figure 1–3. Price equals marginal cost at an output of Q_1. Prove that this output will *not* maximize profit.

5. Put a firm demand curve on a graph like Figure 1–2. Identify the profit maximizing output, the total profit, and the total fixed costs for the firm.

6. Construct a diagram like Figure 1–4. Draw a $d_5 = MR_5$ line below P_4. Show with appropriately drawn rectangles that the loss produced where $MC = MR_5$ is larger than the loss associated with zero output.

7. "A competitive firm will never operate where marginal cost is less than average variable cost." True or false? Discuss.

8. Suppose that the retail grocery industry is comprised of identical firms. Is the long-run supply curve of groceries positively sloped? If so, why?

9. Why do economists prefer competitive market structures?

10. What is the virtue of competitive prices being equal to marginal costs?

11. What is the role of perfect knowledge in the theory of competition? What should we expect to happen when we introduce imperfect information?

12. Analyze the following: "If a market is competitively organized, it is inconceivable that customers buying large quantities will pay lower prices."

13. Under what circumstances is it socially desirable for final good prices to fall below average total costs?

14. "Any firm that is paying out more money than it is taking in should shut down its operations at once." Is this sound advice?

15. "A price increase may not increase a competitive firm's profits because at a higher rate of output the firm will be incurring a higher marginal cost." True or false? Explain.

16. Many years ago, the Illinois legislature passed legislation requiring merchants to possess a license in order to sell alcoholic beverages. Licenses were issued for existing merchants. New licenses are rarely

issued, although existing licenses may be sold. Liquor licenses in Chicago sell for $60,000 each.

a. What does this $60,000 represent?

b. What does this imply about the number of liquor licenses?

c. Are consumers better off or worse off after the legislation that caused this situation?

d. Are liquor store owners better off or worse off after the legislation? Discuss two cases:

(1) Owners at the time of the legislation.

(2) New owners subsequent to the legislation.

e. Why would politicians (1) pass the legislation and (2) not repeal it in subsequent years?

17. Describe the long-run equilibrium for a competitive firm and industry. Now, suppose that the demand for the product increases but that the government forbids entry. Sketch out the adjustments by the firm and the industry.

18. Suppose that industry supply and demand interact to produce a short-run equilibrium price of $70. Consider a firm that has a total cost curve given by

$$TC = 200 + 25Q - 6Q_2 + (\tfrac{1}{3})Q^3$$

and a corresponding marginal cost curve of

$$MC = 25 - 12Q + Q^2$$

Find (a) the firm's optimal output and (b) the amount of the firm's short-run profits or losses.

19. Suppose the paper industry is in long-run competitive equilibrium. Draw the graphs for the industry and for a typical firm assuming that all firms are identical. Now, suppose that industry demand falls. Trace out the short-run and long-run effects under the assumption of constant input prices.

20. Suppose that megafoil is produced in a competitive industry comprised of identical firms. Starting from a position of long-run equilibrium, trace out the short-run and long-run effects of a decrease in production costs under the assumption of constant input prices.

2

The case against monopoly

2–1   INTRODUCTION

As we shall see in the next chapter, public policy as expressed in the antitrust laws is designed to promote competition and prevent monopoly. Our earlier discussion of competition indicated why that market structure is desirable. Now, we shall examine monopoly to see why public policy has been framed to discourage monopoly.

By definition, monopoly exists when a single firm produces a commodity for which there are no close substitutes. This, of course, does not mean that substitution is impossible. Rather, it means that the prices of other goods and services can decrease significantly without causing substantial substitutions away from the monopolist's product. This is the polar opposite of competition since each competitive firm's output is a perfect substitute for the outputs of other firms in that industry. Whereas the competitive firm has no control over price, the monopolist has considerable control over the price through its output decisions. This ability to control price is a measure of the firm's market power and is at the heart of the economic objection to monopoly.

In this chapter, we want to do several things. First, we shall develop the standard monopoly model.[1] Next, we will examine the influence of monopoly on allocative efficiency and discuss the social welfare losses

---

[1] Most introductory economics textbooks have a thorough discussion of the monopoly model. Consequently, our review shall be fairly brief.

attributable to monopoly. Third, we will look at the theory and evidence on the relationship (if any) between monopoly, productive efficiency, and technical progress.

2–2 DEMAND AND MARGINAL REVENUE UNDER MONOPOLY

For a monopolist, the firm demand function and the industry demand function are identical. This is because a monopolist, by definition, is the only firm in the industry. Since there is a single firm, it can hardly suffer the delusion that its actions have no effect upon price. In fact, it must recognize that its output decision determines the equilibrium price. The firm can operate at any point on the demand curve by selecting the appropriate quantity. We assume that the firm will choose that position on the demand curve that maximizes the monopolist's profit.

The monopolist's price can be increased or decreased by adjusting the quantity of output. The benefit to the firm of producing one more unit of output is the resulting change in the total revenue that the firm receives, which is the firm's marginal revenue. Because a monopolist faces a downward-sloping demand curve, the monopolist's marginal revenue is less than the price at which the product sells.

An example will help to show why this is the case. Suppose that the manager can sell 1,000 units of output at a per unit price of $5, thereby generating a total revenue of $5,000. Because the monopolist's demand curve has a negative slope, the firm can sell 1,001 units of output only if the price falls to, say, $4.98. The 1,001st unit of output adds $4.98 directly to the firm's total revenue. But in order to sell 1,001 units of output, the firm must charge $0.02 less per unit. This costs the firm $20 in lost revenue on the 1,000 units it was already able to sell. On balance, the marginal revenue associated with the 1,001st unit of output is negative:

$$\$4.98 - 20.00 = -\$15.02$$

Consequently, the marginal revenue at the 1,001st unit of output is −$15.02 even though the product sells for $4.98 per unit. As a result, the firm will be acutely aware of the effect of its output decisions on price. In contrast, for the competitive firm, price and marginal revenue are identical. This is because the competitive firm's demand curve is horizontal.

We could derive the marginal revenue that corresponds to each point on the demand curve. For a linear demand curve, however, there is a very simple relationship between the demand curve and the marginal revenue curve. Suppose that the demand curve can be written as[2]

$$P = 100 - Q$$

---

[2] In a more general formulation, we can write demand as $P = a - bQ$, where a and b are positive constants. Total revenue is then $PQ = aQ - bQ^2$, and marginal revenue is $MR = a - 2bQ$.

FIGURE 2–1

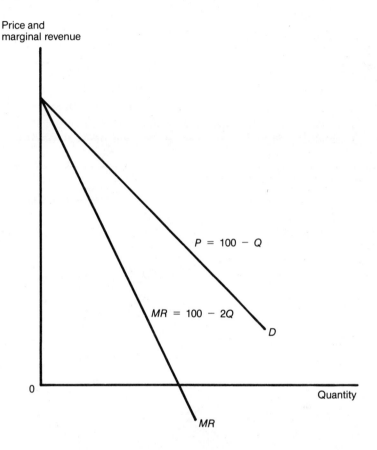

Price and
marginal revenue

$P = 100 - Q$

$MR = 100 - 2Q$

D

0

Quantity

MR

which we have plotted in Figure 2–1 and labeled as D. The intercept on
the price axis is 100, and the slope of the demand curve is -1. The total
revenue for the firm is

$$PQ = (100 - Q)Q$$
$$= 100Q - Q^2$$

By the definition of marginal revenue, we find that

$$MR = \frac{\Delta TR}{\Delta Q} = 100 - 2Q$$

Notice that the intercept remains at 100, but the slope is twice as steep:
-2 compared to -1.

We have plotted the marginal revenue curve in Figure 2–1 along with
the demand curve and labeled it MR. Since MR and D have the same

intercept while *MR* is twice as steep as *D*, the marginal revenue curve will bisect the horizontal distance between the price axis and the demand curve. We also notice that at low prices marginal revenue is negative. When the marginal revenue is negative, total revenue falls as output increases.

2–3 SHORT–RUN MONOPOLY PROFIT MAXIMIZATION

The manager of a monopolistic firm wants to do the same thing as the manager of a competitive firm: maximize profits. In order to do this, he must select that output where the difference between total revenue and total cost is largest. In Figure 2–2, we have graphed the demand (*D*),

FIGURE 2–2

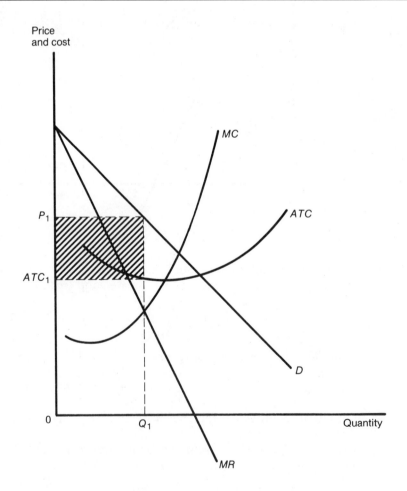

marginal revenue (*MR*), average total cost (*ATC*), and marginal cost (*MC*) curves of a monopolist. Profits are maximized when the incremental effect on profit of a small change in output is zero. Since profit is defined as the difference between total revenue and total cost,

$$\frac{\Delta \Pi}{\Delta Q} = \frac{\Delta TR}{\Delta Q} - \frac{\Delta TC}{\Delta Q}$$

$$= MR - MC$$

If this is set equal to zero, we find that the monopolistic firm, as well as the competitive firm, maximizes profits by producing where marginal revenue equals marginal cost: *MR* = *MC*. The difference between the competitive and monopolistic solutions is found in the marginal revenue curve. For the competitive firm, the marginal revenue curve is a horizontal line at the market price. In contrast, the marginal revenue curve of the monopolistic firm is negatively sloped and lies below the demand curve. The firm in Figure 2–2 maximizes the monopoly profits by producing Q_1 units of output, which will be sold at a price of P_1. The profit can be calculated as

$$\Pi = (P_1 - ATC_1)Q_1$$

This maximum profit is represented by the shaded rectangle in Figure 2–2.

We can be sure that these profits are maximized by considering other outputs around Q_1.[3] A small increase in output will increase total revenue by less than total cost since *MC* exceeds *MR* to the right of Q_1. Thus, expanding output will reduce profit. Similarly, if an output less than Q_1 were produced, an increase toward Q_1 would increase total revenue more than it would increase total cost because *MR* exceeds *MC*. Thus, reducing output from Q_1 would decrease profit. Consequently, we must conclude that Q_1 maximizes profit.

Although the profits in Figure 2–2 look large relative to the total sales revenue, there is no theoretical reason for supposing that all monopolists earn exorbitant profits. The fact that there is only one firm in the industry is no guarantee that the monopolist will make a positive profit, much less an exorbitant one. If the production costs are high relative to the demand for the product, profits will tend to be low. As a simple example, consider a publisher who holds a copyright on a book, *101 Ways of Preparing Brussels Sprouts*, that is not terribly popular. Although the publisher has a monopoly on that particular book, the profit could be low, zero, or even negative. In panel *a* of Figure 2–3, we have a case where the monopolist earns just a competitive rate of return. Its optimal output is found where marginal cost equals marginal revenue (i.e., out-

---

[3] This is precisely the same analysis that we developed in the preceding chapter for the competitive firm.

FIGURE 2–3

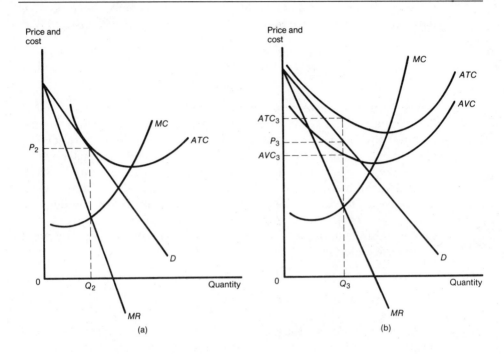

(a)

(b)

put Q_2). At this output, the firm must charge a price of P_2. Unfortunately for the firm, the average cost of production equals that price at output Q_2. Consequently, the monopolist earns no excess profits.

Even more distressing is the case depicted in panel *b* of Figure 2–3 where the monopolist is losing money. Marginal cost and marginal revenue are equal at output Q_3. The price that clears the market at an output of Q_3 is P_3. This price is clearly less than the per unit cost of production, which is ATC_3. Since per unit revenue is less than per unit cost, the firm will suffer a loss equal to $(P_3 - ATC_3)Q_3$. Notice, however, that P_3 is greater than the average variable cost of producing Q_3 units of output. If the firm produced zero output, its loss would be equal to the total fixed costs. In panel *b* of Figure 2–3, we can measure total fixed cost as $(ATC_3 - AVC_3)Q_3$. This loss is clearly larger than the loss incurred by producing an output equal to Q_3. Thus, the firm minimizes its loss by producing Q_3. The reason that this occurs is because price exceeds average variable cost. When this is the case, producing where marginal cost equals marginal revenue yields enough sales revenue to cover all of the variable costs and some of the (inescapable) fixed costs. Thus, production reduces the loss below the level of total fixed costs.

In summary, we can see that the output decision criteria are similar for monopolistic and competitive firms. The manager of a monopoly firm will produce where marginal cost equals marginal revenue, provided that the corresponding price is at least as large as average variable cost. Thus, the short-run equilibrium conditions for the firm are

$$MC = MR$$

and

$$P \geq AVC$$

Otherwise, the firm will produce zero output. A manager who does not meet these conditions is failing to maximize profit.

2-4 LONG–RUN MONOPOLY PROFIT MAXIMIZATION

Since we have assumed that there is only one firm in this industry, when the firm is in long-run equilibrium, the industry is also in long-run equilibrium. Typically, we assume that no entry is possible in this industry. We shall examine this assumption in the next section, but for now we should recall that entry drove excess profits to zero in the competitive model. In the absence of entry, positive profits are consistent with long-run industry equilibrium for the monopolist. Consequently, it is entirely possible to have a situation like the one represented in Figure 2–4.

Long-run profit maximization for the monopolist requires that long-run marginal cost (LMC) be equal to marginal revenue (MR), which occurs at Q_4 units of output. The firm will produce and sell Q_4 units of output at the profit maximizing price of P_4. The long-run average cost of producing Q_4 is LAC_4. Consequently, long-run profits are $(P_4 - LAC_4)Q_4$. When the firm decides on an output of Q_4, it must make commitments on some inputs that then become fixed for a certain period of time. These fixed inputs generate the short-run average cost curve (SAC_4) which is tangent to the long-run average cost curve at Q_4. The short-run marginal cost curve associated with SAC_4 (labeled SMC_4) intersects LMC at Q_4, and goes through the minimum point of the SAC_4 curve. Thus, we can see that the conditions for long-run profit maximization are

$$MR = LMC = SMC$$
$$SAC = LAC$$
$$P \geq LAC$$

The essence of long-run equilibrium is that the firm is producing where long-run marginal cost equals marginal revenue, and the manager has no incentive to alter the size of his plant.

FIGURE 2–4

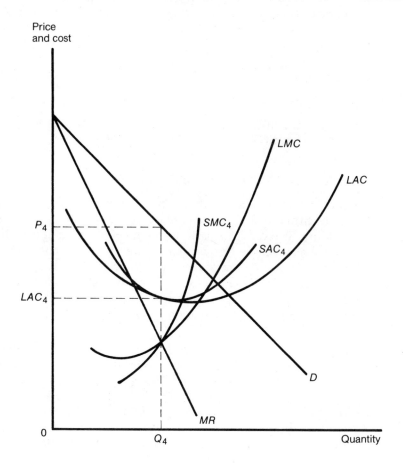

2–5 MONOPOLY PROFIT AND ENTRY

As we have seen, with the passage of time, a monopolist's short-run profits become long-run profits. These excess profits provide an incentive for outsiders to enter the monopolized industry. If the monopolist's profits are to persist in the long run, there must be some obstacle to the entry of these profit-seeking outsiders. These obstacles or impediments are called *entry barriers*, which prevent outsiders from encroaching on the monopolist's turf. We shall consider several examples.

1. Patents, copyrights, and trademarks.   Under the U.S. patent law, a firm may be granted the exclusive right to produce a certain commodity or to use a specific production process for a 17-year period. Patents are offered as rewards to stimulate inventive or creative efforts, which advance knowledge and make information available to society. It is feared that a person would have little incentive to invent a better mouse trap if he or she were not going to reap some reward for doing so. Consequently, our society provides a legal monopoly for a limited time. There is nothing magic about 17 years as the patent life—it is essentially arbitrary.

The grant of a patent is supposed to ensure that no one will copy the inventor's invention during the life of the patent. Although the patent affords the inventor legal protection against blatant copying, it does not provide absolute protection. The monopoly power which comes from a patent is limited because patents are often narrowly defined, which allows other firms to approximate closely the patented process or product. The analysis of copyrights and trademarks is similar as each enjoys some legal protection from infringement.

The economic value of patent protection depends upon the economic value of the protected item in the marketplace. For example, a patent on a hand-powered lawn mower would not be worth much today. Similarly, copyright protection on a film that no one wants to see is worthless. In contrast, a patent on a cure for cancer would be worth a fortune. In instances where a monopolist is earning excess profits, patents, copyrights, and trademarks offer legal protection and prevent entry by outsiders.

2. Control of an essential raw material.   It is obvious that if one firm controls the supply of an essential input, then other firms will be unable to compete. The classic example of this is Alcoa's alleged control of bauxite reserves in the 1930s and 1940s. Through purchases and long-term contracts, Alcoa was supposed to have preempted the available supplies of bauxite ore, which is absolutely necessary for the production of aluminum.

Another example is provided by U.S. Steel's control of commercially viable iron ore deposits.[4] Charles Schwab, president of Bethlehem Steel, testified as follows: "I do not believe there will be any great developments in iron and steel by new companies, but rather by the companies now in business." Asked for an explanation, Mr. Schwab replied, "For the reason that the possibility of a new company getting a sufficiently large supply of raw materials would make it exceedingly difficult if not impossible."

There is good evidence that U.S. Steel vigorously pursued the control of iron ore deposits even though it had iron ore holdings equal to 44 times its annual requirements. Ultimately, its efforts failed to protect its monopoly position.

---

[4] This is recounted by D. O. Parsons and E. J. Ray, "The United States Steel Consolidation: The Creation of Market Control," *Journal of Law and Economics* 18 (April 1975), pp. 181–220.

3. Natural monopoly. A natural monopoly exists when the forces of competition cause all firms but one to leave the industry. This is a result of the interaction between technological conditions that require large scale for efficient production and demand conditions that make one firm of minimum efficient size approximately sufficient to supply the entire market at a price that covers full cost. Under these conditions, it is socially most efficient to have a single firm supplying the entire market. This can be seen in Figure 2–5. If there were 10 firms producing the product, each might produce 1/10 of the output where *LMC* equals *D*. The per unit cost of production would be greatly above marginal cost at that point, and all firms would lose money. As a result, exit would occur until the remaining firm would have control over price. At that point, price would be raised and profits would become positive. Public utilities

FIGURE 2–5

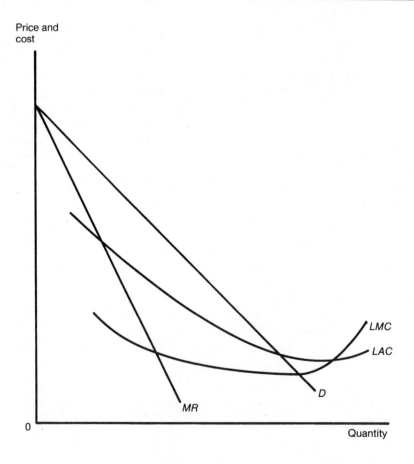

provide the classic examples of natural monopoly. Because of their acknowledged monopoly status, they are generally regulated by society.

4. Market franchise. There are industries where entry is controlled by the government. Consequently, the government agency can confer monopoly power on a firm, at least locally, simply by precluding entry. Examples abound: banking, airline routes, TV and radio frequencies, hospitals, cable TV firms, and so on. Usually some concessions are extracted from the firms in exchange for the protection. In many cases, firms must submit to some form of direct regulation regarding the prices charged, the quality and scope of service, and the rate of return earned on its investment. In these cases, positive profits may be attractive to outsiders, but entry can be barred. This is the most absolute of all entry barriers because the police power of the state is used to prevent entry.

2–6 WELFARE EFFECTS OF MONOPOLY

The economic case against monopoly hinges upon the deleterious effects of monopolistic practices on consumer welfare. We can develop the traditional welfare loss measure by comparing the competitive and monopolistic price and output combinations.[5] Initially, let us suppose that an industry is competitively organized. Further, we shall assume that the input markets are such that industry adjustments in output do not affect input prices. Then the entry and exit of separate profit-seeking firms will result in an industry long-run supply function that is horizontal, which is shown in Figure 2–6. At the competitive equilibrium price and output configuration, P_1 and Q_1, the firms earn just enough profit to keep their resources in this particular industry. Furthermore, price is such that any consumer who is willing to pay the cost to society of an additional unit of output can buy that extra output. Now, let us suppose that the industry becomes monopolized. If this industry were under control of a single firm, the *LRS* curve in Figure 2–6 would be the marginal and average cost curve for the monopolist. Instead of having many separate firms under independent control, one would have a single firm with many separate plants or production facilities. In this case, however, the decision on the quantity of output will be substantially different as will the equilibrium price. The monopolist will equate marginal cost and marginal revenue to determine the optimal output, Q_2, which will then determine the equilibrium price, P_2.

---

[5] The welfare loss triangle is developed from Harold Hotelling's famous paper, "The General Welfare in Relation to Problems of Taxation and of Railway and Utility Rates," *Econometrica* 6 (1938), pp. 242–69. It has been pointed out by many that this is not a precise measure of the welfare loss, but it can be shown that the welfare triangle is bracketed by two unambiguously correct welfare measures. See R. Willig, "Consumer's Surplus Without Apology," *American Economic Review* 66 (September 1976), 589–97.

FIGURE 2–6

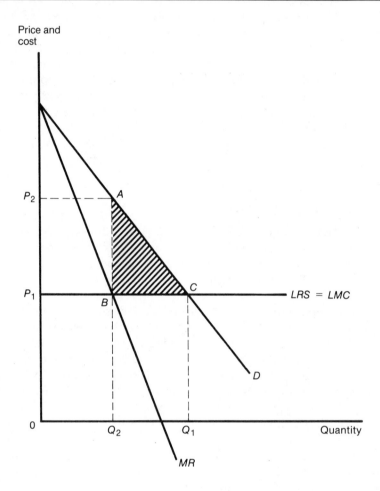

The optimal output shrinks from the competitive optimum of Q_1 to the monopolist optimum of Q_2. Excess profit for the monopolist amounts to $(P_2 - P_1)Q_2 = (P_2 - LAC)Q_2$. This amount is a transfer from consumers to the producer, which is paid by those consumers who continue to buy this product at the higher price P_2. Considered as a transfer within society, economists have nothing to say about such a transfer on social welfare grounds. The economist's main objection to monopoly stems from the resulting misallocation of resources. This can be seen by considering output Q_2. At this output, the marginal value placed upon the output, as measured by price, is P_2. The marginal value to society of the resources used to produce Q_2, as measured by the marginal cost function, is P_1. Thus, the monopolist will refuse to produce an extra unit of output even though consumers are willing to pay more than the social costs of the increase in output. In total, the welfare cost of the monopolist restriction of output is given by the welfare triangle ABC, which is equal to $\frac{1}{2}(P_2 - P_1)(Q_1 - Q_2)$.

Empirical measures of welfare losses

There have been various attempts at empirically measuring the deadweight welfare loss due to monopoly in the U.S. economy. The first, and the best known, is due to Arnold Harberger[6] who started with a simple expression for the welfare triangle:

$$W = \frac{1}{2}(P_2 - P_1)(Q_1 - Q_2) \qquad (2\text{--}1)$$

When doing empirical research on this subject, one is immediately confronted with a serious problem. Specifically, the competitive price and output, P_1 and Q_1, cannot be observed. Consequently, Harberger's first problem was to manipulate this welfare measure to obtain a formulation susceptible to empirical measurement.

First, note that the ratio of the monopoly markup over the competitive price to the competitive price is

$$Z = \frac{P_2 - P_1}{P_1}$$

which can be rearranged to

$$P_1 Z = P_2 - P_1 \qquad (2\text{--}2)$$

Second, we can define the elasticity of demand as

$$E = \frac{\Delta Q}{Q} \cdot \frac{P}{\Delta P} = \frac{Q_1 - Q_2}{Q_1} \cdot \frac{1}{Z}$$

As a result, we may solve for $Q_1 - Q_2$:

$$Q_1 - Q_2 = EZQ_1 \qquad (2\text{--}3)$$

Substituting (2–2) and (2–3) into (2–1), we have

$$W = \frac{1}{2}P_1 Q_1 E Z^2 \qquad (2\text{--}4)$$

Harberger argued that average costs were constant in the long run. In practice, he was willing to assume approximately constant costs that

---

[6] See Arnold C. Harberger, "Monopoly and Resource Allocation," *American Economic Review* 44 (May 1954), pp. 77–87. The Harberger analysis has been criticized effectively in Abram Bergson, "On Monopoly Welfare Losses," *American Economic Review* 63 (December 1973), pp. 853–70. Bergson's simulated results suggest a much higher welfare loss than Harberger's estimate. However, a portion of Bergson's analysis may be incorrect, as discussed in John S. Chipman and James C. Moore, "Compensating Variation, Consumer's Surplus, and Welfare," *American Economic Review* 70 (December 1980), pp. 933–49.

would permit the use of average cost data rather than difficult to obtain marginal cost data. Since costs are apt to be increasing if not constant, any resulting bias in the measure of welfare loss is upward.

Harberger assumed that the elasticity of demand was equal to one. His use of unitary elasticity is convenient computationally. The reasons he advanced are not persuasive, but the empirical results are not apt to change considerably by modifying this assumption.

He used profit data from another source and assumed a competitive rate of return of 10 percent to calculate the amount by which profits diverge from the average. Then he divided excess profit, $(P_2 - P_1)Q_2$ in Figure 2–6, by P_2Q_2 to obtain the percentage by which prices were too high.

By assuming unitary elasticity, the actual total revenue can be used to give optimal quantity by defining units such that price is $1. Thus, for the actual computations, Harberger used actual total revenue for P_1Q_1, $E = 1$, and Z as above. He estimated a total welfare loss for the entire U.S. economy of something less than 0.1 percent of GNP. This was a shocking result, as it implied that the monopoly problem was not worth studying, much less worrying about. The appropriate public policy toward monopoly on this logic would be benign neglect.

Several subsequent studies[7] have found monopoly welfare loss estimates of the same general magnitude as Harberger's. There are, however, two other studies[8] that find much larger estimates—on the order of 4–7 percent. Due to methodological disputes, no clear consensus has been reached on the size of the monopoly welfare losses.[9] In any event, two theoretical developments have emerged that suggest much larger welfare losses due to monopoly.

X-inefficiency

Although the empirical evidence offered by Harberger suggests that the problem of allocative efficiency is trivial, Leibenstein[10] felt that some

---

[7] These studies include David Schwartzman, "The Burden of Monopoly," *Journal of Political Economy* 58 (December 1960), pp. 627–30, and Dean A. Worcester, Jr., "New Estimates of the Welfare Loss to Monopoly, United States, 1956–1969," *Southern Economic Journal* 40 (October 1973), pp. 234–45.

[8] David R. Kamerschen, "An Estimation of the Welfare Losses From Monopoly in the American Economy," *Western Economic Journal* 4 (Summer 1966), pp. 221–36, and Keith Cowling and Dennis Mueller, "The Social Costs of Monopoly Power," *Economic Journal* 88 (December 1978), pp. 724–48.

[9] The estimates by Kamerschen have been criticized by Victor Goldberg, "Welfare Losses and Monopoly: The Unmaking of an Estimate," *Economic Inquiry* 16 (April 1978), pp. 310–12.

[10] The classic paper in this line of reasoning is Harvey Leibenstein, "Allocative Efficiency v. 'X-inefficiency'," *American Economic Review* 56 (June 1966), pp. 392–415. A case study example of the effects of X-inefficiency is provided by John P. Shelton, "Allocative Efficiency v. 'X-Efficiency': Comment," *American Economic Review* 57 (December 1967), pp. 1252–58. What Shelton categorizes as X-inefficiency could be interpreted in other ways, but his effort is interesting in any event.

broad notion of efficiency must be important. Based upon firm-specific evidence, Leibenstein suggested that efficiency losses may stem from nonmaximizing behavior. This source of inefficiency has come to be known as X-inefficiency. If his specific examples are both correct and general, the efficiency losses due to X-inefficiency may be quite significant.

Leibenstein felt that neither individuals nor firms work as hard, nor do they search for information as effectively, as they could. This emphasis on motivation is important because the relationship between inputs and outputs is not determinate for four reasons:

1. Contracts for labor are incomplete (i.e., all performance elements are not specified), which makes monitoring very important.
2. Not all factors of production are marketed or available on the same terms to all buyers (e.g., managerial inputs may not be available and if available, tend to be highly heterogeneous).
3. The production function is neither completely specified nor known.
4. Interdependence and uncertainty lead competing firms to cooperate tacitly with each other in some respects and to imitate each other with respect to technique to some degree.

In other words, Leibenstein surrendered the assumption of cost minimizing behavior. Competitive pressures, however, were a force for greater X-efficiency among firms.

Under these circumstances, a shift from monopoly to competition has two possible consequences: (1) the elimination of monopoly rents and consequent improvement in the allocation of resources and (2) the reduction of unit costs by improved X-efficiency. These consequences can be examined using familiar tools of analysis.

Consider Figure 2–7, where triangle ABC is the traditional welfare loss W based upon the assumption that unit costs C_M are independent of market structure, and the monopoly price and output are P and Q, respectively. Comanor and Leibenstein[11] point to the possibility that the unit costs in a competitively structured market could be C_c. In that event, the true allocative inefficiency is the larger triangle ADE. Under the standard treatment, we normally make no judgments regarding the transfer of rectangle $PABC_M$ from consumers to producers. It is not unambiguously true that we can treat the rectangle C_MBDC_c in the same fashion. If these "costs" are really nonpecuniary income to managers within the firm or its owners, then we may treat this as any other transfer. If, however, this represents "managerial slack" (i.e., wasted resources), then we may not be justified in treating it as a transfer. In

---

[11] William Comanor and Harvey Leibenstein, "Allocative Efficiency, X-Efficiency, and the Measurement of Welfare Losses," *Economica*, August 1969, pp. 304–9, show that the true welfare loss (including the effects of X-inefficiency) is some multiple of the traditional welfare triangle.

FIGURE 2–7

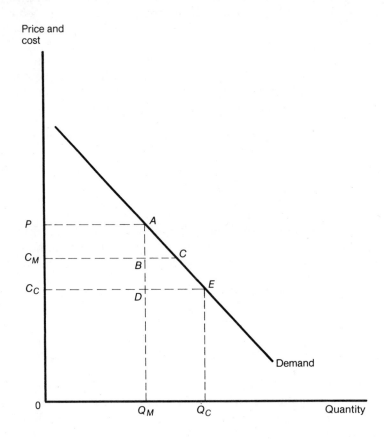

any event, the difference between the conventionally measured welfare loss and the one that includes X-inefficiency may be substantial. For example, in Figure 2–7 the difference between P and C_M equals the difference between C_M and C_c. As a result, the properly measured deadweight welfare loss is four times the apparent deadweight welfare loss.

Pursuit of monopoly profit

Because most analysts have not examined the process of obtaining monopoly status, a significant social cost may have been overlooked. Building on the foundation laid by Tullock[12] and Posner[13], the excess

---

[12] Gordon Tullock, "The Welfare Costs of Tariffs, Monopolies, and Theft," *Western Economic Journal* 5 (June 1967), pp. 224–32.

[13] Richard A. Posner, "The Social Cost of Monopoly and Regulation," *Journal of Political Economy* 83 (August 1975), pp. 807–27.

profit area, P_2ABP_1 in Figure 2–6, has antitrust significance for welfare purposes. Basically, this analysis depends upon the fact that the excess profits enjoyed by a monopolist serve as an inducement for others to compete for those excess profits. This competition requires the investment of resources by each would-be monopolist. The opportunity costs of wasting these resources on socially unproductive efforts are also social costs of monopoly.

In summary, we have developed three efficiency losses associated with monopoly. The traditional measure of welfare loss—the so-called welfare triangle—is a measure of allocative inefficiency due to not employing enough resources as a result of the monopolistic restriction of output. This has been estimated by several economists, and although there is some disagreement about its size, it appears to be positive. The second type of welfare loss is X-inefficiency. This welfare loss is due to wasting resources as a result of no competition. It is extremely difficult to estimate the welfare loss due to X-inefficiency because that would require an estimate of how much extra output the firm should be able to squeeze out of the inputs that it actually employs. In principle, however, this welfare loss could be substantial. Of course, the conceptual foundation for this loss has not gone unchallenged.[14] Finally, we have seen that the monopoly profits, which are usually treated as transfers without normative significance, provide an estimate of the resources that may be expended on efforts to achieve monopoly. Since such efforts are not productive, these resources are in a sense wasted.

2–7 MONOPOLY AND INNOVATION[15]

The relationship between market structure and technical progress is very complex. Economic theory has not provided any unambiguous a priori predictions as to which market structure is most conducive to technological change. Two divergent views on this subject are easily summarized. The traditional view relies upon competition to compel firms to make the best use of all available means to increase their profits. The drive for new and improved products as well as for more efficient production techniques is not much different from price competition. The alternative view is embodied in Schumpeter's hypothesis,[16] which

---

[14] On whether X-inefficiency is distinct from allocative inefficiency, see the interesting exchange between George Stigler and Harvey Leibenstein contained in Stigler's "The Existence of X-Efficiency," *American Economic Review* 68 (March 1978), pp. 203–11.

[15] Handy surveys of the literature in this area are provided by Morton Kamien and Nancy Schwartz, "Market Structure and Innovation: A Survey," *Journal of Economic Literature* 13 (March 1975), pp. 1–37, and by F. M. Scherer, *Industrial Market Structure and Economic Performance*, 2d ed. (Skokie, Ill.: Rand McNally, 1980), Chapter 15.

[16] Joseph A. Schumpeter, *Capitalism, Socialism, and Democracy*, 3d ed. (New York: Harper & Row, 1950).

places great emphasis upon innovation by the firm. In a nutshell, Schumpeter's theory was that the lure of excess profits provides a powerful incentive for undertaking risky and uncertain innovations. Furthermore, Schumpeter seems to have assumed some degree of market power as a precondition because the firm was seen as financing these risky ventures out of previously earned excess profits. These excess profits are not consistent with equilibrium in pure competition.

Neither theory is easy to test empirically and all of the empirical efforts to date suffer from serious defects. For example, many studies rely upon the firm's expenditures on inputs, which is a rather imperfect measure of effort. Although well-intentioned research efforts are of some interest, we must be more concerned with the results. Leibenstein would probably argue that X-inefficiency is apt to plague R&D efforts just as readily as any other endeavor. Some other empirical studies rely upon patent statistics for an output measure. This poses several obvious difficulties (e.g., one cannot easily discriminate between a basic, very important development and another flavor for a soft drink).

We can obtain some slight appreciation for the theoretical difficulties by considering the analyses of Arrow[17] and Demsetz.[18] Arrow began by examining the influence of market structure on the incentive to invent a cost-reducing invention. In Figure 2–8, we denote the preinvention average cost by C, which will be equal to the price in a competitive industry. After the patent holder devises a cost reducing invention, his interest lies in selecting a royalty such that the maximum revenue is extracted for himself. The use of the patent will reduce the producer's average cost from C to $\bar{C}$. As we know, the maximum profit that can be earned is that associated with monopoly behavior. In particular, the patent holder wants the competitive industry to produce the output where $\bar{C}$ equals MR. If the patent holder sets a per unit royalty of $P - \bar{C}$, the competitive industry will perceive a marginal cost equal to P and produce the output that is optimal from the patent holder's perspective. The total royalties then will be $Puv\bar{C}$. Provided that the cost of invention is less than $Puv\bar{C}$, the inventor has an incentive to invent.

We can compare this result with the monopoly case. Under monopoly, the original equilibrium was where marginal revenue equaled marginal cost C. The monopolist was earning excess profits of $wxyC$. When marginal cost falls from C to $\bar{C}$, the new profit, as we saw above, is $Puv\bar{C}$. The *net* improvement for the monopolist is $Puv\bar{C}$ minus $wxyC$. This net amount is the maximum that the patent holder can extract. Since this total is smaller than under competitive conditions, Arrow concluded

---

[17] Kenneth J. Arrow, "Economic Welfare and the Allocation of Resources for Invention," in *The Rate and Direction of Inventive Activity* (Princeton, N.J.: Princeton University Press, 1962).

[18] Harold Demsetz's contrasting view was presented in "Information and Efficiency: Another Viewpoint," *Journal of Law and Economics* 12 (April 1969), pp. 1–22.

FIGURE 2-8

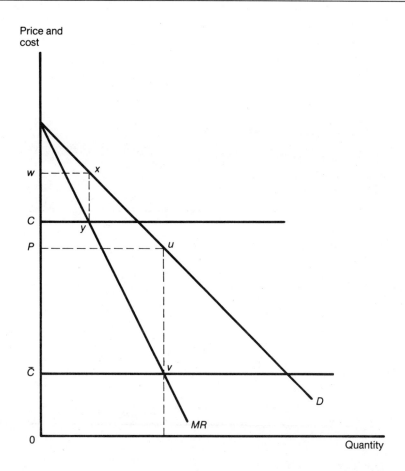

that the incentive to invent is less under monopoly than under competition. Arrow's conclusion, however, has not gone unchallenged.

Demsetz complained that Arrow was confusing the normal restrictive effect of monopoly with incentives for innovation. Since a monopoly restricts output below the competitive level, it will use less of all inputs. This, of course, includes the cost-reducing technology. Since the per-unit costs saved are the same for both the monopolist and the competitive industry, it stands to reason that the invention will generate fewer royalties when it is sold to the monopolist—he wants less of it. In order to analyze the effect of market structure on the incentive to innovate, one must remove the normal restrictive effect of monopoly.

Demsetz insists that we must begin the analysis where the output is the same for both market structures. In Figure 2-9, the demand function

FIGURE 2–9

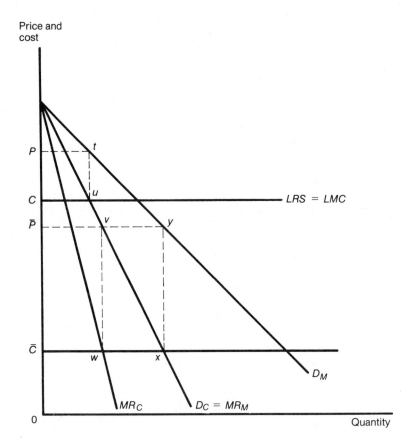

facing the monopolist is D_M while the demand facing the competitive industry is D_C, which was constructed so that it coincided with the monopolist's marginal revenue curve. Given the preinvention marginal cost of C, both the monopolist and the competitive industry produce the same total output. Note that supply equals demand for the competitive industry at precisely the same point that marginal cost equals marginal revenue for the monopolist. Prior to the invention, the monopolist's profit is $PCut$. After the cost-reducing invention, the monopolist's profit could be as large as $\bar{P}\bar{C}xy$. In contrast, the competitive industry enjoyed no excess profits prior to the invention. After the invention, the patent holder can extract a maximum of $\bar{P}\bar{C}wv$ from the competitive industry. In order to evaluate the relative incentives, one must determine whether area $vwxy$ is greater than $PCut$. If P is less than C, this will always be the case. Thus, the incentive to invent will be greater under monopoly than under competition: the exact opposite of Arrow's conclusions.[19]

Even granting Demsetz's initial premise that the relevant analysis must start where the competitive and monopoly outputs are identical, this does not end matters. As Yamey[20] pointed out, Demsetz's analysis implies that the monopolist pays for the invention in the form of a lump-sum payment. This is necessary so that the *MC* curve of the monopolist does not change. This, however, puts the problem into a situation of bilateral monopoly with a lump sum payment because there is only one buyer and one seller.

Bilateral monopoly introduces indeterminacy[21] and bargaining into the pricing process, which changes the inventor's risk. First, if the bargaining occurs *after* the inventor has committed resources to the invention, he would be subject to exploitation. Thus, the incentive to invent would be reduced unless the terms were settled ex ante. Second, even if the terms are to be settled ex ante on the basis of cost reductions, this is not always practicable and reliable when the extent of any cost reduction is difficult to determine ex post. This difficulty arises due to new investment or development costs plus the complications of quality changes. Third, the lump-sum payment puts the purchaser in the position of incurring the same cost no matter what the level of output. Thus, the risk for the buyer is higher, and therefore, the price he is willing to pay is reduced.

QUESTIONS AND PROBLEMS

1. Describe a situation where the monopolist's optimal output is zero.

2. A monopolist's optimal price is $10, and the optimal output is 300 units. If the average cost of production is $7.50 per unit, what is the firm's profit? If a 40 percent profits tax is levied, what is the firm's post tax profit? What happens if it tries to adjust price and output?

3. "The monopolist's price will always exceed his marginal cost." True or false? Explain.

---

[19] Further development of this work was provided by Morton Kamien and Nancy Schwartz, "Market Structure, Elasticity of Demand, and Incentive to Invent," *Journal of Law and Economics* 13 (April 1970), pp. 241–52; S. C. Hu, "On the Incentive to Invent: A Clarificatory Note," *Journal of Law and Economics* 16 (April 1973), pp. 169–78; and Ward Bowman, "The Incentive to Invent in Competitive as Contrasted to Monopolistic Industries," *Journal of Law and Economics* 20 (April 1977), pp. 227–28.

[20] B. S. Yamey, "Competition, Monopoly, and the Incentive to Invent," *Journal of Law and Economics* 13 (April 1970), pp. 253–56.

[21] A concise and clear statement of this problem is provided by J. Gould and C. E. Ferguson, *Microeconomic Theory*, 5th ed (Homewood, Ill.: Richard D. Irwin, 1980), pp. 275–76.

4. Since the resources invested in becoming a monopolist yield a high return, it is unfair to say that such resources are unproductive. Explain why this statement is true or false.

5. The deadweight welfare loss measures are static concepts. If Schumpeter is correct, a little bit of monopoly may get us a lot of technical change and innovation. How does this affect social welfare on balance?

6. Only one firm produces Kellogg's Corn Flakes. Thus, Kellogg's is a monopolist. Is this a useful construction? Does it make economic sense?

7. The courts have referred to *monopoly power* as the power to control price or to exclude competition. Is this consistent with the economic concept of monopoly?

8. Some economists contend that monopoly power is often due to government intervention. In any event, they argue that absent government support, monopoly power will be transitory. Does this mean that there is no cause for concern when we observe monopoly?

9. Is it true that a firm cannot be a monopoly if its shareholders obtain a normal rate of return on their investment in this firm?

10. The Lerner index of monopoly power is

$$\lambda = \frac{P - MC}{P}$$

If a monopolist is maximizing profit, $MC = MR$. Show that Lerner's index is then equal to the reciprocal of the demand elasticity.

11. Suppose that a new production process drives down the price of an input used by a monopolist. What does this do to its average and marginal cost curves? What happens to the profit maximizing price and output?

12. "If a monopolist succeeds in maximizing its profits, the demand for its product cannot be inelastic." True or false? Explain.

13. Why does the monopolist produce where marginal cost and marginal revenue are equal?

14. What sorts of competitive pressures does a monopolist encounter?

15. Use the definition of marginal revenue to explain why marginal revenue is negative over some range of the demand curve.

16. Suppose the industry demand curve is given by

$$P = \$50 - 2Q$$

Plot this demand curve. From this information, plot the corresponding marginal revenue curve.

17. Show a graph depicting a monopolist in a long-run, break-even (i.e., zero profit) situation with positive production. Why would the monopolist continue producing in the long run if its profits were zero?

18. "As long as monopoly power can be transferred, monopolists can continue to receive monopoly profits in the long run." Is this statement true or false? Explain.

19. Will an increase in the demand for a monopolist's product always result in an increase in price and quantity sold?

20. Does a profit-maximizing monopolist typically produce a quantity of output that is optimal from the standpoint of cost and efficiency? Explain.

3

Antitrust response to monopoly

In retrospect, our analysis of competition and monopoly in the preceding chapters provides a sound analytical foundation for the federal antitrust laws. Actual legislation, however, can seldom be attributed to abstract reasoning. Generally, legislation results from a perceived need on the basis of empirical reality. As we shall see in this chapter, much the same can be said for our antitrust laws. The Sherman Act of 1890, the first and most basic antitrust law, resulted from a variety of socioeconomic factors that came together at the end of the last century. The Clayton Act of 1914 was a result, at least in part, of Congress's dissatisfaction with Sherman Act enforcement. Along with the Clayton Act, the Federal Trade Commission Act was passed to fill a perceived void. From time to time, the antitrust laws have been amended as Congress has seen fit.

The purpose of this chapter is to sketch some of the historical factors that motivated the antitrust laws. Further, we shall present and discuss briefly the antitrust statutes. Finally, we shall examine the enforcement efforts of the antitrust authorities.

3-1   HISTORICAL BACKGROUND OF ANTITRUST[1]

Prior to the Civil War, there were very few economic problems caused by monopoly. This is not to say that competition was perfect according

---

[1] Much of this section is based upon Hans B. Thorelli's *The Federal Antitrust Policy*, especially Chapters II and III. Far richer detail is provided by this magnificent historical account.

to the discussion in Chapter 1. In fact, it was decidedly imperfect, primarily due to inadequacies in transportation and the dissemination of information. Any lack of adequate transportation insulates local businessmen and provides some degree of local monopoly power. Similarly, an absence of accurate market information creates information asymmetries that are translated into departures from the competitive results. Such departures from competition were due to violations of the assumptions of the competitive model. Nonetheless, it remains fairly accurate to say that industries were relatively unconcentrated before the Civil War and, for the most part, were populated by small firms.

During the Civil War, the demand for certain products expanded dramatically. At the same time, domestic producers were amply protected by tariffs. The result of this was a marked growth in most industries located in the North and East. Not surprisingly, the industrial expansion during the Civil War did not result in a great deal of industrial concentration. At the end of the war, the U.S. economy was still very competitive.

Although competition was the rule, a few industries began to exhibit certain characteristics of big business. In meat packing, firearms production, machine-made shoes, sewing machines, and farm machinery, inherent economies of scale caused an increasing degree of concentration. Since economies of scale in production caused most of the concentration, there was little combination and a great deal of internal expansion. Interestingly, the only industries demonstrating much in the way of combination were the railroad and the telegraph industries.

Agrarian discontent

The central cause of agrarian discontent in the decades following the Civil War was the almost permanent agricultural depression that prevailed. The pervasive unprofitability of farming made the farm community terribly unhappy. It is little wonder that the farmer suspected that all nonfarm sectors of the economy were conspiring against him. The railroads may have been the most suspect of all. First, the farmer was induced to invest in the railroads. Unscrupulous operators cheated him financially by rewarding him with watered stock and outright fraud. Next, he was required to pay substantial taxes to cover this malfeasance in order to keep the railroad running. Finally, the railroad charged arbitrary and unreasonable rates, or at least the farmer thought so. In fact, the railroad charged competitive rates when it faced competition and could not collude. But on routes where there was little competition, the railroad charged all that the traffic would bear. At the same time, the grain elevator operators exploited their local monopoly position by charging high prices. Thus, the farmer found it very expensive to move his products to market.

When the farmer purchased farm equipment, he found high prices that were insulated from competition by protective tariffs. Local farm equipment dealers had some measure of local monopoly and accordingly charged high retail prices. Adding insult to injury, these local dealers also charged dearly for the credit that was extended to the farmer.

The government seemed to be against the farmer, too. Farmers resented the government grants of land without any apparent return. Moreover, taxes were imposed on real property and thereby increased the price of everything the farmer bought. Tariffs and patents also promoted monopoly power and raised prices to the farmer.

Finally, the ultimate blow was the generally low prices of farm products. The farmer saw no relief on the cost side of his ledger and also saw low prices for his output on the revenue side.

The farmers blamed monopolies and trusts for their problems. In their minds, the low agricultural prices, the high farm equipment prices, the high and discriminatory railroad and grain elevator charges, and so on were the result of monopolies. As a consequence, the large farm population began forming political pressure groups. For example, the National Grange was devoted to obtaining state legislation that would provide some protection for the farmer. This movement enjoyed some short-run success but not much long-run success. Nonetheless, the legislators from the agricultural states were well aware of the farmers' distrust of monopoly.

Behavior of big business

At the same time, a more general public sentiment adverse to big business was developing. This was due in part to a rather steady revelation in the press of offensive business behavior. So-called predatory practices appeared in a few large and very visible industries; a prime example was the petroleum industry. Standard Oil provided a rather unsavory example as it set up sham independents whose mission was to force real independents out of business. It also disparaged its competitors by spreading false rumors about their financial stability and supply reliability, thereby undermining their ability to compete. Further, Standard Oil obtained secret railroad rebates that put its competitors at a competitive disadvantage. Standard Oil was not the only firm guilty of questionable business practices. Clair Wilcox reported that National Cash Register employed similar tactics.[2] Perhaps even more distressing, some firms resorted to political corruption. Both the railroad and petroleum industries apparently corrupted legislators and judges to gain a competitive edge.

---

[2] See Clair Wilcox, *Competition and Monopoly in American Industry*, U.S. Temporary National Economic Committee, Monograph No. 21 (1940), p. 68.

Growth of combinations

Industrial combinations assumed many forms. Some were merely loose-knit price-fixing agreements or pools. Others were more formal—trusts and outright merger. Irrespective of form, however, during the last decades of the 19th century, organized restraints of trade increased substantially. Simple agreements to restrain trade have been noted in a great many industries: petroleum and railroads, of course, but also whiskey distillers, iron and steel producers, mail and stove producers, cottonseed-oil producers, and oatmeal millers. Further evidence suggests that prices were fixed for coal, lumber, ice, beer, tile, gunpowder, and packed meat among others. As we shall see in Chapter 6, such agreements tend to be short-lived. Their success depends upon the co-operation of the participants, as the agreements are not legally enforceable. But each participant can gain at the expense of the others by cheating on the agreement. As a result, these agreements tend to be very unstable due to the greed of the participants.

Unstable price-fixing agreements were replaced by the more structured pool. A pool usually would have some sort of enforcement mechanism. More importantly, it would "pool" production, sales, or profits of the participants and then redistribute them according to some predetermined formula. This reduced, but did not eliminate, the incentive for cheating among the collaborators. Pools appear to have replaced simple price-fixing agreements in the following industries: iron and steel, wallpaper, railroads, coal and grain dealers, candles, salt, meatpacking, glucose, gunpowder, whiskey, and cotton bagging. Although pools were a bit more stable than price-fixing agreements, they also tended to break down due to competitive forces. They were replaced by trusts.

Trusts are cohesive groups of firms that surrender a great deal of individual managerial discretion to a central management. Trusts emerged in petroleum, cotton oil, linseed oil, sugar, whiskey, cordage, and lead. In each instance, the purpose was to gain more perfect control of the industry in order to emulate the monopoly results in terms of prices and profits.

Public opinion

Against this background of economic and political abuse, it is easy to conclude that public opinion must have been quite hostile toward big business. In fact, this appears to have been the case. Letwin[3] provides some convincing evidence that in the late 1880s it was generally conceded that the public deeply hated the trusts. Of course, those who can only be described as radical agitators as well as apologists for the trusts

---

[3] See William Letwin, *Law and Economic Policy in America* (New York: Random House, 1965), especially pp. 54–70.

may have exaggerated the depth of public feeling. But journalists regularly reported news of the trusts which indicates that their readers were interested in the subject. Newspaper interest was not the only index of popular concern. Politicians of that time discussed the question of protective tariffs, the trusts, and the interaction of the two almost constantly. The influence of the trusts on the major issues of the day—federal regulation of railroads, labor unions, low farm income, and poverty generally—was discussed almost constantly.

Hatred and distrust of monopoly has its origins in our Jeffersonian tradition. Historically, monopoly connoted unjustified economic power that usually was associated with some obstacle or barrier to equal opportunity. In the United States, this hatred and distrust was manifested in state statutes prohibiting any grant of monopoly, in opposition to the corporate form of business organization, and in opposition to central banking. In the final years before passage of the Sherman Act, public objections to the trusts grew. There seemed to be a great deal of truth in the charges that trusts (1) corrupted public employees and legislators, thereby threatening political democracy, (2) enjoyed the insulation of protective tariffs, (3) hurt consumers by charging higher prices, (4) engaged in questionable financial practices like watering stock, and (5) caused serious dislocations by suddenly closing plants. The American public felt abused by the trusts and wanted a law that would curtail the power of the trusts. Any law that prohibited the worst abuses of the most visible trusts would be satisfactory. What we got was the Sherman Act.

3–2   THE SHERMAN ANTITRUST ACT

The Sherman Antitrust Act, which was passed on July 2, 1890, is the cornerstone of antitrust policy in the United States. Its two main provisions are contained in sections 1 and 2:

> Sec. 1. Every contract, combination in the form of trust or otherwise, or conspiracy, in restraint of trade or commerce among the several States, or with foreign nations, is hereby declared to be illegal. Every person who shall make any such contract or engage in any such combination or conspiracy shall be deemed guilty of a felony, and, on conviction thereof, shall be punished by fine not exceeding one million dollars if a corporation, or, if any other person, one hundred thousand dollars or by imprisonment not exceeding three years, or by both said punishments, in the discretion of the court.
>
> Sec. 2. Every person who shall monopolize, or attempt to monopolize, or combine or conspire with any other person or persons, to monopolize any part of the trade or commerce among the several States, or with foreign nations, shall be deemed guilty of a felony, and, on conviction thereof, shall be punished by fine not exceeding one million dollars if a

corporation, or, if any other person, one hundred thousand dollars or by imprisonment not exceeding three years, or by both said punishments, in the discretion of the court.[4]

The vague and general prohibition of trade restraints and monopolization provided in sections 1 and 2 of the Sherman Act has caused much mischief. Due to the lack of specificity, the Sherman Act was little more than a legislative command that the judiciary develop the law of antitrust. Since the statute did not provide much guidance, the courts would have to be guided by the apparent legislative intent of Congress.

3–3 LEGISLATIVE INTENT OF THE SHERMAN ACT

Since the language of the Sherman Act is very broad, the courts have been forced to provide specificity through their decisions. The role of the courts is to implement what Congress intended when it passed the legislation in question. Thus, it is important to determine what Congress intended to accomplish when it enacted the Sherman Act. We shall examine Robert Bork's influential interpretation[5] first and then an alternative provided by Robert Lande.[6]

Allocative efficiency

Professor Bork's contention is that the legislative intent of the Sherman Act was to promote consumer welfare through allocative efficiency. His compelling argument is based upon a thorough review of the act's legislative history and its structure. First, explicit policy statements indicate that promoting consumer welfare was the object of the antitrust legislation. Senator Sherman expressed a continuing concern with business behavior that prevented full and free competition and with devices that were designed to raise the price paid by the consumer. Sherman's concern for protecting the competitive process is not consistent with any goal other than the promotion of consumer welfare. If unfettered competition were the order of the day, there would be no way to preserve or promote social values that consumers are unwilling to pay for. Market

---

[4] We have indicated the present sanctions rather than those that appeared in the original statute. Originally, the fines for natural persons and corporations were $5,000, and the maximum imprisonment was one year. Violations were misdemeanors rather than felonies. In 1955, the fines were raised to $50,000. The present sanctions were put into effect in 1974.

[5] See the following two works by Robert H. Bork: "Legislative Intent and the Policy of the Sherman Act," *Journal of Law and Economics* 9 (April 1966), pp. 7–48, and *The Antitrust Paradox* (New York: Basic Books, 1978).

[6] See the intriguing paper by Robert H. Lande, "Wealth Transfers as the Original and Primary Concern of Antitrust: The Efficiency Interpretation Challenged," *Hastings Law Journal* 34 (September 1982), pp. 65–151.

forces do not respect these other social values. Of course, his concern with consumer prices exhibits an appreciation of their relationship to consumer welfare. He seemed to understand that an increase in price caused a restriction in output and a consequent diminution of consumer welfare.

In addition to Senator Sherman, the Senate Judiciary Committee membership apparently endorsed the promotion of consumer welfare. The four Democrats on the committee provided explicit evidence in speech or in their own antitrust bills that they agreed with Sherman's rationale. There were five Republicans on the committee. None of them rejected Sherman's concern for consumer welfare, and two of them demonstrated basic agreement with Sherman.

In the House of Representatives, there was less explicit evidence that consumer welfare should be the central concern of antitrust. There were, however, several spokesmen for this view. Moreover, of all the antitrust bills introduced in the House, none promoted any values other than consumer welfare. Ten of the bills were cast in consumer welfare terms while the rest were not inconsistent with consumer welfare.

A second indication that Congressional concern was with consumer welfare is provided by the rules of law contemplated by Congress. Supporters of the antitrust movement consistently objected to cartels (i.e., loose-knit price-fixing and/or market division conspiracies). In fact, one can infer from some of the political maneuvering that the law was to proscribe all cartels irrespective of the prices set. Amendments to make price fixing illegal only in the event that the price was unreasonable were rejected. Of course, cartels are designed to raise price, restrict output, and otherwise emulate monopoly. Thus, a rule against cartels certainly promotes consumer welfare.

In addition to cartels, Congress intended to prohibit monopolistic mergers and predatory business practices. Monopolistic mergers were seen as close-knit rather than loose-knit combinations. As such, they were just as suspect as the loose-knit conspiracies. At the time (and to some extent now), it was widely believed that a firm could achieve and maintain a monopoly through the use of predatory practices. Accordingly, such predatory practices should be outlawed. The arguments made in favor of bans on cartels, monopolistic mergers, and predatory business practices were based upon the promotion of consumer welfare.

A third indication that Congress had consumer welfare in mind was the distinction drawn between legal and illegal mergers. Those that promoted efficiency were in the consumer's interest and would not be illegal. Sherman went to some trouble to point out that his bill would not interfere with efficiency. Consequently, the law prohibits monopolizing and not the market structure that we term monopoly. If a firm comes to dominate a market by virtue of its superior efficiency, that monopoly is lawful. It is only when a firm achieves the status of monopoly through business practices that are unrelated to efficiency that the firm violates the antitrust law.[7]

Prevention of wealth transfers

Robert Lande argues that Congress was concerned primarily with preventing firms with market power from unfairly transferring wealth from consumers to themselves. This is a distributive issue as opposed to an allocative issue. As between consumers and producers, Congress favored consumers. Now, the intention was not to reallocate wealth in some fashion that Congress perceived to be superior in an overall sense. Instead, Congress was only worried about preventing one transfer of wealth that it considered to be inequitable. It wanted to promote the distribution of wealth that would result from competitive markets. The trusts and monopolies of the late 1800s were condemned because they "unfairly" extracted wealth from consumers.

Lande points out that Bork's argument for a consumer welfare standard is based upon evidence that supports Lande's thesis that Congress wanted to prevent wealth transfers. For example, Senator Sherman's continuing concern with price increases directly supports Lande's position while only providing indirect support for Bork's position. Moreover, Lande points out that few economists understood the consequences of monopoly power for allocative efficiency in 1890. In fact, the prevailing view was that monopoly might be inevitable due to productive efficiency. Consequently, it would be surprising if the legislators had much appreciation for allocative efficiency.

Bork made a powerful argument that consumer welfare is the only sensible goal of antitrust policy. Lande, in contrast, points out that Congress expressed concern for multiple goals. In addition to preventing unfair wealth transfers, Congress wanted to limit the social and political power of large firms. This, of course, is consistent with our Jeffersonian heritage. Further, Congress expressed some concern for protecting small businesses. In particular, the opportunity to compete seemed to be threatened because small firms appeared to be vulnerable to predation by the trusts and monopolies. Consequently, Congress was concerned for their safety and made predatory practices illegal.

3–4 EARLY ENFORCEMENT OF THE SHERMAN ACT

The early enforcement of the Sherman Act was consistent with the legislative intent: promotion of consumer welfare. The history of the

---

[7] Bork also points out that no one who supported Sherman suggested that the courts should give any weight to any values that are inconsistent with the promotion of consumer welfare. Finally, what meager support there is for the notion that small businesses should be preserved at a sacrifice in consumer welfare is highly suspect.

early cases has been recounted by several scholars,[8] and we shall only sketch a brief picture of these early decisions. During the period of 1897–99, Justice Peckham wrote five major opinions in antitrust cases. In the course of these decisions, the Peckham Rule emerged:[9]

> The natural, direct and immediate effect of competition is, however, to lower rates, and to thereby increase demand for commodities, the supplying of which increases commerce, and an agreement, whose first and direct effect is to prevent this play of competition, restrains instead of promoting trade and commerce.[10]

Thus, it is clear that Justice Peckham understood that competition reduced price and expanded output. A direct restraint upon the forces of competition would result in higher prices and reduced output. Consequently, Justice Peckham established that any business practices designed primarily to restrict output would be illegal. This is certainly consistent with the economist's theory of allocative efficiency and thereby consistent with a legislative aim of promoting consumer welfare.

Indirect or incidental restrictions are not necessarily illegal. If a restraint did not increase price or reduce output, usually its purpose was to promote trade. For example, in *Anderson* v. *United States*,[11] Peckham approved of an agreement among the members of an open livestock traders' association not to deal with nonmembers. After reviewing the purpose and effect of the refusal to deal, he explained that the agreement had

> no tendency . . . to limit the number of cattle marketed or to limit or reduce their price or to place any impediment or obstacle in the course of the commercial stream which flows into the Kansas City cattle market.[12]

Because the trade association's agreement did not restrain the flow of commerce, there was no reason to proscribe it. Thus, incidental or indirect restrictions that may increase productive efficiency will not be prohibited. This, too, is consistent with Congress's intention to exonerate efficiency-based monopolies.

In spite of the fact that the early Sherman Act decisions were consistent with the legislative intent, there was almost immediate dissatisfaction with the Sherman Act. As we have seen, the Sherman Act is quite general and a little vague. This seems a bit unfair to those that are

---

[8] Bork, "Legislative Intent," pp. 7–48, and *The Antitrust Paradox*; Letwin, *Law and Economic Policy in America*, pp. 54–70; and John R. Carter, "From Peckham to White: Economic Welfare and the Rule of Reason," *Antitrust Bulletin* 25 (Summer 1980), pp. 275–95, provide brief but convincing accounts of the early enforcement.

[9] See Carter, ibid., p. 278.

[10] *United States* v. *Joint Traffic Assoc.*, 171 U.S. 505, 577 (1898).

[11] 171 U.S. 604 (1898).

[12] 171 U.S. 604, 620 (1898).

regulated by the statute because no sharp line has been drawn between legal and illegal business behavior. Consequently, businessmen are exposed to unwarranted risk of prosecution. Moreover, a general statute like the Sherman Act confers a great deal of discretion upon the judiciary and gives the judges something of a legislative role.

Of course, this criticism is naive in many ways. Most importantly, implicit in this criticism is the belief that Congress could specify exhaustively all the various ways that businessmen could restrain trade. This is not possible because businessmen are very clever when it comes to figuring out how to make a profit. Consequently, a specific list of prohibitions would have to be amended constantly. Nonetheless, as soon as the Sherman Act was passed, there was an expressed desire for a more specific antitrust law. For example, President Roosevelt argued that big business was inevitable due to natural economic forces rather than as a result of convenience or choice. Since Roosevelt read the Sherman Act to forbid all combinations irrespective of economic effect, he opposed the Sherman Act. He felt that the act should be amended so that the business community could be told precisely what behavior was impermissible. In addition, it should receive explicit license to do anything that was not on the list of prohibitions.

Roosevelt was succeeded by William Howard Taft who had written one of the most famous antitrust decisions of all.[13] Unlike Roosevelt, President Taft looked more critically at the Sherman Act's enforcement. Taft recognized that some combinations were formed for purposes of greater efficiency—for example, to exploit economies of scale in production and thereby to reduce costs. Other combinations, however, were formed to gain monopolistic control of an industry. He found that judicial decisions under the Sherman Act had discerned the difference between the two. Where a combination's purpose was to monopolize, it was struck down; where the object was productive efficiency, it was permitted. Taft thought that this was the best that one could expect and that more specific legislation was impractical. Matters might have rested there but for the *Standard Oil* decision in 1911.[14]

Standard Oil and the rule of reason

Justice White's opinion in the *Standard Oil* case announced a theory of Sherman Act enforcement called the "rule of reason." This theory had been invoked in earlier decisions, but White's announcement came as something of a surprise to observers generally.[15] In any event, the rule

---

[13] *United States* v. *Addyston Pipe & Steel Co.*, 85 F. 271 (6th Cir. 1898). See the discussion in Chapter 6.

[14] *Standard Oil Co.* v. *United States*, 221 U.S. 1 (1911).

[15] Bork, "Legislative Intent," pp. 33–41; Carter, "From Peckham to White," pp. 275–95; and Letwin, *Law and Economic Policy in America*, pp. 253–65.

of reason became explicit in White's opinion. White felt that the Sherman Act's language prohibiting every contract in restraint of trade should be read to prohibit every contract that unduly or unreasonably restrained trade. White explained that while the Sherman Act's language was broad so that offenders could not slip through loopholes, the broad language required the exercise of judgment on the part of the judiciary in applying the act. White ruled that the act did not preclude a firm from being the only seller of a commodity, but it did prohibit all firms from using exclusionary practices to preclude others from selling that commodity. Contracts that tended to exclude rival firms were illegal. Life, however, is not simple—a judge is required to exercise discretion (i.e., to use reason) in determining whether any particular contract unduly (i.e., unreasonably) restrained someone's freedom to compete.

White adopted fully the promotion of consumer welfare. Any restraint that hindered consumer welfare was unreasonable, and an unreasonable restraint could not be saved by resorting to other social values.

But White's opinion was misunderstood. The rule of reason confirmed the fears of all opponents of the Sherman Act. Many were very suspicious of judicial discretion. Some feared that the judiciary would be too severe while others feared that it would be too lax. While some groups wanted absolute prohibitions for certain business practices, other groups were more inclined to favor unbridled laissez-faire. The final result was compromise legislation, which was supposed to provide greater specificity.

3–5 THE CLAYTON ACT

The Clayton Act, which was enacted on October 15, 1914, was an expression of Congress's desire to outlaw specific business practices that were thought to be anticompetitive. Although our subsequent discussion of how the law has been applied will be critical at times, the law itself expressed Congress's concern for consumer welfare and the distributive problems caused by market power. This can be seen in the specific practices that were condemned. These business practices fall into three main categories: (1) price discrimination, (2) exclusionary practices, and (3) mergers. We shall examine each of these very briefly.

1. Price discrimination.[16] Section 2 of the Clayton Act, as amended by the Robinson-Patman Act in 1936, deals with price discrimination. Congress banned price discrimination in circumstances where it was believed to have anticompetitive effects:

> Sec. 2(a) That it shall be unlawful for any person engaged in commerce, . . . either directly or indirectly, to discriminate in price between different

---

[16] Chapter 10 provides an economic analysis of price discrimination along with a development of the cases.

purchasers of commodities of like grade and quality, . . . where the effect of such discrimination may be substantially to lessen competition or tend to create a monopoly in any line of commerce, or to injure, destroy, or prevent competition with any person who either grants or knowingly receives the benefit of such discrimination, or with customers of either of them.

Since Congress did not want to penalize efficiency where the consequent cost savings were passed on to the consumer in the form of lower prices, there is a proviso in Section 2(a) that permits a cost justification defense. In practice, the cost justification proviso has rarely proved to be of much use to businesses because the standard of proof is so high. Nonetheless, in principle, a firm may be able to justify price differences on the basis of differences in costs. For example, volume discounts may be justified due to economies in delivery costs.

Section 2(b) provides a "good faith" defense of meeting competition. This allows a seller to protect himself against offers of low prices to selected customers without having to cut his price to all customers. The language of Section 2(b) allows a threatened seller to meet—but not beat—a low price offer of a rival irrespective of the effect upon competition among the customers.

Congress was alert to the fact that businessmen are clever people who are capable of offering lower prices through indirect means. In order to make the prohibition meaningful, Congress sought to exclude these indirect efforts. For example, one way of obtaining a discriminatorily low price is to pretend that a discount is a brokerage commission. Section 2(c) forbids such a sham transaction.

Another way that a buyer may receive discriminatorily favorable treatment is through the provision of promotional allowances and services. These allowances and services include (*a*) cooperative advertising in the local media (e.g., an automobile manufacturer may pay for part of the local dealer's newspaper advertising); (*b*) provision of a demonstrator in the buyer's retail facility; and (*c*) provision of display materials for retail sales. Sections 2(d) and 2(e) prohibit discriminatory behavior in providing promotional allowances and services. In Section 2(d), the seller is prohibited from making discriminatory payments to a favored buyer so that the buyer can perform the promotional function on behalf of the seller. In Section 2(e), the seller is prohibited from supplying the promotional services themselves on a discriminatory basis.

Finally, the act recognizes that a large buyer may have a considerable bargaining advantage over a small, specialized supplier. To the extent that a supplier is heavily dependent upon the sales to a single buyer for its existence, that buyer can, under certain conditions, extract significant concessions from the supplier. Unlike the traditional price discrimination model of economic theory, the seller may be reluctant to offer a lower price to a particular buyer or class of buyers. Nonetheless, he may do so because of the economic sanctions that the large buyer may impose. Such pressure is prohibited by Section 2(f), which imposes liability upon the large buyer that extracts illegal concessions from relatively smaller sellers.

2. Exclusionary practices.[17] Section 3 of the Clayton Act prohibits conditional sales where such sales have an adverse effect on competition. This section has been used to forbid *tying arrangements* where the purchaser can buy product A only if he also buys product B, *requirements contracts* where the buyer agrees to purchase all of his requirements for a particular commodity from a single seller, *exclusive dealing* where the buyer agrees not to handle competing lines of merchandise, and imposition of *territorial confinement* where a buyer is not allowed to resell the product outside a carefully delineated territory. Note that the act requires a substantial, adverse effect on competition before the business practice violates the law:

> Sec. 3. That it shall be unlawful for any person engaged in commerce . . . to lease or make a sale of goods, wares, merchandise, machinery, supplies, or other commodities, whether patented or unpatented, . . . on the condition, agreement, or understanding that the lessee or purchaser thereof shall not use or deal in the goods, wares, merchandise, machinery, supplies, or other commodities of a competitor or competitors of the lessor or seller, where the effect . . . may be to substantially lessen competition or tend to create a monopoly in any line of commerce.

3. Mergers. Section 2 of the Sherman Act deals in a remedial way with problems of market structure. In contrast, Section 7 of the Clayton Act, which was amended by the Cellar-Kefauver Act of 1950, provides some preventive measures. More specifically, Section 7 forbids a merger where a possible substantial lessening of competition or tendency toward monopoly would accompany the merger. This can be a useful tool of public policy to prevent the sort of market structure that is conducive to collusive behavior or single-firm dominance. In the language of Section 7, notice the requirement for determining appropriate geographic market and product-line definitions:

> Sec. 7. That no corporation engaged in commerce shall acquire, directly or indirectly, the whole or any part of the stock or other share capital and no corporation subject to the jurisdiction of the Federal Trade Commission shall acquire the whole or any part of the assets of another corporation engaged also in commerce, where in any line of commerce in any section of the country, the effect of such acquisition may be substantially to lessen competition, or tend to create a monopoly.

---

[17] Tying arrangements are examined in Chapter 15, exclusive dealing is developed in Chapter 16, and territorial restrictions are discussed in Chapter 14. Each chapter provides both an economic analysis and a case development.

As we shall see in subsequent chapters, Section 7 of the Clayton Act applies to horizontal, vertical, and conglomerate mergers.[18]

3–6 THE FEDERAL TRADE COMMISSION ACT

In addition to the Sherman Act's broad prohibitions, there was another feature that disturbed some people: the lack of an agency specifically designed to implement and enforce the act. Prior to the Sherman Act, we had the Interstate Commerce Act, which did provide for an administrative agency that would develop the expertise necessary to aid enforcement of that act. Thus, there was ample precedent for such an agency. Dissatisfied with the performance of the Department of Justice in enforcing the Sherman Act, there was growing sentiment for some form of interstate trade commission to supplement the Department of Justice's efforts. Interestingly, there was support for this notion from those hostile to big business and from big business itself. This should have alerted one and all to the dangers of such a commission, but the Federal Trade Commission Act was enacted on September 26, 1914. The major provision of the act empowers the FTC to discipline business behavior:

> Sec. 5(a)(1) Unfair methods of competition in or affecting commerce, and unfair or deceptive acts or practices in or affecting commerce, are hereby declared unlawful.

The primary economic rationale for a prohibition of unfair methods of competition resided in the belief that monopoly power was transitory without the exercise of unfair business practices. Accordingly, by outlawing such unfair methods of competition, society would be free of entrenched monopolies. Additionally, a specialized agency with delegated rulemaking authority can respond more effectively than Congress to new abuses and new unfair practices. Moreover, a specialized agency can shape remedies with greater flexibility than the judiciary. It can employ experts to advise the commissioners on a continuing basis during both the rulemaking and adjudicative phases of the proceedings.

3–7 PUBLIC ENFORCEMENT

There are two federal government antitrust authorities: the Antitrust Division of the Department of Justice and the Federal Trade Commission. The Antitrust Division can enforce the Sherman Act through civil suits or through criminal suits. As we have seen, violations of Sections 1

---

[18] A separate chapter is devoted to each type of merger. Both the economic analysis and case development for horizontal mergers is provided in Chapter 9, for vertical mergers in Chapter 12, and for conglomerate mergers in Chapter 17.

and 2 of the Sherman Act can result in criminal penalties of fines up to $100,000, imprisonment of individuals up to three years, or both. The actual fines and prison sentences that follow from criminal prosecution rarely are very severe.[19] In fact, the deterrent effect of the criminal penalties probably is not too large. Of course, we cannot be sure of this because an adequate assessment requires knowing how many potential violations actually were deterred, which we cannot determine very easily.[20] The Clayton Act does not provide for criminal sanctions. Thus, the Antitrust Division proceeds through civil suits in enforcing the Clayton Act.

The headquarters of the Antitrust Division is in Washington, and there are field offices in Chicago, Cleveland, Los Angeles, New York, Philadelphia, and San Francisco. More than 300 lawyers are employed by the Antitrust Division and about the same number of other professionals. Its budget is about $30 million.

The Federal Trade Commission has no power to proceed in criminal suits. It does, however, have concurrent responsibility for enforcing the Clayton Act. As one might expect, the commission also enforces Section 5(a) of the Federal Trade Commission Act. Since many business practices that violate the Sherman Act may also be challenged as unfair methods of competition, the FTC's concurrent jurisdiction is even broader than is immediately apparent. In order to avoid duplication and conflict between the Antitrust Division and the FTC, formal liaison procedures have been established.

A remark on case selection

Precious little in life is free. Consequently, the antitrust enforcement agencies cannot pursue every possible antitrust case. Choices have to be made and the most serious offenses selected for prosecution. We would hope that the cases are selected on a rational basis in an effort to further the goals of antitrust. Fortunately, there is some empirical evidence on this point.

To some extent, the deadweight welfare loss due to monopoly provides the rationale for our antitrust policy. Since this policy is implemented through the enforcement agencies, it is of some interest to find out whether their case selection is influenced by welfare losses. Long, Schramm, and Tollison were the first to take a systematic look at this

---

[19] For a discussion of antitrust penalties, see Kenneth Elzinga and William Breit, *The Antitrust Penalties* (New Haven, Conn.: Yale University Press, 1976), or Roger D. Blair, "Antitrust Penalties: Deterrence and Compensation," *Utah Law Review* 1980, no. 1, pp. 57–72.

[20] More will be said about this in the final chapter.

question.[21] They attempted to explain the case-bringing activity of the Justice Department in broadly defined industries. First, they calculated two different formulations of the welfare triangle and then used each of these as an explanatory variable in two separate regression equations. In each regression equation, the dependent variable was the number of cases brought. What they wanted to determine was whether the Antitrust Division tended to bring more cases in those broadly defined industries where the potential for improved consumer welfare was greatest. Even though such a test is fairly crude, their statistical results were rather disappointing. In one equation, the size of the welfare loss was not even statistically significant, and the explanatory power of both equations was quite low. This cast some doubt as to whether the Antitrust Division was selecting its cases appropriately.

Long, Schramm, and Tollison, however, neglected one rather important factor: nonprice competition. In many industries that have an oligopolistic structure, costs are raised as a result of nonprice competition. This makes the apparent profit look smaller than it should for purposes of calculating social welfare losses. We sought to correct this by calculating the average advertising expenditures for the 20 broad industries that were used and adding this to the average industry profits. While it is true that not all advertising is nonprice competition, it is also true that not all nonprice competition is advertising. Our purpose was to make an effort to account for the higher costs in those industries that engage in substantial nonprice competition. When the corrected profit figures were used and the regressions repeated, the statistical results were greatly improved. Both welfare loss measures were highly significant statistically. Moreover, the explanatory power of both equations was greatly improved. Crude as they are, these statistical results suggest that the Antitrust Division does make some attempt to maximize the consumer welfare gains from its limited budget.

Criminal prosecution and civil action

After the Antitrust Division decides that there may be an antitrust violation, it must choose between criminal prosecution and civil action. This selection will be influenced by what the Antitrust Division hopes to accomplish. A criminal case punishes offenders for their past behavior. Accordingly, it provides a powerful deterrent to further transgressions.

---

[21] See W. F. Long, R. Schramm, and R. Tollison, "The Economic Determinants of Antitrust Activity," *Journal of Law and Economics* 16 (October 1973), pp. 351–64. The discussion here depends upon Roger D. Blair and David L. Kaserman, "Market Structure and Costs: An Explanation of the Behavior of the Antitrust Authorities," *Antitrust Bulletin* 21 (Winter 1976), pp. 691–702.

Most antitrust offenders, however, are not people whom others would characterize as hard-core criminals. In fact, they are usually considered to be pillars of the community with unsullied reputations. As a result, criminal sanctions are not necessary to protect society from continued violations. Moreover, the antitrust criminal generally is not in need of rehabilitation. But the dominant theory of the antitrust criminal sanction is neither retribution nor rehabilitation. Instead, it is deterrence, and criminal prosecution with corresponding sentencing provides for general deterrence. Severely punishing today's defendant will discourage others from committing similar acts. The lack of moral culpability or a need for rehabilitation should not make the Antitrust Division reluctant to seek stiff penalties. In fact, the character of the crime rather than the character of the offender should determine the decision to proceed with a criminal prosecution.

While criminal prosecution may provide a powerful deterrent, it does not change the status quo in the industry involved. For example, if a firm were found guilty of illegally monopolizing an industry, fines would not alter the structure of the industry. If the government would like to obtain some remedial action, it must proceed in a civil suit. An illegally obtained monopoly could be dismantled as a result of a successful civil suit. In some instances, the Antitrust Division will challenge the same offense both civilly and criminally to punish the offender and to prevent future recurrence of the antitrust violation.

3–8 ANTITRUST EXEMPTIONS

The broad language of the Sherman Act embraces all sectors of our economy. Consequently, any exceptions must be specified in amending legislation. In fact, several sectors of our economy have been exempted from antitrust coverage for a variety of reasons. The central goal of antitrust policy is the promotion of consumer welfare through reliance upon competitive market forces. Exemptions to the law's insistence upon competition are necessary whenever Congress decides that competition is not appropriate in a particular sector of the economy. This may occur when society wants to grant monopoly power as in the case of patents. It may also occur when competition is impractical, as when technology dictates that a single firm will produce the necessary output more efficiently than would several firms. In those instances, the industries are usually regulated directly to protect the consumer. In addition, there are other sectors where Congress has decided to permit deviations from competition to benefit the members of those sectors—for example, labor and agriculture. We shall mention several of these exempted areas to provide a little better feel for the limits of antitrust policy.

Labor

Unorganized labor is naturally competitive. As with any other productive input, the price of labor services would be dictated by supply and demand. The result of this process is that some people will receive low incomes and thereby suffer a low standard of living. One response to this has been to form labor unions to organize the efforts of the workers. Once organized into a union, the workers have some measure of monopoly power. But a union restrains trade and thereby violates the Sherman Act. Congress, however, did not intend to forbid labor unions and enacted an exemption to permit their development.

In 1914, the Clayton Act (Section 6) specifically removed labor services from antitrust coverage through a legal maneuver. It declared that "the labor of a human being is not a commodity or article of commerce." This defines away the problem for labor unions. Later, in Section 20, the Clayton Act protects union activity from injunctions that would forbid traditional union activities such as strikes. Subsequent legislation, the Norris–La Guardia Act of 1932, reinforced the protection provided by the Clayton Act.

Labor's exemption is not absolute. But as long as a labor union is pursuing its own interest and those of its members, it is exempt from antitrust policy. Even in the event that a union's success will impair the competitive process, that union's activity is still exempt provided that the union is not colluding with the employer. If, however, a union conspires with one employer to put another employer out of business, the conspiracy is subject to antitrust enforcement.

Agricultural cooperatives

In the past, buyers of agricultural products often exploited asymmetries of information and obtained low prices from farmers with perishable products to sell. In response to this, farmers formed marketing cooperatives to sell their output. By combining their outputs, the farmers obviously were not competing with each other. Section 6 of the Clayton Act and the Capper-Volstead Act of 1922 provide an antitrust exemption for this kind of activity. The Secretary of Agriculture is supposed to make sure that these marketing cooperatives do not increase prices too much.

There are several limits to this exemption. First, a cooperative cannot conspire with competitors to set prices or restrain trade. It can only set price for the output of its members. Second, a cooperative cannot employ predatory practices that are geared to stifling competition. Third, the Secretary of Agriculture can step in if the cooperative is too successful in raising price. Finally, raising price does a minimal amount of good without corresponding reductions in the volume of output. It is not clear that a concerted reduction of output among the cooperative's members would be legal.

Regulated industries

Many industries seem to be technologically incompatible with competition. This occurs when a firm of minimum efficient scale[22] is very large relative to the size of the market. In other words, we are faced with a natural monopoly. A blind insistence upon competition would lead to pricing below average cost. The result, of course, would be continual exit until only one firm remained. Antitrust prosecution of the natural monopolist is not sensible because a more competitive market structure is not possible. The public policy response to this situation has been direct regulation of prices, outputs, and entry.

Those industries that are or have been regulated due to natural monopoly include telecommunications, transportation, electric power generation, and petroleum pipelines. These industries are subject to regulation by agencies specifically empowered to limit their exercise of monopoly power. As a result, each industry enjoys some antitrust immunity. The precise scope of the immunity depends upon the language of the statute that established the regulatory agency. Each industry must discover the limits of its antitrust exemption.

Patents

The patent law explicitly confers a monopoly upon an inventor to encourage inventive effort. Patent rights extend for 17 years and prevent others from producing the inventor's product. Obviously, this is inconsistent with the competition fostered by the antitrust laws. Nonetheless, public policy exempts patent holders from antitrust prosecution as they exploit their monopoly.

QUESTIONS AND PROBLEMS

1. How does inadequate transportation lead to local monopoly?

2. Unreliable market information provides some monopoly power. Why?

3. During the Civil War, demand for many products grew substantially. Industries expanded as a result. Why did concentration within these industries fail to increase?

---

[22] A plant is said to be of "minimum efficient scale" if it is large enough to produce output at the lowest per unit cost that is technically feasible.

4. How can economies of scale in production plus competition among business firms lead to increases in concentration and a decrease in competition?

5. Suppose that the Lightning Bolt provided the only rail transportation between Cedar Rapids, Iowa, and Chicago in 1883. Farmers had to ship their corn to Chicago on the Lightning Bolt. Some have claimed that the railroad would charge all that the traffic would bear. What rate would you have charged? Show this rate determination graphically. Is this "all the traffic will bear"?

6. How was Standard Oil in a position to extract secret rebates from the railroads when its competitors could not obtain similar price concessions? Is this power of the big buyer called monopsony?

7. Suppose that the Sherman Act was implemented such that full and free competition reigned. Some people feel that the preservation of small economic units (e.g., "Mom and Pop" grocery stores) is a desirable social goal. First, why might this be inconsistent with consumer welfare? Second, why might the social goal be inconsistent with the Sherman Act as we have supposed it to be implemented?

8. Under White's rule of reason, only unreasonable restraints of trade violate the Sherman Act. Suppose some defendants explain that they fixed reasonable prices (i.e., prices that avoided ruinous competition). In evaluating fixed prices, how would you determine whether fixed prices were reasonable or not?

9. Suppose the widget industry was composed of eight firms. Dismayed at racial discrimination in the United States, the chief executives decided to do something about it through a vigorous recruitment effort. But this program required some excess profit which the firms did not have since competition was fierce. Consequently, the firms fixed prices above the competitive level and used all of the profits generated to combat racial discrimination. How should a court rule?

10. As an economic proposition, price discrimination exists when the price-marginal cost ratio for one customer is different from the price-marginal cost ratio for another customer. Does the Robinson-Patman Act (Section 2 of the Clayton Act) cover all instances of price discrimination?

11. A conglomerate merger is a merger between two firms that are in wholly unrelated businesses. For example, a taxicab company might

buy an ice-cream producer. In principle, this merger is covered by Section 7 of the Clayton Act. Can you think of a way in which such a merger could substantially lessen competition or tend to create a monopoly? Be sure to decide on the product market—cabs or ice-cream cones.

12. Suppose a seller has unexploited economies of scale (i.e., he is producing on the negatively sloped portion of this average cost curve). Show that a large buyer can pay a price below cost and that the seller will be better off as a result.

13. The economic value of a firm is equal to the present value of the future stream of profits that the firm will generate. For the owner of a firm to capitalize fully the profit stream, it may be necessary for him to promise not to compete with the new owners. Should such a promise be illegal under the Sherman Act? If so, what are the consequences?

14. Why would Standard Oil set up sham independents to force real independents out of business? How else could Standard Oil have neutralized these rivals?

15. Explain the economic argument in favor of an antitrust policy opposed to monopoly.

16. Suppose small producers are inefficient producers. If antitrust policy seeks to promote small producers, will this be inconsistent with the promotion of consumer welfare?

FURTHER READINGS

Blair, Roger D., and David L. Kaserman. "Market Structure and Costs: An Explanation of the Behavior of the Antitrust Authorities." *Antitrust Bulletin* 21 (Winter 1976), pp. 691–702.

Bork, Robert H. "Legislative Intent and the Policy of the Sherman Act." *Journal of Law and Economics* 9 (April 1966), pp. 7–48.

———. *The Antitrust Paradox.* New York: Basic Books, 1978.

Lande, Robert H. "Wealth Transfers as the Original and Primary Concern of Antitrust: The Efficiency Interpretation Challenged." *Hastings Law Journal* 34 (September 1982), pp. 61–151.

Letwin, William. *Law and Economic Policy in America.* New York: Random House, 1965.

Thorelli, Hans B. *The Federal Antitrust Policy.* Winchester, Mass.: Allen & Unwin, 1954.

4

Private enforcement

4–1 INTRODUCTION

Since each individual is presumed to make decisions in an effort to maximize utility, it is difficult to legislate behavior that is not consistent with the self-interest of those involved. As we have seen, the antitrust laws make certain types of business activity and behavior illegal to the detriment of would-be monopolists. Accordingly, this legislation would not accomplish much without some sort of penalty for violating the law. With respect to Sections 1 and 2 of the Sherman Act, violations are crimes; in fact, they are felonies. The maximum personal fines and jail sentences are not trivial and could serve as a powerful deterrent to antitrust violations. In practice, however, the deterrent effect is much reduced because of two important factors. First, the evidentiary standards are high in criminal cases; thus, placing the blame on specific individuals is not easy in most antitrust cases. Second, even when individual violators can be identified, the courts have been reluctant to impose much more than token penalties. During the 1966–74 period when the maximum sentence was one year, there were 90 individuals named in 18 cases where jail sentences or probation were imposed. Of these, 65 served no time at all, 20 served 30 days or less, and only 5 served in excess of 30 days.[1] Given that an antitrust violation is detected, that the

---

[1] These data were extracted from Kenneth Elzinga and William Breit, *The Antitrust Penalties* (New Haven, Conn.: Yale University Press, 1976), pp. 34–37.

individual violator is convicted, and that the judge elects to impose a prison sentence or a probationary period, the average time to be served was 12.8 days. Thus, the *conditional* expected prison term appears to be something less than two weeks for a deliberate violation of the antitrust laws. Considering the fact that price fixing is a clandestine activity so that not all violations are detected and jail sentences are not imposed in every case, the potential price fixer appropriately could assign a low probability to serving any time for price fixing.

Fines similarly have been low in antitrust cases. Although the maximum fine was $50,000 for both corporations and individuals from 1955 to 1974, the full maximum was rarely imposed. For example, during the 1955–68 period, the average individual fine was just over $3,000.[2] The spectre of a $50,000 personal fine could not have been very haunting in light of this evidence.

Supplementing the public enforcement sanctions is Section 4 of the Clayton Act, which provides an incentive for private enforcement. This provision allows anyone who has been injured by price fixing to sue in federal court and recover treble damages plus the costs of the suit, including a reasonable attorney's fee:

> Sec. 4. That any person who shall be injured in his business or property by reason of anything forbidden in the antitrust laws may sue therefore in any district court of the United States in the district in which the defendant resides or is found or has an agent, without respect to the amount in controversy, and shall recover threefold the damages by him sustained, and the cost of suit, including a reasonable attorney's fee.

The impact of judicial interpretation of Section 4 has had a mixed effect on its viability as an adjunct to public enforcement. For example, there are complex and confusing issues regarding a potential plaintiff's standing to sue. These issues serve mainly to limit the classes of plaintiffs with standing. Most commentators seem to feel that developments in private suits since 1960 have tended to strengthen the impact of the antitrust prohibition of price fixing. But this consensus is not based upon empirical evidence of deterrence at work. Rather, it is based upon the conclusion that the private plaintiff's chances of a successful suit have improved.

These developments have resulted in an explosion of private antitrust actions in recent years. From 1890 until 1940, very few private actions were initiated and even fewer were successful.[3] Things did not get much better in the decade of the 1950s.[4] Since 1960, however, things changed

---

[2] See Richard A. Posner, "A Statistical Study of Antitrust Enforcement," *Journal of Law and Economics* 13 (October 1970), pp. 365–420, at pp. 365 and 392.

[3] From 1890 to 1940, only 175 private damage cases went to trial, and the plaintiffs prevailed in only 13.

[4] From 1952 to 1958, plaintiffs prevailed in only 20 of 144 cases.

dramatically for several reasons: (1) the Supreme Court reduced the procedural hurdles for private plaintiffs, (2) the Supreme Court broadened liability during the 1960s, and (3) there were changes in the rules governing class action suits, which will be discussed later in this chapter. The impact upon the incentives for private suits can be seen in the number of private cases filed, which is shown in Table 4–1. As a conse-

TABLE 4–1   Private antitrust cases

Fiscal year filed	Number filed*	Fiscal year filed	Number filed*
1960	228	1972	1,203
1961	341	1973	1,089
1962	266	1974	1,162
1963	283	1975	1,334
1964	317	1976	1,416
1965	443	1977	1,528
1966	444	1978	1,321
1967	536	1979	1,208
1968	659	1980	1,457
1969	740	1981	1,292
1970	877	1982	1,037
1971	1,003	1983	1,192

* There were a large number of private suits that followed in the wake of the government's successful suit involving the electrical equipment conspiracy. These were deleted to make the comparison more meaningful.
Source: Annual Reports of the Director of the Administrative Office of the United States Courts.

quence, private enforcement through the treble damage provision may have assumed the major burden of deterring price fixing. In the balance of this chapter, we shall examine the legal and economic problems surrounding private enforcement.

4–2 ANTITRUST STANDING[5]

The term "antitrust standing" denotes the status of being a proper party to pursue a private antitrust suit. If one lacks antitrust standing, one does not have the right to sue for treble damages. Thus, it is crucial to determine the dimensions of antitrust standing.

The language of Section 4 of the Clayton Act seems fairly clear. It appears to confer a property right on any person who has been injured due to an antitrust violation. But this apparently clear language has been

---

[5] There is a massive literature on antitrust standing. The best single source is Daniel Berger and Roger Bernstein, "An Analytical Framework for Antitrust Standing," *Yale Law Journal* 86 (April 1977), pp. 809–83.

muddied by the rulings of several lower courts. We shall examine several criteria for standing: who is a "person," what is "business or property," what is "antitrust injury," the requirement of direct injury, and *in pari delicto.*

Who is a "person"?

The statutory language, "person," refers to natural persons as one might suppose. In addition, it includes corporations, partnerships, and other businesses. Moreover, the Supreme Court ruled that municipalities are "persons" for purposes of antitrust standing.[6] It turns out the United States government is not a "person" in its capacity as an injured customer for purposes of treble damage actions.[7] In contrast, individual states[8] and foreign governments,[9] as injured consumers, are considered to be "persons." Apparently, the Court reasoned that permitting damage recoveries by states and by foreign governments would provide compensation to antitrust victims and would assist in deterring future violations.

What is "business or property"?

Section 4 permits a person to be compensated when an antitrust violation has caused injury to his "business or property." Precisely what constitutes business or property is not abundantly clear. For the most part, an injury to a person's financial interests are compensable. This includes the financial interests of a consumer who has been overcharged by a seller pursuant to an antitrust violation. This last issue was resolved categorically by the Supreme Court in its *Reiter* v. *Sonotone Corp.* decision.[10]

Reiter was a retail purchaser of hearing aids for personal use who brought a suit for treble damages against five hearing-aid manufacturers. The manufacturers argued that Reiter lacked standing to sue because the statutory language "business or property" means "business activity or property related to one's business." The Court was unim-

---

[6] *Chattanooga Foundry & Pipe Works* v. *City of Atlanta,* 203 U.S. 390, 396 (1906).

[7] *United States* v. *Cooper Corp.,* 312 U.S. 600 (1941). Congress subsequently amended Section 4A to permit suits for *single* damages:

> Sec. 4A. Whenever the United States is hereafter injured in its business or property by reason of anything forbidden in the antitrust laws, it may sue therefore in the United States district court for the district in which the defendant resides or is found or has an agent, without respect to the amount in controversy, and shall recover actual damages by it sustained and the cost of the suit.

[8] *Georgia* v. *Evans,* 316 U.S. 159 (1942).

[9] *Pfizer, Inc.* v. *Government of India,* 434 U.S. 308 (1978).

[10] 442 U.S. 330 (1979).

pressed by this "strained construction" of the statutory language. It ruled that ". . . a consumer not engaged in a 'business' enterprise, but rather acquiring goods or services for personal use, is injured in 'property' when the price of those goods or services is artificially inflated by reason of the anticompetitive conduct complained of." Thus, consumers have standing to sue for treble damages when an antitrust violation results in noncompetitive prices being paid.

The judiciary has required that a plaintiff's injury must be the direct result of an antitrust violation and not an incidental result. For example, suppose that a new entrant into the fast-food restaurant business, B&K Burgers, was driven out of the industry through predatory activities of the established firms. Based upon the plain language of Section 4, B&K Burgers would have standing to sue. There are a host of others, however, who could suffer economic injury and be denied standing to sue. For example, the landlord who owned the building being used by B&K Burgers would suffer lost revenue but be unable to sue. In addition, the former employees of B&K, who are now out of jobs, would suffer an economic loss that they could not recover. Sullivan[11] suggests that these potential plaintiffs, along with suppliers, stockholders, and creditors, are denied standing due to an increasing reliance on rules of evidence that simplify the proof of a violation to such an extent that no one can be sure that any significant competitive injury has occurred. The lower courts have responded by denying standing to private plaintiffs as a crude way of screening out suits that may have little merit. This approach is not satisfactory because it is not refined enough, but little can be done until standing issues are resolved by the Supreme Court.

Antitrust injury

The Supreme Court introduced the concept of "antitrust injury" in its *Brunswick* decision.[12] This concept is useful in defining compensable injuries. It is not really an element of standing in the narrow sense of who can recover for an injury. Nonetheless, the antitrust injury doctrine is used as a limiting device, which reduces the number of private suits.

In the late 1950s, Brunswick's sales of bowling lanes, automatic pinsetters, and related equipment soared along with interest in bowling generally. Most of Brunswick's sales were on credit to the bowling alley operator. When the popularity of bowling waned in the 1960s, Brunswick's sales fell, and it was faced with defaulting bowling centers. Sell-

---

[11] Lawrence Sullivan, *Handbook of the Law of Antitrust* (St. Paul, Minn.: West Publishing, 1977), pp. 772–74.

[12] *Brunswick Corp.* v. *Pueblo Bowl-O-Mat, Inc.* 429 U.S. 477 (1977). For an economic analysis of antitrust injury, see William H. Page, "Antitrust Damages and Economic Efficiency: An Approach to Antitrust Injury," *University of Chicago Law Review* 47 (Spring 1980), pp. 467–504.

ing or leasing repossessed equipment met with limited success, and Brunswick was in great financial difficulty. As a result, it began to acquire and operate the failing bowling centers in order to salvage as much as it could financially.

Pueblo, a rival bowling center that was not affiliated with Brunswick, filed suit claiming that the acquisitions violated Section 7 of the Clayton Act, which prohibits mergers that may have an anticompetitive effect. The theory was that Brunswick's size enabled it to reduce competition by driving smaller rivals out of business. A jury agreed that Brunswick's acquisitions violated Section 7. Pueblo then claimed damages on the grounds that if Brunswick had allowed the failing bowling centers to close, then Pueblo's profits would have been larger. In other words, except for Brunswick's actions, Pueblo would have had a larger share of the total market and the increased profits that would have accompanied that larger share.

The Supreme Court agreed that Pueblo's profits were lower than they would have been absent Brunswick's illegal merger. But it ruled that Pueblo had not suffered an injury that was compensable under the antitrust laws. Since the antitrust laws were enacted to protect competition, not competitors, it would be bizarre to compensate Pueblo for the profits it would have earned had competition been reduced.

The Court provided some further guidance on the nature of antitrust injury:

> Plaintiffs must prove *antitrust* injury, which is to say injury of the type the antitrust laws were intended to prevent and that flows from that which makes defendants' acts unlawful. The injury should reflect the anticompetitive effect either of the violation or of anticompetitive acts made possible by the violation.

Thus, the antitrust injury doctrine is quite simple to apply in practice. First, one must determine what the anticompetitive effects of a particular violation are. Then, one must infer the logical consequences of those anticompetitive effects. If a plaintiff has been injured in his property or person due to the anticompetitive effects of an antitrust violation, then he would have suffered antitrust injury under the *Brunswick* rule. Any injury that is not a consequence of the anticompetitive effects of an antitrust violation would not be antitrust injury. Such an injury, therefore, would not be compensable under the remedial provisions of Section 4 of the Clayton Act.

The requirement of direct injury

The Supreme Court introduced the requirement that a plaintiff be injured directly in order to have standing to sue in its *Hanover Shoe* and

Illinois Brick decisions.[13] Its purpose in doing so was to reduce complicated matters of proving damages when the guilty parties do not sell directly to final consumers. These complications can be appreciated by examining a simple example.

Suppose that bread is baked and sold to retail grocery stores by four bakeries which act independently in setting their prices. Let us assume that the retail grocery industry is competitively organized. Initially, the competitive equilibrium price and quantity of bread at retail are P_1 and Q_1, respectively, in Figure 4–1. Now, suppose that the four bakeries get together and raise the price of a loaf of bread. This causes the supply curve of retail bread to shift in Figure 4–1 with the result that the quantity demanded falls to Q_2 while the retail price increases to P_2. By com-

FIGURE 4–1

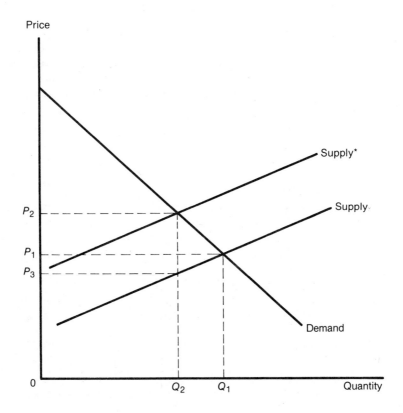

---

[13] *Hanover Shoe* v. *United Shoe Machinery Corp.*, 392 U.S. 481 (1968) and *Illinois Brick Co.* v. *Illinois*, 431 U.S. 720 (1977).

paring the two supply curves at Q_2, we can see that the price of the bread to the grocery stores increased by $P_2 - P_3$. Part of the price increase, $P_2 - P_1$, was passed on to the final consumers while part of the price increase, $P_1 - P_3$, was absorbed by the grocery stores. If everyone who was injured by the illegal price increase were granted standing to sue, proof of how much was passed on would have to be offered. In the illustration presented in Figure 4–1, this does not appear to be terribly difficult. The extent of the passing on, however, is influenced by both supply and demand elasticities. In addition, the problem is complicated when the illegal activity is far removed from the final consumer stage. For example, the producers of a raw material may set an illegal price that is charged to a processor who produces an intermediate good which is used by another manufacturer. If that manufacturer sells its output to wholesalers who sell to retailers who sell to the final consumer, one begins to appreciate the problems of proof.[14] Further problems are encountered when the illegal price is imposed upon an input that is combined in variable proportions with other inputs in the production process.[15]

The Supreme Court decisions have limited standing to direct purchasers. In *Hanover Shoe*, a producer of shoes who leased shoe machinery from United Shoe claimed that United's lease policy was an instrument of illegal monopolization of the shoe machinery industry. Hanover argued that it was entitled to receive the difference between what it paid in rentals and what it would have paid if United had sold its machines. In response, United argued that Hanover suffered no cognizable injury because the illegal overcharge was passed on to Hanover's customers in the form of higher shoe prices. The Supreme Court was unimpressed with United's argument and held that Hanover was entitled to the full overcharge. The Court expressed concern that, if permitted, the passing-on defense would be used by defendants with the result that "[t]reble-damage actions would often require additional long and complicated proceedings involving massive evidence and complicated theories."

The *Illinois Brick* decision made the rule regarding passing-on symmetric. Whereas *Hanover Shoe* precluded the use of passing-on as a defense, *Illinois Brick* precluded its use offensively. The defendants manu-

---

[14] Two articles that analyze this issue and reach opposite conclusions are William M. Landes and Richard A. Posner, "Should Indirect Purchasers Have Standing to Sue under the Antitrust Laws? An Economic Analysis of the Rule of Illinois Brick," *University of Chicago Law Review* 46 (Spring 1979), pp. 602–35, and Robert G. Harris and Lawrence A. Sullivan, "Passing on the Monopoly Overcharge: A Comprehensive Policy Analysis," *University of Pennsylvania Law Review* 128 (December 1979), pp. 269–360.

[15] For an economic analysis, see Robert Cooter, "Passing on the Monopoly Overcharge: A Further Comment on Economic Theory," *University of Pennsylvania Law Review* 129 (June 1981), pp. 1523–32.

factured and sold concrete block primarily to masonry contractors in the Chicago area. These contractors submitted bids to general contractors for the masonry portion of construction projects. In turn, the general contractors submitted bids to the State of Illinois and some 700 local government entities. Thus, the state and these 700 governmental entities were indirect purchasers of concrete block. The issue before the Supreme Court was whether these indirect purchasers could sue for treble damages. On the one hand, the plaintiffs wanted to prove that some of the alleged illegal overcharges had been passed on to them. On the other hand, the manufacturers pointed out that permitting indirect purchasers to do so would lead to duplicative awards unless *Hanover Shoe* were overruled.

The Supreme Court refused to overrule its *Hanover Shoe* decision and went on to point out that

> [p]ermitting the use of pass-on theories under §4 essentially would transform treble-damage actions into massive efforts to apportion the recovery among all potential plaintiffs that could have absorbed part of the overcharge—from direct purchasers to middlemen to ultimate consumers. However appealing this attempt to allocate the overcharge might seem in theory, it would add whole new dimensions of complexity to treble-damage suits and seriously undermine their effectiveness.

Thus, the Supreme Court's rule regarding a pass-on argument is symmetric. Only direct purchasers have standing to sue.

In pari delicto[16]

The *in pari delicto* defense essentially is an assertion that the plaintiff was a willing participant in the illegal scheme and, therefore, should be barred from suing. A variation of this is an assertion that the plaintiff was engaged in an independent antitrust violation that led to the defendant's activities. It is understandable that a plaintiff with unclean hands is not a sympathetic character. Accordingly, the courts have been a little reluctant to reward such a plaintiff with treble damages.

In its *Perma Life*[17] decision, however, the Supreme Court made it clear that an *in pari delicto* defense would not be looked upon with much favor. Unless the plaintiff is a fully equal participant in an illegal scheme, claims of unclean hands will not bar the plaintiff from pursuing *treble damages*. The rationale for this attitude is that such suits will further the overriding public policy in favor of competition by enhancing the deterrent effect of the antitrust laws.

---

[16] *In pari delicto* means "of equal fault."

[17] *Perma Life Mufflers, Inc.* v. *International Parts Corp.*, 392 U.S. 134 (1968).

4–3 DAMAGES

The language of Section 4 provides for the recovery of three times the damages suffered as a result of an antitrust violation. This provision serves as a powerful financial inducement for injured parties to press their claims. As a result, private actions assist in the enforcement of the antitrust laws due to the deterrent effect of treble damages.[18] A large amount of time and effort goes into proving damages and estimating their dollar volume in private antitrust suits. In this section, we shall examine the reasons for this as well as the legal authority for the approaches to damage calculations that have been employed.

Properly measuring damages

The courts have focused upon damages as a means of compensating antitrust victims when addressing the question of how to measure damages properly. If an antitrust violation causes a business to lose profits, it can sue for the value of the lost profits. If a firm or a consumer has paid too much for a good or service due to an antitrust violation, the suit will be for the overcharges. In either case, the measure of damage is roughly equal to the wealth transferred to the monopolist from the buyers. This, of course, is not the "correct" amount in terms of social welfare. To see this, consider Figure 4–2, which depicts industry demand D, marginal revenue MR, and industry marginal cost MC. The competitive price and output are given by P_C and Q_C, respectively, while the monopoly price and output are P_M and Q_M. Assuming that the monopoly price is illegal, the customary measure of damage is the difference between P_M and P_C times the number of units sold: $(P_M - P_C)Q_M$. This is clearly the monopoly profit, which represents a wealth transfer from consumers to the producers. As a means of compensating those who were overcharged, this is appropriate.

The social welfare loss associated with monopolistic pricing is given by the welfare triangle ABC. This area represents the *social* cost of monopoly, but it plays no role in the calculation of *private* antitrust damages. To the extent that the antitrust laws are supposed to improve social welfare, this is a flaw in the law's construction.

Damage theories[19]

There are three basic theories of how one goes about measuring lost profits or overcharges: (1) the "before and after" theory, (2) the "yard-

---

[18] For an alternative approach to deterrence, see Roger D. Blair, "Antitrust Penalties: Deterrence and Compensation," *Utah Law Review* 1980, no. 1 (1980), pp. 57–72, which advocates putting price fixers in jail.

[19] A compact survey of these theories is provided by Richard C. Hoyt, Dale C. Dahl, and Stuart D. Gibson, "Comprehensive Models for Assessing Lost Profits to Antitrust Plaintiffs," *Minnesota Law Review* 60 (1976), pp. 1233–56.

FIGURE 4–2

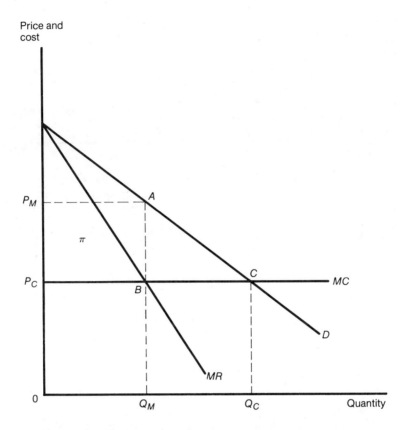

stick" theory, and (3) the "market share" theory. Each theory proceeds upon the assumption that an antitrust violation has been proven. In other words, these theories do not deal with the liability issue of whether a violation occurred. Instead, they focus exclusively upon the extent of the injury and what data can be used to estimate it.

The *before and after approach* to calculating damages examines prices (or profits) during a nonconspiracy period and uses that experience to estimate what prices (or profits) would have been but for the antitrust violation. For example, in Figure 4–3, we show the preconspiracy price pattern for the 1965–76 period. The conspiracy started in 1977, and prices rose dramatically. Based upon the prices during 1965–76, one might estimate prices for the 1977–82 period as shown by the horizontal line.[20] The difference between the prices actually charged and the esti-

---

[20] A discussion of estimation techniques is outside the scope of this text, but the estimates should be based upon sound statistical techniques.

FIGURE 4–3

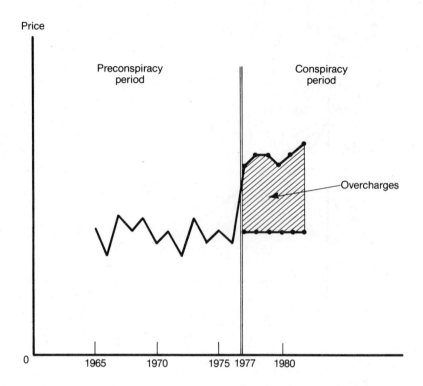

mated prices represent an estimate of the overcharge.[21] The theory behind these estimates is that the only thing that caused prices to rise was
the conspiracy on price. Economic experts employed by the defendants
will attempt to show that the price rise was due at least in part to normal
market forces. Since we have assumed that a conspiracy took place
during 1977–82, we cannot know with certainty what the prices would
have been if the conspiracy had not taken place. Thus, each side will
present evidence based upon an analysis of past history and contemporaneous events. The conflict will be resolved by the jury's wisdom.

The before and after approach requires that the plaintiff has a track
record to demonstrate lost profits, but it does not demand absolute
precision. The Supreme Court has made it clear that the lack of precision
in any damage estimate was due to the defendant's wrongful conduct.
In its *Eastman Kodak*[22] decision, the Court ruled that a plaintiff did not

---

[21] The same approach can be used for estimating lost profits in appropriate cases. We
limited our example to prices for simplicity.

[22] *Eastman Kodak Co.* v. *Southern Photo Co.*, 273 U.S. 359 (1927).

have to prove its actual cost of doing business in order to calculate damages. In effect, the Court approved the use of cost estimates. Shortly thereafter, the Court approved the use of estimated prices in its *Story Parchment*[23] decision.

In summary, the Supreme Court's rulings are fairly liberal toward the precision necessary in calculating the extent of the damages. The before and after approach is restrictive, however, in the sense that the plaintiff must have an established track record to serve as a benchmark for estimating damages. In other words, this procedure will not work for a firm that has been excluded from the market. But where there is a track record, the firm can use this method of proving damages.

The *yardstick approach* to damage estimation is based upon a comparison of the plaintiff's experience with that of a firm or market that was unaffected by the illegal activity. A firm that is claiming lost profits may compare its performance with that of another firm that is similar in all respects except that its performance was not impaired by an antitrust violation. A plaintiff that is claiming damages due to overcharges may attempt to compare the prices it paid with those charged in similar markets where there was no antitrust violation.

The yardstick theory can be very useful when a suitable yardstick can be found. The problems inherent in finding a yardstick are fairly obvious. First, one must locate a firm that is in the same industry. Second, that firm must be unaffected by the antitrust violation. Third, the yardstick firm must be similar to the plaintiff in terms of cost functions, demand conditions, and relative position in the local market. If these conditions are not satisfied, then the yardstick firm will not provide a suitable comparison for damage calculations.[24]

The yardstick theory was attempted in the *Bigelow* case, but before and after evidence was also presented to the Court.[25] Without rejecting the yardstick approach, the Supreme Court ruled in favor of the plaintiff on the before and after award. Following *Bigelow*, the yardstick theory was used in a series of cases involving the movie industry.

The *market share theory* of damages developed as a variant of the before and after and the yardstick theories as they apply to business plaintiffs. It is implemented by estimating the lost market share of the plaintiff. This lost market share is translated into lost total revenue, which can then be translated into lost profit by using the firm's historical

---

[23] *Story Parchment Co.* v. *Paterson Parchment Paper Co.*, 282 U.S. 555 (1931).

[24] The courts seem to prefer damage calculations based upon the before and after approach. When both are offered, the courts usually select the before and after calculation rather than the yardstick estimate. In some way, it must seem less speculative to use actual, firm-specific data rather than the experience of a similar firm.

[25] *Bigelow* v. *RKO Radio Pictures, Inc.*, 327 U.S. 251 (1946). The *Bigelow* decision also reiterated the desirability of a liberal attitude toward the precision of damage calculations. The court noted that the defendant ". . . by his own wrong has prevented a more precise computation."

profit margin. Although the market share theory surfaced in the lower courts in earlier years, the Supreme Court first approved of the theory in its *Zenith*[26] decision. Originally, Hazeltine had sued Zenith for patent infringement, and Zenith filed a counterclaim under the antitrust laws alleging that it had been excluded illegally from the Canadian market by Hazeltine. Zenith presented evidence that but for the exclusionary practices it would have had a 16 percent share of the Canadian market. The Court subtracted Zenith's actual share of 3 percent and proceeded with the damage calculation. This procedure was approved by the Supreme Court.

The market share theory requires a sound data base and a sophisticated analysis. To be a viable theory, four types of data are necessary. First, the analyst must be able to define the relevant geographic and product market. This, as we will discover in subsequent chapters, is more difficult than one might suppose. Second, the analyst will need historical sales volume data for that market. Third, it will be necessary to develop the past trends in the relevant market. Finally, the plaintiff will have to be able to demonstrate the ability to enter and compete in the relevant market. If these data and evidence cannot be gathered and relied upon in the damage calculations, the final opinion of the expert may be too speculative. A damage calculation that is too speculative will be rejected by the court.

Contribution[27]

When two or more firms are found guilty of collusive behavior in violation of the antitrust laws, they share joint and several liability. In practical terms, this means that the plaintiff can demand the payment of damages from one of the firms and ignore the rest. Suppose, for example, that a plaintiff lost his business as a result of the unlawful collusion of four rivals. Having demonstrated to the jury's satisfaction that it was injured by, say, $5 million, the plaintiff is entitled to collect $15 million from the defendants. Now, the plaintiff can collect all of it from a single firm and none from the remaining three. Alternatively, it could collect an equal amount from each defendant or any other allocation that it desires. The defendant who is required to pay more than its "fair" share of the $15 million has no recourse against the other defendants.

---

[26] *Zenith Radio Corp.* v. *Hazeltine Research, Inc.*, 401 U.S. 321 (1971). Zenith was a manufacturer of radio and TV sets. Hazeltine owns and licenses domestic patents. When Zenith stopped licensing Hazeltine's patents, this suit began.

[27] Recently, the issue of contribution in antitrust cases has received a lot of attention. For two excellent analyses, see Frank H. Easterbrook, William M. Landes, and Richard A. Posner, "Contribution among Antitrust Defendants: A Legal and Economic Analysis," *Journal of Law and Economics* 23 (October 1980), pp. 331–70, and A. Mitchell Polinsky and Steven Shavell, "Contribution and Claim Reduction among Antitrust Defendants: An Economic Analysis," *Stanford Law Review* 33 (February 1981), pp. 447–71.

This situation strikes some people as unfair since some wrongdoers may not have to pay any damages. Several lower courts have considered whether a defendant that has paid a disproportionate share of the damages may obtain contribution from the other defendants. Since these lower courts reached conflicting results, the Supreme Court resolved the matter in its *Texas Industries* decision.[28]

Texas Industries and three other concrete suppliers allegedly engaged in an unlawful price-fixing scheme. The Wilson P. Abraham Construction Corporation filed suit against Texas Industries. During the discovery process, Texas Industries learned the identities of the firms that Abraham believed had conspired with Texas Industries. As a result, Texas Industries filed suit against the alleged coconspirators requesting contribution in the event that it should lose the suit filed by Abraham. Both the District Court and the Circuit Court of Appeals held that the antitrust laws should not provide a right of contribution. In its decision, the Supreme Court pointed out that the proponents of contribution invoke principles of equity under the assumption that Congress wanted the firms violating the law to draw upon equitable principles to mitigate the consequences of their wrongdoing. Then the Court shifted the burden to Congress:

> The policy questions presented by petitioner's claimed right to contribution are far reaching. In declining to provide a right to contribution, we neither reject the validity of those arguments nor adopt the views of those opposing contribution. Rather, we recognize that, regardless of the merits of the conflicting arguments, this is a matter for Congress, not the courts, to resolve.

As a result, there is no right to contribution under the antitrust laws. Currently, proposals are circulating in Congress that will provide contribution in some form.

4–4 CLASS ACTIONS AND *PARENS PATRIAE*[29]

In its case against the U.S. gasoline producers, the State of Hawaii alleged that some 300,000 motorists were injured by a price-fixing conspiracy.[30] If we suppose that the average purchase of gasoline was 14 gallons per week and that the conspiracy raised the price by a penny per gallon, the total overcharge in Hawaii would amount to $2,184,000. In principle, the treble-damage provision would expose the conspirators to a potential award of $6,552,000 per year for the duration of the conspiracy. The average consumer, however, would suffer an injury of $7.28,

---

[28] *Texas Industries, Inc.* v. *Radcliff Materials, Inc.,* 451 U.S. 630 (1981).

[29] Some of these thoughts were presented in Roger D. Blair, "The Sherman Act and the Incentive to Collude," *Antitrust Bulletin* 17 (Summer 1972), pp. 433–44.

[30] *Hawaii* v. *Standard Oil Co. of California,* 301 F. Supp. 982 (D. Hawaii 1969).

which could be trebled to $21.84. As we can see, the *total* injury is not inconsequential, but the average *individual* injury is too small to warrant a private suit. Given such small individual claims, it is unlikely that a flood of private suits would be forthcoming. Unless these small individual claims can be aggregated, the offenders will not be deterred from committing further antitrust violations. There are two ways that these individual claims can be aggregated: class action suits and *parens patriae* suits.

Class action suits

Class action suits are supposed to provide the means for individuals with small claims to seek redress in the courts. The courts have generally accepted class action suits where the class can show that the legal issue is common to all members of the class.[31] In addition, the court must be satisfied that a class action is the best way to obtain the fair and efficient adjudication of the issue. There are four criteria that the court must consider in this regard:

> (1) the interests of members of the class in individually controlling the prosecution of separate actions; (2) the extent and nature of any litigation concerning the issue already started by members of the class; (3) the desirability of concentrating the litigation in the particular forum; and (4) the difficulties likely to be encountered in the management of a class action.[32]

All members of the class who can be identified through reasonable effort must receive "individual notice" of the action.[33] Since this has usually meant notice by personal service or by mail, this procedural rule imposes substantial costs and dampens the effectiveness of class actions. In defense of the notice requirement, it must be observed that a constitutional issue is involved. To ensure due process, all parties who are bound to the fate of the representative plaintiff must be informed of the pending action. All interested parties should have the opportunity of deciding whether they want their interests pursued. This presents an interesting question in legal philosophy. If one can assume that a number of interested parties want their interests furthered and the notice requirement prevents litigation, then the *certain* desires of some parties are denied to protect the constitutional rights of others who may not be

---

[31] The common legal issue is also supposed to predominate over all other questions which affect only individual members of the class. Predominance, however, has been relegated to secondary importance: *commonality has been sufficient.* See note, "Wrongs without Remedy: The Concept of *Parens Patriae* for Treble Damages under the Antitrust Laws," *Southern California Law Review* 43 (Summer 1970), pp. 570–95, especially p. 580.

[32] FRCP 23(b)(3).

[33] FRCP 23(c)(2).

in disagreement. In such a situation there exists no conflict of wills but the effort to avoid conflict results in no one being able to seek redress. At any rate, the notice requirement may render the class action impotent as a means of seeking redress. The courts have been unmoved by this consequence. In fact, the courts have held that such notice is required even if the requirement results in abandoning the litigation for financial reasons.

Parens patriae suits

Parens patriae suits can be an effective alternative to either individual or class action suits. The doctrine of *parens patriae* has had two separate developments in the law. The first derives from the "royal prerogative" of the English King as "the general guardian of all infants, idiots, and lunatics."[34] It has been contended that Blackstone's reference to infants, idiots, and lunatics was a complete description of the scope of the royal prerogative.[35] This certainly may have been true when Blackstone composed his *Commentaries*, but there is no real need to cling to Blackstone's words. The royal prerogative seems to have been invoked on behalf of those who were incapable of protecting their own interests. It is surely not unreasonable to argue that an individual consumer is incapable of protecting his interests when he may be matched against the giants of American industry in an antitrust suit. Moreover, when the individual cannot be protected by state action on his behalf, the deterrent effect of the law is reduced. This notion, however, has never been claimed successfully.

The second development of *parens patriae* pertains to the quasi-sovereign interests of the states. Prior to the amendment to Section 4 of the Clayton Act, *parens patriae* suits had been successful only when seeking injunctive relief to protect the interests of a state's citizenry in general. A state had never been permitted to sue to recover damages under the concept of *parens patriae* when the injured parties had standing to sue in their own right. In the words of Malina and Blechman, opponents of *parens patriae* suits for treble damages, "States can sue as *parens patriae* only to enjoin wrongs which affect the *patria* as a whole, and never to benefit particular individuals, *regardless* of how impotent the latter may be."[36] But the point is that when individuals are impotent, the treble-damage provision is certainly less potent than it first appears. This issue was resolved legislatively when the Clayton Act was amended.

---

[34] W. Blackstone, *Commentaries* 47–48 (12th ed., E. Christian, ed., 1794).

[35] M. Malina and M. D. Blechman, "*Parens Patriae* Suits for Treble Damages under the Antitrust Laws," *Northwestern University Law Review* LXV (May–June 1970), pp. 193–231, especially p. 197.

[36] Ibid., p. 214. Emphasis added.

Section 4C of the Clayton Act permits each state to file *parens patriae* suits on behalf of its citizens to protect their property rights:

> Sec. 4C(a)(1) Any attorney general of a State may bring a civil action in the name of such State, as *parens patriae* on behalf of natural persons residing in such State, in any district court of the United States having jurisdiction of the defendant, to secure monetary relief as provided in this section for injury sustained by such natural persons to their property by reason of any violation of [The Sherman Act]. The court shall exclude from the amount of monetary relief awarded in such action any amount of monetary relief (*a*) which duplicates amounts which have been awarded for the same injury, or (*b*) which is properly allocable to (*i*) natural persons who have excluded their claims pursuant to subsection (b)(2) of this section, and (*ii*) any business entity.
>
> (2) The court shall award the State as monetary relief threefold the total damage sustained as described in paragraph (1) of this subsection, and the cost of suit, including a reasonable attorney's fee.

Section 4E provides for the distribution of any monetary damages awarded in a *parens patriae* suit:

> Sec. 4E. Monetary relief recovered in an action under section 4C(a)(1) shall—
>
> (1) be distributed in such manner as the district court in its discretion may authorize; or
> (2) be deemed a civil penalty by the court and deposited with the State as general revenues;
>
> subject in either case to the requirement that any distribution procedure adopted afford each person a reasonable opportunity to secure his appropriate portion of the net monetary relief.

Sections 4C and 4E were added to the Clayton Act by the Hart–Scott–Rodino Antitrust Improvements Act in 1976.

Although the *parens patriae* suit is similar to a class action suit, it may pose fewer problems. Since the suit is not brought by private attorneys, settlement decisions are less apt to be tainted by the self-interest of the attorney. The attorney general does not have the same notice burden that the representative has in a class action suit. This will make more suits possible and add to the deterrent effect of the antitrust laws. The statute permits part or even all of the award to be deemed a civil penalty. This avoids some of the difficult problems encountered in distributing class action damage awards. In summary, the *parens patriae* provision is a welcome addition to the antitrust arsenal available to enforce the law.

4–5 ATTORNEY'S FEES[37]

A successful treble-damage plaintiff is entitled to receive a reasonable attorney's fee. What is "reasonable" is often in the eye of the beholder.

---

[37] For a compact discussion of this issue, see Sullivan, *Handbook of the Law of Antitrust*, pp. 792–96.

Obviously, the attorney for the successful plaintiff will be looking forward to a substantial fee. In contrast, the unsuccessful defendant will not be anxious to pay any more than is absolutely necessary. This conflict is resolved at a hearing after the main trial. At the hearing, the plaintiff has to present evidence regarding the value of the legal services provided. Usually, the attorneys submit affidavits that set out in some detail the services that were performed and the time spent on the case.

In assessing the value of the legal services provided, the courts have relied upon traditional indicia of the value of legal services: time spent on the case, the reputation of the successful attorney, the size and complexity of the litigation, the result achieved, and the rates charged by others for comparable efforts. Increasingly, fee awards are being based upon the time spent by the successful attorney. As a result, the trial courts are insisting upon detailed accounts of the time spent. In particular, the courts want to know which attorneys performed which chores and how much time was spent on unsuccessful parts of the case. Some courts have demonstrated a willingness to disregard time that was spent on duplicative or repetitive tasks or on efforts that were unsuccessful.

When an attorney represents a class, his compensation is contingent upon success. If the case is lost, so is the fee. But when the class prevails, the attorney should be compensated for his legal skills and effort in the usual way. In addition, he should be compensated for bearing the risk inherent in a contingent fee arrangement. If the attorneys are not compensated for bearing risk, we cannot expect them to do so, and some meritorious claims will not be pursued. This, of course, will reduce the deterrent effect of private actions.

QUESTIONS AND PROBLEMS

1. When a plaintiff attempts to estimate his damages, there is some amount of uncertainty surrounding the final figure. The law usually puts the burden of the uncertainty upon the defendant. Does this seem "fair"?

2. In disputes over damages, what is the distinction between the "fact" of injury and the "amount" of damage?

3. Was Pueblo Bowl-O-Mat hurt by Brunswick's acquisition of several defaulting bowling centers? If so, why did the Supreme Court not allow its claim for damages?

4. If the passing-on defense were allowed, how would an economist explain in qualitative terms the problem of measuring the injury suffered by various potential claimants?

5. In our discussion of individual sanctions, we noted that fines averaged some $3,000 during the 1955–68 period. If a convicted price

fixer experienced employment difficulties in the future, how would we measure the full sanction?

6. Would you expect decision makers to take into account statutory maximum penalties or the average penalties actually imposed in making business decisions?

7. A state attorney general can file a *parens patriae* suit on behalf of natural persons but not on behalf of businesses. Does this make any sense?

8. Suppose you are a stockholder in ABC Electronics, a brand new computer firm. As a result of predatory behavior by Megabucks, Inc., ABC goes into bankruptcy. Who has standing to sue—you or ABC Electronics?

9. For purposes of providing a deterrent to antitrust violations, does it matter who actually sues? For example, suppose a price-fixing violation results in $1 million of overcharges. For deterrent purposes, couldn't just anybody sue for treble damages? Why does it have to be the people who were overcharged?

10. Suppose your firm supplies components to a computer manufacturer which is driven out of business by illegal exclusionary practices. Your firm made an average of $200,000 profit on sales to the computer manufacturer. Has your firm been injured? Does it have standing to sue for treble damages?

11. If the purpose of treble damages is to deter antitrust violations, why did the Supreme Court deny Pueblo the right to sue Brunswick for lost profits?

12. United Shoe argued that Hanover passed on all of the monopoly overcharge and, therefore, was not injured by United Shoe's prices on its machinery. What must be true for United Shoe's assertions to be correct? Are these conditions likely?

13. Suppose that the long-run supply curve in a competitive industry is horizontal. Suppliers of an essential input collude and raise price to the competitive industry, which shifts the supply curve. How much of the monopoly overcharge is passed on to customers of the competitive industry?

14. Suppose that B&K Electronics Outlet wanted to sell top-quality computer equipment at discount prices. At the request of its estab-

lished customers, the suppliers of computer equipment agreed not to supply B&K. Assume that this exclusionary scheme is illegal. How could B&K's expert witness estimate damages?

15. Is there any way that treble-damage suits or the threat of such suits could be used to dampen the competitive aggressiveness of a firm's rivals? How?

16. If Pueblo Bowl-O-Mat lacks the ability to recover damages from Brunswick, what incentive does it have to assist in the enforcement of the antitrust laws?

17. How could you use the yardstick theory of computing damages in a case where a consumer is complaining about prices being illegally high?

18. How would unexploited economies of scale influence the damage calculations under the market share approach to damages?

19. Suppose that Jolly Roger's Office Supply suffered lost market share due to an illegal exclusionary practice. As a result, sales revenue was reduced by $2 million in 1985 and $3 million in 1986. As an economic expert hired by Jolly Roger's attorneys, you determine from accounting records that Jolly Roger's experienced historical profit margins of 20 percent in 1981, 24 percent in 1982, 18 percent in 1983, and 26 percent in 1984. What profit margin would you use in calculating lost profits due to lost market share?

20. Some critics of class action suits contend that the class members receive very little of any award at the same time that the attorneys representing the class become wealthy. Assuming that this is true, what are the likely effects?

FURTHER READINGS

Berger, Daniel, and Roger Bernstein. "An Analytical Framework for Antitrust Standing." *Yale Law Journal* 86 (April 1977), pp. 809–83.

Blair, Roger D. "The Sherman Act and the Incentive to Collude." *Antitrust Bulletin* 17 (Summer 1972), pp. 433–44.

————. "Antitrust Penalties: Deterrence and Compensation." *Utah Law Review* 1980, no. 1 (1980), pp. 57–72.

Blair, Roger D., and Virginia Maurer. "Umbrella Pricing and Antitrust Standing: An Economic Analysis." *Utah Law Review* 1982, no. 4 (1982), pp. 763–96.

Easterbrook, Frank H.; William M. Landes; and Richard A. Posner. "Contribution among Antitrust Defendants: A Legal and Economic Analysis." *Journal of Law and Economics* 23 (October 1980), pp. 331–70.

Elzinga, Kenneth G., and William Breit. *The Antitrust Penalties.* New Haven, Conn.: Yale University Press, 1976.

Harris, Robert G., and Lawrence A. Sullivan. "Passing on the Monopoly Overcharge: A Comprehensive Policy Analysis." *University of Pennsylvania Law Review* 128 (December 1979), pp. 269–360.

Landes, William M., and Richard A. Posner. "Should Indirect Purchasers Have Standing to Sue under the Antitrust Laws? An Economic Analysis of the Rule of Illinois Brick." *University of Chicago Law Review* 46 (Spring 1979), pp. 602–35.

Page, William H. "Antitrust Damages and Economic Efficiency: An Approach to Antitrust Injury." *University of Chicago Law Review* 47 (Spring 1980), pp. 467–504.

Polinsky, A. Mitchell, and Steven Shavell. "Contribution and Claim Reduction among Antitrust Defendants: An Economic Analysis." *Stanford Law Review* 33 (February 1981), pp. 447–71.

PART II

Horizontal antitrust issues

In this section of the book, we examine the law and economics of horizontal antitrust issues. We have already seen that the primary purpose of antitrust is to protect and promote consumer welfare. Now, we will focus our attention on the application of the antitrust laws to horizontal problems (i.e., those problems that appear to promote monopoly). Initially, we develop the antitrust treatment of monopoly. We will find that the structural condition of monopoly is not unlawful. Instead, it is the act of monopolizing that is unlawful. This will cause some serious enforcement problems for the antitrust authorities.

The next three chapters deal with multi-firm approximations of monopoly. First, we explore the classic cartel model to provide an analytical foundation for our discussion of price fixing. Next, we turn our attention to other forms of horizontal collusion, such as market division, bid rigging, boycotts, and information exchanges. For these business practices, the law and economics are consistent in most instances. Finally, we examine a very difficult antitrust problem: oligopoly and tacit collusion. This problem involves an industry structure that may yield noncompetitive results without any overt collusive behavior. As we shall see, the law is not well-equipped to deal with this.

The next chapter addresses horizontal mergers (i.e., mergers of competitors). These mergers change the industry structure by eliminating some firms. In this instance, the law is preventive in nature and tries to prevent a deterioration of market structure from one that is competitive to one that is oligopolistic or monopolistic.

Finally, we examine price discrimination and the antitrust treatment of it. We shall see that the legal treatment has not been very successful in promoting consumer welfare.

5

Antitrust treatment of monopoly

Section 2 of the Sherman Act does not forbid the structural condition of monopoly. Instead, it forbids the process of becoming a monopoly. This includes three related offenses: monopolization, conspiracies to monopolize, and attempts to monopolize. In principle, these offenses are distinct, but in practice the legal standards of proof blur together to some extent. Moreover, conspiracies to monopolize often involve actions that are clear violations of Section 1 of the Sherman Act. When both sections are cited in cases charging conspiracy to monopolize, it is not always apparent which section is catching the violators.

In this chapter, we shall examine the judicial interpretation of Section 2 of the Sherman Act. As we shall see, what the law condemns is not necessarily the same as what economists condemn. First, we will examine a few practical reasons for not condemning unequivocally the structural condition of monopoly. Next, we turn to the legal developments in the monopolization cases. After examining a few economic issues raised by these cases, we turn our attention to the offenses of attempting to monopolize and conspiring to monopolize. The landmark decisions on monopoly will be critiqued from an economic perspective. Finally, we shall discuss a concept that has received much recent attention: predatory pricing.

5–1 SECTION 2 AND STRUCTURAL MONOPOLY[1]

The language of Section 2 carefully omits the structural condition of monopoly. Section 2 condemns "[e]very person who shall monopolize, or attempt to monopolize, or combine or conspire with any other person or persons to monopolize." This language focuses the law on the business conduct that either results in structural monopoly or maintains that state. It does not condemn monopoly as such. But why not? Our discussion in Chapter 2 of the welfare loss due to monopoly revealed objections to the monopoly structure. The law, however, seems to focus on the means of achieving that structural condition. But we shall see that the statutory language is enlightened because there are several reasons for not condemning the structure of monopoly.

Natural monopoly

As discussed earlier, technologically, there may not be enough demand to support more than one firm at an efficient level of operation. Given the size of the market, the minimum efficient scale of production may be so large that only one firm can survive the competitive process. This can be seen in Figure 5–1 where industry demand D and marginal revenue MR are shown along with the average cost AC and marginal cost MC curves of a single firm. The competitive process forces price to equal marginal cost, but even for one firm, any price equal to marginal cost will fail to cover average cost. Consequently, marginal cost pricing will lead to permanent losses because total revenue will fall below total costs. The natural result of the competitive process will be exit from the industry until price exceeds the competitive level by enough to eliminate the losses. In Figure 5–1, the survivor of the competitive process will produce Q_1 and sell it for the market clearing price of P_1. In doing so, the firm will incur per unit costs of C_1. Thus, the firm's profits will be $(P_1 - C_1)Q_1$, which are positive.

The profits in this case are excessive in the sense that they are larger than necessary to keep this firm's resources employed in the industry. We can see that society suffers a welfare loss in this instance, but there is no way that antitrust enforcement can improve matters. Fines will not alter the market structure or the pricing behavior of the firm. If the Court attempted to remedy the situation by restructuring the industry, that would prove to be inefficient and futile. First, the firm may have only one production facility. In that event, no restructuring is possible. Second, if the firm had several production facilities and the overall econo-

---

[1] This section depends upon Phillip Areeda and Donald Turner, *Antitrust Law* III (Boston: Little, Brown, 1978), pp. 35–71; A. D. Neale and D. D. Goyder, *The Antitrust Laws of the U.S.A.*, 3d ed. (Cambridge, Mass.: Cambridge University Press, 1980), pp. 90–110; Robert Bork, "Legislative Intent and the Policy of the Sherman Act," *Journal of Law and Economics* 9 (April 1966), pp. 7–48.

FIGURE 5–1

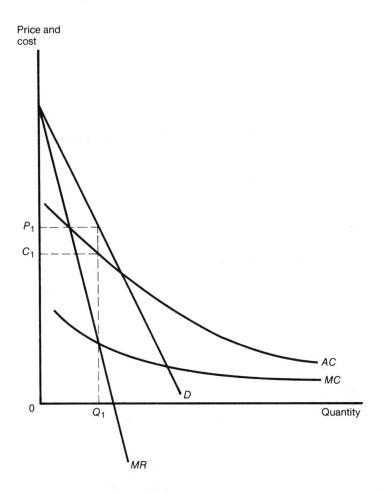

mies of scale depicted in Figure 5–1, breaking up the monopolist would force each resulting firm to operate at a higher point on its average cost curve. This would simply increase the per unit cost to society and probably the price as well. Usually, instances of natural monopoly are recognized, and society largely exempts them from antitrust policy and instead subjects them to direct regulation as a substitute for competition.

Superior efficiency

A firm can come to dominate an industry through superior skill, foresight, and industry. In that case, it may not make much sense to prosecute the successful firm. As Judge Hand said in his *Alcoa* decision, "[t]he successful competitor, having been urged to compete, must not be turned upon when he wins."[2] First, it would strike most observers as being rather unfair to reward the successful competitor with an antitrust suit. If a firm enters the competitive fight and is just too good for its rivals, antitrust prosecution seems an inappropriate response. Second, successful prosecution of a more efficient firm would have unfortunate effects on incentives for productive efficiency. The firm that is challenged will be inclined to avoid future prosecution by refraining from producing as efficiently as possible. This, of course, raises costs to society and increases prices to consumers. More importantly, perhaps, prosecution of the successful competitor will have disincentive effects for all other firms. The results of such a policy could be devastating. Domestic industry would become less efficient and thereby become vulnerable to economic attack from imports.

Finally, there is no obvious antitrust remedy in this situation. The market demand D and associated marginal revenue MR are shown in Figure 5–2. The average and marginal cost curves of the superior firm are shown as AC_1 and MC_1, respectively. Profit maximization leads the superior firm to produce Q_1 units of output and sell it for P_1 per unit. The average cost curve of the most efficient rival is depicted by AC_2. Thus, the profit maximizing price of the superior firm is below the less efficient rival's average cost. Again, the antitrust remedy of splitting up the superior firm cannot work if that firm has only one plant. If it is a multiplant operation, splitting up the firm will make it less efficient and may permit a second firm to survive. Over time, this will only work if the first firm constrains its superior efficiency.

Patent monopoly

If a firm receives a patent on a product that it produces, the patent grant confers monopoly by legal license. For the patent's 17-year life, all rivals are precluded from producing that product.[3] The purpose of the patent system is to promote the progress of science by conferring upon the inventor the exclusive right to his discovery for a limited period of time. In this way, the lure of monopoly profits for the life of the patent will induce some additional inventive effort and enhance the progress of science. Accordingly, it would not make any sense to mount an antitrust attack upon a patent monopolist.

Summary

We have examined several instances where antitrust prosecution of single-firm monopoly seems to be inappropriate. No doubt, as in ab-

---

[2] *United States* v. *Aluminum Co. of America,* 148 F. 2d 416, 430 (2d Cir. 1945).

[3] More specifically, 35 U.S.C. & 154 (1976 & Supp. 1978) defines a patent as "the right to exclude others from making, using, or selling the invention throughout the United States."

FIGURE 5–2

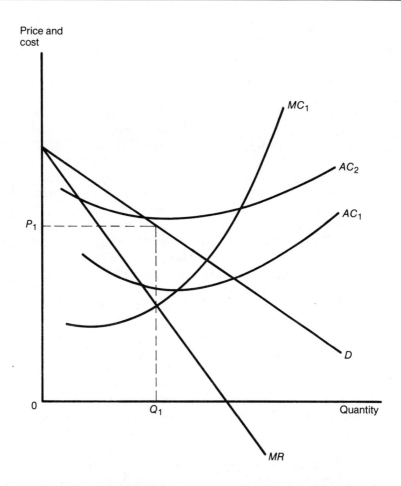

stract cases, the courts would agree that it makes no sense to prosecute patent monopolists, natural monopolists, or super-efficient firms. In practice, of course, life is not so simple, and the situations may not be so clear. We shall explore some of the ambiguities in the rest of this chapter.

5–2 LEGAL DEVELOPMENT OF MONOPOLIZATION

The major emphasis in Section 2 cases has been on monopolization. In order to develop an appreciation of the judicial view of monopolization cases, we shall examine briefly the major decisions that outline this view. In addition to the legal discussion, we shall offer some economic analysis as well.

Standard Oil Co. *v.* United States.[4] Our review starts with the
Standard Oil decision. Beginning in 1870, John D. Rockefeller, William
Rockefeller, and Henry M. Flagler began a conspiracy that unified the
petroleum industry in the United States. In 1870, the two Rockefellers,
Flagler, and several other petroleum refiners formed the Standard Oil
Company of Ohio. By 1872, Standard Oil had acquired all but a handful
of the 35 to 40 refineries in the Cleveland area. Using its buying power,
Standard Oil then extracted concessions from its suppliers that gave
Standard Oil competitive advantages not shared by its rivals. For example, it received low preferential rates and secret rebates from the railroads. With the resulting cost advantage, independent refiners could
not compete with Standard Oil. Consequently, most of its competitors
were driven out of business or were acquired by Standard Oil.

Additionally, Standard Oil acquired refineries elsewhere in Ohio,
Pennsylvania, and New York. Standard Oil and affiliated corporations
gained control of the pipelines linking the eastern oil fields to its refineries. According to the government's complaint, the combination succeeded in controlling some 90 percent of the petroleum business. The
alleged purpose of gaining this control was to permit monopolistic behavior: raising price and restricting the quantity sold.

In 1882, the Standard Oil Company of New Jersey was formed. This
device was used to expand the combination to include more independent petroleum companies. Between 1899 and 1906, Standard Oil of
New Jersey expanded its activities into some of the western states. Its
use of unreasonable business practices included extracting rebates, preferences, and other discriminatory favors from the railroads, monopolization of pipelines, unfair practices against competing pipelines, local
price cutting to suppress competition, industrial espionage, geographic
market allocation, and the operation of bogus independents to give the
appearance of competition.

Standard Oil had achieved a dominant position astride the domestic
oil industry. For all practical purposes, it had effectively monopolized
that industry. In his landmark opinion, Chief Justice White pointed out
that the Sherman Act did not proscribe the structural condition of monopoly. Rather, the purpose of Section 2 was to prohibit "all attempts to
reach the end prohibited by the first section, that is, restraints of trade,
by any attempt to monopolize, or monopolization thereof, . . ."[5]
White went on to point out that Standard Oil had reached its lofty peak
through oppressive business behavior and coercion.[6]

---

[4] 221 U.S. 1 (1911).

[5] 221 U.S. 1, 61 (1911).

[6] There was also an allegation that Standard Oil had engaged in predatory pricing (i.e.,
pricing below cost, to drive out competitors). We shall examine predatory pricing in some
detail in Section 5–8.

The giant size attained by Standard Oil was found to be an abnormal method of industrial development. In other words, the dominance of Standard Oil resulted from a new method of combination that yielded greater power than would otherwise have resulted if normal methods had been employed. The object of Standard Oil's methods was to exclude others from the petroleum industry and provide Standard Oil with perpetual control. These presumptions were reinforced by a review of the firm's conduct, which seemed to White to be plainly exclusionary. As a result, White supported the lower court's finding that Standard Oil was guilty of monopolization.

In Standard Oil, White found a monopoly that had been achieved by abnormal methods with an intent to restrain trade and exclude others. We shall see this theme repeated in later decisions.

United States v. American Tobacco Co.[7] Two weeks after the *Standard Oil* decision, Chief Justice White handed down the Court's decision in *American Tobacco*. In 1890, five firms that accounted for some 95 percent of the total cigarette production merged and formed the American Tobacco Company. Thus, the new firm held a dominant position in the industry. Upon examining the facts, White found that the history of the combination was replete with acts that were designed to monopolize the trade by driving competitors out of business. White inferred wrongful purpose and thereby illegal combination from a series of acts that indicated an intention to use the power of the combination to further monopolize the industry. In addition, American Tobacco had expanded into other aspects of the tobacco industry. By initiating destructive price wars and buying up its bankrupt, former competitors, American Tobacco dominated snuff and cigar production. American Tobacco produced 95 percent of all plug (chewing) tobacco by 1906 based upon its acquisition of nearly all the producers of licorice paste, which is necessary for plug production. Finally, the Court was offended by American Tobacco's practice of acquiring rivals and then closing them down.

United States v. U.S. Steel Corp.[8] In 1901, United States Steel was organized to combine 180 independent steel producers. There was ample evidence that price fixing resulted from this combination. It used the so-called Gary Dinners, set up by the president of U.S. Steel, E. H. Gary, in an effort to stabilize and fix prices through a system of price leadership. At these meetings, all producers were coaxed and cajoled into cooperation, but they were not coerced. There were no subsequent allegations of predatory pricing, secret rebates, coercion of customers, or other "brutalities or tyrannies."

Upon its formation, U.S. Steel controlled some 80–95 percent of U.S. production of some iron and steel products. Subsequently, its share of

---

[7] 221 U.S. 106 (1911).

[8] 251 U.S. 417 (1920).

overall iron and steel production had fallen to some 40 percent. In spite of its initial dominance, U.S. Steel had to enlist the aid of other firms in the industry. It had to rely upon cooperation rather than coercion or compulsion. Consequently, the Court was persuaded that U.S. Steel did not have much monopoly power.[9] In addition, it had abandoned its price-fixing activities before the suit was filed. Since there was no monopoly to dissolve and no current business behavior to discipline, the Court ruled in favor of U.S. Steel.

One interesting quote was contained in the opinion: "the law does not make mere size an offence, or the existence of unexerted power an offence. It . . . requires overt acts."[10] This view persisted until the *Alcoa* decision.[11]

United States *v*. Aluminum Co. of America.[12]   In order to make aluminum, a firm first must extract alumina from bauxite ore. Then it must remove the oxygen from the alumina, a process that yields aluminum. Alcoa acquired the Hall patent that made it commercially feasible to produce aluminum. A subsequent development by Bradley made the Hall patent economically obsolete. Alcoa acquired the production rights to the Bradley patent through a licensing agreement. Thus, Alcoa was a patent monopolist until the Bradley patent expired in 1909. It perpetuated its monopoly until 1912 by employing several restrictive practices. For example, Alcoa agreed with foreign producers of aluminum not to compete in their respective home markets. Additionally, Alcoa obtained concessions from several of its electric power suppliers that they would not supply any other aluminum producer. Such practices were challenged by the government, and in 1912, Alcoa entered into a consent decree with the government which prohibited any further use of restrictive practices.

From 1912 through 1940, Alcoa remained the sole domestic producer of virgin aluminum ingot in spite of having to operate under the consent decree of 1912. Moreover, it had no patent protection. Alarmed by the structural monopoly, the government filed suit against Alcoa under two different theories. It claimed alternatively that (1) Alcoa's continued

---

[9] George Stigler, "The Dominant Firm and the Inverted Umbrella," *Journal of Law and Economics* 8 (October 1965), pp. 157–71, analyzed the formation and performance of the U.S. Steel Corporation. He characterized its formation as a "master stroke of monopoly promotion."

[10] 251 U.S. 417, 451 (1920).

[11] In *United States* v. *International Harvester Co.*, 274 U.S. 693, 708 (1927), the Court said that: "The law . . . does not make the mere size of a corporation, however impressive, or the existence of unexerted power on its part, an offense, when unaccompanied by unlawful conduct in the exercise of its power."

[12] 148 F. 2d 416 (2d Cir. 1945). The *Alcoa* decision in the District Court went against the government. The case was appealed directly to the Supreme Court. Unfortunately, four Justices had to disqualify themselves. As a result, there were too few Justices to constitute a quorum, and the case had to be heard elsewhere. Congress decided that cases like these should be handled by the three most senior judges from the appropriate Court of Appeals.

dominance constituted unlawful monopoly, or (2) Alcoa's dominance plus some new exclusionary practices violated Section 2 of the Sherman Act.

The *Alcoa* decision shows how sensitive a finding of monopoly power can be to the market definition selected. Judge Learned Hand considered three market definitions: (1) production of virgin aluminum ingot, (2) production of virgin and secondary (or recycled) aluminum ingot, and (3) sales to outsiders of virgin and aluminum ingot. The shares for these three definitions were as follows:

	1	2	3
Alcoa virgin production	90	64	—
Alcoa virgin sales	—	—	33
Secondary production	—	29	54
Imports	10	7	13
	100	100	100

The definition selected was a critical issue as Judge Hand felt that 90 percent of a market "is enough to constitute a monopoly; it is doubtful whether 60 or 64 percent would be enough; and certainly 33 percent is not."[13]

In selecting among these alternatives, Judge Hand explained that the rationale of the first definition is that secondary aluminum can be ignored because Alcoa controlled the quantity of virgin aluminum produced. Thus, an enlightened firm would make current production decisions with the knowledge that some part of that production will be reclaimed and compete with virgin aluminum in the future. Consequently, Alcoa's production decisions will be influenced by that consideration, and therefore, one may ignore secondary aluminum.

Having rejected the second definition, we may consider the third. Alcoa urged Judge Hand to count only ingot that was sold to third parties. In this way, all secondary aluminum would be counted, but it would exclude all internal transfers of ingot to Alcoa's fabrication facilities. But Hand recognized that "the ingot fabricated by 'Alcoa' necessarily had a direct effect upon the ingot market. All ingot . . . is used to fabricate intermediate, or end, products; and therefore all intermediate, or end products which Alcoa fabricates and sells . . . reduce the de-

---

[13] This is broadly consistent with Supreme Court decisions in *United States* v. *U.S. Steel Corp.*, 251 U.S. 417 (1920), and *United States* v. *International Harvester Co.*, 274 U.S. 693 (1927), which held that 50 percent and 64 percent control, respectively, did not constitute monopoly power.

mand for ingot itself . . . ." As a result, Hand rejected the third definition.

Using the first definition, Hand had no trouble finding that Alcoa
enjoyed a structural monopoly. But he went further than earlier decisions: "Having proved that 'Alcoa' had a monopoly of the domestic
ingot market, the plaintiff had gone far enough; if it was an excuse, that
'Alcoa' had not abused its power, it lay upon 'Alcoa' to prove that it had
not." This suggests a structural test for monopoly. Hand went on to
discuss the relationship between Sections 1 and 2 of the Sherman Act:

> Starting . . . with the authoritative premise that all contracts fixing prices
> are unconditionally prohibited, the only possible difference between them
> and a monopoly is that while a monopoly necessarily involves an equal, or
> even greater power to fix prices, its mere existence might be thought not
> to constitute an exercise of that power. That distinction is nevertheless
> purely formal; it would be valid only so long as the monopoly remained
> inert; it would disappear as soon as the monopoly began to operate; for,
> when it did—it must sell at some price and the only price at which it could
> sell is a price which it itself fixed. Thereafter the power and its exercise
> must needs coalesce. Indeed it would be absurd to condemn such con-
> tracts unconditionally, and not to extend the condemnation to monopo-
> lies; for the contracts are only steps toward that entire control which
> monopoly confers: they are really partial monopolies.

Hand summarized his views as follows:

> there can be no doubt that the vice of restrictive contracts and of monop-
> oly is really one: it is the denial to commerce of the supposed protection of
> competition. To repeat, if the earlier stages are proscribed, when they are
> parts of a plan, . . . the realization of the plan itself must also be pro-
> scribed.

But Hand retreated from a purely structural test by analyzing Alcoa's
behavior.

Hand pointed out that Alcoa may not have achieved monopoly; instead, monopoly may have been thrust upon it. He recalled that in past
decisions the courts have recognized that "the origin of a monopoly may
be critical in determining its legality." Hand did not reject this principle,
but when he examined Alcoa's behavior, he rejected the idea that Alcoa's dominance was inevitable. He decided that Alcoa was not the
passive beneficiary of a monopoly thrust upon it. From 1912 until 1934,
Alcoa's production increased nearly eightfold while there was no entry
into the industry. Alcoa's continued control resulted from its persistent
determination to maintain control. While it was true that Alcoa stimu-
lated demand for aluminum by developing new uses for it, Alcoa always
made sure that it could supply the additional demand:

> It was not inevitable that it should always anticipate increases in the
> demand for ingot and be prepared to supply them. Nothing compelled it

to keep doubling and redoubling its capacity before others entered the field. It insists that it never excluded competitors; but we can think of no more effective exclusion than progressively to embrace each new opportunity as it opened, and to face every newcomer with new capacity already geared into a great organization, having the advantage of experience, trade connections and the elite of personnel.

Hand pointed out subsequently that

no monopolist monopolizes unconscious of what he is doing. So here, 'Alcoa' meant to keep, and did keep, that complete and exclusive hold upon the ingot market with which it started. That was to 'monopolize' that market, however, innocently it otherwise proceeded.

Thus, Alcoa was found to have violated Section 2.

The most obvious reading of the *Alcoa* decision is that a structural monopoly violates Section 2 of the Sherman Act unless the monopoly was thrust upon the firm. Sound business practices that would usually be perfectly legal may condemn a firm that has a dominant position.[14] It is important to understand that Alcoa maintained its position without merger or any sort of predatory behavior. Judge Hand, therefore, presumably would approve of someone who becomes a monopolist by sheer chance but would condemn someone who achieved monopoly through carefully calculated market behavior.[15] We shall see that subsequent decisions have continued *Alcoa's* hostility toward structural monopoly.

United States *v*. Griffith.[16]   The defendants owned movie theaters in some 85 towns in Oklahoma, Texas, and New Mexico. In 53 towns, there was no competition, while there were competing theaters in 32 towns. In negotiating with the various film distributors, the defendants negotiated for their system or circuit as a whole. Due to the buying power that they enjoyed, they negotiated some exclusive privileges that prevented their competitors from obtaining enough first-run or second-run films to operate successfully. For example, the defendants could preempt the selection of films where they faced competition. The District Court found no monopolistic purpose in Griffith's agreements and ruled against the government.

The Supreme Court, however, held that a specific intent to build a monopoly is not necessary. "It is sufficient that a . . . monopoly results

---

[14] The Supreme Court used *American Tobacco Co.* v. *United States*, 328 U.S. 781 (1946), to endorse Judge Hand's *Alcoa* decision. In particular, it found that a firm acts in an exclusionary way when it takes advantage of each new opportunity. Moreover, it accepted Hand's view that price setting by a monopolist was the same as price fixing by competitors.

[15] See Robert Bork, *The Antitrust Paradox* (New York: Basic Books, 1978), pp. 163–75 for a devastating critique of *Alcoa*.

[16] 334 U.S. 100 (1948).

as the consequence of a defendant's conduct or business arrangements.
. . . To require a greater showing would cripple the Act." Justice
Douglas went on to say that

> Section 2 . . . makes it a crime for any person to monopolize or attempt to
> monopolize any part of interstate or foreign trade or commerce. So it is
> that monopoly power, whether lawfully or unlawfully acquired, may itself
> constitute an evil and stand condemned under §2 even though it remains
> unexercised. For §2 of the Act is aimed, inter alia, at the acquisition or
> retention of effective market control. . . . It follows a fortiori that the use
> of monopoly power, however lawfully acquired, to foreclose competition,
> to gain a competitive advantage, or to destroy a competitor is unlawful.

Douglas went on to apply this general standard to the Griffith facts:

> When the buying power of the entire circuit is used to negotiate films for
> his competitive as well as his closed [monopoly] towns, he is using monop-
> oly power to expand his empire. And even if we assume that a specific
> intent to accomplish that result is absent, he is chargeable in legal contem-
> plation with that purpose since the end result is the necessary and direct
> consequence of what he did.

As a result, he found that the defendants had violated Section 2 of the
Sherman Act.

United States *v*. United Shoe Machinery Corp.[17] United Shoe supplied shoe manufacturers with the machinery necessary for their factories. The demand of some 1,460 shoe manufacturers for machine services
was defined to be the relevant product market. United Shoe faced at
least 10 domestic competitors and some foreign competitors in various
aspects of the shoe machinery market. In fact, the court found that an
entire shoe factory could be organized efficiently without using a single
United Shoe machine. Nonetheless, United Shoe still had over 75 percent of the market. This market dominance was not due to any predatory practices. Nor was it due to fundamental patents as those had
expired long ago, and a rival said that it was possible to invent around
United Shoe's remaining patents.

The principal sources of United Shoe's monopoly were (1) its original
constitution, which had been found legal, (2) the superiority of its products and services, which is not to be condemned, and (3) its system of
never selling, but only leasing, its machines. The Court did condemn
the final source of United Shoe's monopoly in spite of the fact that no
consumer expressed any dissatisfaction with that system.

Judge Wyzanski felt that United Shoe's leasing system created barriers to entry into the shoe machinery industry. The term of the lease was
10 years and United Shoe required its lessees to use the machines to full
capacity if sufficient work were available. Moreover, if the machine was

---

[17] 110 F. Supp. 295 (D. Mass. 1953).

returned before the lease expired, the lessee would have to pay a return charge equal to the balance of the lease payments. These lease terms were found to deter entry because they deterred a shoe manufacturer from switching to the machines of a new entrant. Whenever a customer wanted to replace a machine, United Shoe gave him better terms if he replaced one United Shoe machine with another United Shoe machine rather than with a competitive machine. Finally, as part of the leasing agreement, United Shoe repaired, without separate charge, all of its machines. This allegedly had the effect of hindering the development of independent repair companies. Thus, potential rivals also were compelled to offer repair services, which increased the costs of entering the industry.

United Shoe's network of long-term leases with over 90 percent of the shoe factories "assured closer and more frequent contacts between United Shoe and its customers than would exist if United [Shoe] were a seller and its customers were buyers." Moreover, Wyzanski felt that the leases were designed and implemented so as to increase United Shoe's power to exclude competitors. He found that "[m]uch of United's market power is traceable to the magnetic ties inherent in its system of leasing, and not selling, its more important machines."

Judge Wyzanski found that United Shoe's activities were honestly industrial but did not foster competition on pure merit. Instead, they furthered the dominance of one firm. These activities constituted unnatural barriers, unnecessarily excluded actual and potential competition, and restricted a free market. He interpreted earlier decisions as forbidding market control unless it was economically inevitable. As a result, he ruled that "United [Shoe] is denied the right to exercise effective control of the market by business policies that are not the inevitable consequences of its capacities or its natural advantages." As a result, United Shoe was found guilty of monopolizing the shoe machinery market.

Section 2 offense of monopolization: Summary. In the preceding section, we saw that monopoly by itself should not sensibly violate Section 2 of the Sherman Act. This, of course, raised the question of just what does constitute an example of monopolization. In the course of interpreting the Sherman Act, the Supreme Court had devised a two-prong test for unlawful monopolization. This test is stated succinctly by the Supreme Court in *Grinnell:*

> The offense of monopoly under §2 of the Sherman Act has two elements: (1) the possession of monopoly power in the relevant market and (2) the willful acquisition of maintenance of that power as distinguished from growth or development as a consequence of a superior product, business acumen, or historic accident.[18]

---

[18] *United States* v. *Grinnell Corps.*, 384 U.S. 563, pp. 570–71 (1966).

Thus, to establish the Section 2 offense of monopolization, one must define a relevant market and find the presence of monopoly power in that market.[19] Once this effort has been successful, one must show some general purpose or intent to exercise that monopoly power. This latter requirement is not a difficult standard to meet. In *United Shoe*, for example, Judge Wyzanski decided that the "[d]efendant intended to engage in the leasing practices and pricing policies which maintained its market power. That is all the intent which the law requires when both the complaint and the judgment rest on a charge of 'monopolizing' . . . Defendant having willed the means has willed the end."

5-3 DEFINING THE RELEVANT MARKET[20]

There are two aspects to defining the relevant market for purposes of Section 2 enforcement. First, we must isolate the product of interest and, second, we must identify the geographic area in which the trade takes place. Since economists blithely talk about markets, one might suppose that any economist could define a relevant market quite easily. In fact, that is not the case. Economists have not contributed greatly to our ability to define product and geographic markets. Nonetheless, we must define the relevant market because without a market definition, there is no way to measure a firm's ability to reduce or destroy competition. Our definition may not be as precise as one would like, but the approach will be functional and grounded in economic principles.

Areeda and Turner proceed in an interesting way. For them a market encompasses "a firm or a group of firms which, if unified by agreement or merger, would have market power in dealing with any group of buyers."[21] Presumably, they would use a similar definition for the buyer's market. The boundaries of a market can be delineated by observing price correlations over time supplemented by contemporaneous sales patterns.

Our interest in price correlations is fairly obvious. If an increase in the price of a specific commodity in one area does not lead to a price increase in another area, those two areas are not likely to be in the same geographic market. Similarly, in a single area, if the price of one commodity increases and the price of a second commodity is unaffected, then those

---

[19] In the next section, we discuss market definition. The focus of the section after that is market power.

[20] This section depends upon Areeda and Turner, *Antitrust Law*, pp. 346–88. See also Ira Horowitz, "Market Definition in Antitrust Analysis: A Regression-Based Approach," *Southern Economic Journal* 48 (July 1981), pp. 1–16.

[21] Areeda and Turner, ibid., p. 347. A similar approach was adopted by Kenneth D. Boyer, "Industry Boundaries," in *Economic Analysis and Antitrust Law*, eds. T. Calvani and J. Siegfried (Boston: Little, Brown, 1979), pp. 88–106, who defines "the industry in which a firm operates as the ideal collusive group, from the firm's point of view." See ibid., p. 88.

two commodities are not close enough substitutes to be in the same product market. These presumptions about market delineation follow from the basic proposition that price (net of transportation costs) tends toward uniformity within a market.[22] If there are several producers of sugar in a geographic area, they cannot charge divergent prices for very long. Those with the lower prices will get all of the business while those with the higher prices will make no sales. Consequently, there will be upward pressure on the prices of the low-price producers and downward pressure on the prices of the high-price producers. As a result, the prices of sugar in the market will tend toward uniformity.

The most serious problem that results from relying upon price correlations is inferring causality. For example, suppose that ice cream is produced in local markets. One may observe that the price of an ice-cream cone rises in New York and in San Francisco at the same time. We might be a little uncomfortable with the conclusion that the geographic market for ice-cream cones was national in scope. A more plausible reason for the close price correlation is that the cost of producing ice cream has gone up everywhere. This cost inflation forces all sellers of ice-cream cones to adjust their prices upward. Consequently, a naive look at simple correlation coefficients will mislead the viewer. This, however, is not a fatal flaw because statistical techniques permit the analyst to remove inflationary effects and to focus on the real relationship between the prices.

When the price relationships are ambiguous, an examination of sales and purchasing patterns over time should clear things up. If there is a single market, a significant number of buyers should shift their purchases to the lower-priced product or area. Similarly, producers should shift to the higher-priced commodity or area. These ideas may become a bit more concrete when we discuss geographic and product market delineation below.

Geographic market delineation

Suppose we are trying to decide whether two geographic areas are in the same market. If both prices and price changes of a specific commodity in the two areas are closely correlated, there is a strong presumption that they are in the same geographic market. Analogously, if the price of a given commodity differs across the two areas and the price changes are not positively correlated, we should suspect that the two areas are in separate markets.

Sales patterns can supplement the information on price movements. Suppose we have areas A and B, and we are considering the sales of a

---

[22] See George Stigler, *The Theory of Price* (New York: Macmillan, 1970), pp. 85–87.

well-defined product—say, cans of Maxwell House coffee. Let the prices for the two areas during various weeks be as follows:

	Week 1	Week 2	Week 3	Week 4
Area A	$3.29	$3.29	$3.32	$3.36
Area B	3.32	3.42	3.42	3.39

The two areas are not obviously in the same market. They begin and end with approximately a 1 percent difference in price, which could be explained by transportation cost differences or a similar factor. The fact that a price rise in area B was followed by both a price rise in area A and a gradual return to a 1 percent price differential could indicate that the two areas are in the same market. The positive correlation between the prices also could be spurious. If the two areas are in the same market, we should see a sales pattern that reflects this. As the price of coffee in area B increases above the previous differential in week 2, customers should begin shifting to area A in week 3. This would tend to push up the price in A and pull down the price in B. This process would continue in week 4 until the price differential in week 1 is resumed. In contrast, if the two areas were not in the same market, we would not see any substantial change in the sales patterns across geographic areas.

Product market delineation

Two products do not have to be physically identical or even perfect substitutes to be in the same product market for antitrust purposes. But for two products, X and Y, to be in the same market, consumers must substantially shift their purchases from X to Y when the price of X rises relative to the price of Y. In essence, we are looking for commodities that have a high cross-elasticity of demand, which is defined formally as

$$\theta = \frac{\Delta Q_X / Q_X}{\Delta P_Y / P_Y}$$

(i.e., the percentage change in the quantity of X divided by the percentage change in the price of Y).[23] Due to the competition among all products for the consumer's dollar, the cross-elasticity of demand between remote substitutes is not apt to be zero. For example, if the price of jeans

---

[23] A more precise definition of cross-elasticity for the mathematically inclined is

$$\theta = \frac{\partial Q_X}{\partial P_Y} \cdot \frac{P_Y}{Q_X}$$

falls, students will have more money to spend on beer. Intuitively, we are reluctant to put jeans and beer in the same product market for antitrust purposes. Thus, using cross-elasticities requires some judgment and the assistance of price correlations.

If two products have uncorrelated prices, we should suspect that they are not in the same product market. Whenever price changes for two products are uncorrelated, this means that the producers of each product feel no need to adapt to the price changes of the producers of the other product.

Another key to product market delineation involves how producers respond to price changes. If two products are not close substitutes in consumption, they may still be in the same product market if they are produced from the same production facilities. For example, suppose the Blair Card Company is the sole producer of IBM cards. Other paper companies make stationery. Users of IBM cards cannot use stationery in place of Blair's cards, but this does not mean that IBM cards constitute a separate market. If any competent paper company can make IBM cards, the Blair Card Company will face a substantial influx of new competitors if its price of IBM cards rises relative to the price of stationery.

The clearest expression of the Supreme Court's interest in cross-elasticity of demand is provided in the *Cellophane* case.[24] In this case, Du Pont produced about 75 percent of all cellophane sold in the United States. The bulk of this was moisture-proof cellophane. Sylvania sold the rest under a patent licensing agreement that severely penalized sales in excess of 20 percent of the total market. The Supreme Court conceded that if cellophane constituted the relevant product market, then Du Pont surely had monopoly power in that market. But Du Pont contended that the relevant market was flexible packaging materials, which included wax paper, greaseproof paper, glassine, foil, and Pliofilm among others. The court pointed out that

> Every manufacturer is the sole producer of the particular commodity it makes but its control . . . of the relevant market depends upon the availability of alternative commodities for buyers, (i.e., whether there is a cross-elasticity of demand between cellophane and the other wrappings). This interchangeability is largely gauged by the purchase of competing products for similar uses considering the price, characteristics, and adaptability of the competing commodities.

In appraising the cross-elasticity of demand, the court was looking at the responsiveness of the sales of one product to price changes of the other. In addition, it was looking at more subjective indicators: ". . . no more definite rule can be declared than that commodities reasonably interchangeable by consumers for the same purposes make up that 'part of the trade or commerce,' monopolization of which may be illegal."

---

[24] *United States* v. *E. I. du Pont de Nemours & Co.*, 351 U.S. 377 (1956).

The Court found that although cellophane had the most desirable combination of product characteristics, it faced serious competition in nearly all of its end uses. Only for packaging cigarettes was it clearly the dominant product with some 75–80 percent share. In addition, evidence was presented showing that the buyers of flexible packaging materials were very sensitive to changes in price or quality. The court concluded accordingly "that cellophane's interchangeability with the other materials mentioned suffices to make it a part of this flexible packaging material market." Thus, Du Pont was not guilty of a Section 2 violation.

The Supreme Court's use of cross-elasticity of demand has not escaped criticism.[25] First, the Court's focus on demand ignores the possibilities of substitution in production. If substitution possibilities are great on the supply side, any increase in price above the competitive level will elicit a quick entry response. More importantly, perhaps, the Supreme Court did not specify the relative prices at which two products' reasonable interchangeability is to be evaluated. Suppose cellophane and, say, wax paper are reasonably interchangeable at cellophane's current (and perhaps monopolistic) price. This may be proof that Du Pont had a monopoly because Du Pont's price for cellophane may have been raised above the competitive level in recognition of buyer preferences for cellophane's superiority. Reasonable interchangeability must be evaluated at competitive prices, too. If cellophane is vastly superior to the alleged substitutes, then everyone will buy cellophane at competitive prices.

5–4 DEFINING MARKET POWER

If a firm has market power, it can raise the price for its product by restricting output. Competitive firms do not have market power because each one is quite small relative to the size of the total market and the product is homogeneous across firms. Consequently, changes in one firm's output will have no impact upon the market price. In all markets that are not perfectly competitive, each firm has some degree of market power—each can increase its price to some extent without a total loss of sales. For antitrust purposes, however, we cannot be concerned with trivial amounts of market power. For example, if the price of Burger King's "Whopper" increases by a nickel, its sales will not go to zero because a number of customers will still prefer Whoppers even at the higher price. But there are a huge number of market alternatives for consumers. The consumer preferences for Whoppers that permit a small price rise without a substantial fall in sales volume cannot concern us too much. In contrast, the seller of a product that has no close substitute may be able to raise its price substantially without an enormous decline

---

[25] Richard A. Posner, *Antitrust Law: An Economic Perspective* (Chicago: University of Chicago Press, 1976), pp. 127–28.

in sales. In deciding monopolization cases, the courts have to draw a line somewhere between the trivial and the economically serious.

Lerner index of monopoly power

Economists have proposed various measures of monopoly power. Perhaps the best known of these is the Lerner index,[26] which measures the divergence of the market price from the social optimum that is attained by the competitive price system. You will recall that the competitive solution will have price equal to marginal cost. Accordingly, the essence of monopoly is the divergence between marginal cost and price. Specifically, the Lerner index is defined as

$$\lambda = \frac{\text{Price} - \text{Marginal cost}}{\text{Price}}$$

The value of the index is zero in perfect competition and positive whenever a firm has the power to price above marginal cost. Numerically, the upper limit of the Lerner index is one because marginal cost will never be negative. In application, however, the upper limit depends upon the shapes of the demand and cost curves.

For the monopolist, profit maximization requires producing where marginal cost equals marginal revenue. Thus, we can write the Lerner index as

$$\lambda = \frac{P - MR}{P}$$

where MR is the firm's marginal revenue. In fact, we can use the relationship between price and marginal revenue to express the Lerner index as[27]

$$\lambda = 1/\eta$$

---

[26] See Abba Lerner, "The Concept of Monopoly and the Measurement of Monopoly Power," *Review of Economic Studies* 1 (June 1934), pp. 157–75. In addition, see William M. Landes and Richard A. Posner, "Market Power in Antitrust Cases," *Harvard Law Review* 94 (March 1981), pp. 937–96.

[27]

$$MR = \frac{\Delta TR}{\Delta Q} = \frac{\Delta(PQ)}{\Delta Q} = P + Q\frac{\Delta P}{\Delta Q}$$

Factoring P out of the final expression yields

$$MR = P\left\{1 + \frac{Q}{P} \cdot \frac{\Delta P}{\Delta Q}\right\}$$

Recall that price elasticity of demand is

$$\eta = -\frac{P}{Q} \cdot \frac{\Delta Q}{\Delta P}$$

Thus, $MR = P(1 - 1/\eta)$.

Substitution yields

$$\lambda = \frac{P - MR}{P} = \frac{P - P(1 - 1/\eta)}{P}$$
$$= 1 - 1 + 1/\eta$$
$$= 1/\eta$$

Thus, the index is the reciprocal of the price elasticity of the firm's demand. The less elastic the demand curve, the greater will be the index of monopoly power.

In practice, the Lerner index is not as helpful as we might like because measuring demand elasticity is not terribly easy. A single-firm monopoly may not have the data to measure elasticity. Resorting to the original formulation of the Lerner index is no more helpful because it is quite difficult to measure marginal cost.

Second, we may examine the *Bain index of monopoly*, which focuses our attention on excess profits.[28] Bain argued that persistent excess profits would indicate the presence of monopoly, and therefore, he suggested looking at profit rates over time. At first blush, the Bain index is appealing because profit statistics are easier to obtain than good estimates of marginal cost or the price elasticity of demand. But this advantage is easy to overstate because accounting profits are not the same as economic profits. In order to measure excess profits, we must deduct all relevant costs from total revenue:

$$\Pi = PQ - C(Q) - D - iV$$

where PQ is price times quantity or total revenue, $C(Q)$ is the current cost of generating the income, D is the depreciation on fixed capital investment, and iV represents the opportunity cost on the owned assets of the firm (i.e., the implicit costs of the firm). Thus, transforming the accounting profits into economic profits is not a trivial exercise.

If profit is greater than zero, the firm is earning a return greater than what is necessary to keep its resources employed in the current occupation. In that sense, the profits are excessive. Ordinarily, excess profits attract entry, which stops only when the excess profits vanish. Consequently, *persistent* excess profits signal some barrier to entry that prevents the erosion of monopoly power.

One problem with Bain's measure of monopoly power is that it can miss some structural monopolies. In Figure 5–3, we depict a monopoly that is earning a normal return. Since average cost AC is tangent to demand D at the profit-maximizing price P, excess profit is zero. Using Bain's analysis without any further inquiry would lead us to conclude that there was no monopoly.[29]

Another problem with Bain's approach is in determining the presence of excess profit. First, profit is the difference between total revenue and total costs; thus, profit will depend upon the shapes of the demand and cost functions. Suppose that demand in Figure 5–4 is given by D_1 with

---

[28] Joe S. Bain, "The Profit Rate as a Measure of Monopoly Power," *Quarterly Journal of Economics* 55 (February 1941), pp. 271–92.

[29] We might ask in this case what the antitrust response should be. If there is no entry barrier, no one will enter unless the monopolist's cost curve is too high.

FIGURE 5–3

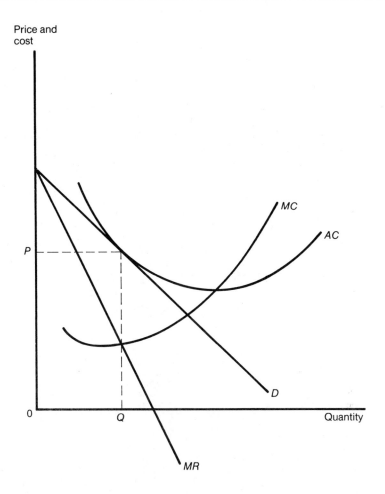

Price and cost

P

MC

AC

D

0

Q

Quantity

MR

the associated marginal revenue MR_1. With the cost functions depicted, the profit will be

$$\Pi = (P_1 - C_1)Q_1$$

and the profit rate will be this profit divided by the firm's investment. In contrast, suppose that the demand and marginal revenue curves were the flatter curves labeled D_2 and MR_2, respectively. Then the same investment would yield a much smaller profit,

$$\Pi = (P_2 - C_1)Q_1$$

and a correspondingly lower profit rate.

FIGURE 5–4

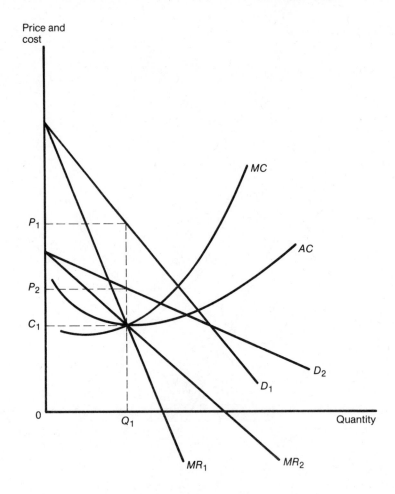

Second, to determine whether the observed profit is excessive or not, we must adjust the profit figures for risk. This can be done, but it is a considerable job. The reason for adjusting the profit for risk is that most investors are risk averse, which means that they do not enjoy bearing risk. Consequently, they must be paid something for risk bearing. Thus, part of the observed profit is really a cost incurred by the firm because the investor will move his assets elsewhere if he is not paid for bearing risk.

Third, when someone buys a going concern, it is obvious that the physical assets are acquired. But the buyer is usually most interested in purchasing a stream of excess profits. Accordingly, the price of a going concern exceeds the market value of the physical assets by an amount that reflects the present value of the excess profits. In this way, the excess profit becomes capitalized in the value of the firm. Thus, we will be unable to observe monopoly profits in many cases.

Finally, we turn to the *Rothschild index of monopoly*, which is particularly useful in an oligopolistic setting.[30] Consider the demand curves in Figure 5–5. The demand curve for firm A's output is given by the rela-

FIGURE 5–5

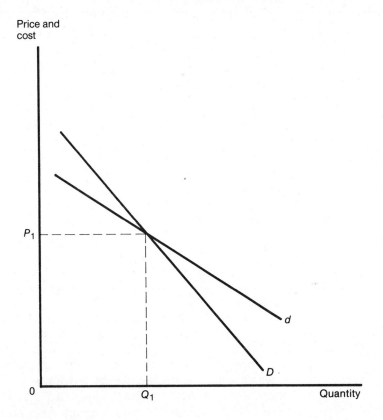

tively flat curve labeled d if the prices of all other firms are held constant. In contrast, the demand curve labeled D describes the options available to firm A if its rivals follow all price changes. If the firm in question were a competitive firm, its d curve would be a horizontal line at height P_1. If the firm were a pure monopolist, there would be no difference between

[30] K. W. Rothschild, "The Degree of Monopoly," *Economica* 9 (February 1942), pp. 24–39. By "oligopoly," we mean a market that has only a few sellers.

the two demand curves. Thus, Rothschild proposed measuring the degree of monopoly by the ratio of the slope of d to the slope of D. For the pure competitor, d is horizontal, and the Rothschild index will be zero. For the pure monopolist, the curves are identical, and the index will equal one.

The Rothschild index is close to measuring what the antitrust courts have been concerned with: the ability of one firm to raise its price above its rival's prices without suffering enormous losses in sales volume. Unfortunately, it is very difficult to measure the d and D curves. Consequently, it is very hard to use the Rothschild index for empirical purposes including antitrust cases.

Judicial accommodation

The Supreme Court has defined monopoly power to be "the power to control market prices or to exclude competition." Thus, a plaintiff could prove monopoly power by offering evidence of actual control over price or the actual exclusion of competitors. Usually, however, such evidence is not unequivocal, and a more complete analysis of structure is desirable. The main criterion for inferring the existence of monopoly power, however, has been the market share of the firm in question. As the Supreme Court remarked in *Grinnell*: "[t]he existence of such power ordinarily may be inferred from the predominant share of the market."[31] As we have seen, this resort to market share has a long history. In the *Standard Oil* and *American Tobacco* cases of 1911, the Court was impressed by the fact that these trusts each controlled over 90 percent of their respective markets. This made it easy to infer the existence of monopoly power. Similarly, in *Alcoa* Judge Hand recognized explicitly that a 90 percent share was clearly monopoly while a lower share in the 60–64 percent range probably was not.

Subsequent Supreme Court decisions have followed in the same vein. For example, in *Grinnell*, the Court defined the market to be accredited central station protective services, which included burglar and fire alarm services. It excluded unaccredited central station protective services, guard dogs, watchmen, and on-site alarms. With this product market definition, the Court found that Grinnell controlled over 87 percent of the market, which was felt to be large enough to confer monopoly power on Grinnell. Finally, we should mention Judge Wyzanski's decision in *United Shoe*. Although other factors played an important part in his decision, he was disturbed by United Shoe's 75 percent control of the shoe machinery market.

---

[31] *United States* v. *Grinnell Corp.*, 384 U.S. 563, 571 (1966). This reliance upon market share is consistent with the Lerner index of monopoly power as Landes and Posner showed. See Landes and Posner, "Market Power in Antitrust Cases," pp. 944–47.

In summary, the case law suggests that some threshold market share in the neighborhood of 75 percent is sufficient for a finding of monopoly power. As the *Cellophane* case makes clear, however, that share must be of a well-defined market.

5–5 THE CONDUCT ELEMENT OF MONOPOLIZATION

The mere existence of monopoly power generally is not sufficient to condemn a firm. After all, the market may be too thin to support more than one or a few firms. Alternately, a single firm may dominate its industry by virtue of a crucial patent or because it was the first firm in the industry and continues to enjoy the benefits of greater experience.[32] In these situations, the firm has not violated Section 2 unless it has acted in such a way as to protect, enhance, or extend its monopoly power. Judicial decisions require that a structural standard be met—usually through a substantial market share—and that a behavioral standard be satisfied. The behavioral aspect of monopolization is supposed to capture the essence of the firm's purpose or intent. But evidence of intent is not apt to be readily available. Consequently, the courts have looked at the firm's conduct and inferred motive on the logical proposition that a firm intends the consequences of its actions.

The behavioral component of the monopolizing offense reflects intent or purpose, but it cannot be defined that way. Instead, it is defined in terms of conduct. Business behavior that can be characterized as "monopolizing conduct" may involve exclusionary practices or it may result from an abuse of monopoly power. Exclusionary conduct is behavior that is not competition on the merits. It may involve restraints that are not reasonably necessary to compete on the basis of price, quality, service, and so on. A monopolist abuses its power when it charges a monopoly price, impairs competition in another market in which it deals, or impairs competition in a market in which it does not participate.

In *Alcoa*, the firm was guilty of exclusionary behavior because it engaged in a deliberate course of conduct. It expanded capacity in anticipation of increases in demand on purpose. There was no compulsion to do so. Although this behavior may have been honestly industrial and may not have been part of a plan to prevent competition, the firm chose to follow this course of conduct.

In *United Shoe Machinery*, Judge Wyzanski formulated an exclusionary conduct test. A Section 2 violation occurs whenever a firm acquires monopoly power through predatory behavior or maintains monopoly power by erecting entry barriers. United Shoe Machinery allegedly did

---

[32] For the benefits of greater experience, see Armen Alchian, "Costs and Outputs," in *The Allocation of Economic Resources*, ed. M. Abramovitz (Palo Alto, Calif.: Standard University Press, 1959).

this through its lease-only policy, the duration of its leases, and United's provision of "free" maintenance service, among other things.

There are many business practices that can turn a structural monopoly into a firm guilty of monopolizing. For example, large *horizontal mergers* with actual or potential competitors may be exclusionary. Certainly, a horizontal merger that confers monopoly power on the firm is avoidable. *Concerted action* that permits the firms collectively to act like a monopolist will, of course, violate Section 1 of the Sherman Act. In addition, it will be proscribed as a Section 2 violation. *Predatory practices* are designed to exclude existing competitors and to discourage potential entrants. Accordingly, such conduct is readily branded as exclusionary. When a firm *raises entry barriers* in an artificial way, it is seeking to exclude potential rivals and insulate its monopoly position. These examples are not meant to be exhaustive. Many others can be provided.[33]

5–6 CONSPIRACIES TO MONOPOLIZE

If two or more persons conspire to monopolize a market, Section 2 of the Sherman Act will be violated. In principle, this is a separate offense distinct from monopolization. In practice, however, there are not many substantive differences. The legal tests for collusive monopolization are much the same as for monopolization resulting from internal expansion. The basic difference stems from the need to prove the existence of a conspiracy.

Based upon the law of criminal conspiracy, there are two elements to proving an illegal conspiracy to monopolize. First, it must be proved that two or more persons deliberately took concerted action with a specific intent to monopolize a market. Second, these persons must have made at least one overt act in furtherance of the illegal scheme. Technically, it is not necessary to prove that the would-be monopolists actually succeeded or had any reasonable prospect of success. One must only prove that an illegal end motivated their agreement. In practice, however, the antitrust enforcers are not going to be too concerned about a scheme that has little chance of success.

Usually, a variety of motives can be inferred from business behavior. Consequently, after proving the existence of a conspiracy (i.e., a concerted agreement), the Antitrust Division must establish a specific intent to monopolize. This does not require reading the minds of the conspirators. Their intent can be inferred from their conduct. For example, when a combination of firms has acquired monopoly power, proof of intent follows automatically since monopoly power is not thrust upon the con-

---

[33] For a more extended discussion, see Areeda and Turner, *Antitrust Law*, pp. 101–288, and L. Sullivan, *Handbook of the Law of Antitrust* (St. Paul, Minn.: West Publishing, 1977), pp. 106–31.

spiring firms. They conspired to acquire that power, and firms do not do that without an intention to use it. Some of these concerns spill over into the final offense under Section 2 of the Sherman Act: attempts to monopolize.

5–7 ATTEMPTS TO MONOPOLIZE

In addition to monopolization and conspiracies to monopolize, even attempts to monopolize violate Section 2. The Supreme Court has provided an interpretation of this violation: "[t]he phrase 'attempt to monopolize' means the employment of methods, means and practices which would, if successful, accomplish monopolization, and which, though falling short, nevertheless approach so close as to create a dangerous probability of it . . . ."[34] In other words, the behavior of a single firm constitutes an illegal attempt to monopolize when (1) the firm has exhibited a specific intent to monopolize, and (2) the firm is dangerously close to unlawful monopolization. The majority of current judicial decisions supports this interpretation.[35] As a result of this interpretation, the Antitrust Division is faced with determining market power in the context of a relevant market as well as presenting evidence of an unlawful specific intent.

Specific intent

An attempt to monopolize requires a specific intent to control price in a relevant market or to exclude competitors from this market. In essence, there must be an intent to achieve monopoly power. But there is a problem with this formulation, because a specific intent to monopolize may not be inferred when the firm's activities are primarily motivated by legitimate business purposes. For example, some markets cannot support more than one efficient firm (i.e., they are characterized by natural monopoly). If there are several firms in such a market, each may fully intend to be the successful firm. In this situation, none of the firms is guilty of an attempt to monopolize. For example, in *Union Leader*, Judge Wyzanski pointed out that "a person does not necessarily have an exclusionary intent merely because he foresees that a market is only large enough to permit one successful enterprise, and intends that his enterprise shall be that one and that all other enterprises shall fail. . . ."[36] This, however, does not excuse the use of unfair means of being the winner: "[i]n a situation where it is inevitable that only one competitor

---

[34] *American Tobacco Co.* v. *United States*, 328 U.S. 781, 785 (1946).

[35] See the definitive article by Edward H. Cooper, "Attempts and Monopolization: A Mildly Expansionary Answer to the Prophylactic Riddle of Section Two," *Michigan Law Review* 72 (March 1974), pp. 373–462.

[36] *Union Leader Corp.* v. *Newspapers of New England*, 180 F. Supp. 125 (D. Mass. 1959).

can survive, the evidence which shows the use . . . of unfair means is the very same evidence which shows the existence of an exclusionary intent."[37]

But this is not all. If a firm intends to be the sole survivor of the competitive struggle through pure competitive superiority, this does not mean that it is attempting to monopolize the industry. When the law speaks of a specific intent to monopolize, it does not refer to a subjective intent to succeed in the market. Rather, it refers to the intent to employ means to that end which are unfair or unseemly. Thus, the courts are not trying to prevent or condemn business practices that are honestly industrial or have a legitimate business purpose.

Dangerous probability

As we have seen, the judiciary's pragmatic approach to determining the existence of market power has been to examine a firm's share of a relevant market. Accordingly, in an attempt situation, the Court will look for a dangerous probability of acquiring monopoly power in a relevant market. Although some commentators feel that defining a relevant market is unnecessary in attempt cases,[38] the Supreme Court was fairly clear on this point:

> To establish monopolization or attempt to monopolize a part of trade or commerce under §2 of the Sherman Act, it would then be necessary to appraise the exclusionary power . . . in terms of the relevant market for the product involved. Without a definition of that market there is no way to measure [a firm's] ability to lessen or destroy competition.[39]

Of course, the relevant market has a *geographic* dimension as well as a *product* dimension, as we discussed earlier.

Once we know what market we are talking about, we must look for a dangerous probability of actually achieving monopoly. This dangerous probability of monopoly can exist only if the firm has attained sufficient power to establish a reasonable likelihood that it can achieve actual monopoly status. In other words, we are looking for *potential* monopoly power as opposed to actual monopoly power. It is fairly clear that a court must measure the extent of the firm's current market power if it is to ascertain whether the firm is dangerously close to achieving monopoly power. This effort proceeds in precisely the same way as when the

---

[37] Ibid.

[38] Donald Turner, "Antitrust Policy and the Cellophane Case," *Harvard Law Review* 70 (February 1956), pp. 281–310: "If defendants are attempting to drive someone out of the market by foul means rather than fair, there is ample warrant for not resorting to any refined analysis as to whether . . . the defendants would still face effective competition from substitutes." Do you agree with Turner? If so, what precisely are the defendants attempting to monopolize?

[39] *Walker Process Equipment, Inc.* v. *Food Machinery and Chemical Corp.*, 382 U.S. 172, 177 (1965).

charge is actual monopolization. Accordingly, the Court will usually consider the following factors:

1. The relative size of the firm in question in terms of its market share.
2. The structure of the industry (i.e., the number and size distribution of firms in the industry).
3. The firm's conduct and business practices.
4. The performance of the firm and industry.

Foremost among these factors is the market share of the firm in question. Generally, when the government has successfully prosecuted an attempt-to-monopolize case, substantial market shares have been found.

5–8 PREDATORY PRICING

For many years, predatory pricing played a substantial role in our antitrust folklore. After all, Standard Oil had been condemned for this business practice in 1911. The image conjured up is of a large, financially powerful monopolist that slashes its prices below cost in the market area of a smaller rival. The rival tries valiantly to compete, but prices below cost eventually drive him from the industry. In the meantime, the monopolist finances this local skirmish from past profits and/or from profits earned in other areas. This scenario is supposed to describe how Standard Oil achieved and maintained its monopoly in the petroleum industry. By systematically using predatory pricing, Standard Oil's monopoly spread geographically until it blanketed the country. Whenever a firm dared to enter the industry, Standard Oil would drive the price down below cost in the entrant's market and thereby bankrupt the smaller firm.

Professor McGee[40] tested this conventional wisdom by economic logic and by empirical facts. In both regards, he found it deficient. First, let us review the theory.[41] Our description of how predatory pricing works makes it clear that a predator must have some market power before it embarks upon predation because the profits necessary to finance below cost pricing must come from somewhere. Standard Oil, therefore, could not have used predatory pricing from scratch. The evidence suggests that Standard Oil got started through a series of mergers and acquisitions. Of course, this is one way of monopolizing an industry—consolidate all of the former competitors into one giant firm. Industry profits

---

[40] John S. McGee, "Predatory Pricing: The Standard Oil (N.J.) Case," *Journal of Law and Economics* 1 (October 1958), pp. 137–69.

[41] Our theoretical discussion depends upon McGee's analysis. His paper has a richness of detail that repays reading in the original. We also draw upon Lester Telser, "Cutthroat Competition and the Long Purse," *Journal of Law and Economics* 9 (October 1966), pp. 259–77.

are larger once monopoly is achieved so all of the former competitors can be made better off than they were before the merger. In other words, the aspiring monopolist may find it sensible to share his monopoly profits with his former rivals.

Suppose that the would-be monopolist has merged with some of his rivals and acquired some others, but quite a few firms are still independent and want to remain so. Now, the aspiring monopolist may have the financial resources and the geographic dispersion to permit predatory pricing in local markets. A local price war can be financed by excess profits earned in markets where the monopolist faces no competition. After a certain period of time during which prices are below average cost, the local firm will expire. We should note, however, that during the price war, the monopolist will be losing money, too. Unfortunately, the only way that he can impose predatorily low prices is to be willing to sell his own output at those prices. If he had been able to purchase his rival, his monopoly profit in that local market would have begun immediately. Instead, these profits do not begin until after the price war. Consequently, the predator could pay his local rival more than the competitive value of the rival's firm. The bonus could be as much as the expected losses incurred during the price war.

A price war delays the starting date for the receipt of monopoly revenues and cannot make those revenues higher after the price war is over. If the predator were to buy the rival firm instead, then the monopoly revenues would begin immediately. Thus, the present value of the monopoly profits would seem to be higher in the purchase case than in the predation case. As a result, one would expect enlightened firms like Standard Oil to buy out their rivals rather than trying to drive them out of the industry.

In addition to being cheaper, the purchase option has another advantage: The rival's assets are neutralized. If the rival were driven to bankruptcy, someone else could buy the assets, and the predator would have another price war to fight. A final disadvantage is the fact that a predatory price war is apt to alienate the key technical and managerial personnel employed by the rival firm. But it is sensible for the aspiring monopolist to hire these personnel and share the monopoly profits with them. Otherwise, the monopolist is likely to see them again working for someone else.

There are two arguments in favor of predation as opposed to purchase. First, a serious bout of predatory pricing may reduce the purchase price of the firm's assets that will be acquired eventually. McGee feels that this is unlikely because others (i.e., third parties) will recognize that the assets of bankrupt firms are valuable because the monopolist must neutralize them if he is to maximize profit. Thus, third parties will compete with the monopolist at the auction block and drive the prices of the bankrupt firm's assets up to their competitive level. This is only a sensible strategy, however, if the third parties are convinced that the aspiring monopolist will not continue or will not renew its predatory ways.

Second, predatory pricing may be pursued for its demonstration effect. Consider a potential entrant who is weighing the costs and benefits of entering the industry. A bout of predatory pricing will raise the costs of entering and may make entry less likely. This is especially true if the long-run average cost curve of the predator is lower than the average variable cost curve of the entrant. In that case, the entrant's assets are really of no value in the sense that a competitive price would not cover variable cost. Moreover, a history of dealing with entrants in predatory fashion may slow down the flow of future rivals.

In spite of McGee's conviction that predation is inferior to the alternative strategies, we have seen that there may be some reasons for using predation. Moreover, the McGee analysis implicitly assumes that merging to create a monopoly is legal.[42] This, however, is not the case now. It has been settled for some time that the antitrust law does not permit such mergers. Although predatory pricing is not legal, it is easier to hide than a merger. If we couple this with the observation that the threat of predation may deter entry, one cannot reject predatory pricing as economically irrational. Let us consider the empirical evidence that has been gathered so far.

First, based upon his analysis of the Standard Oil case, McGee concluded that, in fact, Standard Oil had not practiced predatory pricing. Standard Oil had attained its monopoly through a series of mergers and acquisitions. McGee examined every instance of alleged predation at the refinery level, the wholesale (jobbing) level, and at the retail level. None of them appeared to be instances of actual predation.

Next, Kenneth Elzinga reviewed the trial record involving the Gunpowder Trust.[43] In this case, the government alleged that 14 companies were faced with predatory pricing by the Gunpowder Trust. Elzinga reviewed the trial record to see if he could find any instances of pricing below marginal cost in local markets in order to exclude actual competitors and/or to discourage new entry. This review provided support for at most two instances of predatory pricing. Elzinga pointed out that if predatory pricing were really effective in damaging rivals, then one should not observe much entry. In contrast, if the large firm tended to buy out the new entrants at attractive prices, then one should observe entry. In fact, Elzinga found several instances of owners who were supposed to have been driven out of the industry reentering the indus-

---

[42] See Posner, *Antitrust Law: An Economic Perspective*, pp. 184–87, for a skeptical view of McGee's analysis.

[43] See Kenneth G. Elzinga, "Predatory Pricing: The Case of the Gunpowder Trust," *Journal of Law and Economics* 13 (April 1970), pp.223–40, for more detail on this interesting case.

try. This is not consistent with the predatory pricing thesis but is consistent with the acquisition thesis.

Roland Koller[44] recognized that predation could be used to exclude competitors or to persuade them to collude or merge with the predator. He defined predation to be pricing below average total cost with a predatory intent (i.e., to exclude a rival or force collusion or merger upon him). Koller found 26 cases where the government alleged predatory pricing, where the government won, and where the trial record, briefs, and so on permitted an adequate empirical search. He found 16 cases where predation seems not to have occurred and another 3 where he could not tell. In the remaining seven cases, Koller felt that predatory pricing had been attempted for one reason or another. In four of the seven cases, the predation appears to have been successful—either the rival was excluded or it acquiesced to a merger or collusion.

The major problem with the research methodology of McGee, Elzinga, and Koller is its reliance upon subjective analyses of specific instances of alleged predation. Recently, Malcolm Burns has used a fundamentally different approach.[45] Burns used data on 43 acquisitions by the old American Tobacco Company during the 1891–1906 period. He started by assuming that the allegations of predation were true and tested the data to determine whether American Tobacco was able to buy out its former rivals at distress prices. Using modern finance theory, Burns found that the predatory price cutting of American Tobacco systematically reduced its acquisition costs. This favorable result operated through the reduced prices paid for the victims and through a reputation effect. Once American Tobacco established a reputation for predation, the price that American Tobacco had to pay for former rivals acquired peacefully fell. Thus, Burns provides some empirical evidence that predatory pricing can be an economically sensible business strategy in striving for monopoly.

In summary, neither the theory nor the empirical evidence clearly rules out predatory pricing as a tactic for preserving and enhancing monopoly power. But one thing is certain: It cannot be used from scratch to create market power because the predatory war must be financed from excess profits earned somewhere else.

Definition of predatory pricing

To this point, we have not settled on a precise definition for predatory pricing. In response to the empirical investigations of predatory pricing

---

[44] Roland H. Koller II, "The Myth of Predatory Pricing: An Empirical Study," *Antitrust Law and Economic Review* 5 (Summer 1971), pp. 105–23. Many would quarrel with Koller's definition of predation.

[45] Malcolm R. Burns, "The Effects of Predatory Price Cutting on the Acquisition Cost of Competitors," mimeo, March 1984. We appreciate Professor Burns's kindness in sharing his research efforts with us.

that confirmed few instances of such a practice, Professor Yamey[46] argued that temporary price cutting may be predatory even when price is not below cost. He felt that requiring price to be set below marginal cost or below average variable cost before classifying it as predatory was too restrictive. But suppose a monopolist lowers price when a new rival enters and raises price when the new firm gets discouraged and leaves. Without some sort of a cost-based standard, it is very difficult to determine whether this pricing is predatory because it is not clear how else the monopolist should behave. Professors Areeda and Turner set out to resolve this issue by providing a cost-based rule.

In their provocative article, Areeda and Turner[47] specified a cost-based rule for classifying pricing as predatory. Consider Figure 5–6. For a monopolist, profit maximization requires producing where marginal cost equals marginal revenue (Q_1). The profit-maximizing price (P_1) is the price on the demand curve for that level of output. At times, this price will be below average total cost but at or above average variable cost, as in Figure 5–6. This price is not predatory since the firm is maximizing short-run profits. While it is true that price does not cover average total cost, the firm is doing the best that it can without regard to the impact upon its rivals.

If the demand and cost curves in Figure 5–7 prevail, profit maximization would call for a price and output of P_1 and Q_1, respectively. The firm may elect to charge less than P_1 but more than the per unit cost of production and distribution. It may do this intermittently when rivals enter a market or it may do this as a permanent pricing strategy to forestall entry. In either case, the price is always above unit cost, and therefore, the firm always earns positive profits. It is clear, however, that the firm adopts this sort of pricing behavior in order to protect its market share by deterring its actual or potential rivals. But as long as prices cover average total costs and marginal costs, they should not be deemed predatory. Prices between P_1 and P_2 satisfy these criteria and are not predatory because such pricing is competition on the merits. If rivals cannot survive when price is above the monopolist's average cost, the rivals should not survive because they are too inefficient.

Now, suppose that the monopolist sets price below marginal cost. In that case, he is losing money on at least some units of output. Moreover, he is charging a price below the social cost of the marginal units. This is predatory pricing provided that the price is also below the average cost. Areeda and Turner, however, would exempt prices below marginal cost but above average cost. While we do not want such prices on social

[46] Basil S. Yamey, "Predatory Price-Cutting: Notes and Comments," *Journal of Law and Economics* 15 (April 1972), pp. 129–42.

[47] Phillip Areeda and Donald Turner, "Predatory Pricing and Related Practices under Section 2 of the Sherman Act," *Harvard Law Review* 88 (February 1975), pp. 697–733. This paper has spawned a host of related papers that have shed as much heat as light on the subject.

FIGURE 5–6

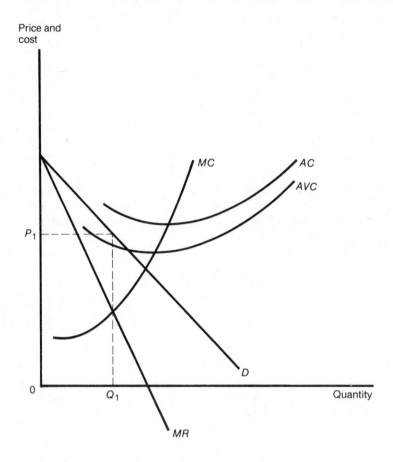

welfare grounds, actual or potential rivals cannot be deterred by prices above average cost unless they are inefficient relative to the monopolist. In summary, then, Areeda and Turner classify as nonpredatory all prices above marginal cost to the left of point Z in Figure 5–8 and above average cost to the right of point Z. Thus, when average cost is falling, marginal cost provides the permissible lower bound. When average cost is rising, average cost is the permissible lower bound.

Areeda and Turner have recognized the difficulty of obtaining data on marginal cost. Accordingly, they have suggested a practical alternative—average variable cost. Thus, any price above average cost is presumptively lawful while any price below average variable cost is predatory. This substantially changes the test for predation and weakens the economic argument for their standard.

FIGURE 5–7

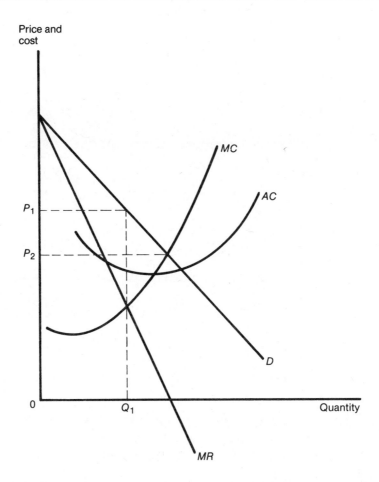

At this point, there has been no Supreme Court decision on the standards for determining the existence of predation. Most lower court decisions have endorsed some version of the Areeda-Turner standard either alone or in conjunction with some other indicators of predation or predatory intent.[48] At this time, no one can ignore the Areeda-Turner

---

[48] See the following decisions: *International Air Industries* v. *American Excelsior Co.*, 517 F. 2d 714 (5th Cir. 1975); *Pacific Engineering & Production Co. of Nevada* v. *Kerr-McGee Corp.*, 551 F. 2d 790 (10th Cir. 1977); *Chillicothe Sand & Gravel Co.* v. *Martin Marietta Corp.*, 615 F. 2d 427 (7th Cir. 1980); *Northeastern Telephone Co.* v. *American Telephone & Telegraph Co.*, 651 F. 2d (2d Cir. 1981); *William Inglis & Sons Baking Co.* v. *ITT Continental Baking Co.*, 668 F. 2d 1014 (9th Cir. 1981); *O. Hommel Co.* v. *Ferro Corp.*, 659 F. 2d 340 (3d Cir. 1981); and *MCI Communications* v. *American Telephone & Telegraph Co.*, 708 F. 2d 1081 (7th Cir. 1983).

FIGURE 5–8

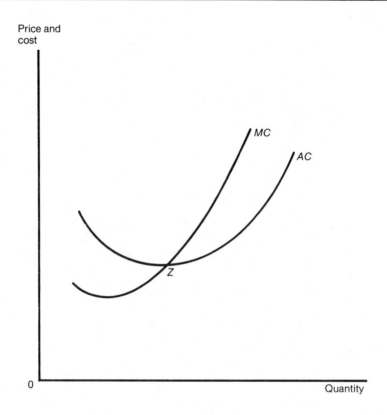

standard, but we will not know precisely how it will be received judi-cially until we get a Supreme Court ruling.

QUESTIONS AND PROBLEMS

1. Suppose the producers of Jones Juice have a monopoly in the non-carbonated soft drink market because consumers have a strong pref-erence for its taste. The drink is made from a secret recipe that is guarded carefully. This monopoly could be remedied by forced dis-closure of the recipe. What are the economic effects on the pro-ducers of Jones Juice? On the behavior of third parties?

2. Blair Bus Manufacturing Company has monopolized the school bus market by virtue of extraordinarily low production costs. The source of low costs is the brilliance of the founder's managerial skills. If

Blair can only manage one firm at a time, is there an antitrust remedy?

3. Suppose that Alcoa's sole source of monopoly in the production of virgin ingot was its control of bauxite reserves all over the world. Alcoa's efforts were conscious—it explored for and discovered the bauxite deposits and entered into long-term extraction agreements with the host governments. Can Alcoa's monopoly be dismantled by requiring that it sell to other aluminum producers? How will this affect Alcoa's investments in exploration in the future? How does it affect Exxon's decision to search for petroleum?

4. In the case of natural monopoly, there is only one survivor of the competitive process. Who will it be?

5. Suppose that General Motors refrained from exploiting all of its production and distribution efficiencies because it was afraid that Ford, Chrysler, and AMC would have failed as a result. Anticipating an antitrust suit if its domestic rivals failed, GM constrained its market share. Can you explain the present incursion of Japanese imports as a result of GM's constrained behavior?

6. Areeda and Turner have agreed that a monopoly resting upon an unexpired patent that first created it should be immune from structural criticism. But they argue that there should be no immunity for a monopoly that is *perpetuated* by subsequent patents that follow naturally from the original. Defend and attack their position.

7. You are the manager of a firm that introduced a new product called "gortons," which are fabricated out of copper sheets. The fabrication equipment is specialized and fairly expensive. As gortons gain greater consumer acceptance, the demand expands accordingly. Being a responsible manager you have expanded production capacity to keep up with the demand. Since no one else makes gortons, your firm has monopoly power. Are you and your firm guilty of monopolizing?

8. In 1972, Amalgamated Features, Inc. opened the first movie theatre in Lone Pine, Montana. Was Amalgamated guilty of monopolization in 1972? In 1981, Lone Pine had grown enough to support a second movie theatre, which Amalgamated constructed and put into operation. Why did this make Amalgamated's lawyers nervous?

9. Suppose that two areas are separated by transportation costs of $10 per unit. In other words, to move a unit of Z from area A to area B

costs $10. Generally, the difference between prices in the two areas is less than $10. Are these two areas in the same geographic market?

10. Shell regular gasoline contains "platformate" while Gulf regular does not. The two gasolines are physically differentiated, but slight differences in price cause large changes in quantities sold. Are the two gasolines in the same product market?

11. Independent (unbranded) gasoline sells for five cents per gallon less than the gasoline sold by the so-called majors (e.g., Exxon or Texaco). Since a one-cent price differential between Exxon and Texaco gasoline cannot be sustained, unbranded gasoline must be in a separate product market from brand name gasoline. Discuss and critique.

12. Robert Bork claims that the *Alcoa* decision exhibits "an illogical stress upon the importance of allocative efficiency without regard to productive efficiency." What does Bork mean? Why is it a problem?

13. Promotional pricing is a temporary, low price designed to attract new business. Sometimes these prices are well below cost and are even zero in some instances. Is promotional pricing predatory? If not, how does one distinguish promotional from predatory pricing?

14. Suppose Firm A has 20 percent of the market for industrial strapping, firm B has 15 percent of the market, and firm C has 10 percent. They agree to follow a course of conduct that will divide a regional market among them. Are they guilty of conspiring to monopolize the industrial strapping market?

15. Suppose that Harvey Hustle is the chief executive of Hustle Hamburgers, a fast-food chain. Harvey's aggressive price competition and his product's superior quality have wounded the rival fast-food chains. Harvey's announced intention is to dominate the fast-food field. Is Harvey guilty of a Section 2 violation?

16. Suppose that someone complained to the Antitrust Division that Blair Bottlers and the Kaserman Korporation were conspiring in an attempt to monopolize the soft drink market. What is the likely reaction of the Antitrust Division?

17. Suppose that B&K Amalgamated used predatory price cutting with the result that it acquired its nearly bankrupt rivals at distress prices. Is this sufficient evidence that predation is an economically sound business strategy?

18. What is the two-prong test for illegal monopolization? Does it have much foundation in economic theory?

19. How do economists use price correlations and sales patterns to define product and geographic markets? Is the cross-elasticity of demand relevant? If so, how?

20. Why is a "dangerous probability of success" important in an attempt-to-monopolize case? How is such a probability determined?

FURTHER READINGS

Areeda, Phillip, and Donald Turner. *Antitrust Law* III. Boston: Little, Brown, 1978.

_____. "Predatory Pricing and Related Practices under Section 2 of the Sherman Act." *Harvard Law Review* 88 (February 1975), pp. 697–733.

Bork, Robert H. *The Antitrust Paradox.* New York: Basic Books, 1978.

Boyer, Kenneth D. "Industry Boundaries." In *Economic Analysis and Antitrust Law,* ed. T. Calvani and J. Siegfried. Boston: Little, Brown, 1979, pp. 88–106.

Landes, William M., and Richard Posner. "Market Power in Antitrust Cases." *Harvard Law Review* 94 (March 1981), pp. 937–96.

McGee, John S. "Predatory Pricing: The Standard Oil (N.J.) Case." *Journal of Law and Economics* 1 (October 1958), pp. 137–69.

6

Collusion: Horizontal price fixing

In Chapter 2, we developed the economic case against monopoly, which hinged upon the misallocation of resources that results from the monopolist's output restriction. Section 2 of the Sherman Act is directed at monopoly. As we shall see, ostensibly competitive firms have devised ingenious methods for coordinating their efforts in an attempt to emulate the monopolist. Accordingly, Section 1 of the Sherman Act prohibits "[e]very contract, combination . . . , or conspiracy in restraint of trade. . . ." This vague language means that collective efforts to increase price, reduce output, prevent entry, exclude actual competitors, and a host of other business practices are illegal.

The classic violation of Section 1 is a horizontal price-fixing conspiracy or cartel.[1] For our purposes, a cartel is just a formal (overt) price-fixing agreement like OPEC (Organization of Petroleum Exporting Countries), but collusive agreements are analytically equivalent. The major difference is that cartels meet in Vienna and are reported in the press, while collusion may occur more frequently in the locker rooms of exclusive country clubs. In this chapter, we shall develop the economic consequences of such a conspiracy to show its similarity to monopoly. We will also discuss some dissimilarities that make price-fixing conspiracies

---

[1] By "horizontal," we mean that the conspirators operate at the same level and would be rivals in the absence of an agreement.

more fragile than monopoly and at the same time more damaging to society. Other forms of conspiracy are examined in the next chapter.

6–1 CARTEL THEORY[2]

We begin our discussion with a simple model that focuses upon price agreements that are aimed at industry profit maximization. Throughout the analysis, we assume that firm and industry demand is linear and remains stable. All production is carried out by employing unspecialized inputs. This, of course, means that input prices do not change in response to changes in industry output, which is apt to occur whenever specialized inputs are employed. In turn, this means that the firm and industry cost functions do not shift as total output changes. Finally, we limit our attention to a single product.

Competitive solution

Suppose there are 100 firms in an industry that is competitively organized. This means that entry is free, but it does not mean that there are no costs to entering (recall our discussion in Chapter 1). Instead, the assumption requires that there are no entry barriers for new firms. In this model, we assume that each existing firm operates a single plant. Since the same technology is available to all firms and input prices are the same for all firms, the cost functions for all plants are the same. In other words, the 100 plants are identical. The cost functions of a typical firm are shown in panel (a) of Figure 6–1.

Under the assumed conditions, the long-run supply (LRS) function for the industry will be perfectly elastic (i.e., it will be horizontal) at a height equal to the minimum point on each firm's average total cost curve. We can aggregate the cost functions of the 100 firms in panel (a) of Figure 6–1 to depict the long-run equilibrium of the industry in panel (b). Even though each firm may have a U-shaped long-run average cost curve, the entry and exit of firms of optimal size will lead to the horizontal long-run supply that interacts with industry demand (D) to determine the equilibrium price and output, P_2 and Q_2, respectively. We should note that the industry output Q_2 is equal to $100q_2$. This result can be compared to the results for a monopoly and for a cartel.

Monopoly solution: Short run

Suppose that a single firm monopolized the industry by buying all 100 of the previously independent (and competitive) firms. For that new

---

[2] This section depends upon the classic paper by Don Patinkin, "Multiple-Plant Firms, Cartels, and Imperfect Competition," *Quarterly Journal of Economics* 61 (February 1947), pp. 173–205.

FIGURE 6–1

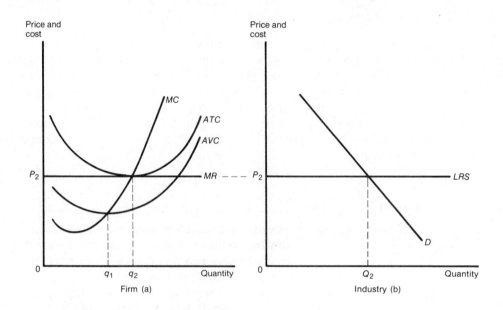

Firm (a)

Industry (b)

firm, which has 100 plants at its disposal, the long-run supply (*LRS*) of Figure 6–1 is its long-run average and marginal cost function, *LAC* and *LMC*, respectively.

Upon acquiring the 100 plants, however, the monopolist's first problem is to select a price and output that will maximize the firm's short-run profits. To see how this can be accomplished, we need the monopolist's *short-run* cost functions.

Since the monopolist has 100 plants, it must allocate output responsibility among these 100 plants. First, notice that q_1 is the output level that minimizes each plant's average variable cost. If the monopolist selects an output level that exceeds Q_1, which is equal to $100q_1$, then the output will be evenly divided among the 100 plants in order to minimize costs. To see the logic of this, suppose output were not evenly divided among the plants. In that event, the marginal cost in one plant would then exceed the marginal cost in another plant—say, $MC_1 > MC_2$. Now look at the consequences of moving one unit of output responsibility from plant 1 to plant 2. The cost *reduction* in plant 1, MC_1, would exceed the cost *increase* in plant 2, MC_2. Consequently, profits are improved simply by reallocating production responsibility among the plants because costs are not minimized unless marginal costs are equal across plants. Now, suppose the monopolist were to select an output smaller than Q_1. It is not economic to operate any plant at an output level below q_1, and therefore, any output Q that is less than Q_1 will be allocated equally among Q/q_1 plants. Each of the plants in operation will produce q_1, while the remaining $100 - Q/q_1$ plants will be idle. Any other solution would have higher variable costs and lower profits. Since total fixed costs are constant and total revenue is fixed once the output is selected, maximizing profits requires minimizing total variable costs.

For the monopolist, the average variable cost (AVC) function is a horizontal line at a height equal to the minimum point on the average variable cost curve in panel (a) of Figure 6–1 until Q_1 is reached. At that point, AVC is positively sloped. The monopolist's short-run marginal cost coincides with AVC until Q_1, and then it is positively sloped and is above the AVC curve. These relationships are depicted in Figure 6–2,

FIGURE 6–2

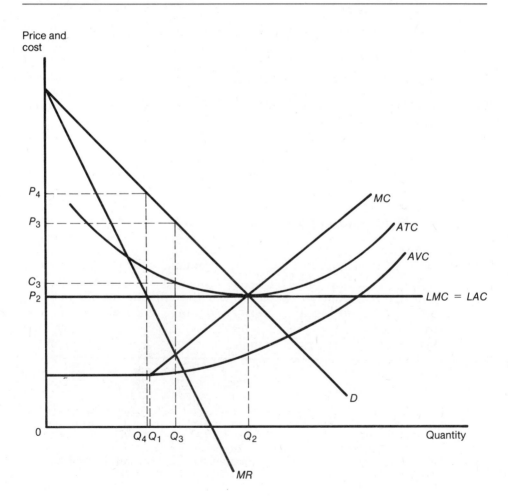

which reproduces panel (*b*) of Figure 6–1 and adds the short-run functions. Note that the average total cost and the average variable cost curves are drawn by combining the cost and output information for the monopolist's 100 plants.

In the short run, the monopolist maximizes profit by producing the output where marginal cost and marginal revenue are equal. Of course, price must exceed average variable cost at that output. In this case, a total output of Q_3 will be produced and sold at the short-run profit maximizing price of P_3. The excess profit is given by the rectangle of area $(P_3 - C_3)Q_3$.

Cartel solution: Short run

Suppose that instead of having a single firm own the 100 plants, the plants continued to be operated under independent ownership. These firms, however, are assumed to form a cartel and then collude upon price and output.[3] The cartel steering committee would be responsible for selecting a price and output that would maximize total industry profits. Once again, this will require the allocation of production responsibility such that total costs are minimized. For simplicity, we shall assume that the 100 firms share equally in any excess profits that are earned.[4] It is easy to see that the short-run cartel solution is identical to that of the monopolist. In this case, the profit of $(P_3 - C_3)Q_3$ is divided equally among the 100 separate firms as is the production responsibility. This division of the spoils is facilitated by the fact that production and, therefore, sales revenue are evenly divided among the firms. Thus, each firm simply keeps what it earns.

Monopoly solution: Long run

If one examines Figure 6–2, it is apparent that the monopolist is not in long-run equilibrium. At the short-run optimal output of Q_3, the average cost C_3 exceeds the long-run average cost of P_2. This means that some long-run adjustment can be made that will improve the monopolist's profits by reducing its costs. For example, if the number of plants were reduced to Q_3/q_2, which is less than 100 because Q_2/q_2 equals 100, then the monopolist's short-run average total cost curve would be tangent to its long-run average cost LAC. As a result, the profit associated with an output of Q_3 would increase from $(P_3 - C_3)Q_3$ to $(P_3 - P_2)Q_3$. But

---

[3] Here, and in the rest of this section, we assume total cooperation among the cartel members. This, of course, is unrealistic, and the implications of incomplete cooperation are explored in subsequent sections of this chapter.

[4] This assumption is a gross simplification because each firm has an obvious incentive to request (demand?) a disproportionate share of the ill-gotten gains. The rest of the firms have an equally obvious incentive to resist. As a result, the negotiations may be stormy.

the former optimal output of Q_3 no longer would be optimal because the short-run marginal cost curve would shift to the left with fewer plants. Of course, we knew that Q_3 was not the long-run profit maximizing quantity for the monopolist because long-run marginal cost LMC does not equal MR at an output of Q_3. In the long-run, the monopolist will reduce the number of plants to Q_4/q_2 and raise the price even further to P_4. Now profit will be equal to the area $(P_4 - P_2)Q_4$. The final equilibrium is displayed in Figure 6–3. By way of comparison, note that the competitive output is twice the monopolist's long-run profit maximizing output, and the competitive price is substantially lower than the monopolist's price.

FIGURE 6–3

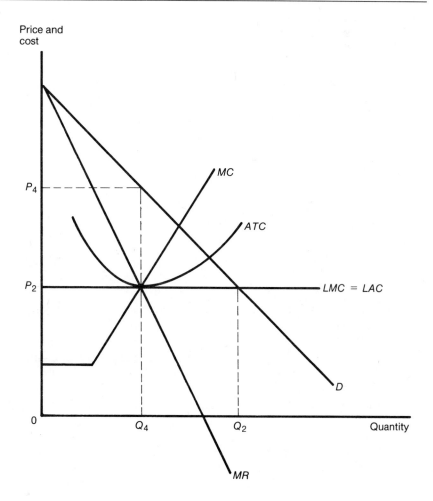

Cartel solution: Long run

The equivalence of the monopoly and cartel decisions in the short run was due to the fact that neither entry nor exit could occur in the short run. Implicit in our discussion of the monopolist's long-run solution was the assumption that no entry could occur in response to the excess profits that were being enjoyed. Without the entry barriers, the monopoly would not last. We did not examine the source of the entry barriers, but one could assume that the government decreed that only a single firm would be permitted to operate. In that case, there would be no need to worry about entry. For the cartel, however, we shall assume that entry remains free (albeit not costless). As a result, the excess profits that the cartel enjoyed in the short run will attract the entry of new firms. As we shall see later, the best that the cartel can hope for is that the new entrants will join the cartel and adhere to the price and output decisions of the cartel steering committee.

In Figure 6–4, we duplicate the short-run equilibrium price and output for the cartel of P_3 and Q_3, respectively. As firms enter in response to the lure of excess profits, the *industry* short-run marginal cost curve changes. All of the new entrants will have cost functions like those in panel (a) of Figure 6–1. As a result, the industry short-run marginal cost function will be horizontal over a wider range of output. In fact, with each entrant, the horizontal range is extended by q_1 units of output. As entry occurs, the cartel's optimal output expands because the intersection of the (shifting) marginal cost and marginal revenue shifts to the right. This, of course, involves corresponding decreases in price since the demand curve does not change. The maximum cartel output occurs at Q_5 where the horizontal portion of the marginal cost curve extends all the way to the marginal revenue function. If there are still excess profits at Q_5 and P_5, further entry will occur in response to these excess profits.

In Figure 6–4, suppose that there are excess profits at P_5 and Q_5 when there are Q_5/q_1 firms in the industry. Industry equilibrium, however, requires zero excess profits because entry will continue as long as excess profits persist. The cartel steering committee will never decrease price or increase output from P_5 and Q_5, respectively, but the excess profits will continue to attract additional firms beyond Q_5/q_1. In order to maximize profits, the cartel will split up the production responsibility equally among Q_5/q_1 firms with each producing q_1 units of output. The remaining firms will be idle but will have to share equally in the excess profits if their cooperation is to be retained. Entry will stop when the *ATC* curve for the *industry* shifts to the point that it is tangent to the demand function at an output of Q_5. At that point, excess profits will be zero, and there will be no incentive for any further entry.

Thus, the long-run equilibrium of the cartel under the hypothesized assumptions will be characterized by excess capacity and overinvest-

FIGURE 6–4

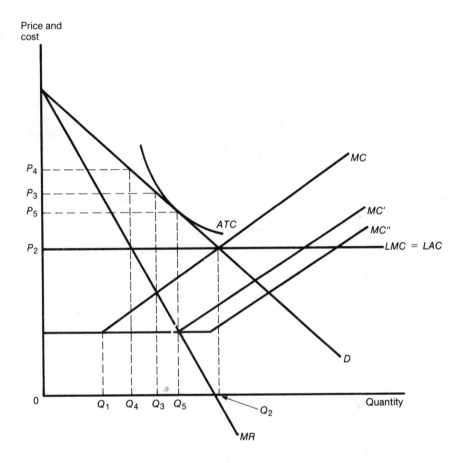

ment. The excess profits have attracted socially useless investment in productive capacity, which stays idle. As a result, the industry has excess capacity, and investors obviously have overinvested in this industry. Several comparisons can now be made. First, relative to the monopoly solution, price will be lower and output will be higher, as can be seen by comparing P_5 with P_4 and Q_5 with Q_4. Naturally enough, this means that the monopolist's profits of $(P_4 - P_2)Q_4$, which are positive, exceed the long-run cartel profits, which are zero. Second, relative to the competitive solution, there will be *more* firms in the industry, but price will be higher and output will be lower as can be seen by comparing P_5 and P_2 and Q_5 and Q_2, respectively. One cannot say which organization (monopoly or cartel) is least desirable because the welfare effects are muddled by the presence of the excess capacity.

6–2 THE PROBLEM OF ENTRY

The cartel's difficulties in the long run stem from the inability to control entry. As we have seen, the cartel's success is threatened by two assumptions: (1) free entry and (2) the presumed existence of an infinite number of firms with identical cost curves. We can discuss each of these in turn.

Free entry. In the real world, successful cartels have solved the entry problem in a number of ways. For example, some have enlisted the aid of the government to compel membership in the cartel and to enforce the cartel decisions. At the federal level, the Interstate Commerce Commission and the Civil Aeronautics Board have performed this function admirably. Although many states provide similar protection in banking, the states do their best work in controlling entry through licensing restrictions. Licensing is used to control many economic activities: (1) the number of taxicabs operating in large cities, (2) the number of barbers, (3) the number of liquor stores, and (4) the number of acres devoted to growing tobacco, to mention just a few examples. Government control of entry is an extremely efficient source of control because the police power of the state can be brought to bear upon any who dare enter without approval.[5]

Another way of controlling entry is through patent control. Du Pont was able to do this through its control of the cellophane patent. You may recall from the previous chapter that Du Pont permitted Sylvania to produce (i.e., enter) under a licensing agreement. In some industries, control over entry through patent control is exerted by several firms jointly through patent pools. Finally, one may limit entry through the ownership and control of raw materials as Alcoa did through its control of bauxite deposits.

Infinite number of identical firms. The cartel's problems were partly the by-product of our assumption that there was an infinite number of firms with identical cost curves. But it is not necessarily true that all firms have the same cost curves. Some firms may be more efficient producers than other firms and therefore may be able to produce at lower prices than other firms. That is, the more efficient firms have lower marginal and average cost curves than other firms. This is because the more efficient firms have either better managerial abilities or more productive resources. For example, one oil company may discover a particularly productive set of oil fields while others are not as lucky or as talented at discovery. Similarly, some companies are blessed with more insightful managers or owners than other companies.

What does all of this have to do with cartels? If the relatively efficient firms in an industry attempt to increase their profits by reducing their

---

[5] For an interesting analysis of the consequences of licensing, see Sidney L. Carroll and Robert J. Gaston, "Occupational Restrictions and the Quality of Service Received," *Southern Economic Journal* 47 (April 1981), pp. 959–76.

production and thereby increasing prices, the higher prices in the industry will attract only a limited number of new firms. The increase in total quantity supplied by these new firms will not be sufficient to drive the price back to the original price, for the new firms are less efficient than the original firms and are unable to survive at the original low price. In other words, the new entrants can only survive as long as the cartel is successful. The relatively efficient firms in the industry therefore will be successful in increasing their profits through collusion if they do not cheat on each other and force prices back down through their own actions.

6–3   THE PROBLEM OF CHEATING

So far, we have assumed that every cartel member obeys the dictates of the cartel steering committee. Unfortunately for the cartel, this turns out to be a heroic assumption. In fact, economic history has shown that cartels tend to be highly unstable unless some means is found to compel adherence to the price and output quotas set for each firm. This is due to greed, not to stubbornness. Cartel members will tend to cheat on their own agreement and thereby cause the whole deal to break down. We can see the incentives for this by examining the situation facing a typical firm. It will prove helpful to introduce the firm's proportional demand curve. Suppose that the industry demand function is given by

$$Q = 1,000 - 2P \tag{1}$$

The proportional demand function for each of the 100 firms is given by

$$Q/100 = 10 - (2/100)P \tag{2}$$

In other words, for each price, each firm's share is 1 percent of the market quantity demanded at that price. On our usual price-quantity diagram, the proportional demand function will have the same intercept on the price axis as the market demand has. The intercept on the quantity axis will be 1/100 of the intercept for the market demand function.

The proportional demand function (d) for a cartel member can be put in a diagram similar to panel (a) of Figure 6–1. Consider the impact of the cartel's short-run decision to set price and quantity equal to P_3 and Q_3, respectively, in Figure 6–5. The typical firm is expected to produce q_3 and to sell it at P_3. But each of these firms has always believed that its output decision had no impact upon the industry price. Each firm used to produce where its marginal cost was equal to the market price. Accordingly, this firm may take P_3 as given and attempt to expand its output to q_6, which is considerably larger than q_2. Since the profit is substantially higher at this quantity, the temptation to cheat on the agreement by producing extra output will be almost irresistible. If this were true for only one firm, little damage would be done, but all members of the cartel will face similar temptations. As each cheats on the

FIGURE 6–5

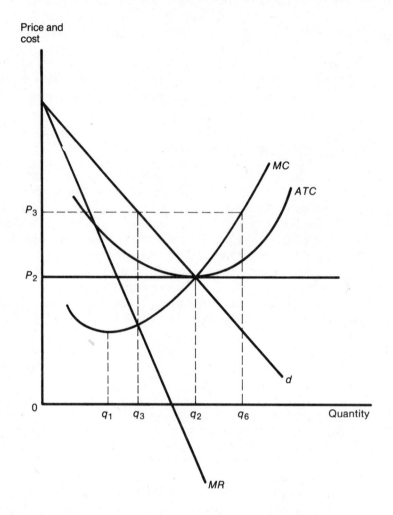

agreement, total output expands considerably beyond Q_3, and price will plummet toward the competitive level.

Although each firm surely appreciates the benefit from an aggregate decrease in industry output, it will prove difficult to resist the increased profits available by expanding its own output. As we have seen above, individual profits are higher at the larger output of q_6 provided that no one else cheats. Moreover, the production people in the firm will also be anxious to expand output due to the unexploited economies of scale that exist. These can be seen in Figure 6–5 by examining the average total cost curve (ATC) at an output of q_3. The fact that the ATC curve is negatively sloped at the restricted output of q_3 indicates that an expansion of output beyond q_3 will reduce the per unit cost.

Unfortunately for the colluders but not for consumers, there is no inexpensive way of disciplining cheaters.[6] Since agreements to fix price are not enforceable contracts, the cheater cannot be sued for failing to keep his part of the bargain. The cartel has no official police power and, therefore, cannot really impose fines on the cheaters. Other methods for punishing cheaters, such as severely depressing prices, will impose substantial costs on the loyal members of the cartel. Thus, there are strong incentives for cheating and very few deterrents. As a result, we should not be surprised to discover that cartels tend to be somewhat fragile.

George Stigler[7] has developed a cartel model with a simple enforcement mechanism. In his model, enforcement takes the simple form of detection. Once significant departures from the agreed upon prices are detected, they will vanish because other firms will match the lower price if it is not withdrawn. This will get the cartel back on track temporarily, but it will not solve the cheating problem. As long as there is some time lag between cheating and getting caught at it, there will be benefits to cheating.

Fixing market shares may be the most efficient means of combatting price cuts because fixing shares will force the price cutter to move along the industry demand curve. But adherence to market shares or quotas is hard to enforce in a clandestine manner. For example, departures from the quota will require interfirm transfers to restore the proper balance, but such transfers are easily detectable. An alternative to fixing market shares is customer allocation.[8] This procedure is not without problems. First, customer allocation also can be detected easily. Second, in the long run, the participants are bound not to be satisfied with the customers allocated to them. This is an inevitable result of random variations in the fortunes of those customers. Some will expand and prosper while others are destined to flounder and die.[9] Internal squabbles are bound to follow. Finally, price cutting (cheating!) has a long-run payoff if the customers are competing firms. If one firm cuts price, its customers will have lower costs and will expand at the expense of the customers assigned to the colluders that refrain from price cutting. Since the cheater's customers are growing relative to the rest of the industry, the cheater's

---

[6] For a very complicated look at this problem, see Daniel Orr and Paul W. MacAvoy, "Price Strategies to Promote Cartel Stability," *Economica* 32 (May 1965), pp. 186–97.

[7] See George J. Stigler, "A Theory of Oligopoly," *Journal of Political Economy* 72 (February 1964), pp. 44–61, for the analytical details.

[8] In a customer allocation scheme, each customer is assigned to a specific supplier, and the other suppliers will not compete for that customer's business. We discuss customer allocation in the next chapter.

[9] F. M. Scherer has an interesting simulation of a random process that provides vastly different outcomes for an industry. This points up the importance of luck. See his *Industrial Market Structure and Economic Performance* (Skokie, Ill.: Rand McNally, 1980).

share of total sales will increase, and it will expand relative to its rivals. Consequently, there are long-run gains from price cutting, and once again, the cartel agreement is subject to breakdown.

Collusion is apt to be especially effective against small buyers and government entities. First, secret price cuts to small buyers are apt to be detected just because of the large numbers that are involved. Suppose that p is the probability that any given price cut will be detected. It follows that $(1 - p)$ must be the probability of not getting caught cutting price once. If reduced prices are offered to n customers, the probability of not getting caught in any of these price cuts is $(1 - p)^n$. Consequently, $1 - (1 - p)^n$ is the probability of detecting at least one price cut if there are n such price cuts. To get a feel for the likelihood of detecting price cuts, suppose that the probability of detecting any one price cut is 0.01 and that there are 100 price cuts. The probability of at least one price cut being detected is 0.634, which may be large enough to deter cheating on small sales to small buyers.

Second, policing a collusive agreement is most efficient when transaction prices can be obtained from the buyers. Collusion is always more effective against buyers who report correctly and fully the prices offered to them. Government entities, which are compelled by law to use competitive sealed bidding for contract awards, are most susceptible to collusive pricing because they assist in the policing effort. It would be interesting to see the reactions of the bidders if awards were made on some sort of random basis whenever collusion or identical bidding were suspected.

In Stigler's model, the detection of secret price cuts depends upon:

1. The behavior of a firm's old customers.
2. The attraction of old customers of rival firms.
3. The behavior of new customers.

In other words, the basic way of detecting price cuts is by inference. If one seller appears to be enjoying business that he should not be getting if he were not cutting prices, the rest of the firms will infer that he is cheating. Each firm knows that there will be some turnover among its customers. If it suddenly starts losing too many of its old customers, however, it should suspect the existence of a price cutter. In addition, each firm expects to attract a certain number of its rivals' old customers. If it fails to get the expected number, suspicions will surface. Finally, each firm will anticipate getting a fair share of new customers and if its expectations are not fulfilled, it may suspect price cutting.

The incentives for secret price cutting depend upon a number of factors. First, the incentive increases with the number of rival sellers. As that number increases, the impact of any price cutting will be spread over a large number of rival firms. Thus, it will be harder to detect than if there were fewer rivals. Second, the incentive to cut price falls as the number of customers per firm increases. This was shown above with a simple probability calculation. In essence, the gain per price cut is small, and therefore, one must cut price to many customers in order to enhance profits appreciably. This, however, increases the probability of detection. Finally, the incentive to cut price increases as the probability of repeat sales falls. The absence of price competition can be inferred by buyer loyalty. Thus, collusion is limited when a firm's significant customers constantly change identity. This conclusion follows because there is insufficient experience with any one customer to detect price cuts.

6–4 THE PROBLEM OF UNEQUAL COSTS

The cartel model has assumed that the cost functions are identical for all firms. In actuality, the costs may not be the same, and this causes

FIGURE 6–6

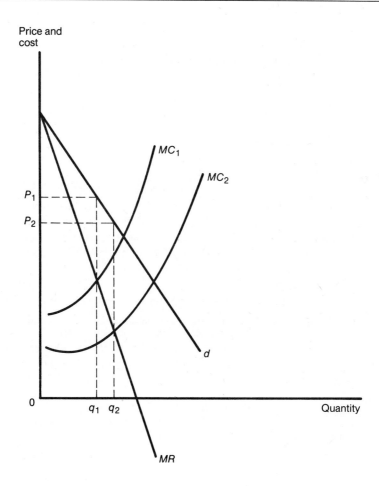

added difficulties. Even if each firm is willing to respect its proportional demand curve as in Figure 6–5, it is unlikely that a common price will satisfy all of the firms. In Figure 6–6, suppose there are two firms that have marginal cost curves MC_1 and MC_2. Let d represent the proportional demand function for each firm, and let mr represent the associated marginal revenue. Profit maximization will lead firm 1 to prefer a price of P_1 for both firms and outputs of q_1 for each of them. In contrast, for firm 2, marginal revenue exceeds MC_2 at an output of q_1, and therefore, firm 2 prefers the larger output q_2 at the lower price of P_2. This difference in preferences can cause a breakdown of the cartel and, in any event, causes negotiating difficulties among the cartel members.

One way out of this difficulty is to rely upon market division. If it is possible to implement, the cartel may split up the total market on a geographic basis. Under such an arrangement, each firm would be free to set any price it deems optimal in its own territory. Other problems, however, surface in this setting. We shall discuss market division in the next chapter.

6–5 PARTIAL CONSPIRACIES[10]

Many price-fixing conspiracies are not industrywide. In other words, the conspiracy may not include every firm in the industry. On occasion, one of the large firms in an industry may be a maverick and refuse to participate directly. Perhaps a more common scenario is for the large firms to cooperate while the small, so-called competitive fringe firms are ignored by the conspirators. There are a number of reasons why it may be desirable to leave out the fringe firms. For one thing, price fixing is an illegal activity, and it is therefore desirable to make it a clandestine activity as well. The smaller the number of active conspirators, the easier it will be to keep their illegal activity concealed. For another thing, there are costs associated with group decision making: coordination costs, negotiation costs, and so on. These costs rise as the number in the group increases, and consequently, it makes some sense to limit the number of conspirators. There are, however, some costs associated with a policy decision to ignore a fringe of competitive firms. Since these firms are not bound by the cartel agreement, they have no obligation to curtail their output. This means that the requisite output restriction falls completely on the shoulders of the conspirators. In addition, the short-run cartel profits will be smaller than they would be if the competitive fringe had been included. Thus, it is apparent that there are both costs and benefits to leaving out the fringe. In an optimal decision, these costs will be

---

[10] Nearly every standard, intermediate microeconomics text contains a discussion of the so-called dominant firm price leadership model. See, for example, J. Gould and C. E. Ferguson, *Microeconomic Theory*, 5th ed. (Homewood, Ill.: Richard D. Irwin, 1980). This section is an application of that model.

balanced: the incremental cost of omitting an industry member will be just equal to the incremental benefit of doing so.

To analyze the effect of a conspiracy involving a core of dominant firms in an industry that excludes a competitive fringe, we employ a variant of the dominant firm price leadership model. Initially, let us examine the preconspiracy price and output. In Figure 6–7, the con-

FIGURE 6–7

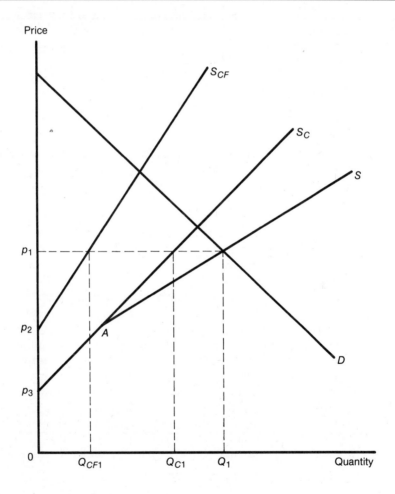

sumer demand for the product is represented by the negatively sloped line labeled D. This shows the quantity that consumers are willing to buy at various prices. The curve denoted S_{CF} is the sum of the competitive fringe firms' marginal cost curves. Accordingly, it shows the amount that the competitive fringe will supply at various prices. Similarly, S_C shows the supply response of the dominant firms to various prices. The industry supply curve is obtained by adding these supply curves together:

$$S = S_C + S_{CF}$$

For prices between P_2 and P_3, only the dominant firms will supply any output. Consequently, the industry supply coincides with S_C. For all prices above p_2, however, the two supply curves are added horizontally. This results in an industry supply curve of p_3AS.

Assuming that there is no collusion, the market will clear at a competitive price of p_1 and an output of Q_1. We can see that the dominant firms produce Q_{C1} while the competitive fringe produces Q_{CF1}. The sum of these two is necessarily Q_1:

$$Q_{C1} + Q_{CF1} = Q_1$$

Collusion of the dominant firms

Suppose that the dominant firms decide to collude in an effort to increase their profits. If they decide to treat the competitive firms passively, their task is a strange one: They must determine the optimal price to charge without having any control over the competitive fringe. One way of accomplishing this end is to determine the profit maximizing price while explicitly recognizing that the competitive fringe will respond to the collusive price as it would to a market determined price. The way that such a price is determined is depicted in Figure 6–8.

We have reproduced the industry demand (D) and the three supply curves (S_{CF}, S_C, and S) of Figure 6–7. The cartel's demand is a residual demand, which is determined by subtracting the competitive fringe supply (S_{CF}) from the industry demand (D). At a price of P_3, the competitive fringe will produce where S_{CF} intersects D, thereby leaving nothing for the dominant firms to produce. At the other extreme, if the cartel selects a price equal to P_4 or less, the competitive fringe will produce nothing at all thereby leaving all of the demand (D) for the conspirators. For all prices between P_3 and P_4, the competitive fringe supply must be subtracted from the industry demand to determine the quantity that the conspirators can sell. Thus, the net demand available to the conspiring dominant firms is the industry demand less the competitive fringe supply:

$$\text{Net demand} = D - S_{CF}$$

This net demand is labeled P_3dD in Figure 6–8. The marginal revenue curve associated with this net demand curve has been constructed and labeled *mr*.

FIGURE 6–8

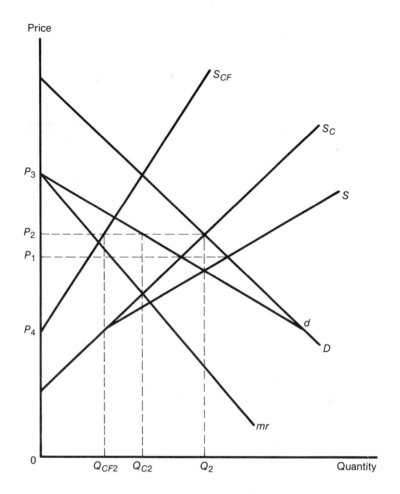

If the conspirators are to maximize their profits, they must select an output where marginal revenue (*mr*) equals marginal cost (S_C). When the cartel selects its output in Figure 6–8 where *mr* intersects S_C, it charges a price of P_2 and produces Q_{C2}. Comparing Figures 6–7 and 6–8, we see that the cartel members have restricted their output from Q_{C1} in Figure 6–7 to Q_{C2} in Figure 6–8. In contrast, the competitive fringe will respond to the higher price of P_2 by expanding its output to Q_{CF2} from Q_{CF1}. On balance, industry output will decline from Q_1 to Q_2, and as a consequence, the market will clear at the price of P_2. Not surprisingly, the cartel members will increase their profits as a result of their conspiratorial efforts. Interestingly, the competitive fringe is a beneficiary of the conspiracy as its profits also are increased. Due to our interest in the stability of collusive arrangements, we shall examine the impact of the conspiracy on the fringe firms.

Impact on competitive fringe

We can see the impact of the price conspiracy on a typical firm in the competitive fringe by examining Figure 6–9. At the initial price of P_1, the

FIGURE 6–9

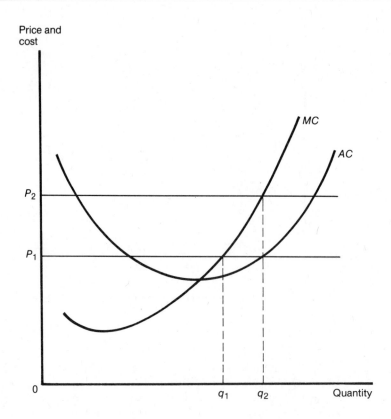

firm had expanded its output to the point where a further increase would have caused a reduction in profits. When the cartel elevated the price to P_2, the fringe firm expanded its output to the point where its marginal cost (MC) intersected the horizontal price line at P_2. Consequently, its output expanded from q_1 to q_2. As all fringe firms do the same sort of thing, the collective effect is to raise output from Q_{CF1} to Q_{CF2} in Figure 6–8.

We can see in Figure 6–9 that the gap between price and per unit cost (AC) has widened. Consequently, the typical fringe firm will enjoy greater profits as per unit profit is greater and output is also greater. This results in a familiar story: More fringe firms will enter, which causes the competitive fringe supply to shift to the right. Since the residual demand is the difference between the market demand and the fringe supply, the residual demand shifts to the left. This obviously makes the cartel firms worse off, as their profits will decline. If nothing is done to block entry, the stream of entrants will not stop until the excess profits disappear.

6–6 EMPIRICAL EVIDENCE

Conditions conducive to collusion

There are a number of structural conditions that facilitate collusion, and therefore, their presence is said to be conducive to collusion. Consequently, other things being equal, we should expect collusion to occur most often when these conditions are satisfied. For example, most government buyers are required by law to ask for sealed bids and have formal bid openings. This, of course, makes collusion easier because a cheater cannot hide his price cut or his identity. Accordingly, we should anticipate an incentive to collude where there are large government buyers.

Product homogeneity is also an important characteristic because it simplifies a collusive price agreement. In the models we have developed in this chapter, we have assumed perfect homogeneity so that a single price would maximize cartel profits. If heterogeneity is the order of the day, however, profit maximization requires a collusive price structure of some complexity. Full homogeneity is rather unlikely in the real world because it actually requires perfect substitutability among purchase commitments as well as among products. In other words, both buyers and sellers must be considered in a determination of homogeneity. Differences among purchasers may result from differences in the order size, promptness of payment, ease of sale, and the likelihood of repeat purchases. These differences clearly influence the desirability of specific sales and make agreement more difficult.

Demand elasticity is important because it affects the relative rewards to successful collusion. Specifically, the less elastic the industry demand curve is at the competitive price and output, the larger will be the profits due to collusion. Thus, demand inelasticity may prompt collusion in the industry.

A fourth factor is fewness of sellers. The smaller the number of sellers, the lower the costs of group decision making and the easier it will be to police the agreement. Moreover, the mutual interdependence among firms is obvious when markets are highly concentrated. In fact, tacit collusion, that is, collusion without the need for actual meetings, may emerge through some form of price leadership when concentration is high.

There is some empirical evidence that these factors are important. Hay and Kelley[11] examined the files and records of all Section 1 Sherman Act cases that were filed and won from January 1963 to December 1972. They counted as victories all cases won at trial and all that were settled by a plea of *nolo contendere*, which is not really a plea, but a statement that the defendant will not contend a charge made by the government. Some 65 cases were examined. In 79 percent of the cases there were 10 or fewer conspirators. If one excludes four cases with over 50 firms, the average number of colluders was 7.25. Concentration ratios[12] were not available for all cases, but in 38 out of 50 cases, the four-firm concentration ratio was over 50 percent. Their subjective assessment of product homogeneity was that the products involved were highly substitutable. Bid rigging proved to be a popular violation, but Federal government agencies were explicitly excluded from some price fixing agreements. As to demand elasticity, Hay and Kelley were unable to discover any empirical evidence on that from the case files. On the whole, Hay and Kelley's results suggest that our a priori suspicions are well-founded.

John Palmer[13] provided further empirical evidence on the conditions conducive to collusion. He based his analysis on antitrust suits involving horizontal restraints (primarily price fixing) during the 1966–70 period. He also confirmed the a priori suspicion that firms in very highly concentrated industries had a higher propensity to collude than firms in less concentrated industries. Additionally, Palmer tested the hypothesis that firms in declining industries are more likely to collude than firms in growing industries. The economic logic of this is fairly clear. When an industry is expanding, demand is apt to shift faster than capacity can be adjusted, and therefore, price will be above average cost, and excess profits will be positive. When demand is declining, the economic pie is getting smaller. In order to maintain excess profits, overt collusion must become more formal and, therefore, more susceptible to detection. Palmer also confirmed this suspicion: Firms in declining industries are more apt to collude than those in expanding industries.

---

[11] See George Hay and Daniel Kelley, "An Empirical Survey of Price Fixing Conspiracies," *Journal of Law and Economics* 17 (April 1974), pp. 13–38.

[12] The concentration ratio measures the percentage of industry sales accounted for by the four largest firms. Similar calculations are also available for the 8 largest, 20 largest, and 50 largest firms.

[13] John Palmer, "Some Economic Conditions Conducive to Collusion," *Journal of Economic Issues* 6 (September 1972), pp. 29–38.

Profitability of collusion

We have developed our models of collusion from the presumption that the object was to enhance profits. No doubt, profit is important to real-world conspirators, but an interesting question involves a determination of how profitable collusion actually is. Palmer's finding that collusion is more apt to occur in declining industries suggests that collusion may be a response to falling profits. Moreover, under those economic conditions, one might suppose that collusion cannot increase profit too much. Asch and Seneca[14] have shed some welcome empirical light on this question. Asch and Seneca looked at a set of 51 firms that were convicted of collusion or entered a plea of *nolo contendere* in a Section 1 Sherman Act case during the 1958–67 period and a control group of 50 noncollusive firms. Most of the 101 firms are on the *Fortune* 500 list, so they are not too small.

Asch and Seneca found that the collusive firms did not have high profits relative to other firms in their industry. In fact, they found a negative and statistically significant relationship between a firm's profit during the conspiracy period and the existence of collusion. Those firms that resorted to collusion experienced significantly lower profits than those that did not conspire. In another test, those firms that experienced below average profits for their industry tended to collude.

There are several explanations for the Asch-Seneca results. First, it seems to be true that the enforcement of Section 1 of the Sherman Act requires proof of conspiracy. As a result, we are more likely to catch the least effective collusive efforts. If this is true, then their results make sense: Those firms that are identified as colluders tend to come from the group of least effective (i.e., least profitable) colluders. Second, managers in declining industries may feel greater pressure to improve the firm's performance by fixing prices. Managers are judged and rewarded on the basis of their firm's performance. When the firm performs below the industry average, a manager may feel greater pressure and find price fixing more tempting.

6–7 CASE DEVELOPMENT

Section 1 of the Sherman Act forbids "[e]very contract, combination . . . , or conspiracy in restraint of trade. . . ." From the beginning, the courts have held that price fixing was just the kind of restraint of trade that the Sherman Act was designed to prevent.[15] There have been a few

---

[14] Peter Asch and Joseph Seneca, "Is Collusion Profitable?" *Review of Economics and Statistics* 58 (February 1976), pp. 1–10.

[15] A remarkable survey of the law and economics is provided by Robert H. Bork, "The Rule of Reason and the Per Se Concept: Price Fixing and Market Division," *Yale Law Journal* 74 (April 1965), pp. 775–847 and *Yale Law Journal* 75 (January 1966), pp. 373–475. This huge, two-part article is still valuable reading.

stumbles along the way, but the central thrust of the case development has been to establish the per se illegality of price fixing. When a business practice has been declared a per se violation, the plaintiff merely has to prove that the forbidden behavior has occurred. In those cases, there is no defense.

Trans-Missouri Freight Association.[16] A group of 18 railroads formed the Trans-Missouri Freight Association for the purpose of establishing and maintaining reasonable rates, rules, and regulations on all freight traffic. This agreement covered all traffic subject to competition between any two or more members. It was decided that rate changes normally should be agreed upon at a monthly meeting. In between meetings, independent rate cuts were permissible as necessary for "meeting competition." If an independent rate cut was in violation of the agreement, however, the violator was fined $100 by the group. This was the sanction for cheating on the price-fixing agreement.

The Justice Department contended that this agreement violated Section 1 of the Sherman Act. The defendants, of course, denied that there were any anticompetitive effects or any adverse effects on consumers resulting from their agreement. In fact, they claimed that the collusive rates were reasonable and no more than necessary to avoid ruinous competition.

The Supreme Court rejected both the reasonable rate argument and the ruinous competition argument. Wisely, the Court asked rhetorically, "[w]hat is a proper standard by which to judge the fact of reasonable rates?" Justice Peckham pointed to the literal wording of Section 1 and held that there were no exceptions—all restraints of trade violated the act. Peckham's language has drawn the criticism of several commentators, but some of the criticism is unjustified as Peckham clarified much of the ambiguity the following year in a similar case.

Joint-Traffic Association.[17] The facts of this case were remarkably similar to those in the *Trans-Missouri* case. This time, however, Justice Peckham clearly articulated that not all restraints of trade are illegal. Restraints that are necessary to promote business, he said, are legal.[18] It is only those restraints whose "direct and immediate effect is a restraint upon interstate commerce" that are banned by the Sherman Act. Since the railroads' agreement "directly and effectually stifles competition, [it] must be regarded under the statute as one in restraint of trade. . . ." Peckham's concept of the statute was applied and developed further by Judge Taft in the *Addyston Pipe & Steel* case.

---

[16] *United States* v. *Trans-Missouri Freight Assoc.*, 166 U.S. 290 (1897).

[17] *United States* v. *Joint-Traffic Association*, 171 U.S. 505 (1898).

[18] The distinction involves ancillary restraints that are generally permissible under the common law. See the discussion on this point in Bork, "The Rule of Reason," pp. 377–90. In addition, see L. Sullivan, *Antitrust* (St. Paul, Minn.: West Publishing, 1977).

Addyston Pipe & Steel.[19]   The manufacturers of cast iron soil pipe in one section of the country formed an association to reduce competition among its members. One important element of the scheme was to assign certain cities to specified producers. This is a customer allocation plan, which will be discussed in more depth in the next chapter. Another important facet of the scheme was bid rigging, which is a variant of price fixing as we shall see. For business outside the allocated cities, the association selected the price to be charged to the customer. Production responsibility was assigned to the association member that was willing to pay the largest amount into a bonus pool. Subsequently, this bonus pool was divided among the members according to each firm's proportion of total productive capacity. The winner would submit a bid equal to that selected by the association, and the other firms would submit higher bids.

The association offered a smorgasbord of defenses. First, they argued that their intention was not to charge unreasonable prices but to avoid ruinous competition. Since ruinous competition injures the public, contracts to check ruinous competition should not be deemed illegal. Judge Taft was unpersuaded that the courts should try to determine how much restraint should be tolerated to protect against ruinous competition or for any other reason:

> It is true that there are some cases in which the courts . . . have set sail on a sea of doubt, and have assumed the power to say, in respect to contracts which have no other purpose and no other consideration on either side than the mutual restraint of the parties, how much restraint of competition is in the public interest, and how much is not.

Second, the defendants argued that the contributions to the bonus pool were deductions from reasonable prices to prevent each member from being too greedy. The logic of this argument is not entirely obvious. Third, the fixed prices were not only reasonable, but they were also subject to competition from outsiders. Finally, the association was not a monopoly, as it involved only some 30 percent of national capacity. These arguments were designed to support the contention that the association lacked the power to fix prices, but Judge Taft disposed of this disingenuous assertion quite easily: "The most cogent evidence that they had this power is the fact, everywhere apparent in the record that they exercised it." In the end, Judge Taft ruled against the association's restraints.[20]

Trenton Potteries Co.[21]   The rule against price fixing acquired more specificity in the *Trenton Potteries* case, which involved 23 producers of

---

[19] *United States* v. *Addyston Pipe & Steel Co.*, 85 F. 271 (6th Cir. 1898). The Supreme Court affirmed Taft's decision: 175 U.S. 211 (1899).

[20] On appeal, Taft's ruling was upheld by the Supreme Court; see 175 U.S. 211 (1899).

[21] *United States* v. *Trenton Potteries Co.*, 273 U.S. 392 (1927).

vitreous pottery fixtures for bathrooms. These firms accounted for over 80 percent of such business in the United States. The Supreme Court did not have to decide whether the evidence was sufficient to find that the defendants had combined to fix prices because that was admitted. Instead, the question was procedural. Was it proper for the trial court to instruct the jury that "if it found the agreements or combinations complained of, it might return a verdict of guilty without regard to the reasonableness of the prices fixed?"

The Supreme Court took this opportunity to clarify its view on price fixing agreements:

> The aim and result of every price-fixing agreement, if effective, is the elimination of one form of competition. The power to fix prices, whether reasonably exercised or not, involves power to control the market and to fix arbitrary and unreasonable prices. The reasonable price fixed today may through economic and business changes become the unreasonable price of tomorrow. Once established, it may be maintained unchanged because of the absence of competition secured by the agreement for a price reasonable when fixed. Agreements which create such potential power may well be held to be in themselves unreasonable or unlawful restraints, without the necessity of minute inquiry whether a particular price is reasonable or unreasonable as fixed.

Thus, price fixing clearly became a per se violation of the Sherman Act. No proof of economic effect was necessary. Price fixing as a business practice was deemed an inherently unreasonable restraint of trade. This view was reaffirmed by Justice Douglas in the case that is the established precedent until this day.

Socony-Vacuum Oil Co.[22] During the 1920s and 1930s, "hot oil" and "hot gasoline" (i.e., oil and gasoline produced in violation of state prorationing laws) were sold at prices substantially below the prices for legally produced oil and gasoline. In addition, there seemed to be a considerable amount of "distress" gasoline on the spot market. The distress gasoline was due to the inadequate storage facilities of independent refiners who could not sell all of their output through normal outlets. Distress sales, of course, were made at substantially reduced prices on the spot market.

The major oil companies were vitally interested in spot market prices because their contracts with jobbers involved formula prices that depended on the spot market price. Alarmed at the deterioration in spot market prices, the major oil companies formed a Tank Car Stabilization Committee to deal with the problem. The committee's plan had each major oil company select one or more of the independent refiners with distress gasoline as its "dancing partner." The major was responsible for buying the distress supply of its dancing partner. By eliminating the

---

[22] *United States* v. *Socony-Vacuum Oil Co., Inc.*, 310 U.S. 150 (1940).

distress supply from the spot market, the spot price was higher than otherwise would have been the case, and therefore, the prices paid by jobbers to the major oil companies were also higher. Thus, by acting collusively to purchase a very small portion of the total supply, the majors could have a substantial effect on their total sales revenue.

Justice Douglas reviewed the Supreme Court decisions dealing with Section 1 and found no relief for the major oil companies:

> Thus for over 40 years this court has consistently and without deviation adhered to the principle that price-fixing agreements are unlawful per se under the Sherman Act and that no showing of so-called competitive abuses or evils which those agreements were designed to eliminate or alleviate may be interposed as a defense.

The issue then turned to whether the per se rule of *Trenton Potteries* applied to the present situation. In this case, the major oil companies had not agreed on uniform and inflexible prices as was the case in *Trenton Potteries*. The oil companies argued that price fixing was illegal per se only where the conspirators set uniform and inflexible prices. Douglas disposed of this distinction as irrelevant. Since the program had the purpose and effect of raising prices, it was a violation of Section 1:

> Any combination which tampers with price structures is engaged in an unlawful activity.

> * * * * *

> Congress has not left with us the determination of whether or not particular price-fixing schemes are wise or unwise, healthy or destructive. It has not permitted the age-old cry of ruinous competition and competitive evils to be a defense to price-fixing conspiracies. It has no more allowed genuine or fancied competitive abuses as a legal justification for such schemes than it has the good intentions of the members of the combination.

To add even further clarity, Douglas wrote:

> Under the Sherman Act a combination formed for the purpose and with the effect of raising, depressing, fixing, pegging, or stabilizing the price of a commodity in interstate or foreign commerce is illegal per se.

This remains the rule of law to the present. Every case that involves a question of price fixing cites and/or quotes Justice Douglas's *Socony-Vacuum* opinion with obvious approval.

6–8 ECONOMIC EFFECTS OF ENFORCEMENT[23]

We have just seen that judicial decisions have made price fixing a per se violation of Section 1 of the Sherman Act. This means that the anti-

---

[23] Much of this section depends primarily upon George Stigler, "The Economic Effects of the Antitrust Laws," *Journal of Law and Economics* 9 (October 1966), pp. 225–58.

trust enforcement agencies only need to prove the existence of price fixing and need not prove economic impact. Defendants cannot offer any explanation for their conduct—no excuses can be accepted. It is tempting to conclude that this must provide a powerful deterrent to potential price fixing, but the success of the law must be measured in terms of its actual achievements in combatting price fixing. Unfortunately, such measurement requires a census of collusion—both detected and undetected. Moreover, we need this census with and without an antitrust law forbidding price fixing. For example, the Antitrust Division has filed many antitrust cases and has won a little over 75 percent of them. Should this performance be applauded as evidence of success, or is this really a measure of antitrust's failure? Clearly, an argument could be made for either proposition.

As one might expect, we have only a few scraps of empirical evidence on the economic effects of antitrust enforcement. Due to the devastating effects of cheating upon the success of a cartel, it is important to employ a collusive mechanism that minimizes the opportunities for cheating. These forms of collusion will be efficient in the sense that they yield greater total profits. The most efficient forms of collusion involve the use of a joint sales agency in which industry output is pooled for sale or the assignment of customers to specific producers. Stigler has pointed out that the per se rule against price fixing has taken away the most efficient forms of collusion, because these forms are so easily detected by the victims. This, of course, reduces the returns from colluding and accordingly should reduce the amount and effects of price fixing. In testing this proposition, Stigler selected a rather small sample of price-fixing cases and divided them into efficient and inefficient forms of collusion. His empirical analysis of these cases was quite interesting as it confirmed his a priori reasoning. He found that the Department of Justice won a larger percentage of the cases where efficient forms of collusion were used. Moreover, he found that the time lag between the inception of the price fixing and the filing of the complaint was significantly shorter for efficient methods of collusion than for the inefficient forms. As a result, the profitability of colluding efficiently is reduced. Consequently, the enforcement of Section 1 has a beneficial effect upon business behavior by reducing the returns to collusion.

Feinberg[24] provided some further evidence that antitrust enforcement has desirable effects. He looked at data on 288 firms in 1970 and examined the effect of *previous* antitrust indictments on each firm's price-cost margin in 1970. He hypothesized that previous antitrust experience would temper a firm's behavior and reduce its price-cost margin. In fact, this is precisely what the evidence showed. If a firm had an antitrust

---

[24] Robert M. Feinberg, "Antitrust Enforcement and Subsequent Price Behavior," *Review of Economics and Statistics* 62 (November 1980), pp. 609–12.

indictment between 1955 and 1970, its price-cost margin was some 2 percent lower than if it did not have an antitrust indictment during the previous 15 years. Thus, Sherman Act indictments have the beneficial effect of curtailing a firm's subsequent pricing behavior.

Block, Nold, and Sidak[25] provided a theoretical foundation for Feinberg's empirical results as well as some empirical results of their own. They begin by assuming that industry profits will be random once a price-fixing conspiracy is put in place because the actual profits will depend upon whether the antitrust enforcers catch them. If they are not caught, their profits will be above the competitive level. If they are caught, their profits will be reduced by the civil and criminal penalties that are imposed. Assuming that the firms are risk neutral, the objective then becomes maximizing expected profit, which is

$$E[\Pi] = p\Pi_S + (1 - p)\Pi_U$$

where p denotes the probability of avoiding detection, Π_S represents the profits associated with successful and undetected price fixing, $(1 - p)$ represents the probability of being detected, and Π_U is the profit if the price fixing is detected and the firms are punished. It is obvious that the expected profit depends heavily upon the probability of being detected. This probability is influenced strongly by the enforcement effort of the Antitrust Division. In addition, Block, Nold, and Sidak argue that the collusive markup over cost[26] influences the probability of detection for two reasons. First, higher markups are more likely to result in customer complaints to the Antitrust Division. Second, due to the incentives for cheating, high markups are apt to be associated with the most visible forms of collusion and, therefore, the most easily detected forms.

As a theoretical matter, they found that maximizing expected profit required selecting a price below the monopoly price but above the competitive price. In other words, the effect of antitrust enforcement is to reduce the optimal markup below the level that would maximize profits in the absence of antitrust penalties. They also found that increasing enforcement efforts or increasing the penalties would reduce the optimal markup.

For their empirical study, they found that the market for white pan bread had several desirable characteristics. The product is homogeneous, it is regionally produced and consumed, and there were a large number of price-fixing cases involving bread. In addition, they were able to estimate the markup tolerably well. In this industry, they found that antitrust enforcement had beneficial results. First, as the Antitrust Division's enforcement effort increased, the markups observed declined.

---

[25] Michael K. Block, Frederick C. Nold, and Joseph G. Sidak, "The Deterrent Effect of Antitrust Enforcement," *Journal of Political Economy* 89 (June 1981), pp. 429–45.

[26] They defined the collusive markup as $(P - MC)/P$ where P denotes price and MC represents marginal cost.

Second, antitrust prosecution had a deterrent effect elsewhere. When the Antitrust Division filed suit against price fixing in one city, the markups declined in other cities. Finally, when a case was filed in a city, the markup declined in the following year in that city. Thus, we are led to the result that antitrust enforcement efforts appear to have beneficial results on the behavior of potential colluders.

6–9 SUMMARY

In this chapter, we have developed a model of cartel behavior for both the short run and long run. The results of the model were compared to the price and quantity combinations for a monopolist and for a competitive industry. We found that under ideal conditions, a cartel could replicate the monopolistic results in the short run. In the long run, however, cheating and entry would undermine the cartel's stability. Moreover, we examined some factors that complicate the operation of a successful cartel such as unequal costs among the cartel members.

We also examined some empirical evidence regarding the conditions conducive to cartel activity. This examination revealed that collusive activity is associated with homogeneous products, relatively less elastic demand, large government buyers, and few sellers. Of course, collusion does not occur whenever these conditions are present, but these conditions facilitate collusion.

Next, we turned our attention to the legal development of Section 1 enforcement. We discovered that the judiciary has adopted a very hostile attitude toward price fixing. In fact, price fixing is a per se offense, which means that the plaintiff need not prove anything more than the existence of the conspiracy. Our economic analysis supports this hostility because price fixing is an effort to emulate the socially undesirable pricing behavior of a monopolist.

Finally, we focused on the empirical evidence regarding the effects of antitrust enforcement. This investigation revealed several reassuring things. First, the very nature of the law and its enforcement takes away the most effective forms of collusive behavior. This, in turn, reduces the gains to collusive behavior and will increase the deterrent effect of the law. Second, we found that previous antitrust prosecution tended to reduce the price-cost margins of the firms. Finally, a study of the bread industry revealed that antitrust enforcement had socially beneficial effects on price-cost margins.

QUESTIONS AND PROBLEMS

1. A freeze in Florida drastically reduced the supply of oranges for making juice concentrate. As a result, the price of oranges shot up and caused the profits of the frozen juice concentrate producers to

fall. In an effort to offset this price rise, the frozen juice concentrate producers joined forces and mutually agreed to "water down" their product. Did these producers violate Section 1 of the Sherman Act? [*National Macaroni Manufacturers Association* v. *Federal Trade Commission*, 345 F. 2d 421 (1965)].

2. It has been argued that collusion is more likely the less elastic the demand at the competitive price and output. Prove that the profits due to collusion are larger under these conditions.

3. On occasion, defendants in price-fixing suits have claimed that price fixing was necessary because price competition resulted in "destructive competition." This refers to a situation where the prices are below average total costs, and therefore, everyone incurs losses. Should this defense ever be persuasive? [*Appalachian Coals, Inc.* v. *United States*, 228 U.S. 344 (1933)]

4. In the partial conspiracy analysis, show the effects of entry. Use a graph similar to Figure 6–8.

5. Examine the proportional demand curve in Figure 6–5. If *mr* equals *MC* at an output of q_3, why would the firm want to expand production past q_3? Is this an exception to the rule that profit maximization requires producing where marginal cost equals marginal revenue?

6. If the long-run solutions for a multiplant monopolist and a cartel diverge, why are the short-run solutions the same?

7. Suppose two taxi drivers agree to raise their fares above the rest of the competition in Chicago. Obviously, their action cannot have any real effect on prices, but they have, in fact, conspired to violate Section 1 of the Sherman Act. If brought to court, should they be excused because their transgression had negligible economic effect?

8. In *United States* v. *American Tobacco Co.*, 221 U.S. 106 (1911), the court was offended by the fact that American Tobacco spent large sums to acquire some 40 tobacco firms, which were promptly closed upon acquisition. Why did American Tobacco do this?

9. On the basis of short film clips or nothing at all, movie theater owners must bid for exhibition rights to new films. This so-called blind bidding has been characterized as commercial roulette. The theater owners must pay guarantees in advance plus some percentage of the box office receipts. To protect themselves, the theater owners have gotten together before the bidding begins and split up

the movies that they expect to do well. This provides some assurance that they will not get into a bidding war. The film producers complain that the bids are depressed. Is this an antitrust violation? ("Hollywood Roulette," *Newsweek,* January 4, 1982, p. 57)

10. Describe the incentives that exist for rival firms to collude on price. Do the antitrust laws eliminate the benefits available to colluders? If so, how? If not, how does the law prevent collusion?

11. Why is price fixing illegal per se (i.e., why are the conspirators denied an opportunity to present mitigating evidence)?

12. In what ways was the scheme in *Addyston Pipe & Steel* an approximation of the cartel model developed in this chapter?

13. Suppose that there are six firms in an industry, and five of them have agreed to fix prices. Use the dominant firm model to show how the colluders will behave if the sixth firm will not participate. Will the price charged by the noncolluder be affected by the conspiracy? How could the noncolluder prove that it did not participate in the conspiracy?

14. Examine the long-run cartel solution in Figure 6–4. What will happen if the cartel breaks down completely and each firm begins to act competitively?

15. In the *Trans-Missouri* case, cheaters were fined $100 by the loyal members of the collusive group. How much of a deterrent would you expect this to be? How much would the fine have to be in current dollars to be equivalent to $100 in 1895 dollars?

16. Is it likely that the "dancing partner" solution to excess gasoline would have been successful? Examine the incentives of and the economic impact upon the major firms and upon their "dancing partners."

17. When several firms fix price above the competitive level, have they caused "antitrust injury" to their customers? How about to those former customers who are willing to pay the competitive price but not the collusive price?

18. In the cartel variant of the dominant firm model, the customers of the fringe firms pay prices above the competitive price. Have they suffered "antitrust injury"? If so, should they collect from the colluders or from the fringe firms?

FURTHER READINGS

Asch, Peter, and Joseph J. Seneca. "Is Collusion Profitable?" *Review of Economics and Statistics* 58 (February 1976), pp. 1–10.

Comanor, William, and M. Schankerman. "Identical Bids and Cartel Behavior." *Bell Journal of Economics* 7 (Spring 1976), pp. 281–86.

Fraas, Arthur G., and Douglas F. Greer. "Market Structure and Price Collusion: An Empirical Analysis." *Journal of Industrial Economics* 26 (September 1977), pp. 29–33.

Mund, Vernon. "Identical Bid Prices." *Journal of Political Economy* 68 (April 1960), pp. 150–60.

Posner, Richard A. *Antitrust Law: An Economic Perspective.* Chicago: University of Chicago Press, 1976.

Worcester, Dean, Jr. "Why 'Dominant' Firms Decline." *Journal of Political Economy* 65 (August 1957), pp. 338–47.

7

Other forms of horizontal collusion

The preceding chapter dealt with the classic antitrust violation of price fixing. In the present chapter, we shall turn our attention to three other forms of horizontal collusion, which may be just as serious as price fixing. First, the firms in an industry may allocate markets or groups of customers among themselves. This so-called market division has been held to be illegal in most instances. We shall see, however, that a blanket per se rule of law may not be appropriate. Second, the firms in an industry may decide not to deal with a particular firm. In such an instance, we must consider whether the concerted refusal to deal, or boycott, is an unreasonable restraint of trade. Once again, a per se rule may not make good sense. Finally, we shall examine information exchanges or data dissemination among competitors within an industry. Since information is usually assumed to be perfect for competition to work well, one might suppose that improved information would be socially beneficial. We shall see, however, that information exchanges can be misused in a noncompetitive way.

7-1 ECONOMIC ANALYSIS OF MARKET DIVISION

When a price-fixing cartel selects an industry profit maximizing price, it becomes necessary for all firms in the industry to restrict output if the increased price is to be maintained. As you will recall from the last chapter, there is a substantial incentive for each firm to cheat on the collusive agreement—those who cheat benefit at the expense of the "honorable" firms that do not cheat. Cheating takes the form of producing more than a fair share of the collusive output. In this case, the burden of restricting output falls on those who do not cheat if the fixed price is to be maintained. This can be seen with the aid of Figure 7–1.

FIGURE 7–1

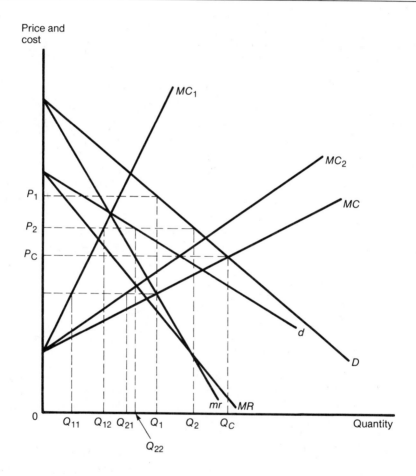

Suppose that the sum of the marginal cost curves of one group of firms is shown as MC_1 in Figure 7–1, while MC_2 is the sum of the marginal cost curves of another group. The industry marginal cost (MC) is the horizontal sum of MC_1 and MC_2. Given industry demand (D) and the associated marginal revenue (MR), the industry profit maximizing price is P_1. This price clears the market for the quantity Q_1 where marginal cost equals marginal revenue. For profit maximization, the first group of firms should produce Q_{11}, and the second group should produce Q_{21}. This division is found by searching for that allocation of production responsibility such that

$$MC_1 = MC_2 = MC$$

and total quantity is Q_1.

The firms in group 1 may decide to cheat by expanding their production beyond Q_{11}. It will be tempting for them to expand production until MC_1 equals P_1. But the impact of such an expansion would force the "honorable" firms to take this behavior into account in selecting the cartel price. If group 2 recognizes that group 1 will produce where MC_1 equals P, then the amount that group 2 can sell at any price is equal to the quantity demanded (given by the demand curve) less the quantity supplied by group 1 (given by their marginal cost). This residual demand curve facing the honorable firms (d) is then constructed by taking the horizontal difference between the demand curve (D) and the marginal cost curve of group 1 (MC_1). The honorable firms will maximize their profits by equating their marginal cost (MC_2) to the marginal revenue (mr) of their residual demand curve (d). Accordingly, they produce Q_{22} at a price of P_2 while the cheaters produce Q_{12}. The industry production is Q_2, which equals the sum of Q_{12} and Q_{22}. The optimal price (P_2) will lie somewhere between the competitive price (P_c) and the monopoly price (P_1). Similarly, the optimal quantity (Q_2) will fall between the monopoly output (Q_1) and the competitive output (Q_c). The optimal price will move closer to P_1 (the profit maximizing price) as cheating becomes less important. We must remember, however, that the cheaters gain at the expense of the honorable firms. Consequently, we should expect group 1 to grow and group 2 to shrink as more and more firms defect. Thus, the ultimate result of unfettered defection is unfettered competition.

One solution to this problem is *market division*. By assigning geographic territories to each firm, each geographic market will be characterized by local monopoly. Now, each firm can decide upon its own price and output strategy, which will avoid the need for negotiating a common price.

Avoiding nonprice competition. There is another benefit of market division: the absence of nonprice competition. In the normal world of real price-fixing agreements, the collusive price may be specified without a firm understanding of market shares. The colluders agree, at least tacitly, that market shares will be determined by nonprice competition. Expenditures on nonprice variables, however, are offsetting to some extent within the industry, which means that the nonprice competition may shift the cost function more than it shifts the demand curve. Consequently, cartel profits tend to be dissipated by nonprice competition. As long as customers are not geographically mobile, however, there will be no incentive to engage in this sort of nonprice competition when markets have been divided.[1]

Avoiding the unequal costs problem. In the last chapter, we saw that unequal costs caused some dissension among the colluding firms.[2] There is no single price that is optimal for all firms when profit pooling is prevented by practical considerations and costs are unequal. Market division can reduce some of the tension in this situation. Assume that there are two markets which are geographically distinct but identical in other respects. As a result, there will be identical demand functions in the two areas. In Figure 7–2, D represents the total industry demand over both markets, and $d_{1,2}$ represents the identical demand functions in markets 1 and 2. The marginal revenue function associated with $d_{1,2}$ is mr. Marginal cost functions for firms 1 and 2 are denoted by MC_1 and MC_2, respectively. If the two firms decide to allocate market 1 to firm 1 and market 2 to firm 2, then the price and output configurations will be P_1 and Q_1 for market 1 and P_2 and Q_2 for market 2. The consumers in market 2 clearly benefit from firm 2's greater efficiency: Price is lower and output is higher than in market 1. Given that each firm adheres to the agreed upon market division, there is no incentive for nonprice competition. Both firms are local monopolies, and each is maximizing its profit constrained by the market division.

Three things may be noted. First, there is still the usual incentive for cheating on the agreement. Consider firm 2's situation: It is maximizing the profits that it can extract from its assigned territory, but there is a possibility for additional profits. The price in market 1 (P_1) exceeds firm 2's marginal cost at quantity Q_2. Consequently, if firm 2 were to charge a price in market 1 just under P_1, it could steal some of firm 1's customers and expand its own profits. Even though firm 1 is the less efficient producer, one can show that the same incentive exists for firm 1. Thus, greed rears its ugly head once again, and the cartel must be vigilant in its policing efforts to ensure that cheating does not occur. Obviously, if firms 1 and 2 succumb to the temptation of further profits, the agreement will collapse and price competition will exist. Both firms wish to avoid this result.

Second, the cartel must also prevent arbitrage among the customers, which is the practice of buying in the cheap market and selling in the expensive market. An enterprising customer might recognize that buying in market 2 at P_2 and reselling in market 1 at P_1 or just below can be profitable. A contemporary example involves the difference in retail

---

[1] Advertising may still be a sensible way to shift the demand function and/or change the elasticity of demand for the firm's product. This incentive to advertise will not disappear.

[2] In addition to the complication caused by unequal cost functions, product differentiation can also cause difficulties in coordinating an appropriate price.

FIGURE 7–2

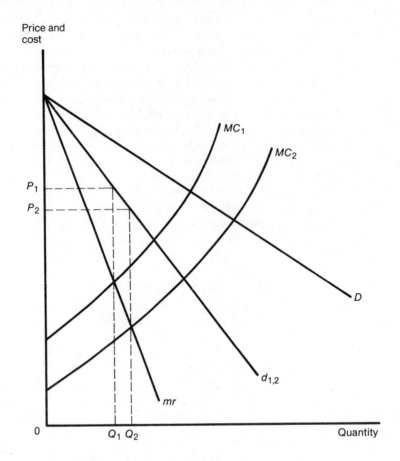

Price and cost

P_1

P_2

MC_1

MC_2

D

$d_{1,2}$

mr

0

Q_1 Q_2

Quantity

prices of cigarettes across different states due to differential state excise taxes. There are profits to be made by buying large quantities of cigarettes in states with low excise taxes and smuggling them into states that levy high excise taxes. Just as the states that have low excise taxes have no incentive to prevent these exports, firm 2 in Figure 7–2 has no incentive to prevent arbitrage. Cartel stability, however, demands that it be prevented.

The third thing to notice about this equilibrium is that *industry* profits are not maximized. This can be seen in Figure 7–2 by noting that MC_1 at Q_1 does not equal MC_2 at Q_2. Thus, keeping prices and quantity sold the same in both markets, one could increase total profits by increasing output in firm 2's plant and decreasing output in firm 1's plant. The market division alternative to price fixing seeks to avoid this sort of interaction. In these instances, market division is an imperfect substitute for the joint profit maximization that requires full cooperation of the firms in the industry.

Another alternative is *customer allocation*, which is not without problems of its own. First, customer allocation is easily detectable and, therefore, is hard to conceal from the antitrust authorities. Second, the participants will not be satisfied with the customers allocated to them in the long run. This is an inevitable result of random variations in the fortunes of those customers. Some will expand and prosper while others are bound to flounder and die. Internal squabbles among the cartel members over who gets which customers are bound to follow. Most serious of all, however, is the unfortunate fact that price cutting (cheating!) has a long-run payoff. If a firm cuts price, its customers will expand at the expense of the customers assigned to the colluders that refrain from price cutting. Consequently, there are long-run gains from price cutting, and we should expect it to occur.

Market division versus price fixing. Although market division is not a perfect substitute for a cartel, when market division works well, there is no competition at all. Usually, price-fixing agreements do not regulate all dimensions of a firm's behavior. In fact, nonprice competition is often used to allocate market shares when prices have been fixed. A successful division of markets precludes any need for nonprice competition. If the assigned territory corresponds to a sensibly defined market, the firm will be insulated from competition. It can set the profit maximizing price, quantity, and combination of services: credit, delivery service, return policy, sales promotion, and so on. As long as there is no cheating and no entry, there will be no competition whatsoever. In this sense, market division is even worse than price fixing and certainly deserves equally harsh treatment in antitrust terms.

7–2 JUDICIAL TREATMENT OF MARKET DIVISION

When market division serves as a substitute for price fixing, it deserves harsh treatment. Historically, it has gotten precisely what it deserves under these circumstances. Unfortunately, some recent decisions have been rendered without any careful economic analysis. Consequently, the Supreme Court's current position on market division paints the good and the evil with the same brush.

In *Addyston Pipe & Steel*,[3] we have an early application of the Sherman Act to an instance of market division. Six cast-iron pipe manufacturers were sued for the way in which they conducted their business of selling cast-iron pipe to municipal water works in several cities. Due to the high

---

[3] *United States* v. *Addyston Pipe & Steel Co.*, 85 F. 271 (6th Cir. 1898).

freight cost incurred in shipping cast-iron pipe from their competitors' locations in New England, these six firms were protected from competition by outsiders. To ensure that no real competition emerged within their own ranks, the firms allocated certain cities among themselves. These cities wanted competitively determined prices for the cast-iron pipe that they bought and requested competitive bids. The six firms, however, met in advance of the bidding and made sure that those firms that were supposed to be unsuccessful submitted higher bids than the firm that was supposed to win. These purposely high bids were submitted to provide an illusion of competition.

It is fairly obvious that the only reason for the customer allocation was to enable the firms to charge noncompetitive prices. Judge Taft noted that the conspirators had sufficient power to set the price as they controlled 30 percent of national output and essentially all of the output in the area served by the Birmingham, Alabama, plants. Their agreement to allocate customers served to override market forces. The important point, of course, is that market division served to promote the producers' goal of earning monopoly profits.[4] As a consequence, it was decided correctly that this behavior violated Section 1 of the Sherman Act.

The next important decision on market division was *Timken Roller Bearing*.[5] The Timken Roller Bearing Company and British Timken, Ltd. divided world markets for antifriction bearings and formed a joint venture, which was organized as French Timken. In conjunction, the three Timkens engaged in a variety of anticompetitive activities. First, they allocated trade areas among themselves on a worldwide basis. Second, they fixed prices on the products that one sold in the allocated territory of the others. Third, they cooperated to protect each other's markets and to eliminate outside competition. Finally, they participated in cartels to restrict imports to, and exports from, the United States. The power of the firms was such that these agreements were effective in raising price above the competitive level.[6] Given the aggregation of trade restraints found here, it is not surprising that the government won the case. Once again, however, we should note that the market division was part of a larger effort to secure monopoly profits.

---

[4] An interesting analysis of this case is provided by George Bittlingmayer, "Decreasing Average Cost and Competition: A New Look at the Addyston Pipe Case," *Journal of Law and Economics* 25 (October 1982), pp. 201–29.

[5] *Timken Roller Bearing Co.* v. *United States,* 341 U.S. 593 (1951).

[6] Timken argued that its conduct was reasonable because it was ancillary to a legitimate joint venture. The court easily dismissed this argument: "Nor do we find any support in reason or authority for the proposition that agreements between legally separate persons and companies to suppress competition among themselves and others can be justified by labeling the project a 'joint venture.' Perhaps every agreement and combination to restrain trade could be so labeled."

The next case, *United States* v. *Sealy, Inc.*,[7] continues to support the idea that market division is illegal where an unreasonable restraint can be found. Sealy licensed mattress manufacturers to make and sell mattresses under the Sealy name and trademarks. The government claimed that Sealy, which was owned by its licensees, conspired with its licensees (1) to fix the resale price to retail customers and (2) to allocate mutually exclusive territories among its manufacturer-licensees. Since the licensees owned Sealy, its agreement not to license other firms in an existing licensee's area constituted a horizontal rather than a vertical agreement. Each licensee specifically agreed not to manufacture or sell Sealy products outside its designated area.

Sealy argued that the territorial restrictions were incidental to its lawful program of trademark licensing. The Court, however, saw it as part of an illegal resale price-fixing scheme: "It may be true . . . that territorial exclusivity served many other purposes. But its connection with the unlawful price fixing is enough to require that it be condemned as an unlawful restraint. . . ." Consequently, the *Sealy* decision does not hold that market division is a per se violation of the Sherman Act. Rather, it holds that when territorial allocation is part of an aggregation of trade restraints, then it is illegal.

The *Sealy* decision is subject to some serious criticism. First, with only 20 percent of the market, the Sealy licensees were too small to have much impact upon competition generally or upon price. Accordingly, there was substantial competition in all markets from other mattress producers. This fact apparently was ignored by the Court. Second, the real purpose of the entire arrangement seems to have been to gain the advantages of national sales promotion and advertising. To do this, the group of manufacturers had to produce a uniform product and sell it under a common name. The Sealy license required a producer to follow certain standards and specifications and thereby provided the uniformity. Of course, the Sealy trademark provided the common name. Each producer has an incentive to supplement the national sales efforts. To some extent, however, the producer in an adjacent area may try to get a free ride on his neighbor's efforts. The use of exclusive territories reduces the possibility of a free ride.[8] As a result, the market division scheme in *Sealy* may have been designed to gain efficiencies in sales promotion.

In other words, the Sealy restraints may have been ancillary to a lawful agreement. Market division, it could be argued, was reasonably necessary to facilitate the main purpose of the agreement, which was to

---

[7] 388 U.S. 350 (1967).

[8] More will be said about the free-rider problem and resale price maintenance in a subsequent chapter on vertical price fixing.

promote and distribute a uniform product on a national basis. If so, the restraint should have been deemed legal. That it was not appears to be due to the Court's preoccupation with the price-fixing aspect of the case.[9]

Until *United States* v. *Topco Associates, Inc.*,[10] the Supreme Court decisions on market division were not pure per se rulings because there was always an element of price fixing or substantial market power present. The *Topco* ruling, however, removed all doubt—horizontal market division, pure and simple, became a per se violation of Section 1.

Topco was a cooperative association of about 25 small and medium-sized regional supermarket chains, which operated in 33 states. Topco was founded in the 1940s by a group of small chains that were independently owned. Their goal was to retain their independence while developing a cooperative private label program that would compete with the large supermarket chains. A&P, for example, had Ann Page products, which it purchased from food packers and distributed exclusively through their A&P stores. The Supreme Court recognized that a chain can experience substantial cost economies in purchasing, transportation, warehousing, promotion, and advertising. As a result, independents that are too small for their own private label line of products were at a significant competitive disadvantage relative to the larger chains.

Topco developed a line of private label products: canned goods, dairy products, frozen foods, fresh produce, nonfood merchandise, and meat. The program was a striking success: In 1964, Topco members had sales of $2 billion. By 1967, sales had risen to $2.3 billion, which was fourth among supermarket chains. The local strength of Topco members was equal to that of any other chain. This enviable position was due, in large part, to the success of the Topco brand products.

One of the ways that Topco members encouraged their mutual success was through the designation of exclusive territories. Each Topco member signed an agreement with Topco designating its exclusive territory. No member was permitted to sell outside the territory in which it was licensed. An outsider could become a Topco member only if the existing members did not object. In effect, the Topco members were protected from each other: No Topco member would have to compete with another Topco member. This would preclude a free-rider problem on local advertising of the Topco brand.

The Antitrust Division complained that Topco's scheme of dividing markets violated Section 1 because it prevented competition in Topco brand products among grocery chains engaged in retail operations.

---

[9] For brief, provocative analyses of *Sealy*, see Robert Bork, *The Antitrust Paradox* (New York: Basic Books, 1978), pp. 270–75; Richard Posner, *Antitrust Law* (Chicago: University of Chicago Press, 1976), pp. 165–66; and Lawrence Sullivan, *Handbook of the Law of Antitrust* (St. Paul, Minn.: West Publishing, 1977), pp. 214–15.

[10] 405 U.S. 596 (1972).

Without any economic analysis, the Supreme Court agreed: "This Court has reiterated time and time again that '[h]orizontal territorial limitations . . . are naked restraints of trade with no purpose except stifling of competition.' Such limitations are per se violations of the Sherman Act."

Topco argued that the restrictions had procompetitive results on balance. First, even though there was a reduction in intrabrand competition, that reduction was of marginal significance in the retail grocery business due to the presence of many competitors in any local market. Second, the Topco restraints permitted the development of private label merchandise for the Topco members, which enabled them to engage in substantial competition with the large chains: A&P, Safeway, Kroger, and others.[11] Thus, Topco's restraints reduced intrabrand competition and promoted interbrand competition. The District Court concluded that the latter outweighed the former. But on this question of sacrificing intrabrand competition for enhanced interbrand competition, the Supreme Court begged off: "If a decision is to be made to sacrifice competition in one portion of the economy for greater competition in another portion, this too is a decision which must be made by Congress and not by private forces or by the courts." More specifically, the majority held that ". . . courts are ill equipped and ill-situated for such decision making."

In a concurring opinion, Justice Blackmun demonstrated the central anomaly of the *Topco* decision:

> Today's decision in the Government's favor will tend to stultify Topco members' competition with the great and larger chains. The bigs, therefore, should find it easier to get bigger and, as a consequence, reality seems at odds with the public interest. The per se rule, however, now appears to be so firmly established by the Court that, at this late date, I could not oppose it.

It is somewhat difficult to reconcile this open admission of anticompetitive effect with the central purpose of the antitrust laws, which is to promote consumer welfare. This is especially true in light of the fact that Topco provided an avenue of entry into the retail grocery business as many budding chains entered by becoming Topco associates. When these new entrants developed to the point where they could maintain their own private label programs, they broke away from Topco, thereby making room for someone else. If the Topco label withers, the Topco associates will not provide as attractive an alternative to the chains and will not promote entry into the industry.

The importance of *Topco* is that it provided the Supreme Court with an opportunity to rule on a pure market division case without any elements of price fixing in a structural situation where there was no signifi-

---

[11] The District Court explicitly considered this and found procompetitive results. The Supreme Court rejected the rule of reason analysis and opted for a per se approach.

cant market power. The Court seized that opportunity to enunciate a per se rule against market division. Thus, at the present time, price fixing and market division receive equally harsh treatment in the antitrust courts.

7–3 BOYCOTTS: AN ECONOMIC ANALYSIS[12]

In the preceding chapter, we saw that all cartels face two serious threats to their stability: cheaters and new entrants. Both groups of firms upset the optimal price-quantity combination for the industry and cause profits to fall. One way of coping with this problem is to exclude some firms from the industry through the use of a boycott and thereby prevent an increase in supply. When a boycott is employed for this reason, it deserves and receives very harsh treatment from the antitrust authorities and the courts. In fact, boycotts are often said to be per se violations of Section 1 of the Sherman Act, although, as we shall see, this statement is not quite correct. Indeed, it is fortunate that boycotts are permitted at times because they can be used for socially valuable purposes. As Professor Posner has pointed out, boycotts should only come under antitrust attack when they are being used to promote a business practice that is offensive on grounds of substantive antitrust policy.[13]

We can use some familiar economic models to examine the economic effects of boycotts. First, we shall consider a case where the structure of the industry appears to be competitive. Interestingly, there is still a return to excluding some of the industry members. Second, we shall use the dominant firm model to examine the effects of a boycott that excludes the competitive fringe.

Boycotts with a competitive structure

In Figure 7–3, we have industry demand drawn as D, and industry supply is shown as S. The equilibrium price and quantity are P_1 and Q_1, respectively. One might suppose that the exclusion of some firms would hold little interest for the remaining firms due to the competitive market structure, but such is not the case. The industry supply (S) is determined by the horizontal summation of the marginal cost curves of the separate firms. We have disaggregated the industry supply into two pieces, which are labeled ΣMC_A and ΣMC_B. Now, we can see the effect of excluding one of the groups—say, the A firms with supply denoted by ΣMC_A.

---

[12] In antitrust discussion, the terms *group boycott* and *concerted refusal to deal* are used interchangeably by most analysts. Sullivan, however, cautions against this practice. See Sullivan, *Handbook of the Law of Antitrust*, pp. 231–32.

[13] See Posner, *Antitrust Law*, pp. 207–11.

FIGURE 7–3

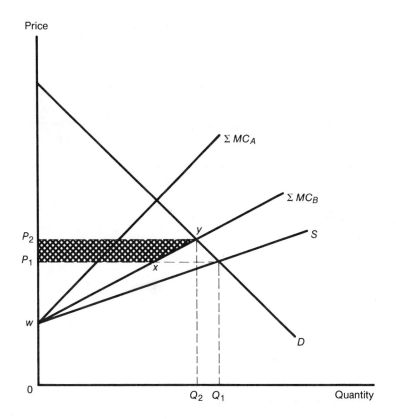

The new price-quantity configuration is determined by the intersection of demand and the new industry supply, which is ΣMC_B. This is P_2 and Q_2 in Figure 7–3. The B firms that remain in the industry now make more profit.[14] Before the exclusion of the A firms, the B firms earned profits equal to the triangular area WP_1X. Now, however, their profits expand to WP_2Y as the price rises from P_1 to P_2, and the B firms produce more output. The increased profits are represented by the cross-hatched area P_1XYP_2.

In this case, the boycott did not exclude enough firms to permit cartel (or monopoly) pricing, but the favored firms that remained in the indus-

---

[14] When total cost is quadratic, it may be written as $C = bQ + cQ^2$. Marginal cost is then linear: $MC = \Delta C/\Delta Q = b + 2cQ$. In Figure 7–3, b equals W. Graphically, total cost is the area under the marginal cost bounded by the price axis and the quantity produced. Profit, then, is the area bounded by the horizontal price line, the marginal cost, and the price axis.

try earned higher profits. Thus, there was a clear incentive for them to engage in this practice even though monopoly did not result. Of course, consumers are worse off as a result of the boycott since price is higher and quantity is lower.

Boycotts in a dominant-firm setting

We can also examine the case where a cartel wants to expel a competitive fringe of firms that have not joined the cartel in its efforts to restrict quantity and raise price. In Figure 7–4, industry demand and marginal revenue are shown as D and MR. The sum of the marginal cost curves of the fringe firms is MC_1 while that of the cartel is denoted MC_2. In the

---

FIGURE 7–4

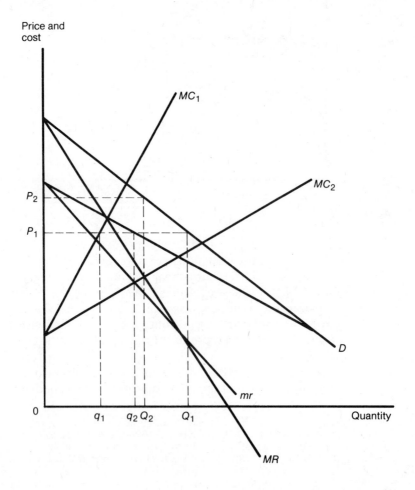

presence of the noncolluding fringe firms, the cartel's optimal price will be P_1. At this price, the fringe will produce q_1, the cartel will produce q_2, and industry output will be $Q_1 = q_1 + q_2$.

If the cartel members can exclude the uncooperative firms, it will determine the joint profit maximizing output by the intersection of MC_2 and MR. Thus, the output of the cartel members increases to Q_2, which is now the industry output. The price that consumers pay rises to P_2 from P_1, and as a result, consumers are worse off. In this case and in the preceding one, it is easy to see that boycotts can have adverse effects on consumers and should be treated harshly when that is the case.

7–4 JUDICIAL TREATMENT OF BOYCOTTS

The Supreme Court has developed a per se approach to dealing with boycotts. When the boycotts are "naked" (i.e., unaccompanied by any possible efficiences), this approach is sound. As we shall see, however, there are several questionable decisions in cases where the boycott could have been ancillary to a legitimate pursuit of efficiency. In still other cases, the courts have recognized the fact that some group refusals to deal (boycotts) benefit consumers by enhancing economic efficiency.

In *Eastern States*,[15] we have the first very clear, naked boycott to reach the Supreme Court. That case involved retail lumber dealers who resented having to compete with some of their wholesale suppliers for retail sales. As a result, they decided to circulate among all retailers a list of those wholesalers who had made retail sales to final consumers. It was obvious to the Court that the "circulation of such information among the hundreds of retailers as to the alleged delinquency of a wholesaler with one of their number had and was intended to have the natural effect of causing such retailers to withhold their patronage from the concerns listed."

The Court found ample evidence in the record that the scheme had worked according to this design. As to the necessary element of conspiracy, the Court had little trouble:

> It is elementary, however, that conspiracies are seldom capable of proof by direct testimony and may be inferred from the things actually done; and when, in this case, by concerted action the names of wholesalers who were reported as having made sales to consumers were periodically reported to the other members of the associations, the conspiracy to accomplish that which was the natural consequence of such action may be readily inferred.

In essence, the Court found an implicit agreement among the retailers.

The Court recognized the absolute right of a retailer to decide *unilaterally* to stop dealing with a wholesaler for any reason whatsoever. In

---

[15]*Eastern States Retail Lumber Dealer's Assoc.* v. *United States*, 234 U.S. 600 (1914).

particular, he may decide to stop dealing with any wholesaler who makes retail sales, but retailers may not agree *collectively* to withhold their business from offending wholesalers. It is the use of the collective market power of the group to force each wholesaler to conform to the retailers' wishes that is the evil of a boycott.

The movie industry provided two cases that suggest a hostile judicial attitude but are of questionable wisdom. In *Paramount Famous Lasky*,[16] 10 film producers and distributors agreed to a standard contract that each would impose upon all exhibitors. The contract contained a provision that any dispute between a distributor and an exhibitor would be submitted to arbitration. If an exhibitor failed to comply with one contract, all distributors would suspend service on their contracts with that exhibitor.

The 10 distributors controlled 60 percent of the entire film business, and their agreement restricted their freedom of action to negotiate contracts on more competitive terms. The Court felt that the agreement was "unusual" and necessarily and directly tended to restrict the sort of competition that the antitrust laws were designed to protect. The Court went on to say:

> It may be that arbitration is well adapted to the needs of the motion picture industry; but, when under the guise of arbitration parties enter into unusual arrangements which unreasonably suppress normal competition, their action becomes illegal.
>
> In order to establish violation of the Sherman Act, it is not necessary to show that the challenged arrangement suppresses all competition between the parties. . . . The interest of the public in the preservation of competition is the primary consideration. The prohibitions of the statute cannot be evaded by good intentions.

There was no doubt that the collective monopsony power of the major distributors was being used to coerce the movie theaters to adhere to uniform contractual terms, but this may have reduced the costs of the distributors. In the normal course of events, these cost savings would be reflected in lower prices and greater quantities for consumers.

Potential cost savings are even more obvious in *First National Pictures*.[17] In that case, a group of film distributors formed local credit committees to assess the financial soundness of the theater owners. They were especially concerned with the new owners of established theaters. As part of this plan, the distributors agreed to refuse to supply films to new owners if (1) the new owner failed to assume and complete all existing contracts of the former owners and (2) if the new owner refused to pay a cash deposit determined by the credit committee.

---

[16] *Paramount Famous Lasky Corp.* v. *United States*, 282 U.S. 30 (1930).

[17] *United States* v. *First National Pictures*, 282 U.S. 44 (1930).

The credit committee agreement clearly limits the freedom of each distributor to compete for the business of new owners by offering more attractive terms. This did not escape the Court's attention:

> The obvious purpose of the arrangement is to restrict the liberty of those who have representatives on the film boards and secure their concerted action for the purpose of coercing certain purchasers of theaters by excluding them from the opportunity to deal in a free and untrammeled market.

Once again, this agreement may reduce the costs associated with selling to theater owners that are bad risks, which in turn should lead to lower prices for consumers. Nonetheless, the Supreme Court ruled against the distributors.

A large step toward a per se rule was taken in *Fashion Originators' Guild*.[18] The Fashion Originators' Guild of America (FOGA) was comprised of firms that design, manufacture, and sell women's clothing and firms that manufacture, convert, or dye textiles for women's clothing. Some of their original designs were copied once they hit the market and proved to be popular. The copies usually sold for lower prices than the originals. Although these designs had no legal protection, the creators claimed that copying them was an unfair trade practice. As a result, FOGA was formed to combat and destroy all competition from copyists, which were referred to as "style pirates."

To achieve their goal, FOGA members boycotted retailers who adopted a policy of selling copies of designs produced by FOGA members. As a result, retailers had been coerced into cooperating with FOGA. Enforcement effort included the use of "shoppers" who would examine the stocks of retailers to determine whether copies were being sold. In addition to its efforts against "style pirates," FOGA limited its members' freedom to engage in retail advertising, to discount their prices, to sell at retail, and to follow other business practices.

The Supreme Court found that the FOGA activities violated the Sherman and Clayton Acts and thereby violated Section 5 of the FTC Act:

> The purpose and object of this combination, its potential power, its tendency to monopoly, the coercion it could and did practice upon a rival method of competition, all brought it within the policy of the prohibition declared by the Sherman and Clayton Acts.

Further, the Court held that "even if copying were an acknowledged tort under the law of every state, that situation would not justify petitioners in combining together to regulate and restrain interstate commerce in violation of federal law." Since the Supreme Court analyzed the likely effect of the scheme developed by the FOGA members, one

---

[18] *Fashion Originators' Guild of America* v. *Federal Trade Commission*, 312 U.S. 457 (1941).

might suppose that a rule of reason analysis had been employed. This, however, is not really the case because the Court refused to weigh the benefits of the program against its costs to consumers. In fact, the Court felt that such an inquiry was irrelevant. Thus, a further step toward per se illegality had been taken.

Whatever residual doubt regarding the status of boycotts that may have existed vanished with the Supreme Court's ruling in *Klor's*,[19] which was a civil case. Klor's was a retail appliance store in San Francisco, and Broadway-Hale Stores was a chain of department stores, one of which was adjacent to Klor's. These two competed in the sale of radios, television sets, refrigerators, and other household appliances. In this case, Klor's complained that manufacturers and distributors of well-known brands like General Electric, RCA, Admiral, and Zenith had conspired among themselves and with Broadway-Hale "either not to sell to Klor's or to sell to it only at discriminatory prices and highly unfavorable terms." Presumably, Broadway-Hale wanted to eliminate Klor's because it was a discount retailer.

The defendants did not dispute the allegations but claimed that there was no antitrust violation because there was no public injury. They demonstrated that there were hundreds of other appliance dealers who sold all brands of household appliances. Some of these retailers were within a few blocks of Klor's. Thus, there was ample opportunity for consumers to buy at retail. As a result, the District Court found this to be a "purely private quarrel" between Klor's and Broadway-Hale. The Ninth Circuit felt that "a violation of the Sherman Act requires conduct of the defendants by which the public is or conceivably may be ultimately injured." Since the price, quantity, and quality offered the public was unaffected, and there did not appear to be any purpose or intent to change or influence price, quantity, or quality, there was no public injury. In other words, consumer welfare was unaffected by the boycott of Klor's.

The Supreme Court disagreed:

> The holding, if correct, means that unless the opportunities for customers to buy in a competitive market are reduced, a group of powerful businessmen may act in concert to deprive a single merchant, like Klor, of the goods he needs to compete effectively.
>
> We think Klor's allegations clearly show one type of trade restraint and public harm the Sherman Act forbids, and that defendants' affidavits provide no defense to the charges.

In essence, there seemed to be no offsetting efficiency gain, and there was an actual loss of a preferred retailer.

In this case, the Court found a wide combination of firms that took away Klor's freedom to buy appliances in an open competitive market

---

[19] *Klor's* v. *Broadway-Hale Stores*, 359 U.S. 207 (1959).

and drove it out of business. The agreement deprived the manufacturers of their freedom to sell to Klor's on the same terms as they sold to Broadway-Hale. It interfered with the natural flow of interstate commerce. As a result, this agreement

> is not to be tolerated merely because the victim is just one merchant whose business is so small that his destruction makes little difference to the economy. Monopoly can as surely thrive by the elimination of such small businessmen, one at a time, as it can by driving them out in large groups.

Summary of boycott cases

It is common to observe that boycotts are per se illegal. This view, as we have seen, has a rich tradition and history. The reason for this harsh treatment is that a boycott usually inflicts some competitive injury. If whatever good comes from a boycott may be obtained in a less restrictive way, the harsh treatment may not cause much social damage and may lead to social gains in the form of lower prices.

7–5 SOME ECONOMIC ASPECTS OF INFORMATION

Nearly all economic models assume that information is perfect and freely available to anyone who would benefit from having it. For example, we usually assume that consumers have complete information on the availability, the prices, and the precise consumption characteristics of all commodities. Producers are presumed to know the existing production technologies, the optimal plant locations, precise consumer demands, and the prices of all inputs. A split second's reflection will convince you that the perfect information assumption is heroic to say the least. In fact, imperfect or incomplete information is the rule rather than the exception. In this section, we shall discuss the problem posed by imperfect information on prices.[20]

The usual competitive model predicts a single price at which all transactions will occur. But we observe some dispersion of prices among sellers in the real world and, in fact, this dispersion of prices is pervasive even for homogeneous commodities. A glance at the supermarket advertisements in the newspaper will provide an example of this phenomenon.

One measure of ignorance in the market is provided by the dispersion of prices. Ignorance is costly, and we should expect buyers and sellers to attempt to reduce the level of ignorance. In a famous study, Allen Jung measured the dispersion of automobile prices in metropolitan Chicago.[21]

---

[20] Much of this section depends upon George J. Stigler, "The Economics of Information," *Journal of Political Economy* 69 (June 1961), pp. 213–25.

[21] Allen F. Jung, "Price Variations among Automobile Dealers in Metropolitan Chicago," *Journal of Business* 33 (January 1960), pp. 31–42.

For identical models with identical equipment, prices varied as much as 8.5 percent. Certainly, the buyers who paid relatively high prices and the sellers who charged relatively low prices would have benefited from more perfect information. As a result, we see consumers searching for the lowest price and sellers attempting to find out what their competitors are charging.

In spite of efforts by buyers and sellers to eliminate price dispersion, we continue to see such dispersion. This is because information is not free. Some search will often lead to cost savings for buyers, but it will seldom be sensible to canvass every seller. As with any other costly activity, one engages in search until the marginal benefits equal the marginal costs. For search, the marginal benefits involve cost savings while the marginal costs involve expenditures of resources on the search activity. Some dispersion of price is optimal due to the costs incurred by sellers in determining the asking prices of their rivals and due to the costs incurred by buyers in conducting more extensive search. In other words, it will not be optimal to reduce dispersion to zero because the costs will outweigh the benefits of doing so.

Even when searching is not terribly expensive, considerable price dispersion can persist because knowledge of prices rapidly becomes obsolete. Both supply and demand change continually over time, which necessitates continual search. As one might expect, the less stable the demand and/or supply, the greater will be the price dispersion. Moreover, the flow of new buyers and sellers into the market provides a constant component of ignorance—these newcomers are bound to be somewhat uninformed initially. Finally, the extent of price dispersion will be smaller the larger the market is. This follows because when markets are large enough, specialized firms will emerge to collect and sell information.

Information as a commodity

When information is not free, it becomes a commodity. In some respects, it is just like any other commodity, but in other respects, information poses special problems.[22] The most pressing economic problem associated with information concerns its appropriability. When information is used, it does not disappear. Thus, the purchaser of information can sell it to someone else or someone else may simply observe it for free when a purchaser uses the information. As a result, information may

---

[22] A provocative exchange of views is presented by Kenneth J. Arrow, "Economic Welfare and the Allocation of Resources for Invention" in *The Rate and Direction of Inventive Activity*, National Bureau of Economic Research (Princeton, N.J.: Princeton University Press, 1962); and Harold Demsetz, "Information and Efficiency: Another Viewpoint," *Journal of Law and Economics* 12 (April 1969), pp. 1–22.

not be produced in the optimal quantity because the supplier of the information may not be able to extract enough revenue for it.

When sellers recognize that each can be better off with superior information about prices in the market, there will be some demand for the collection and dissemination of price data. If a specialized firm does not emerge to provide the price reporting service, producers may simply exchange price information among themselves. In many cases, the exchange is not highly organized, but there is some agreement that one firm's response today imposes a reciprocal obligation on the recipient of the information to provide data in the future. In other instances, the exchange is more formalized through membership in a trade association or subscription to a statistical reporting service.

Each producer can be more competitive if he knows what he is confronting. Ideally, he would like to know the price and quantity of his rivals' outputs, the quality of the products offered, the services that each provides, and so on. Each producer can make a more sensible price, output, and quality decision when he fully comprehends his competitive environment. The antitrust laws, however, curtail the exchange of price information.[23]

7–6 JUDICIAL TREATMENT OF DATA DISSEMINATION

Generally, we should not be concerned when a businessman makes every effort to be well-informed. On occasion, however, these efforts mask an attempt to fix prices. When this is the case, the antitrust law properly condemns this activity. Recent cases reflect an increasing hostility toward exchanges of price information.

In *American Column & Lumber*,[24] the government complained about the activities of a trade association, the American Hardwood Manufacturers' Association, which had 400 members when the suit was filed. Some 365 members participated in the so-called Open Competition Plan. These firms accounted for approximately one third of the total hardwood production in the United States.

After the "Plan" was developed, the trade association urged its members to join by pointing out that "[k]nowledge regarding prices actually made is all that is necessary to keep prices at reasonably stable and normal levels." Although any agreement to charge the same prices or curtail production was always disclaimed, the Plan was promoted as a way of achieving a "certain uniformity of trade practice."

---

[23] For a recent analysis and critique of the antitrust treatment of information provision, see Richard A. Posner, "Antitrust and Information: Reflections on the *Gypsum* and *Engineers* Decisions," *Georgetown Law Journal* 67 (June 1979), pp. 1187–1203.

[24] *American Column & Lumber Co. v. United States*, 257 U.S. 377 (1921).

The Plan included an elaborate scheme for the exchange of business data. Each member was required to file a substantial number of detailed reports:

1. A daily report of all sales actually made by customer and by product.
2. A daily shipping report.
3. A monthly production report.
4. A monthly inventory report.
5. Price lists and all price changes.

In addition, an effort was made to ensure uniform grading through an inspection service. The declared purpose of the inspection service was not to change any member's grading but to furnish each member a basis upon which to compare prices with those of other members.

All of these reports by members were subject to complete audit by representatives of the association. Any member who failed to report would be denied the reports of the trade association. Furthermore, failure to report for 12 days in six months would be grounds for expulsion from the Association.

Each participating member received reports from the Association:

1. A monthly summary showing the production of each member for the previous month.
2. A weekly report of all sales, giving each sale, the price, and the name of the purchaser.
3. On Tuesday of each week, a report of each shipment by each member, complete up to the evening of the preceding Thursday.
4. A monthly report showing the individual stock on hand of each member.
5. A monthly summary of the price lists furnished by all members, showing the prices asked by each.

Immediate updates were provided whenever a price change was reported.

The elaborate plan for the interchange of reports did not simply supply each member with the data necessary for judging the market. It went much farther by reporting the views of each member as to "market conditions for the next few months," what the production of each would be for the next "two months," and frequent analyses of the reports by an expert with advice on future prices and production. In addition, the members were subjected to repeated exhortations to limit production.

Within a month of formulating the Plan, the membership began cooperating and suppressing competition by restricting output. This restriction naturally led to increases in lumber prices. This conclusion follows from an examination of the association's meetings.

The Supreme Court saw the association's efforts for what they were.

> Genuine competitors do not make daily, weekly, and monthly reports of the minutest details of their business to their rivals, as the defendants did; they do not contract, as was done here, to submit their books to the discretionary audit and their stocks to the discretionary inspection of their rivals for the purpose of successfully competing with them. . . . This is not the conduct of competitors but is so clearly that of men united in an agreement, express or implied, to act together and pursue a common purpose under a common guide that, if it did not stand confessed a combination to restrict production and increase prices in interstate commerce as we have seen that it is, that conclusion must inevitably have been inferred from the facts which were proved. To pronounce such abnormal conduct on the part of 365 natural competitors, controlling one third of the trade of the country in an article of prime necessity, a "new form of competition" and not an old form of combination in restraint of trade, as it so plainly is, would be for this court to confess itself blinded by words and forms to realities which men in general very plainly see and understand and condemn, as an old evil in a new dress and with a new name.

The Court went on to point out that "the fundamental purpose of the Plan was to procure 'harmonious' individual action among a large number of naturally competing dealers with respect to the volume of production and prices, without having any specific agreement with respect to them."

In 1925, the Supreme Court ruled in favor of a different lumber association.[25] The Maple Flooring Manufacturers Association was a trade association of firms that produced maple, birch, and beech flooring. Nearly all of them were located in Michigan, Minnesota, and Wisconsin. In 1922, the defendants accounted for some 70 percent of the total production of these types of flooring. The government complained about several things:

1. Information on the average cost of production for all products was distributed to all members.
2. A booklet was provided to each member showing freight rates on flooring from Cadillac, Michigan, to 5,000–6,000 different destinations.
3. Information on prices, quantities sold, and inventories of all members were summarized and distributed to each member.
4. Meetings of the trade association afforded individuals the chance to meet and discuss the industry's problems.

In this case, however, the court found the government's arguments wanting. First, there was no evidence that the clear opportunity for

---

[25] *Maple Flooring Manufacturers Assoc. v. United States*, 268 U.S. 563 (1925).

basing point pricing actually resulted in the uniformity of delivered prices.[26] In fact, the firms would sell on an FOB (free on board) mill basis if requested. Second, there was no evidence that the freight book and the average cost data were used to fix prices. Finally, all of the association's reports were available to buyers as well as to sellers. Moreover, these reports contained the same sort of trade statistics as those available in many industries.

The Court recognized that the collection and dissemination of information could make markets work more smoothly. As a result, such activity may lead to stabilized production and price. But this does not mean that the association is guilty of restraining trade. The court stated this specifically:

> the natural effect of the acquisition of wider and more scientific knowledge of business conditions . . . and its consequent effect in stabilizing production and price, can hardly be deemed a restraint of commerce, or, if so, it cannot, we think, be said to be an unreasonable restraint, or in any respect unlawful.

The distinction between *American Column & Lumber* and *Maple Flooring* lies in the court's inference of collusion in the former case. In the latter case, the court was not persuaded by the evidence presented on collusion.[27] This distinction continued to be the rule until the *Container*[28] decision.

In *Container*, the defendants accounted for about 90 percent of the shipments of corrugated containers (cardboard boxes) from plants in the southeastern United States. Since the products were ordered according to precise specifications, the products were identical across different suppliers. All producers were capable of producing according to the buyer's specifications so that one firm's output was a perfect substitute for that of another firm. This case was different from earlier information exchange cases because not much was involved:

> Here all that was present was a request by each defendant of its competitor for information as to the most recent price charged or quoted, whenever it needed such information and whenever it was not available from another source. Each defendant on receiving that request usually furnished the data with the expectation that it would be furnished reciprocal information when it wanted it.

---

[26] In a basing point pricing system, the delivered price to the customer equals the price at the basing point plus freight from the basing point to the customer's location no matter what the actual location of the seller. We shall discuss this pricing system in some detail in the next chapter.

[27] Sullivan, *Handbook of the Law of Antitrust*, pp. 269–70, offers a more critical view of the *Maple Flooring* decision and, in fact, concludes that it was decided incorrectly.

[28] *United States* v. *Container Corp. of America*, 393 U.S. 333 (1969).

There was of course freedom to withdraw from the agreement. But the fact remains that when a defendant requested and received price information, it was affirming its willingness to furnish such information in return.

There was to be sure an infrequency and irregularity of price exchanges between the defendants; and often the data were available from the records of the defendants or from the customers themselves. Yet the essence of the agreement was to furnish price information whenever requested.

The importance of this part of the decision is that an agreement was found to exist among the firms in the industry. For antitrust purposes, once an agreement is found, its effects can be analyzed to determine if it restrains trade. If so, the agreement is not lawful. In this instance, the court found an illegal effect on price:

The exchange of price information seemed to have the effect of keeping prices within a fairly narrow ambit. Capacity has exceeded the demand from 1955 to 1963, the period covered by the complaint, and the trend of corrugated container prices has been downward. Yet despite this excess capacity and the downward trend of prices, the industry has expanded in the Southeast from 30 manufacturers with 49 plants to 51 manufacturers with 98 plants. An abundance of raw materials and machinery makes entry into the industry easy with an investment of $50,000 to $75,000.

The result of this reciprocal exchange of prices was to stabilize prices though at a downward level. Knowledge of a competitor's price usually meant matching that price. The continuation of some price competition is not fatal to the government's case. The limitation or reduction of price competition brings the case within the ban, for as we held in *United States* v. *Socony-Vacuum Oil Co.*, interference with the setting of price by free market forces is unlawful per se. Price information exchanged in some markets may have no effect on a truly competitive price. But the corrugated container industry is dominated by relatively few sellers. The product is fungible and the competition for sales is price. The demand is inelastic, as buyers place orders only for immediate, short-run needs. The exchange of price data tends toward price uniformity. For a lower price does not mean a larger share of the available business but a sharing of the existing business at a lower return. Stabilizing prices as well as raising them is within the ban of §1 of the Sherman Act. As we said in *United States* v. *Socony-Vacuum Oil Co.*, "in terms of market operation stabilization is but one form of manipulation." The inferences are irresistible that the exchange of price information has had an anticompetitive effect in the industry, chilling the vigor of price competition. The agreement in the present case, though somewhat casual, is analogous to [that] in *American Column & Lumber Co.* v. *United States*.

Price is too critical, too sensitive a control to allow it to be used even in an informal manner to restrain competition.

Consequently, the court ruled against the firms in *Container*. While there was some discussion about economic analysis of market structure, the court failed to execute a sensible analysis.[29] The market structure was not highly concentrated. There was no evidence of a poor economic performance of the industry. There was no evidence of a wrongful purpose or of anticompetitive effects of the information exchanges. Finally, the conduct of the firms involved no agreement regarding price. In spite of these factors, Justice Douglas and his majority ruled against the firms.

A final remark on information exchanges

When price data are exchanged among rival firms, two effects are possible: (1) the average price could rise, and/or (2) the dispersion of prices could fall. If the average price was to rise, that would be an undesirable result. If, however, the dispersion of prices was to narrow, that would not be undesirable. In fact, it would be beneficial, as the actual prices would be closer to ideal price of perfect competition. Accordingly, exchanges of price information should serve only as circumstantial evidence of a Section 1 violation. The burden would still be on the plaintiff to show that the average price rose as a result of the information exchange.[30]

QUESTIONS AND PROBLEMS

1. Dunk Jones was suspended from his team and the National Basketball Association when it was discovered that he had gambled on his team. Such bets were in violation of Dunk's contract and NBA rules. When the league would not lift his suspension, Dunk claimed that the teams were guilty of a concerted refusal to deal. Were they? If so, what were the damages? [*Molinas* v. *National Basketball Association*, 190 F. Supp. 241 (S.D.N.Y. 1961)]

2. The Professional Golfer's Association refused to permit Henry Hacker to play in professional tournaments because he could not play very well. Henry claimed that the tour players were guilty of boycotting him. Were they? [*Deesen* v. *Professional Golfer's Association*, 358 F. 2d 165 (9th Cir.)]

3. Why does product heterogeneity provide an incentive for market division in preference to price fixing?

4. In the idealized case, market division creates a series of local monopolies and leads to noncompetitive pricing. Is this what happened to *Topco*?

---

[29] Lawrence Sullivan, *Handbook of the Law of Antitrust*, pp. 271–73 succinctly criticizes *Container*.

[30] This analysis was suggested by Richard A. Posner, *Antitrust and Information*, pp. 1187–1203.

5. After the pipe manufacturers were convicted of price fixing and market division in *Addyston Pipe & Steel* they merged into the U.S. Cast Iron Pipe & Foundry Company. Why did they do this?

6. Examine Figure 7–2, which shows the price-output combinations selected by two firms with different costs. Does either firm have an incentive to cheat on the market division agreement? How can the high-cost firm cheat on the low-cost firm?

7. In Figure 7–1, the supply response of the firms that are cheating on a collusive agreement is represented by MC_1, while the marginal cost of those firms that obey the collusive agreement is MC_2. What happens when a firm defects from the cartel and joins the cheaters?

8. Since the competitive model assumes perfect information, why should there be any antitrust rules against the dissemination of information? How can the provision of accurate information be anti-competitive?

9. The Nationwide Trailer Rental System organized trailer rental operators to make one-way, intercity rentals easier and cheaper. The organization restricted its membership to one operator per city. Its members dealt only with each other. They claimed the right to deny membership to outsiders on the grounds that they built up a valuable organization and should not have to share it. The courts disagreed in *United States* v. *Nationwide Trailer Rental System, Inc.*, 156 F. Supp. 800 (D. Kan. 1957). Why? What is the likely result of this decision?

10. In the analysis of Figure 7–3, we saw that a boycott could benefit the remaining members of an industry even when monopoly pricing did not result. Is there an incentive for the remaining firms to expand their productive capacity? If so, show it. How could the remaining firms prevent such expansion?

11. During the 1920s there was chronic overproduction of sugar and intense price competition that included secret rebates. The sugar refiners formed the Sugar Institute to administer its code of ethics. In part, the Sugar Institute required that an announced price would be adhered to and no secret concessions would be made. As a result, the frequency of price changes dropped, refiners' margins improved, and profits rose in the face of continued excess capacity. [*Sugar Institute, Inc.* v. *United States*, 297 U.S. 553 (1936)]. How can these results be explained?

12. "Although price dispersion is a measure of ignorance in the market, it is a biased measure because of product differentiation." What does this mean?

13. "In a world of scarce resources, perfect information is not optimal." Why not?

14. When a supplier of reinforcing bars enters a specific job contract, he promises to deliver whatever reinforcing bars are necessary for a specific piece of construction. The contract specifies a maximum price for the reinforcing bars. The buyer need not take any if the spot market price falls. These contracts permit contractors to bid on construction jobs with full assurance that the necessary reinforcing bars will be available at a predetermined maximum price.

    Some contractors entered into several of these contracts for the same job. If the market price fell during the construction period, they just did their job. If the price rose, however, they would order full shipments from all suppliers and sell the excess, thereby earning a profit. Since the specific job contract stipulates that all reinforcing bars delivered are to be used solely on the job specified, no supplier was obligated to supply excess reinforcing bars. A problem arises because the suppliers cannot determine whether excess reinforcing bars were being ordered. A trade association was formed to gather and disseminate information on specific job contracts. This would inform each supplier of multiple contracts for the same job. In turn, it put the manufacturers in a position to refuse delivery when excess reinforcing bars were ordered.

    Have the suppliers violated Section 1 by exchanging information? [*Cement Manufacturers Protective Assoc.* v. *United States*, 268 U.S. 588 (1925)]

15. In Houston, the mayor informed four prospective cable television operators that he did not want to choose among them. Instead, he wanted them to present him with a plan to service Houston. In due course, the four split up the Houston market into four disjoint pieces. A fifth cable television operator complained that it was excluded from the market and that the four franchisees had shared the market. Is this a per se violation of Section 1 of the Sherman Act? Do the mayor's preferences make any difference? [*Affiliated Capital Corp.* v. *City of Houston*, No. 81–2335, CA5 (1983)]

16. Promoters at the four major automobile race tracks in the Northeast and the New England Drivers and Owners Club agreed to use the Hoosier "Budget" tire during the 1982 auto racing season. As a result, the other three major racing tire manufacturers were ex-

cluded from this market. One of the excluded manufacturers, M&H Tire Co., Inc., charged that this was an illegal boycott. What do you think? Why would the drivers make one of the firms a monopoly? [*M&H Tire Co., Inc.* v. *Hoosier Racing Tire Corp.*, No. 82–0697–C, D. Mass. (1983)]

17. In the Milwaukee area, the owners of movie theaters competed vigorously for the exhibition rights to first-run films. As a result, the percentage terms, the playtimes, the guarantees, and the advances increased substantially. The exhibitors (theaters) found that competitive bidding forced them to pay unreasonable prices. The owners of the theaters found a solution to this problem: They simply got together and split the first-run films so that competition was unnecessary and prices fell. Is this a restraint of trade? Where is the competitive harm if a theater reduces its costs in this way? [*United States* v. *Capital Services, Inc.*, No. 80–C–407, ED Wis. (1983)]

FURTHER READINGS

Bork, Robert H. "The Rule of Reason and the Per Se Concept: Price Fixing and Market Division." *Yale Law Journal* 74 (April 1965), pp. 775–847.

Posner, Richard A. "Antitrust and Information: Reflections on the Gypsum and Engineers Decisions." *Georgetown Law Journal* 67 (June 1979), pp. 1187–1203.

————. *Antitrust Law: An Economic Perspective.* Chicago: University of Chicago Press, 1976.

8

The problem of oligopoly

We have seen in Chapter 6 that price fixing can be very beneficial to the firms in an industry. Through collusion, they can set a price that a monopolist would select and share the resulting monopoly profits. We have also seen, however, that collusion is not costless to the colluders. For one thing, there are costs incurred in coordinating the efforts of the separate firms. In addition, the conspirators must police and enforce their agreement because cheating is such an attractive proposition. As a consequence, it is unlikely that price fixing will be successful when there are many firms in the industry. Small numbers of firms are much more conducive to collusion than large numbers. When we have a small number of firms producing a homogeneous output, the market structure is called an oligopoly. Just how small the number of firms must be to constitute an oligopoly does not have a precise answer. But we know that the number must be small enough so that the firms recognize their "mutual interdependence." In other words, each firm in the industry is aware of the other firms' presence, and each is concerned about the price and output decisions of those firms.[1] Some analysts have pointed out that an oligopoly may not need to engage in overt collusion that can be challenged readily by the antitrust laws. Instead, the firms may

---

[1] Economists refer to "rivalry" under these conditions. To many businessmen, however, such concern about the behavior of fellow industry members signifies a "competitive" industry.

achieve the results of overt collusion by tacit collusion, which is not so readily challenged.

In this chapter, we shall review a few simple[2] oligopoly models to develop the concepts of mutual interdependence and tacit collusion. Our purpose in presenting these models is not to develop a thorough treatment of oligopoly, which is far beyond the scope of this text. Rather, we want to provide some feeling for the range of outcomes that are possible in an oligopolistic industry. In addition, we want to convey the idea that noncompetitive price-quantity solutions may emerge without any overt conspiracy. For antitrust purposes, this is the oligopoly problem. After examining two views on the suitability of the present laws for dealing with noncompetitive outcomes absent overt collusion, we shall look at three consequences of small numbers: conscious parallelism, delivered pricing, and price leadership. In each instance, we will discuss the economic theory and summarize the case law.

8-1 SOME SIMPLE MODELS

Unlike monopoly and competition, there is no central theory of oligopoly. Instead, there are several theories that have almost countless variations. For antitrust purposes, we shall be concerned with parallel business behavior. To this end, we may start with Cournot's naive theory and increase the degree of sophistication in stages.

The Cournot duopoly model

A French economist, Augustin Cournot, developed the first duopoly model in 1838.[3] In the simplest version of the Cournot model, both firms have identical marginal and average cost functions, which are constant at zero. Moreover, the products of the two firms are assumed to be completely homogeneous and therefore are perfect substitutes. The final structural assumption is that the industry demand function is linear and does not change during the course of the analysis. To these, we add the customary assumption that each firm seeks to maximize its profits. But a rather curious form of myopia is attributed to each firm: Each firm is assumed to act in the belief that the output of his rival will not change. As we shall see, this is myopic because it is never true until the final equilibrium.

Suppose that initially there is a single firm in the industry. In Figure 8-1, we see firm 1's optimal price and output as P_M and Q_M, which is

---

[2] While these models are "simple" relative to other oligopoly models, some readers may find them to be tough going. In that case, the reader should just get the essence of the price-quantity solution.

[3] By duopoly, we mean an industry with two firms. Cournot's work was translated into English in 1897 by Nathaniel T. Bacon as *Researches into the Mathematical Principles of the Theory of Wealth* (New York: Macmillan, 1897).

FIGURE 8–1

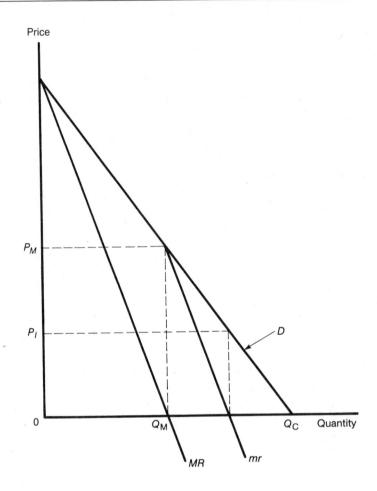

easily recognized as the monopoly solution. There are excess profits equal to $P_M Q_M$ because the costs are assumed to be zero, and therefore, the profit equals the total revenue. In contrast, the competitive solution would require zero excess profits. In this simple model, competitive equilibrium requires a zero price and an output of Q_C, which is twice the monopoly output Q_M.

Now, let firm 2 enter. Firm 1 has produced Q_M and anticipates profits of $P_M Q_M$. The best that firm 2 can do is maximize profit according to the residual demand function, which is the lower half of the industry demand representing sales that have not been made by firm 1. Accordingly, firm 2 will sell one half of $Q_C - Q_M$ at a price of P_1. In essence, we have moved the origin in Figure 8–1 to Q_M for the determination of firm 2's optimal price and output, given its assumption that firm 1 will continue to supply Q_M. The marginal revenue associated with the residual demand is shown as the line labeled mr in Figure 8–1. We can see that mr equals MC (which is zero) at an output of $\frac{1}{2}(Q_C - Q_M)$ which is $(\frac{1}{4})Q_C$. Thus, total output is $(\frac{3}{4})Q_C$, and the market clearing price will be P_1.

Firm 1's profits turned out to be $P_1 Q_M$ rather than the anticipated $P_M Q_M$. According to the behavioral assumption, firm 1 believes that firm 2 will continue to sell $(\frac{1}{4})Q_C$. Consequently, the profit maximizing quantity for firm 1 is one half of the residual $(\frac{3}{4})Q_C$ or $(\frac{3}{8})Q_C$. When firm 2 sees that firm 1 has reduced its output to $(\frac{3}{8})Q_C$, firm 2 recognizes that its residual demand is now $(\frac{5}{8})Q_C$. Consequently, firm 2 produces $(\frac{5}{16})Q_C$. This process will be iterated until there is no further incentive for a firm to revise its production plans. Given our assumption of identical and constant costs, this will occur when firm 1 has reduced its output to $(\frac{1}{3})Q_C$ and firm 2 has increased its output to $(\frac{1}{3})Q_C$. Table 8–1, shows

TABLE 8–1   Quantity adjustment for Cournot duopolists

| Period | Firm 1 | | Firm 2 | | Total |
	Residual D	Optimal Q	Residual D	Optimal Q	Output
1	Q_C	$\frac{1}{2}Q_C$	$\frac{1}{2}Q_C$	$\frac{1}{4}Q_C$	$\frac{3}{4}Q_C$
2	$\frac{3}{4}Q_C$	$\frac{3}{8}Q_C$	$\frac{5}{8}Q_C$	$\frac{5}{16}Q_C$	$\frac{11}{16}Q_C$
3	$\frac{11}{16}Q_C$	$\frac{11}{32}Q_C$	$\frac{21}{32}Q_C$	$\frac{21}{64}Q_C$	$\frac{43}{64}Q_C$
⋮	⋮	⋮	⋮	⋮	⋮
∞	$\frac{2}{3}Q_C$	$\frac{1}{3}Q_C$	$\frac{2}{3}Q_C$	$\frac{1}{3}Q_C$	$\frac{2}{3}Q_C$

the pattern of output changes that will occur in this model. In principle, it will take forever to reach the final equilibrium as we have described the process. In equilibrium, the total industry production will be $(\frac{2}{3})Q_C$, which is clearly greater than the monopoly output of $(\frac{1}{2})Q_C$. Total industry profits are $P_D \cdot Q_D$, where duopoly output Q_D equals two thirds of the competitive output and P_D is the market-clearing price at the duopoly output. Thus, the Cournot equilibrium involves a price and output between the monopoly and competitive price and output combinations.

The restrictiveness of the Cournot model lies in its behavioral assumption regarding the continuing belief that one's rival will always produce the quantity that is currently being produced. The fact that marginal and average cost are constant and zero can be relaxed quite easily. It complicates the calculations a bit, but does no real damage to the basic conclusion. The simple Cournot model can also be generalized to accommodate more than two firms. The addition of a third firm would result in the equilibrium output expanding to $(\frac{3}{4})Q_C$ where each of the three firms would produce one fourth of the competitive output. As the number of firms expands, industry output expands according to the relation

$$Q = (n/(n + 1))Q_C$$

where n denotes the number of firms. Clearly, as the number of firms gets larger, $n/(n + 1)$ will approach one, and the industry output will approach the competitive level.

The Stackelberg duopoly model

Most critics and commentators focus on the extraordinary stupidity of the Cournot duopolists. No matter how often their expectations regarding their rival's output are disappointed, they never surrender their beliefs. In the Stackelberg duopoly model,[4] one of the two firms behaves just like a Cournot firm, but the other firm is aware of its rival's myopic behavior. Thus, the contribution of Stackelberg is to smarten up one of the duopolists. The smart duopolist is assumed to be sophisticated enough to recognize that his rival will behave according to the Cournot assumption. As a result, the sophisticated firm is able to anticipate the reaction of its rival. This anticipation allows the sophisticated firm to maximize its profit subject to the reactions of the other firm. By being able to do this, the sophisticated firm makes more profit than it would as a naive Cournot duopolist. Total industry profits may decline further from the monopoly level than was true in the Cournot case, but because the profits are not shared equally, the sophisticated firm makes more profit. In spite of the fact that the two firms have identical cost functions, the sophisticated firm's greater awareness is rewarded by a bigger piece of the action. Thus, the sophisticated firm gets a sufficiently larger share of a smaller total profit so that the sophisticated firm's profit is greater than under the naive Cournot assumptions.

If both firms become sophisticated and each attempts to incorporate the reactions of the other, they both lose because price wars result. A way of preventing such losses is to agree to refrain from price warfare—in other words, to collude.

A numerical example may be helpful in tying together the results of the various market structures that we have been discussing. Suppose that the demand function for the industry is given by

$$P = 100 - \frac{1}{2}Q \tag{8-1}$$

---

[4] Heinrich von Stackelberg, *The Theory of the Market Economy*, trans. A. T. Peacock (London: William Hodge, 1952).

We shall continue to assume that the average and marginal costs are constant and equal to zero. As usual, a monopolist would attempt to set price P and output Q such that its profits were maximized. The necessary condition for maximizing profit

$$\Pi = PQ = 100Q - \tfrac{1}{2}Q^2 \tag{8-2}$$

is obtained by producing that output where the increment in profit is zero:

$$\frac{\Delta\Pi}{\Delta Q} = 100 - Q = 0 \tag{8-3}$$

Solving the profit maximizing condition (8–3) for Q, we discover that the optimal output is 100 units. Substituting 100 for Q in equation (8–1) reveals that the optimal price is $50. By substituting for P and Q in (8–2), we find that the maximum profit is $5,000.

In contrast, the competitive solution requires that price be equal to average cost, which is zero in this example. If price is not equal to average cost, it must be above or below average cost, thereby creating incentives for entry or exit. Since average cost is zero by hypothesis, we may set the right-hand side of (8–1) equal to zero and solve for Q. This yields the competitive output of 200. Of course, this is not an unexpected result based upon the graphical discussion surrounding the Cournot model.

In the Cournot model, each firm believes that the other will always produce the quantity it is currently observed to be producing. Consequently, the industry demand function is seen by each firm as

$$P = 100 - \tfrac{1}{2}(Q_1 + Q_2) \tag{8-4}$$

where Q_1 and Q_2 are the outputs of firms 1 and 2, respectively. Obviously, (8–4) and (8–1) are identical demand functions; we have just disaggregated the industry quantity into the amounts produced by each firm. The profit functions Π_1 and Π_2 for the firms are

$$\begin{aligned} \Pi_1 &= PQ_1 = [100 - \tfrac{1}{2}(Q_1 + Q_2)]Q_1 \\ \Pi_2 &= PQ_2 = [100 - \tfrac{1}{2}(Q_1 + Q_2)]Q_2 \end{aligned} \tag{8-5}$$

Given the behavioral assumption, the optimal output for each firm is found where the increments in Π_1 and Π_2 are zero:

$$\frac{\Delta\Pi_1}{\Delta Q_1} = 100 - Q_1 - (\tfrac{1}{2})Q_2 = 0$$

$$\frac{\Delta\Pi_2}{Q_2} = 100 - Q_2 - (\tfrac{1}{2})Q_1 = 0 \tag{8-6}$$

If we solve these profit maximizing conditions for Q_1 and Q_2, we find that each firm behaves according to its respective reaction function:

$$Q_1 = 100 - (\tfrac{1}{2})Q_2$$
$$Q_2 = 100 - (\tfrac{1}{2})Q_1 \qquad (8\text{--}7)$$

In other words, firm 1 will produce 100 minus one half of the quantity produced by firm 2. Similarly, firm 2 also will produce 100 minus one half of the quantity that firm 1 produces. Thus, each firm will react to the behavior of its rival as it attempts to maximize profit. The essence of oligopoly is reflected in equations (8–5), (8–6), and (8–7). Specifically, we can see that the output of each firm influences the output and profit of the other firm. In fact, this is what economists mean by "mutual interdependence." Given the small number of firms in the industry, the firms recognize their mutual interdependence and behave accordingly.

Substituting firm 2's reaction function into firm 1's reaction function, we find that the optimal output is

$$Q_1 = 100 - \tfrac{1}{2}(100 - \tfrac{1}{2}Q_1) = 66.67 \qquad (8\text{--}8)$$

Similarly, firm 2's optimal output is

$$Q_2 = 100 - \tfrac{1}{2}(100 - \tfrac{1}{2}Q_2) = 66.67 \qquad (8\text{--}9)$$

Not unexpectedly under our assumptions, we find that each Cournot duopolist produces the same as the other firm, and together they produce two thirds of the competitive output. Arithmetic reveals that the industry profit, which is shared equally, is $4,443.89 on total sales of 133.33 units at $33.33 per unit. This is consistent with our graphical discussion above.

In Stackelberg's model, we shall let firm 1 be the sophisticated firm. Consequently, it incorporates firm 2's reaction function into its profit function. Thus, firm 2's reaction from (8–7) is a constraint upon firm 1's profit function and is incorporated directly:

$$\begin{aligned}
\Pi_1 = PQ &= 100Q_1 - \tfrac{1}{2}(Q_1 + Q_2)Q_1 \\
&= 100Q_1 - \tfrac{1}{2}[Q_1 + (100 - \tfrac{1}{2}Q_1)]Q_1 \qquad (8\text{--}10) \\
&= 50Q_1 - \tfrac{1}{4}Q_1^2.
\end{aligned}$$

This firm's optimal output is found where

$$\frac{\Delta\Pi_1}{\Delta Q_1} = 50 - (\tfrac{1}{2})Q_1 = 0 \qquad (8\text{--}11)$$

or an output of 100. Substituting this into firm 2's reaction function, $Q_2 = 100 - \tfrac{1}{2}Q_1$, we find that the firm lacking in sophistication sells only 50 units. For the industry, total output is 150, which is three fourths of the competitive output. As a consequence, the price is $25, and industry profit is $3,750. In this case, however, profits are not shared equally: firm 1's profit is $2,500, and firm 2's profit is $1,250. Table 8–2 summarizes the results of these various market structures.

TABLE 8–2   Comparisons among various market structures

Market structure	Price	Q_1	Q_2	$Q_1 + Q_2$	Π_1	Π_2	$\Pi_1 + \Pi_2$
Competition	0	$200/n$	$200/n$	200	0	0	0
Monopoly	50	100	0	100	5,000	0	5,000
Cournot							
duopoly	33.33	66.67	66.67	133.33	2,221.95	2,221.95	4,443.90
Stackelberg							
duopoly	25	100	50	150	2,500	1,250	3,750

The Chamberlian duopoly model[5]

Chamberlin recognized that the firms in the duopoly models were not really behaving in a profit maximizing way. For example, one can hardly imagine actual firms behaving according to the Cournot assumptions because Cournot duopolists never learn. In addition, each firm fails to take account of its total impact upon price because the firms in the simple models ignore the indirect effects of their actions. A noncollusive duopoly model assumes that the firms behave independently in their efforts to maximize profits. Independence of action, however, cannot sensibly refer to firm behavior that requires each firm to believe that its fortunes are independent of the other. Each duopolist must see that its profit depends upon the output decisions of its rival and that its own decision affects the rival firm's profit. In this context, then, independence of action refers to the absence of agreement between the firms. Chamberlin suggested that we should let each firm be aware of its impact upon its rival and see how that logically influences our theoretical expectations.

Suppose, as before, there was initially a monopoly. In Figure 8–1, the optimal output under our previous cost assumptions was Q_M, which the firm would sell at the market clearing price of P_M. We saw that the best a new entrant can do is to produce one half of $Q_C - Q_M$, which is equal to one half of Q_M. If firm 2 produces this quantity, its entry results in price falling to P_1. If firm 1 is enlightened, it will recognize firm 2's presence and understand the consequences for the industry. As a result, firm 1 sensibly will reduce its output to one half of Q_M, which is equal to firm 2's output. The previous (monopoly) level of output Q_M now will be restored if firm 2 continues to produce at its initial level. Firm 2 should realize that this is best for both of them collectively. It also recognizes that one half of the monopoly profit is better than one half of the profit at any other output. Thus, firm 2 will, in fact, continue producing one half of Q_M. The total industry output is Q_M, and price is restored to P_M.

---

[5] Edward H. Chamberlin, *The Theory of Monopolistic Competition*, 8th ed. (Cambridge, Mass.: Harvard University Press, 1962). See Chapter III, pp. 30–55 for his review of duopoly and oligopoly.

Firms 1 and 2 each produce $(\frac{1}{2})Q_M$ and share the monopoly profits of $P_M Q_M$ equally. Chamberlin's analysis extends to more than two firms. In fact, it holds no matter how many firms there are as long as each firm recognizes that its behavior affects price and acts accordingly. Once the firms ignore their effect on price, the price will fall immediately to the competitive level.

We should recall that in both the Cournot and the Stackelberg duopoly models there is neither overt nor tacit agreement. In Chamberlin's case, however, it is arguable that there was at least tacit agreement. After firm 2's entry, firm 1 made a show of "good faith" or acquiescence by reducing its previous output. Firm 2 subsequently did not try to take advantage of the output reduction. Instead, it reciprocated the good faith by holding its output at one half of the monopoly output. Presumably, the two firms live happily ever after. This behavior raises two fundamental antitrust questions:

1. Is this behavior collusive?
2. If it is collusive, can it be challenged successfully by Section 1 of the Sherman Act?

We turn to these issues in the next section.

8–2 MUTUAL INTERDEPENDENCE AND TACIT COLLUSION

Fundamentally, the mutual interdependence among firms in an oligopolistic industry is recognized by all firms due to the industry structure itself. When only a few firms populate an industry, the firms inevitably must recognize that the industry structure causes interdependent pricing. Each firm knows that its optimal price is a function of the price charged by its rivals. Under these circumstances, it would be silly to expect the firms to ignore the obvious and blithely act as though they were totally independent. Since the firms cannot avoid recognizing their mutual interdependence, we shall take notice of it, too.

Where the firms are vividly aware of one another, we could get the result described by Chamberlin. Without any collusion or express agreement, a price output combination very close to that of monopoly is a conceivable outcome. As long as no one gets too greedy, each firm can see that it is better off with its fair share of the maximum industry profit than with a proportional share of a much smaller profit. This price and output result offends the basic purpose of the antitrust laws, which is to promote consumer welfare. When the monopoly result is the product of tacit collusion, however, antitrust challenges have not been very successful.

In part, our inability to deal with tacit collusion stems from the interpretation of the law on price fixing. As we saw in Chapter 6, the Supreme Court decided early on that collusively determined prices were unreasonable and therefore violated Section 1 of the Sherman Act. The early applications of the rule against collusive prices emphasized the impact on market price of any challenged conduct. While the court did not require a demonstration of the conduct's actual effect on market price, it did insist that one be able to draw a logical inference that the challenged behavior would raise the market price. In drawing such inferences, the Court would rely upon economic factors (e.g., market structure and the collective power of the firms in question).

This changed with the *Socony-Vacuum* decision where the mere attempt to charge a monopoly price became a violation. The majority held that the power necessary for likely success need not be demonstrated by the plaintiff. This turned the rule against price fixing into a part of the law of criminal conspiracy.[6] As a result, the Antitrust Division could prosecute criminal cases on a familiar basis by presenting evidence of actual agreement. Best of all (from their perspective), they did not have to ramble through the wilds of economic analysis because they did not have to present evidence of economic impact. In the process, however, it became more necessary to obtain proof of actual agreement. Consequently, some critics maintain that the antitrust authorities are most successful against those conspiracies that are least likely to succeed. In the case of tacit collusion, however, there is no overt agreement, and some analysts contend that such "agreements" are beyond the reach of Section 1. Consider the Chamberlinian duopolists that reached the monopoly solution without any overt or even covert communication. Neither firm provided any information to the other about its intentions. If what happened can be called collusive, it must be termed "tacit" as well because no words were exchanged. In other words, one might claim that the duopolists arrived at the monopoly solution without an express contract or agreement (i.e., tacitly). Others would simply conclude that the duopolists reached their mutually advantageous result by recognizing their mutual interdependence and by behaving optimally. Describing what has transpired as an "agreement" might strike those observers as metaphysical. There is, however, an economic argument for stretching antitrust to cover tacit collusion. We shall look at both sides of the argument.

8–3 TACIT COLLUSION AND ANTITRUST LIABILITY

There are two opposing views on the suitability of the antitrust laws for attacking tacit collusion. These views are held by two of the most respected antitrust scholars: Donald Turner and Richard Posner. We

---

[6] Richard A. Posner has made this point forcefully. See his *Antitrust Law: An Economic Perspective* (Chicago: University of Chicago Press, 1976), pp. 24–26.

shall examine these views briefly before moving on to three specific examples of what some have termed tacit collusion.

Turner's view[7]

Professor Turner was concerned about what has come to be known as "conscious parallelism" in antitrust circles. This is an ill-defined doctrine holding that if two or more firms have behaved in the same fashion in mutual recognition of one another, then one may infer the existence of a conspiracy. In the next section, we shall take a close look at a series of cases and conclude that consciously parallel conduct has never been deemed sufficient in and of itself to establish agreement. In every successful case, there were some additional facts that established the interdependence of the firms' decisions. In other words, the courts have required that there be additional evidence that the decisions are consistent with the individual self-interest of the individual firms only if all firms behave similarly.

Consider several cases. At one extreme, we have the case where behavior appears to be parallel because each firm acts the same way. But it may be that each firm would have done the same thing even if all the others had done something else. Supose one observes that all U.S. automobile manufacturers advertise in *Time* magazine. This is parallel behavior, but it is not outlandish to think that each of the firms would have advertised in *Time* even if the others had not. In such cases, there is nothing that can reasonably be called an agreement.

At another extreme, the best price for each individual firm will be the same, and all firms know it. For example, suppose we have the case where three firms of equal size have identical cost functions. In Figure 8–2, D is the industry demand function, and MR is the corresponding marginal revenue. Each firm has a marginal cost function like MC_i. These can be summed horizontally and labeled ΣMC_i. The price and output that will maximize industry profits are found by equating industry marginal revenue (MR) and industry marginal cost (ΣMC_i). On the graph, these are labeled P_1 and Q_1, respectively.

If we use the reasoning that underlies the Chamberlin model, we may conclude that each of these three firms will recognize the optimality of P_1 and produce accordingly. Recognizing that a fair share (in this case, one third) of maximum industry profit is better than a fair share of any other profit level, each firm will look at its proportional demand curve. In Figure 8–2, the proportional demand curve (d) represents one third of the industry quantity at each price. The marginal revenue curve associated with the proportional demand is labeled mr. Each firm will maxi-

[7] Donald F. Turner, "The Definition of Agreement under the Sherman Act: Conscious Parallelism and Refusals to Deal," *Harvard Law Review* 75 (February 1962), p. 655–706.

FIGURE 8–2

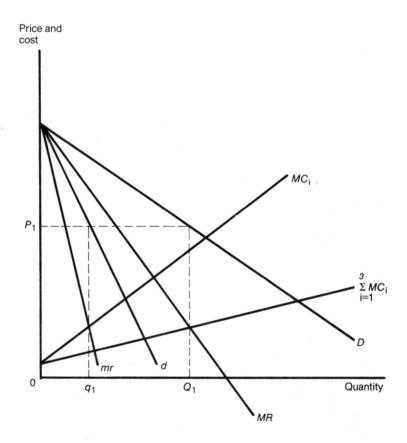

mize profits by producing an output of q_1, which is precisely one third of Q_1.

Turner feels that in a situation like this each firm is so aware of the optimal price and output that "hardly a shade of even a 'meeting of minds' could be said to be involved." But this is not quite true. Each of the three firms depicted in Figure 8–2 is producing where its own marginal cost MC_i is below the *industry* marginal revenue curve. Thus, each has an incentive to cheat (i.e., expand output beyond its "quota" at the expense of other industry members). Mutual forbearance may not be more than an indication of mature judgment and a concern for long-run profit maximization, but it cannot be conceded readily that no "meeting of minds" is necessary. Each must be convinced by something that its rivals will confine themselves to their proportional demand. Otherwise, self-restraint makes no sense at all because those who exercise self-restraint will lose market share to those who do not restrain their quest for higher profits.

Turner, however, is willing to go even further. Suppose that products are not perfectly homogeneous, cost conditions are not identical across firms, and uncertainties upset simple calculations. Nonetheless, identical prices may still emerge as a result of some form of price leadership.[8] In this case, all firms follow the price leader in full knowledge that the others will also follow. Turner describes such conduct as rational oligopoly behavior. He feels that a rational oligopolist behaves just like a competitive firm behaves. A rational oligopolist prices its output and determines the optimal quantity so as to maximize its profit just as the competitive firm does. The oligopolist, however, has to take one more thing into account, namely, the reactions of his rivals. It goes without saying that one cannot dictate myopia to the firm—a rational oligopolist cannot be made to ignore its rivals. Turner's conclusion is that if conscious parallelism results in noncompetitive prices, such conduct is beyond the reach of Section 1 of the Sherman Act.

Posner's views[9]

Posner's main argument is that Section 1 of the Sherman Act can be useful in dealing with noncompetitive pricing in oligopolistic industries. He adopts a view that is precisely opposite that of Turner's. Conscious of Turner's position, Posner argues that Turner's analysis depends critically on a theory of oligopoly behavior that is unsatisfactory in several important respects. Basically, the theory is that oligopolists will be reluctant to cut price because they know that any price cut will have such a significant impact upon their rivals that a matching price reduction will follow and everyone will be worse off. According to Posner, there are several deficiencies with such a belief. First, it assumes implicitly that no appreciable time lag will exist between the initial price reduction and the subsequent response. But a time lag will make a price cut *potentially* profitable, and only the present value calculations can determine whether a particular situation is ripe for a price cut. Second, price cuts may not have such a big impact upon rivals. Some of the expanded output will come from new buyers rather than from the old customers of the rival firms. Third, by focusing on the fear of price *reduction*, one must assume that price is already supracompetitive. The interdependence theory offered by Turner has no explanation for how the price initially rose above marginal cost. If price leadership is the answer, Turner should have to explain why a price leader fails to emerge when prices are spiraling downward after some foolish firm cuts its price.

---

[8] We will discuss price leadership in Section 8–6.

[9] Richard A. Posner, "Oligopoly and the Antitrust Laws: A Suggested Approach," *Stanford Law Review* 21 (June 1969), pp. 1562–1606.

Posner points out that collusion is a rational business strategy only if its returns exceed its costs. Returns and costs are influenced by (1) the price elasticity demand, which measures the responsiveness of the quantity demanded to changes in price; (2) the condition of entry, which provides some indication of how much price can exceed the competitive level before outsiders will enter the industry and disrupt the collusion; and (3) whether and how long widespread cheating can be prevented. We must recognize that collusion is like other contracts in that there are costs of bargaining in reaching an agreement and of enforcing the agreement to prevent cheating. Section 1 of the Sherman Act can be viewed as a device for increasing the costs involved in establishing and maintaining noncompetitive prices. Since bargaining and enforcement costs are quite sensitive to the number of firms, oligopoly emerges as a necessary condition to successful price fixing.

Posner then goes on to say that

> each seller must make a deliberate choice not to expand output to the point where the cost of the last unit of output [marginal cost] equals the market price, or, if he is at that point, to reduce output. There is a real choice here. It is not irrational for an oligopolist to decide to set a price that approximates marginal cost. It is not an unprofitable point at which to sell.

This, of course, will generally be true. Marginal cost will normally be above average cost where demand intersects marginal cost. But Posner is stretching things a bit when he attributes rationality to behavior that results in less than maximum profits. If a firm elects to earn less than maximum profits, we must wonder about the firm's objectives.

Posner argues further that tacit understandings and completely concealable explicit acts should not be distinguished. Both can be considered tacit collusion, which is very like express collusion, and Section 1 is obviously the appropriate remedy. There is no vital difference between formal cartels and tacit collusive arrangements. Since Section 1 is supposed to deter collusion by increasing its costs, the tacit colluder should be punished like the express colluder in order to deter tacit collusion. Since tacit collusion is voluntary behavior, appropriate punishments will deter the tacit colluders. It is not an unconscious state. Consequently, no firm should have a problem in determining when they are behaving noncompetitively.

As a matter of semantics, tacit collusion is a form of concerted rather than unilateral activity. In forbearing to seek short-run gains at each other's expense in order to share monopoly benefits that require mutual forbearance, the firms act like the parties to a unilateral contract. As far as judicial precedent is concerned, the Supreme Court has declared that Section 1 does not require proof of express collusion. Finally, we should consider the statutory purpose of the Sherman Act. Section 1 attacks collusion because it is a joint effort to reap monopoly profits, and tacit collusion has a very similar impact. Thus, Posner's proposal is consistent with the spirit of the Sherman Act.

Posner recognizes that the problem of proof is not trivial because sufficient evidence to an economist may not suffice in court. In his view, however, there are several types of evidence that could be offered:

1. Evidence of systematic price discrimination leads to an inference of noncompetitive pricing. This includes the case where $P_i = P_j$ but $MC_i \neq MC_j$ because colluders often decide upon a simple price scheme to reduce coordination and enforcement costs.
2. Persistent excess productive capacity leads to a similar inference because cartel members may maintain excess capacity for strategic purposes (i.e., to preempt entry opportunities or to warn potential entrants that sufficient capacity exists to fight a price war.[10]
3. Prices of noncompeting sellers should change less frequently than the prices of competing firms. Moreover, a cost change will affect the market price proportionately less in a noncompetitive market than in a competitive market.
4. Abnormal profit is a symptom of noncompetitive results, but excess profits can exist with marginal cost pricing.
5. Price leadership, which is examined below, is a means of achieving pricing coordination.
6. Refusal to offer discounts in the face of excess capacity provides some indication that a firm is passing up a profitable opportunity.
7. Extremely early announcements of price changes provide a means of communicating intentions among rivals and permit time for adjustments.
8. Public statements are made by a firm as to what it considers the right price for the industry to maintain.

8–4 CONSCIOUS PARALLELISM

Collusion can be inferred from circumstantial evidence. In other words, even if there is no hard evidence of an actual agreement, one can reach the conclusion that an agreement must have occurred based upon circumstantial evidence. We have already discussed the economist's notion of mutual interdependence in connection with oligopoly. The legal counterpart to mutual interdependence is conscious parallelism, which occurs when several rival firms act in the same way and each is aware of what the others are doing. The antitrust question is whether this common course of action coupled with mutual awareness is sufficient for an inference of collusion. The answer to this question is not obvious, but we can examine a few cases that shed some light on the issue.

---

[10] For an analysis of this strategy, see A. Michael Spence, "Entry, Capacity, Investment, and Oligopolistic Pricing," *Bell Journal of Economics* 8 (Autumn 1977), pp. 534–44.

Interstate Circuit, Inc. _v_. United States.[11]   A film distributor owns a copyright on its films and distributes them in interstate commerce. It earns profit through license fees and rental charges collected from exhibitors like Interstate Circuit and Texas Consolidated. Interstate Circuit operated 43 first-run and second-run movie theaters in six Texas cities. For the most part, it had a complete monopoly of the first-run theaters in those cities. Interstate did, however, face competition in the second-run market. Texas Consolidated, an affiliate of Interstate, operated 66 theaters in Texas and New Mexico. None of these theaters were located in the cities covered by Interstate. Texas Consolidated had several first-run monopolies among its towns and cities. In combination, Interstate Circuit and Texas Consolidated accounted for 74 percent of all the license fees collected by the film distributors in the geographic market.

O'Donnell, who was the general manager of both Interstate Circuit and Texas Consolidated, sent a letter to the branch managers of eight film distributors simultaneously. Each letter had all eight addressees identified, and therefore, each branch manager knew that all of his rivals were receiving the same letter. The O'Donnell letter made two demands of any distributor that wished to continue doing business with Interstate. First, each distributor must require that subsequent-run theaters charge at least 25 cents for adults in the evening. Since the prevailing charge in most locations was 10–15 cents, this would have represented a dramatic departure in the current pricing scheme. Second, O'Donnell wanted the distributors to prevent double features at the subsequent-run theaters. This, too, was a substantial change in the current practice since many subsequent-run theaters offered double features.

After consultation with their superiors, the branch managers of the eight film distributors came to terms with Interstate. These terms were not precisely those demanded by the O'Donnell letter, but they were substantially the same.

The trial court inferred that the simultaneous and unanimous adherence to the terms were not reached unilaterally. On the contrary, the trial court found that the distributors conspired among themselves to take uniform action on Interstate's demands. The distributors and Interstate had conspired to impose the restrictions on subsequent-run theaters to their detriment and to Interstate's benefit. The court found that these agreements were in restraint of trade and, therefore, violated Section 1 of the Sherman Act.

On appeal, the Supreme Court noted that it is not unusual for the government to proceed without direct testimony that the defendants agreed with each other. But the Supreme Court felt that an inference of agreement was not out of line given the nature of the O'Donnell letter, the unanimity of the actions taken, and the fact that none of the defendants testified that there was no agreement.

---

[11] 306 U.S. 208 (1939).

Thus, the Court was convinced by all of the circumstantial evidence that an agreement must have existed. The Court went on to say, however, that even if an actual *agreement* had not existed, an unlawful *conspiracy* would still have existed:

> It was enough that, knowing that concerted action was contemplated and invited, the distributors gave their adherence to the scheme and participated in it. Each distributor was advised that the others were asked to participate; each knew that cooperation was essential to successful operation of the plan. They knew that the plan . . . would result in a restraint of commerce . . . and knowing it, all participated.

Thus, the decision in *Interstate Circuit* stands for the proposition that when a group of competitors enters into a series of similar but separate agreements with competitors or others, one can reasonably infer that the agreements resulted from collusion.

A series of decisions endorsed the logic of *Interstate Circuit*. For example, in *Masonite*,[12] the Supreme Court found a series of contracts restraining trade illegal because the firms knew at some point that the contracts were not isolated transactions but were, in fact, part of a broader arrangement. Similarly, in *Paramount Pictures*,[13] a horizontal price-fixing conspiracy was inferred from the uniform pattern of business practices in the record. The Court remarked that evidence of an express agreement was not necessary to establish a Section 1 violation. "It is enough that a concert of action is contemplated and that the defendants conformed to the arrangement." Finally, consider the language in *Milgram* v. *Loew's, Inc.*[14] Eight major film distributors each refused to grant first-run status to a brand new and very attractive drive-in theater. Since Milgram was prepared to pay a premium over the existing rental paid by other first-run theaters, these refusals looked suspicious. The court found that "[e]ach distributor has thus acted in apparent contradiction to its own self-interest. This strengthens considerably the inference of a conspiracy, for the conduct of the distributors is . . . inconsistent with decisions independently arrived at." Thus, parallel business conduct that is inconsistent with apparent self-interest may be sufficient for a finding of conspiracy. We must be clear about one thing, however. There are no cases in which mere parallel behavior was found by the courts to constitute collusion.

Theatre Enterprises, Inc. *v.* **Paramount Film Distributing Corp.**[15] The owner of a suburban theater, the Crest, repeatedly requested films on a first-run basis from all of the major producers and distributors. The

---

[12] *United States* v. *Masonite Corp.*, 316 U.S. 265 (1942).

[13] *United States* v. *Paramount Pictures, Inc.*, 334 U.S. 131 (1948). For another decision consistent with *Interstate Circuit* and *Masonite*, see *United States* v. *U.S. Gypsum*, 333 U.S. 364 (1948).

[14] 192 F. 2d 579, 583 (3d Cir. 1951).

[15] 346 U.S. 537 (1954).

Crest was located in a neighborhood shopping district about six miles from downtown Baltimore. All of the major distributors granted first-run status only to downtown theaters, and none would grant first-run status to the Crest. In this case, however, there was no direct evidence of illegal agreement among the distributors.

Each major distributor offered a similar explanation: The Crest is in substantial competition with the downtown theaters, and simultaneous first-run showings are economically infeasible. Moreover, no downtown theaters would waive its clearance right. Thus, the Crest would have to have been granted exclusive first-run status in the area, which is economically unsound because it is a suburban theater, served by limited public transportation facilities, and has a drawing area less than one tenth that of a downtown theater.

As in the other conscious parallelism cases, the Court was faced with the following legal question: Did the distributors' attitude toward the Crest stem from independent decisions or from an agreement, tacit or express? There was no doubt that the action was parallel, but the Court was unwilling to infer conspiracy in this case. The Court stated that

> business behavior is admissible circumstantial evidence from which the fact finder may infer agreement. But this Court has never held that proof of parallel business behavior conclusively establishes agreement. . . . Circumstantial evidence of consciously parallel behavior may have made heavy inroads into the traditional judicial attitude toward conspiracy; but "conscious parallelism" has not yet read conspiracy out of the Sherman Act entirely.

The distinction between *Interstate Circuit* and *Theatre Enterprises* stems from the fact that it would make economic sense for any distributor to deny the Crest first-run status on an independent basis. Moreover, there was no "plus" factor like an invitation to participate in a restraint of trade.

United States *v*. Charles Pfizer & Co., Inc.[16] This is a confusing decision in the development of the conscious parallelism doctrine. The government alleged that Pfizer, Cyanamid, Bristol-Meyers, Squibb, and Upjohn conspired to exclude competitors and fix prices. These pharmaceutical firms allegedly accomplished this through limited licensing of various tetracycline patents and through the continuation of noncompetitive prices dating from pretetracycline days.

During the pretetracycline days, no licenses or cross-licenses for broad spectrum antibiotics were issued. Nonetheless, a stable and parallel price structure for the three antibiotics emerged because each manufacturer wanted to be competitive with his other two rivals. This, the Court decided, was due to the fact that sales "are largely dependent upon the physician's opinion of their effectiveness in treating the specific patient."

---

[16] 367 F. Supp. 91 (S.D.N.Y. 1973).

Pfizer invented tetracycline by processing aureomycin, which was patented by Cyanamid. Pfizer and Cyanamid got into a patent squabble because tetracycline was a superior antibiotic. Although it appears that Pfizer could have won the squabble, it would still have been dependent upon Cyanamid for the aureomycin supply. Thus, they got together and settled the patent dispute. Cyanamid withdrew to Pfizer's benefit, and Pfizer agreed to license Cyanamid to produce tetracycline.

Bristol-Meyers filed a patent application for a variant of tetracycline and agreed to supply Squibb and Upjohn, who in turn agreed to indemnify Bristol-Meyers in any patent infringement action. Pfizer started infringement proceedings against Bristol-Meyers but settled them when a potentially embarrassing development came to light involving a Pfizer agent's wiretapping of Bristol-Meyers. As a result, Bristol-Meyers got a piece of the tetracycline action along with its licensees, Squibb and Upjohn.

The undisputed facts in the case were as follows:

1. Patent licensing agreements are not illegal.
2. Substantially similar and parallel prices on tetracycline were maintained.
3. Only five firms made or sold tetracycline to the exclusion of all others.

The legal question in *Pfizer* was whether the government had shown that the defendants agreed or conspired to fix price and to exclude competitors. The alternative is that the facts demonstrate only the natural and normal consequences of independent business judgment. The government offered circumstantial proof and argument. The defendants offered vigorous denials. They asserted that "the proof demonstrates nothing more than 'conscious parallelism' and similarity of business practices, neither of which is illegal standing alone."

The court found that the government failed to sustain its burden of proof. This decision raises an obvious question: Can circumstantial evidence of agreement be discredited by vigorous denials? At this point, it is not terribly clear just how much guidance *Pfizer* offers for conscious parallelism.

8–5 DELIVERED PRICING[17]

Delivered (or basing point) pricing can be a collusive oligopolistic pricing policy that serves to maximize industry profits under certain

---

[17] The present discussion depends upon George Stigler, "A Theory of Delivered Price Systems," Chapter 14 in *The Organization of Industry* (Homewood, Ill.: Richard D. Irwin, 1968), and F. M. Scherer, *Industrial Market Structure and Economic Performance*, (Skokie, Ill.: Rand McNally, 1980), pp. 325–34.

economic conditions. In particular, suppose an oligopoly produces a physically homogeneous product that has a high weight to market value ratio. For such products, transportation costs are significant, and spatial differentiation of products emerges. Spatial differentiation is important because it creates natural geographic markets within which a particular seller will have an advantage.

Under these conditions, suppose that all firms practice FOB mill pricing. This means that a customer pays the seller his mill price plus the actual freight charges from the mill to the customer's location. As a result, each seller receives the same mill net price irrespective of the customer's identity or distance from the actual seller. In Figure 8–3, we

FIGURE 8–3

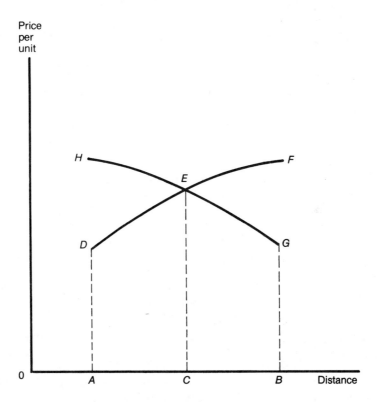

can see a further result of this pricing practice. The price at mill A is *AD*. As a unit of output is sold and transported eastward, we add the freight cost to get the total delivered price along *DEF*. Similarly, the price at mill B is *BG*, which we have assumed to be equal to the price at A. As a unit is sold and transported westward, we add the freight cost to obtain the delivered price along *GEH*. If the sellers adhere to their FOB mill pricing policies, mill A will make all of the sales to those customers located between *A* and *C* while mill B will make all of the sales to the customers located between *B* and *C*. At the center, customers will be indifferent between buying from mill A or from mill B because the mill price plus freight will be identical. Each mill has a natural market area that is delineated by the advantage in transportation costs that it enjoys. This area is referred to as a freight advantage territory. As long as each mill follows its FOB mill pricing policy, neither can sell in the other's territory. We can see that *DEF* is below *GEH* between *A* and *C*, while *GEH* is below *DEF* between *B* and *C*.

If mill A wants to sell to a customer in B's natural territory, it has two options. First, it could reduce its mill price below *AD*. This has a decidedly unfortunate side effect: Mill A will receive a lower price on all of its sales, not just on those in B's natural market area. In addition, one should expect mill B to retaliate, which means that the strategy might fail, and A will sell the same volume at a lower price. Alternatively, mill A could discriminate in price by offering price cuts to selected customers. This would be a policy of ad hoc, unsystematic price discrimination. If various producers do this, it can lead to an outbreak of vigorous price competition that would reduce everyone's profits. The basing point pricing system is an alternative that reduces the pressures for rivalrous price reactions.

In industries where products are physically homogeneous, transportation costs are high relative to the product's market value, and where marginal production cost is low relative to average total cost, basing point pricing can deal satisfactorily with demand instability. Basing point pricing exists when each seller, irrespective of its location, quotes the same price at a customer's door which is equal to the base price plus the freight calculated from the base to the customer's location. The classic example of a single basing point system is the "Pittsburgh plus" system employed in the steel industry.[18] All sales of steel were made at delivered prices equal to the mill price in Pittsburgh plus the rail freight from Pittsburgh. We can see the effects of this in Figure 8–4. All customers pay the mill price at Pittsburgh *(PA)* plus freight costs along *AEB*. Thus, a customer in Gary, Indiana, pays a delivered price of *GB*. When a Pittsburgh producer makes a sale, the customer pays the actual freight. When a producer in Gary makes the sale, the customer pays so-called phantom freight of *CB*. Phantom freight is freight that is charged to the buyer but is not incurred by the seller.

---

[18] The basing point system of pricing has been used in steel, cement, lead, cast-iron pipe, plywood, and rigid steel conduit.

FIGURE 8–4

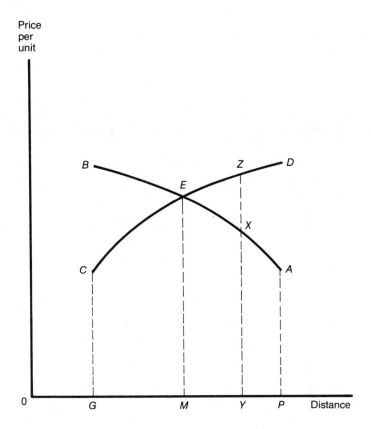

This system will not necessarily lead to random sales all over the map. Each producer will tend to concentrate its sales around its production center because these are most profitable. This strategy reduces the costs of making the sales and servicing the customers. But when demand around Gary drops off, this system allows the Gary producer to invade the natural territory of the Pittsburgh producer. Suppose a sale is made in Youngstown by the Gary producer. The delivered price is *YX* according to the Pittsburgh plus system. The combination of a mill price equal to *GC* and actual freight is *YZ*. Thus, the Gary producer has absorbed freight equal to *ZX*, and its mill net price is *GC* minus *ZX*. But the producer was able to make this sale without extending this lower mill net price to all customers.

Economic analysis of basing point pricing[19]

It is fairly clear that basing point pricing reduces competition among the rival sellers. Each firm must agree to respect certain production centers as basing points. Then they must follow a set of pricing rules that results in no price competition. Consequently, all competition is of the nonprice variety.

There is a popular conception that excessive transportation resources will be consumed because buyers have no incentive to minimize the use of such resources. But we should expect sellers to focus their efforts around their own production centers where they receive phantom freight. It is only when demand instability entices distant sales that we should see much freight absorption.

The pricing system depends upon substantial conformity by all sellers. As a result, there is great reluctance among the sellers to do anything that will upset the system. One aspect of this is a resistance to using the most efficient mode of transportation. Many basing point systems use rail freight rates because they are most easily incorporated in a mechanical way. When other means of transport are more efficient, there is a tendency to stick with rail because substitutions cause uncertainties that could undermine the system.

The plant locations of both buyers and sellers may be socially inefficient due to basing point pricing. Buyers have little incentive to locate near production sites that are not basing points. Instead, they have a strong incentive to locate near production sites that are also basing points. Moreover, producers need not move in response to demand shifts. Due to the pricing mechanism, when demand increases in an area where there is no production capability, existing producers can ship their output into the area at no cost disadvantage. Of course, there is some incentive to move because of the additional phantom freight that can be earned.

Judicial treatment of basing point pricing

The landmark decisions on basing point pricing are in cases brought by the Federal Trade Commission under §5(a)(1) of the FTC Act, which states that "[u]nfair methods of competition in or affecting commerce . . . are hereby declared unlawful." It should be noted that judicial interpretation has empowered the FTC "to restrain practices as 'unfair' which, although not yet having grown into Sherman Act dimensions,

---

[19] Two recent papers have expanded our understanding of basing point pricing: David D. Haddock, "Basing-Point Pricing: Competitive versus Collusive Theories," *American Economic Review* 72 (June 1982), pp. 289–306, and Dennis W. Carlton, "A Reexamination of Delivered Pricing Systems," *Journal of Law and Economics* 26 (April 1983), pp. 51–70. Both authors express some skepticism about the automatic conclusion that delivered pricing is necessarily collusive.

would most likely do so if left unrestrained." Consequently, these decisions do not have quite the force that they would have if they had been Sherman Act cases.

Federal Trade Commission v. Cement Institute.[20] At the time of the FTC decision, there were some 80 cement manufacturers operating 150 plants in the United States. Ten firms controlled more than half of these plants. Due to the standardized nature of the product, the firms have believed historically that price competition is ill-advised. As a result, a multiple basing point system[21] was used to eliminate price competition. In furtherance of this pricing mechanism, the Cement Institute (a trade association) obtained promises of the producers not to permit sales FOB mill to customers who provided their own trucks. Moreover, whenever a producer cheated by cutting the delivered price, that producer was made an involuntary basing point. The base price was then cut, which imposed heavy losses on the cheater but relatively light losses on the other producers.[22]

The FTC found that the members of the Cement Institute had restrained competition in the sale and distribution of cement by means of a combination among themselves made effective through a mutual understanding or agreement to employ the multiple basing point system of pricing. In spite of testimony by economic experts that such a system could result from competition, the FTC found otherwise. The Supreme Court, deferring to the expertise of the FTC, held that the FTC "was authorized to find understanding, express or implied, from evidence that the industry's Institute actively worked, in cooperation with various members, to maintain the multiple basing point delivered price system." The Court endorsed the FTC's conclusion that the delivered price system provided an effective means of completely destroying competition and establishing a monopoly in the cement industry.

Triangle Conduit & Cable Co. v. Federal Trade Commission.[23] Some 14 manufacturers of rigid conduit steel were charged by the FTC with violating §5 "through their concurrent use of a formula method of making delivered price quotations with the knowledge that each did likewise, with the result that price competition between and among them was unreasonably restrained." In this instance, both Pittsburgh and Chicago served as basing points. Freight was calculated from the nearest basing point to the customer's location.

The court found that this pricing system had some unfortunate results: (1) delivered prices were uniform, and there were no price ad-

---

[20] 333 U.S. 683 (1948).

[21] In a multiple basing point system, there are several basing points. The customer pays the mill price plus the rail freight from the nearest basing point irrespective of the origin of the product. This is an obvious variant of the single basing point system.

[22] See Problem 12 in this chapter.

[23] 168 F. 2d 175 (7th Cir. 1948).

vantages for any of the buyers, and (2) selection of location decisions was not optimal.

Conscious use of the basing point system in one's own natural market area is an invitation to share the business in return for a reciprocal invitation. The uniformity and simultaneity of action on the part of individual firms underscores the consciousness of what is going on. Thus, the court found that the producers had violated §5 of the FTC Act.

8–6 PRICE LEADERSHIP

Price leadership can be a way of communicating prices and price changes within an oligopolistic industry. Several types of price leadership have been identified and criticized.[24] We shall examine four types of price leadership: dominant firm, low-cost firm, barometric, and collusive. Fine lines can be drawn in theory, but we must recognize that in practice these types are not always distinguishable.

Dominant firm price leadership

We saw the cartel variant of this model in Chapter 6. In the dominant firm model, there is a large firm whose presence dominates the industry. In addition, there is a competitive fringe of smaller firms that will take the dominant firm's price as given and will respond as though they were competitive firms. This means that they will produce where their marginal cost equals the price selected by the dominant firm. In this sense, they are said to follow the price leadership of the dominant firm. In order to maximize profits, the dominant firm will recognize the behavior of the smaller firms and will incorporate that behavior into its own decision calculus. We can see how this is accomplished in Figure 8–5.

Industry demand is labeled D, the dominant firm's marginal cost curve is MC, and the supply capability of the fringe firms is S. In this regard, note that S is the sum of the small firms' marginal cost curves (Σmc). If the dominant firm is going to take into account the supply response of the small firms to any price that it sets, then it must subtract that supply from the market demand. The result will be the portion of the market that the dominant firm can satisfy. The kinked curve labeled P_0AD represents the difference between the market demand (D) and the small firms' supply (S). At P_0, those small firms will supply all that the

---

[24] See Kenneth Boulding, *Economic Analysis*, rev. ed. (New York: Harper & Row, 1948), pp. 582–87; George Stigler, "The Kinky Oligopoly Demand Curve and Rigid Prices," *Journal of Political Economy* 55 (October 1947), pp. 432–49; and Jesse W. Markham, "The Nature and Significance of Price Leadership," *American Economic Review* 41 (December 1951), pp. 891–905.

FIGURE 8–5

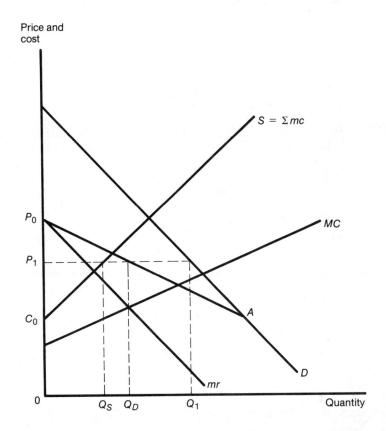

market demands. If price falls below C_0, none of the small firms will supply anything, and the dominant firm will have the entire market.

Given his share of the market demand, P_0AD, the dominant firm will maximize profits by producing where marginal revenue equals marginal cost. The marginal revenue associated with P_0AD is mr. Thus, the dominant firm will produce Q_D and set a price of P_1. The competitive fringe firms follow this price and produce where their collective supply equals P_1, which is at an output of Q_S in Figure 8–5. The sum of Q_D and Q_S necessarily equals Q_1, which is the market clearing quantity for a price of P_1.

Since the competitive price in this industry is found where the sum of all of the marginal cost curves crosses the market demand curve, the price (P_1) is higher than the competitive price.[25] Consequently, we must

---

[25] See Problem 15 at end of chapter.

object to this price and output configuration on social welfare grounds, but the socially suboptimal price and output are not due to collusion. Instead, they are due to the market structure. Accordingly, the appropriate public policy response depends upon whether the industry can be restructured. There is no way to impose competitive pricing on this industry without restructuring the industry. Consequently, this form of price leadership should not be attacked by Section 1 of the Sherman Act.

Low-cost firm price leadership[26]

In an oligopoly, we have seen that problems may arise when costs vary across firms. The most efficient firm (i.e., the one with the lowest costs) is in a position to impose its preferences on the other firms in the industry. It is convenient to examine this form of price leadership in a duopoly setting. In Figure 8–6, we have the high-cost firm in panel a and the low-cost firm in panel b. We have assumed that the two firms have

FIGURE 8–6

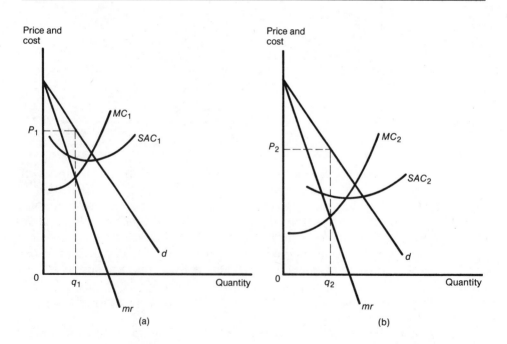

(a)

(b)

split the market evenly. Accordingly, the proportional demand curves labeled d in both panels are the same and equal to one half of the market demand.

The high-cost firm will find that P_1 and q_1 are the optimal price and quantity. In contrast, the low-cost firm will want a lower price equal to P_2 and a larger quantity equal to q_2. This, of course, is not possible in a single market. There must be a single price and the more efficient firm clearly can impose its will upon the high-cost firm.

Two remarks on this model are in order. First, the agreement to split the market on an equal basis is clearly illegal. As we saw in Chapter 7, market sharing is a per se violation of Section 1 of the Sherman Act. Second, this agreement is unstable. There is no reason for the low-cost firm to surrender a full half of the market to a less efficient firm. Consequently, there will always be a temptation for the low-cost firm to usurp more than one half of the market, which can lead to serious price cutting.

Barometric price leadership[27]

The concept of barometric price leadership proceeds from the sensible observation that one firm may be more adept at reading market conditions than the other firms in the industry. This firm will serve the industry as a barometer of market conditions. Consequently, its rivals follow the lead of the barometric firm only because its price reflects market conditions. In other words, the barometric firm's price serves as information for the other firms in the industry. This form of price leadership does not depend upon market power or superior productive efficiency. Rather, it is voluntary behavior on the part of the followers due to the barometer's superior sensitivity to market conditions. If the barometric firm's ability to perceive changes in the market slips a bit, the other firms will stop following. In any event, barometric price leadership looks very much like competitive behavior. To the extent that the barometric firm successfully anticipates or perceives changes in market conditions and other firms follow its lead, the industry will move from one equilibrium to another more quickly. Generally, this will be desirable and is of no antitrust interest.[28]

---

[27] For critiques of barometric price leadership, see Joe S. Bain, "Price Leaders, Barometers, and Kinks," *Journal of Business* 33 (July 1960), pp. 193–203, and Robert F. Lanzillotti, "Competitive Price Leadership—A Critique of Price Leadership Models," *Review of Economics and Statistics* 39 (February 1957), pp. 56–64.

[28] Barometric price leadership is a "free-rider" phenomenon. Since information is costly to acquire and assimilate, some firms will elect to let someone else bear that burden and will simply follow along. In this sense, these firms take a free ride on the efforts of others.

Collusive price leadership[29]

In some industries, price leadership may emerge as an alternative to an overt agreement. When several conditions are satisfied, the firms in the industry will tend to behave as Chamberlin suggested. These conditions are: (1) there must only be a few large firms in the industry, (2) there must be serious entry barriers, (3) although products need not be homogeneous, output of the industry members must be good substitutes, (4) demand is relatively inelastic at the competitive price, and (5) the cost curves of industry members are quite similar. When these conditions are fulfilled, the situation is ripe for a conspiracy of some kind.[30] Successful price fixing, bid rigging, market sharing, or whatever also requires the same sorts of conditions. But collusive price leadership should be viewed as an alternative to the more frequently observed forms of price fixing. In this instance, we see price leadership as a form of conscious parallelism. Some firm is at least tacitly nominated as the price leader. The others then follow the leader in full recognition of their community of interests. For antitrust purposes, it would seem to be a difficult task to determine when price leadership reached collusive dimensions absent an explicit agreement.

Judicial view of price leadership

There are very few cases on price leadership to review. The theme of the existing cases, however, is familiar: Without some reasonable inference that an agreement existed, no inference of collusion will be drawn. For example, in *International Harvester*,[31] the Supreme Court ruled that simple price leadership did not violate Section 1 of the Sherman Act. The government alleged that International Harvester ruled its industry by virtue of its superior efficiency. It coerced its rivals into line by the threat of selling at its cost, which was below the cost of its rivals. Faced with this sort of disciplinary action, the rival firms followed International Harvester's prices. The Court was not offended by that industry practice: ". . . the fact that competitors may see proper, in the exercise of their own judgment, to follow the prices of another manufacturer, does not establish any suppression of competition or show any sinister domination."

Although this is a very old case, this remains the law on price leadership until today. Something extra must be shown in order to condemn price leadership. For example, if some circumstantial evidence of agreement can be offered or some evidence that the followers were coerced,

---

[29] See Markham, "The Nature and Significance of Price Leadership," pp. 891–905, and Lanzillotti, "Competitive Price Leadership," pp. 56–64.

[30] See Section 6–6 for the empirical relevance of these conditions.

[31] *United States* v. *International Harvester Co.*, 274 U.S. 693 (1927).

there is a better chance of conviction. But if an industry's members "independently and as a matter of business expediency" have found it sensible to follow the prices of one of their rivals, the court will be reluctant to find a conspiracy. The logic of this decision is fairly clear: If a price follower unilaterally elects to follow the price charged by one of its rivals, the price leader cannot be held responsible for that action.

In contrast to this view, one could argue[32] that a price leader sets some price and anticipates cooperation from its rivals. It expects the others to follow. If they did not follow and instead charged a lower price, the leader could not maintain its initial price. Similarly, when the rivals follow the leader's price, they know that the leader expected that behavior. By following, they signal their agreement to the scheme. Everyone in the industry is participating with a full understanding of the end desired. On this logic, some dictum in *Interstate Circuit* suggests that price leadership may be vulnerable to antitrust attack. In that case, the court said that overt agreement was not a prerequisite for finding an illegal conspiracy. "It is enough that, knowing that concerted action was contemplated and invited, the distributors gave their adherence to the scheme and participated in it."[33] On this logic, one could proceed against price leadership of the collusive variety. Unfortunately, one cannot distinguish easily among the various types.[34]

8–7 SUMMARY REMARKS

In this chapter, we have been concerned with the oligopoly "problem" (i.e., the fact that a noncollusive oligopoly can yield noncompetitive results). On social welfare grounds, we may object to the noncompetitive price-output configuration, but in the absence of a demonstrable agreement to restrict output or to raise price, the antitrust laws are not well equipped to deal with oligopoly. As we learned earlier in this chapter, some economists feel that successful price coordination does not require anything more than tacit collusion in highly concentrated oligopoly. The more modern view is that this is unlikely without some sort of restraints that prevent each oligopolist from promoting its self-interest at the expense of its rivals.[35]

The law fails to deal with tacit collusion very effectively. In examining the case law on conscious parallelism, basing point pricing, and price leadership, we found that no case has held purely tacit behavior to be

---

[32] This argument is implicit in Posner, note 6 above. It was made explicitly by Lawrence A. Sullivan, *Handbook of the Law of Antitrust* (St. Paul, Minn.: West Publishing 1977), p. 357.

[33] *Interstate Circuit, Inc.* v. *United States*, 306 U.S. 208, 226 (1939).

[34] See Scherer, *Industrial Market Structure*, pp. 177–83 for various brief examples.

[35] See, for example, Steven C. Salop, "Practices that (Credibly) Facilitate Oligopoly Coordination," mimeo, 1982; and George A. Hay, "Oligopoly, Shared Monopoly, and Antitrust Law," *Cornell Law Review* 67 (March 1982), pp. 439–81.

illegal. The basic problem seems to be that the law on collusion has developed around the fact of agreement rather than the economic effects of collusion. Economic theory is not terribly helpful in these circumstances. The sad fact is that economic theory does not predict when vigorous rivalry does or does not occur in industries with few firms.

QUESTIONS AND PROBLEMS

1. In *Interstate Circuit*, the court said "[a]cceptance by competitors, without previous agreement, of an invitation to participate in a plan, the necessary consequence of which, if carried out, is restraint of interstate commerce is sufficient to establish an unlawful conspiracy under the Sherman Act." Should this extend to price leadership?

2. In *Interstate Circuit*, why should the distributors have done anything that O'Donnell requested?

3. The existence of first-run and second-run showings can be interpreted as intertemporal price discrimination. Explain this phenomenon. Analyze the effects of an increase in the price of admission to a second-run showing.

4. Intertemporal price discrimination was involved in *Theatre Enterprises.* How would granting the Crest a first-run license upset the conditions for successful price discrimination?

5. Suppose one of the distributors had given the Crest first-run status. Would the other distributors be helped or hindered?

6. In *Pfizer*, the court seemed to think that parallel pricing was adequately explained by the dependence of sales on doctors' prescriptions. Does this make sense?

7. Although Pfizer had a patent on tetracycline, it was dependent upon Cyanamid's patented aureomycin. Explain Pfizer's dilemma.

8. Why is delivered pricing superior to FOB mill pricing from the firm's perspective?

9. How does systematic freight absorption lead to price discrimination in a basing point pricing scheme?

10. In the *Cement Institute* case, 11 firms bid $3.286854 per barrel on an order of 6,000 barrels. What does this indicate?

11. How important was the decision to refuse sales on an FOB mill basis to consumers with their own trucks?

12. In *Cement Institute,* the collusive use of the multiple basing point system was policed by making cheaters an involuntary basing point. How would this work as a policing mechanism? What is the cost to the noncheaters of this policing mechanism?

13. Could a basing point pricing system emerge without collusion? Could it be the result of competition?

14. Cross-hauling occurs when a customer in Gary buys from a Pittsburgh mill and a customer in Pittsburgh buys from a mill in Gary. If basing point pricing is due to demand instability, are we likely to see much cross-hauling?

15. In Figure 8–5, construct the industry supply, which is $S + MC$. Find the competitive price and output. Compare these to the solution in the text.

16. There are four U.S. producers of lead antiknock compounds. Whenever a price change is contemplated, it is announced more than 30 days in advance. These announcements appear in newspapers. Is this a method of price signaling by which the producers can collude tacitly?

17. New prices are announced in the cement industry by mailing price lists to customers some 60 to 90 days in advance of the effective date. Inevitably, each seller finds out what prices its rivals are charging. Being a homogeneous product, cement must sell at a single price, and in fact, we observe uniform prices. Can you tell from this whether an antitrust violation has occurred? If not, what other information do you need?

18. In the Chamberlinian duopoly case, has an "agreement" been reached? If so, how would the law instruct the firms to behave in the future so as to avoid reaching such an "agreement"?

19. In the Cournot, Stackelberg, and Chamberlin duopoly models, are there excess profits in the short-run equilibrium? If so, would you expect entry to occur? Why? Is it possible for entry to correct the structural problem that leads to the noncompetitive (albeit noncollusive) results? If so, why is there an antitrust problem?

20. Suppose that there are several firms in an industry, and they are producing and pricing at the monopoly level. If a firm "cheats" by producing a larger quantity and offering price concessions to move the larger volume, the price cuts will be matched after some time lag. Given that reactions are *not* instantaneous, can "cheating" be profitable? If so, how would the potential cheater determine whether it was profitable?

21. Suppose that each production site is a basing point for calculating delivered prices. Will there be any "phantom" freight? Will there be freight absorption? Could this pricing system emerge without any collusion? What might distinguish this from the "Pittsburgh plus" system?

22. Suppose that B&K Enterprises is a dominant force in the manufacture of electronic sensing devices. As a result, the remaining firms in the industry generally follow B&K's prices on similar products. There is no evidence of any agreement within the industry, but the Antitrust Division has filed suit. Is this a sensible suit based upon earlier decisions? How could B&K prevent its rivals from copying its prices? If it cannot, what could B&K be guilty of?

23. In the figure below, suppose that mills exist in each of the three cities. Transportation costs between these cities are shown. Assume that the mill prices are equal at $5 per unit. Also assume that basing point pricing is used with Chicago as the base.

Seattle $.75   Chicago $.50   New York

a. What is the delivered price to New York if purchased from the mill in Seattle?
b. What is the delivered price to Seattle if purchased from the mill in New York?
c. What is the delivered price to Seattle if purchased from the mill in Seattle?
d. Does phantom freight exist in any of these cases? If so, in which one, and how much is the phantom freight?

FURTHER READINGS

Brodley, Joseph F. "Oligopoly Power under the Sherman and Clayton Acts—From Economic Theory to Legal Policy." *Stanford Law Review* 19 (January 1967), pp. 285–366.

Carlton, Dennis W. "A Reexamination of Delivered Pricing Systems." *Journal of Law and Economics* 26 (April 1983), pp. 51–70.

Chamberlin, Edward H. *The Theory of Monopolistic Competition*, 8th ed. (Cambridge, Mass.: Harvard University Press, 1962), esp. Chapter III.

Hay, George A. "Oligopoly, Shared Monopoly, and Antitrust Law." *Cornell Law Review* 67 (March 1982), pp. 439–81.

Lanzillotti, Robert F. "Competitive Price Leadership—A Critique of Price Leadership Models." *Review of Economics and Statistics* 39 (February 1957), pp. 56–64.

Markham, Jesse W. "The Nature and Significance of Price Leadership." *American Economic Review* 41 (December 1951), pp. 891–905.

Posner, Richard A. "Oligopoly and the Antitrust Laws: A Suggested Approach." *Stanford Law Review* 21 (June 1969), pp. 1562–1606.

Spence, Michael. "Tacit Coordination and Imperfect Information." *Canadian Journal of Economics* II (August 1978), pp. 490–505.

Stigler, George. "A Theory of Delivered Price Systems." chapter 14 in *The Organization of Industry* (Homewood, Ill.: Richard D. Irwin, 1968).

Turner, Donald. "The Definition of Agreement under the Sherman Act: Conscious Parallelism and Refusals to Deal." *Harvard Law Review* 75 (February 1962), pp. 655–706.

9

Horizontal mergers

Nearly all of our antitrust law is corrective or remedial.[1] Generally speaking, the Sherman Act was designed to eliminate monopoly power already in existence or to restrict the application of existing power and much the same can be said for the Clayton Act. Section 7 of the Clayton Act, however, provides an important exception in its treatment of mergers. In 1914, the Clayton Act was passed in order "to arrest the creation of trusts, conspiracies and monopolies in their incipiency and before consummation."[2] Thus, the Clayton Act's prohibition of certain mergers was intended to be *preventive* in nature.

In its original form, Section 7 left a gaping loophole that permitted firms to avoid the law's proscriptions.[3] Consequently, Section 7 was almost wholly ineffective in dealing with anticompetitive mergers. The Celler-Kefauver Act amended the original Section 7 so that it would provide

> [t]hat no corporation engaged in commerce shall acquire, directly or indirectly, the whole or any part of the stock or other share capital and no

---

[1] For a brief discussion, see George J. Stigler, "Mergers and Preventive Antitrust Policy," *University of Pennsylvania Law Review* 104 (November 1955), pp. 176–84.

[2] Senate Report no. 698, to accompany H. R. 15, 657, 63d Congress, 2d session, 1914, p. 1.

[3] The original language of Section 7 prohibited the acquisition of a rival's stock, but it did not prohibit the acquisition of a rival's assets. There is, of course, no economic difference between the two strategies.

corporation subject to the jurisdiction of the Federal Trade Commission shall acquire the whole or any part of the assets of another corporation engaged also in commerce, where in any line of commerce in any section of the country, the effect of such acquisition may be substantially to lessen competition, or to tend to create a monopoly.

As the law now reads, Section 7 covers all types of mergers: horizontal, vertical, and conglomerate. In this chapter, we focus on horizontal mergers.[4]

The language "in any line of commerce" requires a product market definition. We have already encountered difficulties in this area in Chapter 5, which dealt with monopolization. In the present chapter, we shall see that these problems are just as vexing when dealing with mergers. Similarly, the language "in any section of the country" calls for a geographic market definition. Problems in this area for merger enforcement will also be examined.

9–1 TYPES OF MERGERS

Although we are concerned only with horizontal mergers here, it is useful to describe briefly the several types of mergers so we know what we are not concerned with as well. There are three general types of mergers: horizontal, vertical, and conglomerate. The conglomerate category is comprised of three subgroups.

Horizontal mergers. A horizontal merger occurs whenever two firms in the same industry are merged. For a merger to be deemed horizontal, the firms involved must have been rivals prior to their combination. Consequently, the two firms must sell the same product in the same geographic market for their merger to be deemed horizontal. An example of a horizontal merger that we shall discuss later is provided by the acquisition of Shopping Bag by Von's Grocery.[5] In this case, one grocery store chain, Von's Grocery, acquired one of its direct competitors in the Los Angeles area, Shopping Bag. Since each firm sold the same product in the same market, this was a horizontal merger.

Vertical mergers. A vertical merger occurs when a firm merges with one of its suppliers (backward integration) or when a firm merges with one of its customers (forward integration). An example of a vertical merger was Ford's acquisition of Autolite.[6] Ford, of course, is the second largest producer of automobiles in the United States. Autolite was a large producer of spark plugs, which could be used in Ford automobiles. Thus, this merger is an example of backward integration because Ford acquired one of its input suppliers.

---

[4] Vertical mergers are examined in Chapter 12, while conglomerate mergers are treated in Chapter 17.

[5] *United States* v. *Von's Grocery Co.*, 384 U.S. 270 (1966).

[6] *Ford Motor Co.* v. *United States*, 405 U.S. 562 (1972).

Conglomerate mergers. Under the general rubric of conglomerate merger, there are three distinct subcategories: product extension, market extension, and pure. A *product extension* merger occurs when the acquiring firm is a multiple-product firm that fills out its product line in a natural way by acquiring an established producer of the added commodity. The classic example of a product extension merger is Procter & Gamble–Clorox.[7] Prior to the merger, Procter & Gamble had an extensive line of household cleansers and detergents, but no household bleach. It elected to add a household bleach by acquiring Clorox, an established supplier, rather than by producing a new brand of bleach. A *market extension* merger involves firms in the same industry but not in the same geographic market. The acquiring firm elects to enter a new geographic market by acquiring an established firm in that market rather than by entering from scratch. Falstaff's acquisition of Narragansett[8] provides an example of a market extension merger. Both Falstaff and Narragansett sold beer, but they did not compete in the same geographic market. Falstaff wanted to enter the geographic market comprised of the six New England states, a market in which Narragansett was dominant. Falstaff elected to acquire Narragansett rather than to enter anew. Finally, a *pure* conglomerate merger involves two firms that are wholly unrelated in any obvious way. The Ling–Temco–Vought acquisition of the Jones and Laughlin[9] Steel Corporation is an example since LTV's business activities were wholly unrelated to the steel industry prior to the merger.

9–2 INCENTIVES FOR MERGERS

There are many specific incentives for mergers. Based upon the standard theory of the firm, however, the main motivation for a merger is to enhance profits. Since profit is the difference between total revenue and total cost, profits will rise whenever revenues increase, costs decrease, or both occur. A merger can yield greater revenues when market power is enhanced and noncompetitive pricing results. Costs may decrease when operating efficiency is improved due to the exploitation of scale economies or the replacement of an inefficient management. We shall discuss four of these possibilities.

1. Merging to monopoly[10]

For antitrust purposes, we are primarily concerned with mergers that increase profits by enabling the industry to price at noncompetitive lev-

---

[7] *Federal Trade Commission v. Procter & Gamble Co.* (*Clorox*), 386 U.S. 568 (1967).

[8] *United States v. Falstaff Brewing Corp.*, 410 U.S. 526 (1973).

[9] *United States v. Ling–Temco–Vought, Inc., Jones and Laughlin Steel Corp., and Jones and Laughlin Industries, Inc.*, 1970 Trade Cases, par. 73, 105 (W. D. Pa. 1970).

[10] For a provocative discussion, see George J. Stigler, "Monopoly and Oligopoly by Merger," *American Economic Review* 40 (May 1950), pp. 23–34.

els. A merger among all the firms in an industry can be seen as a perfect form of collusion. There can be no cheating and no disputes over territories, customers, or market shares because a single firm monopoly has resulted. The only remaining difficulty is controlling entry, which will prove to be far from easy due to the presence of excess profits. More importantly, however, merging to monopoly will seldom succeed due to the profit incentives for firms to remain outside the consolidation.

In merging to monopoly, it will become increasingly more expensive to acquire independent firms. This can be seen in Figure 9–1 where the average and marginal cost curves are labeled AC and MC, respectively, and the *proportional* demand function and the associated marginal revenue are d and mr. Prior to the merger activity, each firm would have

FIGURE 9–1

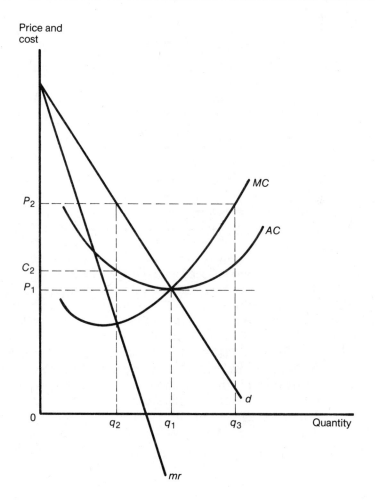

produced the competitive output of q_1 and sold it at the competitive price of P_1. In the short run, the ultimate goal of a merger to monopoly in this industry is to have each plant producing q_2. As a result of the reduced production, price would rise to P_2, and excess profits per plant would be $(P_2 - C_2)q_2$. But the value to the independent firm if it refuses to merge will be much larger than that. If the firm depicted in Figure 9–1 were to remain independent, then it could act as a price taker and view P_2 as its marginal revenue function. As a price taker, the optimal output for this firm would be q_3 where its marginal cost equals P_2. Its profit in this case is much larger than $(P_2 - C_2)q_2$. Thus, it is more profitable to remain outside the consolidation. In order to convince the recalcitrant firm that merger is in its best interest, the merged firm may have to resort to some predatory behavior. An alternative would be to simply ignore those firms that refuse to sell out. The optimal price and output would then follow the dominant firm model that we have encountered several times.

2. Mergers for improved efficiency[11]

For mergers that result in monopoly power without any increase in efficiency, the welfare effects are easy to assess—at least on a conceptual level. These mergers should not be permitted because consumer welfare is impaired. But some mergers are induced by a quest for greater profits through reduced costs. If such mergers occur, there will be short-run excess profits. In this instance, however, the excess profits are desirable because greater efficiency is properly rewarded. Moreover, these excess profits will provide the correct signals to other firms. Unless some entry barrier is erected, entry of new firms or further mergers within the industry will restore competition in the industry. The welfare results of such a merger are unambiguously positive. Real resources are saved for society, and prices will be correspondingly lower to reflect those cost savings. This effect is so strong that welfare can be improved even in cases where costs are reduced as the result of efficiencies, but prices are increased as a result of an increase in concentration. We shall consider such a case in Figure 9–2.

Industry demand is shown as D, and average costs prior to the merger are AC_1. Assuming that competition prevailed initially, price would reflect the costs of production and would be equal to P_1 (and AC_1). Suppose that the merger yields a reduction in costs due to production or promotional efficiencies that save on resources. As a result, the average cost of production falls from AC_1 to AC_2. At the same time, market power increases, and price rises from P_1 to P_2. There is clearly a

---

[11] The importance of efficiencies in antitrust analysis was pointed out by Oliver E. Williamson, "Economies as an Antitrust Defense: The Welfare Tradeoffs," *American Economic Review* 58 (March 1968), pp. 18–34.

FIGURE 9–2

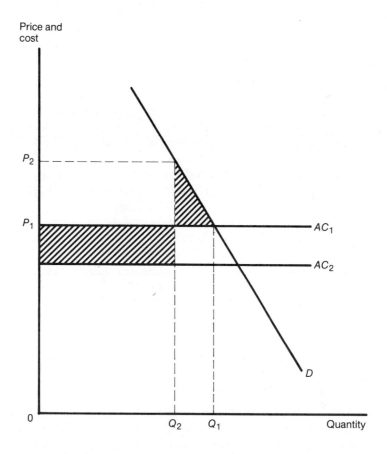

loss in consumer surplus, which is shown as the shaded triangle in Figure 9–2. This area, which is equal to $\frac{1}{2}(P_2 - P_1)(Q_1 - Q_2)$, must be compared to the shaded rectangle, which represents the reduced costs of producing the output Q_2. This cost saving is equal to the area $(AC_1 - AC_2)Q_2$. If the cost saving exceeds the loss in consumer surplus, then the merger can be deemed socially beneficial. Thus, we want to know whether

$$(AC_1 - AC_2)Q_2 - \frac{1}{2}(P_2 - P_1)(Q_1 - Q_2)$$

$$\text{Cost saving} \qquad \text{Consumer welfare loss}$$

is positive. After some algebraic manipulation, we find that this condition will be satisfied if

$$\frac{\Delta AC}{AC_1} - \frac{1}{2} \cdot \frac{Q_1}{Q_2} \eta \left(\frac{\Delta P}{P_1}\right)^2 > 0$$

where $\eta = (\Delta Q / \Delta P)(P/Q)$ is the price elasticity of demand. Therefore, we may conclude that the allocative effects of the merger are positive if the percentage decrease in average cost exceeds one half the ratio of pre-merger quantity to postmerger quantity times the product of the demand elasticity and the percentage price increase squared. There is no intuitive meaning that one can attach to this expression. The virtue of this alternative expression lies solely in the fact that one may be able to measure it empirically.

An illustrative numerical example of this efficiency argument may be instructive. If the demand function were of constant, unitary price elasticity, then it would be of the form $PQ = k$, which says that total revenue is constant. In particular, let price be $1 and quantity be 10,000 prior to the merger. Of course, k (total revenue) will be $10,000. Williamson has argued that a modest cost reduction will be more than sufficient to offset even a fairly large price increase. In our case, let the per unit cost decrease by 1 percent and the price increase by 10 percent. The new price will be $1.10, and the new quantity will be 9,091 units sold. If the original cost was equal to total revenue, then the cost saving amounts to (.01)(9,091) or $90.91 on the new production level. The deadweight welfare loss is approximately equal to $\frac{1}{2}(\Delta P)(\Delta Q)$ or $\frac{1}{2}(\$.10)(909)$ or $45.45. It is clear that the efficiency gain is double the welfare loss in spite of the fact that the price increase was 10 times the size of the per unit cost reduction. This result is not unique—the efficiency gains from a horizontal merger exceed the accompanying welfare loss for most parameter combinations.

3. Profits to merger promoters

When two firms merge, there is usually a promoter who does much of the arranging. In some cases, the promoters put mergers together for the firms without being invited. For example, suppose the hydrofoil industry has three big firms—Apex, Nadir, and Dynamic—with 25, 35, and 20 percent of total sales, respectively. The remaining 20 percent is spread among 12 other firms. A promoter might recognize that a merger of Apex, Nadir, and Dynamic would end vigorous competition among them. As a result, price would rise, quantity would shrink, and excess profits would come into being. The stock of the new firm, AND, Inc., would be worth more than the stock of Apex, Nadir, and Dynamic separately. The promoter who put the AND, Inc. merger together could take a block of the AND shares as compensation for his efforts. A stunning example of how much one might earn from this activity is provided by the fee that the Morgan syndicate earned when the U.S. Steel Corporation was put together in 1901: $62.5 million, which would be worth about $720 million in 1982 dollars.

Many investors are ready to jump at a chance to earn excess profits.

This greed makes them welcome targets for unscrupulous merger promoters. Preying upon the unsophisticated, unscrupulous promoters will arrange mergers that will not be unusually profitable. Upon receipt of their block of newly issued stock, they will sell it to unwary investors before its value plummets. Two historical studies of merger activity suggest fairly extensive abuses by merger promoters.[12] But many of the big ones appear to have been profitable.[13]

4. Takeovers

Ownership of the modern corporation is usually quite diffused: Many people own very small portions of our largest firms.[14] The fact of ownership diffusion has led to the suspicion that there is a separation of ownership and control in the modern corporation. In other words, when ownership is sufficiently dispersed, one suspects that the managers will take control of the firm. Managers who are in control of a firm may put their own interests ahead of the stockholders' interests. The extent to which managerial utility maximization is inconsistent with stockholder wealth maximization depends partly upon the costs to the owners of monitoring the manager's performance. An example of the costs is the time and effort required to evaluate the quality of the manager's performance relative to what other managers might have been able to achieve. The reason for some concern over the diffusion of ownership is the suspicion that there is a consequent reduction in the ability of the owners to revoke and reassign decision-making authority within the firm. This loss of control could have a significant effect on the value of the firm.

There are good grounds for this concern. The probability of forming a majority to reassign authority diminishes as there is greater diffusion of stock ownerships. For one thing, the fact of negligence or inefficiency of the manager is more expensive to disseminate over a dispersed majority. In addition, recognition of deleterious managerial decisions will tend to be less important to each stockholder as the number of owners increases. This means that a manager's substitution of his personal goals for those of the firm's owners is less likely to be monitored.

---

[12] Shaw Livermore, "The Success of Industrial Mergers," *Quarterly Journal of Economics* 49 (November 1935), pp. 68–96, and Jesse Markham, "Survey of the Evidence and Findings on Mergers," in *Business Concentration and Price Policy*, National Bureau of Economic Research (Princeton: Princeton University Press, 1955).

[13] For interesting analyses of the U.S. Steel example, see George J. Stigler, "The Dominant Firm and the Inverted Umbrella," *Journal of Law and Economics* 8 (October 1965), pp. 167–71, and Donald Parsons and Edward Ray, "The United States Steel Consolidation: The Creation of Market Control," *Journal of Law and Economics* 18 (April 1975), pp. 181–220.

[14] The most recent evidence is chronicled in P. Burch, *The Managerial Revolution Reassessed* (Lexington, Mass.: D. C. Heath, 1972), but the seminal work was by A. Berle and G. Means, *The Modern Corporation and Private Property* (New York: Macmillan, 1932).

The potential conflict of interest between managers and stockholders is recognized in corporate law. The shareholder elects the board of directors which has the authority to hire and fire management. In principle, then, ownership and control need not be vested in the same person to ensure efficient management. All that is necessary is that some method exists by which investors can obtain control of the board of directors and fire any manager who fails to perform satisfactorily. Since the existing management may dominate the board of directors, drastic changes in the composition of the board may be necessary before an inefficient management team can be replaced.

A takeover is one way of accomplishing this drastic change. In a takeover, alert investors buy a sufficient number of shares to obtain a controlling interest, elect a new board of directors, and fire the existing management.[15] Unfortunately, the law hampers such takeover efforts. Specifically, the Securities and Exchange Commission requires that an investor announce his or her intentions when buying a large portion of a firm's common stock. This serves to reduce the incentives for a takeover. In this regard, Hay and Morris summarize some empirical evidence indicating that takeovers provide surprisingly weak discipline for incompetent or wrongly motivated management.[16]

In summary, we have examined four motivations for horizontal mergers. A quest for monopoly power and the profits that go along with it are of antitrust concern. To the extent that a promoter can only profit from a merger that leads to market power, this motivation also has antitrust overtones. When mergers result from efficiency considerations, the consequences for consumer welfare are ambiguous. Finally, when a merger results from a takeover bid, the outcome is usually benign because an inefficient management team is being replaced.

9–3 MARKET POWER AND CONCENTRATION

The purpose of Section 7 of the Clayton Act is to maintain market structures that are consistent with vigorous competition. In other words, this law is designed to prevent oligopolistic or monopolistic market structures from forming through merger activity. Industrial organization economists have focused considerable attention on market structure in the belief that firm conduct and industry performance follow inexorably from market structure.[17] In practice, this focus has carried over to the judiciary as an examination of actual cases leads to the

[15] For a more complete discussion, see Henry G. Manne, "Mergers and the Market for Corporate Control," *Journal of Political Economy* 73 (March/April 1965), pp. 110–20.

[16] See Donald A. Hay and Derek J. Morris, *Industrial Economics: Theory and Evidence* (New York: Oxford University Press, 1979), at pp. 491–94, 498.

[17] The modern treatise on this is F. M. Scherer, *Industrial Market Structure and Economic Performance*, 2d ed. (Skokie, Ill.: Rand McNally, 1980). For a brief overview, see pp. 1–7.

striking fact that concentration in the relevant markets has played a large role in judicial decisions on mergers. Much has been alleged regarding the consequences of industrial concentration including the following: (1) concentration may retard (or alternatively increase) the rate of technological change; (2) concentration may alter the goals of the firm away from profit maximization; (3) concentration leads to an unequal distribution of political power; and (4) concentration increases the inequality of income distribution. For antitrust purposes, however, the most important allegation is that concentration will lead to noncompetitive pricing and, as a consequence, resources will be misallocated. Neither the theoretical nor the empirical foundation for these allegations is unambiguous.[18] Nonetheless, the assumed evil of concentration has dominated the thinking with respect to public policy regarding mergers.

It is possible to use any economic variable as the basis for a measure of concentration. Some, however, may pose problems of interpretations. For example, concentration measures that are based upon employment, total assets, or net capital assets could be biased if the capital intensity of large firms differs from that of small producers. As a consequence, value added or total sales may be the most appropriate economic variable to use. The numerical measure of concentration also can vary, but only two measures have a substantial following among industrial organization or antitrust scholars: the n-firm concentration ratio and the Herfindahl index.

Concentration ratio

Historically, the most popular measure of concentration among industrial organization and antitrust economists has been the concentration ratio. Its main virtue from a mechanical perspective is its simplicity. The n-firm concentration ratio simply reports the percentage of industry sales accounted for by the n largest firms. From a practical perspective, it is of some note that the federal government publishes concentration ratio data on a somewhat aggregated basis. Due to disclosure rules, the government provides 4-firm, 8-firm, 20-firm, and 50-firm concentration ratios for a very large number of aggregated industries which contain products that may not be substitutes in consumption. Although these "industries" do not conform to the economist's usual definition of an industry, the data are the best that can be obtained for large-scale empirical studies.

As a consequence of ready availability, most economists and antitrust lawyers are more familiar with concentration ratios than with any other measure. In addition, concentration ratios have been used extensively in

[18] For a thorough discussion of these issues, see Tibor Scitovsky, "Economic Theory and the Measurement of Concentration," in *Business Concentration and Price Policy*, National Bureau of Economic Research (Princeton, N.J.: Princeton University Press, 1955).

empirical efforts to control for market structure. Although it is not so easy to tell from their actions, "everyone" recognizes that a one-parameter measure to express the shape of the distribution of an industry's total sales is unavailable. Nonetheless, the concentration ratio has been used quite often as a summary statistic to represent market structure.

Saving developed a theoretical link between the Lerner index of monopoly power and the concentration ratio based upon the dominant firm model.[19] Suppose that the largest n firms act cooperatively to dominate the industry. The remaining firms constitute a competitive fringe and act as price takers. Assuming that the dominant firms adopt a peaceful coexistence strategy, the n-firm cartel will set price in full recognition that the competitive fringe will supply a portion of the total demand. This portion will be determined by the supply function of the competitive fringe. The n-firm cartel will set price to maximize their profits subject to the constraint imposed by the competitive fringe supply.

Based upon this model, a measure of monopoly power for the industry is

$$\bar{\lambda} = \frac{C_n^2}{\eta + \varepsilon(1 - C_n)}$$

where C_n is the n-firm concentration ratio, η is the price elasticity of market demand, and ε is the elasticity of the fringe supply function.[20] It can be shown that an increase in the n-firm concentration ratio will increase monopoly power. In other words, that[21]

$$\frac{\Delta\bar{\lambda}}{\Delta C_n} > 0$$

Herfindahl index

The Herfindahl index (H) is the sum of the squared market shares of every firm in the industry:

$$H = \sum_{i=1}^{n} S_i^2$$

where S_i denotes the fraction of total industry sales accounted for by firm i, and n is the number of firms in the industry.[22] This measure of

---

[19] You will recall from Chapter 5 that the Lerner index, $\lambda = (P - MC)/P$, can be written as $\lambda = 1/\eta$ and measures the divergence of monopoly price from the socially optimal competitive prices. We encountered the dominant firm model in Chapters 6 and 8. For the theoretical derivation of the relationship summarized here, see Thomas R. Saving, "Concentration Ratios and the Degree of Monopoly," *International Economic Review* 11 (February 1970), pp. 139–46.

[20] This expression is derived in the Appendix to this chapter.

[21] To prove this one must evaluate the derivative of $\bar{\lambda}$ with respect to C_n and note that η, ε, and $(1 - C_n)$ are all positive.

[22] The Herfindahl index has been derived from a theory of oligopoly. See George J. Stigler, "A Theory of Oligopoly," *Journal of Political Economy* 72 (February 1964), pp. 44–61.

concentration has not been used widely in empirical research because its construction requires data on the market shares of every firm in the industry. In most instances, such detailed data are unavailable. In addition, the Herfindahl index does not have a clear intuitive meaning. Its popularity rose dramatically when the Antitrust Division of the Department of Justice revised its merger guidelines in 1982.

Adelman provided some intuition when he derived the numbers equivalent.[23] In particular, Adelman discovered that the number (N) of equal-sized firms that would generate any particular value of H is the reciprocal of H: $N = 1/H$. For example, if H is equal to 0.125, then N will be equal to eight, which is the number of equal-sized firms that would yield an H of 0.125.

One convenient aspect of H and therefore of N is that useful approximations can be made for an industry without full knowledge. For example, suppose one had market share data on the top four firms only and knew that $S_1 = 0.08$, $S_2 = 0.07$, $S_3 = 0.06$, and $S_4 = 0.05$. These four firms account for 26 percent of total sales. Since these are the four largest, the highest value that H can assume will occur when the other 74 percent of the industry is made up of 14 firms with a 5 percent share and 1 with a 4 percent share. In that case, the value of H is 0.054 and N is 18.5. If we were to look further and discover that the market shares of the next four firms were $S_5 = S_6 = 0.04$ and $S_7 = S_8 = 0.03$, then the maximum value of H would require 20 more firms each with a 3 percent share of the market. In that event, H would be 0.0404 and N would be 24.8. It is clear that the added effort sharpens the estimate of H and of N, but our initial determination that the Herfindahl index had a maximum value of 0.054 may indicate that no further research is necessary. This, of course, will depend upon the purpose to which the index will be applied.

One unfortunate property of the Herfindahl index is that there are no statistical tests of significance. This is a rather serious handicap when one is concerned with drawing inferences, say, about the changes in H over time.

9–4 JUDICIAL TREATMENT OF HORIZONTAL MERGERS

In assessing the legality of a merger between two firms, the courts must decide whether the merger will result in a substantial lessening of competition or tendency to create a monopoly in any line of commerce in any section of the country. Thus, there is a need to define product and geographic markets. If the two firms are found to be competitors within the same product and geographic markets, the merger is horizontal. The next question is whether that particular merger substantially reduces competition. Our review of the cases will highlight this question.

---

[23] See M. A. Adelman, "Comment on the 'H' Concentration Measure as a Numbers Equivalent," *Review of Economics and Statistics* 51 (February 1969), pp. 99–101.

Product market definition

We examined the difficult issue of defining the relevant product market in Chapter 5 when we discussed monopoly. As we discussed, an analyst must rely upon price correlations and purchase patterns as a practical way of drawing inferences about the cross-elasticity of demand. For the most part, the Court has not relied upon such evidence. In fact, the Supreme Court has not handled product market issues very well.

In its *Columbia Steel*[24] decision, the Court put U.S. Steel and Consolidated in the same product market even though the two firms had product lines that did not completely overlap. At this point, it is difficult to say whether this was correct or not. The Court failed to provide much information and no discussion.

The concept of a relevant submarket surfaced in *Brown Shoe*.[25] As in the *Du Pont (Cellophane)*[26] case, the Court recognized explicitly that the dimensions of a product market are drawn by the reasonable interchangeability of use or by the cross-elasticity of demand between the item in question and its potential substitutes. The Court ruled, however, that within a broad market there may also exist one or more well-defined submarkets, which can constitute a relevant line of commerce for antitrust purposes.

> The boundaries of such a submarket may be determined by examining such practical indicia as (1) industry or public recognition of the submarket as a separate economic entity, (2) the product's peculiar characteristics and uses, (3) unique production facilities, (4) distinct customers, (5) distinct prices, (6) sensitivity to price changes, and (7) specialized vendors.

Critics of the submarket concept point out that serious errors can be committed when it is implemented in a particular case.[27] If a submarket is defined that omits products that curb the market power of the merging firms, then the analysis of competitive effect will be too severe. When one examines cross-elasticity of demand and finds that a broad array of products are reasonably interchangeable, an analysis of competitive impact involving only a portion of that array will be misleading. No useful purpose is served by preventing unobjectionable mergers on the basis of faulty economic analysis.

The submarket concept has led to much mischief by the Court. Relying upon the *Brown Shoe* indicia, the Court has distinguished some products from a broader group of products and treated the resulting sub-

---

[24] *United States v. Columbia Steel Co.*, 334 U.S. 495 (1948).

[25] *Brown Shoe Co., Inc. v. United States*, 370 U.S. 294 (1962).

[26] *United States v. E. I. du Pont de Nemours & Co.*, 351 U.S. 377 (1956).

[27] A stunning critique is provided by Lawrence C. Maisel, "Submarkets in Merger and Monopolization Cases," *Georgetown Law Journal* 72 (December 1983), pp. 39–71.

market as economically relevant. This has resulted in the denial of what may have been innocent mergers. The abuse of the submarket concept was obvious in *Alcoa (Rome)*.[28] In that case, Alcoa acquired Rome Cable. Alcoa produced bare aluminum wire and cable and insulated aluminum wire and cable. While bare aluminum conductor is a separate line of commerce, insulated conductor must compete with its copper counterpart. The Court, however, rejected this lower court finding of commercial reality and separated insulated copper and aluminum conductor into separate product markets. This approach makes gerrymandering of markets possible.[29]

The Court's excesses were particularly objectionable in the *Continental Can* case.[30] Continental Can, which made metal containers, acquired Hazel Atlas, which made glass jars. Although the lower court felt that metal and glass were separate, the Supreme Court grouped them together because they competed in some uses. Discarding the niceties of reasonable interchangeability of use and cross-elasticity of demand, the Court ruled that the relevant line of commerce was metal and glass containers. The majority was not "concerned by the suggestion that if the product market is to be defined in these terms it must include plastic, paper, foil, and any other materials competing for the same business." This logic cannot be dismissed lightly. Given these precedents, it is clear that the Court can manipulate the market definition to obtain any desired result in a merger case.

Geographic market definition

As we saw in Chapter 5, the tools that proved useful in defining the relevant product market will also be useful in defining the relevant geographic market. Not surprisingly, the Court's treatment of geographic markets has been unsatisfactory. In *Pabst*,[31] the Court adopted a rather casual attitude toward geographic market definition. This case involved a merger between Pabst and Blatz, which the Antitrust Division challenged under Section 7. Using either the state of Wisconsin alone or the states of Illinois, Michigan, and Wisconsin as the relevant geographic market, the government claimed that the merger substantially lessened competition. The district court ruled in favor of Pabst because the government had failed to prove that either Wisconsin or the three-state area was a relevant geographic market. The Supreme Court reversed the lower court and expressed a lack of concern for carefully

---

[28] *United States* v. *Aluminum Co. of America (Rome Cable)*, 377 U.S. 271 (1964).

[29] L. Sullivan, *Handbook of the Law of Antitrust* (St. Paul, Minn.: West Publishing, 1977), p. 608 expressed this concern.

[30] *United States* v. *Continental Can Co.*, 378 U.S. 441 (1964).

[31] *United States* v. *Pabst Brewing Co.*, 384 U.S. 546 (1966).

defining the market. According to the Court, Section 7 "requires merely that the Government prove the merger has substantial anticompetitive effect somewhere in the United States." Just how the government would go about proving this without defining a relevant geographic market was never made explicit.

The *Pabst* decision was rendered by the Warren Court in an era of extreme hostility toward mergers. A much different Court addressed the geographic market definition question in *Marine Bancorporation*,[32] which involved the merger of two banks in the State of Washington. The National bank of Commerce (NBC) was located principally in Seattle and had no branch offices in Spokane. NBC wanted to acquire the Washington Trust Bank, which operated in Spokane. These banks did not compete with each other, and state banking laws precluded any practical way for NBC to enter the Spokane market except by acquiring one of the existing banks. The Court ruled against the government and recanted some of the unfortunate language in *Pabst*.

In its *Marine Bancorporation* decision, the Court tried to resurrect the requirement that a plaintiff establish a substantial anticompetitive effect within a sensible geographic market. This effort resulted in an operationally empty pronouncement that a relevant geographic market is an area in which the "goods and services at issue are marketed to a significant degree by the acquired firm." Although resurrecting the necessity for establishing a relevant market should be applauded, the Court provided little guidance on the sort of proof that will satisfy the requirement.

Establishing anticompetitive effect

At the Supreme Court, the standard for proving anticompetitive effect has revolved around market shares for many years. At least as early as the *Columbia Steel* decision in 1948, market shares have been important.[33] Following the Celler-Kefauver Amendment to Section 7 of the Clayton Act in 1950, the importance of market shares took a big leap forward.

The *Brown Shoe*[34] case involved a merger between the Brown Shoe Company and G. R. Kinney in 1956. The two firms both manufactured and retailed shoes. In 1955, Brown Shoe was the fourth largest domestic shoe producer with about 4 percent of national output. Kinney owned four shoe factories, which accounted for one half of 1 percent of national

---

[32] *United States* v. *Marine Bancorporation, Inc.*, 418 U.S. 602 (1974).

[33] *United States* v. *Columbia Steel Co.*, 334 U.S. 495 (1948). The Court stated a vague rule of reason standard for judging mergers. Among the relevant considerations was "the percentage of business controlled" by the parties. This was the last government defeat for some 25 years.

[34] *Brown Shoe Co., Inc.* v. *United States*, 370 U.S. 294 (1962).

output, thereby making Kinney the 12th largest shoe producer. As one would suspect from these data, shoe production was highly fragmented. The 4-firm concentration ratio was about 23 percent while the 24-firm concentration ratio was only some 35 percent. It was true that there seemed to have been a decreasing number of plants and firms at the manufacturing level. Nonetheless, in 1954, there were still some 970 independent shoe manufacturers.

Shoe retailing was even more fragmented than shoe production. In the mid-1950s, there were about 70,000 shoe outlets in total, 22,000 of which were classified as shoe stores. Brown Shoe either owned or controlled through its franchise plan some 1,230 shoe stores while Kinney, of course, was primarily a shoe retailer with over 400 family-style shoe stores.

In its decision, the Supreme Court felt compelled to review the legislative history of the Celler-Kefauver Amendment of Section 7. Among the factors that the Court described as being instrumental in the passage of the legislation was Congress's desire to provide the power to halt a merger trend. Moreover, Congress wanted to make it easier for the government to prevail in court by providing a lower standard of proof than the Sherman Act demanded. The Court noted that Congress did not propose any particular tests for defining the relevant markets nor did it define "substantially." Congress, however, did intend that a merger be viewed functionally in the context of the relevant industry. Finally, the Court noted that the language of Section 7 clearly indicates a concern with probabilities rather than with certainties.

Turning to the case at hand, the Supreme Court noted that a horizontal merger completely eliminates any competition between the partners. Section 7 is concerned with that loss of competition as well as the broader effect that a merger may have on "competition generally in an economically significant market." In this instance, Brown's acquisition of Kinney resulted in a horizontal combination at both the manufacturing and the retailing levels of their businesses. The merger of the manufacturing facilities was too insignificant to come under Section 7. But the merger of the retail outlets was found to violate the Clayton Act.

For purposes of the case, there were three relevant lines of commerce or product markets: men's shoes, women's shoes, and children's shoes. The geographic market definition was interesting. It included every city with a population exceeding 10,000 and its immediate contiguous area in which both Brown and Kinney retailed shoes through their own outlets. This market constituted less than one half of all cities in which either Brown or Kinney sold shoes through their own outlets. The validity of the entire merger was judged by the horizontal competition that existed in these cities.

The Court went on to evaluate the probable effect of the merger. In some cities, either Brown or Kinney had a large share and together had big shares (e.g., 33–57 percent). In 118 separate cities, the combined shares of Brown and Kinney in one of the relevant lines of commerce exceeded 5 percent. In 47 cities, their share exceeded 5 percent in all three lines. These data were important determinants of the Court's decision.

Market share of the merged firms is "one of the most important factors to be considered when determining the probable effects . . . on effective competition in the relevant market." The Court went on to find that a 5 percent share was important in a market as fragmented as shoe retailing. Moreover, a small share is still significant if the store is part of a strong national chain. Just what transforms a small share into something more significant is a mystery.

Although the shoe retailing industry was not concentrated, the Court noted a historical tendency toward concentration in the industry through merger. Admittedly, this merger did not involve huge market shares. Nonetheless, there was a danger that if this merger were approved others also would have to be approved and oligopoly would result. In any event, the Brown-Kinney merger resulted in Brown's controlling some 1,600 shoe outlets or 7.2 percent of the nation's retail "shoe stores" or 2.3 percent of total retail shoe outlets. The Court was compelled to rule against Brown Shoe: "[w]e cannot avoid the mandate of Congress that tendencies toward concentration in industry are to be curbed in their incipiency."

The importance of market shares received a further boost in the following year when the Court decided the *Philadelphia National Bank* case.[35] The Philadelphia National Bank (PNB), second largest commercial bank in the Philadelphia area, merged with the Girard Trust Corn Exchange Bank, third largest commercial bank of the 42 commercial banks in the four-county area around Philadelphia. PNB had assets over $1 billion in 1959 while Girard had assets of $750 million. The merger would make the resulting bank the largest in the area with 36 percent of the assets, 36 percent of the deposits, and 34 percent of the net loans. The market was already fairly concentrated with the following concentration ratios:

	Assets	Deposits	Net loans
PNB	36	36	34
2-firm CR	59	58	58
4-firm CR	78	77	78

The premerger size of PNB and Girard was partly due to several previous mergers. The Court detected a noticeable trend toward concentra-

---

[35] *United States* v. *Philadelphia National Bank*, 374 U.S. 321 (1963).

tion in the Philadelphia area. In 1947, there were 108 banks, but by 1963, there were only 42 left. Unfortunately, the Supreme Court did not offer any explanation for the decrease in the number of banks. Nor did it determine whether we could have effective competition with 42 banks.

The Court defined the relevant line of commerce as "the cluster of products (various kinds of credit) and services (such as checking accounts and trust administration) denoted by the term 'commercial banking'."

The Court's definition of the relevant geographic market was the city of Philadelphia and three contiguous counties. The logic of this definition followed from a Pennsylvania law which permitted branching into contiguous counties. Moreover, the Court reasoned that banking is a service industry, and therefore, convenience of location is essential to effective competition. Consequently, the factor of inconvenience localizes banking competition. Not wanting to get mired down in a lot of analysis, the Court struck a pragmatic compromise in defining the geographic market.

The Court decided not to do any economic analysis. In fact, it wanted to simplify the test of illegality. According to the Court, Congress was concerned about a rising tide of economic concentration in the economy.

> This intense congressional concern with the trend toward concentration warrants dispensing, in certain cases, with elaborate proof of market structure, market behavior, or probable anticompetitive effects. Specifically, we think that a merger which produces a firm controlling an undue percentage share of the relevant market, and results in a significant increase in the concentration of firms in that market is so inherently likely to lessen competition substantially that it must be enjoined in the absence of evidence clearly showing that the merger is not likely to have such anticompetitive effects.

Incredibly, the Court felt that this "test is fully consonant with economic theory." Given this test of illegality, the PNB-Girard merger stood no chance whatever. Moreover, the Court observed that "[t]here is nothing in the record of this case to relent the inherently anticompetitive tendency manifested by these percentages." PNB tried to argue that a larger bank in Philadelphia would bring business to the area and stimulate its economic development, but the Court rejected that argument: "[w]e are clear . . . that a merger the effect of which 'may be substantially to lessen competition' is not saved because, on some ultimate reckoning of social or economic debits and credits, it may be deemed beneficial." So much for social welfare.[36]

---

[36] The logic of PNB was applied in *United States* v. *Aluminum Co. of America*, 377 U.S. 271 (1964), and in *United States* v. *Continental Can Co.*, 378 U.S. 441 (1964). In both cases, the government presented some market share data, and the Court ruled in its favor without a scrap of economic analysis. In *Continental Can*, the Court observed that "[w]here a merger is of such size as to be inherently suspect, elaborate proof of market structure, market behavior and probable anticompetitive effects may be dispensed with in view of Section 7's design to prevent undue concentration."

The Court's reluctance to conduct any meaningful economic analysis before deciding a merger case was continued in *Von's Grocery*.[37] In terms of sales, the Von's Grocery Company was the third largest retail grocery chain in the Los Angeles area with 30 stores. The sixth largest chain in terms of sales was Shopping Bag Food Stores, which had 36 stores. In the decade prior to the merger, both chains had been successful and were growing rapidly.

For purposes of the case, the relevant line of commerce was retail groceries, and the relevant section of the country was the Los Angeles area. The majority opinion employed a very simplistic logic. Essentially, five industry facts were found:

1. The merger created the second largest retail grocery chain with 66 stores and 7.5 percent of the total sales.
2. The number of owners operating single stores had declined from 5,365 in 1950 to 3,818 in 1961 and further to 3,590 in 1963.
3. From 1953 to 1962, the number of chains with two or more stores rose from 96 to 150.
4. Nine of the top 20 chains acquired 126 stores from their smaller competitors from 1949 to 1958.
5. There appeared to be a lot of merger activity in the retail grocery industry in the Los Angeles area.

The Court followed this recitation with a bombshell: "These facts alone are enough to cause us to conclude contrary to the District Court that the Von's–Shopping Bag merger did violate §7."

Von's contended that Section 7 of the Clayton Act does not prohibit the merger because the retail grocery business in Los Angeles was, is, and probably always will be competitive despite the merger. The Court rejected this contention and relied upon the incipiency argument. In its view, the facts suggested a "threatening trend toward concentration which Congress wanted to halt."

At this point in the development of Section 7's interpretation, the government could simply play a numbers game. Their case involved nothing more than defining a market in such a way that concentration rose following a merger. The Court did no economic analysis in assessing the probable competitive significance of horizontal mergers. For example, the majority in *Von's Grocery* was not swayed by the facts that (1) the actual structure of the retail grocery market was competitive, (2) new stores, aided by cooperative private brands, were entering the market, (3) many of the stores that were failing were specialty stores that were economically obsolete, and (4) there were no substantial barriers to entry. In his dissent, Justice Stewart was moved to complain that "[t]he

---

[37] *United States* v. *Von's Grocery Co.*, 384 U.S. 270 (1966).

sole consistency that I can find is that in litigation under §7, the Government always wins."

In the late 1960s the composition of the Supreme Court began to change. President Nixon attempted to alter the character of the Court through the appointment of conservatives. The effect of this was felt in the merger area with the *General Dynamics*[38] decision. The Material Service Corporation, which mined deep reserves, owned the Freeman Coal Mining Corporation, which also had deepshaft mines. It began acquiring control over the United Electric Coal Companies, which mined open-pit or strip coal. By 1959, Material Service effectively controlled United Electric through the ownership of 34 percent of the common stock. General Dynamics acquired Material Service and subsequently acquired all of United Electric's stock. Within a year, the government challenged Material Service's acquisition of the United Electric stock.

The Justice Department attempted its usual ploy, which had proved so successful in the past. It defined the line of commerce as coal and the geographic market as Illinois or the Eastern Interior Coal Province Sales Area. The concentration data were then displayed. Since coal production was concentrated in either geographic market and it was increasing over time, the merger, which increased concentration even further, should be prohibited according to the government's complaint.

In this instance, the government's trusty formula for success failed. The Court recognized that coal is an exhaustible resource. Unlike manufacturing, present production does not give a good indication of a firm's future ability to compete. Competition among producers is for long-term requirements contracts and, by the time of the suit, United Electric had committed all of its reserves. Thus, it was not a competitive factor in the market. The evidence was convincing that United Electric had little ability to acquire new strip reserves. The Court felt that United Electric should not be compelled to enter a new endeavor to mine deep reserves as this would require different equipment, different personnel, and different expertise. Given the fact that United Electric had no uncommitted reserves, divestiture would not benefit competition because its long-term supply contracts had neutralized its competitive impact. In effect, it was removed from the competitive fray.

It would be easy to misread *General Dynamics*. This decision did not reverse the Court's earlier reliance on concentration data in horizontal merger cases.[39] Under the structural rules of *Philadelphia National Bank* and *Von's Grocery*, the government had shown that the coal industry

---

[38] *United States* v. *General Dynamics Corp.*, 415 U.S. 486 (1974). Since Justice Stewart was so distressed over the *Von's Grocery* decision, it was fitting that he be allowed to write the majority opinion in this case.

[39] For an analysis of *General Dynamics* and some other cases, see Roger D. Blair and Arnold A. Heggestad, "Some Remarks on Recent Merger Decisions," *Industrial Organization Review* 5 (1977), pp. 109–14.

was concentrated; the industry had exhibited a definite trend toward increasing concentration; and the merger would increase concentration substantially. Since precedent would suggest that the merger should have been held illegal (but was not), one might infer that the judicial climate had changed. Such a reading is unjustified. In *General Dynamics*, the Supreme Court had to decide "whether the District Court was justified in finding that other pertinent facts affecting the coal industry and the business of the respondents mandated a conclusion that no substantial lessening of competition occurred or was threatened by the acquisition of United Electric." Clearly, the Court had stated in earlier cases (such as *Brown Shoe*) that additional evidence could be considered. Whatever the additional evidence ever considered in other merger cases, it had never carried the day.

The significant departure in *General Dynamics* was that the Court really examined what the concentration data purported to show. In this case, the government neglected to show the requisite change in the "true" market concentration. Thus, one should not interpret *General Dynamics* as a rejection of the structural approach to horizontal merger cases. The Court ruled for the defendant because, after properly measuring competitive strengths in the coal industry, the acquisition did not fall within the proscriptions of *Philadelphia National Bank* and *Von's Grocery*. In other words, it seems likely that the Court would have decided in favor of the government if the *uncommitted* reserves had mirrored the production statistics. The important lesson seems clear: The government will have to be more careful in selecting the appropriate measure for estimating market power in the future.

9–5 MERGER GUIDELINES OF JUSTICE DEPARTMENT

In 1968, the U.S. Department of Justice published its first set of merger guidelines, which were designed to provide clear signals to the business community regarding the Antitrust Division's attitude toward mergers.[40] These guidelines revealed a hostility toward horizontal mergers that paralleled that of the Supreme Court. By 1982, the Department of Justice was in the hands of people who were more sympathetic to the business community. The 1982 revised guidelines reflected this change in attitude as do the newest set of guidelines, which were published on June 14, 1984.[41] The purpose of the guidelines continues to be to improve predictability of the department's merger enforcement policy. Nonetheless, the department will use the guidelines in conjunction with

---

[40] See Department of Justice Release, May 30, 1968; reprinted on p. 360, *Antitrust and Trade Regulation Report*, pp. x–1 et seq. (June 4, 1968).

[41] See *Justice Department Merger Guidelines*, June 14, 1984, in Special Supplement, *Antitrust and Trade Regulation Report*, S-1–S-16 (June 14, 1984).

informed judgment regarding the factual setting and competitive conditions that surround the specific merger in question.

Product market definition

In general, the department will include in the product market a group of products such that a hypothetical firm that was the only present and future seller of those products ("monopolist") could profitably impose a "small but significant and nontransitory" increase in price.

Specifically, the department will begin with each product (narrowly defined) produced or sold by each merging firm and ask what would happen if a hypothetical monopolist of that product imposed a "small but significant and nontransitory" increase in price. If the price increase would cause so many buyers to shift to other products that a hypothetical monopolist would not find it profitable to impose such an increase in price, then the department will add to the product group the product that is the next-best substitute for the merging firm's product and ask the same question again. This process will continue until a group of products is identified for which a hypothetical monopolist could profitably impose a "small but significant and nontransitory" increase in price. The department generally will consider the relevant product market to be the smallest group of products that satisfies this test.

In evaluating product substitutability, the department will consider all relevant evidence but will give particular weight to the following factors:

1. Evidence of buyers' perceptions that the products are or are not substitutes, particularly if those buyers have actually considered shifting purchases between the products in response to changes in relative price or other competitive variables.
2. Differences in the price movements of the products or similarities in price movements over a period of years that are not explainable by common or parallel changes in factors such as costs of inputs, income, or other variables.
3. Similarities or differences between the products in customary usage, design, physical composition, and other technical characteristics.
4. Evidence of sellers' perceptions that the products are or are not substitutes, particularly if business decisions have been based on those perceptions.

Geographic market definition

The purpose of geographic market definition is to establish a geographic boundary that roughly separates firms that are important factors in the competitive analysis of a merger from those that are not. Depending on the nature of the product and the competitive circumstances, the geographic market may be as small as part of a city or as large as the entire world. Also, a single firm may operate in a number of economically discrete geographic markets.

In general, the department seeks to identify a geographic area such that a hypothetical firm that was the only present or future producer or seller of the relevant product in that area could profitably impose a "small but significant and nontransitory" increase in price.

In defining the geographic market or markets affected by a merger, the department will begin with the location of each merging firm (or each plant of a multiplant firm) and ask what would happen if a hypothetical monopolist of the relevant product at that point imposed a "small but significant and nontransitory" increase in price. If this increase in price would cause so many buyers to shift to products produced in other areas that a hypothetical monopolist producing or selling the relevant product at the merging firm's location would not find it profitable to impose such an increase in price, then the department will add the location from which production is the next-best substitute for production at the merging firm's location and ask the same question again. This process will be repeated until the department identifies an area in which a hypothetical monopolist could profitably impose a "small but significant and nontransitory" increase in price. The "smallest market" principle will be applied as it is in product market definition.

In evaluating geographic substitutability, the department will consider all relevant evidence but will give particular weight to the following factors:

1. The shipment patterns of the merging firm and of those firms with which it actually competes for sales.
2. Evidence of buyers having actually considered shifting their purchases among sellers at different geographic situations, especially if the shifts corresponded to changes in relative price or other competitive variables.
3. Differences in the price movements of the relevant product or similarities in price movements over a period of years that are not explainable by common or parallel changes in factors, such as the cost of inputs, income, or other variables in different geographic areas.
4. Transportation costs.
5. Costs of local distribution.
6. Excess capacity of firms outside the location of the merging firm.

Horizontal merger standards

In examining horizontal mergers, the Department of Justice will use the Herfindahl-Hirschman index (HHI), which it calculates by summing the squares of the individual market shares of all firms in the market. It ignores the decimal point in the calculation so that if there were four firms with market shares of 10, 25, 30, and 35 percent, the HHI would be $(10)^2 + (25)^2 + (30)^2 + (35)^2 = 2,850$. The department divides the spectrum of market concentration as measured by the HHI into three regions that can be broadly characterized as unconcentrated (HHI below 1,000), moderately concentrated (HHI between 1,000 and 1,800), and highly concentrated (HHI above 1,800). An empirical study by the department of the size dispersion of firms within markets indicates that the critical HHI thresholds at 1,000 and 1,800 correspond roughly to four-firm concentration ratios of 50 percent and 70 percent, respectively.

The general standards for horizontal mergers are as follows:

1. *Post-merger HHI below 1,000.* Markets in this region generally would be considered to be unconcentrated. Because implicit coordination among firms is likely to be difficult and because the prohibitions of Section 1 of the Sherman Act are usually an adequate response to any explicit collusion that might occur, the department will not challenge mergers falling in this region, except in extraordinary circumstances.

2. *Post-merger HHI between 1,000 and 1,800.* Because this region extends from the point at which the competitive concerns associated with concentration are raised to the point at which they become quite serious, generalization is particularly difficult. The department, however, is unlikely to challenge a merger producing an increase in the HHI of less than 100 points. The department is likely to challenge mergers in this region that produce an increase in the HHI of more than 100 points, unless the department concludes that the merger is not likely substantially to lessen competition.

3. *Post-merger HHI above 1,800.* Markets in this region generally are considered to be highly concentrated. Additional concentration resulting from mergers is a matter of significant competitive concern. The department is unlikely, however, to challenge mergers producing an increase in the HHI of less than 50 points. The department is likely to challenge mergers in this region that produce an increase in the HHI of more than 50 points, unless the department concludes that the merger is not likely substantially to lessen competition.

Other considerations

The department has no interest in a mechanical approach to analyzing horizontal mergers. Thus, it will examine and consider other factors before making a final decision on whether to challenge a particular merger. These factors include changing market conditions, ease of entry, homogeneity of the product, special buyer characteristics, the ability of fringe firms to expand sales, the conduct of the firms in the market, and considerations of efficiency.

9-6 THE FAILING FIRM DEFENSE[42]

The purpose of Section 7 is to prevent a substantial lessening of competition due to a merger between two firms. Suppose, however, that one of the firms is failing. Absent the merger, the failing firm will cease operations. Consequently, that firm cannot provide much competitive force, and the merger may not reduce competition to any substantial degree.

The failing firm doctrine is a judicially created doctrine that can be traced to the *International Shoe*[43] decision of 1930. In that case, International Shoe had purchased the stock of the W. H. McElwain Company, which was on the brink of financial ruin. The Supreme Court held that even if the two firms were in substantial competition, McElwain's failure would terminate that competition. Thus, a merger that would usually violate the Clayton Act due to anticompetitive effects may be permissible:

> In the light of the case thus disclosed of a corporation with resources so depleted and the prospect of rehabilitation so remote that it faced the grave probability of a business failure with resulting blow to its stockholders and injury to the communities where its plants were operated, we hold that the purchase of its capital stock by a competitor (there being no other prospective purchaser), not with a purpose to lessen competition, but to facilitate the accumulated business of the purchaser and with the effect of mitigating seriously injurious consequences otherwise probable, is not in contemplation of law prejudicial to the public and does not substantially lessen competition or restrain commerce within the intent of the Clayton Act.

In implementing the failing firm doctrine, a court must determine whether one of the firms was, in fact, failing. This is not a trivial proposition because all firms face temporary reverses that do not cause the firm to leave the industry. For example, a reduction in price below average total cost will not close down a firm as long as the price is above average variable cost. Even though the firm is experiencing negative profits, it will remain in the industry in the short run. Not until it is time to renew its long-run commitment to the industry will these short-run losses be important. At that time, the firm will leave the industry if it believes that price will not cover average total cost.

In *International Shoe*, the Court pointed out that International Shoe was the only prospective purchaser of McElwain. Since International Shoe was the largest shoe manufacturer in the industry, it would have

---

[42] An excellent historical survey is provided by Marc P. Blum, "The Failing Company Doctrine," *Boston College Industrial and Commercial Law Review* 16 (November 1974), pp. 75–113. A contemporary analysis is contained in Phillip Areeda and Donald F. Turner, *Antitrust Law* IV (Boston: Little, Brown, 1980), at pp. 100–30.

[43] *International Shoe Co.* v. *Federal Trade Commission*, 280 U.S. 291 (1930).

been preferable for someone else to have purchased McElwain. In later cases involving mergers that would otherwise violate Section 7, the Court has required proof that some good faith effort was made to find the least offensive merger partner. In other words, a merger between two firms may be prohibited if a second merger partner exists that is significantly better in terms of competitive impact. For example, in its *Citizen Publishing*[44] decision, the Supreme Court pointed out that "[t]he failing company doctrine plainly cannot be applied . . . unless it is established that the company that acquires the failing company . . . is the only available purchaser. For if another person or group could be interested, a unit in the competitive system would be preserved and not lost to monopoly power."

In its Merger Guidelines, the Justice Department has expressed a rather lukewarm attitude toward the failing firm defense. The guidelines set out the department's policy in this regard. The department is unlikely to challenge an anticompetitive merger in which one of the merging firms is allegedly failing when: (1) the allegedly failing firm probably would be unable to meet its financial obligations in the near future, (2) it probably would not be able to reorganize successfully under Chapter 11 of the Bankruptcy Act, and (3) it has made unsuccessful good faith efforts to elicit reasonable alternative offers of acquisition of the failing firm that would both keep it in the market and pose a less severe danger to competition than does the proposed merger.

9–7 FINAL REMARKS

We have covered a lot of ground in this chapter, but the main thing that we have learned is that the major merger precedents were set during the 1960s by the Warren Court, which was very hostile toward mergers. These decisions demonstrate a fixation on market shares and concentration data. At times, the market definition was gerrymandered so the Court could rationalize its disapproval of a particular merger (e.g., *Alcoa-Rome* and *Continental Can*). In other cases, the Court boldly refused to engage in any economic analysis and just dismissed the need for analysis (e.g., *Philadelphia National Bank* and *Von's Grocery*). In all cases, however, the Court pointed to some market share data and expressed concern about concentration.

As we saw in the last chapter, the major theories of oligopoly indicate that prices will be higher in more concentrated industries. Most dominant firm models predict noncompetitive prices, at least in the short run. A cartel variant of the dominant firm model can be used to relate the Lerner index of monopoly power to concentration in the market. This body of theoretical work indicates that concentration does, indeed, have some antitrust significance.

---

[44] *Citizen Publishing Co. v. United States*, 394 U.S. 131 (1969).

The empirical work on the importance of concentration is not as clear. For the most part, empirical work focuses on the question of whether concentration leads to higher profits. This is a more confusing issue because of nonprice competition, which tends to be offsetting within an industry.[45] For example, competitive advertising within an industry is an expensive means of determining market shares. Even though price may exceed marginal cost by a considerable amount, these rivalrous advertising expenditures may reduce profits greatly. Nonetheless, many empirical studies have examined the influence of concentration—as a proxy for market power or market structure—on profits. The results of some 75–80 separate studies have been synthesized in an excellent survey by Leonard Weiss.[46] The bulk of these studies provides empirical confirmation of the theoretical prediction that concentration and profits are positively correlated. The policy implication that has been drawn from these empirical findings is that collusion—tacit or explicit—is facilitated by high concentration. Accordingly, a vigorous antitrust policy prohibiting horizontal mergers among financially healthy firms in concentrated industries appears to be quite sensible. This, of course, is the path that the Antitrust Division and the courts have followed in the past.

The empirical results surveyed by Weiss have not gone unchallenged. A major attack on the concentration doctrine was started by Harold Demsetz.[47] He pointed out that absent serious entry barriers, concentration can only result from the superiority of a few firms in manufacturing and marketing their products. This superior performance may be due to luck or to superior managerial efficiency. It may be due to being first in line with a good idea. In any event, concentration will develop if some firms obtain greater rewards for expanding output.

If the concentration doctrine is correct, then the largest firms in a concentrated industry will collude either tacitly or overtly, charge higher prices, and will earn excess profits. The smaller firms in the industry also will benefit from the collusion. If they are part of the conspiracy (tacit or overt) or form a competitive fringe, they benefit from receiving a higher price for their output. If the small firms are as cost efficient as the large firms, they ought to earn excess profits, too. The data, however, do not support this conclusion. Demsetz found that the small firms do

---

[45] For a brief discussion, see George Stigler, "Price and Nonprice Competition," *Journal of Political Economy* 76 (February 1968), pp. 149–54.

[46] Leonard W. Weiss, "The Concentration-Profits Relationship and Antitrust," in *Industrial Concentration: The New Learning*, eds. Harvey J. Goldschmid, H. Michael Mann, and J. Fred Weston (Boston: Little, Brown, 1974), pp. 184–232.

[47] See the following papers by Demsetz: *The Market Concentration Doctrine* (Washington: American Enterprise Institute, 1973); "Industry Structure, Market Rivalry, and Public Policy," *Journal of Law and Economics* 16 (April 1973), pp. 1–9; and "Two Systems of Belief about Monopoly," in *Industrial Concentration: The New Learning*, eds. H. Goldschmid, H. M. Mann, and J. F. Weston (Boston: Little, Brown, 1974).

not earn impressive profits irrespective of industry concentration, but the large firms in concentrated industries earn higher profits than the large firms in unconcentrated markets. The inference drawn from these data is that the large firms are more efficient than the small firms. They got to be large because they were more efficient than other firms.

There are only two serious criticisms of the Demsetz view of market concentration.[48] First, his results are consistent with the view that non-competitive pricing provides an umbrella for less efficient firms. Inefficient firms that could not survive at competitive prices can enter and thrive when the dominant firms in an industry are pricing above the competitive level. Consequently, no one should be surprised that the small firms have lower rates of return than the large firms. Second, this pattern is not inconsistent with the hypothesis that the dominant firms are colluding either tacitly or explicitly. Accordingly, a vigorous anti-merger policy is still warranted.

One way of separating these effects would be to examine rates of return while statistically controlling for size and for market structure.[49] Carter reports that this has been done and that very little of the excess profit can be attributed to collusion.[50] Consequently, the Demsetz challenge is quite serious for the formation of a sensible antitrust merger policy.

APPENDIX

The expression for the Lerner index as a function of the n-firm concentration ratio can be derived without too much difficulty. When the n-firm cartel sets its optimal price and output, the quantity supplied by the competitive fringe will be a function of that price, $Q_S(P)$. The quantity demanded by the market will also be a function of that price $Q_M(P)$. As a result, the quantity demanded from the n-dominant firms is a function of price $Q_n(P)$ and is equal to the difference between the market demand and the fringe supply:

$$Q_n(P) = Q_M(P) - Q_S(P)$$

It follows that

$$\frac{\Delta Q_n}{\Delta P} = \frac{\Delta Q_M}{\Delta P} - \frac{\Delta Q_S}{\Delta P}$$

---

[48] For a synthesis of this literature and a critique of the critics, see John R. Carter, "Antitrust, Competition, and the Demise of the Concentration Doctrine," *University of Toledo Law Review* 12 (Winter 1981), pp. 243–67.

[49] Weiss, "The Concentration-Profits Relationship," pp. 184–232 suggested this approach.

[50] See Carter, "Antitrust, Competition," pp. 255–59, and Sam Peltzman, "The Gains and Losses from Industrial Concentration," *Journal of Law and Economics* 20 (October 1977), pp. 229–64.

Multiplying by $-P/Q_n$ yields

$$\frac{-\Delta Q_n}{\Delta P} \cdot \frac{P}{Q_n} = -\frac{\Delta Q_M}{\Delta P} \cdot \frac{P}{Q_n} + \frac{\Delta Q_S}{\Delta P} \cdot \frac{P}{Q_n}$$

Algebra permits the following manipulation:

$$-\frac{\Delta Q_n}{\Delta P} \cdot \frac{P}{Q_n} = -\frac{\Delta Q_M}{\Delta P} \cdot \frac{P}{Q_n} \cdot \frac{Q_M}{Q_M} + \frac{\Delta Q_S}{\Delta P} \cdot \frac{P}{Q_n} \cdot \frac{Q_S}{Q_S}$$

By the definitions of demand and supply elasticities, we may write this as

$$\eta_n = \eta_M \frac{Q_M}{Q_n} + \varepsilon \frac{Q_S}{Q_n}$$

The n-firm Lerner index is $\lambda = 1/\eta_n$ under the assumption that the n-firm cartel is maximizing its profits. By substituting for η_n, we get

$$\lambda = \frac{1}{\eta \dfrac{Q_M}{Q_n} + \varepsilon \dfrac{Q_S}{Q_n}}$$

The n-firm concentration ratio (C_n) shows the share of total sales made by the n firms. Thus, $C_n = Q_n/Q_M$. Consequently,

$$\frac{Q_M(P)}{Q_n(P)} = \frac{1}{C_n} \text{ and } \frac{Q_S(P)}{Q_n(P)} = \frac{(1 - C_n)}{C_n}$$

By substituting these into λ, we will find that in the n-firm version of the dominant firm model the Lerner index of monopoly power is

$$\lambda = \frac{C_n}{\eta + \varepsilon(1 - C_n)}$$

In other words, the n-firm Lerner index of monopoly power is a function of the n-firm concentration ratio, the price elasticity of demand, and the elasticity of the competitive fringe supply.

A relevant measure of monopoly power for the industry can be obtained by weighting the Lerner index for the n largest firms and for the competitive fringe by their respective market shares:

$$\bar{\lambda} = C_n \lambda + (1 - C_n)\lambda_F$$

The competitive fringe firms, however, act as price takers and produce where marginal cost equals price. As a result, λ_F will be zero. Then,

$$\bar{\lambda} = C_n \lambda$$
$$= \frac{C_n^2}{\eta + \varepsilon(1 - C_n)}$$

Since $\eta > 0$, $\varepsilon > 0$, and $(1 - C_n) > 0$, we know that $\Delta\bar{\lambda}/\Delta C_n > 0$, $\Delta\bar{\lambda}/\Delta\eta < 0$, and $\Delta\bar{\lambda}/\Delta\varepsilon < 0$, but a proof requires the use of differential calculus.

QUESTIONS AND PROBLEMS

1. The expression for monopoly power in an n-firm dominant firm model was given as

$$\bar{\lambda} = \frac{C_n^2}{\eta + \varepsilon(1 - C_n)}$$

By using calculus, we can determine the effect on $\bar{\lambda}$ of changes in η and ε. In fact, $\Delta\bar{\lambda}/\Delta\eta$ is negative. What does this mean? Does it square with your intuition? In addition, it is true that $\Delta\bar{\lambda}/\Delta\varepsilon$ is negative. Interpret this, and explain the economic intuition behind it.

2. Consider the cartel variant of the dominant firm model. Suppose one of the cartel members defects and joins the fringe. Trace through the effect on price, output, and the allocation of output.

3. Suppose there are no serious entry barriers. Does it follow that there is no need for a vigorous antimerger policy?

4. Suppose that all you know is that the Herfindahl index is 0.36 in industry A and 0.42 in industry B. Do those facts provide enough information to decide on the advisability of a merger in either industry?

5. Suppose the four-firm concentration ratio in industry R is 0.65, while the four-firm concentration ratio in industry S is 0.80. Is it possible that industry S will be more competitive than industry R?

6. The Department of Justice has objected to a merger between the Atlas T-Shirt Company and Sports Jerseys, Inc. It has been stipulated that the two firms operate in the same geographic and product markets. The lawyers for Atlas want to argue that the merger will result in the exploitation of economies of scale in production. Can you help them with the economic argument? Is it easier to discuss economies of scale in distribution?

7. Prior to the *Alcoa* decision, structural monopoly was treated differently than was behavioral monopoly (i.e., price fixing). What effect should such divergent treatment have on the incentive for mergers?

8. Suppose the manufacturer of Levi's jeans wanted to merge with the manufacturer of Botany 500 suits. Is that a horizontal merger? Why or why not? What about a merger between Levi's and Calvin Klein? If you are having trouble deciding, what additional information would you find helpful?

9. In *Continental Can*, why did the Court expand the product definition to cross industry lines and then carve out an artificial submarket? Is this consistent with the promotion of consumer welfare?

10. What sorts of mergers are "of such size as to be inherently suspect"? Why is proof of market structure, market behavior, and probable anticompetitive effect unnecessary?

11. Examine the Court's practical indicia for defining a submarket. Are they all independent? Are they all equally important?

12. Suppose that Phil's Pharmacies operates primarily in Florida with 150 stores while Don's Drugs operates primarily in Alabama with 97 stores. In Mobile, Alabama, Phil's has two stores, and Don's has a dozen. In Pensacola, Florida, Don's has one store while Phil's has eight. Should a merger between the two drugstore chains violate Section 7 of the Clayton Act? Defend your conclusion. What facts would you want to answer the question?

13. How should one measure concentration in exhaustible resource industries like coal, natural gas, and petroleum?

14. There is a "failing firm" defense in merger cases. What is the defense? What is the competitive significance of a failing firm? In *General Dynamics*, why was United Electric less than a failing firm?

15. In some industries, say, retail groceries, large chains have replaced small, independent grocery stores. Some people have argued that it is appropriate for §7 enforcement to protect competitors (rather than competition) because our society values small economic units. A conservative economist pointed out that the chains replaced the independents because they were more efficient and offered lower prices. He concluded that this proved that society did not value small economic units. What was he talking about? Do you agree?

16. The confusion between protecting competition and protecting competitors has been a vexing problem in antitrust. How might these goals conflict? Under what circumstances would protecting competi-

tors be the best way to protect competition? How do competitors force each other to "perform well"?

17. Suppose that the PNB-Girard merger had been allowed. Is it likely that the prime rate that PNB would have charged its major borrowers would have risen as a result of the merger? If not, why not?

18. In most urban locations, there are slums and there is the high rent district. Often these areas stand in stark contrast right next to each other. For purposes of estimating the competitive effect of a merger between two retail stores, should these two areas be combined in the same geographic market? Explain.

19. Do you think that suburban (shopping mall) shoe stores are in the same retail market as downtown stores? Where do you buy your shoes? How large would a price difference have to be to induce you to switch geographic locations?

20. How do you think the Supreme Court would deal with a merger that was motivated by and resulted in increased efficiency (i.e., lower costs)? How *should* it deal with such a merger?

FURTHER READINGS

Bork, Robert H. *The Antitrust Paradox.* New York: Basic Books, 1978, Chapters 9 and 10.

Landes, William M., and Richard A. Popner. "Market Power in Antitrust Cases." *Harvard Law Review* 94 (March 1981), pp. 937–96.

Maisel, Lawrence C. "Submarkets in Merger and Monopolization Cases." *Georgetown Law Journal* 72 (December 1983), pp. 39–71.

Peltzman, Sam. "The Gains and Losses from Industrial Concentration." *Journal of Law and Economics* 20 (October 1977), pp. 229–63.

Peterman, John L. "The Brown Shoe Case." *Journal of Law and Economics* 18 (April 1975), pp. 81–146.

Posner, Richard A. *Antitrust Law: An Economic Perspective.* Chicago: University of Chicago Press, 1976, Chapter 6.

"Symposium: 1982 Merger Guidelines." *California Law Review* 71 (March 1983), pp. 280–672.

10

Price discrimination

Price discrimination is a common practice. It occurs every time a seller charges different prices to different customers for the same product. For example, when a movie theater charges $2 for children and $4 for adults, price discrimination has occurred. It also occurs every time that the same price is charged to two different customers when the costs of serving them are different. For example, a cup of coffee with cream and sugar usually carries the same price as a cup of black coffee. The costs of providing these two cups of coffee are obviously different. In most cases, price discrimination has little competitive significance. Nonetheless, when Congress passed the Clayton Act in 1914 to buttress the Sherman Act's ability to deal with the monopoly problem, it included a prohibition of price discrimination. At the time, Congress was concerned that large firms could bankrupt their smaller local rivals through local price cutting. For example, it was alleged that Standard Oil used its monopoly profits from some markets to finance deep price cuts in markets where it faced competition. If necessary, it would cut price below cost in order to drive its competitors out of business. Thus, this sort of price discrimination was seen as a means of attaining and maintaining monopoly power.

In this chapter, we develop the economic theory of price discrimination by a monopolist and contrast this with legal definitions of price discrimination. We review the price discrimination provisions in the Clayton Act as amended by the Robinson-Patman Act. We will also examine the case law along with some defenses. Finally, we provide a critique of Robinson-Patman Act enforcement.

10–1 ECONOMICS OF PRICE DISCRIMINATION

In many cases, monopolists will sell their output in a single market and charge the same price to each customer. Sometimes, however, a monopolist may find it profitable to charge different prices to different customers for precisely the same commodity. When this occurs, we say that the monopolist has engaged in price discrimination. More precisely, we define price discrimination as the practice of selling the same product at two or more prices, and the price differences do not reflect cost differences. More formally, if $(P/MC)_1 \neq (P/MC)_2$, then price discrimination exists. There are numerous examples of price discrimination. Movie theaters, amusement parks, and airlines charge lower prices for children than for adults. Industrial customers pay lower electricity rates than the utility company charges its residential customers. Senior citizens get discounts on golf course privileges, pharmacy prescriptions, and eyeglasses. Each of these price differences reflects differences in demand rather than differences in costs. Let's see why.

Profit maximization

Suppose a monopolist sells its output in two separate markets with quite different demand curves. In addition, suppose that the monopolist has only one production facility. In order to maximize its profits, the monopolist must decide (1) how much to produce and (2) how much to sell in each market. Prices will be set in each market according to demand.[1] The principles of profit maximization that we have used before will prove useful here. In each market, sales should be expanded to the point where marginal revenue is equal to marginal cost. But output is

---

[1] Under these conditions, profit is as follows:

$$\Pi = P_1 Q_1 + P_2 Q_2 - C(Q)$$

where $Q_1 + Q_2 = Q$. In order to maximize profit, the firm must satisfy the following conditions simultaneously:

$$\frac{\Delta \Pi}{\Delta Q_1} = MR_1 - MC = 0$$

and

$$\frac{\Delta \Pi}{\Delta Q_2} = MR_2 - MC = 0$$

Thus, these two conditions require that

$$MR_1 = MR_2 = MC$$

Of course, the analysis can be extended to more than two markets in an obvious way.

produced in a single production facility. Thus, a sales increase in one market will cause an increase in marginal cost, which influences optimality in both markets. In order to deal with this complication, we shall decide upon an optimal total output and then allocate that quantity between the two markets. To this end, examine Figure 10–1, which

---

FIGURE 10–1

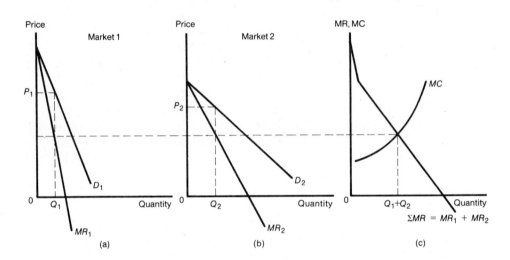

(a)   (b)   (c)

---

displays the demand and corresponding marginal revenue curve for market 1 in panel a and the same curves for market 2 in panel b. In panel c, we have drawn the firm's marginal cost curve along with the horizontal summation of the two marginal revenue curves. The firm's profit maximizing output is found by equating the summed marginal revenue curve (ΣMR) and the marginal cost curve (MC). Once this optimal output is produced, the firm has incurred all of its costs. In order to maximize its profits, the firm must allocate sales to the two markets in such a way that its total revenue will be maximized. This requires equating the marginal revenues in the two markets. To see this, suppose, for example, that MR_1 exceeded MR_2. A reallocation of output from market 2 to market 1 would decrease total revenue by MR_2 and increase total revenue by MR_1. Since MR_1 exceeds MR_2, this reallocation will increase total revenue. This, in turn, will increase profits because total costs do not change. Thus, profit maximization requires producing and allocating output such that

$$MR_1 = MR_2 = MC$$

In Figure 10–1, profits are maximized by allocating Q_1 to market 1 and Q_2 to market 2. The profit maximizing prices are P_1 and P_2, respectively. As we can see, P_1 is higher than P_2 while the marginal cost of production is the same for both markets. This is a clear case of price discrimination: When a firm sells a homogeneous output simultaneously to two different markets such that the price-marginal cost ratios are not equal, the firm is engaging in price discrimination.

When we examine Figure 10–1, we notice that D_1 is less elastic than D_2 at each price. Moreover, we see that the profit maximizing price is higher in market 1 than in market 2. Intuition suggests that this may be more than a coincidence. Although we cannot always rely upon our intuition, this time it is pointing us in the right direction. A higher price is charged in the market that is less responsive to price increases while a lower price is charged in the market that is more responsive to price increases. We can see this in a more formal way by writing the optimality condition as[2]

$$P_1(1 - 1/\eta_1) = P_2(1 - 1/\eta_2) = MC$$

where η_1 denotes the price elasticity of demand in market 1 and similarly for η_2. Suppose the elasticity of demand in market 1 is 2, while that in market 2 is 3. Then we know that

$$P_1(1 - \tfrac{1}{2}) = P_2(1 - \tfrac{1}{3})$$

which means that P_2 equals $(\tfrac{3}{4})P_1$. As we can see, price is higher in the market with the less elastic demand curve.

Conditions for successful price discrimination

The firm discriminates in price because it earns higher profits by doing so. In spite of this, not all products are sold at discriminatory prices. Consider groceries, magazines, beer at the local pub, everything in Sears, and so on. If price discrimination is profitable, why isn't it practiced more frequently?

First, the firm must be able to identify the separate markets. In some cases, this is easy: adults versus children, foreign versus domestic markets, males versus females. In other cases, however, the identification of separate markets is far more difficult.

Second, arbitrage may prevent successful price discrimination. Arbitrage is the very clever practice of buying in the low-price market and reselling in the high-price market. This practice may thwart the monopolist's efforts at price discrimination. Consider a firm that sells its output

---

[2] This is a legitimate substitution because $MR = P(1 - 1/\eta)$ as a general proposition.

in several geographic locations. A firm's ability to charge different prices in different locations is determined by the cost of transportation between locations. If a good sells in different markets at a price differential that exceeds the cost of transportation between the two markets, arbitrageurs would find it profitable to buy in the cheap market, ship the item to the expensive market, and resell it. Of course, this would drive the price down in the expensive market. For instance, suppose oranges were sold to retailers in Miami for $2.00 per bushel and to retailers in New York for $2.50 per bushel. If it cost less than 50 cents per bushel to ship oranges from Miami to New York, clever merchants would buy oranges in Miami, ship them to New York, and sell them at a profit for a price below $2.50 per bushel. Unless these efforts were constrained, competition among these clever merchants eventually will drive the price to New York retailers down to $2.00 plus the cost of transportation.

Similar incentives exist to arbitrage away price differences among groups. For example, children would try to resell their cheaper movie tickets to adults. In response, the price discriminating firms would try to stamp out such arbitrage by forbidding the product's resale. For example, airlines and theaters can easily monitor who ultimately uses plane and movie tickets; an adult is simply not allowed to enter a theater with a child's ticket. In other markets, it may be more difficult to reduce the incidence of resale. For example, Heinz sells ketchup to the retail grocery market as well as to the restaurant market. The restaurant market has a higher price elasticity of demand for ketchup and is charged a lower price. The bottles of ketchup that are sold to restaurants are labeled "not for resale," which facilitates policing against arbitrage between the two markets. If a Heinz representative were to see a restaurant bottle (labeled "not for resale") in a grocery store, he could punish the grocery store for its activities by withholding Heinz products.

Of course, the firm is better off if it does not have to pay for policing against resale. One way to accomplish this is to persuade the government to make resale of the firm's product illegal. Through lobbying, a firm may be able to enlighten politicians on the "evils" of resale. As an example, milk producers at the turn of the century were able to get laws passed that banned the resale of milk. These efforts at preventing arbitrage are costly and are not socially productive. When resources are expended to separate markets that are not naturally distinct, nothing of social value is produced. Of course, if the costs of preventing arbitrage exceed the increased profits due to price discrimination, the firm will decide not to engage in price discrimination.

It is true that not every firm will engage in price discrimination. Where two or more markets with different demand curves can be identified and arbitrage can be prevented, however, a monopolist can expand its profits through discriminatory pricing.

Difference in costs

So far, we have focused on instances where prices differ, but costs of production and distribution are the same across customers. As we shall see in the next section, this corresponds to the focus of the Robinson-Patman Act. Our definition of economic price discrimination also covers the instances where marginal costs differ while prices are the same. For example, if the price is $10 in markets 1 and 2 while marginal cost is $8 in market 1 and $7 in market 2, then

$$\frac{P}{MC_1} \neq \frac{P}{MC_2}$$

and price discrimination exists.

For the most part, the Robinson-Patman Act does not deal with this complication. Thus, the antitrust law focuses on only a subset of all forms of price discrimination.[3]

10–2   THE LAW OF PRICE DISCRIMINATION

Originally, Section 2 of the Clayton Act prohibited the sort of predatory price discrimination that Standard Oil was suspected of employing. The large firm could still reduce price in response to local entry by a small competitor, but the lower prices would have to be extended to all areas. Thus, the cost of driving out small rivals would rise. Congress recognized, however, that some price reductions were not really discriminatory. For example, buyers who bought in large quantities were granted discounts. This recognition was incorporated in the original Section 2 language with the result that a seller could always explain price differences on the basis of quantity differences. Originally, there was no need to show any sort of cost difference that would justify the particular quantity discount that was given.

Many small businesses failed during the Depression of the 1930s. Contributing to the demise of many local retail stores was the superior efficiency of the chain stores, which exploited economies in centralized buying. The resulting cost advantages were reflected in lower retail prices, which put tremendous competitive pressure on inefficient local retail outlets. These local businessmen appealed to Congress for assistance and got it in the form of the Robinson-Patman Act amendment to Section 2 of the Clayton Act.

Passed in 1936, the Robinson-Patman Act forbids price discrimination where it has the potential for lessening competition:

> Sec. 2(a) That it shall be unlawful for any person engaged in commerce, . . . either directly or indirectly, to discriminate in price between different

---

[3] But see our discussion of indirect price discrimination in Section 10–5.

purchasers of commodities of like grade and quality, . . . where the effect of such discrimination may be substantially to lessen competition or tend to create a monopoly in any line of commerce, or to injure, destroy, or prevent competition with any person who either grants or knowingly receives the benefit of such discrimination, or with customers of either of them: Provided, that nothing herein contained shall prevent differentials which make only due allowance for differences in the cost of manufacture, sale, or delivery resulting from the differing methods or quantities in which such commodities are to such purchasers sold or delivered.

Thus, Section 2(a) recognizes explicitly that some price differentials result from cost differences. To the extent that this is so, such price differences are not illegal. The cost justification proviso has rarely proved to be of much use to businesses because the standard of proof is so high. Nonetheless, in principle, a firm may be able to justify price differences on the basis of differences in costs. For example, volume discounts may be justified on the basis of economies in delivery costs. This defense will be examined later in this chapter (see Section 10–7).

In addition to the cost justification defense, Section 2(b) provides the meeting competition defense. To use this defense, the supplier must show that its lower price was offered in good faith to *meet* an equally low price of a competitor. Note that the seller can only meet, not beat, the rival's price. We examine this defense later in the chapter (see Section 10–6).

10–3 PRIMARY–LINE INJURY

When we speak of primary-line injury, we are referring to injury suffered by competitors of the firm practicing the price discrimination. For example, suppose that Lackluster Steel offers a discriminatorily low price to a customer of B&K Enterprises, which is also in the steel industry. In this case, the price discrimination occurs because Lackluster offers a lower price to a potential new customer than the price charged to its established customers. The primary-line injury is suffered by B&K, which is a rival of Lackluster.

The legal theory of the primary-line injury cases depends upon the assumption that a multimarket firm can reduce its price in one geographic market to harm a localized rival. The idea is to price predatorily in one market and finance this venture with profits earned in the other markets. The localized rival cannot employ similar tactics because it does not operate in any other markets and, therefore, has nowhere to earn excess profits. As a result, the localized firm will fail. After its exit, the predatory price cutter will then raise its price and recover its investment in acquiring monopoly profit. One problem with this theory is that we have already seen that predatory pricing does not make much sense.[4] In

---

[4] See our discussion of predatory pricing in Chapter 5.

fact, conditions under which predatory pricing is a sensible business practice are rare. With this caveat in mind, let us examine the leading primary-line decision.

Utah Pie Co. *v*. Continental Baking Co.[5]   In the 1950s the market for frozen dessert pies was small but growing. The Salt Lake City market was supplied by distant plants in California that were owned by Carnation, Continental Baking, and Pet Milk. Until 1957, these three firms accounted for almost all of the frozen fruit pies sold in the Salt Lake City market.

The Utah Pie Company had been baking dessert pies in Salt Lake City and selling them fresh for 30 years. This family-owned and family-operated business entered the frozen pie market in 1957. It was successful immediately and grabbed a huge share of the Salt Lake City market. During the relevant years, the market shares were as follows:

	1958	1959	1960	1961
Utah Pie	67	34	46	45
Pet Milk	16	36	28	29
Carnation	10	9	12	9
Continental	1	3	2	8
All others	6	19	13	8

Utah Pie's strategy for penetrating the market was to set its price below those of its competitors. Due to its immediate success, it built a new plant in 1958. Its local plants gave Utah Pie a locational advantage over its competitors. For most of the time in question, Utah Pie's prices were the lowest in the Salt Lake City market. The incumbent firms, of course, responded to Utah Pie's entry and lower prices by reducing their own prices. As a result, each of the defendants sold frozen pies in Salt Lake City at prices that were lower than those charged for pies of like grade and quality in other markets considerably closer to its California plants. Utah Pie sued these firms, claiming price discrimination. Ultimately, the case was reviewed by the Supreme Court, which took a dim view of such pricing behavior: "Sellers may not sell like goods to different purchasers at different prices if the result may be to injure competition in either the sellers' or the buyers' market unless such discriminations are justified as permitted by the Act." It appears that price discrimination does not have to have an obviously predatory impact. All the Court saw in this case was a pattern of falling prices. It feared that

---

[5] 386 U.S. 685 (1967).

such a pattern ultimately could result in a lessening of competition if one or more competitors fell out of the market.

Justice Stewart's dissent raised the appropriate objection to the majority's decision. He asked rhetorically whether the defendants' actions had any anticompetitive impact. The answer had to be negative. In 1958, Utah Pie had a near monopoly market share of 66.5 percent. By 1961, after a few years of vigorous price competition, Utah Pie still had a commanding share with 45.3 percent. To Stewart, the market appeared to be more competitive in 1961 than it had been in 1958. He felt that the majority "has fallen into the error of reading the Robinson-Patman Act as protecting competitors, instead of competition."

In addition to the change in market shares, consider what was happening to prices in the Salt Lake City market:

	Early 1958	1961
Utah Pie	$4.15	$2.75 (August)
Pet Milk	4.92	3.46 (April)
Carnation	4.82	3.46 (August)
		3.30 (lowest)
Continental	5.00	2.85 (lowest)

Thus, the vigorous price competition reduced the wholesale price of frozen fruit pies to retail grocers in the Salt Lake City market. Presumably, retail competition will lead to lower retail prices to consumers.

Postscript on Utah Pie.[6] Most critics of the *Utah Pie* decision argue that it protected Utah Pie from competition by companies outside the Salt Lake City area. As a result, it would be able to exploit its locational advantage and dominate the Salt Lake City market. This argument appears logical since the outsiders would not want to cut prices everywhere and would be afraid to do so again in Salt Lake City.

The actual scenario is quite different: Utah Pie went out of business in 1972. Its capital equipment was repossessed by its creditors. Its building was purchased by a firm that uses it to make women's lingerie. No one uses the frozen pie labels of Utah Pie. It appears that Utah Pie failed because of significant managerial deficiencies. As for the rest of the actors, Continental (Morton) has been successful; Pet's share in 1975 was less than 3 percent; and Carnation left the industry in 1967.

---

[6] Kenneth G. Elzinga and Thomas F. Hogarty, "*Utah Pie* and the Consequences of Robinson-Patman," *Journal of Law and Economics* 21 (October 1978), pp. 427–34.

10–4 SECONDARY–LINE INJURY

Suppose a producer sells its output to some of its customers at one price and to other customers at a lower price. If these customers compete among themselves in the resale market, those that paid the lower price will have a competitive advantage over those that paid the higher price. To the extent that a competitive injury is suffered, we have an example of secondary-line injury. In these cases, the concern is with competitive injury to some of the customers of the firm that is practicing price discrimination. Instances of secondary-line price discrimination raise the question of why the seller would want to disadvantage any of its customers. The judiciary, however, has not been concerned with this question.

Federal Trade Commission *v.* Morton Salt Co.[7] The *Morton Salt* case provided the classic secondary-line price discrimination decision. Morton Salt manufactured various brands of table salt which it sold to wholesalers and to large retailers. The wholesalers resold the salt to retail grocery stores that were in direct competition with the large retailers that bought directly from Morton Salt. Blue Label was Morton Salt's finest brand of table salt, which it sold to all of its customers according to its standard quantity discount system. These discounts were available to all of its customers—large and small alike. Under this discount plan, the buyer pays a delivered price, and the cost to both wholesale and retail purchasers of Blue Label salt varies according to the quantities purchased. The price schedule was as follows:

Less-than-carload purchases	$1.60/case
Carload purchases	1.50/case
5,000-case purchases in any consecutive 12 months	1.40/case
50,000-case purchases in any consecutive 12 months	1.35/case

Although these discounts were available to all purchasers in principle, only five firms ever qualified for the $1.35/case price. Not surprisingly, these buyers were large grocery chains. Given the low margin on retail sales, these chains could sell Blue Label salt at retail cheaper than wholesale purchasers could resell Blue Label to its customers, which were independently operated retail stores.

---

[7] 334 U.S. 37 (1948).

The Supreme Court did not have much trouble with this case. First, the Court noted that the discounts were not functionally available to all customers because only the very largest chains can use 50,000 cases of table salt. Moreover, "[t]he legislative history of the Robinson-Patman Act makes it abundantly clear that Congress considered it to be an evil that a large buyer could secure a competitive advantage over a small buyer solely because of the large buyer's quantity purchasing ability." Accordingly, the Court decided that such discounts are illegal unless they can be cost justified.

Morton Salt argued that table salt is not a big revenue factor for any grocery store and that its discounts were not shown to have caused injury to competition. The Court dismissed this argument: ". . . we have said that 'the statute does not require that the discriminations must in fact have harmed competition, but only that there is a reasonable possibility that they "may" have such an effect.'"

Morton Salt indicates that proof of a price difference between purchasers that compete in the resale market may be sufficient to establish a prima facie case of illegal price discrimination. Of course, the price differential may be defended on cost justification or meeting competition grounds.

10–5 INDIRECT PRICE DISCRIMINATION

Congress was well aware of the fact that price discrimination may not be direct and obvious. De facto price differentials can exist through indirect means. Most of these avenues are foreclosed by the act, as we shall see.

Brokerage commissions

A broker's function is to bring buyers and sellers together. Depending upon custom, the broker is paid a commission by either the buyer or seller. One way for a buyer to receive an indirect price concession is to set up a sham broker. The buyer insists that this broker be paid a commission for services that actually were never performed. When the broker turns the commission over to the buyer, the buyer has received a discount indirectly. This sort of sham transaction is covered by Section 2(c):

> That it shall be unlawful for any person engaged in commerce, in the course of such commerce, to pay or grant, or to receive or accept, anything of value as a commission, brokerage, or other compensation, or any allowance or discount in lieu thereof, except for services rendered in connection with the sale or purchase of goods, wares, or merchandise, either to the other party to such transaction, or to an agent, representative, or other intermediary therein where such intermediary is acting in fact for or in

behalf, or is subject to the direct or indirect control, of any party to such transaction other than the person by whom such compensation is so granted or paid.

Discriminatory allowances and services

Another way that a buyer may receive discriminatorily favorable treatment is through the provision of promotional allowances and services. These allowances and services include (a) cooperative advertising in the local media (e.g., an automobile manufacturer may pay for part of the local dealer's newspaper advertising), (b) provision of a demonstrator in the buyer's retail facility, and (c) provision of display materials for retail sales. Sections 2(d) and 2(e) prohibit discriminatory behavior in providing promotional allowances and services. In Section 2(d), the seller is prohibited from making discriminatory payments to a favored buyer so the buyer can perform the promotional function:

> Section 2(d). That it shall be unlawful for any person engaged in commerce to pay or contract for the payment of anything of value to or for the benefit of a customer of such person in the course of such commerce as compensation or in consideration for any services or facilities furnished by or through such customer in connection with the processing, handling, sale, or offering for sale of any products or commodities manufactured, sold or offered for sale by such person, unless such payment or consideration is available on proportionally equal terms to all other customers competing in the distribution of such products or commodities.

In Section 2(e), the seller is prohibited from supplying the promotional services themselves on a discriminatory basis:

> Section 2(e). That it shall be unlawful for any person to discriminate in favor of one purchaser against another purchaser or purchasers of a commodity bought for resale, with or without processing, by contracting to furnish or furnishing, or by contributing to the furnishing of, any services or facilities connected with the processing, handling, sale, or offering for sale of such commodity so purchased upon terms not accorded to all purchasers on proportionally equal terms.

These prohibitions of indirect price concessions are more severe than open price cuts in that they are per se illegal. There is no need to show any probable injury to competition. Since these are means for disguising price cuts, the harsh treatment is justified as a deterrent.

10–6 AFFIRMATIVE DEFENSE OF MEETING COMPETITION

If a plaintiff can show that a seller offers a product of like grade and quality at two different prices and that competition may be affected adversely by that price differential, it has established a prima facie case of unlawful price discrimination. The defendant can escape Robinson-Patman liability by offering one of two affirmative defenses: the "good faith" meeting competition defense or the cost justification defense, which will be discussed in the next section.

"Good faith" meeting competition defense

The language of Section 2(b) provides for a meeting competition defense:

> nothing herein contained shall prevent a seller rebutting the prima facie case thus made by showing that his lower price or the furnishing of services or facilities to any purchaser or purchasers was made in good faith to meet an equally low price of a competitor, or the services or facilities furnished by a competitor.

It should be emphasized that the burden of proof is on the defendant. Once the plaintiff makes its prima facie case, the burden of proof shifts to the defendant. The plaintiff has no obligation to show that the discriminatory prices were not offered in good faith to meet competition; rather, the defendant must show that they were.

The purpose of this defense is straightforward. Congress wanted each seller to be able to respond competitively to price raids by a competitor without having to lower its price to all of its customers. If this defense were not available, a seller might refrain from cutting price in response to a price raid. Eventually, this would have an adverse effect on competition at the buyer's level because some buyers would continue to suffer a competitive disadvantage.

For quite some time, the Court has held that the meeting competition defense is absolute. In other words, when a seller offers a discriminatory price as a counteroffer made in good faith to meet a rival's equally low price, the discriminatory price is lawful irrespective of the effect on competition. This was decided in unqualified terms by the Supreme Court in the following case.

Standard Oil (of Indiana) Co. v. Federal Trade Commission.[8] Standard Oil sold gasoline to jobbers in the Detroit area at 1.5 cents per gallon less than the price charged to retail service stations. This price differential could not be justified on the basis of lower costs of dealing with the jobbers. The effect of the discriminatory price, however, was anticompetitive. The favored jobbers or their customers were able to sell gasoline at retail for prices below those that would be profitable for Standard Oil's retail customer stations. As a result, some competitors were injured by the discriminatory pricing, and the Federal Trade Commission claimed that Standard Oil was guilty of price discrimination.

---

[8] 340 U.S. 231 (1951).

The four large jobbers were particularly attractive customers because they had the storage capacity to take huge deliveries, they distributed the gasoline to retail service stations, they bought substantial quantities on an annual basis, and they posed little credit risk. As a result, other gasoline suppliers made competitive attempts to lure them away from Standard Oil. In fact, Standard Oil

> presented evidence tending to prove that its tank-car price was made to each "jobber" in order to retain that "jobber" as a customer and in good faith to meet a lawful and equally low price of a competitor. Standard Oil sought to show that it succeeded in retaining these customers, although the tank-car price which it offered them merely approached or matched, and did not undercut, the lower prices offered them by several competitors of Standard Oil.

The Federal Trade Commission maintained that the meeting competition defense was not absolute if an injury to competition resulted. The Court rejected this contention categorically:

> there has been widespread understanding that, under Robinson-Patman Act, it is a complete defense to a charge of price discrimination for the seller to show that its price differential has been made in good faith to meet a lawful and equally low price of a competitor. . . . We see no reason to depart now from that interpretation.

Thus, it is clear that this defense is absolute.

It is crucial that the accused seller make "good faith" price reductions in response to competitive probes by its rivals if the meeting competition defense is to be viable. If there is any evidence of bad faith or a lack of good faith, the courts are apt to reject the defense. Generally, a defendant will satisfy the good faith requirement by showing that it acted just as any prudent businessman would in responding fairly to what he believes is a situation of competitive necessity. It is not necessary to prove that the prices are in fact equal to prices offered by competitors. All that is necessary is a good faith belief that the prices are equal. This, of course, is a sensible way to interpret the "good faith" requirement. Buyers are interested in the lowest price possible and, in trying to obtain low prices from one supplier, they may suggest or hint that lower prices are available from a rival when this is not true. If the courts insisted upon absolute accuracy, interseller price verification would be encouraged. The effect of such information exchanges is apt to be a reluctance to compete in prices. Such a result is clearly in conflict with the purpose of the antitrust laws. In this connection, the Supreme Court has ruled that interseller price verification was unnecessary and undesirable.

The defendants in *United States* v. *United States Gypsum Co.*[9] had established a systematic practice of exchanging presale price quotations.

---

[9] 428 U.S. 422 (1978).

When challenged, they claimed that it was necessary to verify competitive prices to maintain eligibility for a meeting competition defense to price discrimination charges. The Supreme Court acknowledged that earlier cases contained some unfortunate language that may have misled some of the lower courts into thinking that this was necessary. For example, the *Staley* decision[10] used the words "investigate or verify," while the *Corn Products* decision[11] focused on "personal knowledge of the transactions." This suggests that direct price verification is necessary to meet the burden of proof under Section 2(b), but the Court wanted to dispell that notion in its *Gypsum* decision. In particular, the Court held that

> a good-faith belief, rather than absolute certainty, that a price concession is being offered to meet an equally low price offered by a competitor is sufficient to satisfy the Robinson-Patman's §2(b) defense. While casual reliance on uncorroborated reports of buyers or sales representatives without further investigation may not be sufficient . . . , nothing in the language of §2(b) . . . indicates that direct discussions of price between competitors are required.

Suppose that B&K Blue Jeans offers to supply K mart with its full jeans requirement for the next year. Its offer is attractively priced below that of K mart's usual supplier, Kalvin Levy. In responding to this competition, can Kalvin Levy cut price below the B&K offer and still claim a Section 2(b) defense? The language of Section 2(b) indicates that a seller may meet but not beat the price concessions offered by its rivals. This, however, cannot be construed too severely due to vagaries in the market place, product differentiation, and all-or-nothing bidding situations.

Defensive versus offensive tactic

For some time, there has been lower court disagreement regarding the purpose of the price reduction. Some courts have held that the meeting competition defense is only available when it is used defensively (i.e., to retain existing customers). These courts would reject the defense if the price cut had been made to obtain new business. In its *Vanco*[12] decision, the Supreme Court explicitly dealt with this issue. The Court ruled that "Section 2(b) . . . does not distinguish between one who meets a competitor's lower price to retain an old customer and one who meets a competitor's lower price in an attempt to gain new customers." All that is necessary is a good faith belief that the new customer can obtain an equally low price from a rival supplier.

---

[10] *Federal Trade Commission v. A. E. Staley Manufacturing Co.*, 324 U.S. 746 (1945).

[11] *Corn Products Refining Co. v. Federal Trade Commission*, 324 U.S. 726 (1945).

[12] *Falls City Industries, Inc. v. Vanco Beverage, Inc.*, 103 S. Ct. 1282 (1983).

10–7 AFFIRMATIVE DEFENSE OF COST JUSTIFICATION

There is a second affirmative defense to a charge of unlawful price discrimination: cost justification, Section 2(a), specifically exempts price differentials that "make only due allowance for differences in the cost of manufacture, sale, or delivery resulting from the differing methods or quantities in which such commodities are to such purchasers sold or delivered." As with the meeting competition defense, the burden of proof is on the defendant. If the plaintiff establishes a prima facie case of illegal price discrimination, the burden of proving that the price difference was due to differences in costs falls upon the defendant. It is not up to the plaintiff to prove that no such cost justification exists.

The purpose of this defense is sensible. Congress did not want to deny the benefits of lower prices to consumers. Thus, it did not want to force a seller to reduce its price to all buyers in order to pass on a cost saving to one buyer. This was accomplished through the cost justification proviso in Section 2(a). But this proviso does not extend to all cost differences. For example, suppose a firm was producing an output of Q_1 in Figure 10–2 and incurring an average cost of C_1. A large potential

---

FIGURE 10–2

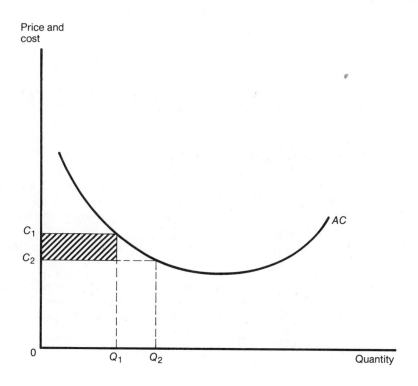

customer could point out that its purchase of $Q_2 - Q_1$ units would push down the average cost of all units sold to C_2. As a result, this buyer wants to pay only C_2 per unit. The seller could afford to do this because its profits on sales to its original customers would rise by $(C_1 - C_2)Q_1$, which is the shaded rectangle in Figure 10–2. This sort of price concession was expressly not meant to be covered by the cost justification proviso. Of course, this is a sensible position because there is nothing special about the favored buyer in this case. All purchasers contribute to the reduction in unit costs to the level of C_2.

Cognizable costs

The cost proviso protects price differentials that are closely related to savings in the supplier's costs of production or distribution that resulted from the differing methods or quantities in which such goods were sold or delivered. The courts and the FTC have held several types of costs to be legally cognizable for purposes of invoking the cost proviso: (1) freight and delivery costs, (2) catalog expenses, (3) depreciation of facilities used exclusively to support sales to one customer or class of customers, (4) brokerage allowances if passed on to an entire class of customers, and (5) manufacturing costs. Whenever a defendant can show that the price differential is explained by differences in these sorts of costs, an otherwise illegal price differential will be excused.

Customer grouping

The literal language of the cost proviso suggests that any price differential between any two purchasers must be individually justified. Fortunately, the antitrust authorities and the courts have recognized the impracticality of such a requirement. In its *Borden*[13] decision, the Supreme Court dealt with this problem. Borden sold milk to retail grocery stores. The independents paid prices according to a system of volume discounts. Two chains, A&P and Jewel, received a discount that was larger than the maximum that an independent could earn. Borden sought to justify this price differential by comparing the costs of dealing with A&P and Jewel as a group with those incurred in dealing with the independents as a group.

The Court explicitly approved of cost justification on the basis of customer grouping:

> to completely renounce class pricing as justified by class accounting would be to eliminate in practical effect the cost justification proviso as to sellers having a large number of purchasers, thereby preventing such sellers from passing on economies to their customers.

---

[13] *United States v. Borden Co.*, 350 U.S. 460 (1962).

In that instance, however, Borden had grouped customers in an arbitrary way on the basis of ownership rather than on a rational basis. The Court held that Borden's classes were not "composed of members of such self-sameness as to make the averaging of the cost of dealing with the group a valid and reasonable indicium of the cost of dealing with any specific group member." In other words, Borden's classes were not sufficiently homogeneous. Nonetheless, the principle of grouping received judicial approval.

10–8 ROBINSON–PATMAN TREATMENT OF THE BIG BUYER

One curious aspect of Robinson-Patman Act enforcement is its focus on sellers. In nearly every instance, it is the discriminating seller who is under attack. Given the historical importance of the chain stores—large buyers—in the act's formulation, it is interesting that large buyers are seldom charged. The act explicitly recognizes that a large buyer may have a considerable bargaining advantage over a small, specialized supplier. To the extent that a supplier is heavily dependent upon the sales to a single buyer for its existence, that buyer can, under certain conditions, extract significant concessions from the supplier. Unlike the traditional price discrimination model of economic theory, the seller may be reluctant to offer a lower price to a particular buyer or class of buyers. Nonetheless, he may do so because of the economic sanctions that the large buyer can impose. Such pressure is covered by Section 2(f):

> Section 2(f). That it shall be unlawful for any person engaged in commerce, in the course of such commerce, knowingly to induce or receive a discrimination in price which is prohibited by this section.

This provision has been used only rarely because the plaintiff must show that the buyer was aware of the fact that it extracted an illegal price concession from the seller. Moreover, the "good faith" defense of the seller is available to the buyer.

10–9 FINAL REMARKS

Generally, most observers have been highly critical of the Robinson-Patman Act and its enforcement. Its proscription of primary-line price discrimination inhibits competition in most cases. In the *Utah Pie* situation, for example, the multimarket firms had two choices: (1) surrender the Salt Lake City market to Utah Pie and maintain prices elsewhere, or (2) reduce prices all over the country in order to compete in Salt Lake City. The most likely reaction is to simply abandon the Salt Lake City market. This outcome certainly would benefit a small firm like Utah Pie, but it does nothing to promote consumer welfare. As a matter of fact, consumers are denied the benefits of lower prices that vigorous price competition provides. In fact, the *Utah Pie* decision depends wholly upon the decrease in market price that occurred. Thus, price competition may be unlawful under the Robinson-Patman Act.

When we turn to secondary-line considerations, the story does not get any better. The main objection to the proscription of secondary-line price discrimination is that it prevents sellers from passing on cost differences that are difficult to prove. The cost justification defense has been hard to use because of FTC and judicial interpretations that demand extraordinary precision. When sellers are reluctant to pass on cost savings, consumers obviously are injured by higher prices and reduced levels of consumption. Moreover, society's resources are going to be wasted because incentives for cost reductions are dampened if their competitive value is reduced.

QUESTIONS AND PROBLEMS

1. Most local telephone service permits the customer to make as many calls as he wishes for a flat monthly fee. The Smith family has three teenage children who make many more calls than the Jones family with no children. Both families pay the same monthly charge. Is this price discrimination? Does it violate the Robinson-Patman Act?

2. Suppose the chain stores cut out the middlemen by performing the middleman function internally (i.e., the chain stores vertically integrated backward). How would this give them a cost advantage over their rivals?

3. The *Utah Pie* case involved "primary-line" price discrimination. What is this? How is it supposed to affect competition adversely?

4. Recall in *Topco* that what made Topco an important competitive force was the private brands that were offered. In *FTC* v. *Borden,* 383 U.S. 637 (1966), the issue was whether Borden's national brand and its private brand were of like grade and quality because they sold at different prices. Why do producers offer private brands? Why do resellers want private brand merchandise? Does a simple price difference constitute price discrimination when the two products are physically identical?

5. A hardcover text sells for $21.95 while a paperback version sells for $8.95. Suppose that the two books are identical except for the cover and that the cost difference is $1.00. Is this price discrimination? Would it be illegal? Why would a publisher select such a pair of prices?

6. Cement is sold to large contractors at a price below the list price, which is charged to ready-mix concrete companies. Is this two-tier pricing an example of price discrimination? Is it unlawful? Is there any competitive effect?

7. Since a monopolist can increase its profits by discriminating in price, why don't competitive firms adopt this lucrative business practice? Is it because they are not interested in additional profits?

8. If you were attempting a cost justification defense, where would you obtain the cost information? In practice, how would you measure marginal costs? Is there a difference between economic costs and accounting costs?

9. In the price discrimination model, show that a reallocation of the quantity produced will increase profits if MR_1 is not equal to MR_2.

10. Suppose B&K Manufacturing has a monopoly over the production of a new diet supplement. Several of its customers complain that B&K is providing preferential pricing to their competitors. A spokesman for B&K said, "There is no reason for us to allow a group of our customers to be disadvantaged competitively, because they will fail, and we will be worse off as a result." Is this sound economics?

11. Why would Morton Salt give a substantial discount to a handful of grocery store chains? As a result of the Supreme Court decision, would you expect Morton Salt to raise its price to everyone or reduce its price to everyone?

12. The standard charge for mailing a letter anywhere in the United States is the same. Is the U.S. Postal Service charging discriminatory prices?

13. Utah Pie entered the Salt Lake City frozen pie market based upon the pricing structure that it observed. Upon entering, the prices fell. Did Utah Pie suffer any antitrust injury?

14. Suppose that all cement producers in Gotham City charge the announced list price to all cement purchasers. On the advice of B&K Consultants, the LDL Cement Company won a few large contracts by cutting price significantly below its list price, which it continued charging to most of its customers. Has LDL discriminated in price on economic grounds? Has it violated the Robinson-Patman Act? How would you expect LDL's rivals to respond? Will that be socially beneficial or socially harmful?

15. Who was injured by the price discrimination in *Morton Salt*? Did anyone suffer antitrust injury? If not, why was the firm guilty?

16. Consider the price discrimination model in Figure 10–1. Suppose D_2 increases. What happens to the prices and quantities in markets 1 and 2?

17. Suppose that a monopolist faces two demand curves

$$P_1 = 200 - Q_1$$

and

$$P_2 = 100 - 3Q_2$$

in markets 1 and 2, respectively. His total cost function is

$$C = 20 + 4Q.$$

   a. Find the profit maximizing prices and quantities in the two markets.
   b. What are the total profits for the firm?

18. There are times when the price of a Sony TV set is lower in the United States than it is in Japan. Can you explain why that occurs?

19. "Since price discrimination will lead to higher profits, every monopolist will practice price discrimination." True or false? Explain.

20. Why should we expect to see more instances of price discrimination in the sale of services than in the sale of commodities?

FURTHER READINGS

Bowman, Ward. "Restraint of Trade by the Supreme Court: The *Utah Pie* Case." *Yale Law Journal* 77 (November 1967), pp. 70–85.

Edwards, Corwin. *The Price Discrimination Law*. Washington, D.C.: Brookings Institution, 1959.

Elzinga, Kenneth G., and Thomas F. Hogarty. "*Utah Pie* and the Consequences of Robinson-Patman." *Journal of Law and Economics* 21 (October 1978), pp. 427–34.

Machlup, Fritz. "Characteristics and Types of Price Discrimination." In *Business Concentration and Price Policy*. Princeton, N.J.: Princeton University Press, 1955, pp. 400–23.

Phlips, Louis. *The Economics of Price Discrimination*. New York: Cambridge University Press, 1983.

Posner, Richard A. *The Robinson-Patman Act.* Washington, D.C.: American Enterprise Institute, 1976.

Schmalensee, Richard. "Output and Welfare Implications of Monopolistic Third-Degree Price Discrimination." *American Economic Review* 71 (March 1981), pp. 242–47.

Taggert, H. E. *Cost Justification.* Ann Arbor, Mich.: University of Michigan Press, 1959.

PART III

Vertical antitrust issues

In this section of the book, we focus our attention upon a set of seriously misunderstood business practices between vertically related firms (i.e., between firms that have a customer-supplier relationship). Initially, we provide a survey of the economic theory of vertical integration. This reveals that vertical integration has effects that may promote consumer welfare or that may not. The predominant effect is a matter of analysis and empirical measurement in most cases.

Following the theoretical survey, we examine the antitrust policy toward vertical mergers. We shall see that this policy tends to be somewhat hostile. The balance of this section of the book deals with contractual alternatives to vertical integration: vertical price fixing, customer and territorial restraints, tying arrangements, and exclusive dealing. We shall see that these contractual alternatives are economically equivalent to vertical integration. Although one might expect economically equivalent practices to receive similar antitrust treatment, such is not the case. Some practices receive per se treatment while others receive rule of reason treatment.

11

The theory of vertical integration

11–1 INTRODUCTION

As a product moves from being a collection of raw materials to being a finished good in the hands of a consumer, many distinct production and distribution functions are performed. Basic raw materials must be extracted and transported. Intermediate products that are employed as inputs in the later stages of production must be fabricated from these raw materials and these, too, must be transported. Finally, the various intermediate inputs must be combined or assembled into a final good which must then be distributed and sold to the ultimate consumer.

In principle, each of these myriad functions could be performed by separate specialized firms, or they could all be performed by a single vertically integrated firm. In the former case, the raw materials and intermediate products would each be sold on the open market with downstream producers (those nearer the final product stage) purchasing their inputs from upstream producers (those nearer the raw material stage). In the latter case, the vertically integrated firm would simply transfer the raw materials and intermediate products internally from its upstream divisions to its downstream divisions with little or no participation in raw material or intermediate product markets.

Although a precise definition may be elusive, we shall say that a firm is vertically integrated if that firm transfers internally from one department to another a commodity which could be sold in the market without major adaptation.[1] From this definition, two important observations emerge. First, virtually all firms are vertically integrated to some degree. That is, most firms carry out some function or manufacture some tool or part that could, "without major adaptation," be purchased from another firm. And second, no firm is totally vertically integrated. That is, all firms purchase some inputs or services that they could, in principle, manufacture or provide themselves.

For example, the independent service station on the corner that purchases its oil, tires, gasoline, tools, water, and electricity from upstream suppliers may appear to exhibit no vertical integration. But it is a virtual certainty that this firm will provide some product or service that could, if it so desired, be purchased from some other firm. Perhaps the owner keeps the books when this function could be performed by a separate accounting firm. Or the owner may clean the rest rooms when it would be feasible to contract with a janitorial service for this function. At the same time, the service station across the street may be owned by a major oil corporation that also owns crude-oil wells, oil tanker ships, refineries, and tanker trucks. The parent corporation may also provide the accounting service to its own stations and may even have a janitorial crew to clean the rest rooms at these stations. Yet this highly integrated station is not likely to have its own tool manufacturing facilities, electrical generating equipment, or water plant. It, too, will purchase some inputs on the open market. Consequently, we are not ever likely to observe the extremes of zero or total vertical integration. But, as our service station example indicates, we do observe a wide variation in degrees of vertical integration between these extremes.

If an upstream firm (e.g., a coal company) acquires productive capacity at a downstream stage (e.g., an electric utility), we refer to this as *forward* integration. The acquisition of downstream productive capacity may be accomplished by the purchase of or merger with existing firms or by the construction of completely new facilities. In contrast, if a downstream firm purchases upstream input suppliers or constructs its own input supply facilities, we refer to this as *backward* integration. In either case, the firm in question has elected to replace a market transfer that is governed by arm's-length bargaining and market prices with an internal transfer that is governed by the administrative decisions of the firm's managers.

In this chapter, we will examine some of the economic reasons why a firm might select the latter option over the former (i.e., why a firm vertically integrates). We shall see that a variety of reasons exist. For convenience, we categorize these reasons into three groups: (1) those involving government actions; (2) those that may arise even if intermediate and final product markets are competitive; and (3) those that are

---

[1] See M. A. Adelman, "Integration and Antitrust Policy," *Harvard Law Review* 63 (November 1949), p. 27.

spawned by monopoly power at one or more of the stages of production.[2] In the following chapter, we investigate public policy in this area and provide a critique of the current policy.

In order to simplify our analysis, in this chapter we will limit the options available to the firm for the allocation of the intermediate product to two: market transactions and vertical integration. In practice, however, the firm faces a variety of other options that involve contractual agreements between upstream and downstream firms. Long-term contracts that specify prices, quantities, or a host of other performance criteria allow the firm at one stage of production to influence the behavior of firms at another stage without actually acquiring productive capacity at that stage. Through such agreements, then, firms are often able to achieve many of the same ends served by vertical ownership integration. The economics of vertical control through contract will be examined in four subsequent chapters.

11-2 VERTICAL INTEGRATION DUE TO GOVERNMENT ACTIONS

Governmental policies and programs often have pervasive effects upon business, which can lead to modification in the way that business is conducted. Our immediate concern is with government policies that lead to vertical integration. Although there may be many, we shall consider three examples: taxation, price controls, and regulation.

Taxation

If an external (market) transaction is taxed or penalized more than an internal (integrated) transaction, there will be an obvious incentive for vertical integration. For example, by removing the intermediate product transfer from the open market, vertical integration may insulate the transaction from sales taxes, thereby reducing the effective cost of the input to the downstream firm. In addition, the income of firms at different stages of production is sometimes taxed at different rates. When marginal tax rates depend upon the production level at which the profit is earned, vertical integration may permit some accounting adjustments that reduce overall taxes. In essence, vertical integration allows the firm to reallocate its income from the relatively higher taxed stage to the relatively lower taxed stage simply by charging itself an appropriate transfer price.[3] In order to shift income from the downstream stage to

---

[2] This organizational scheme was suggested by F. R. Warren–Boulton, *Vertical Control of Markets: Business and Labor Practice* (Cambridge, Mass.: Ballinger Publishing, 1978).

[3] The "transfer price" is the price of the intermediate product or service that the upstream division charges the downstream division in the firm's accounting records. Since the firm pays this price to itself, it obviously has no effect (other than the tax effect described above) on the overall profits of the integrated operation.

the upstream stage, the vertically integrated firm would employ a high transfer price for the intermediate good or service. A low transfer price shifts the firm's income in the opposite direction.

Common examples of this phenomenon involve multinational corporations that may be organized, in part, to exploit differential taxation. If tax rates are lower in a country where one stage of production takes place (e.g., raw material extraction) than in another country where some other stage of production is performed (e.g., fabrication), then the vertically integrated multinational firm may be able to reduce its overall tax burden through its choice of an appropriate transfer price.[4] In addition, some economists have argued that the depletion allowance that was applied to crude oil production for many years encouraged vertical integration in the petroleum industry.[5] By shifting income to the upstream (crude oil production) stage through its choice of a high transfer price to its own refineries, the vertically integrated firm could subject a greater portion of its overall income to the favorable tax treatment provided by the depletion allowance.

Price controls

From time to time, the government has imposed price controls on intermediate product markets for a variety of reasons, both political and economic. Under some circumstances, these controls can provide an economic incentive for vertical integration by the firms participating in these markets. Consider, for example, the market depicted in Figure 11–1. Suppose that this product is an intermediate good (e.g., crude oil) that is employed by a downstream industry (refining) in the production of some final product (gasoline). From microeconomic principles, we know that the derived demand curve for this input (D) represents the downstream producers' willingness to pay for each additional unit of this intermediate product at various levels of output.[6] The supply curve (S) represents the upstream producers' willingness to produce and sell additional quantities of the input at various prices.

Without any government intrusion, the supply of and the demand for the intermediate product are equal at a price of P_1 and a quantity of Q_1.

---

[4] In the situation described here, would a low or a high transfer price be to the firm's advantage? Why?

[5] See B. Bolch and W. W. Damon, "The Depletion Allowance and Vertical Integration in the Petroleum Industry," *Southern Economic Journal* 45, (July 1978), pp. 241–49. The depletion allowance ended in 1975 for large oil and gas producers.

[6] In fact, the derived demand for an input is equal to the value of the marginal product (or, in the case of monopoly at the downstream stage, the marginal revenue product) of the input. In either case, it is the addition to the downstream firm's revenues generated by the employment of an additional unit of the input. See C. E. Ferguson and S. C. Maurice, *Economic Analysis: Theory and Applications* (Homewood, Ill.: Richard D. Irwin, 1978), or almost any intermediate microeconomics text.

FIGURE 11–1

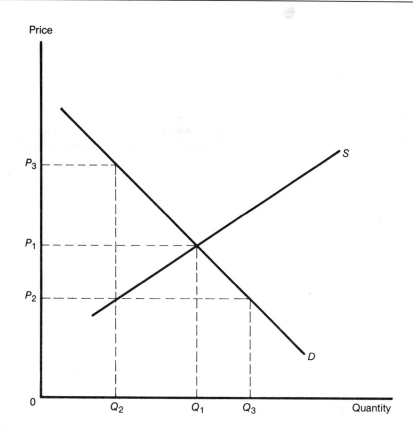

With the downstream firms' willingness to buy equated to the upstream firms' willingness to sell at P_2, no incentive for vertical integration exists. But, if the government decides, for whatever reason, that P_1 is too high, a ceiling price equal to P_2 may be imposed on the market. Now, at a price equal to P_2, only Q_2 units of output will be supplied by the upstream industry. This, of course, assumes that the governmental policy cannot (or does not) compel the upstream firms to supply quantities off the supply function. Generally, in an otherwise free market economy, this is a reasonable assumption.

Although only Q_2 will be supplied at P_2, the downstream industry would like to purchase Q_3 at this ceiling price. Thus, an excess demand of $Q_3 - Q_2$ is created. That is, buyers would like to purchase Q_3 units, but sellers are willing to provide only Q_2 units. Consequently, some buyers will be frustrated in their attempt to purchase the intermediate product as the upstream firms exercise some sort of nonprice rationing device.[7]

Looking again at Figure 11–1, when the supply of the intermediate product is limited to Q_2, downstream buyers are willing to pay as much as P_3 for the product. Then, if downstream firms can avoid rationing by vertically integrating backward into the supply of this intermediate product, the gap between the ceiling price, P_2, and the downstream firm's willingness to pay, P_3, creates an incentive for such vertical integration. As integration proceeds, more and more transactions are removed from the market and thereby are rendered immune to the price controls. Eventually, all downstream firms will integrate backward, and the open market for this intermediate product will cease to exist.[8] At that point, the internal (effective) transfer price will gravitate toward P_1, and the quantity transferred from the integrated firms' upstream divisions to their downstream divisions will expand to Q_1. Consequently, the price control can be rendered ineffective through vertical integration.

In order to analyze the social welfare effects of vertical integration that result from the evasion of price controls, one must consider the social welfare effects of the price controls that are being circumvented as well as any costs or benefits attributable to the vertical integration itself. If the price controls are socially beneficial (a rather dubious presumption) and vertical integration increases the costs of production through, for instance, managerial diseconomies, then integration spawned by this incentive reduces overall social welfare. But if the price controls were, in fact, an ill-advised response to political pressures (perhaps a more plausible presumption), then vertical integration that renders them ineffective could improve overall social welfare even if production costs are thereby increased. Clearly, the social welfare effects cannot, in general, be determined on a priori grounds.

Regulation

A natural monopoly can be said to exist when the production technology and market demand are such that a single firm can produce a sufficient quantity of output to satisfy the entire market demand and still be on the declining portion of its long-run average cost curve.[9] Figure

---

[7] What sorts of rationing devices are employed in practice to allocate available supply in the face of excess demand?

[8] This tendency for the intermediate product market to disappear because of complete vertical integration (by which we mean downstream firms produce all their requirements of the intermediate good internally) under rationing is analyzed formally in J. R. Green, "Vertical Integration and Assurance of Markets," Harvard Institute of Economic Research, Discussion Paper Number 383, October 1974.

[9] This is a sufficient but not a necessary condition for natural monopoly to exist. The necessary condition carries the somewhat weaker requirement that one firm be able to produce enough to satisfy market demand at a lower cost than could two or more firms. See Chapter 3 for a brief discussion of the theory of natural monopolies.

FIGURE 11-2

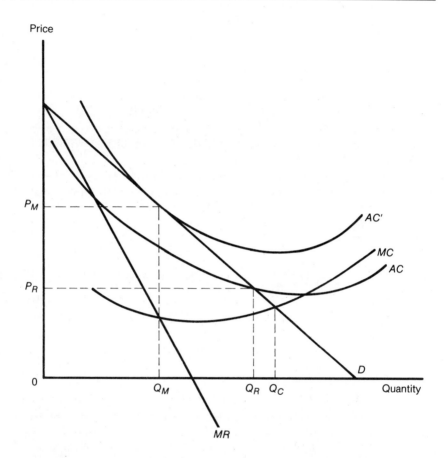

11-2 depicts the natural monopoly situation. Here, the market demand curve is given as D with associated marginal revenue MR. The natural monopolist's long-run average cost curve is AC, and long-run marginal costs are MC.

In the case of natural monopoly, a public policy of antitrust enforcement is fruitless. The *natural* market structure is monopoly in the sense that the process of competition leads to losses for all firms in the industry. As long as competitive pricing persists (i.e., prices are equal to marginal costs), these losses will continue. This is apparent in Figure 11-2 because marginal cost is below average cost at all levels of output that consumers would be willing to take off the market with price equal to marginal cost. These losses induce exit from the industry, and eventually, there will be only one firm left.

This remaining firm would then be a monopolist and could price its product above marginal cost in order to maximize its profits. Such behavior would lead the firm to produce the monopoly output, Q_M, and charge the monopoly price, P_M, as shown in Figure 11–2. Since P_M exceeds the firm's average costs at the monopoly output, this firm could earn positive economic profits.

The traditional public policy response to a natural monopoly situation has been to grant some firm an exclusive franchise to participate in the industry and, in exchange for this franchise, impose regulations on the firm's operations.[10] In setting the price that the regulated firm is allowed to charge, the objective generally has been to approve a price (or price schedule) that is sufficiently high to generate just enough revenue to provide the firm with a competitive rate of return at the market-clearing output. This means that the regulators attempt to set the price at the point where the firm's long-run average cost curve intersects the market demand curve. Such a price is shown as P_R in Figure 11–2. At P_R, the regulated firm earns the competitive ("normal" or "fair") rate of return on its invested capital, which implies that it earns zero economic profit.[11]

Regulation of this sort, which is referred to as rate of return regulation and is designed to curb the output restriction of a profit-maximizing monopolist, can create an incentive for backward vertical integration by the regulated firm.[12] Specifically, if the regulated firm can completely integrate backward into an unregulated input supply industry, it can, by charging itself a high enough transfer price, inflate its average costs at the downstream (regulated) stage to AC' in Figure 11–2. If regulators are sufficiently myopic, they will now set the regulated price at P_M, the profit-maximizing monopoly price. The regulated division of the vertically integrated firm will earn zero economic profit, but the input supply division will collect the full monopoly profit. Thus, through the selection of an appropriate transfer price, the regulated firm can shift the locus of excess profits from its regulated business to its unregulated subsidiary and thereby circumvent the effect of rate of return regulation. Consumers end up buying the monopoly output at the monopoly price.[13]

---

[10] Generally, the government agrees to refrain from antitrust action against the monopolist and to protect the firm from entry by potential competitors. In exchange, the government claims the right to set prices and to require that output satisfy market demand at those prices, review investment plans, and generally oversee the operations to try to ensure socially acceptable performance.

[11] Also note that, at P_R, the firm produces output equal to Q_R. This output is closer to (but still short of) the competitive output, shown as Q_C, than is the unregulated monopolist's output Q_M.

[12] A rigorous treatment of backward vertical integration by a regulated monopolist is provided in D. Dayan, "Behavior of the Firm under Regulatory Constraint: A Reexamination," *Industrial Organization Review* 3 (1975), pp. 61–76.

[13] Bell Telephone was a regulated natural monopoly that had integrated backward into the supply of telephone equipment. It bought its equipment from its wholly owned subsidiary, Western Electric.

This possibility, of course, has been recognized by regulatory authorities, and they go to great lengths to prevent the avoidance of regulation. Basically, two alternative approaches are available. First, regulators may simply prohibit backward integration by the regulated firm. And second, regulation may be extended to cover the transfer price of the internally supplied input. The first approach runs the risk that possible economies of vertical integration (which we will discuss later in this chapter) may be lost, thereby increasing costs in the regulated industry. The second approach, however, involves the imposition of regulation on an industry that may not be a natural monopoly. Since regulation itself is not costless, the extension of the regulatory constraint to an additional stage of production is certain to increase society's costs.[14] Consequently, the socially optimal policy response involves selecting the alternative that increases costs less than the others, and this cannot be determined on purely theoretical grounds. Specific features of the regulated industry must be examined to determine whether economies of vertical integration are likely to be realized and whether such economies outweigh the incremental cost of extending the regulatory network to an additional stage of production.

11–3 VERTICAL INTEGRATION WITH COMPETITIVE MARKETS

Incentives for vertical integration can arise when intermediate product markets are competitively organized, even in the absence of any incentives provided by government actions. Assuming that neither buyers nor sellers of an input are able to exercise any monopoly power, vertical integration can, under certain conditions, improve the firms' profits. Generally, we shall see that vertical integration under these circumstances also has a positive effect on consumer welfare (i.e., results in lower prices for the final product). Therefore, with both consumers and producers made better off, vertical integration that occurs in response to these incentives must improve overall social welfare. In this section, we shall discuss two such incentives: technological interdependencies and transaction costs.

Technological interdependencies

Many production processes involve a flow in which inputs are combined in a virtually continuous movement toward the final product, such as an assembly line in an automobile manufacturing plant. To break this flow by imposing an intermediate product market at some

---

[14] A typical rate case for a moderately large electric utility, for instance, costs between $300,000 and $500,000 in out-of-pocket expenses and may run double that amount when fixed costs such as staff salaries are counted. See "Legal Expenses and Utility Ratemaking," *Public Utilities Fortnightly* 102 (October 26, 1978), pp. 58–60.

point would likely increase the overall costs of production by adding transportation, handling, and start-up charges. In other processes, more distinct stages of production can be discerned, but certain physical relationships exist between these stages which make it cheaper for one firm to carry out the successive tasks internally. For instance, in the steel industry, blast furnaces, converters, and reduction mills are typically owned by a single firm. This vertical integration of the successive stages minimizes production costs by avoiding the necessity of reheating the steel as it moves from one stage to the next.

In principle, the market mechanism could be employed in either of the above situations to allocate the intermediate products between the separate stages. The degree of coordination required between these stages to minimize costs, however, would place a severe strain on real world markets. The contractual arrangements that would be required to achieve such coordination would be prohibitively complex, and the enforcement of these arrangements would also contribute to cost increases. Thus, vertical integration under these conditions reduces costs and should not be discouraged by public policy.

Transaction costs

Transaction costs refer to any expenditure of resources associated with the use of the market mechanism in transferring a good or service from one party to another. Keep in mind that since we are discussing the use of the market in lieu of vertical integration, we must be referring to intermediate product markets where upstream producers sell some input to downstream producers. Ronald Coase described three categories of costs (in addition to governmentally imposed costs such as sales taxes) that are associated with use of the price system.[15]

First, there are search costs that must be borne in order to discover the relevant prices. Since it is in the buyer's interest to pay the lowest price possible and in the seller's interest to charge the highest price possible, both parties involved in a given transaction must carry out some search activity in order to ensure that they are not being taken advantage of by the other party. A sizable portion of the budgets of the purchasing and marketing departments of many corporations may be due to the presence of search costs involved in buying inputs and selling outputs.

Second, use of the market mechanism often necessitates the negotiation (and, later, enforcement) of contracts that stipulate precisely what

---

[15] See R. H. Coase, "The Nature of the Firm," *Economica* 4 (November 1937), pp. 386–405. A later, more extended treatment of this same topic is provided in O. E. Williamson, *Markets and Hierarchies: Analysis and Antitrust Implications* (New York: Free Press, 1975).

the buyer and seller are agreeing to do. These contracts often specify not only the price and quantity of the product to be traded, but also such myriad items as product quality, warranties, delivery dates, buy-back agreements, escalator clauses, and so on. Careful elaboration of all such items affecting the sale is required to ensure that both parties will live up to the terms of the agreement because performance incentives may change drastically after the sale. Generally, the longer the term of such contracts, the greater will be the costs of negotiation and enforcement.

And third, in addition to negotiation and enforcement costs, there are costs of reduced flexibility associated with market transactions that make use of long-term contracts. If the market price of the input falls during the term of the contract, the buyer will bear an opportunity cost in being unable to take advantage of the lower price due to the contractual obligation to purchase the input at the higher price specified in the contract. A similar opportunity cost will be borne by the seller of the input if the market price increases unexpectedly during the term of the contract. Changes in market conditions involving aspects other than price (e.g., the introduction of a superior intermediate product) can impose analogous costs on either party. The basic point here is that, by entering into the contractual agreement, each party locks itself into a predetermined pattern of behavior in order to assure the other party that it has not misrepresented its intended postsale performance. An unexpected alteration of market conditions often makes this behavior costly.

Vertical integration, by replacing the system of market exchanges with internal transfers, may reduce substantially these transactions costs. Instead of having buyers and sellers negotiate the sale of an intermediate product, we have managers arrange for the transfer of this product from the upstream division to the downstream division of the integrated firm. As Oliver Williamson has persuasively argued, this replacement of market by bureaucratic allocation devices can be expected to result in a reduction of transaction costs for two fundamental reasons.[16]

First, internalization of the transfer alters the relationship between the affected parties (buyer and seller) from one of being largely adversaries to one of being partners. Without vertical integration, one firm often stands to gain profits at the expense of the other firm. If firm A can increase its profits by $1 by pursuing a certain course of action, it may be expected to do so even if such action reduces firm B's profits by $100. Williamson refers to this sort of behavior as opportunistic. By joining together the profits of the two firms, vertical integration brings about a

---

[16] See O. E. Williamson, "The Economics of Antitrust: Transaction Cost Considerations," *University of Pennsylvania Law Review* 122 (May 1974), pp. 1439–96; and O. E. Williamson, "The Vertical Integration of Production: Market Failure Considerations," *American Economic Review* 61 (May 1971), pp. 112–23.

convergence of goals and thereby eliminates (or greatly reduces) the incentive for such behavior. This, in turn, reduces the costs of completing the given transaction because the parties involved will no longer find it necessary to expend resources designing and negotiating contracts to protect themselves from the opportunism of the other party.

The second reason that vertical integration is expected to reduce transaction costs is that the incentive and control options available to the firm are much more extensive for intrafirm as opposed to interfirm transfers. It is far easier for the manager of a firm to discover and, as necessary, reward or penalize the behavior of employees than it is to exercise similar controls over the behavior of another firm. In the former case, access to the relevant data (e.g., through internal audits) is improved, and rewards or penalties (e.g., through promotions, firings) are more easily administered. In the latter case, discovery of opportunistic behavior is relatively costly, and haggling or litigation may be the only means available for encouraging more desirable performance. Consequently, vertical integration increases the amount of information available to the parties to the transaction and sharpens the incentives of all parties to behave in a manner that promotes the profitability of the overall operation. The net effect of the added information and improved incentive structure is a reduction in the costs of carrying out the transfer of the intermediate product from upstream to downstream producers.

Since transaction costs are associated with most real world markets, the incentive to integrate which stems from this source is expected to be pervasive. Yet firms do continue to utilize intermediate product markets. This is because vertical integration may itself increase the firm's costs. Expanding the firm's operations to an additional industry increases the problems of coordinating all of the firm's production activities. As more and more intermediate products are brought within the firm's control, efficient management of the total operation becomes increasingly difficult. Eventually, the additional costs of trying to coordinate one more stage of production will exceed the transaction cost savings that result from internalization of this additional stage. At that point, the firm will refrain from further vertical integration and will make use of the intermediate product market for the allocation of this input. Thus, while transaction costs provide a major incentive to vertically integrate, managerial diseconomies of scale place a limit on the extent to which such integration will occur.

Clearly, where vertical integration occurs in response to the presence of transaction costs, social welfare is improved by such integration. Cost reductions that do not themselves lead to any increase in market power will result in price reductions for final product consumers. Both producers and consumers can be made better off by avoidance of the costs of using the market mechanism to transfer the intermediate product from one stage of production to the next. Consequently, public policy should do nothing to discourage vertical integration under these circumstances.

11–4   MONOPOLY AND VERTICAL INTEGRATION

Although it is probably true that more vertical integration occurs in response to transaction cost considerations than for any other single reason, a disproportionate share of the economics literature has been devoted to analyses of the incentives for and effects of vertical integration that occurs in response to market power at one or more of the stages of production.[17] This focusing of attention on what may well be an empirically less prominent source of observed behavior may be explained by the greater and more complex policy implications that are raised when vertical integration is combined with monopoly power. As we shall see, the presence of market power can lead to a variety of specific incentives to integrate vertically, and the social welfare implications of the vertical integration that results from these incentives vary greatly from one situation to the next.

In the sections that follow, we shall examine six different incentives to vertically integrate that depend upon the presence of market power at one or more of the vertically related stages of production. In order to keep our attention focused on the economic aspects of vertical integration, we shall assume throughout this section that the monopoly power that provides the underlying incentive to integrate is legal (e.g., due to a patent). Otherwise, the appropriate antitrust policy would be to attack the horizontal market power directly through dissolution of the monopoly, regardless of the vertical structure of the industry. Thus, unless we assume that the monopoly power in question is immune to antitrust attack, the social welfare effects of vertical integration itself are without interest. We turn now to the specific models.

Successive monopoly

We begin our analysis with a model in which no incentive to vertically integrate exists. To generate such a model, we must make certain assumptions about the market structure and production technology at each stage of production. Assume, then, that we have two vertically related stages of production. In the first stage, an intermediate product, A, is manufactured. In the second stage, this intermediate product is used to produce a final product, X. Initially, we assume that both indus-

---

[17] After reviewing the incentive to integrate that is provided by rate of return regulation, one author writes: "While I do not wish to minimize the importance of such considerations in individual industries, I submit that these are rather special cases and that the main incentive for vertical integration is that integration serves to economize on transaction costs." See O. E. Williamson, "The Economics of Antitrust: Transaction Cost Considerations," *University of Pennsylvania Law Review* 122 (May 1974), p. 1461.

tries (A and X) are competitive, that they exhibit constant marginal costs, and that the production of one unit of X requires exactly one unit of the input A.[18]

That this set of assumptions leads to no incentive for vertical integration is demonstrated in Figure 11–3.[19] Here, we measure the quantities

---

FIGURE 11–3

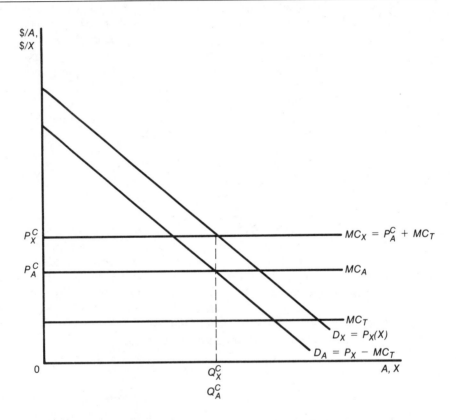

---

of both A and X on the horizontal axis (keeping in mind that $A = X$), and we measure prices and marginal costs on the vertical axis. The curve labeled D_X represents the total market demand for the final product. The

---

[18] We also assume zero transaction costs. The assumption of constant marginal cost and the assumption that the constant input-output ratio is equal to one are made for simplicity of exposition and are not crucial to the analysis. A useful example of fixed proportions production involves retailing. For each TV set that is sold at retail, one TV set must be manufactured.

[19] The analysis here draws heavily from J. J. Spengler, "Vertical Integration and Antitrust Policy," *Journal of Political Economy* 58 (August 1950), pp. 347–52.

marginal cost of producing the intermediate product A is given by MC_A, and the marginal cost of transforming one unit of this intermediate product into one unit of the final product X is MC_T. The marginal cost of producing output X, then, is the vertical summation of the price that the downstream producer must pay for the intermediate product A plus the marginal cost of transforming this input into output. Therefore, the marginal cost of output X is given by

$$MC_X = P_A^c + MC_T \qquad (11\text{--}1)$$

With competition at the downstream stage, the final product X will be priced at its marginal cost MC_X. The total industry output will then be given by Q_X^c in the graph.

The derived demand for the intermediate product A is found by subtracting the marginal cost of transforming A into X, MC_T, from the final output price. Thus, the derived demand for A is given by

$$D_A = P_X - MC_T \qquad (11\text{--}2)$$

With competition at the upstream stage, the price of the intermediate product will equal its marginal cost ($P_A^c = MC_A$), and the competitive output Q_A^c will be produced.

If producers of input A were to vertically integrate with the producers of output X, no change in the market outcome would result. If the market for X remains competitive, price will continue to equal MC_X. Under vertical integration, MC_X will equal the vertical summation of MC_A and MC_T. But since $P_A^c = MC_A$ without integration, MC_X will not be affected by vertical integration. Moreover, with output price equated to constant marginal (and, therefore, average) cost, economic profits are zero with or without vertical integration. Consequently, no incentive to integrate exists.

Now, suppose that the upstream industry is monopolized. If all of our other previous assumptions continue to hold, there will still be no incentive for vertical integration. Figure 11–4 demonstrates this result. Here, we have reproduced D_X, D_A, MC_T, MC_A, and MC_X from Figure 11–3. With monopoly in the production of the intermediate product A, the upstream producer will no longer equate price to marginal cost but will instead choose that level of output where marginal revenue is equal to marginal cost. The marginal revenue of the derived demand for input A is given as MR_A in the graph. The nonintegrated intermediate product monopolist will, therefore, produce Q_A^M units of output and will charge P_A^M per unit. As a result, this firm will earn a positive economic profit equal to

$$\pi_A = (P_A^M - MC_A)Q_A^M \qquad (11\text{--}3)$$

FIGURE 11–4

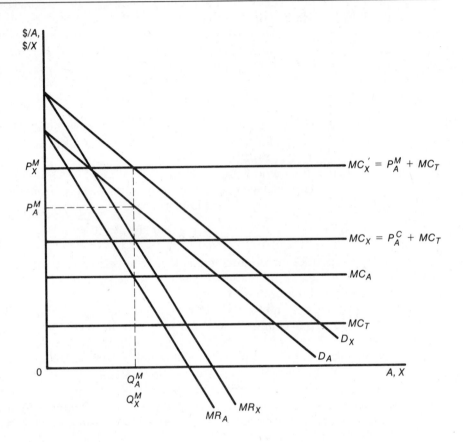

The downstream producers of final product X will now have marginal costs equal to

$$MC'_X = P^M_A + MC_T \qquad (11\text{–}4)$$

and will, therefore, be forced to price X at P^M_X. Profits at this downstream stage remain at zero.

If the upstream monopolist were to vertically integrate, then the final product industry would be monopolized. The integrated monopolist would then produce that level of final output for which the marginal revenue of the final product (given as MR_X in the graph) is equal to the marginal cost of the integrated operation, which is MC_X. Thus, the vertically integrated monopolist would produce Q^M_X and charge P^M_X, which is the same output and price that resulted in the nonintegrated case. Profits from this integrated operation are

$$\pi_X = (P_X^M - MC_X)Q_X^M \qquad (11\text{--}5)$$

which are equal to the profits of a nonintegrated input monopolist that sells its output to a competitively organized final product industry.[20] Therefore, there is no incentive for an input monopolist to integrate forward when the downstream industry is competitive and subject to a production technology that requires a fixed quantity of the input for each unit of output.

Suppose now, however, that we have *successive monopoly*. That is, both the A industry and the X industry are monopolized but are not vertically integrated. In addition, suppose that the X monopolist exercises no monopsony power in purchasing the A input (i.e., the downstream firm accepts the price of the intermediate product as a parameter). Under these conditions, an incentive exists for either the upstream or the downstream firm to integrate. That is, both firms can increase their profits through vertical integration.

This case is depicted in Figure 11–5, which reproduces the basic demand and cost curves of Figures 11–3 and 11–4. With monopoly at the downstream stage, the effective demand for input A becomes the MR_A curve, and the corresponding marginal curve is MMR_A.[21] The reason for this is that the final product monopolist will produce where its marginal cost is equal to its marginal revenue. But the downstream firm's marginal cost is the price that this firm must pay for the intermediate product plus the marginal cost of transforming this intermediate product into a unit of final output. Thus, for any given price of input A, the downstream firm will purchase an amount that is given by the intersection of MR_X with this price plus MC_T. Consequently, $MR_X - MC_T = MR_A$ is the downstream firm's derived demand for input A. The A monopolist's effective marginal revenue, then, is MMR_A.

---

[20] To show the equality of profits under the integrated and nonintegrated market structures, we need to show that $\pi_A = \pi_X$. Substituting from equations (11–4) and (11–5), this requires that $(P_A^M - MC_A)Q_A^M = (P_X^M - MC_X)Q_X^M$. We know that $Q_A^M = Q_X^M$ by our assumption regarding the production technology. Thus, the above equality requires that $P_A^M - MC_A = P_X^M - MC_X$. From Figure 11–4, we know that $P_X^M = P_A^M + MC_T$, and $MC_X = MC_A + MC_T$ (since $P_A^C = MC_A$). Substituting these on the right-hand side of the above equality, we have $P_A^M - MC_A = P_A^M + MC_T - MC_A - MC_T$ or $P_A^M - MC_A = P_A^M - MC_A$, which completes the proof.

[21] The downstream monopolist will equate MR_X with MC_X. But with the upstream monopolist charging the monopoly price for the intermediate product, $MC_X = P_A^M + MC_T$. Thus, $MR_X = P_A^M + MC_T$ or $P_A^M = MR_X - MC_T$. Thus, the derived demand for input A is the marginal revenue curve for output X minus the marginal cost of transforming A into X, which is the marginal revenue curve for input A that would result if the downstream industry were competitive, MR_A. The curve marginal to this, MMR_A, then, is the marginal revenue of input A with monopoly at the downstream stage.

FIGURE 11–5

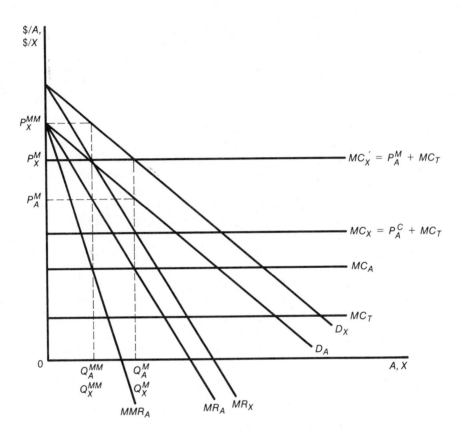

To maximize its profits, the upstream monopolist equates MMR_A with MC_A and produces Q_A^{MM} in the successive monopoly case. The input monopolist then charges the downstream firm a price equal to P_A^M for the intermediate product.[22] The downstream monopolist then experiences marginal costs equal to $MC_X' = P_A^M + MC_T$. To maximize its profits, the X monopolist equates the marginal cost to its marginal revenue MR_X, producing Q_A^{MM} units of final output. Thus, with a separate monopolist at each of the two successive stages of production, consumers are worse off than they were with a single monopolist at either stage or an inte-

---

[22] Note that this price is equal to the price charged when the input monopolist sold its output to a competitive downstream industry, though output is cut in half. This result is not general but is due to the assumption that MC_A is constant and the fact that, with linear demand, D_A and MR_A have the same elasticity at any given price.

grated monopolist that controls both stages. Final output price is higher, and quantity is lower.

In addition, the sum of the profits of the two separate monopolists is less than the profits that could be earned by a single vertically integrated monopolist. Under successive monopoly, the A monopolist earns profits of

$$\pi_A^{MM} = (P_A^M - MC_A)Q_A^{MM} \tag{11-6}$$

and the X monopolist earns profits of

$$\pi_X^{MM} = (P_X^{MM} - MC_X')Q_X^{MM} \tag{11-7}$$

Since $MC_A = MC_X - MC_T$ and $MC_X' = P_A^M + MC_T$, the total profits of the two firms combined are

$$\pi_A^{MM} + \pi_X^{MM} = (P_X^{MM} - MC_X)Q_X^{MM} \tag{11-8}$$

Comparing the areas indicated by equations (11–5) and (11–8) in Figure 11–5, it is clear that

$$\pi_X > \pi_A^{MM} + \pi_X^{MM} \tag{11-9}$$

That is, the profits earned by a single integrated monopolist exceed the total profits that can be earned by two successive monopolists.[23] Consequently, given the successive monopoly situation, there will be a profit incentive for the two firms to integrate.

Thus, under successive monopoly, vertical integration increases total profits while reducing output price and increasing the quantity of the final product sold. Both producers and consumers are made better off through vertical integration. Clearly, public policy should do nothing to discourage vertical integration of this sort.

For many years, several economists were willing to halt the analysis of vertical integration at this point and recommend an overall antitrust policy that, at best, looks favorably upon vertical integration and, at worst, ignores it. The basic argument used to support this policy recommendation is that (1) in the absence of successive monopoly, the only reason that firms will vertically integrate is to reduce transaction costs; and (2) with successive monopoly, social welfare is unambiguously improved by vertical integration. Therefore, any vertical integration that occurs is socially beneficial and should not be discouraged. While there is still some justification to support this general attitude, more recent analyses of the incentive to integrate when monopoly power exists at one or more of the vertically related stages of production have caused this overall policy recommendation to be tempered somewhat. We turn now to these other analyses.

---

[23] See the Appendix to this chapter for a numerical example.

Upstream monopoly with variable input proportions

Above, we found that an input monopolist has no incentive to integrate forward into the production of the final commodity when the downstream industry is competitive and subject to a production technology that requires a fixed quantity of the intermediate product per unit of final output. Suppose now, however, that the competitive downstream industry is able to combine the monopolized input A, in variable proportions with some other input, B, that is competitively supplied. That is, for any given level of final output, X, downstream producers are able to employ various combinations of inputs A and B. This is known as a variable proportions production technology and is generally descriptive of most real world production processes. There are few inputs for which no substitution opportunities exist, at least in the long run.

The introduction of input substitutability at the downstream stage creates a definite incentive for an intermediate good monopolist to vertically integrate forward.[24] This incentive is most easily explained with the aid of Figure 11–6. Here, we have drawn an isoquant representing all combinations of inputs A and B that may be employed by the downstream industry in producing a final output of x_0 units. Given a competitive price for input B and a monopolistic price for input A, the downstream industry will face the isocost curve DD', where the slope of this curve is given by $-P_A^M/MC_B$.[25]

Faced with these input prices, the downstream industry will minimize the cost of producing x_0 units of final output by selecting the input combination indicated at point Z where the relevant isocost curve is tangent to the x_0 isoquant. Since the intercept of the isocost curve on the B axis at point D shows how many units of B could be purchased if downstream producers expend all of their costs on input B (purchasing none of input A), the height of this intercept may be used to measure the level of costs represented by any given isocost curve in units of input B.

The isocost curve given by EE' goes through point Z but has a slope reflecting the input price ratio that would result if both inputs were competitively priced (i.e., the slope of EE' is $-MC_A/MC_B$). The vertical intercept of this isocost curve on the B axis at point E indicates the total cost of producing x_0 units of final output (measured in units of B) if input A's price falls to its marginal cost and the same input combination as before is employed. Since the entire difference in isocost curves DD'

---

[24] This incentive to vertically integrate was originally described in Meyer L. Burstein, "A Theory of Full-Line Forcing," *Northwestern University Law Review* 55 (March/April 1960), pp. 62–95. It was rediscovered and graphically analyzed in John M. Vernon and Daniel A. Graham, "Profitability of Monopolization by Vertical Integration," *Journal of Political Economy* 79 (September/October 1971), pp. 924–25.

[25] With the price of A equal to P_A^M and B priced at MC_B, the total cost of producing X is $C = (P_A^M \cdot A) + (MC_B \cdot B)$. Holding this cost constant at C_0 and solving for B, the equation of the isocost curve is $B = C_0/MC_B - (P_A^M/MC_B) \cdot A$.

FIGURE 11–6

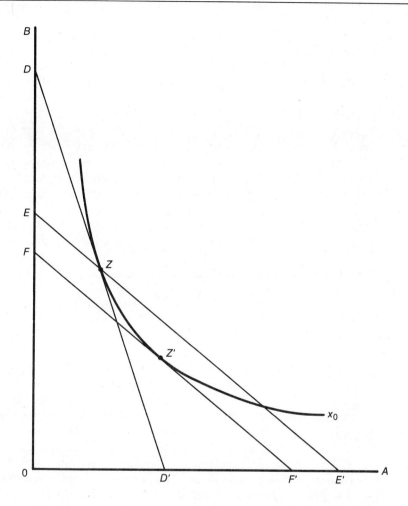

and EE' is due to the monopolistic price increase for input A, the difference between the vertical intercepts of these two curves (i.e., $D - E$) measures the A input monopolist's profits in units of B in the absence of vertical integration.[26] In other words, the downstream industry experiences a total cost of E when input combination Z is employed to produce x_0 and input A is priced at marginal cost. These costs increase to D when A's price is raised to the monopoly level and the same input combination

---

[26] Since the intercept of a given isocost curve is C_0/MC_B, this measure of the monopolist's profits could be translated into dollars simply by multiplying by MC_B.

is used. Since the price of input B remains the same in both cases, this cost difference corresponds to the total profits earned by the A monopolist (in units of B) from selling its output to the competitive downstream industry.

Suppose, now, that the A monopolist integrates forward into the production of final output X. Also, suppose that such integration is complete (i.e., the final product market is monopolized by the upstream firm).[27] If the integrated monopolist decides to continue producing X_0 units of final output, it will now employ the input combination indicated at point Z' where the FF' isocost curve is tangent to the x_0 isoquant. This alteration of input combinations occurs because the input mix indicated at point Z is inefficient. It resulted from the competitive producers substituting away from the relatively higher-priced input A. By shifting to input combination Z', the vertically integrated firm increases the efficiency of input utilization at the downstream stage and thereby reduces the cost of producing x_0 units of final output. Due to this cost reduction, the monopolist's profits, measured in units of B, increase from $D - E$ to $D - F$. Consequently, the increase in profits attributable to vertical integration is given by $E - F$.[28] This increase provides the incentive for vertical integration by an input monopolist when the final good production process is characterized by variable input proportions.

The social welfare effects of vertical integration in this model are indeterminate on theoretical grounds.[29] At the final product stage, we have traded a competitive market for a monopolistic market with lower costs. The welfare effects of this trade may be positive or negative, depending primarily on the elasticity of demand for the final good and the extent of the cost reduction experienced. Consequently, in the absence of more specific information on the actual market demand curve and the production technology at the downstream stage, we cannot say whether vertical integration by an input monopolist is socially beneficial. The mere possibility that negative welfare effects will arise, however, casts some doubt on the advisability of adopting a public policy that either encourages or ignores completely vertical integration by an intermediate product monopolist.

---

[27] Richard Schmalensee, "A Note on the Theory of Vertical Integration," *Journal of Political Economy* 81 (March/April 1973), pp. 442–49, shows that, in the variable proportions model, the upstream monopolist will have an incentive to completely monopolize the downstream industry.

[28] This increase in profits is a lower-bound measure of the actual increase attainable. This is because we are holding final output constant under the two alternative market structures. If the monopolist finds it optimal to alter the level of final output after vertical integration, the actual increase in profit will exceed $E - F$.

[29] See Frederick R. Warren-Boulton, "Vertical Control with Variable Proportions," *Journal of Political Economy* 82 (July–August 1974), pp. 783–802; and Fred M. Westfield, "Vertical Integration: Does Product Price Rise or Fall?" *American Economic Review* 71 (June 1981), pp. 334–46.

Disequilibrium and vertical integration

As a general principle, all firms have an economic interest in the performance of industries with which they deal either as buyers or sellers. Poor performances at one stage of production can devalue the assets of firms at another stage. When that occurs, the firm or firms suffering the damage may be able to take some corrective actions to improve industry performance at the related stage. In particular, when a competitive industry fails to achieve a position of long-run equilibrium following some exogenous change in market demand, profits at some vertically related stage of production may be affected. This, in turn, may create an incentive for vertical integration by the affected firm or firms.

Assume that we have an intermediate product monopolist that sells its output to a competitively structured final good industry. To abstract from any additional incentive for vertical integration provided by variable proportions production at the downstream stage, we shall assume that the final good industry employs the monopolized intermediate good, A, in fixed proportion to final output, X. The individual firms' marginal and average costs of transforming the input A into output X, however, are assumed to be U-shaped. Thus, while each unit of final output requires a fixed number of units of input A, transformation costs per unit change as more output is produced, first falling and then rising.

If the downstream competitive industry is in a position of long-run equilibrium, then the market clearing price (where quantity demanded equals quantity supplied) will be equal to the minimum point on the long-run average cost curve for every firm in the industry. At such an equilibrium, there will be no incentive for the intermediate product monopolist to vertically integrate forward. This result was demonstrated in the section above that dealt with the successive monopoly model and need not be repeated here.

Suppose, however, that an exogenous increase in final good demand occurs and that because of imperfect information, frictions, or the inherent inertia of productive resources, the necessary entry required to restore long-run equilibrium at the downstream stage is not immediately forthcoming. Then, the input monopolist will have an incentive to integrate forward into the production of final output. To show this result, we make use of Figures 11–7 and 11–8.

The first figure demonstrates the outcomes experienced by the individual firms and the total industry at the final product stage, while the second figure depicts the implications of these outcomes for the upstream monopolist. In Figure 11–7, we show the individual firms' long-run average and short-run marginal cost curves and output in panel (a), and the total industry demand and short-run supply curves are shown in panel (b).

FIGURE 11-7

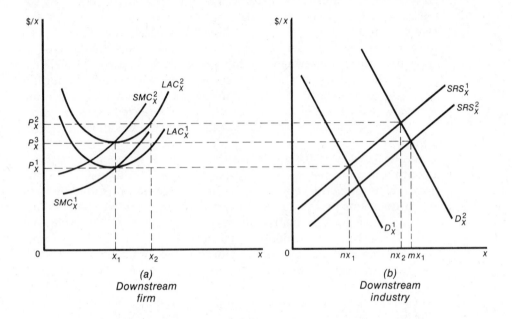

(a)
Downstream
firm

(b)
Downstream
industry

The original equilibrium price is given by P_X^1, where the market demand curve D_X^1 intersects the industry short-run supply curve SRS_X^1.
The individual firms' long-run average and short-run marginal cost
curves are given as LAC_X^1 and SMC_X^1, respectively. Thus, each of the n
firms in the industry produces X_1 units of final output and earns zero
economic profit, and the total industry output of nx_1 clears the market at
the equilibrium price P_X^1.

This equilibrium at the downstream stage will generate a derived
demand curve for the monopolized intermediate product A. In order to
keep Figure 11-8 as uncluttered as possible, we do not draw this original
demand for A. At this point, suffice it to say that the upstream monopolist, which we assume experiences constant marginal costs equal to
MC_A, will produce where marginal revenue from the derived demand
curve equals MC_A. The profit maximizing monopoly price of input A,
then, is already reflected in the cost curves of firms at the downstream
stage (i.e., LAC_X^1 and SMC_X^1 incorporate the price of input A).

Now, suppose that market demand at the downstream stage increases to D_X^2 in panel (b) of Figure 11-7. In the short run (i.e., with no
entry of new firms at the downstream stage), the market clearing price
of the final product will increase to P_X^2 where the new demand curve
intersects the original short-run supply curve, SRS_X^1. This increase in

FIGURE 11–8

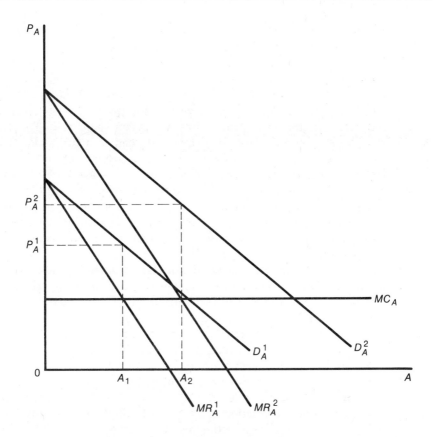

price will lead the individual firms in the industry to expand their output to x_2, moving along their respective short-run marginal cost curves in panel (a). This expansion of each of the n firms' output from x_1 to x_2 accounts for the expansion of total industry output from nx_1 to nx_2.[30] This output expansion at the downstream stage shifts the derived demand curve for the monopolized input outward to D_A^1 in Figure 11–8. The upstream monopolist, then, maximizes profits by producing A_1 units of the intermediate product which are sold at P_A^1 to the downstream firms. This firm's profits, then, are given by the area $(P_A^1 - MC_A)A_1$.

---

[30] Actually, as downstream firms expand output from x_1, the upstream monopolist's derived demand curve will shift outward, and the profit-maximizing price of input A will increase. This, in turn, will cause an upward shift in the individual firms' cost curves in Figure 11–7(a). We abstract from this adjustment here to keep our analysis as uncluttered as possible.

Notice, however, that firms at the downstream stage are also earning economic profits while the industry is in short-run (but not in long-run) equilibrium. These profits will equal the difference between P_X^2 and short-run average costs (which are not shown but must be less than P_X^2) times output x_2 for each firm. The existence of these profits will attract the entry of new firms at the downstream stage *if entry barriers are absent.* Such entry, if it occurs, will cause the short-run industry supply curve in panel *(b)* of Figure 11–7 to shift outward to SRS_X^2 pushing the market clearing price of the final product downward to P_X^3 and the market clearing output upward to mx_1, where m is the number of firms in the industry after the entry process has run its course $(m > n)$. This entry of new firms at the downstream stage will lead to a further shift in the derived demand curve for the monopolized input to D_A^2 in Figure 11–8, increasing the intermediate good monopolist's profits to $(P_A^2 - MC_A)A_2$. The new higher price for the monopolized input, P_A^2, shifts the downstream firms' cost curves upward to LAC_X^2 and SMC_X^2 in panel *(a)* of Figure 11–7. At that point, profits at the downstream stage are eliminated and the final good industry is restored to a position of long-run equilibrium.

Suppose, however, that some barriers to entry prevent the adjustment process described above from taking place so that the downstream industry remains in short-run equilibrium for an extended period with n firms each producing x_2 units of output at price P_X^2. It is clear from the above analysis that this failure of the final good industry to adjust back to a position of long-run competitive equilibrium reduces the profits available to the intermediate good monopolist. The additional profits that result from the expansion of output that entry brings about at the downstream stage provide an incentive for the upstream firm to enter into final good production (i.e., to vertically integrate forward). Although all owners of productive resources have an incentive to enter the downstream industry in order to share in the profits that exist at that stage during the period of adjustment back to long-run equilibrium, the monopolist input supplier has the *additional* incentive provided by the expansion of derived demand. Consequently, where significant barriers to entry exist, they are most likely to be surmounted by the firm that has the most to gain from entry—the intermediate product monopolist.[31]

The welfare effects of vertical integration in this model are unambiguously positive. Output of the final good is larger and price is lower with forward integration than without it. The monopolist, of course, is not motivated by undiluted altruism. We have seen that upstream profits

---

[31] The upstream monopolist may be the most likely potential entrant not only because of this additional profit incentive but also because of informational advantages that stem from its close proximity to the downstream industry. In other words, the input supplier is in a strategic position to detect the presence of profit opportunities at the downstream stage.

are increased by vertical integration that restores a position of long-run competitive equilibrium in the downstream industry. Since total industry output expands with such integration, however, the final good consumers benefit as well. The interests of the monopolist and the consumer happily coincide in this instance. If entry into the downstream industry is not forthcoming (or, in a dynamic model, if it is forthcoming but slow) the input monopolist can increase profits and simultaneously improve overall social welfare by forward vertical integration. Finally, the positive welfare effects stemming from forward integration will be greater: (1) the larger the shift in final good demand, (2) the greater the price elasticity of this demand, (3) the steeper the slope of the downstream firms' short-run marginal cost curves, and (4) the slower the rate of entry by other firms.

Monopsony and vertical integration

Market power, where it exists, does not always reside with the *seller* of a product. Particularly in intermediate product markets, it is possible to have a *buyer* whose purchases are sufficiently large in relation to the total market output that its purchasing decisions will have a perceptible effect on the price of the intermediate good. Generally, as such a buyer expands its purchases, the market price of the intermediate product is increased (i.e., the supply curve of the input slopes upward). In this case, the buyer is said to have monopsony power. Where monopsony power exists, there will be an incentive for backward vertical integration to occur. In other words, the monopsonist will have an incentive to integrate into its input supply industry.

To demonstrate this incentive, we assume that a competitive intermediate good industry sells its output to a single buyer at the downstream stage. The situation is depicted in Figure 11–9. Here, AC_A is the average cost curve of the upstream industry, and MC_A is the corresponding marginal cost curve. Since the input supply industry is competitive, it will price its output at marginal cost. Thus, MC_A is the supply curve of the input faced by the downstream firm.

As we know from microeconomic principles, the monopsonist confronted with an upward sloping input supply curve will maximize profits by employing the input up to the point at which the additional revenue generated by the last unit hired equals the additional cost of the last unit hired.[32] The additional revenue from hiring one more unit of an input is called the marginal revenue product of the input. It is equal to the marginal revenue of output (additional revenue per additional unit of output) times the marginal product of the input (additional output per

---

[32] Readers who are not familiar with the monopsony model should consult an intermediate microeconomics text.

FIGURE 11–9

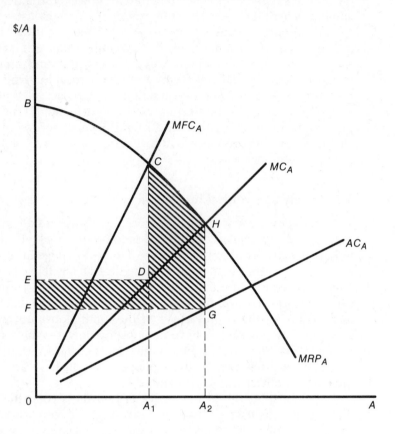

additional unit of the input). Since both marginal revenue and marginal product are expected to be downward sloping, marginal revenue product, which is shown as MRP_A in Figure 11–9, is also expected to be downward sloping. Given an upward sloping supply curve, the addition to total cost of hiring one more unit of the monopsonized input is equal to the price that the downstream firm must pay for the additional unit plus the incremental price required to bring forth this additional unit times the number of units already employed. This is known as the marginal factor cost of hiring the input and is shown as MFC_A in Figure 11–9. Since MFC_A includes the incremental price paid to inframarginal units as employment expands, it will lie above the input supply curve.

The nonintegrated monopsonist, then, will locate its equilibrium employment of the intermediate product at point C where $MRP_A = MFC_A$. It will hire A_1 units of the input and, according to the input supply curve, will pay OE per unit. Since the total revenue generated by employing this input is given by the area under the MRP_A curve from O to A_1 units, and the total cost of employing this input is OE times OA_1, the nonintegrated monopsonist's total profit will be equal to the area $BCDE$ in the graph.

Now, suppose that instead of purchasing this input from firms at the upstream stage, the monopsonist produces its entire requirements of input A internally. In other words, the downstream firm integrates backwards into the production of input A. Then, when the firm increases its use of the input, it will not have to pay the incremental price to the inframarginal units. In other words, the addition to the vertically integrated firm's total costs from hiring one more unit of input A at the downstream stage becomes the marginal cost of producing that additional unit, MC_A. The integrated firm, then, will expand its employment to A_2 units, with a corresponding increase in output of the final product. Total revenues expand by the area CHA_2A_1, and total costs are changed from $OEDA_1$ to $OFGA_2$. Consequently, total profits are increased by the shaded area $CDEFGH$ under vertical integration.

This increase in profits provides an incentive for the monopsonist to integrate backward. The extent to which such integration will occur depends upon the costs of acquiring productive capacity at the upstream stage. Since input suppliers are earning an economic profit under the nonintegrated market structure (price exceeds average cost at the upstream stage), they will not be ready to sell their productive assets at a competitive price. Some premium to compensate these resource owners for foregone future profits will be required. Martin Perry has shown, however, that for almost any reasonable assumption regarding acquisition cost, *some* backward integration will always be profitable.[33]

The social welfare effects of whatever backward integration does occur are unambiguously positive in this case. Since optimal employment of the monopsonized input expands with vertical integration, final good output also will expand. Thus, consumers will be able to purchase a greater quantity at a lower price. Once again, the interests of the firm and the consumer are simultaneously served by vertical integration.

Price discrimination and vertical integration

A firm possessing monopoly power in an intermediate product market may often sell its output to downstream firms with differing elasticities of input demand, particularly in situations in which the latter group sells their products in more than one output market. Multiple output markets at the downstream stage may result from the existence of sepa-

[33] See Martin K. Perry, "Vertical Integration: the Monopsony Case," *American Economic Review* 68 (September 1978), pp. 561–70.

rate geographic markets for the final product or from employment of the monopolized input by more than one final good industry. In either case, differences in the price elasticities of final product demands can easily lead to corresponding differences in price elasticities of derived demands for the monopolized input.

Under such circumstances, the input monopolist can increase profits by practicing price discrimination, selling the intermediate product at a lower price to downstream firms with relatively high demand elasticities. Suppose, for example, that a monopolist over the production of input A sells its output to two different final good industries, which we label industries 1 and 2. The derived demands for input A exhibited by these two industries are assumed to be given by D_A^1 and D_A^2 in Figure 11–10, with corresponding marginal revenues MR_A^1 and MR_A^2. With marginal costs given by MC_A,[34] the intermediate product monopolist will maximize profits by selling A_1 units of the input to industry 1 at a price of P_A^1 and A_2 units of the input to industry 2 at a price of P_A^2.

To be successful in carrying out such discriminatory pricing, however, the upstream monopolist must be able to prevent arbitrage at the downstream stage. In other words, the A monopolist must somehow prevent firms in industry 2 (who buy the input at the lower price) from reselling the intermediate good to firms in industry 1 (who face the higher price from the upstream supplier). Otherwise, the price differential between these firms will not persist, and the discriminatory pricing scheme will break down.

One means of preventing arbitrage is for the upstream monopolist to vertically integrate forward into the relatively price elastic industry.[35] In the above example, the A monopolist would integrate into industry 2. Through merger with the firms in this industry, the upstream monopolist effectively can eliminate incentives for arbitrage at the downstream stage. In effect, vertical integration is used to achieve a consensus between the parties to the merger regarding the price to be paid for the intermediate product by the lower-elasticity firms in industry 1. The increased profits available from effectuating the price discrimination scheme may be shared by the parties to the merger so that the input monopolist as well as the high-elasticity downstream firms can both realize net gains from integration.

---

[34] The assumption of constant marginal costs at the upstream stage greatly simplifies the solution. With increasing marginal costs, we would need to sum horizontally the marginal revenue curves of industries 1 and 2 and equate this summation to marginal cost. Then, the intersection of a horizontal line drawn from this point with the individual marginal revenue curves would indicate the optimal outputs in the two markets.

[35] This incentive for vertical integration is mentioned in George J. Stigler, *The Theory of Price*, 3d ed. (New York: Macmillan, 1966), p. 237. It is analyzed at greater length in J. R. Gould, "Price Discrimination and Vertical Control: A Note," *Journal of Political Economy* 85 (October 1977), pp. 1063–71; and Martin K. Perry, "Price Discrimination and Forward Integration," *Bell Journal of Economics* 9 (Spring 1978), pp. 209–17.

FIGURE 11–10

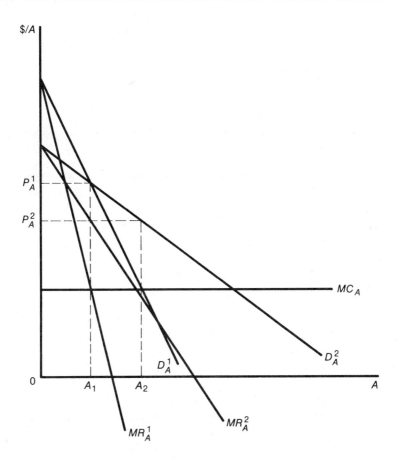

Even where arbitrage can be prevented easily without vertical integration (where, for example, the intermediate good is a service that is physically impossible to resell), the input monopolist may choose to adopt a vertically integrated market structure when practicing price discrimination. This is because the Robinson-Patman Act makes price discrimination a virtual per se violation of the antitrust laws.[36] Since actual market exchange at different prices is required to establish the existence

---

[36] You will recall from Chapter 10 that this law states that it is unlawful for any seller to discriminate in the price charged to buyers on the sale of goods of like grade and quality where the effect may be to injure competition. In many cases, the firms at the downstream stage may be in direct or indirect competition with one another so that charging different prices to them for an input might convey a competitive advantage to those firms receiving the lower price. In this case, the requirement that competition be injured is fulfilled.

of price discrimination, the input monopolist may eliminate the threat of detection by removing the lower priced exchanges from the market through vertical integration. Thus, merger of the input monopolist with the high-elasticity firms serves not only to eliminate arbitrage incentives but also to conceal the act from the antitrust authorities.

The welfare effects of vertical integration undertaken to facilitate price discrimination are indeterminate on theoretical grounds. Successful implementation of discriminatory pricing results in an expansion of output in the more elastic market and a contraction of output in the less elastic market as compared to the uniform price solution. Its net effect on overall social welfare, therefore, will depend upon the magnitudes of these conflicting effects which, in turn, depend upon the specific demand curves that exist in the affected markets. Consequently, we are once again confronted with a model of vertical integration that provides rather ambiguous policy directives. In some circumstances, vertical integration to achieve price discrimination should be allowed while in others it should not.

Vertical integration and barriers to entry

Whether and to what extent vertical integration increases barriers to entry into a given industry has been debated for some time.[37] The pertinent questions surrounding this debate are: (1) Does the vertical market structure of existing firms affect the ability of potential entrants to successfully enter the industry at a single stage of production? and (2) If so, does simultaneous entry at more than one stage cause the *per unit* cost of capital to the potential entrant to be higher than it would be if single stage entry were feasible? If the response to both of these questions is in the affirmative, then existing firms can increase barriers to entry through vertical integration. Let us examine each in turn.

First, if vertical integration is to exert an influence on entry barriers, new firms must feel compelled to enter at more than one stage simultaneously. That much is tautological; for if potential entrants could produce at any one stage independently, without penalty, then the vertical structure of existing firms would be irrelevant to the condition of entry. But multistage entry may be necessary for two potential reasons. First, if the industry is totally vertically integrated in the sense that all existing firms manufacture their entire requirements for the intermediate product and transfer internally their entire output of this product, then no market will exist for the input, and single-stage entry will be completely forestalled unless the potential entrant can expect simultaneous inde-

---

[37] For the predominant opposing views, see Robert H. Bork, "Vertical Integration and Competitive Processes," in *Public Policy Toward Mergers*, eds. J. F. Weston and S. Peltzman (Pacific Palisades, Calif.: Goodyear Publishing, 1969), pp. 139–49; and Williamson, "The Economics of Antitrust: Transaction Cost Considerations," pp. 1439–96.

pendent entry at the other stage. Similarly, if vertical integration is incomplete but pervasive, then the size of the intermediate product market may be severely constrained. If so, economies of scale or indivisibilities in the production of the intermediate good may inhibit independent single-stage entry; nonintegrated firms may suffer bargaining difficulties, particularly if they must transact with integrated firms on either the supply or demand side of the market; and the threat of being subjected to rationing will be increased if the intermediate product market should fail to clear.

Second, if production costs are lower for vertically integrated firms, either because of transaction cost savings or the ability to circumvent monopoly pricing in the input market, then potential entrants may feel obliged to undertake entry at both stages simultaneously. Otherwise, the extra costs associated with single-stage entry may prohibit the achievement of a competitive rate of return.

If, for any of these reasons, new firms are forced to enter at more than one stage of production, then vertical integration can conceivably exert an influence on entry barriers. Such an influence may result from two basic sources. First, if some barrier to entry exists at one stage but is absent at the other, then the necessity of multistage entry will transmit this barrier, *a fortiori*, from the former to the latter. Then, integrated entry can be expected to be at least as difficult as single-stage entry at the most restricted stage. And second, a requirement that entry occur simultaneously at more than one stage necessarily increases the capital needs of potential entrants. Such an increase may or may not impede entry, depending upon the existence of an imperfection in the capital market (defined as a situation in which the terms of finance deteriorate with the quantity of funds raised). Vernon Smith has shown that lender risk aversion and a positive probability of borrower default will yield such a result if funds are raised by debt flotation.[38] Also, Oliver Williamson argues that difficulties of monitoring the performance of large integrated firms may result in higher returns being required by investors if funds are raised in the equity market.[39] Therefore, it is plausible, but not certain, that vertical integration impedes entry by increasing the capital requirements of potential entrants, thereby causing the per unit cost of capital to be higher than it would be if entry could occur independently at a single stage.

If an existing firm (or group of firms in a concentrated industry) can impede the entry of new firms by adopting a vertically integrated market structure, then we should expect that firm (or firms) to do so whenever sufficient market power exists to allow profits to rise above the competi-

---

[38] See Vernon L. Smith, "The Borrower-Lender Contract under Uncertainty," *Western Economic Journal* 9 (March 1971), pp. 52–56.

[39] See Oliver E. Williamson, "The Vertical Integration of Production: Market Failure Consideration," *American Economic Review* 61 (May 1971), p. 119.

tive level. When such profits exist, any action that forestalls entry has the effect of prolonging the period of time over which these profits will remain available. Consequently, firms with market power may engage in vertical integration even in situations in which short-run profits suffer (through, for example, an increase in costs that result from managerial diseconomies). Such integration, then, may be viewed as an "investment in entry barriers"[40] that will enable the firm to earn somewhat lower profits but over a longer period of time.

Since the entry of new firms into concentrated markets in which supracompetitive profits are being realized is the principal process through which competition occurs in the long run, any vertical integration undertaken for the purpose of impeding such entry clearly has negative social welfare effects. To the extent that such integration slows the entry of new firms, it maintains the market price above the competitive level by preventing output expansion in the industry. Consequently, public policy should discourage vertical integration that stems from this source.

11–5 SUMMARY AND CONCLUSIONS

In this chapter, we have examined the firm's motives for vertical integration. We found three incentives for vertical integration that could be attributed to governmental actions: taxation, price controls, and profit regulation. Two additional incentives—technological interdependencies and transaction costs—were also examined in a competitive market structure. These five incentives have no antitrust significance because market power is not an issue. Accordingly, the appropriate antitrust response to vertical integration in these situations is silence.

Turning our attention to situations where monopoly power exists, we analyzed six incentives for vertical integration: successive monopoly, variable proportions production, disequilibrium in the downstream market, monopsony, price discrimination, and barriers to entry. If we continue to accept consumer welfare as the appropriate standard for evaluating the social desirability of any given business practice, then the appropriate antitrust response to vertical integration in the presence of market power depends upon the impact on consumer welfare. We have seen that in only one instance (involving entry barriers) are the consumer welfare effects of vertical integration negative on a priori grounds. Accordingly, a per se prohibition of vertical integration clearly would be inappropriate. Without further information, we cannot be sure of the impact on consumer welfare of vertical integration due to variable proportions production or price discrimination. In these instances, a

---

[40] See William S. Comanor, "Vertical Mergers, Market Power, and the Antitrust Laws," *American Economic Review* 57 (May 1967), p. 261.

rule of reason analysis would appear suitable. Finally, the welfare effects of vertical integration are unambiguously positive when successive monopoly, monopsony, or disequilibrium provides the incentive. In these cases, vertical integration should be applauded and encouraged.

APPENDIX   MARKET OUTCOMES UNDER INTEGRATED AND SUCCESSIVE MONOPOLY

Suppose we have a market demand curve for the final product, X, that is given by

$$P_X = \$100 - 2X$$

with associated marginal revenue given by

$$MR_X = \$100 - 4X$$

Also suppose that the marginal cost of transforming the intermediate product, A, into output X is

$$MC_T = \$10$$

and the marginal cost of producing A is

$$MC_A = \$50$$

A vertically integrated monopolist would then have total marginal costs of

$$MC_X = MC_A + MC_T = \$60$$

In order to maximize profit, this integrated monopolist would equate the marginal revenue of output to marginal cost, or

$$100 - 4X = 60$$

This yields an optimal output for the vertically integrated firm of $X^* = 10$, a market price of $80, and total profit of $200 $[(P_X \cdot X) - (MC_X \cdot X)]$.

Under successive monopoly, the intermediate product monopolist will face a derived demand for its output that is given by

$$\begin{aligned} P_A &= MR_X - MC_T \\ &= \$90 - 4X \\ &= \$90 - 4A \end{aligned}$$

with associated marginal revenue given by

$$MMR_A = \$90 - 8A$$

The upstream monopolist will maximize profits by equating this marginal revenue to its marginal cost,

$$\$90 - 8A = \$50$$

This yields an optimal output of $A^* = 5$, a price for the input of \$70, and a profit to the upstream monopolist of \$100.

The downstream monopolist, then, has marginal costs of

$$MC_X = \$70 + \$10 = \$80$$

Equating these marginal costs to the marginal revenue of output X,

$$100 - 4X = 80$$

This yields an optimal output at the downstream stage of $X^* = 5$, a market price of \$90, and a profit to the downstream monopolist of \$50.

Thus, vertical integration of these successive monopolists increases their combined profits by \$50 while, at the same time, reducing final output price by \$10 and increasing final output by five units. Both consumers and producers are made better off by vertical integration under these circumstances.

QUESTIONS AND PROBLEMS

1. Pfizer invented tetracycline and received a patent on its production and sale. In order to make tetracycline, however, Pfizer had to use aureomycin, which was patented by Cyanamid. Explain Pfizer's problem in maximizing its profits.

2. Historically, the distributors of motion pictures appear to have made each first-run theater a local monopoly. What problem does this create for the distributors? Why would a distributor do this? Can the distributor set the contract terms so that full monopoly profits can be extracted? Would such terms require the grant of local monopoly?

3. Critics of vertical mergers contend that internal expansion is preferable to vertical merger. Assume that demand for the final product does not change and that the downstream industry was originally in competitive equilibrium. If the vertical integration is motivated by efficiency considerations, trace the short-run and long-run effects of internal expansion and vertical merger.

4. Ignoring any incentives for vertical integration provided by government policies, it has been said that where competitive markets prevail, any vertical integration that occurs must be socially beneficial. Explain this statement.

5. "Transaction costs cannot exist in the absence of uncertainty." Is this statement true or false? Explain.

6. In the successive monopoly model, is the assumption that no monopsony power exists crucial to the results? What would be the outcome of relaxing this assumption?

7. Suppose that we have the successive monopoly situation. What would be the market outcomes if we (a) allowed the successive monopolists to vertically integrate; (b) dissolved the monopoly at the downstream stage; (c) dissolved the monopoly at the upstream stage; or (d) dissolved monopoly at both stages?

8. Assume that you have a monopoly over the production of crude oil. Why might you decide to vertically integrate forward into refining? Give more than one reason.

9. Suppose you have a monopoly over an input that is employed in variable proportions with some other input to produce final output. The final good industry and the other input industry are both competitive. (a) Show graphically the minimum increase in profit that you could obtain by integrating into the final product industry. (b) Why is this profit increase a minimum of what could actually be obtained?

10. Why might a large utility company decide to enter the coal business? Would the social welfare effects of such backward integration be positive or negative?

11. Why would an upstream monopolist have more of an incentive to enter a downstream competitive industry that is earning excess profit than any other firm?

12. Why are the welfare effects of vertical integration undertaken to facilitate price discrimination theoretically indeterminate? If there are costs to integrating, such as managerial diseconomies, might we be better off allowing the firm to price discriminate?

13. It is possible that vertical integration can increase the barriers to entry into an industry. First defend this position, and then attack it. Which position do you find more appealing theoretically?

14. Suppose a downstream monopolist faces a demand for final output, X, that is given by

$$P_X = \$1,000 - 4X$$

Also suppose that the production of one unit of X requires the use of one unit of input A. The marginal cost of producing input A is \$35, and the marginal cost of transforming A into X is \$5. Find the market price, quantity, and profit that would result if: (a) the input A industry is competitive; (b) the input A industry is monopolistic; (c) the A industry and the X industry are vertically integrated; and (d) both industries were made competitive.

FURTHER READINGS

Allen, Bruce T. "Vertical Integration and Market Foreclosure: The Case of Cement and Concrete." *Journal of Law and Economics* 14 (April 1971), pp. 251–74.

Blair, Roger D., and David L. Kaserman. "Vertical Integration, Tying, and Antitrust Policy." *American Economic Review* 68 (June 1978a), pp. 397–402.

―――――. "Uncertainty and the Incentive for Vertical Integration." *Southern Economic Journal* 45 (July 1978b), pp. 266–72.

―――――. "Vertical Control with Variable Proportions: Ownership Integration and Contractual Equivalents." *Southern Economic Journal* 46 (April 1980), pp. 1118–28.

―――――. "Optimal Franchising." *Southern Economic Journal* 48 (October 1982), pp. 494–505.

Bork, Robert. "Vertical Integration and the Sherman Act: The Legal History of an Economic Misconception." *University of Chicago Law Review* 22 (Autumn 1954), pp. 157–201.

Burstein, Meyer. "A Theory of Full-Line Forcing." *Northwestern University Law Review* 55 (March/April 1960), pp. 62–95.

Coase, Ronald. "The Nature of the Firm." *Economica* 4 (November 1937), pp. 386–405. Reprinted in *Readings in Price Theory*, eds. George J. Stigler and Kenneth Boulding. Homewood, Ill.: Richard D. Irwin, 1952, pp. 331–51.

Comanor, William S. "Vertical Mergers, Market Power, and the Antitrust Laws." *American Economic Review* 57 (May 1967), pp. 254–65.

Gould, J. R. "Price Discrimination and Vertical Control: A Note." *Journal of Political Economy* 85 (October 1977), pp. 1063–71.

Hay, George. "An Economic Analysis of Vertical Integration." *Industrial Organization Review* 1 (1973), pp. 188–98.

Kaserman, David L. "Theories of Vertical Integration: Implications for Antitrust Policy." *Antitrust Bulletin* 23 (Fall 1978), pp. 483–510.

McGee, John S., and Lowell R. Bassett. "Vertical Integration Revisited." *Journal of Law and Economics* 19 (April 1976), pp. 17–38.

Spengler, Joseph J. "Vertical Integration and Antitrust Policy." *Journal of Political Economy* 58 (July/August 1950), pp. 347–52.

Schmalensee, Richard. "A Note on the Theory of Vertical Integration." *Journal of Political Economy* 81 (March/April 1973), pp. 442–49.

Vernon, John, and Daniel Graham. "Profitability of Monopolization by Vertical Integration." *Journal of Political Economy* 79 (July/August 1971), pp. 924–25.

Warren-Boulton, Frederick R. "Vertical Control with Variable Proportions." *Journal of Political Economy* 82 (July/August 1974), pp. 783–802.

Williamson, Oliver E. "Economies as an Antitrust Defense: The Welfare Trade-offs." *American Economic Review* 58 (March 1968), pp. 18–34.

―――――. "The Vertical Integration of Production: Market Failure Considerations." *American Economic Review* 61 (May 1971), pp. 112–23.

12

Vertical merger policy

12–1 INTRODUCTION

Section 7 of the Clayton Act forbids a merger "where in any line of commerce or in any activity affecting commerce in any section of the country, the effect of such [merger] may be substantially to lessen competition, or to tend to create a monopoly." The law's proscription extends to all types of mergers including *vertical* mergers. As we shall see, it is not obvious just how a vertical merger can have the proscribed effect on competition. In spite of this, the judiciary has adopted a fairly hostile attitude toward vertical mergers.[1]

The foundation for the judicial hostility toward mergers between customers and suppliers resides in the market foreclosure doctrine. When a supplier buys one of its customers (forward integration), the former customer's business is foreclosed to outsiders. Similarly, when a customer acquires one of its suppliers (backward integration), its business is foreclosed to outsiders. Moreover, the acquired supplier is foreclosed as a source of supply to the acquiring firm's rivals. These possibilities of foreclosure form the basis for legal objections to vertical mergers. In the next section, we shall provide an economic analysis of the vertical market foreclosure doctrine. This analysis will expose the serious weaknesses that are inherent in the theory.

---

[1] In subsequent chapters, we shall see that the judiciary is similarly hostile to vertical control through contractual alternatives as well.

321

In subsequent sections, we shall examine the case law and provide a critique of the most important decisions. In addition, we shall describe and analyze the merger guidelines of 1968 and 1983. Finally, we will provide a public policy proposal for analyzing vertical mergers.

12–2 THE VERTICAL MARKET FORECLOSURE DOCTRINE

Legal analysis of vertical integration has focused primarily on the concept of vertical market foreclosure. Consequently, prior to examining the case history in this area, we will pause to examine this concept in some detail. The basic idea behind the foreclosure doctrine is that an input supplier, by merging with one of its customer firms (or an input customer, by merging with one of its suppliers), effectively removes that firm's purchases (or sales) from the open market. By so doing, vertical integration reduces the size of the market that is left available to the other nonintegrated firms in the industry. This is alleged to have anticompetitive consequences.

Although discussions of the evils of foreclosure are notable for their level of obfuscation, we may infer from them two anticompetitive effects that are alleged to result. First, by decreasing the size of the "open" market, vertical merger may increase the level of concentration in the nonintegrated segment of the market. For example, suppose we have three firms at the upstream stage, each with one third of the intermediate product market. If one of these firms merges with all of its downstream customers, the remaining two firms that have not vertically integrated will now share the "open" market equally. The single-firm concentration ratio in the "open" market has increased from one third to one half as a result of the foreclosure that results from vertical merger.[2] The second anticompetitive effect that is alleged to occur is that by foreclosing access to the integrated segment of the market to nonintegrated firms but not foreclosing access to the nonintegrated segment of the market to the integrated firms, vertical mergers place the nonintegrated firms at a competitive disadvantage. This, in turn, is expected to lead to exit by the nonintegrated firms over time, thereby increasing the level of concentration in the overall market as well.

The foreclosure doctrine has not been generally well received by economists. This cool reception is due to the fact that the fundamental presumption underlying this doctrine—that vertical merger entirely removes a given set of transactions from the pressure of market forces—does not make economic sense. The basic flaw in the legal analysis of

---

[2] If the firm that vertically integrates enjoys a relatively large share of the market prior to the merger, it is quite possible that concentration in the "open" segment of the market will fall as a result of foreclosure. Can you devise an example in which this occurs?

vertical integration was most clearly exposed in a paper by Bruce Allen.[3] Allen's analysis is repeated here with the aid of Figure 12–1.

FIGURE 12–1

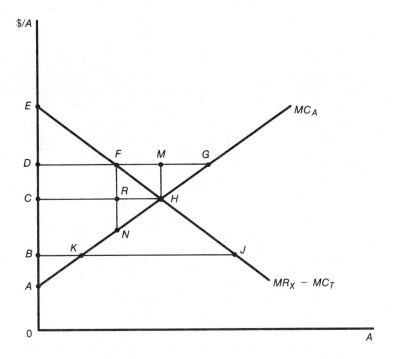

This figure pertains to the situation faced by a vertically integrated firm that manufactures an input A that is employed by the firm's downstream division in the production of output X. The curve labeled MC_A represents the marginal cost of producing input A. The curve labeled $MR_X - MC_T$ is the downstream division's derived demand for the input, which is given by the marginal revenue of output, MR_X, minus the marginal cost of transforming the input into output, MC_T. This curve will slope downward because of a downward sloping demand for the final product, an upward sloping MC_T curve, or both.

---

[3] See Bruce T. Allen, "Vertical Integration and Market Foreclosure: The Case of Cement and Concrete," *Journal of Law and Economics* 14 (April 1971), pp. 251–74. Also, see Jack Hirschleifer, "On the Economics of Transfer Pricing," *Journal of Business* 29 (July 1956), pp. 172–84; and Wesley J. Leibeler, "Toward a Consumer's Antitrust Law: The Federal Trade Commission and Vertical Mergers in the Cement Industry," *UCLA Law Review* 15 (June 1968), pp. 1153–1202.

Now, suppose that there are nonintegrated firms at both stages of production so that an active intermediate product market for input A exists. Then, will the fact that this firm is vertically integrated remove its operations from the influences of this market? The answer is clearly no. The vertically integrated firm will always find it optimal to set the transfer price of the intermediate good equal to the market price of the input. It will then participate in the intermediate product market if the market price differs from the level OC in the graph, selling input A if its price exceeds OC and buying it if its price falls short of OC.

To see this, first suppose that the open market price is equal to the distance OC. Then, to maximize profits, the upstream division will transfer CH units of the input to the downstream division at the market price OC. In this case, the integrated firm does not participate in the intermediate product market at all. It manufactures internally its entire requirements and utilizes its entire output of the intermediate good. Total profits to the downstream division are given by the triangle CHE (the area under the marginal revenue product curve and above the transfer price), and total profits to the upstream division are CHA (the area above the marginal cost curve and below the transfer price). Consequently, total profits to the overall integrated operation are AHE.

Given the market price of OC, any other combination of transfer price and input quantity will result in less (or no more) profit being earned by the integrated firm. For example, suppose that the upstream division forces the downstream division to pay a price equal to the distance OD, despite a market price of OC. If the downstream division is not coerced into buying more, it will purchase DF units of the input and earn a profit of only DFE as compared to area CHE, which is what it earned before the upstream division raised its price above the market level. Thus, the downstream division experiences a reduction in profit of $CHFD$. From this loss, the upstream division will gain back only $CRFD$, leaving a net reduction in profit on sales to the downstream division of NHF. Part of this loss may be offset if the upstream division sells RH units on the open market at the market price of OC. But this still leaves a loss of RHF that is not offset.

Now, suppose that the upstream division forces the downstream division to purchase DG units of the input at the price OD. This increases the profits of the upstream division by the area $CHGD$. But this entire increase is paid for by the downstream division. In addition, production costs are increased so that total profits are once again reduced. With an open market price of OC, the best the integrated firm can do if it insists on charging a transfer price of OD is to force the downstream division to purchase DM units of the input (the same amount it would have purchased willingly at the market price OC). The downstream division then loses $CHMD$, and the upstream division gains *CHMD* as compared to the situation in which the transfer price is set at the market level. Thus, total profits are the same. The only thing that is accomplished in this case is a redistribution of profits from the downstream to the upstream stage.

What happens if the open market price of the intermediate product is not equal to *OC*? For instance, suppose this price rises to *OD*. By the same line of reasoning used above, the vertically integrated firm facing an open market price of *OD* will set the internal transfer price at *OD*. Then, the downstream division will purchase *DF* units of the input, and the upstream division will sell an additional *FG* units on the open market. Profits to the downstream division are *DFE*, and profits to the upstream division are *AGD*. No other solution can yield greater total profits to the integrated operation. Conversely, if the open market price falls below *OC*, say to *OB*, then the transfer price will be reduced to that lower level. Here, the downstream division will purchase *BK* units from the upstream division and an additional *KJ* units on the open market. Profits to the upstream division are *ABK*, and profits to the downstream division are *BJE*.

Therefore, we conclude that (in the absence of some other incentive provided by one or more of the economic theories reviewed in the preceding section) the profit-maximizing vertically integrated firm will always set the transfer price of the internally supplied input at the level determined by the open market. This firm will continue to participate in that market (either as a buyer or a seller) so long as the market price differs from the level at which the internal supply and demand curves intersect. It follows from this that the foreclosure doctrine has no foundation in microeconomic theory.

12–3 VERTICAL MERGER POLICY: CASE HISTORY

Despite disfavor on the part of economists concerning the market foreclosure doctrine and the existence of alternative and more logically appealing explanations of observed integration, the antitrust authorities and the courts have consistently relied on the foreclosure concept in dealing with vertical mergers. This fundamental inconsistency between the legal and the economic approaches to vertical integration has persisted for a long time. As Robert Bork noted in 1954: "A comparison of the law and the economics of vertical integration makes it clear that the two bear little resemblance."[4] Nearly two decades later, George Hay, who was the Director of Economics of the Antitrust Division of the U.S. Department of Justice wrote: "There is probably more disagreement

---

[4] Robert H. Bork, "Vertical Integration and the Sherman Act: The Legal History of an Economic Misconception," *University of Chicago Law Review* 22 (1954), p. 201.

among lawyers and economists on the subject of vertical integration, especially vertical mergers, than in any other area of antitrust."[5]

The virtual fixation of enforcement officials on the foreclosure doctrine as the appropriate basis for judging the competitive effects of vertical integration can be seen in both the case history and the 1968 merger guidelines provided by the Department of Justice. We will review the cases here and the guidelines in a subsequent section.

Early (pre-1950) case history

Prior to the 1950 Amendment of Section 7 of the Clayton Act, vertical mergers seemed to be subject only to Sherman Act prosecution. Three vertical merger cases decided before 1950 addressed the legality of vertical integration as such. These cases are worth a brief review because of the judicial focus on vertical integration at that time.

United States *v.* Yellow Cab Co.[6] The Checker Cab Manufacturing Company acquired control of the Yellow Cab Co. and a few other taxicab companies. Following the acquisitions, it required these subsidiaries to purchase their cabs from Checker. The Justice Department filed suit under the Sherman Act on the theory that Checker's actions illegally foreclosed a substantial fraction of the market for taxicabs. The lower court observed quite sensibly that such foreclosure was commonplace in vertically integrated firms.

The Supreme Court, however, felt otherwise: "The fact that these restraints occur in . . . a vertically integrated enterprise does not necessarily remove the ban of the Sherman Act. The test of the Act is the presence or absence of an unreasonable restraint on interstate commerce." The Court felt that if the government could show that Checker's activity was a "deliberate, calculated purchase for control" and its "dominating power" resulted in "an undue restraint of interstate trade," then it could prevail under the Sherman Act.[7]

United States *v.* Paramount Pictures.[8] In this case, the government argued that vertically integrating the production, distribution, and exhibition of motion pictures is a per se violation of the Sherman Act. The Supreme Court, however, rejected per se treatment of vertical integration. Instead, vertical integration violates the Sherman Act when it is "a calculated scheme to gain control over an appreciable segment of the

---

[5] George A. Hay, "An Economic Analysis of Vertical Integration," *Industrial Organization Review* 1 (1973), p. 188.

[6] 322 U.S. 218 (1947). An interesting analysis of this case is provided by Edmund W. Kitch, "The Yellow Cab Antitrust Case," *Journal of Law and Economics* 15 (October 1972), pp. 327–36.

[7] When the case was remanded for a new trial, the lower court found that Checker had no intention to restrain competition and, therefore, found them not guilty.

[8] 334 U.S. 131 (1948).

market and to restrain or suppress competition, rather than an expansion to meet legitimate business needs. . . ." In addition, a vertically integrated firm will constitute an illegal monopoly if it has the power to exclude competitors coupled with a purpose or intent to do so.

Whether a particular instance of vertical integration created monopoly power was found to depend upon "the nature of the market to be served . . . and the leverage on the market which the particular vertical integration creates or makes possible."[9]

United States *v*. New York Great Atlantic & Pacific Tea Co.[10]   For many years, A&P had used its power as a large buyer to get preferential prices from its suppliers. This was made possible because it was partially vertically integrated. To ensure compliance with its demands, A&P threatened further vertical integration. In this case, the government's burden was to show that A&P's vertical integration was used to bring about inevitably unreasonable advantages over competitors not similarly integrated.

Later (post-1950) case history

These pre-1950 cases express a concern with foreclosure possibilities, attempts to monopolize, and unfair advantages that flow from vertical integration. We shall see that the post-1950 cases lend further support to the foreclosure theory of vertical mergers.

In 1950, Section 7 of the Clayton Act was amended to extend its prohibition to vertical and conglomerate mergers, as well as to close the asset loophole, as discussed in Chapter 9. The amended Section 7 prohibits a vertical merger whenever its effect may be substantially to lessen competition or tend to create a monopoly. A review of the legislative history of the amendment sheds no light on the standards that the courts were expected to use in evaluating vertical mergers. The statute is similarly unenlightening. Thus, it was left to the courts to interpret the statute as best they could. Unfortunately, this exercise was not terribly successful. A review of the *Du Pont (GM)*, *Brown Shoe*, and *Ford (Autolite)* decisions will confirm this suspicion.

United States *v*. E. I. du Pont de Nemours & Co.[11]   This case challenged the legality of Du Pont's acquisition of 23 percent of General Motors' stock. The Supreme Court decision did not rest upon the empirical market facts as they existed during the 1917–19 period when Du Pont was in the process of acquiring the General Motors stock. Instead, it was based upon the market facts *at the time of the suit*, which was some 30 years later. This, by itself, made the case noteworthy. For our present

---

[9] 334 U.S. 131, 174 (1948).

[10] 67 F. Supp. 626 (E. D. Ill. 1946), affirmed 173 F. 2d 79 (7th Cir. 1949).

[11] 358 U.S. 586 (1957).

purposes, however, we are interested in the Court's reasoning regarding the notion of vertical market foreclosure.

The objection to Du Pont's stock acquisition resides in the fact that Du Pont supplied a substantial portion of the automotive fabrics and finishes that General Motors required. In percentage terms, Du Pont supplied 67 percent of General Motors' requirements for finishes in 1946 and 68 percent in 1947. In fabrics Du Pont supplied 52.3 percent of General Motors' needs in 1946 and 38.5 percent in 1947. Since "General Motors [was] the colossus of the giant automobile industry" with a 50 percent market share, its requirements for fabrics and finishes had to account for a substantial share of the market.

In analyzing the competitive significance of Du Pont's stock acquisition, the Court noted that Du Pont was not a major GM supplier until just after its purchase of a large block of GM stock. Further, the Court observed that

> The fact that sticks out in this voluminous record is that the bulk of Du Pont's production has always supplied the largest part of the requirements of the one customer in the automobile industry connected to Du Pont by a stock interest. The inference is overwhelming that Du Pont's commanding position was promoted by its stock interest and was not gained solely on competitive merit.

The Court went on to express its concern about vertical market foreclosure:

> The statutory policy of fostering free competition is obviously furthered when no supplier has an advantage over his competitors from an acquisition of his customer's stock likely to have the effects condemned by the statute. We repeat, that the test of a violation of §7 is whether at the time of suit there is a reasonable probability that the acquisition is likely to result in the condemned restraints. The conclusion upon this record is inescapable that such likelihood was proved as to this acquisition.

The foreclosure doctrine was sharpened in the Court's first decision under the amended section 7 of the Clayton Act.

Brown Shoe Co. _v._ United States.[12] You will recall from Chapter 9 that the Brown Shoe case involved horizontal as well as vertical aspects. Our present concern is with the vertical part of the Supreme Court's decision. To refresh our memories, let's examine the facts involved in the Brown-Kinney merger. The Brown Shoe Company was the fourth largest shoe manufacturer in the country with about 4 percent of the total domestic footwear production. Brown was also a major retailer with about 1,230 retail outlets that it owned, operated, or otherwise

---

[12] 370 U.S. 294 (1962). A thorough analysis and critique of this decision was provided by John L. Peterman, "The Brown Shoe Case," _Journal of Law and Economics_ 18 (April 1975), pp. 81–146.

controlled. G. R. Kinney Company, Inc. was primarily a retailer of shoes. It operated the largest family-style shoe store chain in the United States. Its 400 stores, located in over 270 cities around the country, accounted for about 1.2 percent of all retail shoe sales by dollar volume. In addition to its retail operations, Kinney also manufactured men's, women's, and children's shoes. This manufacturing operation made Kinney the nation's 12th largest producer with 0.5 percent of total domestic production. The Kinney stores obtained approximately 20 percent of their shoe requirements from Kinney's own production facilities. At the time of the merger, Kinney bought no shoes from Brown.

It is important to place Brown and Kinney in the proper perspective relative to the industry as a whole. The four largest producers—International, Endicott-Johnson, Brown (including Kinney), and General Shoe—accounted for 23 percent of total domestic production. The next 20 largest producers accounted for only 12 percent of total output. In 1954, there were 970 independent shoe manufacturers, which represented a 10 percent decrease from the 1,077 that existed in 1947. By 1958, the number had declined another 10 percent to 872 independents.

Shoe retailing was highly fragmented: In all, there were some 70,000 retail outlets. Of these 70,000, about 22,000 were defined by the Census Bureau as shoe stores because they derived over 50 percent of their sales volume from the sale of shoes. Shoe departments of clothing and department stores represented a considerable share of the remainder.

In evaluating the Brown-Kinney merger, the Supreme Court expressed a clear concern for vertical market foreclosure:

> The primary vice of a vertical merger or other arrangement tying a customer to a supplier is that, by foreclosing the competitors of either party from a segment of the market otherwise open to them, the arrangement may act as a "clog on competition," which "deprive[s] . . . rivals of a fair opportunity to compete." Every extended vertical arrangement by its very nature, for at least a time, denies to competitors of the supplier the opportunity to compete for part or all of the trade of the customer-party to the vertical arrangement.

After defining the relevant product and geographic markets, the Court noted that to be proscribed it is necessary to find that the merger's effect "may be substantially to lessen competition, or to tend to create a monopoly" as the language of Section 7 of the Clayton Act requires. The Court went on to say that

> Since the diminution of the vigor of competition which may stem from a vertical arrangement results primarily from a foreclosure of a share of the market otherwise open to competitors, an important consideration in determining whether the effect of a vertical arrangement "may be substantially to lessen competition, or to tend to create a monopoly" is the size of the share of the market foreclosed. However, this factor will seldom be

determinative. If the share of the market foreclosed is so large that it approaches monopoly proportions, the Clayton Act will, of course, have been violated; but the arrangement will also have run afoul of the Sherman Act. And the legislative history of §7 indicates clearly that the tests for measuring the legality of any particular economic arrangement under the Clayton Act are to be less stringent than those used in applying the Sherman Act. On the other hand, foreclosure of a de minimis share of the market will not tend "substantially to lessen competition."

* * * * *

Between these extremes, in cases such as the one before us, in which the foreclosure is neither of monopoly nor de minimis proportions, the percentage of the market foreclosed by the vertical arrangement cannot itself be decisive. In such cases, it becomes necessary to undertake an examination of various economic and historical factors in order to determine whether the arrangement under review is of the type Congress sought to proscribe.

The Supreme Court decided that the Brown-Kinney merger should be proscribed because of two factors:

1. There was a trend toward vertical integration in the shoe industry.
2. Brown would use its ownership of Kinney to force Brown shoes into Kinney stores.

These factors require a bit of analysis if we are to evaluate the Supreme Court's *Brown Shoe* decision.[13] We shall take them in turn.

The trend toward vertical integration was undeniable. At the time of the suit, the 13 largest shoe manufacturers operated 21 percent of the shoe stores. But this ignores all of those shoe departments in department stores and clothing stores. Moreover, if 13 manufacturers had accounted for only 21 percent of all retailing, that would still leave room for over 60 equally large manufacturers, which would be ample for effective competition. Of course, we know that there were a substantial number of other outlets and that the next tier of manufacturers involved smaller firms. Consequently, there was plenty of room for at least 100 manufacturers in spite of any trend toward vertical integration. In addition, entry barriers to shoe retailing are almost nonexistent. Accordingly, a new entrant at the manufacturing stage would have no difficulty finding retail outlets.

The Court's concern about Brown's forcing its shoes on the Kinney stores rests on Brown's historical performance. In fact, Brown actually sold some of its production through its own outlets. Before the merger, Kinney bought no Brown shoes. Two years after the merger, Brown supplied almost 8 percent of Kinney's shoe requirements. Thus, Brown

---

[13] For a devastating critique of *Brown Shoe*, see Robert H. Bork and Ward S. Bowman, Jr., "The Crisis in Antitrust," *Columbia Law Review* 65 (March 1965), pp. 363–76.

appeared to exploit its ownership by selling through the Kinney outlets. But why else would it want to merge vertically with a retail chain? Based upon this logic, any vertical merger that is apt to result in actual integration, that is, one with real efficiencies, will be suspect.

As for the foreclosure possibilities, there are two things that should be considered. First, Kinney's production facilities produced 20 percent of its needs, and Kinney only had some 1.2 percent of total sales. Thus, if Brown totally foreclosed access to Kinney stores, the market foreclosure would be about one tenth of 1 percent—hardly a substantial clog on competition.

Second, it cannot be free to Brown to force its shoes upon Kinney. Prior to the merger, Kinney considered the price, quality, styles, and other characteristics of Brown's shoes and elected not to buy them for its retail stores. The merger is not going to make Brown's shoes suddenly more suitable for the Kinney outlets. If Brown forces its shoes on Kinney, that will have to cost Kinney at least as much as it would benefit Brown. This is a straightforward application of the theory presented in Section 12–2 above.

The only time that this can be a sensible strategy is when there is excess capacity in shoe production. Under these circumstances, a shoe producer that "captures" some customers can expand production and reduce its average costs. Those producers that lose sales because of this will have even more excess capacity and suffer even higher average costs. Eventually, some of the firms will leave the industry. But in a market characterized by excess capacity, it is socially desirable for some of the productive capacity to leave the industry.

In brief, the Supreme Court spoke of a trend toward vertical integration and a fear that vertical market foreclosure would deprive rivals of a fair opportunity to compete. Unfortunately, the Court provided no economically sensible reason for prohibiting a merger that carried a maximum foreclosure potential of some 1 percent.

Ford Motor Co. *v.* United States.[14] This is the most recent Supreme Court decision on vertical integration. The preoccupation of the judiciary with market foreclosure appears to continue as the Court ruled against Ford on foreclosure grounds.

Until 1961, the major automobile manufacturers each had a reliable source of supply of spark plugs. General Motors had vertically integrated backward and produced its own AC spark plugs, which it would sell to anyone who wanted them. The Ford Motor Company purchased its spark plugs from Champion, which was the largest independent spark plug manufacturer. Chrysler was supplied by Electric Autolite, another independent manufacturer. Both Champion and Autolite sold

---

[14] 405 U.S. 562 (1972). For a brief but devastating critique of this decision, see Robert Bork, *The Antitrust Paradox* (New York: Basic Books, 1978), pp. 234–37.

to American Motors. In 1961, Ford purchased Autolite, and the Antitrust Division filed suit.

There are two markets for spark plugs: the original equipment (OE) market and the replacement market, which usually is referred to as the aftermarket. Champion and Autolite sold OE spark plugs to the automobile manufacturers at prices that were below cost. They made up these losses through the profits that were earned on replacement sales. The average automobile requires five sets of replacement spark plugs during its lifetime. Automobile mechanics tend to replace spark plugs with the same brand as the OE spark plug. Thus, a spark plug manufacturer invests in establishing a position in the aftermarket by charging OE prices below cost.

Ford decided that it wanted to participate in the aftermarket, but that internal expansion would take some five to eight years. In order to be an effective participant, Ford concluded that it would need an effective distribution system and a recognized brand name. Moreover, it would require a full line of high volume service parts, engineering experience in replacement designs, low volume production facilities, and the opportunity to capitalize on an established automobile population. As a consequence, Ford decided that it would be cheaper to acquire Autolite than to enter de novo. Accordingly, Ford acquired Autolite in 1961.

Following Ford's acquisition of Autolite, Champion lost the Ford account, and Autolite stopped supplying Chrysler. In due course, Champion began supplying Chrysler's OE spark plug requirements. Since Chrysler's share of the automobile market was smaller than Ford's share, Champion's fortunes declined—from a 50 percent share of the market in 1960, Champion's share fell to 33 percent by 1966.

The District Court found (and the Supreme Court agreed) that Ford's acquisition of Autolite violated Section 7 of the Clayton Act for two reasons. First, Ford was a potential entrant and thereby had a procompetitive influence upon pricing in the spark plug market. Second, and more importantly for our purposes, the District Court found that Ford's acquisition of Autolite resulted in "the foreclosure of Ford as a purchaser of about 10 percent of total industry output." In its decision, the Supreme Court emphasized that Ford's acquisition eliminated one of the two major independent spark plug manufacturers and thereby aggravated an already oligopolistic market. In addition, after Ford entered the aftermarket, "it would have every incentive to perpetuate the OE tie and thus maintain the virtually insurmountable barriers to entry to the *aftermarket*."

In evaluating this decision, it is interesting to note that the number of spark plug producers actually increased as a result of Ford's acquisition. This occurred because the former Autolite managers opened a new plant and began selling Prestolite spark plugs. More important, however, is the vertical foreclosure issue. When Ford entered the spark plug industry, it foreclosed some 10 percent of the market to independents. But what is the competitive harm in that? Ford certainly would not voluntarily foreclose itself to its own disadvantage. There cannot be any harm in the OE market because Ford wants its OE spark plugs supplied as efficiently as possible. Consequently, Ford's interests in profit maximization are consistent with those of the ultimate consumer in lower prices. As Bork pointed out, the firm's decision to make an input or to buy it from others always rests upon considerations of costs and effectiveness. Thus, the law should not interfere.

Let's turn to an analysis of the acquisition's impact upon the aftermarket. The Court did not provide or cite any economic evidence that the aftermarket was performing poorly. But it did recognize that mass merchandisers were beginning to be active. For example, Sears had its Allstate spark plug with a 1.2 percent share; Atlas plugs, which were sponsored by Exxon, had a 1.4 percent share; and Montgomery Ward's Riverside plug had a 0.6 percent share. There is no apparent reason why Ford's acquisition of Autolite would reverse this growth.

The Court indicated some concern with the notion that Ford would have an interest in perpetuating the OE tie. But this concern ignores the fact that Ford had this incentive while it was purchasing from Champion. After all, Ford was paying only six cents per spark plug, and this price amounted to just one third of the manufacturing cost. The only reason that Champion (and Autolite) charged such a low price was because of the OE tie.

Thus, the *Ford (Autolite)* decision contains no valid theory of vertical market foreclosure in spite of the Court's expression of concern.

General judicial concern

Areeda and Turner[15] surveyed 43 vertical merger cases and examined the criteria that the courts have used in evaluating the merits of each dispute. In case after case, vertical market foreclosure is a primary concern of the court involved. None of these cases provides a sound economic rationale for the judiciary's fear of foreclosure. In effect, the courts have adopted a presumptive approach to vertical mergers. If either market is highly concentrated and the merger results in foreclosure which is not *de minimus*, then the merger is apt to be held unlawful. Using this approach greatly simplifies the Court's burden—it just rules according to the presumption without having to deal with an economic analysis of the facts.[16]

---

[15] See Phillip Areeda and Donald Turner, *Antitrust Law* IV (Boston: Little, Brown, 1980), pp. 296–319.

[16] Lawrence Sullivan, *Handbook of the Law of Antitrust* (St. Paul, Minn.: West Publishing, 1977), p. 663, remarks "[i]f the share foreclosed is high enough, the prosecutor need not articulate any particular theory about why the merger is injurious; it need only insist that it is."

12–4 MERGER GUIDELINES

To date, two sets of merger guidelines have been issued by the Antitrust Division of the Department of Justice. The first set[17] was published ". . . to acquaint the business community, the legal profession, and other interested groups and individuals with the standards currently being applied by the Department of Justice in determining whether to challenge corporate acquisitions and mergers under Section 7 of the Clayton Act." These guidelines expressed the department's opinion that vertical mergers tend to raise barriers to entry by (1) "foreclosing equal access to potential customers," (2) "foreclosing equal access to potential suppliers," and (3) "facilitating promotional product differentiation." Thus, two of the three sources of alleged anticompetitive effects relied upon the concept of market foreclosure.

The old guidelines did acknowledge the possibility that vertical integration might have been undertaken in some situations to facilitate cost reductions. This possibility, however, was dismissed as a potential justification for large vertical mergers because it was presumed (with no justification provided) that the negative effect of increasing entry barriers usually would predominate. On the basis of this presumption and concern about market foreclosure, the guidelines stated that

> the Department will ordinarily challenge a merger or series of mergers between a supplying firm, accounting for approximately 10 percent or more of the sales in its market, and one or more purchasing firms, accounting in total for approximately 6 percent or more of the total purchases in that market, unless it clearly appears that there is no significant barrier to entry into the business of the purchasing firm or firms.

Having explicitly defined the criteria that, if satisfied, would have led the department to challenge a vertical merger, the guidelines went on to explain that some additional mergers that did not satisfy these criteria might also be challenged ". . . on the ground that they raise entry barriers in the purchasing firm's market, or disadvantage the purchasing firm's competitors, by conferring upon the purchasing firm a significant supply advantage over unintegrated or partly integrated existing competitors or over potential competitors."

Like the judiciary, then, the antitrust enforcement officials were willing to make presumptive rules that applied to all vertical mergers instead of attempting to distinguish among them on the basis of the appropriate economic theories. Moreover, the rules that were established tended to be rather restrictive. The likely consequence of this was that while some resources would be saved by eliminating the need to adjudicate individual cases, many more resources probably were wasted by disallowing mergers that should have been permitted (and permitting a few that should have been disallowed) on social welfare grounds.

The decade of the 1970s witnessed an explosion of academic interest in vertical integration. As a result, much was learned about vertical integration, and some of what was already known became more widely recognized and accepted. This led to a revision in the merger guidelines in 1982.

The 1982 vertical merger guidelines[18]

The new guidelines identify three economic consequences of vertical mergers that could be anticompetitive. First, a vertical merger "could create competitively objectionable barriers to entry." Second, a vertical merger could facilitate collusion. Third, a vertical merger may permit the evasion of rate regulation.

The guidelines recognize that three conditions are necessary for a vertical merger to increase entry barriers to an objectionable level.

> First, the degree of vertical integration between the two markets must be so extensive that entrants to one market (the "primary market") also would have to enter the other market (the "secondary market") simultaneously. Second, the requirement of entry at the secondary level must make entry at the primary level significantly more difficult and less likely to occur. Finally the structure and other characteristics of the primary market must be otherwise so conducive to noncompetitive performance that the increased difficulty of entry is likely to affect its performance.

The guidelines go on to explain how market structure will influence its enforcement actions:

> Barriers to entry are unlikely to affect performance if the structure of the primary market is otherwise not conducive to monopolization or collusion. The Department is unlikely to challenge a merger on this ground unless overall concentration of the primary market is above 1,800 HHI.[19] Above that threshold, the Department is increasingly likely to challenge a merger that meets the other criteria set forth above as the concentration increases.

The guidelines indicate that vertical mergers are most likely to facilitate collusion when a producer vertically integrates into retail distribution:

> A high level of vertical integration by upstream firms into the associated retail market may facilitate collusion in the upstream market by making it

---

[18] An interesting analysis of the revised guidelines is provided by Oliver E. Williamson, "Vertical Merger Guidelines: Interpreting the 1982 Reforms," *California Law Review* 71 (March 1983), pp. 604–17. Also, see Alan A. Fisher and Richard Sciacca, "An Economic Analysis of Vertical Merger Enforcement Policy," *Research in Law and Economics* VI (1983).

[19] HHI is an abbreviation for the Herfindahl-Hirschman index.

easier to monitor price. Retail prices are generally more visible than prices in upstream markets, and vertical mergers may increase the level of vertical integration to the point at which the monitoring effect becomes significant. Adverse competitive consequences are unlikely unless the upstream market is generally conducive to collusion and a large percentage of the products produced there are sold through vertically integrated retail outlets. The Department is unlikely to challenge a merger on this ground unless *(i)* overall concentration of the upstream market is above 1,800 HHI and *(ii)* a large percentage of the upstream product would be sold through vertically-integrated retail outlets after the merger.

Finally, the guidelines recognize that

nonhorizontal mergers may be used by monopoly public utilities subject to rate regulation as a tool for circumventing that regulation. The clearest example is the acquisition by a regulated utility of a supplier of its fixed or variable inputs. After the merger, the utility would be selling to itself and might be able arbitrarily to inflate the prices of internal transactions. Regulators may have great difficulty in policing these practices, particularly if there is no independent market for the product (or service) purchased from the affiliate. As a result, inflated prices could be passed along to consumers as "legitimate" costs. In extreme cases, the regulated firm may effectively preempt the adjacent market, perhaps for the purpose of suppressing observable market transactions, and may distort resource allocation in that adjacent market as well as in the regulated market. In such cases, however, the Department recognizes that genuine economies of integration may be involved. The Department will consider challenging mergers that create substantial opportunities for such abuses.

The current merger guidelines focus exclusively on the structure of the *acquired* firm's industry. It is only when that market is concentrated (i.e., when the HHI exceeds 1,800) that a vertical merger is subject to challenge. This, of course, is an appropriate requirement because foreclosure possibilities are fairly remote in unconcentrated markets. Nonetheless, one can still discern an underlying concern regarding foreclosure possibilities, although the term *foreclosure* is notably absent.

12–5 A POLICY PROPOSAL

As an alternative to continued reliance on the foreclosure doctrine for guidance concerning the competitive effects of vertical mergers, we propose that the economic theories of vertical integration that we have surveyed in the preceding chapter be used as a foundation for antitrust policy in this area. A total of 11 different theories were presented to explain why a firm might choose to supplant market exchange with internal transfers. Of these, three were seen to stem from government actions: taxation, regulation, or price controls. Since enforcement of the policies of other government entities is not generally viewed as a legitimate task of antitrust, we shall ignore these three theories in our attempt to derive an appropriate policy from economic theory.

The remaining eight theories are listed in Table 12–1 along with an indication of the direction of the effect of vertical integration on social

TABLE 12–1   Economic theories of vertical integration and welfare effects

Theory	Effect on social welfare
Technological interdependencies	+
Transaction costs	+
Successive monopoly	+
Upstream monopoly with variable proportions	?
Disequilibrium	+
Monopsony	+
Price discrimination	?
Barriers to entry	−

welfare in each case. In this table, a "+" indicates that welfare is improved by vertical integration, a "−" indicates that it is reduced, and a "?" indicates that it might move in either direction depending on the particular circumstances encountered. The first thing that we notice from this table is that of the eight theories listed, in five cases social welfare is unambiguously improved by vertical integration. In two more, the welfare effect is indeterminate on theoretical grounds. And in only one case can we conclude that social welfare is unambiguously reduced. Consequently, it would appear that an antitrust policy based on economic theory would be somewhat less restrictive of vertical mergers overall than a policy founded on the foreclosure doctrine.

Next, we notice that vertical integration can never reduce social welfare if the relevant markets are competitive. The first two theories listed in Table 12–1 are the only theories presented that assume competitive intermediate product markets. In both cases, vertical integration is undertaken to reduce costs and, as a result, leads to an improvement in social welfare. Consequently, we conclude that where vertical integration is not associated with market power at one or more of the vertically related stages of production, it should be viewed as being presumptively legal. The antitrust authorities should concern themselves with the internalization decisions of firms only when it can be shown that market power is present in one or more of the relevant markets.

Finally, even where such market power exists, it should not be presumed that vertical integration should be opposed. Of the last six theories listed in Table 12–1 (all of which assume some market power at one or more stages), three indicate an unambiguously positive welfare effect stemming from vertical integration. Where the market power that underlies the incentive to integrate is not immune to antitrust attack, the appropriate policy response, of course, is to dissolve the horizontal structure that provides this market power. Then, any incentives to integrate that might remain, by necessity, would be cost-reducing. But where such market power is protected from direct attack, the antitrust authorities should adopt a rule of reason approach to the treatment of vertical integration. They should first attempt to classify given cases according to the appropriate theory or theories that might explain the observed decision to integrate the production process. If it appears that the successive monopoly, the disequilibrium, or the monopsony model is the applicable theory, then no further action should be taken. If the variable proportions or the price discrimination models coincide with the evidence better, then some further analysis should be carried out to determine whether consumers would be likely to benefit from the imposition of a nonintegrated market structure. And if a significant effect on entry barriers is likely to result, hampering the disciplinary effect of potential competition,[20] then the decision to internalize the transaction should be challenged. If social welfare is to be served by antitrust policy, then the foreclosure doctrine must be abandoned and a more logically consistent view of the internalization process put in its place.

QUESTIONS AND PROBLEMS

1. In the *Ford (Autolite)* case, independent spark plug manufacturers sold OE spark plugs to the automobile manufacturers below cost. Why? How would a spark plug manufacturer calculate the value of being the producer of the OE spark plug?

2. Is it likely that the Supreme Court's decision in the *Ford (Autolite)* case will enhance competition in the spark plug industry?

3. What would the ultimate structure of the spark plug market have been if Ford had entered de novo?

4. Robert Bork has characterized the market foreclosure doctrine as a conjuring trick because it leads the analyst to focus on the wrong level of the industry. What does he mean? Is he correct?

5. In *Ford (Autolite)*, the District Court recognized that "[h]ad Ford taken the internal-expansion route, there would have been no ille-

---

[20] Potential competition is not needed where actual competition exists. Thus, the effect on entry barriers only becomes important where some market power is present.

gality; not, however, because the result would have been commendable. . . ." If the ultimate market structure would have been the same, what purpose is served by the proscription of this merger?

6. Robert Bork has complained that "[t]he law against vertical mergers is merely a law against the creation of efficiency." What does this mean? Is Bork correct in his assessment?

7. "Since the market structure of the shoe industry was not even remotely close to monopoly, a trend toward vertical integration in an industry must be evidence that such a change is prompted by efficiency considerations." Discuss.

8. Suppose there are 100 shoe producers of equal size and 10,000 shoe retailers of equal size. Both industries are in long-run competitive equilibrium. Now, the management of Blair's Boots decides to acquire the 100 shoe retailers that used to be independent customers. The goal is to "capture" these customers and then get a fair share of the remaining 9,900 shoe retailers. Can this be a viable strategy for expanding market share? (Hint: What would have to be true about the cost functions in shoe production? Is this consistent with competition?)

9. Suppose that the *Du Pont (GM)* decision stands for the proposition that "any merger, no matter how old or how innocent initially, can be challenged on the basis of a current anticompetitive effect." How would this affect a small firm's ability to sell out? What would be the effect upon acquisition prices?

10. Suppose that B&K, Inc. acquired the C&L Company in 1950. Both firms were relatively young competitors in dynamic industries. From 1950 until 1985, B&K was the sole supplier of C&L, which grew very rapidly. By 1985, C&L dominated its industry with a 60 percent market share. As C&L prospered, so did B&K. The Antitrust Division files suit. Who wins? Evaluate.

11. Robert Bork has suggested that all vertical merger cases should be decided on the basis of *horizontal* merger standards. His suggestion is based upon the belief that a vertical merger cannot have anticompetitive effects without horizontal market power. Do you agree? Explain.

12. There are 100 firms of equal size at the upstream stage and 100 firms of equal size at the downstream stage. If 50 upstream firms each merge with 1 downstream firm, then one half of the market has

been foreclosed to access by the remaining 50 integrated firms at both stages. Assess the competitive implications.

13. An upstream firm that vertically integrates forward can increase its profits by forcing its downstream subsidiary (captive market) to pay a higher price. Is this statement true or false? Explain.

FURTHER READINGS

Areeda, Phillip, and Donald Turner. *Antitrust Law* IV. (Boston: Little, Brown, 1980), pp. 207–319.

Bork, Robert H. "Vertical Integration and Competitive Processes." In *Public Policy toward Mergers*, eds. J. F. Weston and S. Peltzman, Pacific Palisades, Calif.: Goodyear Publishing, 1969.

————. "Vertical Integration and the Sherman Act: The Legal History of an Economic Misconception." *University of Chicago Law Review* 22 (Autumn 1954), pp. 157–201.

Mueller, Willard F. "Public Policy toward Vertical Mergers." In *Public Policy toward Mergers,* eds. J. F. Weston and S. Peltzman. Pacific Palisades, Calif.: Goodyear Publishing, 1969.

Peltzman, Sam. "Issues in Vertical Integration Policy." In *Public Policy toward Mergers,* eds. J. F. Weston and S. Peltzman. Pacific Palisades, Calif.: Goodyear Publishing, 1969.

Peterman, John L. "The Brown Shoe Case." *Journal of Law and Economics* 18 (April 1975), pp. 81–146.

13

Vertical price fixing

13–1 INTRODUCTION

In Chapter 11, we saw that incentives for vertical integration may arise in a variety of situations. As a general proposition, whenever firms can increase their profits by replacing market transactions with internal transfers, there is an incentive for vertical integration. Indeed, it is the potential for increased profits that provides the incentive for previously separate firms to vertically integrate through merger. At the same time, we saw that the social welfare effects of vertical integration are, in many cases, positive. That is, the firms' profits and consumers' welfare are both increased simultaneously (final output price falls while total profits rise). In these circumstances, we concluded that public policy should not discourage such vertical integration from taking place.

We observed, however, that public policy often does discourage vertical integration even in situations where social welfare is likely to improve. In addition, other factors that are unrelated to public policy, such as managerial diseconomies, may make vertical integration a prohibitively costly alternative for the firm to adopt. In these cases, the firm that is pursuing the lure of increased profits may design some sort of contractual arrangement that will achieve the same end as combined ownership of the related stages of production.[1] Fundamentally, these contractual

---

[1] This is a manifestation of the universal law which states that there is more than one way to skin a cat.

arrangements involve the upstream firm's placing some condition on the sale of the intermediate product. The downstream firm, in exchange for the opportunity to purchase the input, agrees to perform in some specified manner stated in the contract. One such arrangement is for the upstream firm (a manufacturer) to specify either a maximum or a minimum price that downstream firms (distributors) can charge. These are forms of what is referred to as vertical price fixing, and under some circumstances, it can be employed as a contractual alternative to ownership integration.

One might suppose that antitrust policy toward vertical price fixing would be similar to the policy toward vertical integration. After all, if they are economically equivalent, they should be legally equivalent. Such a belief would be sadly mistaken. In fact, vertical price fixing is an extremely hazardous avenue to vertical control since it is accorded much the same treatment as horizontal price fixing. We know from our earlier analysis that *horizontal* price fixing leads to a decrease in consumer welfare. Accordingly, it is the proper object of antitrust attack. But the effects of *vertical* price fixing on consumer welfare cannot be determined so easily. In some instances, vertical price fixing is innocuous while in others the effects are positive. That is, vertical price fixing actually can improve consumer welfare and, in those cases, it should be applauded. As we shall see, however, vertical price fixing is always illegal per se.

In some cases, the supplier imposes *maximum* resale prices while in others *minimum* resale prices are set. The motivation for setting either maximum or minimum resale prices is the same: a quest for higher profits. But this does not necessarily mean that the supplier's goals are inconsistent with the promotion of consumer welfare. In the case of fixing *maximum* resale prices, the welfare effects are unambiguously positive. For minimum resale prices, the picture is not quite so clear. We shall analyze each of these in turn.

13–2 FIXING MAXIMUM RESALE PRICES: ECONOMICS[2]

A striking characteristic of many vertical restraints is that they involve products that do not change physically as they move from the manufacturer through the distributor to the retail customer. For example, retail sellers of television sets, refrigerators, automobile tires, electric typewriters, newspapers, stereo equipment, and myriad other consumer goods simply perform a distribution function. These sellers do not alter the product physically, which is not to say that no useful function is performed. In this situation, there is what we referred to in Chapter 11

---

[2] This section and the next depend upon Roger D. Blair and David L. Kaserman, "The *Albrecht* Rule and Consumer Welfare: An Economic Analysis," *University of Florida Law Review* 33 (Summer 1981), pp. 461–84.

as a fixed proportions relationship between one of the inputs and the output. In other words, for every television set sold to a retail customer there must be one television set sold by the manufacturer to the distributor. Given this one-to-one relationship between the input (which is the good sold at the wholesale level) and final output (which is the same good sold at the retail level), the successive monopoly model which we developed in the preceding chapter indicates that an incentive for vertical integration of the two stages (manufacture and distribution) will arise whenever monopoly power is present at both stages. Some (perhaps limited) degree of market power may be present at the upstream stage because of substantial economies of scale relative to market demand (e.g., newspapers), because of significant product differentiation (e.g., many consumer durables), or because of patents or trademarks (e.g. cameras). At the downstream stage, market power is often bestowed upon individual distributors because of the existence of fairly well-defined local markets. For many products, retail distribution is carried out by franchisees who have some local monopoly power. In some instances, the manufacturer assigns exclusive territories to the franchisees. The classic example of this involves the distribution of newspapers. The newspaper publisher has often assigned specific and exclusive routes to distributors for home delivery service. In other cases, exclusivity is not guaranteed, but the manufacturer spaces the franchisees in such a way that each one can be a viable business entity. In other words, the cost structure of the franchisee's business indicates that excessive intrabrand competition among distributors would lead to business failures. An example of this involves the distribution of automobiles. A local market must be larger than some critical size, or it will not support more than one, say, Buick dealer. This is because the minimum volume of sales necessary for financial well-being is fairly substantial. It is not in the interest of General Motors to have so many Buick dealers in one geographic market that each is on the brink of financial ruin. The particular source of market power at the two vertically related stages is really not important for our purposes here. All that is required for the analysis that follows is that both the manufacturer and the individual distributors face downward-sloping demands.

Suppose that the manufacturer sells his output in a national market through a system of distributors to final consumers. The retail demand for the product is represented by D in Figure 13–1 along with the associated marginal revenue MR. We have denoted the marginal cost of retailing as MC_R and the marginal cost of production at the manufacturing stage as MC_P. If the retail distribution stage were competitively organized, the curve labeled $D - MC_R$ would be the derived demand for the manufacturer's output. The curve marginal to $D - MC_R$ is labeled d, which equals $MR - MC_R$. Under competitive distribution, then, the manufacturer will equate its marginal revenue, $MR - MC_R$, to its mar-

FIGURE 13–1

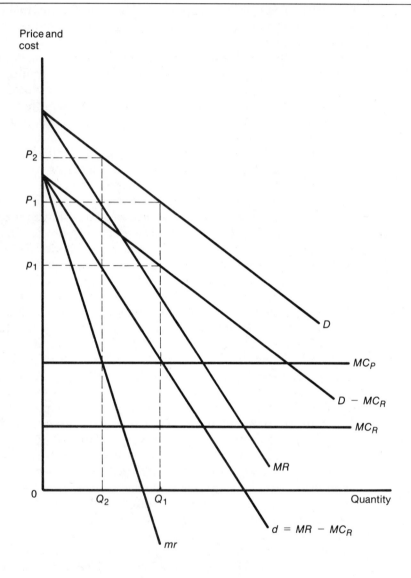

ginal cost, MC_P, and produce Q_1 units of output in order to maximize its profit. It will charge distributors a wholesale price of p_1 for this output, and the distributors, in turn, will charge final customers a retail price of P_1. The manufacturer's profits in this situation is given by the area $(p_1 - MC_P)Q_1$ which, as we saw in Chapter 11, is equal to the maximum profit that could be earned by a vertically integrated monopolist. Distributors in this situation earn zero economic profit since the price they pay for the good plus the marginal cost of performing the retail function equals the retail price (i.e., $p_1 + MC_R = P_1$).[3]

Now assume that due to the nature of the distribution function, only one distributor will be established in each geographic submarket. Since each retail distributor is a local monopolist, each one will maximize its profits by equating its marginal revenue to its marginal cost. The curve labeled $d = MR - MC_R$ is marginal revenue minus the marginal cost of retailing. For the distributor, marginal cost is the sum of the price charged by the manufacturer plus the marginal cost of retailing. Thus, the distributor will select its profit maximizing output by equating the price it has to pay to the manufacturer with the net marginal revenue $MR - MC_R$. Consequently, when the distributor has a local monopoly, the derived demand for the submarket is $d = MR - MC_R$.

The manufacturer exploits its monopoly power by selecting its price and output where its marginal cost (MC_P) and marginal revenue (mr) are equal. Thus, the manufacturer will produce Q_2 units of output for this market and will charge p_1 per unit. This price and output generate profit for the manufacturer of $(p_1 - MC_P)Q_2$, which is clearly less than the profit that could be earned if the distribution stage were competitive.

The distributor will have a marginal cost equal to the price it pays to the manufacturer p_1 plus the marginal cost of retailing MC_R. The distributor maximizes its profit by equating this marginal cost $(p_1 + MC_R)$ to its marginal revenue (MR). Consequently, the distributor will sell Q_2 units of output to retail customers at a retail price of P_2. The distributor now earns excess profits of $(P_2 - p_1 - MC_R)Q_2$. Thus, the distributor benefits from his status as a local monopolist at the expense of the manufacturer and of the consumer.

The role of maximum resale prices

It should be fairly obvious that the manufacturer will resent having his profit reduced below the maximum potential profit by noncompetitive behavior at the distribution stage. One possible response to this state of affairs is for the manufacturer to vertically integrate forward and perform its own distribution. Such integration, however, requires the manufacturer to develop expertise in areas such as marketing that may be relatively unfamiliar. In addition, the daily operation of many retail outlets in various locations may impose difficult problems of coordination upon the managers of the vertically integrated firm. As a result, the total costs of the integrated operation may be greater than the sum of the

---

[3] Keep in mind that zero economic profit implies a normal return for the industry since the relevant cost curves incorporate opportunity costs including a competitive return on the investment in the firm.

costs of the vertically related stages operated independently. In other words, there may be significant costs associated with vertical integration.[4]

As a contractual alternative to vertical integration under these circumstances, the manufacturer may require its distributors to charge no more than some specified price at the retail level (i.e., the manufacturer may establish maximum resale prices). If the manufacturer does, indeed, have market power, it will be able to enforce such a contract by threatening the downstream firms with a refusal to deal. Distributors failing to comply with the terms of the contract (i.e., those that exceed the maximum retail price) may not be able to obtain the product from the manufacturer in the future and may, therefore, be forced out of business. In other words, manufacturers would enforce the maximum resale prices by terminating sales to dealers who failed to comply.

In Figure 13–1, if the manufacturer establishes a maximum resale price of P_1, the distributor's marginal revenue curve becomes equal to P_1 for all outputs between zero and Q_1. For outputs greater than Q_1, the distributor's marginal revenue curve drops to MR. Thus, a maximum resale price of P_1 will prevent the distributor from restricting output below Q_1 because the distributor's marginal cost will equal the effective marginal revenue at Q_1 units of output. Fixing maximum resale prices restores the price and quantity that would result from competition at the distribution stage. For the retail customer, price is lower and a larger quantity is consumed when the manufacturer sets maximum resale prices. This, of course, is a beneficial development for the consumer. In addition, maximum resale prices restore the manufacturer's profits to the level that would be realized if the firm vertically integrated forward. Therefore, in the successive monopoly situation, maximum resale prices and vertical integration are economically equivalent.

One would think that economically equivalent business practices ought to receive equivalent antitrust treatment. If they did, then the manufacturer confronted with the successive monopoly problem would choose between vertical integration and maximum resale prices on the basis of a simple cost comparison. That is, the manufacturer would compare the costs of integrating vertically versus the costs of enforcing maximum resale price contracts. The option that is less costly would then be adopted.[5]

---

[4] An example of how this may occur is provided by J. Shelton, "Allocative Efficiency v. 'X-Efficiency': Comment," *American Economic Review* 57 (December 1967), pp. 1252–58. He analyzed the business results of a franchise operation with company-owned outlets as well as independently owned franchise outlets. Shelton reported that the independent franchisees performed better than the company-owned outlets.

[5] Selection of the lower-cost alternative results in a greater improvement in social welfare. You should be able to explain why.

As we shall see, however, public policy does *not* treat these two alternative strategies equivalently. In practice, maximum resale price contracts have become a per se violation of the antitrust laws. On the other hand, although we concluded in the preceding chapter that vertical integration receives somewhat harsher treatment than can be justified on the basis of economic theory, it is not dealt with on a per se basis. That is, vertical integration is not viewed as being presumptively illegal. Consequently, vertical integration exposes the manufacturer to a smaller risk of antitrust attack than does an economically equivalent maximum resale price contract. As a consequence, the existing public policy will tend to bias the manufacturer's selection process in favor of vertical integration even if that involves some extra costs.

13-3   FIXING MAXIMUM RESALE PRICES: LEGAL DOCTRINE

The legal treatment of fixing maximum resale prices is short but not particularly sweet for the consumer. The earlier mention of maximum prices can be found in the Supreme Court's decision in *Socony-Vacuum*. Although this case did not deal with fixing maximum resale prices, Justice Douglas wrote that "[u]nder the Sherman Act a combination formed for the purpose and with the effect of raising, depressing, fixing, pegging, or stabilizing the price of a commodity in interstate or foreign commerce is illegal per se."[6] For over 10 years, the language regarding "depressing" prices remained nothing more than dictum. In 1951, however, the Supreme Court handed down an important decision in *Kiefer-Stewart*.[7]

Kiefer-Stewart was an Indiana firm that had a wholesaler liquor business. Seagram and Calvert were producers of liquor that was sold to wholesalers in Indiana. Seagram and Calvert agreed not to sell their products to any wholesaler that refused to respect the maximum resale prices set by Seagram and Calvert. Since Kiefer-Stewart refused to respect these maximum resale prices, it was denied access to Seagram and Calvert. As a result, Kiefer-Stewart was injured due to lost profits on lost sales. Seagram and Calvert claimed that the decision to fix maximum resale prices was motivated by a horizontal price-fixing conspiracy among its wholesale customers and presented evidence to support this contention. In spite of this evidence, the Court ruled in favor of Kiefer-Stewart and explicitly reaffirmed the dictum in *Socony-Vacuum* on the grounds that agreements to fix maximum resale prices "cripple the freedom of traders and thereby restrain their ability to sell in accordance with their own judgment."

---

[6] *United States* v. *Socony Vacuum Oil Co., Inc.* 310 U.S. 150 (1940).

[7] *Kiefer-Stewart Co.* v. *Joseph E. Seagram & Sons*, 340 U.S. 211 (1951).

Following the logic developed in *Kiefer-Stewart,* the Court held a maximum price-fixing scheme to be illegal in *Albrecht.*[8] Due to the special nature of the home delivery of newspapers, the publisher of the *Globe Democrat* assigned exclusive territories to its carriers. Within each exclusive territory, the assigned distributor had a monopoly on home delivery. This practice assured that the costs incurred in providing home delivery service would be minimized because duplicate effort was eliminated. These delivery routes were subject to termination if the carrier charged a price in excess of the price advertised by the *Globe-Democrat.* Albrecht was one of the *Globe-Democrat's* distributors. Although he was aware of the maximum price policy, he ignored the policy and charged a higher price. Following the complaints of several customers, the publisher warned Albrecht that he was jeopardizing his distributorship. When Albrecht continued to overcharge his customers, the publisher took action against him by first competing directly and later by substituting another distributor for part of Albrecht's territory. Albrecht sued the publisher and others for injuries suffered. When he filed suit, he was terminated and forced to sell his distributorship.

On review, the Supreme Court explicitly approved its earlier decision in *Kiefer-Stewart:* "We think *Kiefer-Stewart* was correctly decided and we adhere to it." This, of course, doomed the Herald Co. as the Court found that "schemes to fix maximum prices, by substituting the perhaps erroneous judgment of a seller for the forces of the competitive market, may severely intrude upon the ability of buyers to compete and survive in the market." In spite of the fact that the Court was aware that competitive forces may not operate in exclusive territories, it ruled that fixing maximum prices violated Section 1 of the Sherman Act.

Current vitality of the Albrecht rule

The rule against fixing maximum prices persists today. Although the practice may occur in any situation where successive market power exists, most of the recent cases involve newspaper distribution[9] or gasoline dealers.[10] In these cases, the lower courts have heartily endorsed the unambiguous holding of the Supreme Court. Consequently, the vitality of the rule enunciated in *Albrecht* continues despite its questionable economic logic.

Maximum resale price fixing is invariably used by a supplier to prevent its distributors from exploiting whatever market power they possess. In *Kiefer-Stewart,* ostensible horizontal competitors in wholesale

---

[8] *Albrecht* v. *Herald Co.,* 390 U.S. 145 (1968).

[9] See, for example, *American Oil Co.* v. *Arnott,* No. 79–1357 (1980) and *Yentsch* v. *Texaco, Inc.,* Nos. 79–7735 and 79–7746 (1980).

[10] See, for example, *Knutson* v. *The Daily Mirror,* No. C–73–1354–CBR, ND, Cal (1979) and *Auburn News Company, Inc.* v. *Providence Journal Co.,* No. 80–0446, D.R.I. (1980).

distribution were allegedly fixing *minimum* prices. That is, the wholesalers were conspiring to *raise* prices. The actions of Seagram and Calvert can be seen as a means of preventing the inevitable decline in sales that accompanies an increase in price. Although each wholesale distributor may have had precious little monopoly power, collectively the wholesalers were trying to emulate the price and output that a monopolist would select. Fixing maximum prices is a way of thwarting these intentions of horizontal price fixers at the distribution stage.

The analysis of Albrecht is even more direct. The distributor, Albrecht, had an exclusive territory. For home delivery of the *Globe-Democrat*, Albrecht had a complete monopoly in his assigned territory. The publisher wanted to prevent Albrecht from behaving like the monopolist that he was. Fixing the maximum resale price of the *Globe-Democrat* was the publisher's way of doing that.

In both of the cases afforded full Supreme Court review, we see that the manufacturer enjoyed some market power through product differentiation (brand names of Seagram and Calvert) or through being the only seller (of an evening newspaper). The distributor also enjoyed some market power through the collusion of horizontal competitors *(Kiefer-Stewart)* or through exclusive territories *(Albrecht)*. By preventing maximum resale price fixing, the antitrust law promotes the welfare of the local monopolists at the expense of the consumer.

13–4 FIXING MINIMUM RESALE PRICES: ECONOMICS[11]

We have seen that a manufacturer usually benefits most when its distributors charge very low prices. Ordinarily, the producer will be concerned when price rises above the competitive level. Consequently, it is a bit puzzling to find that some manufacturers forbid their distributors from setting the price too low. In effect, these manufacturers specify some minimum price. Several reasons have been proposed for this sort of behavior. We shall examine three of these explanations.

Important product—Specific services

Whenever a product is sold, the customer jointly buys a package of services. These services include the amenities of the sales outlet, the seller's location, the provision of credit, the number of salespeople per customer, the hours of operation, and so on. All of these services relate to the way that a seller does business generally. In the normal course of events, we see that these services usually vary across different sellers. In this way, each seller attempts to cater to the tastes of a particular group

---

[11] This section depends heavily upon Lester Telser, "Why Should Manufacturers Want Fair Trade?" *Journal of Law and Economics* 3 (October 1960), pp. 86–105.

of customers. Those who prefer buying in a fancy store can go to such a store and pay more for the product than those who are indifferent to the purchasing environment and frequent a store with plainer appointments. As a general proposition, there will be many different retailers offering different combinations of services in conjunction with any particular commodity. Consequently, the cost of providing the commodity plus the bundle of services will vary across sellers. Competition, then, will result in an array of prices rather than a single price.

Ordinarily, the manufacturer of a commodity is largely unconcerned with the business practices followed by the retailers of his output. Those who put together the most desirable packages of services will survive and prosper. The manufacturer can trust that competition will eliminate the inefficient and the unscrupulous, but this lack of concern extends only to the distributor's general business practices. It does not extend to services that are product specific. There are numerous examples of product-specific services: an automobile dealer provides test drives for potential buyers; sellers of complicated consumer goods such as cameras or stereo equipment must be able to explain the product's technical features to prospective customers; and some products require proper installation for satisfactory performance. These kinds of services are important to the manufacturer because they affect the demand for his product. It is not hard to see that General Motors is vitally interested in whether the local Pontiac dealer provides test drives and adequate service. If he does not, then fewer Pontiacs will be sold. This follows from the fact that the information contained in a test drive is valuable to the customer.

We can examine the nature of this problem in Figure 13–2. The retail demand for the commodity in question is denoted by D if no product-specific services are provided. The marginal (and average) costs of retailing are given by MC_D. Consequently, the manufacturer's derived demand is $d = D - MC_D$, and the associated marginal revenue is mr. Given the manufacturer's marginal cost of production, MC_P, the optimal price and quantity for the manufacturer are p and Q, respectively. The retail price will be P, which is equal to p plus MC_D. Consequently, the competitive retail distributors will earn zero excess profits while the manufacturer's profits will be $(p - C)Q$.

This outcome can be compared to the results when the product-specific services are provided. The provision of those services shifts the retail demand curve to D^*. Since the additional services are costly, the marginal (and average) distribution costs rise to MC_D^*. Now, the manufacturer's derived demand becomes $d^* = D^* - MC_D^*$, and the associated marginal revenue curve is mr^*. The manufacturer obviously benefits from this shift in demand. His new optimal price and quantity are higher—p^* and Q^*, respectively. The competitive distributors still earn zero excess profit because the new retail price P^* equals p^* plus MC_D^*. In contrast, the manufacturer's profit expands to $(p^* - C)Q^*$. Conse-

FIGURE 13–2

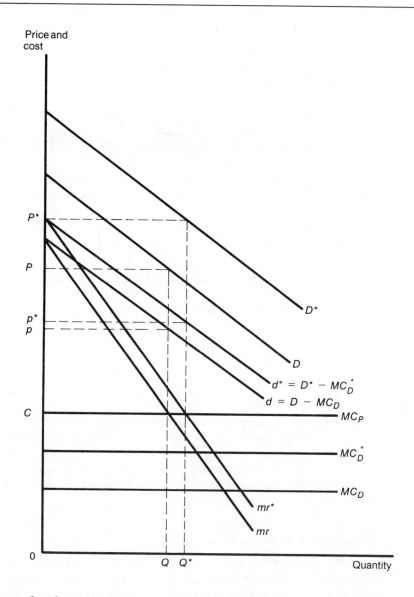

quently, the manufacturer will insist that these services be provided to the customer.

Free-rider problem

The manufacturer may ask each of his distributors to provide the desirable product-specific services. If each of them honors this request, the demand shifts to D^*, and all of the desirable results follow. The problem with product-specific services is that they can often be consumed separately from the product itself. This makes it possible for some distributors to "free ride" on the efforts of others.

Suppose that all distributors are offering the requested services. Each is incurring costs of MC_D^* per unit and selling the product for P^*. None of the distributors is earning any excess profit because the difference between P^* and MC_D^* equals the price charged by the manufacturer. Sooner or later, it will occur to one of the distributors that it can improve its profits by not offering some or any of the product-specific services. As long as the rest of the distributors continue providing those services, the final-good demand will remain at D^*. By cutting out some services, the clever distributor can cut its price just below P^*, thereby increasing its volume of business. In addition, its profits will soar as its distribution costs are reduced considerably. For example, suppose a discount house offered no services in its camera department. Its costs would fall to MC_D from MC_D^*. By offering a price slightly below P^*, it will attract many customers. A full service camera store provides the product-specific services that help the customer decide to buy the camera while the discount house makes the sale by offering a lower price.

At this point, the manufacturer is unconcerned about a single discounter. But the manufacturer will become concerned when a lot of distributors catch on and follow suit. When this happens, the demand curve begins to drift downward from D^* to D. The excess profits of the early defectors will prove to be transitory as competition leads to lower and lower prices. The final equilibrium where none of the product-specific services is offered has been described above. The only long-run losers are the manufacturer and the customers. It is obvious that the manufacturer loses because his profits are reduced from $(p^* - MC_P)Q^*$ to $(p - MC_P)Q$. Although it is not so obvious, it is true nonetheless that the consumers also lose. This follows because the value of the services to the consumer is given by the vertical difference between D and D^*, which exceeds the added costs of providing those services as measured by the difference between MC_D and MC_D^*.

Resale price maintenance

The manufacturer can use resale price maintenance to prevent the free-rider problem. If the manufacturer specifies that all units of his product must be sold at a price of P^* or more, there will be little incentive to stop providing the services. It is still true that a single dealer can reduce his costs by reducing the services provided, but there is no way for him to attract the customer. Thus, a reduction in services will result in lost sales and probably in negative profits. In the absence of retail price competition, the scramble for retail sales will lead to nonprice competition, which is not susceptible to free-rider problems. The retailers will be forced to provide the level of services that leads to maximum profits for the manufacturer.

If a minimum resale price is specified by the manufacturer, a recalcitrant distributor can still *attempt* to be a free rider. In other words, a dealer can try to cut his services and his prices. This just means that the resale price maintenance agreement will have to be policed, which, of course, is true of many contracts. As long as the costs of policing the agreement are smaller than the difference in the profit levels, or

$$\Delta\Pi = (p^* - C)Q^* - (p - C)Q$$

it will be sensible to impose a resale price maintenance agreement.

Vertical integration

Forward ownership integration is an alternative to resale price maintenance. Certainly, if the manufacturer is also distributing his own product, he can be sure that the product-specific services are being provided. In some cases, this is a viable option. For example, when other avenues to vertical control were foreclosed, Schwinn began to distribute its bicycles through its own retail outlets rather than through independent franchisees. In principle, the automobile manufacturers could own all of their dealerships. There are other products, however, that can benefit from product-specific services where forward vertical integration is not a sensible option. For example, the producer of a particularly sophisticated camera could vertically integrate forward and open retail camera shops. But he would have to carry a full complement of products, or there would be very little customer traffic. Thus, the manufacturer may be able to specialize in production but be unable to do so in distribution. Consequently, this may make vertical integration an unrealistic practical option although it remains a theoretical alternative.

Alternative uses for resale price maintenance

Unlike fixing maximum prices where the welfare effects are clearly positive, the effects of resale price maintenance are ambiguous. The ambiguity stems from the fact that minimum price-fixing schemes may not always be due to a need for product-specific services. There are two other motivations for resale price maintenance: (1) retailer cartel and (2) manufacturer cartel. If resale price maintenance emerges as a result of either cartel, the welfare effects will be negative: Consumers will be worse off.

First, suppose that the distributors form a conspiracy to raise prices above the level that provides a competitive return on their investment. The retailers may decide to accept whatever price the manufacturer puts on his product and select the quantity that will maximize joint profits at retail. This scenario is analytically equivalent to the successive monopoly case that was discussed earlier. Moreover, we may recognize the fact pattern as being similar to the *Kiefer-Stewart* case.

We know what the effects of a retailer cartel are. The derived demand changes, price to the consumer rises, and output falls. As a result, the retailers enjoy some excess profits while the manufacturer's excess profits are reduced. Each retailer is in a situation where the retail price exceeds marginal cost. Consequently, each retailer can be better off by behaving strategically. If all of the other colluding retailers were to adhere to the collusive price, any one of them could increase its profits by reducing its price below the cartel price and expanding output. Thus, there is an incentive to cheat on one's fellow conspirators. This, of course, is the cross that every cartel has to bear. Human nature being what it is, there is little honor among thieves. Cartel instability results from the simple fact that each member has an independent incentive to cheat on the agreement. As we have seen before, the colluders must police their agreement and attempt to enforce the agreement to fix price and restrict output. The manufacturer can provide them with some much needed help in this endeavor. Resale price maintenance, ostensibly imposed and actually policed by the manufacturer, is an ideal supplement for an effective conspiracy. The retailers would have the manufacturer impose a resale price equal to the cartel price, which would then be enforced for the benefit of the retailers.

The consequences of resale price maintenance imposed by the retailers are inconsistent with the usual goals of antitrust policy. Fortunately, public policy will tend to be furthered by the manufacturer's pursuit of its own self-interest. Specifically, the manufacturer has an incentive to undermine the effectiveness of the conspiracy. If competition is restored at the retail level, the manufacturer's profits will increase. Consequently, the retailers can hardly expect the manufacturer to be vigilant in policing and enforcing the resale price maintenance agreement. Of even more concern, however, is the recognition that the manufacturer has an obvious motive for reporting the collusive activity to the antitrust authorities. As a result, one should not expect such a conspiracy to endure. Thus, distributor collusion does not provide a satisfactory explanation for sustained efforts at resale price maintenance by the manufacturer.

Second, suppose that the manufacturers form a conspiracy to charge the monopoly price for their output. Each manufacturer has an incentive to reduce its price slightly and expand its output at the expense of its fellow conspirators. One way of dulling this incentive is to impose a resale price maintenance agreement. Such an agreement will prevent the retailers from expanding the sales of the cheater's product. Consequently, secret price concessions may be unmatched by increases in sales volume. But resale price maintenance is a very cumbersome way of preventing cheating among the cartel members, and in addition, it is highly imperfect. A little reflection reveals that the resale price maintenance agreement would have to be buttressed by extensive other controls. For example, secret price cuts could induce a retailer to favor the manufacturer giving the special deal. To offset this possibility, the cartel may have to adopt exclusive dealing (i.e., have a policy that a dealer could only handle one line). In response, the price cutter may offer concessions to lure dealers away from other cartel members, and therefore, this avenue also must be foreclosed. But the list goes on and on. This is an unwieldy way of attempting to deal with policing a cartel arrangement.

In summary, we have examined three roles for resale price maintenance. When it is used for assuring the provision of commodity-specific services, it is beneficial to the manufacturer and to the consumer. The other two uses are to further the aims of cartels—either a dealer cartel or a producer cartel. In these cases, resale price maintenance has undesirable consequences for the consumer. But we have also seen that resale price maintenance probably will not be very effective in those instances.

13–5 FIXING MINIMUM RESALE PRICES: LEGAL DOCTRINE

While the economic analysis of resale price maintenance may not lead to unambiguous conclusions regarding consumer welfare, the judicial history is quite clear. Since 1911, the rule on resale price maintenance has been quite clear and consistent: Such agreements violate Section 1 of the Sherman Act. In the interlude, ways around this harsh rule have been sought. We shall see that two legal gambits—refusals to deal and agency relationships—have not been wholly successful. Moreover, even special legislation has not fared too well.

The controlling case is *Dr. Miles*,[12] which involved the manufacturer of proprietary medicines that were prepared according to allegedly secret formulas. Dr. Miles devised an elaborate pricing system that established minimum prices at which sales of its products would be made throughout the entire distribution chain. The case arose because John D. Park, a wholesale drug concern, refused to enter into the restrictive agreements that Dr. Miles required. Instead, John D. Park obtained the medicines for resale at discount prices from other wholesalers who had accepted the restrictions. Dr. Miles sued John D. Park for maliciously interfering with the contract between Dr. Miles and some of his buyers.

The Supreme Court recognized the issue as being whether the restrictive agreements were valid. If they were, Dr. Miles would win; if they were not, John D. Park would prevail. The Court characterized the

---

[12] *Dr. Miles Medical Co.* v. *John D. Park & Sons Co.*, 220 U.S. 373 (1911).

contractual scheme as "a system of interlocking restrictions" whereby Dr. Miles could control the prices of its products at every stage in the distribution system. As a result, Dr. Miles would ultimately "fix the amount which the consumer shall pay, eliminating all competition" between retailers. Since these agreements obviously restrained trade, the Court's task was to determine whether the restraints violated Section 1 of the Sherman Act.

Dr. Miles made two arguments in its defense. First, it contended that it was entitled to extensive control because the medicines were produced according to a secret process. The Court rejected this argument easily:

> This argument implies that if, for any reason, monopoly of production exists, it carries with it the right to control the entire trade of the produced article, and to prevent any competition that otherwise might arise between wholesale and retail dealers. . . . But, because there is monopoly of production, it certainly cannot be said that there is no public interest in maintaining freedom of trade with respect to future sales after the article has been placed on the market and the producer has parted with his title.

The second argument was disposed of just as easily. Dr. Miles argued that a manufacturer is entitled to control the prices on all sales of his own products. In effect, Dr. Miles claimed that it could produce and sell or not as it saw fit and, therefore, that it could impose conditions as to the prices at which purchasers may resell the item. The Court reasoned that "because a manufacturer is not bound to make or sell, it does not follow in cases of sales actually made he may impose upon purchasers every sort of restriction. Thus, a general restraint upon alienation is ordinarily invalid."

The rule against resale price maintenance is robust. Bobbs-Merrill[13] had a copyright on a book and claimed a right to fix its resale price. In that case, the Court held that the copyright privilege was not designed to provide such prerogatives. In *Bauer & Cie* v. *O'Donnell*,[14] the manufacturer claimed a right to fix resale prices on the basis of a patent. Since a patent provides the right to restrict use and since resale is a use, the manufacturer claimed that it had the right to restrict the resale price. The Court held that when the manufacturer sold a product whose value is in its use, the right to restrict use passes to the purchaser. Thus, neither copyrights nor patents confer authority for resale price maintenance.

In *Dr. Miles*, the Court did not announce that resale price maintenance was a per se violation of the Sherman Act. The Court's reasoning, however, could have been used to reach such a conclusion:

> agreements or combinations between dealers, having for their sole purpose the destruction of competition and the fixing of prices, are injurious to the public interest and void. . . .

---

[13] *Bobbs-Merrill Co.* v. *Straus*, 210 U.S. 339 (1908).
[14] 229 U.S. 1 (1913).

> The complainant's Dr. Miles' plan falls within the principle which condemns contracts of this class. . . . The complainant having sold its product at prices satisfactory to itself, the public is entitled to whatever advantage may be derived from competition in the subsequent traffic.

Subsequent decisions by the Supreme Court have left little doubt that vertical price fixing is a per se violation of the Sherman Act. Recently the Court remarked[15] that "[t]he per se illegality of [vertical] price restrictions has been established firmly for many years."

Fair trade legislation

Some states passed fair trade laws that would permit vertical price fixing. These laws were not very helpful by themselves because of the Federal Antitrust laws that prohibited resale price maintenance. Eventually, the Miller-Tydings Amendment was passed, which permitted resale price maintenance where state law permitted it. When the Supreme Court ruled that nonsigners to a fair trade agreement could not be bound by the established minimum prices, the Miller-Tydings Amendment became ineffective. In an effort to revive the force of state fair trade laws, Congress amended the Federal Trade Commission Act by passing the McGuire Act, which extended fair trade to unwilling resellers.

The purpose of this legislation generally has been to protect small merchants who are threatened economically by mass merchandisers. Many of these small merchants are quite inefficient and cannot survive in competition with large retailers that enjoy the benefits of greater efficiency. This resulted in a campaign in Congress to pass a Federal resale price maintenance law. The admitted rationale for such legislation was the competitive difficulties encountered by small merchants. This effort failed. Subsequently, the tide of public opinion turned as inflation alarmed consumers. During the Ford administration, the Consumer Goods Pricing Act of 1975 was passed. This repealed the McGuire Act and restored the supremacy of the Sherman Act over state fair trade laws.

Refusals to deal

Some manufacturers have attempted to implement a resale price maintenance policy by refusing to deal with those who fail to honor the minimum prices. The Supreme Court explicitly approved of this behavior in its *Colgate*[16] decision. Through its resale price maintenance program, Colgate's producers sold at uniform retail prices. In contrast to the Dr. Miles program, Colgate did not have elaborate contractual agreements. Colgate allowed each of its dealers to sell at whatever price the

---

[15] *Continental TV, Inc.* v. *GTE Sylvania, Inc.*, 433 U.S. 36 (1977).

[16] *United States* v. *Colgate & Co.*, 250 U.S. 300 (1919).

dealer felt appropriate, but Colgate would simply not deal with those dealers who deviated from the minimum prices. Since there were no contractual arrangements, the Court approved of Colgate's behavior:

> In the absence of any purpose to create or maintain a monopoly, the [Sherman] Act does not restrict the long recognized right of trader or manufacturer in an entirely private business, freely to exercise his own independent discretion as to parties with whom he will deal; and, of course, he may announce in advance the circumstances under which he will refuse to sell.

The freedom to engage in resale price maintenance by relying upon *Colgate* has been severely restricted through subsequent decisions. This is not too surprising when one recognized that the *Colgate* decision is incoherent. If the manufacturer unilaterally decides to impose resale price maintenance through explicit contracts, then it violates the law according to *Dr. Miles*. If it achieves the same end without explicit contracts, it may be safe on the *Colgate* logic. This is one of the law's infamous distinctions without a difference.

For some reason, the Supreme Court is reluctant to overrule its *Colgate* decision. Instead, it has narrowed the scope of the rule so severely that a manufacturer should be cautioned that "[t]he line between legal and illegal conduct here is a very narrow one and if a seller chooses to walk that line, he must do so at his peril."[17] Currently, a manufacturer can announce a policy of not dealing with those who do not follow its schedule of minimum prices and actually follow through on this policy. If this results in resale price maintenance, the seller is secure under *Colgate*. If, however, the seller takes any additional steps to enforce its policies, he or she will fall off that "narrow line." Some ways of losing the *Colgate* shield are (1) establishing a policing mechanism to detect violators, (2) reinstating violators who promise to abide by the minimum prices in the future,[18] (3) asking wholesalers to police the retailers,[19] and (4) assuring compliant dealers that it will do something about those who do not comply.[20] In all of these cases, the seller would have overstepped the bounds of its *Colgate* rights.

Agency relationships

In his dissenting opinion to the Dr. Miles decision, Justice Holmes expressed some concern that the majority has confused form with substance because the Dr. Miles program would have been legal if an agency relationship had been established. An agent is one who acts on

---

[17] FTC Advisory Opinion Digest No. 163 (1968), 16 C.F.R. paragraph 15.163 (1973).

[18] See *FTC v. Beech-Nut Packing Co.*, 257 U.S. 441 (1922).

[19] See *United States v. Parke, Davis & Co.*, 362 U.S. 29 (1960).

[20] *United States v. GM Corp.*, 384 U.S. 127 (1966).

behalf of another. In *General Electric*,[21] the agency relationship carried the day for General Electric. In that case, there was no serious dispute about whether General Electric was setting the subsequent prices for its light bulbs. GE argued, however, that the bulbs were sold through wholesale and retail agents. The bulbs went to the agents under consignment and remained the property of GE until they were ultimately sold. The agents were given no discretion to deal with the bulbs in any way other than as directed by GE. If the middlemen had been purchasers, the Court ruled, prices could not be fixed. In contrast, if the middlemen were agents, then GE can fix the prices. The Court found that the independent merchants were agents of GE in the consignment sales.

The *General Electric* decision is another one that has not been expressly overruled, but the Supreme Court's decision in *Simpson* v. *Union Oil*[22] leaves little of substance standing from the GE case. Union Oil had what appeared to be a consignment agreement with dealers like Simpson. Union Oil owned its retail outlets and leased them to its dealers. These leases were used to enforce the retail price structure since renewal was not automatic. The Court found that the lease agreement was used coercively and appeared to be quite effective in maintaining retail prices. Although the consignment agreement was not much different from the one that General Electric used, the Court seemed to be offended by this escape hatch. Justice Douglas said that "a consignment no matter how lawful it might be as a matter of private contract law, must give way before the federal antitrust policy." Further,

> [w]hen, however a "consignment" device is used to cover a vast gasoline distribution system, fixing prices through many retail outlets, the antitrust laws prevent calling the "consignment" an agency for then the end result of *United States* v. *Socony-Vacuum Oil Co.*, would be avoided merely by clever manipulation of words, not by differences in substance.

Thus, the consignment or agency exemption from the dictates of *Dr. Miles* was severely attenuated by the *Union Oil* decision.

13–6 FINAL COMMENTS

The purpose of antitrust policy should be to preserve competition because this promotes consumer welfare. It is clear that the current antitrust policy prohibiting maximum resale prices has perverse effects (i.e., is not proconsumer). It is a form of protection for local monopolists whose welfare is not a legitimate concern of the antitrust laws. Such a policy inhibits the manufacturer's efforts at combatting the successive

---

[21] *United States* v. *General Electric Co.*, 272 U.S. 476 (1962).
[22] 377 U.S. 13 (1964).

restriction of output that follows inexorably from the successive monopoly market structure.

An upstream monopolist will attempt to impose maximum resale prices whenever a successive monopoly situation is present. The producer is not motivated by undiluted altruism to act on behalf of consumers. On the contrary, the producer is motivated by a quest for larger profits. In this case, however, the interests of the firm and the consumer coincide, and as a result, fixing maximum prices promotes consumer welfare. This case presents an obvious structural standard—whenever successive monopoly is observed, constraints on downstream pricing discretion should be permitted.

We have seen that there are two anticompetitive reasons and one procompetitive reason for fixing minimum resale prices. But majority does not rule in this case. For one thing, it would not be easy for a retailer cartel to impose a resale price maintenance agreement on the manufacturer. For another thing, there is a way to distinguish between the procompetitive and anticompetitive motivations. If minimum resale prices are imposed to assure the provision of commodity-specific services, the result should be an expansion of output. In contrast, if either a dealer cartel or a producer cartel is behind the resale price maintenance scheme, the industry output will fall. Consequently, the antitrust authorities can determine whether the resale price maintenance agreement offends the spirit of the antitrust laws. As matters stand now, there is no room for a defense based on procompetitive resale price maintenance.

QUESTIONS AND PROBLEMS

1. Given the successive monopoly situation, assume that vertical integration is not financially feasible because it increases costs more than fixing (and enforcing) maximum resale prices. Show graphically the increase in profits that the manufacturer can earn by adopting the lower-cost strategy. Show also that consumers benefit from the adoption of this strategy.

2. How could sales quotas be used in place of maximum resale prices in the successive monopoly case?

3. Suppose the manufacturer of widgets buys its inputs in a competitive input market. If the producers of one of these inputs start colluding on the price that they will charge, how does this affect the widget manufacturer? How can he cope with this development?

4. It has been suggested that maximum resale prices may be an oligopolistic effort to practice limit pricing and thereby prevent entry. Discuss.

5. Show that the manufacturer will never find it profitable in the long run to force his distributors to provide services that customers are unwilling to pay for. (Hint: In Figure 13–2, show that the vertical difference between D and D^* must be at least as great as the difference between MC_D and MC_D^*.)

6. General Motors distributed Chevrolets exclusively through independent franchised dealers, but automobile discounters began to appear. These sellers bought automobiles from dealers and sold them at very low prices, or they simply referred a customer to a dealer that agreed to sell at an extremely low price and collected a commission from that dealer. An association of dealers complained to General Motors, which, in turn, took some steps to prevent its dealers from doing business with discounters. Was the action of General Motors explicable on the "product-specific service" argument or on the "retailer cartel" argument? [*United States* v. *General Motors Corp.*, 384 U.S. 127 (1966)]

7. Joseph E. Seagram & Sons supplied retail liquor stores through independent wholesalers. One of the wholesalers wanted to offer special discounts to several large retailers. Seagram offered to support this effort by lowering its price to the wholesaler. It conditioned the lower price on the wholesaler's actually passing this on to the large retailers. Is this per se illegal resale price maintenance? (*AAA Liquors, Inc.* v. *Joseph E. Seagram & Sons, Inc.*, No. 82–1512, U.S. Supreme Court, cert. denied, 5/2/83)

8. Many resale price maintenance cases involve simple consumer products such as Russell Stover candy, Levi's jeans, Arrow shirts, and Colgate's toiletries. How can we explain the existence of resale price maintenance for these products?

9. Should a monopolist's freedom to refuse to deal with its dealers be restricted? Suppose a refusal to deal will put a dealer out of business.

10. Suppose a newspaper distributor was prevented from raising its delivered price due to threats of termination by the publisher. The distributor sues for the lost profits. Has the distributor suffered antitrust injury?

11. Since newspapers cannot set maximum resale prices for their distributors, how can they achieve the same result? Does this alternative promote the freedom of independent businessmen?

12. Describe the three motivations for resale price maintenance. Suppose that the empirical evidence showed convincingly that resale price maintenance caused retail prices to be higher than they otherwise would be. Does this provide a clue as to which motivation for resale price maintenance was operative?

13. The Antitrust Division found that resale price maintenance leads to lower sales volume per retail outlet. Is this consistent with any of the motives for resale price maintenance? Explain.

14. In *Albrecht*, the Supreme Court seems to have based its per se prohibition of *maximum* price fixing on the logic that agreements to fix maximum prices "cripple the freedom of traders and thereby restrain their ability to sell in accordance with their own judgment." What does this have to do with consumer welfare? Can the Court's concern for the freedom of traders be inconsistent with consumer welfare?

15. One rationale for a per se rule against maximum resale price fixing is that the producer may set the price too low to permit the distributor to service its customers and still earn a competitive return. Is this a valid concern? Does the manufacturer have any incentive to do this?

16. Since the Herald Company created the successive monopoly problem by establishing exclusive territories, could the problem be solved by simply opening up home delivery to competition among several distributors?

17. Assume horizontal cost curves, linear demand curves, and an upstream monopoly. Compare the monopolist's profits with competitive distribution and successive monopoly. Prove that successive monopoly halves the upstream firm's profits.

18. In *Dr. Miles*, the Supreme Court asserted that a manufacturer has no interest in the disposition of its product once ownership is transferred to the retailer. Does this make sense?

19. In *Dr. Miles*, the Court asserted that vertical price fixing is analogous to horizontal price fixing among retailers. Does this make any sense?

20. Some analysts argue that General Electric set up a bona fide consignment arrangement while the purported consignees in *Union Oil* were really independent businessmen. How can we distinguish between bona fide and sham consignments?

FURTHER READINGS

ABA Antitrust Section. Monograph No. 2. *Vertical Restrictions Limiting Intrabrand Competition*, 1977, pp. 71–98.

Blair, Roger D., and David L. Kaserman. "The *Albrecht* Rule and Consumer Welfare: An Economic Analysis." *University of Florida Law Review* 33 (Summer 1981), pp. 461–84.

Bowman, Ward. "Prerequisites and Effects of Resale Price Maintenance." *University of Chicago Law Review* 22 (Summer 1955), pp. 825–73.

Easterbrook, Frank H. "Maximum Price Fixing." *University of Chicago Law Review* 48 (Fall 1981), pp. 886–910.

Levi, Edward H. "The Parke, Davis—Colgate Doctrine: The Ban on Resale Price Maintenance." In *The Supreme Court and Patents and Monopolies*, ed. Philip B. Kurland. Chicago: University of Chicago Press, 1975, pp. 1–69.

Pitofsky, Robert. "In Defense of Discounters: The No-Frills Case for a *Per Se* Rule Against Vertical Price Fixing." *Georgetown Law Journal* 71 (December 1983), pp. 1487–95.

Telser, Lester. "Why Should Manufacturers Want Fair Trade?" *Journal of Law and Economics* 3 (October 1960), pp. 86–105.

14

Territorial and customer restrictions

14-1   INTRODUCTION

A commonly observed characteristic of many distribution systems is the assignment by the manufacturer of exclusive territories to individual distributors. We see this practice employed in the distribution of such diverse products as newspapers, televisions, fast foods, hardware, and automobiles. While the precise nature of the territorial restrictions may vary from one case to another, the manufacturer of some final product typically will promise the downstream firms that have agreed to distribute the product that it will not authorize any other distributors to locate within the geographic territory specified for each distributor. Thus, McDonald's Corporation may include a clause in the contract that it signs with each of its franchised outlets which stipulates that no other McDonald's franchisees will be permitted to locate within some fixed distance of the existing or proposed restaurant.

The result of this sort of vertical arrangement is to establish each distributor as the sole supplier of that particular manufacturer's product within the specified territory. An alternative (and economically equivalent) form that these types of agreements may take is for the manufacturer to assign specific customers to each distributor. In that case, the distributor assigned to a particular set of customers becomes the sole supplier of the manufacturer's product to those customers.

The obvious purpose that is served by this class of vertical restraints is to eliminate (or at least reduce) competition between distributors of the manufacturer's product. The economic incentives that lead both the manufacturer and the distributors to agree to such an arrangement, however, are not so obvious. Nor is it obvious what the impacts of such arrangements are on the vigor of competition in the overall market in which the manufacturer's product falls. In many cases, it appears that the reduction in competition among the distributors of a given manufacturer's product is accompanied by an increase in competition between them and the distributors of other competing brands of that product. Thus, policymakers and the courts have been faced with a potentially complex trade-off between intrabrand and interbrand competition. As we shall see below, the resulting confusion concerning the economic effects of vertical territorial restrictions has contributed to a somewhat schizophrenic treatment of this type of agreement in the courts.

In this chapter, we investigate the economic incentives that can motivate manufacturers and distributors to agree to vertical territorial restrictions. In surveying the various potential incentives involved, we shall gain some insight concerning the likely effects of such restrictions on the overall competitive process. We shall then turn to a discussion of the mercurial legal treatment that these nonprice vertical restraints have received in the courts. Following that discussion, we will conclude the chapter with some recommendations for public policy in this area.

14–2 ECONOMIC INCENTIVES

In the preceding chapter, we saw that, under certain conditions, a manufacturer may have an economic incentive to exercise some control over the price that its distributors charge for the final product. We also saw that such control could be achieved through either vertical integration or vertical price fixing. The latter, we found, may involve the setting of either a maximum or a minimum resale price, depending upon the precise economic situation that is providing the underlying incentive for the manufacturer to control the distributors' behavior at the downstream stage. Earlier chapters have also demonstrated that horizontal price fixing (collusion) could be used to achieve the same result as horizontal integration (merger to monopoly) and that horizontal market division could, in turn, be used to emulate the results achieved by a collusive agreement.[1] By analogy, then, it follows that vertical contractual agreements restricting distributors to specific geographic markets or customers may provide an alternative to vertical integration or vertical price fixing. This, in fact, is the case.

As a result, we shall find that the same incentives that motivate vertical price fixing (or resale price maintenance) also largely motivate vertical territorial restrictions. Here, however, we have the added com-

---

[1] See Chapter 6 and 7.

plication that the manufacturer agreeing to such restrictions appears to be conferring monopoly status on the distributors of its product. Recalling the successive monopoly model from Chapter 11, however, economic theory tells us that manufacturers experience lower profits when monopoly is substituted for competition at the downstream stage. Consequently, the voluntary use of exclusive territories by the manufacturer appears to present an anomaly. If manufacturers' profits are higher with competition at the distribution stage, why do we observe them creating local monopolists through the use of territorial restrictions? The following sections address this question.

Franchising[2]

Territorial restrictions are a common feature of franchised systems of distribution. In these systems, the upstream firm is not typically a manufacturer but is, instead, the owner of a nationally advertised trademark. To the extent that the trademarked product is viewed by consumers as being distinct from other products in the same industry (i.e., to the extent that the trademark and its associated advertisements lead to product differentiation), the holder of the trademark enjoys some monopoly power, namely, faces a downward-sloping demand. Since the trademark receives protection from the government against infringement much like a patent, any monopoly power resulting from the trademark itself is legal.

Now, the owner of the trademark (the franchisor) licenses firms at the downstream stage (the franchisees) to distribute the trademarked product. The ultimate value of the trademark itself then depends upon the subsequent performance of these distributors in providing the level of quality, speed of service, and cleanliness of surroundings that consumers associate with the trademark. Clearly, all parties have an interest in maintaining the value of the trademark. But each individual distributor, by itself, will have an incentive to reduce costs by allowing the quality of its own outlet to slip. So long as the other distributors continue to provide the higher quality expected by consumers, the lower-quality distributor will be able to maintain its revenues. Consequently, by free riding on the performance of the other distributors in the franchise system, a single distributor can increase its profits by providing a

---

[2] The economic literature concerned with franchising has only recently begun to develop. See R. Caves and W. Murphy II, "Franchising: Firms, Markets, and Intangible Assets," *Southern Economic Journal* 42 (April 1976), pp. 572–86; P. Rubin, "The Theory of the Firm and the Structure of the Franchise Contract," *Journal of Law and Economics* 21 (April 1978), pp. 223–33; B. Klein, "Transaction Cost Determinants of 'Unfair' Contractual Arrangements," *American Economic Review* 70 (May 1980), pp. 356–62; and R. Blair and D. Kaserman, "Optimal Franchising," *Southern Economic Journal* 49 (October 1982), pp. 494–505.

substandard level of service. But all distributors will face the same incentive. As a result, to protect the value of the trademark (and, thereby, the value of the entire franchise system), the franchisor must be assured that each franchisee will maintain some specified standard of performance.

One way to obtain such assurance is to require each franchisee to pay the franchisor a lump-sum fee in exchange for the right to employ the trademark over some specified period of time, where this fee is forfeited in the event that the franchisor cancels the franchisee's contract for nonperformance prior to the contractual date of termination. Thus, the franchise fee that the distributor pays to use the trademark may be viewed as a bond that ensures both the franchisor and the other franchisees that the distributor will maintain the specified quality standards.

Having posted this bond, the distributor, in turn, must be provided some assurance that he will be able to earn at least a competitive rate of return on his investment. If the franchisor subsequently licenses another distributor and allows that distributor to locate just across the street, such a return will not be forthcoming. Consequently, to assure each distributor that it will be able to earn a return that is sufficient to amortize the lump-sum franchise fee, the franchisor specifies an exclusive territory for each franchisee in the contract.

The net result of this type of arrangement is depicted in Figure 14–1. In this graph, D is the demand curve for the trademarked product in one geographic market, and MR is the marginal revenue associated with this demand curve. The franchisee's marginal costs of distributing the product under the quality standards specified in the contract (often, with the aid of lawyers, in exhaustive detail) are given as MC in the graph. The lump-sum entry fee that the franchisee must pay to utilize the trademark is a fixed cost that does not vary with output. Consequently, average costs will lie above marginal costs; and if marginal costs are constant, average costs will fall throughout. The franchisor can raise or lower the franchisee's average costs without affecting its marginal costs simply by increasing or decreasing the fixed fee. Then, by setting the fixed fee at a level that results in average costs of AC in the graph, the franchisor can collect the entire monopoly profit that is due to the trademark through the lump-sum franchise fee. As can be seen in the graph, this fee (and, therefore, the franchisor's profit) is given by area P_Mabc, which is exactly equal to what the total monopoly profits would be at the downstream stage if no fee were collected.

Thus, despite the presence of a monopoly in the trademarked product in each geographic market at the downstream stage, distributors earn zero economic profit (i.e, they just earn a competitive rate of return). The franchisor is not frustrated by the successive monopoly problem because he collects the full monopoly rents through the fixed fee, which does not affect the distributor's marginal costs and, therefore, does not lead to additional output restriction at the downstream stage.

FIGURE 14–1

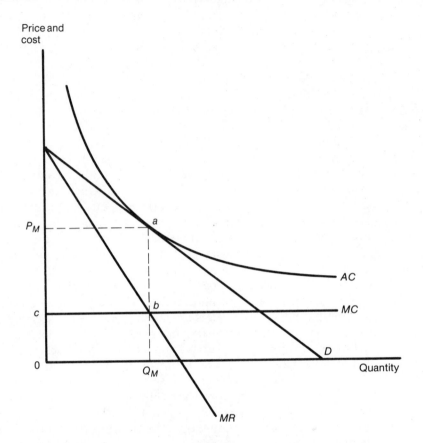

With regard to the public policy implications of this model, a few comments are in order. First, since the trademark itself represents a legal monopoly that is conferred by the government in order to promote product quality and innovation, the profits attributable to that trademark should also be legal. Second, the use of territorial restrictions in the pursuit of those profits appears to represent a relatively efficient approach to solving the free-rider problem, which, if unaddressed, could devalue the trademark and frustrate the very goals that the trademark laws were intended to serve. Finally, to the extent that trademarked products compete with one another (e.g., Wendy's versus McDonald's versus Burger King), the degree of monopoly power actually enjoyed by a given brand is not likely to be of much consequence. As a result, any diminution of intrabrand competition that results from the use of territorial restrictions is also not likely to be of serious concern where interbrand competition is active. Thus, we are led to the conclusion that the use of territorial restrictions in franchise systems of distribution should be of little or no concern to the antitrust authorities.

Economies of scale in local distribution

For some products, technological and market demand conditions may create a natural monopoly situation in each geographic market at the distribution stage. That is, for a given geographic area, it may be efficient to have only one distributor of the product. Consequently, intrabrand competition is economically inefficient.

A good example is the distribution, or delivery, of local newspapers. To minimize transportation costs, it is necessary to have only one delivery person for each neighborhood. To require more than one would increase the total costs of delivering the newspapers because of the duplication of travel over a given route. As a result, newspaper firms generally assign an exclusive territory to each delivery person so that these economies of scale in local distribution can be realized.

Without more, such an assignment of exclusive territories would result in the successive monopoly problem. Each delivery person would purchase the newspapers from the publisher and mark the price up to the monopoly level in the specific geographic market controlled. The resulting restriction in sales at the distribution stage, of course, would reduce the profits of the newspaper publisher, whether or not it enjoys any significant monopoly power at the upstream stage. As we saw in the preceding chapter, one way for the upstream firm to circumvent this problem (without integrating vertically) is to impose maximum resale prices on its distributors (see Section 13–2). In so doing, the upstream firm is responding to the natural monopoly situation in much the same way that governments do. It awards the downstream firm monopoly status, protects it from (intrabrand) entry, and, in exchange, regulates the price. Another method that can be used by the manufacturer to counteract the successive monopoly problem is a simple refusal to renew the contract of a distributor that has been restricting output. Through the refusal to deal, the manufacturer can control the errant distributor.

Clearly, public policy should not interfere with this function of vertical territorial restraints. When we observe such restraints being imposed in conjunction with maximum resale price (or, equivalently, minimum output requirements), we should presume them to be motivated by efficiency considerations at the distribution stage.

Product-specific services

In the preceding chapter, we saw that resale price maintenance may be employed by manufacturers to encourage the provision of advertising, presale information, and postsale service at the distribution stage. The manufacturer wants these services provided because they have a positive influence on the level of demand for the product. Each distributor, however, has an incentive to free ride on the services provided by other distributors. By setting the minimum resale price at a level that is sufficiently high to compensate for the provision of such services, the manufacturer can greatly reduce the free rider-problem (see Section 13–4).

In situations where the product-specific services are also specific to a given geographic market (e.g., where local advertising is more effective than national advertising or where, due to significant transportation costs, the provision of postsale service is limited to customers within a given geographic area), the assignment of exclusive territories to the distributors of the product may be a more efficient method for encouraging the provision of these services. By allowing each distributor to enjoy monopoly status in the relevant geographic market, the manufacturer can be assured that the optimal (profit maximizing) level of services will be provided. With geographically distinct markets and with one distributor of the given manufacturer's product per market, free riding among the distributors can be eliminated or greatly reduced.

Again, however, the manufacturer must take steps to circumvent the successive monopoly problem. Otherwise, the increase in demand that is brought about by the provision of product-specific services may be more than offset by the reduction in the quantity demanded of the manufacturer's product that is due to the monopoly output restriction at the downstream stage. This unfortunate result may be seen in Figure 14–2. This graph is adapted from Figure 13–2, which showed the effect of product-specific services on demand when the provision of such services is fostered by resale price maintenance. Final output demand in a given geographic market is given by D if the distribution stage is competitive, and as a result, no product-specific services are provided. In the absence of such services, the marginal costs of distribution are given by MC_D. Thus, with no product-specific services provided, the derived demand for the manufacturer's product is given by the curve labeled d (which is the demand for final output minus the marginal costs of distribution), with associated marginal revenue given by mr. Thus, without the assignment of exclusive territories (i.e., with intrabrand competition at the downstream stage), the manufacturer's maximum profits are given by the area $abcp$.

Now, suppose the manufacturer attempts to encourage the provision of product-specific services by assigning each distributor to a given geographic market. As a result of its monopoly status in the assigned market, each distributor will now have an incentive to provide product-specific services because free riding by other distributors is forestalled. The provision of such services causes the final product demand curve to

FIGURE 14–2

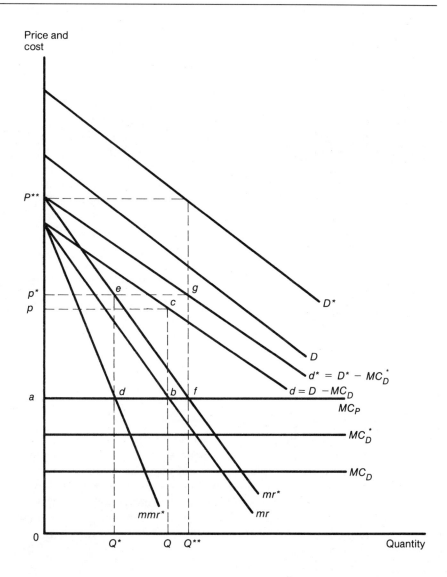

shift to D^*, and the distributor's marginal cost curve shifts to MC^*. If the distributor were to continue to behave competitively, this shift in final product demand would increase the derived demand for the manufacturer's product to d^* in the graph. But since the distributor is now a monopolist in its own geographic market, it will want to restrict sales to the point where marginal revenue equals marginal cost. As a result, the manufacturer's derived demand will fall to mr^*.[3] The marginal revenue associated with this new derived demand is given by mmr^* in the graph. Therefore, the manufacturer will now find the profit maximizing rate of output to be Q^*, with maximum profits given by the area $adep^*$. These profits are less than the profits obtained with no product-specific services provided but with competition at the distribution stage. Consequently, unless the manufacturer can devise a method to prevent the monopolistic output restriction that accompanies the assignment of exclusive territories, he may be better off to maintain intrabrand competition and forego the provision of product-specific services.

If, however, the manufacturer can assign exclusive territories and, at the same time, circumvent the successive monopoly problem, his output can be increased to Q^{**}, and maximum profits can be expanded to the area $afgp^*$ in the graph.[4] To achieve this result, the manufacturer may stipulate a maximum resale price equal to P^{**}. Alternatively, the manufacturer may contractually impose an output quota of Q^{**} on the distributor. In either case, the incentive for the distributor/local monopolist to restrict output and raise price is effectively counteracted.

Thus, we conclude that vertical territorial restrictions may be used in lieu of resale price maintenance to encourage the provision of product-specific services. When used for this purpose, however, we should expect to see some ancillary controls, such as the specification of maximum resale prices, imposed to counteract the successive monopoly problem. To the extent that society benefits from the provision of product-specific services,[5] this use of vertical territorial restrictions should not be discouraged.

Manufacturer cartel

In the preceding chapter, we saw that resale price maintenance may also be used to facilitate the policing of a collusive agreement at the manufacturing stage. The argument was that, by fixing minimum resale prices for each brand, the manufacturers participating in the cartel could detect cheating more easily. Also, the incentive for a given manufacturer to secretly cut price below the cartel level would be reduced if that manufacturer's distributors could not, in turn, lower the resale price. The reason for this is that, in the absence of a price cut at the downstream stage, no additional sales of the manufacturer's product would

---

[3] At this point, it may be helpful (necessary?) to review the successive monopoly model from Chapter 11.

[4] Notice that in this case, the consumers' interests coincide with those of the manufacturer.

[5] The social welfare effects of activities that lead to a shift in the demand curve are analyzed in A. Dixit and V. Norman, "Advertising and Welfare," *Bell Journal of Economics* 9 (Spring 1978), pp. 1–17.

be realized. At the same time, however, we also concluded that this was not a particularly likely use for resale price maintenance (see Section 13–4).

Since, as we have just seen, the assignment of exclusive territories at the distribution stage can be used as a substitute for resale price maintenance to encourage the provision of product-specific services, we might expect that such an assignment could also substitute for resale price maintenance in facilitating the enforcement of a collusive agreement among the manufacturers. This, however, appears to be an extremely unlikely use for vertical territorial restrictions. The reason, once again, is the successive monopoly problem. If the manufacturers have formed a cartel, they will have a profit incentive to promote competition at the distribution level. Otherwise, the additional restriction in sales at the downstream stage will reduce the profits available to the colluding manufacturers. Since the assignment of exclusive territories to distributors results in each downstream firm obtaining some degree of monopoly power, any attempt to employ territorial restrictions as an aid to policing the agreement would frustrate the very purpose the agreement was designed to serve. Of course, the manufacturers participating in the price-fixing conspiracy might attempt to counteract the successive monopoly problem by specifying maximum resale prices. But this, too, would require policing and creates a whole new tier of enforcement problems. Consequently, it is highly unlikely that vertical territorial restraints would ever be employed as a device to facilitate collusion among manufacturers.

Dealer cartel

Suppose, instead, that the firms at the distribution level are able to collude successfully.[6] Of course, to have any impact on competition, the collusive agreement must include the distributors of all (or most) brands of the product in question. Then, interbrand competition will be eliminated at the distribution stage by the collusive agreement.

Having eliminated interbrand competition, the distributor cartel may also want to eliminate intrabrand competition. This goal may be attractive for two reasons. First, with only one dealer of a given brand in each geographic market, it will be easier to detect cheating. And second, with no limit on the number of distributors of a given brand in a given market, the economic profits that result from the collusive agreement will attract the entry of additional distributors. Such entry, in turn, will dilute the profits attributable to the conspiracy and increase the problems of negotiation and enforcement.

---

[6] How likely do you think this is? Recall our discussion of the industry characteristics that facilitate collusion from Chapter 6.

Consequently, we might expect the colluding distributors to enlist the aid of the manufacturers in supporting the price-fixing conspiracy by imposing exclusive territories at the downstream stage. Whether the manufacturers will be willing to oblige this request, however, depends upon whether they enjoy any monopoly power of their own. If they do, then establishing exclusive territories at the downstream stage to support a distributors' cartel will reduce the manufacturers' profits because of the successive monopoly problem. Thus, if interbrand competition is sufficiently weak to present each manufacturer with a downward sloping demand curve, we should expect manufacturers to resist the distributors' requests for vertical territorial restrictions.

If the manufacturing stage is competitive, however, a distributor cartel may be able to convince manufacturers to impose exclusive territories by promising to share the monopoly profits that result from the collusive agreement. But, if there is a sufficient number of manufacturers to permit competition at the upstream stage, it seems rather unlikely that there will be sufficiently few distributors at the downstream stage to make collusion a feasible alternative. Therefore, we conclude that, while vertical territorial restrictions may be used to facilitate policing and prevent entry when a collusive agreement has been reached among the distributors of all brands of a given product, this particular use of such restrictions does not appear likely.

14–3 LEGAL TREATMENT OF VERTICAL TERRITORIAL RESTRICTIONS

The above analysis of the economic incentives for manufacturers to employ vertical territorial or customer restrictions has identified five potential motivations, three of which were efficiency-based and two of which resulted from price-fixing conspiracies. The latter, we concluded, are likely to be relatively uncommon. Moreover, in many respects, we found that the assignment of exclusive territories could be used to serve the same purposes as vertical price fixing, which, in the previous chapter, we concluded should receive a rule of reason treatment under the antitrust laws. Therefore, since the impact of vertical territorial restraints on consumer welfare varies according to which underlying incentive is providing the economic motivation for their use, they, too, should receive a rule of reason treatment.

Such treatment has, in fact, been provided to these restraints since the *Sylvania* decision in 1977.[7] Prior to that landmark case, however, vertical territorial restraints had, for a time, been judged to be a per se violation of the antitrust laws. Thus, the courts have vacillated in their attitude toward this business practice. Apparently, this pronounced in-

---

[7] *Continental TV* v. *GTE Sylvania*, 433 U.S. 36 (1977).

stability in our public policy toward vertical territorial restraints stems from the Court's inability to come to grips with the interbrand versus intrabrand competitive effects of such restraints. A brief survey of the major cases will serve to illuminate the twisted path that has been taken to arrive at the current policy.

White Motor.[8] During the first six decades of Sherman Act enforcement, the lower federal courts had adopted the policy that vertical territorial restraints were legal except when employed with price fixing or upstream monopoly.[9] Starting in 1948, however, the Antitrust Division asserted that such restraints were per se illegal. Rather than risk going to trial, numerous firms negotiated consent decrees with the government that precluded them from using territorial restraints. As a result, there was little case law dealing with this issue until the *White Motor* decision.

White Motor Company had formed an agreement with its dealers requiring them to sell trucks only to customers located within their assigned territories.[10] In exchange, White gave an exclusive distributorship to each of its dealers. White argued that interbrand competition would be fostered by the dealer system, which required the territorial restrictions. The Antitrust Division argued that vertical market division was analogous to horizontal market division and, therefore, was per se illegal.

The lower court granted summary judgment in favor of the government, but the Supreme Court refused to adopt a per se rule. Specifically, the Court held that: "This is the first case involving a territorial restriction in a *vertical* arrangement; and we know too little of the actual impact of both that restriction and the one respecting customers to reach a conclusion on the . . . evidence before us."[11] In Justice Brennan's concurring opinion, he pointed out that restrictions on intrabrand competition that may promote interbrand competition should be weighed in court for their net effect. Per se violations involve practices which are presumed to be unreasonable and therefore illegal without elaborate inquiry as to the precise harm caused by their pernicious effect on competition and lack of any redeeming virtue. In *White Motor*, the Court refused to categorize vertical territorial restrictions as inherently pernicious, due to its lack of experience with them. Thus, the case was remanded to the lower court for a trial on the merits. Prior to that trial, however, the company agreed to a consent decree that required it to abandon the vertical restraints.

---

[8] *United States* v. *White Motor Co.*, 372 U.S. 253 (1963).

[9] See E. F. Zelek, Jr., L. W. Stern, and T. W. Dunfee, "A Rule of Reason Decision Model after *Sylvania*," *California Law Review* 68 (January 1980), pp. 13–47.

[10] In addition, distributors were prohibited from making sales to government agencies, as these sales were reserved for the manufacturing firm. Thus, both territorial and customer restrictions were employed.

[11] 372 U.S. 253 (1963) at p. 261.

Schwinn.[12] Shortly after confessing an inability to fashion a rule of law on vertical territorial restraints, the Court was confronted with the issue again in the *Schwinn* case. In 1951, Schwinn had a 22.5 percent share of the U.S. market for bicycles. Faced with foreign and domestic competition, Schwinn's market share had eroded to less than 13 percent by 1961. Although Schwinn was declining relatively during the decade of the 1950s, its absolute sales volume was increasing. In marketing its bicycles, Schwinn employed a complex distribution scheme. First, it sold bicycles to 22 wholesale distributors who had been granted exclusive territories. There were restrictions on the resale of those bicycles: Each distributor was limited to its own territory and was allowed to sell only to Schwinn franchisees. Second, Schwinn sold to retailers on a consignment basis with the same distributors and the same resale restraints.[13] Finally, and quantitatively most important, Schwinn employed the Schwinn Plan where the bicycles were sold directly to its franchised retailers with commissions going to the distributors. All of the Schwinn franchisees were free to sell other brands so long as the Schwinn bicycles were given equal prominence. Also, the franchisees were permitted to sell only to ultimate customers, not to discount houses. These complex customer and territorial restrictions were enforced by Schwinn through threats of termination.

In hearing the Schwinn case, the Supreme Court claimed that it was engaging in a rule of reason analysis. Although it recognized Schwinn's contention that its system of distribution enhanced interbrand competition, the Court said that "the antitrust outcome does not turn merely on the presence of sound business reason or motive. Our inquiry is whether . . . the effect upon competition in the market place is substantially adverse." Regardless of this assertion, the Court's ultimate decision did *not* rest on an analysis of the overall competitive impact. In reaching its decision, the Court drew an artificial distinction between a case in which the manufacturer parts with title and a case in which it retains ownership (i.e., makes a consignment sale). The Court held that it is "unreasonable without more for a manufacturer to seek to restrict and confine areas or persons with whom an article may be traded after the manufacturer has parted with dominion over it." Restrictions upon resale once title had passed were deemed per se violations of Section 1 of the Sherman Act. This ruling came as a great shock after the Court's candid admission in its *White Motor* decision.[14]

---

[12] *United States* v. *Arnold, Schwinn & Co.,* 388 U.S. 365 (1967).

[13] Under a consignment sale, Schwinn would retain title to the bicycle until it was purchased by the final consumer. The retail outlet making the sale would receive a commission for its services.

[14] It is interesting to note that, following this decision, Schwinn pursued a policy of integrating vertically into distribution.

Sylvania.[15]   For 10 years, academic commentary on the *Schwinn* decision was severely critical. In addition, in the post-*Schwinn* era, the lower courts were trying to sidestep the harsh per se rule of *Schwinn* by distinguishing the facts in the cases under consideration. One of these cases was *Sylvania,* which involved the legality of a location clause.

GTE Sylvania was a rather small producer of television sets which were sold through a network of franchised retailers. These retailers were permitted to sell only from locations specified by Sylvania. Its careful selection of highly competent retailers resulted in a large increase in market share from 1–2 percent to about 5 percent for Sylvania. Continental TV was one of Sylvania's franchisees. Following its termination for violating the location restriction, Continental filed suit against Sylvania, alleging that the location clause was a per se violation of Section 1 of the Sherman Act under the *Schwinn* rule.

The Ninth Circuit Court of Appeals drew a distinction between the *Sylvania* facts and the *Schwinn* facts. It decided that Sylvania was entitled to a rule of reason treatment and ruled in favor of Sylvania.

The Supreme Court, however, recognized that the proverbial distinction without a difference had been drawn by the Ninth Circuit: "Unlike the Court of Appeals, however, we are unable to find a principled basis for distinguishing *Schwinn* from the case now before us." There was no substantive difference between Schwinn's vertical restraints and those of Sylvania. Nevertheless, the Supreme Court refused to apply the *Schwinn* rule, because it felt that that rule was not appropriate under existing antitrust standards. *Schwinn* was being overruled.

In reaching its decision, the Court reviewed the demanding standards for per se illegality and concluded that nonprice vertical restraints simply did not measure up. The Court recognized that such restraints may "promote interbrand competition by allowing the manufacturer to achieve certain efficiencies in the distribution of his products." Moreover, the Court admitted that manufacturers may require the use of such restraints "because of market imperfections such as the so-called 'free-rider' effect."[16] Finally, the Court implicitly appealed to the successive monopoly theory by arguing that "manufacturers have an economic interest in maintaining as much intrabrand competition as is consistent with the efficient distribution of their products." Thus, this enlightened

---

[15] *Continental TV* v. *GTE Sylvania,* 433 U.S. 36 (1977).

[16] At the same time, the Court indicated that the per se rule still applies to vertical price fixing. This distinction between what are economically equivalent practices is currently receiving much criticism. See T. A. Baker, "Interconnected Problems of Doctrine and Economics in the Section One Labyrinth: Is *Sylvania* a Way Out?" *Virginia Law Review* 67 (November 1981), pp. 1457–1520. Also, see R. A. Posner, "The Rule of Reason and the Economic Approach: Reflections on the *Sylvania* Decision," *University of Chicago Law Review* 45 (Fall 1977), pp. 1–20.

decision rests on the fact that vertical restraints may have procompetitive effects on interbrand competition at the same time that they inhibit intrabrand competition. These conflicting effects cannot sensibly be resolved with a per se rule. Consequently, the current rule of law is that nonprice vertical restraints will be judged under the rule of reason.

14–4 CONCLUSION

In this chapter, we have surveyed the economics and the law of vertical territorial and customer restrictions, or what is generically referred to as nonprice vertical restraints. The economic theories that we examined indicated that, while these restraints generally limit or even eliminate intrabrand competition, they may, in many cases, promote interbrand competition. Our analysis also showed that, where interbrand competition is lacking due to the presence of monopoly power at the manufacturing stage, upstream firms will not want to permit any reduction in intrabrand competition at the distribution level. As a result, if territorial restrictions are imposed in this situation, they will generally be motivated by efficiency considerations (e.g., economies of scale in distribution or product-specific services), and they will be combined with some ancillary restraint designed to counteract the successive monopoly problem (e.g., maximum resale prices or minimum output requirements). Moreover, where interbrand competition is strong, the loss of intrabrand competition that accompanies vertical territorial restraints has no effect on consumer welfare. The only situation we found where such restraints have the potential to do significant harm to the competitive process is where interbrand competition has been eliminated by the formation of a cartel at the distribution level. Here, otherwise competitive manufacturers may be bribed into assigning exclusive territories as a method of restricting entry and facilitating enforcement of the price-fixing agreement. We concluded, however, that this is not a particularly likely situation.

Our survey of the law indicated that our public policy dealing with nonprice vertical restraints has bounced around a little bit from rule of reason to per se and back again. One cannot be sure that the rule will not change again. But for now, at least, the antitrust treatment seems appropriate. The procompetitive and anticompetitive consequences of a vertical restraint will be weighed and judged according to the rule of reason. This, of course, does not mean that all restraints will pass muster, but at least they will be given a chance.

The primary public policy problem remaining at this point is the asymmetry of the law as it pertains to vertical integration, nonprice vertical restraints, and vertical price fixing. While the first two receive the appropriate rule of reason treatment, the last remains a per se violation of the antitrust law. Since the three practices are economically equivalent in a variety of situations, they should all be afforded equal treatment under the law. Otherwise, business decisions will be channeled into safe as opposed to efficient choices. The resulting loss in economic efficiency that is fostered by such artificial incentives will be borne by society as a whole.

QUESTIONS AND PROBLEMS

1. Which of the economic theories surveyed in this chapter best explains the distribution practices observed in the automobile industry? Note: Automobile dealers generally have exclusive (or semi-exclusive) territories, but sticker prices can be thought of as maximum resale prices.

2. Recreate Figure 14–2 so that the provision of product-specific services results in so large an increase in demand that the manufacturer's profits are increased despite the output restriction that occurs in response to the monopoly power created at the distribution stage by the assignment of exclusive territories. Would the upstream firm still have an incentive to circumvent the monopolistic output restriction at the downstream stage?

3. Using our discussion of the factors that facilitate the formation and prolong the duration of collusive agreements from Chapter 6, discuss the likelihood that exclusive territories will be used to support either a dealer or a manufacturer cartel.

4. Explain why the imposition of a fixed entry fee in franchise systems that assign exclusive territories does not result in the successive monopoly problem.

5. Currently, nonprice vertical restraints receive a rule of reason treatment under the antitrust laws while vertical price fixing is per se illegal. Is this appropriate? Why or why not?

6. Describe the asymmetry exhibited by the current legal treatment provided the various vertical business practices. Also, describe the potential economic harm fostered by such asymmetry.

7. How can a contractual arrangement between a manufacturer and its distributors promote interbrand competition while, at the same time, eliminate intrabrand competition? How might the courts go about judging such a contractual arrangement?

8. The *Sylvania* decision overruled *Schwinn*. Explain.

9. Suppose that the *Sylvania* case had been decided the other way (i.e., that restrictions on locations were illegal). How would this affect the franchise industry? For example, what problems would McDonald's encounter?

FURTHER READINGS

Blair, Roger D., and David L. Kaserman. *Law and Economics of Vertical Integration and Control.* New York: Academic Press, 1983.

Bork, Robert H. "Vertical Restraints: Schwinn Overruled." In *1977 Supreme Court Review*, ed. Philip Kurland. Chicago: University of Chicago Press, 1978.

Comanor, William S. "Vertical Territorial and Customer Restrictions: *White Motor* and Its Aftermath." *Harvard Law Review* 81 (May 1968), pp. 1419–38.

Liebeler, Wesley J. "Intrabrand 'Cartels' under GET Sylvania." *UCLA Law Review* 30 (October 1982), pp. 1–51.

Pitofsky, Robert. "The *Sylvania* Case: Antitrust Analysis of Non-Price Vertical Restrictions." *Columbia Law Review* 78 (January 1978), pp. 1–38.

Posner, Richard A. "The Rule of Reason and the Economic Approach: Reflections on the *Sylvania* Decision." *University of Chicago Law Review* 45 (Fall 1977), pp. 1–20.

White, Lawrence J. "Vertical Restraints in Antitrust Law: A Coherent Model." *Antitrust Bulletin* 26 (Summer 1981), pp. 327–45.

Mathewson, G. F., and R. A. Winters. "An Economic Theory of Vertical Restraints." *Rand Journal of Economics* 15 (Spring 1984), pp. 27–38.

15

Tying arrangements

15–1 INTRODUCTION

A tying arrangement exists when a seller of product A insists that his customers also buy product B from him. For example, several Subaru dealers recently claimed that Subaru of New England agreed to supply new Subaru automobiles only on the condition that the dealers also buy the distributor's transportation services.[1] This is only one example, as tying arrangements can take many forms. The essence of each such arrangement, however, is a conditional sale: Sales of the tying good are conditioned on sales of the tied good.

Conditional sales are covered by Section 3 of the Clayton Act, which forbids such sales when their effect is to "substantially lessen competition or tend to create a monopoly in any line of commerce." Judicial interpretation of the law on tie-in sales has been very harsh. One of the best known judicial assessments of tying arrangements is contained in Justice Frankfurter's opinion in an exclusive dealing case: "Tying arrangements serve hardly any purpose beyond the suppression of competition."[2] Accordingly, tying arrangements are virtually per se illegal. This hostile attitude stems from the notion that a seller can use economic power in the tying good market to restrain trade in the tied good market.

---

[1] *Chase Parkway Garage, Inc.* v. *Subaru of New England, Inc.*, No. 79–1889–MC, D. Mass., 6/16/82.

[2] *Standard Oil Co. of California (Standard Stations)* v. *United States*, 337 U.S. 293, 305–306 (1949).

Many economists do not share the judiciary's harsh assessment of tying arrangements. There are, in fact, many reasons for the existence of tie-in sales. In the next section, we shall examine several of the purposes served by tie-in sales. We shall see that the harsh judicial treatment provided such sales fails to account for some improvements in economic efficiency and the consequent gains in consumer welfare. As a result, we shall question the appropriateness of the virtual per se rule of illegality.

Following the economic analysis of tying, we shall develop the case history behind the current judicial attitude toward tying. In that section, we shall discuss several defenses that are available that remove tying from the strict per se category. Finally, we contrast the antitrust treatment of tying with that of vertical integration. Since tying is a contractual form of vertical integration,[3] one might suppose that the two practices should receive the same antitrust treatment. As we shall see, however, they do not receive the same treatment.

15–2 ECONOMIC ANALYSIS OF TYING[4]

By now, we are familiar with the idea that firms behave in a way that increases their profits. But another idea that we are also familiar with is that profits can be improved in a number of ways. In this section, we shall examine several motivations for tying arrangements. Each of these will have a positive effect on profits without necessarily raising any antitrust concerns.

Technological interdependence

There are times when the tying and tied goods are technologically interdependent. In these situations, the tying good may not perform satisfactorily unless a complementary good of precise specifications is used with it. For example, at one time, IBM argued that it had to tie its cards to the use of its tabulator because substandard cards would cause the machine to malfunction.[5] The seller's reputation or goodwill is on the line and depends upon the performance of the tying good. In order to protect his reputation, the seller will tie the two goods together. In this way, the seller attempts to guarantee that the tying good performs properly.

---

[3] For a rigorous proof, see Roger Blair and David Kaserman, "Vertical Integration, Tying, and Antitrust Policy," *American Economic Review* 68 (June 1978), pp. 397–402.

[4] A good deal of this analysis is based upon Roger D. Blair and Jeffrey Finci, "The Individual Coercion Doctrine and Tying Arrangements: An Economic Analysis," *Florida State University Law Review* 10 (Winter 1983), pp. 531–68.

[5] The argument was unsuccessful in this case. See *International Business Machines Corp. v. United States*, 298 U.S. 131 (1936). In other cases, however, the technological interdependence argument has succeeded. See *Pick Mfg. Co. v. GM Corp.*, 229 U.S. 3 (1936), and *Dehydrating Process Co. v. A. O. Smith Corp.*, 292 F. 2d 653 (1st Cir.), *cert. denied*, 368 U.S. 931 (1961).

It is interesting to observe that the buyer as well as the seller has an interest in the tying good's proper performance. The tie-in, then, appears to be advantageous to both the seller and the buyer. While the seller protects his reputation, the buyer is guaranteed a product that will operate efficiently. If this is the case, however, one must wonder why a tying arrangement is necessary. Why does the buyer have to be compelled to do what is in his own best interest?

A seller may decide to compel the buyer to do what is in his own best interest simply because it is more efficient to do so. It may be very costly to convey the information that is necessary for the buyer to make the correct decision. When a product is technologically sophisticated, a considerable education may be required to decide correctly. Moreover, mistakes by the buyer have consequences for the seller. It is the seller's reputation that suffers when a large number of complaints surface as a result of the improper use of his or her product. Even though the seller knows that the buyer has an interest in the proper functioning of the product, he may still wish to protect himself. Although it is true that certain buyers will have sufficient information to make the proper decision, the simplest and most efficient way for the seller to protect himself from those buyers who do not take the proper precautions is to tie the two goods together. Nonetheless, it must be recognized that the seller could insist upon the use of complements that met the necessary specifications.

Evasion of government regulations

Whenever the government attempts to regulate market activity to achieve an unnatural economic result, it creates incentives for evading that regulation. Tie-in sales can be used to evade two types of market interferences: ceiling price regulation and profit regulation. In either case, the tie-in is used to increase the seller's return without creating any new market power.

Price ceilings.[6] Suppose that a price ceiling has been imposed on a particular good while the supplier sells another good whose price is not being regulated. The astute seller may tie the good whose price is not regulated to the good subject to price regulation. In this way, the seller can increase the price of the tied good so that the combined profit on the two goods would be no more than what it would have been if the price of the tying good had not been restricted. No monopoly is being extended into the market for the tied good. The seller's share of the market for the tied good may be somewhat larger than it would have been without the tie-in sale, but the output he can sell to maximize his total

---

[6] Ward Bowman, "Tying Arrangements and the Leverage Problem," *Yale Law Journal* 67 (November 1957), pp. 19–36, was one of the first to explain this incentive.

profit is limited. Moreover, the seller may not even produce the tied good. He may simply purchase it on the open market and resell it to buyers of the tying good.

A simple example may be helpful. In the early days of gasoline price controls under President Nixon, some enterprising service station owners recognized that the mandated price was too low. As a result, they were forced to charge a price for gasoline that was lower than the price that buyers were willing to pay. In an effort to extract the full value of the gasoline, they began to fill tanks only on the condition that the customer buy a cheap plastic windshield scraper for $5. The purpose was obvious: to evade the price controls and thereby increase profits.

Profit regulation. When a firm's profits are constrained by regulation, this is often accomplished indirectly by price regulations. The seller must get regulatory approval for its prices, which are supposed to yield no more than the maximum permissible rate of return or profit. If the regulated monopolist sells another product in an unregulated market, it can transfer profit from the regulated to the unregulated sphere. To use an example, assume a regulated monopoly exists in the market for lightbulbs and that this monopolist also sells desk lamps that are sold and priced competitively. Since one uses a desk lamp in fixed proportion with a lightbulb, by tying the two products together, the monopolist can raise the price of the desk lamp to a level that will create the maximum revenue had the price of the bulbs remained unrestricted. Of course, the lightbulb monopolist has not extended his monopoly to the market for desk lamps. But the monopolist has been able to evade the profit constraint through tying.[7] His total profit on the two goods equals the profit he would have earned on the bulbs had that market been unregulated. Although we may not want to applaud this evasion of regulation, it does not appear to raise any substantive antitrust concerns.

Meter pricing

In some cases, a seller may tie two complementary goods[8] in an effort to meter the use of one of them. A concrete example of this motive for tying is provided by the facts in the *IBM* case.[9] IBM produced and leased its card processors to business firms. The value to any firm of having a card processor sitting in the office ready for use depends upon the

---

[7] The evasion of profit constraints was one factor underlying much of the concern over the relationship between AT&T and its wholly owned subsidiary, Western Electric, prior to the 1984 divestiture. For a brief discussion, see Alfred Kahn, *The Economics of Regulation* (New York: John Wiley & Sons, 1970), p. 28, footnote 19. In addition, see Roger Blair, "The Scope of Regulation in the Competitive Telephone Equipment Market," *Public Utilities Fortnightly* 108 (December 17, 1981), pp. 29–34.

[8] Complements are goods that are used together (e.g., hot dogs and mustard, bread and butter, paper towels and towel dispensers).

[9] *International Business Machines Corp.* v. *United States*, 298 U.S. 131 (1936).

frequency and intensity of use (i.e., upon the number of cards processed). IBM leased its card processor at a fixed monthly rate to all customers. This lease was conditioned upon the lessee's agreement to use IBM supplied cards in the card processor.[10] The price of these cards was the same per unit no matter how many were purchased. IBM raised the card price above the competitive level and earned supracompetitive profits on the sale of cards. It should be noted that the user needs a card for each unit of service performed by the processor. Thus, the cards can serve as a way of metering the intensity of use of the processor.

One way of viewing this pricing arrangement is as a variable rental rate contract. The user pays (1) a competitive price for the cards plus (2) a user fee equal to the difference between the nominal card price and the competitive price plus (3) the monthly rental. In effect, the total rental price of the card processor (monthly rental plus user fees on the cards) is a function of the firm's use of the card processor. Figure 15–1 indicates how the total monthly cost of using the card processor varies with different levels of usage. The fixed rental price for the machine is given by the distance OA. This price is paid whether the machine is operated or not. Having paid this fixed rental price, the user's total expenditures then increase linearly with usage because of the user fee placed on the tied good, cards. As a result, the user's total outlay for the processing service is given by the kinked schedule OAB. Given this total outlay schedule, the average or per unit price of the service to the user is shown in Figure 15–2. Due to the presence of the fixed monthly fee and the constant per-unit usage charge of OE, the average price for the processing service declines nonlinearly with increasing usage along the schedule CD. Since heavier users end up paying a lower price per unit, this practice may be seen as a form of price discrimination. Thus, the purpose of tying is clearly *not* to monopolize the card market. It is to make more profit by charging different rental rates to different users.[11]

The tied good acts as a counting device. The buyer who makes greater use of the tying good pays more in total than the buyer with a smaller demand because he buys more units of the service. The seller is not in a position to remove other suppliers of the tied good from the market unless the tied good has no uses other than with the tying good. In all other cases, the sellers of close substitutes for the tied good can still sell them in other markets in which the tied good is demanded. Moreover,

---

[10] IBM tried to claim that quality control of the cards was necessary to protect its goodwill. This argument did not succeed due to the possibility of issuing precise specifications for the cards.

[11] Most antitrust analysts characterize this practice as price discrimination. See, for example, Bowman, "Tying Arrangements," pp. 19–36, and Richard Posner, "Exclusionary Practices and the Antitrust Laws," *University of Chicago Law Review* 41, (March 1974), pp. 506–35. This interpretation is not apt to be correct, however, as Robert Hansen and R. Blaine Roberts, "Metered Tying Arrangements, Allocative Efficiency, and Price Discrimination," *Southern Economic Journal* 47, (July 1980), pp. 73–83, have shown.

FIGURE 15–1

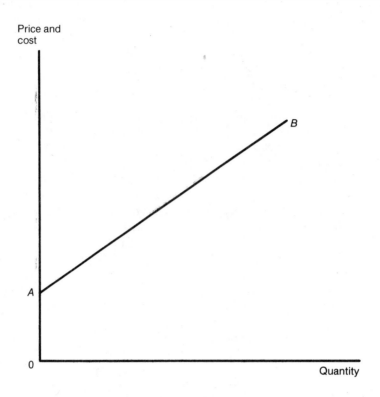

Price and cost

B

A

0

Quantity

the seller imposing the tying arrangement on its customers may buy the tied good from these other firms. Under those circumstances, they will sell to the tying firm rather than directly to the tying good's user.

Those opposed to the use of a tie-in as a counting device suggest that the monopolist might initially charge different prices to different users of the tying good based on expected use by the buyer. Errors, though, are likely to be made by attempting to estimate the intensity of the buyer's use, and any adjustments would be difficult to make. Any mistakes may result in a lower return. The tie-in eliminates the need for estimation and reduces the possibility of error.

Another suggested alternative is to attach a meter to serve as a counting device.[12] The seller can charge the buyer a fixed rate for the good plus a rate that varies with use. This method would be just as effective but not likely to be as efficient for the seller due to the increased costs for

---

[12] See James Ferguson, "Tying Arrangements and Reciprocity: An Economic Analysis," *Law and Contemporary Problems* 30, (Summer 1965), pp. 552–80.

FIGURE 15–2

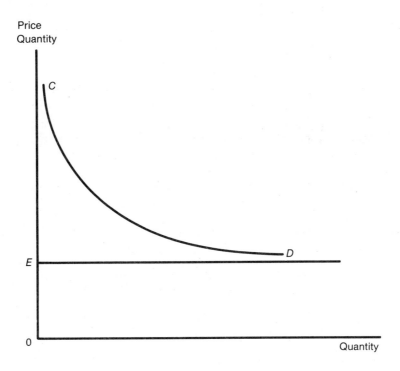

the meters as well as for monitoring the meters. Monitoring the meters would require not only a check to determine if the meter is being tampered with. Of course, there are additional costs when one uses a tying arrangement, but these presumably are lower than those associated with metering. The tie-in must also be monitored to prevent the buyer from substituting cheaper tied goods of lesser quality which he can purchase at the competitive price.[13]

Economies of joint sales

Tie-ins may be intended to take advantage of an economy of scale in either the production or distribution of goods. If two goods can be produced or sold at a lower cost together than they can separately, then a tying arrangement would be an appropriate method of ensuring the maximum return from these goods. By requiring the buyer to purchase the two goods together, the seller can enjoy lower costs and higher

---

[13] The judiciary has recognized the existence of revenue maximizing purposes of tying like metering. But it has never condoned a tie-in sale on that basis.

profits than if he or she were to offer the goods separately. In the absence of any monopoly power, a buyer would obviously be better off purchasing both goods from the same seller because the cost savings attributable to joint production will be passed along in the form of a lower price for the two-product package. Thus, a tie-in requirement forcing the buyer to purchase the two goods together would not appear to be necessary. The buyer, however, may not always choose the seller's tied good for nonprice reasons. For example, he may choose to purchase the tied good from another supplier with whom he has developed a good business relationship. This has an adverse effect on the supplier of the tying good that can be eliminated through the tying arrangement.

Another situation also requires implementation of a tie-in due to economies of combined sales. In the *Times-Picayune*[14] case, for example, the publisher of a morning and an evening newspaper required all advertisers to buy space in both papers. The facts in the case suggest that a major portion of the cost savings would not have been realized unless all advertisers had agreed to purchase space in both newspapers. For example, assume there was no tying arrangement and that one advertiser chose to buy space in the morning edition only. This one difference in the layout of the advertising pages would have made it necessary for the newspaper to rearrange the entire layout to accommodate this one advertiser. In the process, higher costs would have been incurred. A tie-in based on economies of joint sales, then, increases the net return for the seller and presumably leads to lower prices for the buyers.[15]

Uncertainty[16]

It is hardly profound to note that the world in which we live is an uncertain place. Nonetheless, much antitrust analysis is conducted as though risk and uncertainty do not exist. But they do exist and are avoided by risk-averse[17] decision makers. In avoiding or mitigating risk, the decision maker acts cautiously by reducing output and consequently must give up something—namely, profit. Tying can be used to reduce the adverse effects of some kinds of uncertainty. In doing so, output will expand along with profits, and prices will fall.

---

[14] *Times-Picayune Publishing Co.* v. *United States,* 345 U.S. 594 (1953).

[15] When there are obvious economies of joint sales, the judicial response has been to decide that there are not two separate products. Thus, tying is not found because there is only a single product.

[16] This section is based upon R. Blair and D. Kaserman, "Uncertainty and the Incentive for Vertical Integration," *Southern Economic Journal* 45 (July 1978), pp. 266–72, and R. Blair and D. Kaserman, "Tying Arrangements and Uncertainty," *Research in Finance,* Supplement 1, *Management under Government Intervention: A View from Mount Scopus,* 1984.

[17] A risk-averse decision maker will always reject an actuarially fair gamble. The classic discussions of risk aversion are provided by J. Pratt, "Risk Aversion in the Small and in the Large," *Econometrica* 32 (January–April 1964), pp. 122–36, and K. J. Arrow, *Essays in the Theory of Risk Bearing,* (Chicago: Markham Publishing, 1971), pp. 90–120.

A concrete example may be helpful here. The production of a knife requires that one handle and one blade be combined in fixed proportions. Suppose that the production of blades is monopolized due to a legitimate patent.[18] In contrast, the production and sale of handles and knives are competitively organized. Now, the blade monopolist will attempt to maximize his profits through selecting the appropriate price and output of blades. This is a simple optimization problem, which has been solved for some time.[19]

Suppose, however, that the price of the handles is uncertain. The knife producers must commit themselves to specific production levels before they are able to observe the price they will have to pay for the handles. In other words, each firm must plan its future output of knives on the basis of orders for future delivery and some probabilistic notions of what the handle prices will be. Of course, each knife firm will be aware of the actual costs only when the handles and blades are purchased. It has been shown[20] that the risk-averse knife producer will attempt to mitigate the impact of uncertainty by acting cautiously. This results in a reduction in employment of the input with the risky price. The firm's perceived cost of employing an additional handle exceeds the expected price by the risk premium demanded for bearing the risk. This reduces the demand for the monopolized blades since they are used in fixed proportions with the handles. As a direct result, the blade monopolist's profit declines.

The effect of tying

The blade monopolist could offset this impact of uncertainty by selling blades and handles in a package to the knife producers. Specifically, the blade monopolist would buy handles at the competitive, albeit random, price. The knife producers would then buy one handle and one blade at given prices for each knife that they intended to produce. The knife producers will expand their output and thereby their purchases of blades due to the intervention in the handle market and the removal of uncertainty.

The welfare effects of tying in this instance are decidedly positive. The output of knives expands, and the price falls, thereby making consumers better off. Knife producers are no worse off because uncertainty has been reduced for them. Even the handle suppliers are better off

---

[18] This assumption of a legal knife blade monopoly is made only so our attention is not directed to extraneous issues. If the monopoly were not legal, the appropriate public policy response is to prosecute the unlawful monopoly.

[19] See, for example, J. Spengler, "Vertical Integration and Antitrust Policy," *Journal of Political Economy* 58 (August 1950), pp. 347–52.

[20] See Roger D. Blair, "Random Input Prices and the Theory of the Firm," *Economic Inquiry* 12 (June 1974), pp. 214–26.

because the demand for handles has expanded. There appear to be no losers, only gainers.

The need for tying in this case is clear. The knife producer will be only too happy to buy his requirements for handles from the blade producer whenever the actual price of handles exceeds the average price. But when the actual price is below the average, he will try to purchase handles on the open market. The blade producer, however, wants to use the gains from the sales of handles at prices above the average to offset the losses when prices are below the average. Thus, he will have to insist on purchase commitments for all of the handles, irrespective of the spot market price for handles.

Promotional ties

On occasion, conditional sales are made as promotions. For example, a grocery store may offer a five-pound bag of sugar at an extremely low price on the condition that the buyer spend at least $10 in the store. Otherwise, the price of the sugar is the normal price. It is obvious in this case that the seller has no monopoly power. He uses a loss leader (the sugar) to induce customers to buy less attractively priced merchandise. Although the low-priced sugar is nominally a tying good, no one is confused into thinking that this tying arrangement has any monopolistic motive.

Not all promotional ties are so easy to analyze, however, as the *Fortner* litigation demonstrates.[21] The U.S. Steel Corporation, which was trying to sell prefabricated housing, offered Fortner Enterprises, a real estate developer, very attractive credit terms that covered the cost of the houses and the cost of the land, as well as the construction costs. This credit was sufficient to enable Fortner to develop the property without putting up any of his own money. Subsequently, Fortner complained that the U.S. Steel homes were priced above the competitive level. When he filed suit, Fortner alleged that the attractive credit was used as a tying good while the U.S. Steel homes constituted the tied good. In this case, the issue of a promotional tie arises. Was Fortner forced to buy unwanted homes in order to get attractive financing? If so, we have a tie-in sale. Alternatively, was the attractive financing used as an inducement to buy the homes from U.S. Steel rather than from someone else? If so, we have a promotion rather than a tie-in sale.[22] A promotional sale is a means of competing whereas standard antitrust orthodoxy holds

---

[21] *U.S. Steel Corp.* v. *Fortner Enterprises, Inc.*, 429 U.S. 610 (1977). This case lasted for some 15 years.

[22] We owe this succinct distinction to Professor Milton Handler. See his "Changing Trends in Antitrust Doctrines: An Unprecedented Supreme Court Term—1977," *Columbia Law Review* 77, (November 1977), pp. 979–1028.

that tie-in sales are a means of avoiding competition. Thus, the decision is very important to everyone concerned.

Variable proportions

In Chapter 11, we examined the case where an input monopolist had an incentive for forward vertical integration due to its input being used in variable proportions by the competitive downstream industry. We shall see that the input monopolist can achieve the same result through tying. Some of the analysis will be familiar from our discussion of Figure 11–6.

In Figure 15–3, we have drawn an isoquant representing all combinations of inputs A and B that can be used by the downstream industry to produce x_0 units of final output. Given a competitive price for input B

FIGURE 15–3

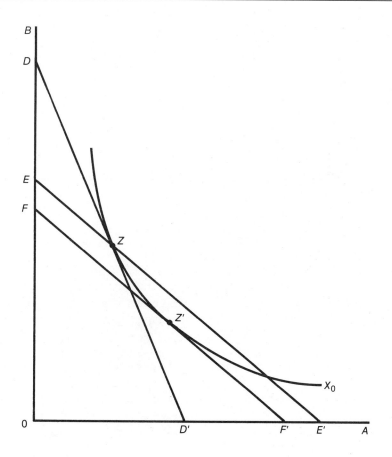

and a monopolistic price for input A, the downstream industry will face the isocost curve DD', where the slope of this curve is given by $-P_A^M/MC_B$.[23]

Confronted by these input prices, the downstream industry will minimize the cost of producing x_0 units of final output by selecting the input combination indicated at point z where the relevant isocost curve is tangent to the x_0 isoquant. Since the intercept of the isocost curve on the B axis at point D shows how many units of B could be purchased if downstream producers expend all of their money on input B (purchasing none of input A), the height of this intercept may be used to measure the level of costs represented by any given isocost curve in units of input B.

The isocost curve given by EE' goes through point z but has a slope reflecting the input price ratio that would result if both inputs were competitively priced (i.e., the slope of EE' is $-MC_A/MC_B$). The vertical intercept of this isocost curve on the B axis at point E indicates the total cost of producing x_0 units of final output (measured in units of B) if input A's price were equal to its marginal cost and the same input combination as before is employed. Since the entire difference between isocost curves DD' and EE' is due to the monopolistic price increase for input A, the difference between the vertical intercepts of these two curves (i.e., $D - E$) measures the A input monopolist's profits in units of B in the absence of vertical integration.[24] In other words, the downstream industry experiences a total cost of E when input combination z is employed to produce x_0 and input A is priced at marginal cost. These costs increase to D when A's price is raised to the monopoly level and the same input combination is used. Since the price of input B remains the same in both cases, this cost difference corresponds to the total profits earned by the A monopolist (in units of B) from selling its output to the competitive downstream industry.

Suppose, now, that the A monopolist recognizes that its customers have substituted away from the monopolized input. One response is to vertically integrate, as we discussed in Chapter 11. An alternative response is to use a tying arrangement. The A monopolist will produce units of B or will buy them from the existing producers of B. Then he will sell both inputs to the producers of the final good. His price on A will be reduced, and the price on B will be raised to the point where

$$\frac{P_A}{P_B} = \frac{MC_A}{MC_B}$$

---

[23] With the price of A equal to P_A^M and B priced at MC_B, the total cost of producing x is

$$C = P_A^M \cdot A + MC_B \cdot B$$

Holding this cost constant at C_0 and solving for B, the equation of the isocost curve is

$$B = C_0/MC_B - (P_A^M/MC_B) \cdot A$$

[24] Since the intercept of a given isocost curve is C_0/MC_B, this measure of the A monopolist's profits could be translated into dollars simply by multiplying by MC_B.

In other words, the tying monopolist's price ratio will be equal to the ratio of competitive prices. This will stop the final goods producers from substituting away from the monopolized input. Now, the competitive producers of final-good x will use the input combination at z' where the FF' isocost is tangent to the x_0 isoquant. Thus, the producers will move back onto the socially efficient expansion path.

The input monopolist will adjust the input prices above marginal cost by an amount that is just enough to extract all of the profit inherent in that downstream demand. In Figure 15–4, D is the demand for the final

FIGURE 15–4

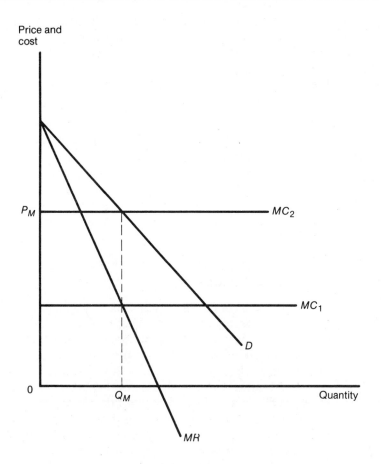

good, and MR is the associated marginal revenue. The horizontal curve, MC_1, represents the constant marginal (and average) cost curve for the final good when all inputs are priced competitively. This industry can generate a maximum profit of $(P_M - MC_1)Q_M$. Under the tying arrangement, the input monopolist will raise all input prices above their competitive levels such that the final-good producers have a marginal cost curve of MC_2. The competitive behavior of the final-good producers will lead them to produce Q_M units and sell them at a price of P_M. As a result, the tying arrangement yields the maximum profit for the input monopolist.

In Chapter 11, we found that the social welfare effects of vertical integration by the input monopolist are indeterminate in this model. Since tying is economically equivalent to vertical integration in this model, the welfare effects of tying must also be indeterminate. In effect, we have the familiar Williamson-type trade-off between productive efficiency and monopoly power at the downstream stage.[25] Consequently, the net effect on social welfare will depend upon the magnitude of the cost reduction and the elasticity of final good demand. Given this indeterminacy, however, it is clear that tying arrangements that are spawned by this incentive should not receive a per se treatment under the antitrust laws.

Summary

We have discussed half a dozen reasons why a producer might want to employ tying arrangements. All of these have to do with making more money (i.e., more profit). Generally, the purpose is not to monopolize or control another market. Instead, the purpose is to use whatever market power currently exists more effectively. After examining the judicial treatment of tying, we shall provide an economic analysis of the judiciary's objections to tying.

15–3 JUDICIAL TREATMENT OF TYING

Prior to the passage of the Clayton Act in 1914, tying cases had to be brought under the Sherman Act. These efforts proved to be largely unsuccessful. For example, the A. B. Dick Company had a patent on the duplicating machine.[26] The users of the patented duplicator were required to use A. B. Dick ink. Henry was charged with contributory infringement of the duplicator patent for making and selling a substitute ink to be used in the A. B. Dick duplicator. In response, Henry argued that the Sherman Act had been violated by this tying arrangement, and this fact should offset the A. B. Dick's claim. This defense failed. Partly in response to this decision, Congress included a specific prohibition of

---

[25] O. W. Williamson, "Economies as an Antitrust Defense: The Welfare Tradeoffs," *American Economic Review* 58 (March 1968), pp. 18–36.

[26] See *Henry* v. *A. B. Dick Co.*, 224 U.S. 1 (1912).

tying in the Clayton Act. The pre-Clayton Act benign attitude toward patent tie-ins was reversed with the first post-Clayton Act case.[27]

The *International Salt* case.[28] The early cases filed under Section 3 of the Clayton Act developed the leverage theory of tying. When the tying good is protected by a patent, the Court's instinct has been that tying is used to lever market power from the tying good market into the tied good market. This can be seen in the *International Salt* case.

The International Salt Company owned a patent on the Lixator, which dissolved rock salt into brine for various industrial purposes. It also owned a patent on the Saltomat, which injects salt tablets into canned products during the canning process. These machines were leased to their users. The leases required the lessees to purchase all unpatented salt and salt tablets used in the machines from International Salt. In essence, International Salt tied salt and salt tablets to its patented machines. Despite this tying arrangement, International Salt never obtained more than 4 percent of the salt market. Hence, the Court's leverage/foreclosure theory does not appear to be consistent with the facts in this case. Moreover, the Court did not appear to examine the market for either the tying goods or the tied good. It made no inquiry into International Salt's market share of the patented salt dispensing machine market. Nor did the Court ascertain the portion of the salt market affected.

The Court inferred the existence of market power from the existence of a patent on the tying machine:

> The appellant's patents confer a limited monopoly of the invention they reward. From them appellant derives a right to restrain others from making, vending or using the patented machines. But the patents confer no right to restrain use of, or trade in, unpatented salt. By contracting to close this market for salt against competition, International has engaged in a restraint of trade.[29]

The Court observed that International Salt sold about 119,000 tons of salt in 1944 for about $500,000. Without regard to the size of the total market, the Court said that "[t]he volume of business affected by these contracts cannot be said to be insignificant or insubstantial. . . ." Moreover, the Court held that "it is unreasonable, per se, to foreclose competitors from any substantial market."

Thus, *International Salt* stands for the proposition that a tying arrangement violates the antitrust law when the tying good is patented and it forecloses a "substantial" market in the tied good. The dimensions of substantiality, however, were not firmly drawn at this point.

---

[27] In *Motion Picture Patent Co.* v. *Universal Film Manufacturing Co.*, 243 U.S. 502 (1917), the Court overruled A. B. Dick and held that tying unpatented items to a patented commodity was illegal.

[28] *International Salt Co* v. *United States*, 332 U.S. 392 (1947).

[29] Ibid., pp. 395–96.

The *Times-Picayune Publishing* case.[30] Because tying restrained trade, it could be challenged under Section 1 of the Sherman Act. But tying involved a conditional sale and thereby also comes under Section 3 of the Clayton Act. In 1953, the Supreme Court laid down the different standards of illegality under the Sherman and Clayton Acts. The *Times-Picayune* case involved a newspaper publisher that owned both the only morning newspaper and one of the two afternoon newspapers in New Orleans. Under the publisher's "unit plan," advertisers were not permitted to buy advertising space in either newspaper separately. Instead, they had to buy space in both or none.

Because the government filed suit under the Sherman Act, the Court felt compelled to distinguish between the Sherman and Clayton Act standards of illegality. After summarizing the previous tying cases decided by the Court, the majority pointed out that

> When the seller enjoys a monopolistic position in the market for the "tying" product, *or* if a substantial volume of commerce in the "tied" product is restrained, a tying arrangement violates the narrower standards expressed in §3 of the Clayton Act because from either factor the requisite potential lessening of competition is inferred. And because for even a lawful monopolist it is "unreasonable, per se, to foreclose competitors from any substantial market," a tying arrangement is banned by §1 of the Sherman Act whenever both conditions are met.[31]

Thus, the Court held that the Sherman Act condemns a tying arrangement whenever (*a*) "sufficient economic power" is shown in the tying good and (*b*) a "not insubstantial" amount of commerce in the tied good is affected. In contrast, the Clayton Act is offended when either of these conditions is satisfied. Subsequent decisions have so attenuated the requirements for proving either condition that there is practically no distinction between the Sherman Act and the Clayton Act.

The *Northern Pacific* case.[32] The first major step in this attenuation process was taken in the *Northern Pacific* case. As part of a program to encourage the private development of railroads, Congress gave Northern Pacific some 40 million acres of land in checkerboard fashion along its proposed line. This permitted intermittent private development and subsequent sale or lease by the railroad. These land grants were made in 1864 and 1870. By 1949, Northern Pacific had sold some 37 million acres and had leased the rest of them. In many of its sales contracts and nearly all of its leases, Northern Pacific had included a "preferential routing" clause. These preferential routing clauses compelled the buyer or the lessee "to ship over its lines all commodities produced or manufactured on the land, provided that its rates (and in some instances its service)

[30] *Times-Picayune Publishing Co.* v. *United States*, 345 U.S. 594 (1953).
[31] Ibid., pp. 608–9.
[32] *Northern Pacific Railway Co.* v. *United States*, 356 U.S. 1 (1958).

were equal to those of competing carriers." Thus, the basic question before the Court was whether the preferential routing clause in the Northern Pacific sale and lease agreements constituted an illegal tying arrangement under Section 1 of the Sherman Act.

To answer this question, the Court began by defining tying arrangements and indicating that competitive harm could result:

> For our purposes a tying arrangement may be defined as an agreement by a party to sell one product but only on the condition that the buyer also purchases a different (or tied) product, or at least agrees that he will not purchase that product from any other supplier. Where such conditions are successfully exacted competition on the merits with respect to the tied product is inevitably curbed.[33]

The Court then went on to explain that tying arrangements reduce competition in the tied-good market by (a) foreclosing competitors from access to those buyers who have entered into such arrangements and (b) denying buyers in that market the opportunity to freely select from among the alternative suppliers on the basis of the prices and qualities of the goods offered for sale. Given these perceived effects, which appeared to be inevitably involved with all tying arrangements, the Court attempted to define the circumstances under which the requisite degree of unreasonableness would be found:

> For these reasons tying agreements . . . are unreasonable in and of themselves whenever a party has sufficient economic power with respect to the tying product to appreciably restrain free competition in the market for the tied product and a "not insubstantial" amount of interstate commerce is affected.[34]

In discussing Northern Pacific's economic power in the tying good (the land), the Court remarked that

> [t]his land was strategically located in checkerboard fashion amid private holdings and within economic distance of transportation facilities. . . . common sense makes it evident that this particular land was often prized by those who purchased it or leased it and was frequently essential to their business activities.[35]

Thus, the Court seemed to say that economic power in the tying-good market could be inferred from the fact that the land involved was desirable property and was unique to certain buyers. As a *reductio ad absurdum*, we might conclude that if someone is willing to pay for a good, then the person who owns it has monopoly power over the sale of that good to the buyer who wants to purchase it. Without going quite this

---

[33] Ibid., p. 5–6.
[34] Ibid., p. 6.
[35] Ibid., p. 7.

far, the Court did say that the fact that buyers were willing to submit to the tying arrangement itself provided evidence that the firm enjoyed monopoly power in the tying good market: "The very existence of this host of tying arrangements is itself compelling evidence of the defendant's great power, at least where, as here, no other explanation has been offered for the existence of these restraints."[36] Finally, the Court weakened the power requirement further by relaxing the indicia of power:

> While there is some language in the *Times-Picayune* opinion which speaks of "monopoly power" or "dominance" over the tying product as a necessary precondition for application of the rule of *per se* unreasonableness to tying arrangements, we do not construe this general language as requiring anything more than sufficient economic power to impose an appreciable restraint on free competition in the tied product (assuming all the time, of course, that a "not insubstantial" amount of interstate commerce is affected.[37]

In other words, the Court was no longer requiring that the seller have significant monopoly power in the market for the tying good in order to find a violation of Section 3 of the Clayton Act or Section 1 of the Sherman Act; a smaller market share might be adequate. By doing so, the Court was approaching an unqualified per se treatment of tying agreements.

The *Loew's* case.[38]   The Supreme Court's standards for proving the existence of market power in the tying good and the quantitative substantiality of the restraint in the tied-good market continued their downward slide in the *Loew's* case. The salient feature of this case was that six major distributors of pre-1948 copyrighted movies for television broadcasting had engaged in block booking. In selling to television stations, the defendants had

> conditioned the license or sale of one or more feature films upon the acceptance by the station of a package or block containing one or more unwanted or inferior films.
>
> [As one example,] Associated Artists Productions, Inc., negotiated four contracts that were found to be block booked. Station WTOP was to pay $118,000 for the license of 99 pictures, which were divided into three groups of 33 films, based on differences in quality. To get "Treasure of the Sierra Madre," "Casablanca," "Johnny Belinda," "Sergeant York," and "The Man Who Came to Dinner," among others, WTOP also had to take such films as "Nancy Drew Troubleshooter," "Tugboat Annie Sails Again," "Kid Nightingale," "Gorilla Man," and "Tear Gas Squad."

---

[36] Ibid., p. 11.

[37] Ibid.

[38] *United States* v. *Loew's, Inc.*, 371 U.S. 38 (1962).

The Court went on to point out the customary antitrust concern regarding tying arrangements: "They may force buyers into giving up the purchase of substitutes for the tied product and they may destroy the free access of competing suppliers of the tied product to the consuming market." Moreover, market dominance need not be shown at all, and economic power may be shown qualitatively:

> Market dominance—some power to control price and to exclude competition—is by no means the only test of whether the seller has the requisite economic power. Even absent a showing of market dominance, the crucial economic power may be inferred from the tying product's desirability to consumers or from uniqueness in its attributes.
>
> The requisite economic power is presumed when the tying product is patented or copyrighted.

The extension of the definition of "sufficient economic power" to include "uniqueness" and "desirability" was essential to successfully overturn the tying agreements since Loew's market share was indeterminate. Moreover, the volume of interstate commerce was as low as $60,800, which must be considered a very small amount.

The _Fortner_ litigation.[39] In 1960, Fortner Enterprises, a real estate developer, obtained a $2 million loan from a U.S. Steel subsidiary to buy prefabricated houses from another U.S. Steel subsidiary, and the land on which they were to be built. In addition, the loan was sufficient to cover all construction costs. Since the credit terms were highly advantageous, Fortner leaped at the unusual bargain, which permitted him to erect 210 houses without spending any of his own money. Fortner Enterprises was not a very good credit risk. It defaulted on the U.S. Steel loan complaining that the houses were too expensive and were not of high quality. Of course, U.S. Steel attempted to obtain a judgment against Fortner Enterprises for the amounts owed. Fortner filed an antitrust suit alleging that U.S. Steel illegally tied its overpriced prefabricated houses to the extraordinary loan.

In _Fortner I_,[40] the issue before the Court was whether Fortner was entitled to his day in court because the lower court had granted U.S. Steel a summary judgment. The majority felt that a tie-in sale had occurred. Since the volume of commerce affected was neither paltry nor insubstantial, half of the two-prong test for per se illegality was satisfied. The majority held that one can infer the existence of market power when "the seller has the power to raise prices, or impose other burdensome

---

[39] The Fortner litigants made three trips to the District Court, three trips to the Circuit Court of Appeals, and two to the Supreme Court. _U.S. Steel Corp._ v. _Fortner Enterprises_, 429 U.S. 610 (1977) was the final Supreme Court decision.

[40] _Fortner Enterprises, Inc._ v. _U.S. Steel Corp._, 394 U.S. 495 (1969). An exceptionally incisive analysis of this decision is provided by Kenneth W. Dam, "_Fortner Enterprises_ v. _United States Steel_: 'Neither a Borrower Nor a Lender Be'," _1969 Supreme Court Review_, pp. 1–40.

terms such as a tie-in, with respect to any appreciable number of buyers within the market."[41] As in *Northern Pacific*, this amounts to saying that the ability of a seller to impose a tying arrangement on its customers provides proof of the market power that makes tying illegal. The fundamental flaw in this approach is apparent in this case. Namely, the proposed rule would imply that U.S. Steel must have had monopoly power over the provision of credit financing to be able to "force" Fortner to accept the prefabricated houses that were tied to the credit. Obviously, this is nonsense. It confuses the favorable credit terms which were offered as an inducement to buy the houses (i.e., which represented an implicit discount in the price of the houses) with the presence of monopoly power over credit. This proposed rule terrified the private antitrust bar who feared that credit-financed sales of all types would become vulnerable to triple-damage claims from dissatisfied buyers under the antitrust laws. Moreover, if this rule were allowed to stand, promotional sales would constitute illegal ties. As a *reductio ad absurdum,* for example, suppose a gasoline station offered a free car wash with the purchase of at least 10 gallons of gasoline. This would be an illegal tying sale if a large number of customers took advantage of the offer. Surely, the majority could not want such a result. In any event, the case was sent back to the District Court.

When *Fortner II* was decided, the Supreme Court apparently recognized that some of the *Fortner I* language left a bit to be desired. In ruling for U.S. Steel, the Court reiterated that the relevant transactions involved a not insubstantial volume of commerce. It then turned to the sufficiency of U.S. Steel's market power in the credit market.

> Although the Credit Corp. is owned by one of the Nation's largest manufacturing corporations, there is nothing in the record to indicate that this enabled it to borrow funds on terms more favorable than those available to competing lenders, or that it was able to operate more efficiently than other lending institutions. In short, the affiliation between the petitioners does not appear to have given the Credit Corp. any cost advantage over its competitors in the credit market.
>
> The fact that Fortner—and presumably other Home Division customers as well—paid a noncompetitive price for houses also lends insufficient support to the judgment of the lower court. Proof that Fortner paid a higher price for the tied product is consistent with the possibility that the financing was unusually inexpensive and that the price for the entire package was equal to, or below, a competitive price.
>
> The most significant finding made by the District Court related to the unique character of the credit extended to Fortner. This finding is particularly important because the unique character of the tying product has provided critical support for the finding of illegality in prior cases.

---

[41] 394 U.S. 495, 504 (1969).

Quite clearly, if the evidence merely shows that credit terms are unique because the seller is willing to accept a lesser profit—or to incur greater risks—than its competitors, that kind of uniqueness will not give rise to any inference of economic power in the credit market. Yet this is, in substance, all that the record in this case indicates.

The unusual credit bargain offered to Fortner proves nothing more than a willingness to provide cheap financing in order to sell expensive houses. Without any evidence that the Credit Corp. had some cost advantage over its competitors—or could offer a form of financing that was significantly differentiated from that which other lenders could offer if they so elected—the unique character of its financing does not support the conclusion that petitioners had the kind of economic power which Fortner had the burden of proving in order to prevail in this litigation.[42]

This decision seems to be a small step back from a myopic per se rule of illegality. Nonetheless, if a plaintiff can show (1) a seller conditions the sale of one good on the purchase of a separate tied good, (2) the supplier has sufficient market power in the tying good to restrain competition in the tied good, and (3) a not insubstantial volume of commerce is affected, then the seller is guilty of an illegal tie under the Sherman Act. In addition to the first requirement, if either of the next two is met, the tie-in sale has violated the Clayton Act. The distinction between these two standards of illegality has become blurred in practice due to the Court's relaxation of the standards of proof.

15–4 FACTORS LEGALLY JUSTIFYING TYING ARRANGEMENTS

Not all tying arrangements are necessarily illegal. First, a plaintiff must prove that two products are concerned. While this would seem simple in most instances, it really is not. For example, a radio is actually a collection of component parts that the manufacturer may refuse to sell separately. Most shoe stores will not sell less than a pair of shoes. Are these tying arrangements? In a sense they are, but these cases can be resolved quite easily. There are, however, more difficult cases. For example, the Ford Motor Company redesigned its dashboard in such a way that its dealers had to use radios installed by Ford.[43] Consequently, independent radio producers were foreclosed from selling to Ford dealers. Is this a tie-in imposed upon the dealers by Ford's design decisions? In this case, the Court said that Ford's design decision was independent of its contracts with its dealers, and consequently there was no tying arrangement. The Court considered and rejected the argument that there were two separate products involved.

[42] 429 U.S. 610.

[43] See *Automatic Radio Manufacturing Co.* v. *Ford Motor Co.*, 242 F. Supp. 852 (D. Mass. 1965).

A very important single-product rationale was raised in *Principe* v. *McDonald's Corporation.*[44] McDonald's is in the business of developing a system of hamburger restaurants, which are operated by franchisees, and collecting royalties from their sales. In doing this, McDonald's selects locations for new restaurants, buys the land, builds the building, and locates a franchisee. The franchisee must contract with McDonald's for the use of the McDonald's trademark and must also lease the building and land. Principe alleged an illegal tie of the building and land to the trademark. The Court, however, ruled that the trademark license and the building lease were really a single product—the franchise. Both the trademark license and the leased property are "integral components of the business method being franchised. Where the challenged aggregation is an essential ingredient of the franchised system's formula for success, there is but a single product, and no tie-in exists as a matter of law."

Second, a defendant may argue that tying is necessary to protect its goodwill. This is a common defense but not one with a particularly encouraging record of success. Generally, the defense is based upon the economic argument associated with technological interdependence. In spite of the fact that tying may be the most efficient way of protecting goodwill, the courts will not accept it when the defendant can insist upon detailed specifications. For example, IBM tried to argue that tying its punch cards to its equipment leases was necessary because the proper operation of the machine depended upon cards of precise specifications. The Court rejected this argument: "[t]here is no contention that others than [IBM] cannot meet these requirements."

A semisuccessful goodwill defense was raised by Jerrold Electronics.[45] The defendant was among the first suppliers of community television antenna equipment in the country. This antenna equipment (the tying good) was tied to the installation and maintenance performed by Jerrold. Due to the complexity and sensitive nature of the products involved, Jerrold defended its tying agreement on goodwill grounds, its reputation of providing quality equipment being at stake. The Court recognized that "a wave of system failures at the start would have greatly retarded, if not destroyed, this new industry and would have been disastrous for Jerrold, who, unlike others experimenting in this field such as RCA and Philco, did not have a diversified business to fall back on." Accordingly, the Court held that the tie-in was reasonable "at the time of its inception . . . but as the industry took root and grew, the reasons for the blanket insistence on a service contract disappeared." Thus, Jerrold's tie-in sale was permissible in principle, but in practice it

---

[44] 631 F. 2d 303 (4th Cir. 1980).

[45] *United States* v. *Jerrold Electronics Corp.*, 187 F. Supp. 545 (E. D. Pa. 1960) affirmed per curiam, 365 U.S. 567 (1961).

was not because it had gone on beyond the necessary time. Thus, while the defense that the tying arrangement is necessary to protect the firm's goodwill in the tying good market has, on occasion, met with success,[46] it is not an easy argument to carry in court.

The only other response to a charge involving a tie-in sale is to argue that the seller does not have the requisite power in the tying-good market. This, of course, is what saved the day for U.S. Steel in the *Fortner* case. The Court found that U.S. Steel did not have any appreciable power in the credit market. Implicit in this finding was the recognition of the tie-in's promotional intent.

15–5   ECONOMIC ANALYSIS OF JUDICIAL CONCERN[47]

Tying arrangements involve two evils that the courts have tried to prevent. First and foremost, tying arrangements deny competitors free access to the market for the tied good. Second, buyers are forced to forego their free choice between competing products in the tied market. In some sense, these concerns are over the same thing: some judicial feeling that it is unfair to use power in one market to influence economic activity in a separate market. When the seller of tying good A requires its customers to also buy tied good B, the Court has assumed that some economic power has been transferred from the A market to the B market. According to this view, somehow the seller expands or levers his monopoly power from one market to another. This, of course, is not possible. A seller cannot get two monopoly profits from one monopoly. The only way that the seller can impose additional requirements on its customers is to reduce the price of the tying good. Thus, the leverage theory of tying is unsatisfactory. But let us consider the two primary evils in turn.

Foreclosure of tied-good market.   There is little doubt that when a buyer agrees to purchase commodity B from his supplier of A the rival sellers of B are foreclosed. The real question is whether this makes any difference to consumer welfare. First, suppose that the monopolist of A is at least as efficient in producing B as the rival seller of B. There is no reason to object to the tying arrangement because the tied good is being produced as efficiently or more efficiently than otherwise. Second, suppose that the rival sellers of B are more efficient than the A monopolist.

---

[46] The goodwill defense was successful in *Pick Mfg. Co.* v. *GM Corp.*, 299 U.S. 3 (1936) and in *Dehydrating Process Co.* v. *A. O. Smith Corp.*, 292 F. 2d 653 (1st Cir.), *cert. denied*, 368 U.S. 931 (1961).

[47] There is a huge, generally critical, literature on this subject. See, for example, Robert H. Bork, *The Antitrust Paradox* (New York: Basic Books, 1978), especially Chapter 19, and Tyler Baker, "The Supreme Court and the Per Se Tying Rule: Cutting the Gordian Knot," *Virginia Law Review* 66 (Nov. 1980), pp. 1235–1319. But a different view is provided by Lawrence Sullivan, *Handbook of the Law of Antitrust* (St. Paul, Minn.: West Publishing, 1977), especially pp. 431–71.

We should expect the A monopolist to buy B from its rivals and resell to its customers. There is no reason to object in this case either. The producers of B compete for sales to the A producer rather than to A's customers. It would not seem to make very much difference where the locus of competition is. The competition still exists.

We should also recognize that the tied good market is often very specialized. For example, in the *IBM* case, the foreclosed sellers were paper companies that could not sell punch cards to IBM customers. But these firms could make any of a large number of other paper products. In most of the other tying cases, no significant foreclosure has occurred in the tied-good market.

Buyers are denied freedom of choice. The customers who are subject to the tying arrangements supposedly are denied freedom of choice. But this is not really of central concern. The purpose of the antitrust laws is to promote consumer welfare. Generally, however, the buyers do have choices to make. The only choice they do not have is to buy the tying good alone. But the tied good can be thrown away if it is unwanted, or it could be sold to a third party.

15–6 CONCLUDING REMARKS

We have seen that tying arrangements serve many purposes. They can be used to protect the goodwill of a business firm concerned that its customers will misuse its primary product, thereby causing it to malfunction. They can be used in lieu of mechanical meters to measure the intensity of use by a customer and thereby permit variable rental rate contracts. Tie-in sales can be used to evade price and/or profit regulation or to exploit economies of joint sales. Tying permits a reallocation of risk in some cases and prevents a socially undesirable combination of inputs from being used in other cases. Finally, tie-ins can be employed as promotional devices. In none of these cases is the purpose to lever monopoly power from the tying-good market to the tied-good market. That is an impossible task.

The Supreme Court, however, has taken a very hostile attitude toward tying arrangements. Its condemnation has focused upon the foreclosure of the tied-good market to rivals and the reduction of choices available to buyers. The decisions do not focus upon tying's impact on the competitive process. It appears that the Court's policy against foreclosure is not based upon a concern for consumer welfare. Rather, it is based upon a concern for protecting firms from an unfair method of competition.[48] The decisions do not seem to be concerned with allocative

---

[48] See note, "The Logic of Foreclosure: Tie-In Doctrine after *Fortner* v. *U.S. Steel*," *Yale Law Review* 79 (November 1969), pp. 86–101.

efficiency and consumer welfare. Some lower courts have even conceded that tie-ins are not inherently harmful and, in fact, can even be beneficial.[49] Nonetheless, the Supreme Court persists in its hostile attitude.

QUESTIONS AND PROBLEMS

1. If IBM used the cards as a meter for its processor, how could it prevent its lessees from using unauthorized cards?

2. F. Cummings and W. Ruhter, "The *Northern Pacific* Case," *Journal of Law and Economics* 22 (October 1979), pp. 329–50, suggest that tying may have been used to monitor a price-fixing scheme among the railroads. How would that work?

3. John Peterman, "The *International Salt* Case," *Journal of Law and Economics* 22 (October 1979), pp. 351–64, observed that International Salt sold its salt at the same price to all buyers. Thus, tying was not being employed to meter the use of its salt dispensers. Why does he conclude this?

4. Suppose B&K Burgers, Inc. offered a franchise at zero cost to all franchisees but required the franchisees to buy their supplies and equipment from B&K. Although B&K Burger, Inc. admits that it charged prices above the competitive level for the supplies and equipment, it claims that the franchisees have suffered no damages. Is B&K correct?

5. In the knife production example for uncertainty, why is monitoring no problem for the blade monopolist?

6. Suppose the demand for knives were uncertain (i.e., the competitive knife price shifted around its mean in a random fashion). Let the competitive price of handles and the monopoly price of blades be known with certainty. Can tying be used to reduce uncertainty in this case? Is there an alternative?

7. The Friendly Family Bakery recently ran a special on carrot cake. "Buy one at the regular price of $1.95, and get a second cake free." Is

---

[49] See *Moore* v. *Jas. H. Matthews & Co.*, 550 F. 2d 1207, 1213 (9th Cir. 1977) for such a concession. This court rejected a rule of reason test because courts are not equipped to deal with complex economic questions, and they have overcrowded calendars.

this a tie-in sale? Why should I have to buy the cake with the regular price to get the one with the zero price?

8. Suppose that Sears will not extend credit to cover your purchases anywhere else (e.g., at Montgomery Wards). Has Sears tied its merchandise to its credit?

9. Shortly after the *Times-Picayune* decision, the second afternoon paper in New Orleans folded. Was the Court's decision a contributing factor? How could one tell?

10. Suppose that a regulatory agency requires that a seller charge no less than $10 for product X. This prevents ABC, Inc. from expanding its market share and enjoying economies of scale through price competition. If ABC, Inc. also sells product Y, can it evade the minimum price regulation through a tying arrangement? If so, explain how. Would such evasion be anticompetitive?

11. The decision in *Fortner II* suggests that if U.S. Steel had been extraordinarily efficient and thereby had a cost advantage over other prefabricated house producers, its credit tie-in could have been illegal. Does this make sense? What effect would this have on the incentives of others to strive for greater efficiency?

12. All of the major petroleum refiners supply tanks and pumps at nominal rentals to their lessee-dealers on the condition that the dealer put only, say, Gulf gasoline in the tank supplied by Gulf. Each dealer can sell other brands of gasoline but use a different pump and storage tank. Is this illegal tying? [*Federal Trade Commission* v. *Sinclair Refining Co.*, 261 U.S. 463 (1923)]

13. The line of Supreme Court decisions made it clear that if a tying good is patented, then the patent itself is proof of sufficient economic power. But the Supreme Court has recognized that "a patent does not always confer a monopoly over a particular commodity." How do we reconcile these two facts?

FURTHER READINGS

Baker, Tyler A. "The Supreme Court and the Per Se Tying Rule: Cutting the Gordian Knot." *Virginia Law Review* 66 (November 1980), pp. 1235–1319.

Blair, Roger D., and David L. Kaserman. "Vertical Integration, Tying, and Antitrust Policy." *American Economic Review* 68 (June 1978), pp. 397–402.

Bowman, Ward. "Tying Arrangements and the Leverage Problem." *Yale Law Journal* 67 (November 1957), pp. 10–36.

Burstein, Meyer. "A Theory of Full-Line Forcing." *Northwestern University Law Review* 55 (March/April 1960), pp. 62–95.

Cummings, F. Jay, and Wayne E. Ruhter. "The *Northern Pacific* Case." *Journal of Law and Economics* 22 (October 1979), pp. 329–50.

Jones, William K. "The Two Faces of *Fortner:* Comment on a Recent Antitrust Opinion." *Columbia Law Review* 78 (January 1978), pp. 39–47.

Peterman, John L. "The *International Salt* Case." *Journal of Law and Economics* 22 (October 1979), pp. 351–64.

16

Exclusive dealing and requirements contracts

16–1 INTRODUCTION

An exclusive dealing contract commits a buyer to deal only with a particular seller. Thus, for the duration of the contract, one supplier has the exclusive right to sell to the customer involved. We shall also analyze a similar arrangement that is called a requirements contract. These contracts involve a commitment by a buyer to take all he needs of a given product for a specified period from the seller, or it may involve a commitment by a seller to supply all of a buyer's needs, or it may involve both. It is clear that either arrangement tends to foreclose a portion of the market from competitors and to reduce free choice during the duration of the agreement. Normally, exclusive dealing and requirements contracts refer to business practices that do not involve tying arrangements, which we have examined in the preceding chapter. Exclusive dealing, however, does invoke Section 3 of the Clayton Act. If the effect of an exclusive dealing arrangement or a requirements contract may be to substantially lessen competition or tend to create a monopoly in any line of commerce, that contract will violate Section 3 of the Clayton Act.

If, for various reasons that we shall discuss below, it is advantageous for a given distributor to handle the output of a single manufacturer, such specialization at the distribution stage can be accomplished either by vertical ownership integration (the manufacturer operates its own distribution outlets) or by an exclusive dealing contract in which otherwise independent distributors agree to limit the range of products offered for resale to those produced by a single manufacturer. Thus, both exclusive dealing and requirements contracts are forms of vertical integration. They are forms of contractual integration as opposed to the more permanent ownership integration discussed in Chapter 11. The antitrust law's concern with such arrangements lies in their alleged capacity for coercing buyers and foreclosing the opportunities of a rival. In this chapter, we shall be concerned with the incentives for entering into such contracts. We will also analyze the usual objections to these contracts. Finally, we will examine the state of the law on exclusive dealing and requirements contracts.

16–2 REASONS FOR EXCLUSIVE DEALING ARRANGEMENTS

Exclusive dealing and requirements contracts often promote efficiency and consequently, in these cases, are procompetitive and consistent with the promotion of consumer welfare. Both parties to the contract may experience improvements in efficiency (i.e., cost reductions).

Cost reductions

The supplier need call on fewer dealers, keep fewer records, and perhaps experience fewer credit problems when he or she opts for a smaller number of nonexclusive distributors. In other words, selling expenses may be greatly reduced or nearly eliminated by exclusive dealing. Moreover, the supplier can plan his operations more effectively and experience efficiency gains in production as well as in his sales efforts. For example, if the buyers with fairly stable requirements agree to buy exclusively from one supplier, that firm will have fairly stable sales and can plan production and distribution more efficiently.

The buyer may also enjoy cost savings due to exclusive dealing. For one thing, the buyer can reduce the transaction costs of dealing with a multitude of competing suppliers. Buyers may agree to exclusive dealing contracts in exchange for the guarantee of frequent (small) deliveries so that they can reduce their inventory costs. In a different vein, exclusive dealing enables a distributor to afford a more extensive inventory of the supplier's full line of products. If a buyer attempted to stock a full line without exclusive dealing, this could cause credit problems and increase default risks for the supplier.

Improved product promotion at the distribution stage

The buyer will have an added incentive to vigorously promote the seller's product if that is all he has to sell to the final consumer. Thus, the supplier can be sure that each of his distributors will work very hard on his behalf. Consequently, it will be worth providing special training to the distributor where the complex character of his product requires special skills. Whenever the supplier's product demands specialized selling or servicing techniques, the supplier will be more interested in exclusive dealing than otherwise.

Areeda has pointed out that this improved product promotion can be carried too far.[1] When a seller obtains the exclusive benefit of a dealer's efforts, the dealer may promote the brand too intensively. We can see the results of this in Figure 16–1. The original demand for and supply of the final good are represented by D_1 and S_1, respectively. At a quantity of Q_1, the market clearing price of P_1 represents the value to consumers

FIGURE 16–1

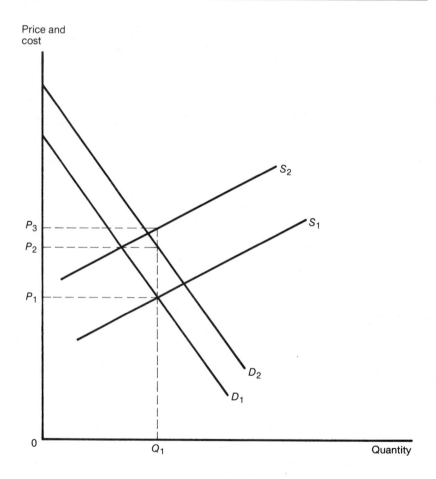

[1] P. Areeda, *Antitrust Analysis*, 2d ed. (Boston: Little, Brown, 1974), pp. 636–37.

and the cost to the distributors of the product. Oligopolistic competition for market share can take the form of promotion and selling efforts. To some extent, these efforts can be mutually offsetting across rival firms. As a result, the supply curve S_2 incorporates the excessive promotion and selling costs. Thus, the supply price for the original output of Q_1 is now P_3. Because the rivalrous efforts are partially offsetting, demand shifts from D_1 to only D_2. As a result, the original quantity of Q_1 is now worth P_2 per unit, which is less than P_3. Obviously, neither P_2 nor P_3 are market clearing prices. The new equilibrium price, which is not shown, would be located at the intersection of S_2 and D_2. Rather, the prices P_2 and P_3 show the valuation and cost to society of the old market clearing quantity, respectively. Since P_3 exceeds P_2, the added costs are greater than the added value. In this sense, the selling efforts have been excessive and wasteful.[2] Thus, the extra promotional efforts garnered by exclusive dealing may not always be socially beneficial.

Improved product promotion at the manufacturing stage

Just as some products are more efficiently promoted by the local sales efforts and product specific services supplied by the individual distributors of the product, the promotional efforts required for the sale of some other products may be most efficiently conducted at the manufacturing stage (e.g., through a national advertising campaign). In Chapters 13 and 14, we saw how the former situation can lead to the use of resale price maintenance and/or the assignment of exclusive territories in order to protect the distributors' property rights in the investment required to provide local promotion and postsale service. A recent paper by Howard Marvel demonstrates how the latter situation can create a strong incentive for exclusive dealing in order to protect the manufacturer's property rights in the fruits of the promotional investments required at the upstream stage.[3]

Promotional efforts undertaken by the manufacturer generate customer flows for the downstream firms which distribute the advertised product. To recoup the costs of promoting the product, the manufacturer must increase the wholesale price paid by its dealers. Then, if the brand choice of final consumers is susceptible to manipulation by the dealers and these dealers are permitted to carry more than one brand of the product, they will have a profit incentive to channel customers to other nonadvertised brands for which the wholesale (but not necessarily the retail) price is lower. Even where the retail price of the nonadver-

---

[2] George Stigler, "Price and Non-Price Competition," *Journal of Political Economy* 76 (January–February 1968), pp. 149–54, unintentionally makes this point in another connection.

[3] Howard P. Marvel, "Exclusive Dealing," *Journal of Law and Economics* 25 (April 1982), pp. 1–25.

tised brand is lower, this incentive will still exist so long as the potential markup above the wholesale price is larger for this brand. By requiring exclusive dealing, the manufacturer can prevent such opportunistic brand switching at the distribution stage and thereby protect the investment in brand promotion.

A simple example will serve to illustrate the incentives involved. Suppose that there exist two brands of a given product, brands A and B. The manufacturer of brand A invests in extensive advertising to inform consumers of the existence of this product and to explain the myriad useful functions that it can perform. To pay for this advertising plus the costs of production, the manufacturer of brand A sets its wholesale price to distributors of the product equal to P_A. The manufacturer of brand B engages in no advertising and, as a result, sets its wholesale price at a lower level equal to P_B. Assume, for simplicity, that the marginal and average costs of distribution are zero. Then, Figure 16–2 shows the profits that can be earned by the distributor who switches customers to brand B but charges a retail price equal to P_A. These profits are shown as the shaded rectangle $P_A abP_B$.

FIGURE 16–2

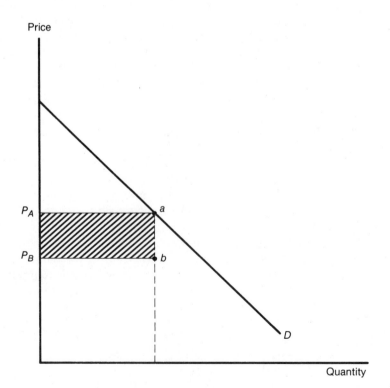

Clearly, if all distributors engage in this profitable brand-switching activity, the brand A manufacturer will be eliminated from the market as will the promotional efforts that generated the postadvertising level of demand, *D*. In effect, both the distributors and the manufacturers of brand B are free riding on the promotional investments made by the brand A manufacturer. Such free riding can be forestalled by the use of an exclusive dealing arrangement. If distributors of brand A are not permitted to sell brand B, they will not be able to switch the customer's selection to the nonadvertised brand. Thus, exclusive dealing serves to protect the manufacturer's property rights in the demand generating investment. To the extent that such promotional investment is beneficial to society, this use of the exclusive dealing arrangement should not be discouraged by public policy.

Risk reduction

Both the supplier and the buyer may be risk averse, which means that risk imposes costs upon them. If supply is uncertain, a risk-averse buyer will guard against the effects of uncertainty by cutting back planned output, which in turn reduces the derived demand for the supplier's output. Similarly, if demand for a supplier's output is random, his risk-averse response will be to plan on producing less. The buyers will be facing a reduced supply schedule. Thus, we see that risk can make both buyers and sellers worse off. This, of course, means that each will be willing to pay a premium to reduce the risk being faced.[4]

Buyers may want the assurance of continuous supply to avoid the disruptions of periodic shortages. For example, an electric utility must have a stable and adequate supply of fuel in order to avoid having to interrupt service. If prices tend to be volatile, a buyer may want a specified price over some time interval for corporate planning purposes. In either event, the seller's quid pro quo may be an exclusive dealing contract. In order to avoid supply problems, buyers may be happy to agree to an exclusive dealing arrangement.

Manufacturer cartels

In Chapter 13, we pointed out that a manufacturers' cartel might adopt a policy of resale price maintenance in order to police its members' performance more easily. To refresh our memories briefly, suppose that a group of manufacturers of some product form a cartel to increase their collective profits. To be successful, the members of the cartel will have to reach an agreement as to what price should be charged for this product.

---

[4] A more formal analysis is provided by Roger D. Blair, "Random Input Prices and the Theory of the Firm," *Economic Inquiry* 12 (June 1974), pp. 214–26.

Then, to maintain this joint profit-maximizing price, all members will have to restrict their individual outputs below the level that each would like to produce at that price. In other words, given the cartel price, each cartel member will be able to increase its own profits if it can secretly reduce its own price and thereby increase its sales (i.e., if it can cheat). Such cheating will be profitable so long as: (1) other firms do not also cheat (in which case the cartel price will fall toward the competitive price); and (2) the firm is not caught cheating (in which case the other cartel members will take some sort of retaliatory action). Since all firms have the same incentive to cheat, there must be some mechanism to discourage this cheating if the cartel is to endure.

By adopting a policy of resale price maintenance in which distributors of the cartel's product are forbidden from charging less than the agreed upon price, the cartel members' incentive to cheat may be lessened. Under such a policy, secret price concessions made to a given distributor are not likely to result in greater sales because of the distributor's inability to reduce price to the final consumer. If such price concessions do not increase sales, the incentive for the manufacturer to reduce price disappears. If the given distributor handles the output of more than one cartel member, however, it may be possible to increase sales of the cheating manufacturer's product without reducing the final output price by increasing the relative sales effort directed toward that particular product. This possibility is eliminated if each distributor specializes in the output of only one manufacturer. Consequently, a manufacturers' cartel that has adopted a policy of resale price maintenance may also adopt exclusive dealing contracts to help discourage cheating by its members.[5] As a result, where we find the two practices (resale price maintenance and exclusive dealing) being used together, the probability that a manufacturers' cartel is present is somewhat increased. Thus, our conclusion from Chapter 13 that resale price maintenance is rarely employed to enhance the stability of a manufacturers' cartel must be modified where exclusive dealing is also involved.

In summary, there are several reasons for buyers and sellers to embrace exclusive dealing contracts. The results of exclusive dealing when the motivation is to reduce costs, reduce risk, or improve product promotion are apt to be beneficial for consumers. On the other hand, when exclusive dealing is adopted in conjunction with resale price maintenance to facilitate a manufacturers' cartel, the results are clearly undesirable. The appropriate role for public policy, then, is to discriminate between these cases, encouraging the former and discouraging the latter. Certainly, the appropriate public policy response is fairly clear in

---

[5] See Lester G. Telser, "Why Should Manufacturers Want Fair Trade?" *Journal of Law and Economics* 3 (October 1960), pp. 86–105. In this article, the author describes the use of this combined strategy of resale price maintenance and exclusive dealing by the light bulb industry cartel in the early 1900s.

two cases: (1) when exclusive dealing facilitates the entry of a new brand which thereby intensifies competition in the final good market and (2) when exclusive dealing permits a relatively weak brand to survive and compete. In both of these cases, the exclusive dealing contract intensifies the competitive process and should, therefore, be applauded.

A supplier may prefer to vertically integrate forward by contract rather than by actual ownership for several reasons. First, the supplier need not make any capital investment in distribution facilities. Second, the supplier avoids tort and other liabilities of an employer at the distribution stage. Finally, the supplier avoids some of the potential managerial diseconomies of scale that we discussed in preceding chapters. Once again, public policy should not bias the firm's choice among economically equivalent strategies. Otherwise, firms will tend to select safe as opposed to efficient alternatives, and consumers will pay the price for the resulting higher costs.

16–3 EXCLUSIVE DEALING AND FORECLOSURE

An exclusive dealing arrangement, by its very nature, must result in market foreclosure. This has an allegedly adverse impact upon the supplier's competitors. It might foreclose the market opportunities of the seller's competitors if the seller preempts all of the outlets. Some analysts have expressed concern that if one supplier captured all of the leading distributors, other producers would be severely handicapped in their efforts to reach consumers—even if their product were better or cheaper. Alternatively, if several leading producers entered into exclusive dealing arrangements with all of the distributors, new suppliers would have a difficult time entering the industry. Existing suppliers would have a tough time expanding their share of the market. In other words, the requirements contract raises the barriers to entry for new firms and limits the expansion of existing firms.

The antitrust concept of monopoly is the power to exclude. We can analyze the power to exclude and examine the relevance of requirements contracts in that regard.[6] What we mean by the power to exclude is the power or ability to prevent competitors from gaining access to the market. Exclusive dealing or a requirements contract cannot create exclusionary power. It can only be a means of implementing such power as already exists. Thus, a requirements contract can only restrict competition in any meaningful sense when the power to exclude is already present. It should be clear that single exclusive dealing contracts are innocent. If such contracts are to pose a problem, it must be true that a seller who already has the ability to exclude insists upon a system of these contracts. Let us examine the sources of exclusionary power.

[6] The ensuing analysis is based upon Gordon Shillinglaw, "The Effects of Requirements Contracts on Competition," *Journal of Industrial Economics* 2 (April 1954), pp. 147–63.

Sources of power to exclude

First, it is possible that one producer enjoys significant cost and/or locational advantages. In essence, it is more efficient than its rivals. If that firm's average costs do not rise sharply as its market share expands and its competitors continue to fail to match the advantage, the firm will have exclusionary power, but it will be due to superior efficiency. In this instance, the requirements contract does *not* contribute to this power nor does it implement this power.

Second, one producer may have significantly more money and resources than its rivals. This "deep pocket" makes predatory behavior possible. If entry barriers are significant, then the stronger firm may have the power to exclude. But once again, requirements contracts are irrelevant.

Finally, one firm's product may be sufficiently differentiated to provide power, and the number of satisfactory outlets may be limited for some exogenous reason. If alternative market outlets are difficult to establish, a firm whose product is greatly preferred to all others will have exclusionary power. Preemption of existing outlets will leave rivals without a means of distributing their products.

Product differentiation is an essential requirement because a buyer will not otherwise prefer one source of supply to another. If alternative sources of supply were available on comparable terms, buyers could not be induced to deal exclusively with a single seller. But when the seller can offer a significantly differentiated product with greater consumer acceptance, the buyers may be happy to deal exclusively with that seller.

Necessary conditions for exclusionary effect

There are three conditions that seem necessary for a requirements contract to have a significant exclusionary effect. These three conditions must hold simultaneously.

First, product differentiation must confer a substantial degree of monopoly power on the firm. Neither exclusive dealing nor requirements contracts themselves will generate any market power. Thus, a small market share is a priori evidence that the seller has insufficient coercive power to induce buyers in large numbers relative to the market to enter into a requirements contract with the seller. Although size is a prerequisite for any restrictive effect, it is not sufficient.

Second, the number of satisfactory sales outlets must be effectively limited for some reason. If the number of satisfactory outlets were not limited, then competitors would simply go to alternative sources. But reasonably effective exclusion may be inferred if the system of exclusive dealing contracts entered into by the seller puts his competitors at a disadvantage that is disproportionate to their relative inefficiency in production and location. In most markets there are "preferred" locations, and these may be preempted by the seller practicing exclusion.[7] This preemption hurts the competitor. For example, suppose there are economies of scale that limit the number of buyers in any particular market area. Preemption of these buyers will foreclose competition in that market.

Third, the contract period must be longer than the buyer's usual purchasing period. The longer the term of the contract, the fewer are the opportunities for competitors to bid for a buyer's business. Of course, industry practice is a mitigating circumstance here. If the buyers usually have a long time horizon, then the contract's term will be longer than otherwise.

A critique of the foreclosure theory

We must remember that exclusive dealing and requirements contracts are contractual forms of vertical integration. The objection to exclusive dealing and requirements contracts relies on the theory that competition may be injured through foreclosure of rivals when a firm vertically integrates by contract. If the foreclosure theory is fallacious as it pertains to ownership integration, then it must be fallacious as it pertains to contractual integration. For example, suppose a seller attempts to monopolize its market by exclusive dealing. If there are no efficiencies, the seller's rivals will match whatever inducements it offered. Under these conditions, exclusive dealing cannot be exclusionary.

Suppose, however, that a superior product is offered at the same price or that a lower price is offered for the same quality product. Most people will agree that superior products or lower prices are to be applauded. Now, the seller must offer an inducement that exists for the life of the contract. Thus, in terms of excluding rivals, the contract offers the seller no advantage that it would not have had without the contract. If productive efficiency or superior products provide an advantage and an ability to exclude rivals, requirements contracts or exclusive dealing provide no added ability.

16–4 EXCLUSIVE DEALING: LEGAL DOCTRINE

Unlike some other business practices, exclusive dealing and requirements contracts have received neither per se nor rule of reason treatment by the courts. Since the courts have recognized beneficial as well as deleterious consequences of exclusive dealing, they have sought a

---

[7] The buyers in the preferred locations and the seller with a particularly desirable product are in a bilateral monopoly situation. It is not obvious that the seller will get the best of the bargain.

means of quickly distinguishing between arrangements where the deleterious effects predominate and those in which the effects are beneficial.
There has been a search for an alternative to a per se approach that
would not consume as many judicial resources as a full blown rule of
reason inquiry requires. This judicial search can be seen in the case
development.

Standard Fashion Co. *v.* Magrane-Houston Co.[8] In this case, Standard Fashion made and distributed patterns for women's and children's
clothes. Magrane-Houston was a retail dry goods store. The two parties
entered into an exclusive dealing contract that required Magrane to
maintain a substantial inventory, to remain in the same location, and to
sell only Standard's patterns at full list price. The price of the patterns to
Magrane was 50 percent of the retail price. Moreover, discarded patterns
could be returned for 90 percent on new patterns. Finally, the term of
the contract was two years. Before the contract expired, Magrane dis-
continued selling Standard's patterns and began selling McCall's patterns. Standard sued for enforcement of the contract.

Since the contract was quite explicit, the Supreme Court held that
there was no question about whether exclusive dealing existed. The real
question was whether this particular contract should be struck down
because the covenant not to sell the patterns of others "may be to substantially lessen competition or tend to create a monopoly." The Court
reasoned that "(t)he Clayton Act sought to reach the agreements em-
braced within its sphere in their incipiency, and . . . to determine their
legality by specific tests of its own. . . ." The Court's test turned out to
be structural.

There were 52,000 pattern agencies in the entire country. A holding
company controlled Standard and two other pattern companies and,
through contractual arrangements, controlled about 40 percent of the
pattern agencies. These facts led the Court to two inferences. First, in
small towns, the pattern business is apt to be monopolized by a single
pattern manufacturer. Second, in large towns and cities, exclusive contracts with the most attractive retailers will lead to monopoly. As a
result, these exclusive dealing contracts violated Section 3 of the Clayton
Act.

Standard Oil Co. of California *v.* United States.[9] This case is
known as the "Standard Stations" case. The lower courts had enjoined
Standard Oil from using exclusive dealing contracts in its relations with
independents.

In 1946, Standard Oil sold 23 percent of the total taxable gallonage of
gasoline sold in the so-called Western Area, which was comprised of
Arizona, California, Idaho, Nevada, Oregon, Utah, and Washington. At

---

[8] 258 U.S. 346 (1922).
[9] 337 U.S. 293 (1949).

the retail level, Standard Oil sold 13.5 percent of the total while its six leading competitors sold some 42.5 percent. All of these companies used similar exclusive dealing arrangements. Most of these contracts were for one year, but both parties envisioned a continuing relationship. Standard Oil had 5,937 independent stations under exclusive supply contracts. This amounted to about 16 percent of all retail gasoline outlets in the area.

Between 1936 and 1946, Standard Oil's sales through independent dealers remained a relatively constant proportion of total sales. Since Standard Oil's contracts clearly involved exclusive dealing, the question was whether the contract had the effect of substantially lessening competition. The District Court inferred a substantial effect. The requirement of showing an actual or potential lessening of competition or a tendency to establish monopoly was adequately met by proof that the contract covered a substantial number of outlets and a substantial amount of products, whether considered comparatively or not. Given such quantitative substantiality, the substantial lessening of competition is an automatic result, for the very existence of such contracts denies dealers the opportunity to deal in the products of competing suppliers and excludes suppliers from access to the outlets controlled by those dealers.

Given the District Court's ruling, the issue before the Supreme Court was obvious: Was the burden of showing a substantial lessening of competition met by proof that a substantial portion of commerce had been affected? Alternatively, must it be shown that competitive activity has actually diminished or probably will diminish? This case was new because Standard Oil could not be considered to occupy a dominant position. But *International Salt*[10] had rejected the necessity of demonstrating economic consequences once it had been established that the volume of business affected is neither insignificant nor insubstantial and that the effect is to foreclose competitors from a substantial market.

The Supreme Court explicitly recognized that requirements contracts may well be of economic advantage to buyers as well as to sellers and thereby may help the consumer. *For the buyer,* requirements contracts may assure supply, guarantee price, enable long-term planning on the basis of known costs, and reduce inventory problems. *For the seller,* they may substantially reduce selling expenses, protect against price fluctuations, and offer the possibility of a predictable market, thereby facilitating entry. In fact, the Court proposed various tests of economic usefulness:

1. Evidence that competition flourished despite the use of the contracts.

---

[10] *International Salt Co. v. United States,* 332 U.S. 392 (1947), was a tying case brought under Section 3 of the Clayton Act.

2. The length of the contract relative to the reasonable requirements of the field of commerce in which they were used.
3. The status of the defendant as a struggling newcomer or as an established competitor.
4. Perhaps most important, the defendant's degree of market control.

Apparently Standard Oil's contracts failed these tests. The Court emphasized that it is the theory of the antitrust laws that the long-run advantage of the community depends upon the removal of restraints upon competition. The Court noted that there were alternative "ways of restricting competition" and remarked that as long as these remained available, "there can be no conclusive proof that the use of requirements contracts has actually reduced competition below the level which it would otherwise have reached or maintained." Nonetheless, the majority felt that

> We are dealing here with a particular form of agreement specified by §3 and not with different arrangements . . . that may tend to lessen competition. To interpret that section as requiring proof that competition has *actually* diminished would make its very explicitness a means of conferring immunity upon the practices which it singles out. Congress has authoritatively determined that those practices are detrimental where their effect *may be* to lessen competition.

The requisite probability was easily satisfied: "We conclude, therefore, that the qualifying clause of §3 is satisfied by proof that competition has been foreclosed in a substantial share of the line of commerce affected."

The problem with the majority's approach is revealed in Jackson's dissent:

> The number of dealers and the volume of sales covered by the arrangement of course was sufficient to be substantial. That is to say, this arrangement operated on enough commerce to violate the Act, provided its effects were substantially to lessen competition or create a monopoly. But proof of their quantity does not prove that they had this forbidden quality.
> I cannot agree that the requirement contract is *per se* an illegal one.

Federal Trade Commission *v.* Motion Picture Advertising Service Co.[11] The Motion Picture Advertising Service Company (MPAS) made advertising films that were shown in movie theaters. MPAS paid the theaters for showing their advertising films on the condition that the theater not show anyone else's films. These exclusive arrangements were prevalent in the industry: MPAS and three competitors had tied up some 75 percent of the theaters that showed such films.

The Federal Trade Commission (FTC) challenged this arrangement as an unfair method of competition in violation of Section 5 of the Federal

---

[11] 344 U.S. 392 (1953).

Trade Commission Act. As a result, the FTC ordered MPAS, et al., to limit their contracts to one year or less on the grounds that longer terms unreasonably restrain competition and tend to create a monopoly situation.

The Supreme Court found that the FTC ruling was appropriate in this case: "The exclusive dealing arrangement which has sewed up a market so tightly for the benefit of a few falls within the prohibitions of the Sherman Act and is therefore an 'unfair method of competition' within the meaning of §5(a) of the FTC Act."

Tampa Electric Co. *v.* Nashville Coal Co.[12] In 1955, Tampa Electric decided to expand its facilities by constructing an additional generating plant with six generating units. Tampa Electric decided to use coal as fuel in the first two units at the Gannon Station. Concerned about having a ready supply of coal for the life of the generating units, Tampa Electric entered into a requirements contract. The supply contract called for Tampa Electric to obtain its "total requirements of fuel . . . not less than 225,000 tons of coal per unit year" for a period of 20 years from Nashville Coal. As Tampa Electric constructed other units at Gannon Station, they would be added to the contract unless they were not designed to burn coal. The minimum price for the coal was $6.40 per ton delivered, subject to an escalation clause based on labor cost and other factors.

Shortly after reaching this agreement, the market price of coal increased, and Nashville Coal came to regret the terms of the contract. When Nashville Coal refused to honor its contract, Tampa Electric had to find another source. The terms were not as good and the price was some $8.80 per ton. Tampa Electric's estimated requirements for the first unit were 350,000 tons in 1958, 700,000 tons in 1959 and 1960, 1 million tons in 1961, and steady increases until an annual average of 2.25 million tons was reached. Consequently, the inferior terms of the new contract imposed substantial costs on Tampa Electric. As a result, Tampa Electric sued Nashville Coal for breach of the supply contract. In response, Nashville Coal argued that the contract violated the antitrust laws and, consequently, was unenforceable.

The Supreme Court recognized several structural facts in this industry. First, total coal consumption in peninsular Florida other than Tampa Electric was 700,000 tons per year. There were 700 coal suppliers in the Nashville Coal producing region. Tampa Electric's demand for 2.25 million tons amounted to some 1 percent of the total production in the Nashville Coal producing region.

With respect to the business practice of exclusive dealing, the Court remarked that "(a)n exclusive dealing arrangement . . . does not violate the section unless the Court believes it probable that performance of the

---

[12] 365 U.S. 320 (1961).

contract will foreclose competition in a substantial share to the line of commerce affected." In order to determine the effect, the Court pointed out that several factors would have to be determined: (1) the line of commerce and (2) the geographic market. The threatened foreclosure of competition must be judged in relation to the market affected. In other words, the competition foreclosed by the contract must be found to constitute a substantial share of the relevant market. Merely showing that the contract itself involves a substantial number of dollars is ordinarily of little consequence.

For purposes of analysis, the Court *assumed* that the contract involved exclusive dealing and that the line of commerce was bituminous coal. The geographic market was that area served by the Appalachian coal area producers. Consequently, the volume of coal affected was only 0.77 percent of total production and, therefore, in the relevant market was "quite insubstantial."

The Court remarked that

> (a)lthough protracted requirements contracts may be suspect, they have not been declared illegal per se. Even though a single contract between single traders may fall within the initial broad proscription of the section, it must also suffer the qualifying disability tendency to work a substantial—not remote—lessening of competition in the relevant competitive market.
>
> There is here neither a seller with a dominant position in the market as in *Standard Fashion;* nor myriad outlets with substantial sales volume and an industrywide practice as in Standard Stations.

Moreover, the 20-year period appeared necessary to assure a steady and ample supply of fuel. Consequently, the Court refused to strike down the requirements contract.

Brown Shoe.[13] The *Tampa Electric* decision appeared to signal a more conciliatory attitude on the part of the Court toward exclusive dealing and requirements contracts. In addition, this decision seemed to imply that economic analysis would assume a more prominent role in future decisions involving such contracts. A short five years later, however, the Court returned to its previous harsh and noneconomic treatment of this type of arrangement.

The Brown Shoe Company had reached an agreement with a number of retail outlets in which the company would provide certain services in exchange for these dealers "concentrating" on Brown shoes and refraining from carrying other brands in those lines of shoes that competed directly with Brown's products.[14] The retail outlets that participated in these agreements accounted for approximately 1 percent of all shoe stores in the United States. Moreover, these outlets remained free to

---

[13] 384 U.S. 316 (1966).

[14] See Robert H. Bork, *The Antitrust Paradox* (New York: Basic Books, 1978), pp. 302–3.

terminate the agreements at any time. Despite the apparent lack of potential competitive harm, however, the Supreme Court struck down the agreements. Returning to its pre-*Tampa Electric* posture, the Court refused to engage in any economic analysis of the alleged consequences of the challenged practice but, instead, fell back on its instinctive distrust of any ". . . contracts which take away freedom of purchasers to buy in an open market." Thus, the respite provided to exclusive dealing arrangements by *Tampa Electric* was soon ended with the *Brown Shoe* decision.

16–5 ASSESSMENT OF LEGAL DOCTRINE

It is clear that the law on exclusive dealing and requirements contracts is based on a judicial concern for vertical foreclosure of markets and restrictions on freedom of choice. This concern is misplaced. First, the foreclosure theory cannot support a prohibition of exclusive dealing because the theory is fallacious.[15] Second, freedom of choice is not constrained by these contracts in any meaningful sense. Both parties reach agreement in advance of signing the contract. Prior to signing, the parties examine the available options and freely choose what each perceives to be in its self-interest. In spite of these observations, there is a lingering concern that a large supplier can coerce its distributors to accept an exclusive dealing arrangement. This residual concern is also unfounded.

If a supplier has a particularly desirable product that most distributors want to sell, he or she can extract the value of that product in the form of higher prices. Alternatively, he can impose exclusive dealing on his distributors. But he cannot do both. Consequently, it is apparent that the supplier cannot get something for nothing. If he wants exclusive dealing, he must purchase it from the distributors in the form of lower prices or the provision of greater efficiencies. The supplier who purchases exclusivity must do so because its costs are reduced as a result. This follows because exclusive dealing cannot be used as a vehicle for monopolization.

Tampa Electric contained a structural analysis and signaled a departure from the earlier reasoning. But this case had some special circumstances. In particular, Nashville Coal was trying to renege on a contract that it had entered into freely because it regretted the terms. Thus, one of the parties was trying to escape the consequences of breaching a contract through the antitrust laws. In *Brown Shoe,* a similar amount of foreclosure subsequently was found to violate the law. Thus, *Tampa Electric* cannot be viewed as a fundamental change in direction. Rather, antitrust policy continues to be generally hostile to exclusive dealing.

---

[15] Refer to the discussion of vertical market foreclosure in Chapter 12. Since exclusive dealing is a form of contractual vertical integration, the analysis is precisely the same.

QUESTIONS AND PROBLEMS

1. Posner has claimed that "(a)n exclusive dealing contract of very long or indefinite duration is unlikely to be an effective method of monopolization." Offer an analytical justification for this position.

2. If exclusive dealing increases the scale necessary for new entry and thereby increases the time required for entry, will the opportunity for monopoly profits be increased?

3. Sullivan has suggested that if a requirements contract extends beyond one year, it could be presumed invalid. Can you defend this suggestion?

4. Several commentators have alleged that exclusive dealing raises entry barriers. How does this occur? Does your answer depend upon what one considers an entry barrier?

5. In *Standard Stations*, Justice Frankfurter rejected a rule of reason analysis because the necessary economic analysis is too difficult for the courts. Is this a sensible way to develop public policy?

6. Shillinglaw has expressed the following concern regarding requirements contracts: "The essence of the competitive system lies in competition *before* each sale. A requirements contract, however, increases the interval between 'sales'. Competition has fewer opportunities to exert its influence. . . ." How does this influence your view of requirements contracts?

7. What do you think was the purpose of the requirements contract in *Tampa Electric?* Was anyone foreclosed from competing with Nashville Coal for the Tampa Electric *contract?*

8. In *Standard Stations*, Justice Douglas dissented because he feared that condemnation would result in forward vertical integration. Would such a change result in any substantive economic change?

9. What was it about the exclusive dealing in *Standard Stations* that made it illegal? Who was foreclosed from which market?

10. How are exclusive dealing and requirements contracts economically different from tying arrangements? Based on your analysis, does tying deserve its status of per se illegality?

11. Is an exclusive dealing contract covering a period of three years any more restrictive than an employment contract covering a similar period? Explain your view.

12. Most of the Brown Shoe contracts contained a clause permitting the dealer to terminate at will. Given this fact, how were those contracts anticompetitive? What does Brown have to do to avoid mass cancellations? Is that anticompetitive? Is anyone disadvantaged by the arrangement?

13. What is the economically appropriate measure of foreclosure resulting from the Tampa Electric requirements contracts? Did the Court use this measure?

FURTHER READINGS

Bork, Robert H. *The Antitrust Paradox.* New York: Basic Books, 1978, pp. 299–309.

Lockhart, William B., and Howard R. Sacks. "The Relevance of Economic Factors in Determining whether Exclusive Arrangements Violate Section 3 of the Clayton Act." *Harvard Law Review* 65 (April 1952), pp. 913–54.

Marvel, Howard P. "Exclusive Dealing." *Journal of Law and Economics* 25 (April 1982), pp. 1–25.

Peterman, John L. "The Federal Trade Commission v. Brown Shoe Company." *Journal of Law and Economics* 18 (October 1975), pp. 361–420.

Telser, Lester G. "Why Should Manufacturers Want Fair Trade?" *Journal of Law and Economics* 3 (October 1960), pp. 86–105.

PART IV

Conglomerate antitrust issues

Our final section deals with conglomerate firms and their potential for causing antitrust problems. For the most part, conglomerate firms are feared because they are large in an absolute sense and not because they hold dominant (monopolistic) positions in any of the industries in which they do business. In the first chapter, we examine the economic and financial motives for conglomeration and for conglomerate mergers. We also examine the legal concerns that have led to antitrust challenges to conglomerate mergers. In the second chapter, we investigate the seriously misunderstood business practice of reciprocity. Although reciprocity has received hostile antitrust treatment, our search for any anticompetitive effect failed to turn up much evidence against this business practice.

17

Conglomerate mergers: Theory and policy

17–1 INTRODUCTION

You will recall from Chapter 9 that our taxonomy of mergers included three major categories: horizontal, vertical, and conglomerate. The characteristic that identifies a conglomerate merger is that the firms involved have not met each other either as direct competitors within a given geographic and product market or as buyer and seller across an intermediate product market. Prior to the conglomerate merger, the firms involved have had no direct commercial contact. In addition, you will recall that, within the general category of conglomerate mergers, we identified three subcategories: product extension, market extension, and pure conglomerate. The product extension merger involved a merger between firms which sell noncompeting goods that fall within the same general product line. The market extension merger involves firms that sell the same product but operate in different geographic markets. Finally, the pure conglomerate merger involves firms that sell completely unrelated products.

The proportion of all mergers falling into the conglomerate category has increased dramatically over time. Table 17–1 demonstrates the upward historical trend in the relative frequency of conglomerate mergers. We can also see in this table that as the share of total merger activity falling into the conglomerate category has risen, the proportion of conglomerate mergers that are classified as pure conglomerate (involving

TABLE 17–1   Relative frequency of various types of mergers

Type of merger	Percentage of assets acquired			
	1948–53	1956–63	1963–72	1973–77
Horizontal	36.8%	19.2%	12.4%	15.1%
Vertical	12.8	22.2	7.8	5.8
Conglomerate				
Product extension	44.8 ⎫	36.0 ⎫	39.3 ⎫	24.2 ⎫
Market extension	2.4 ⎬ 50.4	6.7 ⎬ 58.6	7.3 ⎬ 79.8	5.7 ⎬ 79.1
Pure conglomerate	3.2 ⎭	15.9 ⎭	33.2 ⎭	49.2 ⎭

Source: F. M. Scherer, *Industrial Market Structure and Economic Performance* (Skokie, Ill.: Rand McNally, 1980), p. 124.

firms that sell unrelated products) has experienced the greatest increase. To a large extent, the growth of the pure conglomerate diversified firm has been a post-World War II phenomenon. The growing importance of conglomerate merger activity tentatively has been attributed to the deterrent effect that the Celler-Kefauver Act of 1950 has had on horizontal and vertical mergers.[1] The increased antitrust pressure placed on horizontal and vertical mergers following this act has reduced the incidence of nonconglomerate mergers from 49.6 percent during the 1948–53 period to 20.9 percent during the 1973–77 period.

The rising importance of the large diversified firm in the U.S. economy that has accompanied the trend toward conglomerate mergers raises public policy issues at two levels. First, at the market level, the dominant issue has been whether diversification across markets confers an unfair competitive advantage or facilitates anticompetitive behavior that may lessen the degree of competition realized in a given market and ultimately lead to increased levels of market concentration. Second, at the aggregate level, concerns have been expressed regarding the economic and political consequences of increasing the concentration of ownership of productive assets in general, even in the absence of any effects on concentration or competition in a specific well-defined market. Despite considerable debate over the past three decades, both of these public policy issues remain open at the present time.

In this chapter, we survey some of the major economic theories of conglomerate mergers. Following this survey, we discuss conglomerate merger policy both as revealed in prior merger cases and as advertised in the Antitrust Division's Merger Guidelines. Looking ahead, we shall

---

[1] F. M. Scherer, *Industrial Market Structure and Economic Performance*, 2d ed. (Skokie, Ill.: Rand McNally, 1980), p. 559.

find a distinct absence of any definite policy relating to this category of mergers. The reason for the absence of a systematic policy emerges from our survey: There are numerous potential explanations for conglomerate mergers, only some of which imply anticompetitive effects. Moreover, the existing empirical evidence relating to conglomerate merger incentives is insufficient to distinguish between the competing theories. Thus, an information vacuum exists that makes it difficult to formulate any definite policy toward conglomerate mergers.

17–2 CONGLOMERATE MERGERS: INCENTIVES

If we maintain the usual assumption of microeconomics that firms typically make decisions intending to increase their profits, then any theory of conglomerate mergers based on this assumption must involve some explanation of how two firms operating in different markets (either product or geographic) can increase the sum total of their combined profits by merging. In other words, how does bringing their productive assets under common management control lead to increased profits. Since profits are simply the difference between total revenues and total costs, it follows that increased profits may result from either an increase in the price charged by one or both firms that are party to the merger or by a decrease in the costs of producing the set of goods involved.[2] It is convenient, then, to categorize the existing theories of conglomerate mergers that rely on the assumption of profit maximization according to which of these two avenues is operative. This simple classification scheme is capable of accommodating all but one of the relevant theories. The remaining theory does not depend directly upon profit maximization as the driving force motivating the merger but posits other objectives to explain the observed behavior. We shall first discuss the neoclassical theories that fit into the bifurcated taxonomy (i.e., those theories that assume profit maximization) and then address the exception separately.

17–3 THEORIES INVOLVING LOWER COSTS

1. Economies of scope.   There are certain products for which the total costs of production are lower when these products are produced together within a single firm. The classic example comes from Alfred Marshall's early work on joint products.[3] Here, Marshall pointed out that when two goods (mutton and wool) share some common input (a

---

[2] Clearly, the social welfare implications of these two alternative avenues for increasing profits are not the same.

[3] Alfred Marshall, *Principles of Economics*, 8th ed. (New York: Macmillan, 1949), pp. 388–90.

sheep) efficiency or technical considerations may dictate the joint production of the two goods together. Analogous, though much less obvious, cases can arise in the production of more complex manufactured goods. In any situation where two (or more) different outputs can share or make joint utilization of one (or more) input, cost savings may be realized through joint production. Such a sharing of inputs may result from the imperfect divisibility of certain factors of production. For example, the use of technical or market information for the manufacture of one good does not reduce its availability for use in the manufacture of some other good.[4] The costs of joint production also may be reduced when some common input (e.g., advertising or research and development) is subject to economies of scale.

Recent contributions to the economics literature have introduced some useful cost concepts that are designed to measure the degree to which cost savings may result from multiproduct production.[5] A prominent feature of this work has been the concept of *economies of scope*. Economies of scope are said to exist when one firm is able to produce a fixed level of output of two or more products at a lower total cost than can two or more firms each producing a single product at the same level of output. In other words, the total costs incurred by firm A in producing 100 widgets and 50 gadgets is less than firm B's cost of producing 100 widgets plus firm C's cost of producing 50 gadgets. Conversely, diseconomies of scope exist when the costs of joint production exceed the sum of the costs of producing these products in separate firms. Clearly, if two single-product firms are producing outputs across which there are economies of scope, a merger between these firms can improve the profitability of both firms by reducing the costs of production.[6] Therefore, the existence of economies of scope provides one potential incentive for conglomerate mergers.

2. Political influence. A possible variant of the economies of scope explanation for conglomerate mergers is the political influence theory.[7] Here it is argued that firms may combine ownership in order to influ-

---

[4] D. Teece, "Economies of Scope and the Scope of the Enterprise," *Journal of Economic Behavior and Organization* 1 (September 1980), pp. 223–45, and J. W. Mayo, "The Technological Determinants of the U.S. Energy Industry Structure," *Review of Economics and Statistics* 66 (February 1984), pp. 51–58.

[5] E. E. Bailey and A. F. Friedlaender, "Market Structure and Multiproduct Industries," *Journal of Economic Literature* 20 (September 1982), pp. 1024–48, and W. Baumol, J. Panzar, and R. Willig, *Contestable Markets and the Theory of Industry Structure* (New York: Harcourt Brace Jovanovich, 1982).

[6] The analogy between the single-product concept of economies of scale and the multiproduct concept of economies of scope should be apparent. While the former determines the cost minimizing size of the firm in a given market, the latter determines the cost minimizing breadth of a firm across markets.

[7] J. J. Siegfried, "The Effects of Conglomerate Mergers on Political Democracy: A Survey," in *The Conglomerate Corporation: An Antitrust Law and Economics Symposium*, eds. R. D. Blair and R. F. Lanzillotti (Cambridge, Mass.: Oelgeschlager, Gunn & Hain, 1981).

ence more effectively the political process that, in turn, affects the rules or market conditions under which those firms operate. In effect, this line of reasoning depends upon the existence of economies of scale in the acquisition of a common input—political influence. By pooling their resources, firms with similar objectives in the political arena may be able to achieve some desired goal (e.g., passage of a given piece of favorable legislation) at lower cost if lobbying exhibits economies of scale. Such economies of scale may arise from more intensive utilization of certain inputs into the lobbying process that are fixed in quantity (e.g., computer facilities for mass mailing campaigns or particularly talented lobbying personnel), or from coordination and planning economies that reduce or eliminate duplicative efforts.

For economies of scale in lobbying to provide an incentive to merge, however, it must be relatively expensive for the firms involved to combine lobbying efforts without combining ownership (i.e., to enter joint ventures to influence political outcomes). In the absence of joint ownership, however, there will exist a strong incentive for each firm to free ride on the lobbying efforts of other firms with similar political goals; therefore, an externality problem may be involved. Consequently, it is not unreasonable to speculate that merger is required in order to internalize the externality and provide the proper (from the point of view of the firms involved) incentive to participate in the political process.

While we have considered the political influence theory under the general heading of Theories Involving Lower Costs for purposes of discussion, it is clear that the impact of a successful lobbying effort on the firm's profits may be channeled through either cost reductions or price increases (or both). For instance, legislative exemption from some environmental regulation will serve to reduce production costs, while protective trade regulations limiting competition from imports may enable domestic firms to raise prices. Consequently, the political influence theory might be classified in either category of the taxonomy employed here.

3. Financial diversification. In addition to these technical or scope economies, it is also possible for conglomerate mergers to generate savings of a financial nature through the diversification effect of joining together two profit streams that are less than perfectly correlated.[8] Using elementary statistics, one can demonstrate that, unless the profits earned by two firms are perfectly correlated over time, a merger between these firms will reduce the overall variance of total profits as a percentage of average profits. Moreover, the extent of this reduction in

---

[8] F. M. Scherer, *Industrial Market Structure and Economic Performance,* 1st ed. (Skokie, Ill.: Rand McNally, 1970), pp. 101–2, and M. Monroe, "Conglomerate Mergers: Financial Theory and Evidence," in *The Conglomerate Corporation: An Antitrust Law and Economics Symposium,* eds. R. D. Blair and R. F. Lanzillotti (Cambridge, Mass.: Oelgeschlager, Gunn & Hain, 1981), pp. 116–19.

the variance of profits is inversely related to the degree of positive correlation that exists between the profit streams of the two firms. In other words, the lower the correlation between the two profit streams, the lower the variance of the combined profit stream as a percentage of total average profits. Since a conglomerate merger involves firms that either sell different products or operate in different markets, the correlation between their profits is likely to be relatively low (perhaps even negative). Therefore, the diversification effect is likely to be operative with mergers of this variety.

The risk reduction experienced by the diversified firm as the result of a conglomerate merger may generate two potentially beneficial results. First, if stockholders are risk averse, the stock market's valuation of the combined firm may exceed the sum of the market's valuation of the two individual firms prior to the merger. And second, if lenders are risk averse, the cost of debt capital to the diversified firm may be lower than the weighted average cost of debt capital to the two separate firms prior to the merger. Both of these potential effects of a conglomerate merger, however, depend upon the existence of some so-called imperfection in the capital market.[9] If capital markets are perfect in the sense that transaction and information costs are zero, individual investors will be able costlessly to diversify their portfolios to optimize their risk/return positions. In this case, there is no need for firms to diversify, and the stock market will not place a premium on the shares of a conglomerate firm as a result of any diversification achieved through merger. But if nonzero information and transaction costs limit the ability of the individual investor to diversify to the optimal degree, then this incentive to merge may arise.

4. Takeovers. Another possible motive for conglomerate mergers that relies upon the concept of costly or asymmetric information is the managerial inefficiency theory. Poor management leads to low profitability with the result that the stock market undervalues the firm's productive assets. Obviously, undervalued firms would not exist if the stockholders of these firms were perfectly informed concerning their managers' poor performance. With perfect information, inefficient managers would be replaced immediately by the owners (stockholders) of the firm. With imperfect information, however, poor managerial performance may persist over substantial periods of time, and undervaluation of the firm's assets is theoretically possible. Now, if the management of some other firm recognizes that the stock of the poorly managed firm is undervalued, it can purchase this stock at a bargain price, replace the inefficient management of the acquired firm, and realize an increase in profits. Since any investor or group of investors could do the same

---

[9] See Monroe, "Conglomerate Mergers," p. 116–19. In addition, see J. W. Mayo, "Theories of the Multiproduct Firm: Implications for Antitrust Policy," mimeo, 1983, pp. 12–13.

thing, this theory must also assume an additional asymmetry of information that confers superior knowledge on the managers of the acquiring firm.[10]

5. Efficient reallocation of capital. Still another possible motive for conglomerate merger that relies upon informational asymmetries involves the relative efficiency of two alternative methods for transferring capital from one industry to another.[11] Within the conglomerate firm, such transfers can be accomplished through the hierarchical or bureaucratic decision-making mechanism. In other words, capital may be reallocated from one industry to another through the routine investment decisions affecting the firm's subsidiaries operating in these industries. Outside the conglomerate firm, however, such transfers must be directed through the capital markets. With imperfect (costly or asymmetric) information, the use of the capital market to reallocate capital from one industry to another may involve transaction costs that exceed the benefits of the transfer being sought. Intrafirm transfers may well economize on these transaction costs and thereby bring about a more efficient allocation of capital. Such improved allocations may reduce overall costs and, in turn, increase profitability.

6. Tax reductions. Finally, it may be possible for firms to lower costs by reducing their tax obligations through a conglomerate (or other) merger.[12] The possibility of reducing taxes arises from several features of the U.S. tax laws. First, since capital gains are taxed at a lower rate than income earned through dividends, stockholders are often better off to have their profits reinvested rather than paid out as dividends. Such reinvestment may entail the purchase of another firm if investment opportunities within the acquiring firm's market have dwindled. Due to the tax savings, reinvestment via merger may benefit stockholders even where the total before-tax profits are unaffected by the merger. Second, inheritance and estate taxes may encourage owners of firms with unlisted or thinly traded stocks to sell. By merging with a larger corporation, the firm's owners can avoid the risks of having the Internal Revenue Service do an independent estimation of the firm's worth.[13] Finally, a firm that is losing money may be purchased in order to provide a tax-

---

[10] Since we have described this theory under the heading Theories Involving Lower Costs, we are assuming that the profitability of the acquired firm is improved by reducing costs. This is not the only way that the acquired firm's profits could be improved.

[11] O. E. Williamson, *Markets and Hierarchies: Analysis and Antitrust Implications* (New York: Free Press, 1975). W. S. Comanor, "Conglomerate Mergers: Considerations for Public Policy," in *The Conglomerate Corporation: An Antitrust Law and Economics Symposium,* eds. R. D. Blair and R. F. Lanzillotti (Cambridge, Mass.: Oelgeschlager, Gunn & Hain, 1981), p. 20.

[12] R. Sherman, "How Tax Policy Induces Conglomerate Mergers," *National Tax Journal* 25 (December 1972), pp. 521–30.

[13] Scherer, *Industrial Market Structure,* p. 128, and C. C. Bosland, "Has Estate Taxation Induced Recent Mergers?" *National Tax Journal* 16 (June 1963), pp. 159–68.

loss carry-forward to a firm that is earning profits to reduce the combined tax burden.[14] In these (and, no doubt, other) ways, the tax laws can provide merger incentives.

17–4 THEORIES INVOLVING HIGHER PRICES

There are four principal theories of conglomerate mergers that rely upon price increases to generate higher postmerger profits. These are: (1) the theory of potential competition; (2) cross-subsidization; (3) spheres of influence; and (4) reciprocity. We shall defer our discussion of reciprocity until the following chapter. The first three theories listed above, however, are discussed here. Before we begin, it is important to note that all four theories assume the existence of some horizontal market power on the part of one or both firms prior to the merger. The conglomerate merger, then, becomes a vehicle for making more effective use of the monopoly power that already exists.

1. Potential competition. The theory of potential competition is based on the idea that firms that are not currently producing a given product may provide a restraining influence on firms that are producing that product through their threat of entry. This theory is analytically equivalent to what is known as the theory of limit pricing.[15] In essence, this theory is founded on the idea that a monopolist or a dominant firm may choose to set its price below the short-run profit maximizing level in order to discourage new firms from entering the industry. For example, suppose that a firm with some monopoly power (i.e., a downward-sloping demand) faces a demand curve that is given by D in Figure 17–1. For simplicity, we assume that this firm has constant marginal and average costs that are given by MC_M. Short-run profit maximization would lead this firm to produce the monopoly output, Q_M, and charge the monopoly price, P_M. If barriers to entry into this industry are sufficiently large, then this firm can continue to earn these profits in all future periods.[16]

Suppose, however, that entry barriers are insufficient to deter new firms from entering if the incumbent firm charges a price of P_M. Specifically, assume that there exists a firm not currently in this industry that could produce this product at marginal and average costs equal to MC_{PC}. This outside firm is referred to as a potential competitor. Given this potential competitor, if the incumbent firm charges the monopoly price,

---

[14] Scherer, *Industrial Market Structure*, p. 133, and S. N. Wiggins, "A Theoretical Analysis of Conglomerate Mergers," in *The Conglomerate Corporation: An Antitrust Law and Economics Symposium*, eds. R. D. Blair and R. F. Lanzillotti (Cambridge, Mass.: Oelgeschlager, Gunn & Hain, 1981), p. 63.

[15] Scherer, *Industrial Market Structure*, pp. 232–39.

[16] J. S. Bain, *Barriers to New Competition* (Cambridge, Mass.: Harvard University Press, 1956).

FIGURE 17–1   The limit price theory

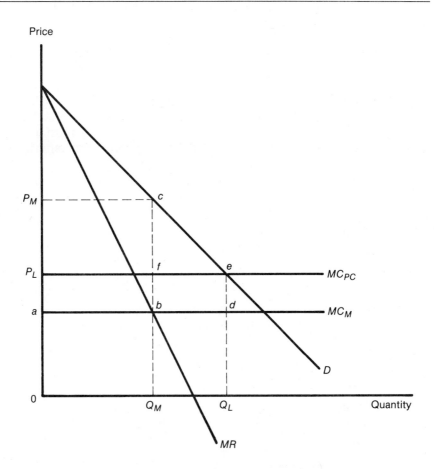

P_M, the new firm will enter the industry and the incumbent firm's profits will decline. Once this firm has entered the industry, the incumbent firm may find it difficult to force the new entrant to exit by reducing price below MC_{PC} because sunk costs may drive the new entrant's average variable costs well below MC_{PC}.

If the incumbent firm is aware of this outsider and its cost structure, then long-run profit maximization may lead the incumbent firm to deter entry by reducing its price to P_L in the graph. Since P_L equals MC_{PC}, the outsider will not be attracted to this industry by excess profits. To make this lower price effective, the incumbent firm must also increase its output to Q_L. Otherwise, unsatisfied demand would exist to attract entry. At this higher output and lower price (the limit price), the poten-

tial competitor can only earn a normal profit in this industry and, therefore, will not enter. As a result, the incumbent earns a lower rate of
profit, $adeP_L$, but it is able to earn this lower profit indefinitely into the
future.

Consequently, the existence of the potential competitor on the fringe
of the market forces the existing firm to expand output and reduce price,
moving it closer to the competitive solution. Obviously, if MC_{PC} is sufficiently close to MC_M, the incumbent firm's long-run monopoly power
will be severely limited by the presence of potential competition, and it
will be forced to charge close to the competitive price (equal to MC_M) in
order to deter entry. For this reason, the antitrust authorities have pursued policies that are intended to preserve potential, as well as actual,
competition.

With regard to conglomerate mergers, the theory of potential competition (alias, limit pricing) provides another avenue through which the
combined profits of the two firms that are party to the merger can be
increased. Going back to Figure 17–1, suppose that there is only one
potential competitor in existence. The incumbent firm now can be seen
to have three alternatives: (1) charge the monopoly price and suffer
entry; (2) charge the limit price and deter entry; or (3) merge with the
sole potential entrant. If the firm selects the third alternative, then the
monopoly price, P_M, can be sustained indefinitely into the future. The
profits that this price generates, $abcP_M$, will then accrue to the merged
firm; but, if these profits are sufficiently greater then the entry-deterring
profits, $adeP_L$, merger may well represent the optimal (profit maximizing) choice for both the incumbent firm and the potential competitor.

Having demonstrated how the theory of potential competition can
provide a possible explanation for some conglomerate mergers, we are
compelled to make two basic observations that are pertinent to the application of this theory to the design of an effective merger policy. First,
potential competition serves a useful role only in situations where actual
competition is inadequate. That is, the limit pricing model necessarily
assumes that the incumbent firm possesses some monopoly power.
Otherwise, it would not have the ability to raise the market price above
its costs by restricting output. And second, a merger between an incumbent (dominant) firm and a potential competitor cannot enhance the
incumbent firm's ability to raise price without attracting entry in situations where there exists a relatively large number of potential entrants
with roughly equivalent cost structures. Thus, for this theory to have
much applicability to conglomerate merger policy, it must be confined to
situations in which the incumbent firm already has monopoly power
and potential competitors are few in number. The second condition is
particularly difficult to substantiate in practice since all firms (and resource owners) are ultimately potential competitors in all industries. We

shall return to this issue later in this chapter when we examine some conglomerate merger cases.

2. Cross-subsidization. The second conglomerate merger theory involving higher prices is the cross-subsidization theory, which is analytically equivalent to the theory of predatory pricing. According to this theory, a conglomerate firm may utilize the profits obtained in one market to subsidize the losses incurred in some other market (which is separated along either geographic or product dimensions), where these losses are the necessary result of predatory pricing in the latter market. Such cross-subsidization/predatory pricing may be seen as an investment of the earnings obtained in one market in the anticipated future earnings to be obtained in the second market, where these future earnings are enlarged by the predation being practiced in that market in the present period.

It has been argued that conglomerate mergers enhance the opportunities for this sort of behavior simply by enlarging the number of separate markets in which a given firm operates. By increasing the breadth of the firm's operations, the conglomerate merger increases both the potential sources of funds to finance predatory pricing and the likelihood that the firm will find itself operating in a particular market that holds the promise of yielding positive returns to predation (i.e., where existing firms may be forced to exit at relatively low cost and where their later reentry appears unlikely). Where conditions conducive to predation are present, a conglomerate merger may provide the most efficient means available for the predator to raise the investment funds needed to wage a successful price war. The outside firm merging with the predator firm provides these funds with the expectation of reaping the future returns of such successful predation.

Recall our discussion of the predatory pricing debate from Chapter 5. After surveying the theoretical arguments and empirical evidence regarding the issue of whether predatory pricing is ever likely to be an economically sensible strategy to employ, we concluded that it may pay the firm to engage in predation but only under certain restrictive circumstances. Given the restrictiveness of those circumstances, however, and the apparent infrequency of actual occurrences of predation uncovered by researchers addressing this issue, we also concluded that predatory pricing is (and is likely to remain) a fairly rare phenomenon.

More importantly, when we combine this conclusion with the observation that predatory behavior is, in practice, very difficult to distinguish from aggressively competitive behavior, we are left with a distinctly uneasy feeling about the applicability of this theory to the formulation of effective conglomerate merger policy. The competitive struggle between rival firms is inherently predatory (particularly in oligopolistic industries) in the sense that any price reductions that are made by one firm reduce the demand for the output of the other firms in the industry regardless of the ultimate motive or underlying intent of such price reductions. To forbid aggressive price cutting on the apparently unlikely chance that significant price increases will eventually follow seems to represent a policy founded on paranoia rather than sound economic reasoning. As we shall see later in this chapter, however, the cross-subsidization (alias predatory pricing) theory has played a significant role in more than one conglomerate merger case. In our opinion, utilization of this theory to block mergers or to discourage price cutting by rival firms comes dangerously close to a policy that sacrifices competition in order to protect competitors.

3. **Spheres of influence.** The final theory of conglomerate mergers that relies upon price increases to provide the profit incentive for joining the two firms together is the spheres of influence theory. As with the two preceding theories, the spheres of influence theory also has an alias—it is often described under the heading of mutual forebearance. The basic idea underlying the economic theory is that a firm that shares more than one market with a rival firm may refrain from aggressive price competition in one or more of these markets in an implicit exchange for restraint on the part of the other firm in one or more of the other markets that they share. The behavior that is posited under this theory, then, closely resembles tacit collusion, where the firms that operate in a given market are able to reach an understanding on what price to charge for their mutual benefit without any explicit negotiation or formal agreement. The distinction between these two theories is that in the spheres of influence theory the cooperation between rival firms extends across different markets.

An incident that is commonly used to exemplify this sort of behavior is the exchange that took place between the Consolidated Food Corporation and the National Tea Corporation in 1965.[17] Consolidated was both a manufacturer and retailer of food products, while National's operations were confined to the retail stage. When Consolidated launched an aggressive retail price campaign in one of National's principal market areas (the Chicago market), National responded by canceling the sale of Consolidated's products in all of their grocery stores throughout the country. Consolidated, in turn, acquiesced by restoring prices and eventually withdrawing from the Chicago retail market altogether. The signal that had been sent by National's retaliatory response to Consolidated's aggressive pricing was clear: If you choose to compete aggressively in my market, I will do what I can to damage you in your market. The signal relayed back by Consolidated's acquiescent response was equally clear: Forget competing; let's live and let live.

---

[17] D. F. Greer, *Industrial Organization and Public Policy* (New York: Macmillan, 1980), pp. 422–23, and W. F. Mueller, "Conglomerates: A Nonindustry," in *The Structure of American Industry*, ed. W. Adams (New York: Macmillan, 1977), pp. 474–75.

Where rival firms meet in a single market, this sort of cooperative behavior may be quite elusive and, if attained, fragile (recall our discussion of the incentive to cheat on a cartel agreement). But where these firms meet in multiple markets, more efficient signaling mechanisms exist that may facilitate cooperation between otherwise rivalrous firms. Given this superior signaling apparatus, the theory of mutual forebearance posits that the likelihood that pricing restraint will emerge increases with the number of separate markets in which the firms meet. While familiarity may breed contempt, contact facilitates communication. Consequently, the conglomerate merger is hypothesized to increase the probability that cooperative behavior across markets will be forthcoming.

Due largely to data limitations, this hypothesis has not been subjected to extensive empirical verification. It has, however, received support from the only study to test it to date. In an analysis of the banking industry, Heggestad and Rhoades[18] found that the intensity of competition in local markets depended not only on the structural characteristics of those markets (primarily the volatility of market shares and entry barriers) but also on the frequency with which the banks in those markets met one another in other local markets. As predicted by the spheres of influence theory, the more frequent the market contact between rival banks, the less intense is the competition between these banks in any given market, other things being equal. While one study conducted on one industry certainly does not confirm the spheres of influence theory as an important factor for all industries, it does provide some support for this theory as a potential explanation of some conglomerate mergers. In effect, it puts the ball in the court of those who dismiss the theory as patently unrealistic.

17–5 THEORY THAT DOES NOT DEPEND UPON AN INCREASE IN PROFIT

Up to this point, the conglomerate merger theories we have discussed all depend upon an increase in the combined profits of the firms which are party to the merger to provide the incentive for the merger to take place. The final theory that we discuss here is an exception. This theory postulates that at least some mergers are the manifestation of the discretionary power of the acquiring firm's managers who are alleged to be seeking to maximize the growth rate of the firm that they control.[19] Since

---

[18] A. Heggestad and S. Rhoades, "Multi-Market Interdependence and Local Market Competition in Banking," *Review of Economics and Statistics* 60 (November 1978), pp. 523–32.

[19] D. C. Mueller, "A Theory of Conglomerate Mergers," *Quarterly Journal of Economics* 84 (November 1969), pp. 643–59. Wiggins, "A Theoretical Analysis of Conglomerate Mergers," p. 63.

merger represents the most rapid avenue to growth, managers of acquiring firms may pursue mergers that do not result in an increase in profits (or, perhaps, even result in a decrease in profits). The alleged reason for managers adopting growth (as opposed to profits) as their objective is that managerial remuneration is sometimes thought to be more closely associated with firm size than with profitability. If this premise is correct,[20] then managers with any discretionary power at all will sacrifice profits (stockholder remuneration) in order to increase growth (and, thereby, their own remuneration).

The degree of latitude that managers have to substitute their own preferences for those of the firm's stockholders has been the subject of considerable debate for some time. It is clear, however, that even in the most widely held (diffuse ownership) corporation, the managers are not allowed complete discretion. If the managers of a given corporation were to ignore profitability altogether in pursuing their own goals, they may well find themselves out of work as a result of a successful takeover bid engineered by the managers of another firm. Moreover, it is also possible for attentive stockholders to replace what they perceive to be inept managers. Thus, growth objectives cannot be pursued with total disregard for profitability. Within the constraints provided by takeover bids and stockholder ire, however, managers may have sufficient discretionary power to pursue some mergers that do not improve profits.

With regard to antitrust policy, the managerial discretion theory would not appear to have a great deal of relevance. Since the goal of antitrust is not to protect stockholders from headstrong managers, any merger that results solely from managerial discretion should be of no concern to the antitrust authorities. Thus, regardless of the merits of this theory (which are subject to considerable doubt), it should not play a major role in conglomerate merger policy.

17–6 CONGLOMERATE MERGER CASES

From the above survey of the economic theories of conglomerate mergers, it is clear that no definitive answer can be provided to the question, "Do conglomerate mergers damage competition?" Our review of the various explanations of this category of merger uncovered several theories that do admit the possibility of anticompetitive effects (e.g., the theories of potential competition, cross-subsidization, and spheres of influence). At the same time, however, some of the other theories that we described rely upon cost reductions that are likely to improve market outcomes (e.g., economies of scope, efficient capital transfers, and takeover bids). Still others have no apparent impact on the competitive

---

[20] R. Masson, "Executive Motivations, Earnings, and Consequent Equity Performance," *Journal of Political Economy* 79 (November/December 1971), pp. 1278–93.

process at all (e.g., the managerial discretion theory). In short, the direction of the impact of a conglomerate merger on competition is theoretically indeterminate on a priori grounds.

In addition to this theoretical indeterminacy of the *direction* of the effect (if any), the distinct impression that one gets in surveying these theories is that, in the majority of cases, the *magnitude* of the effect on competition (where present) is likely to be of relatively minor proportions. Thus, even in situations where a conglomerate merger appears likely to inflict damage on the intensity of competition in a given market, the harm that is done is not likely to be very great. Other factors, such as the degree of horizontal market power already in place, are more likely to determine the ultimate vigor of competition.

While we have not attempted any comprehensive review of the empirical literature pertaining to conglomerate mergers here, the studies that have tried to verify statistically the various hypothesized effects have also failed to reach a consensus.[21] The evidence that has been generated concerning the impact of conglomerate mergers on prices, costs, output, profit, and so on is simply insufficient to distinguish any pronounced systematic effects. This failure of the empirical research to uncover any significant general relationships supports the conclusion that the direction of effects is mixed and the magnitude of effects is small.

Given these theoretical and empirical ambiguities, it is not surprising that conglomerate merger policy remains one of the more unsettled areas of antitrust law. There have not been a great many cases challenging this type of merger. And, from those that have been tried, a clear picture discerning the proscribed from the lawful has yet to emerge. The law in this area is still under construction; and, in the absence of a more definite blueprint, it is not clear what the structure will look like when the last brick is finally put in place. Hopefully, a brief summary of four of the more important cases will provide some idea of the general outline of the current state of the law of conglomerate mergers.

Federal Trade Commission *v.* **Procter & Gamble Co.**[22] This case involved a product extension merger between the Procter and Gamble Company and the Clorox Chemical Company, which occurred in 1957. At the time of the merger, P&G was the dominant producer of household soaps and cleansers, with 54.4 percent of the market for packaged detergents. This industry was highly concentrated, with P&G and the next two largest firms (Colgate-Palmolive and Lever Brothers) accounting for 80 percent of the market. Prior to the merger with Clorox, P&G sold no liquid household bleach, but it had been following a course of diversification into related product lines.

---

[21] See D. C. Mueller, "The Effects of Conglomerate Mergers: A Survey of the Empirical Evidence," *Journal of Banking and Finance* 1 (1977), pp. 315–47, for a review of this literature.

[22] 386 U.S. 568 (1967).

At the time of the acquisition, Clorox was the leading manufacturer of household liquid bleach, accounting for 48.8 percent of the national market with much higher shares in certain regional markets.[23] Moreover, Clorox's market share had been increasing for several years prior to the merger. The next largest firm in this industry was Purex, which accounted for only 15.7 percent of the market.

Advertising and sales promotion were generally conceded to be important components in the marketing of both detergents and liquid bleach. At the time of the merger, P&G was the nation's largest purchaser of advertising, with expenditures on advertising and sales promotion exceeding $127 million. Because of the magnitude of these expenditures, P&G allegedly received volume discounts from the media over which its advertising campaigns were carried.

The FTC challenged the merger under Section 7 of the Clayton Act as amended by the Celler-Kefauver Act. The government's attack was based on two arguments involving anticompetitive effects. First, it was argued that P&G had been the most likely potential entrant into the liquid bleach market and that the reduction in potential competition which resulted from the merger was likely to substantially lessen competition in that market. This argument was buttressed with evidence of the high degree of concentration in the liquid bleach industry (approaching monopoly in certain geographic areas) and evidence from company files that P&G had, in fact, been contemplating entry. Had P&G entered the liquid bleach industry de novo (i.e., through internal expansion) or via a toehold acquisition (i.e., a merger with a nondominant firm), potential competition would have been translated into actual competition, and the antitrust authorities would not have opposed the action. But entry by merger with the leading firm in the industry reduced potential competition without increasing actual competition.

Second, the FTC argued that the merger would entrench Clorox as the dominant producer of liquid bleach by providing access to P&G's overall resources, particularly their massive advertising budget. Because of the discounts received by P&G, the merger reduced the unit costs of advertising Clorox bleach (an economy of scope attributable to pecuniary economies of scale in the common input, advertising). The expected result would be an increase in the intensity of advertising the product of an already dominant firm. In addition, it was felt that the merger would enable Clorox to discourage entry into the liquid bleach industry by predatory pricing efforts funded by the profits from P&G's other household products. Together, these two effects were expected to solidify Clorox's dominant position and increase the barriers to enter

---

[23] Due to high shipping costs, it was not considered profitable to transport this product more than 300 miles from the point at which it was produced. Consequently, local geographic markets were relevant.

into this industry.[24] In conjunction with the loss of P&G as a potential entrant, these effects were expected to substantially lessen competition in the liquid bleach industry.

The Supreme Court ruled in favor of the FTC, and the merger was dissolved. Notice, however, that despite the fact that the merger was conglomerate in nature, the factors determining the outcome of the case all related to the impact of the combination on the intensity of competition in a specific, well-defined market. Had it not been for the dominant positions held by each firm in their respective markets (particularly Clorox's share of the liquid bleach market), it is doubtful that the merger would have been challenged successfully.

United States *v*. Falstaff Brewing Corp.[25] This case involved a market extension merger between the Falstaff Brewing Company and the Narragansett Brewing Company that occurred in 1965. The acquired firm, Narragansett, was the largest seller of beer in New England, with approximately 20 percent of that regional market. The acquiring firm, Falstaff, was the fourth largest producer of beer nationally, with 5.9 percent of total national production. At the same time, however, Falstaff was a regional (as opposed to national) brewer, selling beer in only 32 states. Largely because of economies of advertising on a nationwide basis, Falstaff found it desirable to expand its market geographically in order to be able to compete more effectively with the national brewers that sold beer in all significant regional markets.

The Antitrust Division of the Justice Department opposed the merger on the grounds that the New England beer market would be likely to suffer a substantial lessening of competition as the result of the loss of Falstaff as a potential competitor. The four-firm concentration ratio in this regional market was 61.3 percent at the time of the acquisition and had been increasing steadily in prior years. At trial, the District Court ruled in favor of Falstaff, allowing the merger to stand. This decision appeared to be based upon three considerations: (1) the New England market was judged to be competitive (i.e., actual competition existed); (2) Falstaff's change of status to a national brewer would probably strengthen competition in the industry nationally; and (3) Falstaff's management testified that the company had not considered entering and would not enter the New England beer market de novo. On the basis of this third consideration, the District Court concluded that Falstaff was not, in fact, a potential competitor. As a result, Falstaff's entry through a major acquisition could not have reduced the vigor of competition in this market.

On appeal, however, the Supreme Court ruled that the District Court

---

[24] At the same time, however, the Court noted that the production of liquid bleach was not protected by any patents, the production technology was widely known, there was abundant raw material, and the necessary machinery was available at reasonable cost.

[25] 410 U.S. 526 (1973).

had erred in concluding that Falstaff's presence on the edge of the market could not serve as a restraining influence merely on the basis of (possibly self-serving) management testimony that they would not enter de novo. It was argued that, regardless of management's stated or actual intentions, if the existing firms that occupied the New England market *perceived* Falstaff as a potential entrant, then the desirable effects of potential competition would be realized from Falstaff's presence outside the market. As a result, the Supreme Court remanded the case to the District Court for reconsideration.

Upon reconsideration, however, the District Court once again dismissed the complaint against Falstaff, allowing the merger to stand. In reaching this decision, the District Court applied the broader definition of potential competition advocated by the Supreme Court but concluded that the existing brewers in the New England market had not perceived Falstaff as a potential entrant. This broader definition of potential competition that attempts to include the perceptions of incumbent firms concerning the possibility of entry by an outside firm has not fared any better in later cases. Thus, as the law appears to stand now, some evidence that the firm that has entered through a large-scale merger might have at least considered entry by a more innocuous route is required if the government is to win a potential competition case.

Kennecott Copper Corp. *v.* FTC.[26] This case involved a pure conglomerate merger—the acquisition of Peabody Coal Company by Kennecott Copper Corporation in 1968. Most pure conglomerate mergers have gone unchallenged because the enforcement agencies and the courts have perceived the most likely potential entrants to be those firms that are situated "on the edge of the market" (i.e., engaged in the production of a related product or the same product in another geographic market). As this case demonstrates, however, this category of merger is not completely immune to attack under the doctrine of potential competition.

At the time of the acquisition, Kennecott was the dominant U.S. producer of copper but had no significant energy holdings. Peabody was the largest producer of coal in the United States with a 1967 market share of 10.7 percent of domestic production.[27] The coal industry itself was relatively unconcentrated, with a 1967 four-firm concentration ratio of 29.2 percent. However, the level of concentration in this industry had been increasing since 1954.

In challenging the merger, the FTC relied upon the theory of potential competition. Given the circumstances that are logically required for this

---

[26] 467 F. 2d 67 (10th Cir. 1972).

[27] With nonrenewable resources, market share calculated on the basis of ownership of reserves is probably a better indicator of the firm's market power. This was recognized by the Court in the *General Dynamics* case; see Chapter 9.

theory to have any relevance to market performance,[28] the FTC found it necessary to base its challenge on three lines of argument. First, it was argued that while the coal industry was not yet highly concentrated, the observed trend toward concentration should be of concern to the Court if the Clayton Act's purpose of halting monopoly power in its incipiency was to be served. In this regard, it was argued that Kennecott's financial power might be employed to increase and entrench Peabody's market position as a dominant firm in the coal industry. Thus, the absence of actual competition (on which the theory of potential competition depends) was predicted to be forthcoming in the not too distant future, partly as a result of the challenged merger.

Second, since the loss of a potential competitor through a merger with a dominant incumbent firm can damage market performance only in situations where entry barriers block other outside firms from entering the industry when economic profits materialize, the FTC found it necessary to argue that entry barriers were high in the coal industry. With no prohibitive patents on innovative mining techniques, with abundant reserves available for purchase, and with no overwhelming economies of scale in relation to market demand, this argument had to be based on the magnitude of the absolute capital investment required to enter this industry on an efficient scale. Thus, the FTC argued that only a very large firm with financial strength equivalent to Kennecott's would be likely to command the resources needed for successful entry into coal production.

Finally, since the loss of a potential competitor is relevant only where other potential competitors of equal efficiency and likelihood of entering are absent, the FTC argued that other firms that controlled assets comparable to Kennecott's and that currently owned coal reserves but were not producing coal for sale (which included several major petroleum firms and utility companies) were not likely to enter the industry as active competitors. To carry this argument, the FTC speculated that the utility companies would mine coal for their own plants but would not offer their coal for sale on the open market (recall our critique of the foreclosure doctrine from Chapter 12). Also, they argued that the petroleum companies were holding coal reserves for synthetic fuel production (coal liquefaction and gasification) and that they, too, would not sell their coal in direct competition with other coal producers.

On the basis of these arguments, the Court upheld the FTC's order that Kennecott divest itself of Peabody Coal. At the time of this ruling, this was the largest divestiture order ever issued.[29] The actual sale of

[28] See our discussion of this theory in Section 17–4.

[29] The more recent divestiture of AT&T exceeds the Kennecott-Peabody divestiture by a considerable margin, but it was the result of a settlement. Although it was approved by the Court, it was not ordered by the Court.

Peabody occurred in 1977 at a price of $1.2 billion. It was purchased by a consortium of six firms, several of which had other energy holdings. Thus, the ultimate effect of the case was to increase marginally the level of concentration that exists in the (highly unconcentrated) energy industry.

An interesting aspect of this case is that between the time of the Court's decision affirming the FTC's divestiture order in 1972 (which was based on a record of evidence compiled in 1969) and the actual sale of Peabody in 1977, the coal industry underwent a substantial transition resulting from the 1973 oil embargo and the "energy crisis." The evidence generated by this transition strongly refuted all three of the FTC's arguments justifying the divestiture order. As the price of coal rose in response to the rapid increases in petroleum prices, substantial new entry into coal production occurred. This entry was composed of both those firms that the FTC had predicted would not sell their coal on the open market (utilities and petroleum firms) and other firms that the FTC had failed to consider as potential competitors. Thus, the arguments concerning high entry barriers and the lack of other potential competitors were proven to have been specious. Finally, as a result of this new wave of entry, the four-firm concentration ratio in this industry reversed its trend upward and began to fall. Given these results, the future role for potential competition arguments in pure conglomerate cases is in serious doubt.

United States v. International Telephone and Telegraph Corp.[30] This case involved the acquisition of Grinnell Corporation, a large producer of automatic sprinkler systems and related devices, by International Telephone and Telegraph Corporation (ITT), a large diversified company that had been a major participant in the conglomerate merger activity of the 1960s. Since ITT's product lines did not include sprinkler systems (or any closely related products) prior to the acquisition, the merger was of the pure conglomerate variety. It was an important case in the development of the law pertaining to conglomerate mergers because it served to define the types of arguments and evidence that the Courts were prepared to consider in applying Section 7 of the Clayton Act to such mergers.

At the time of the acquisition, ITT was the nation's ninth largest industrial firm, with 1969 sales revenues of approximately $5.5 billion and assets of $5.2 billion. During the 1960s, the firm had grown substantially by merger, acquiring 85 domestic and 60 foreign corporations. The acquired firm, Grinnell, was the 268th largest industrial corporation, with 1968 sales revenues of $341 million and assets of $184 million. In the four specific product lines delineated in the case (power piping, pipe

---

[30] 324 F. Supp. 19 (D. Conn. 1970).

hangers, automatic sprinkler devices, and automatic sprinkler systems), Grinnell's market share did not exceed 23 percent.

What distinguishes this case is that the government did not base its attack on the theory of potential competition. Although there were some allegations that Grinnell had dominated the automatic sprinkler system market and that the merger with ITT would confer marketing and promotional advantages which would tend to entrench Grinnell's market position, sufficient evidence was not presented to buttress this line of reasoning. Instead, the government attempted to block the merger by an appeal to its effect on aggregate concentration as opposed to competition in a well-defined market:

> The new twist to the government's economic concentration claim is that in the wake of a "trend among large diversified industrial firms to acquire other large corporations," it can be established that "anticompetitive consequences will appear in numerous though *undesignated individual 'lines of commerce'.*"
>
> The Court's short answer to this claim . . . is that the legislative history, the statute itself and the controlling decisional law all make it clear beyond a peradventure of a doubt that in a Section 7 case the alleged anticompetitive effects of a merger must be examined in the context of *specific product and geographic markets;* and the determination of such markets is a necessary predicate to a determination of whether there has been a substantial lessening of competition within an area of effective competition. To ask the Court to rule with respect to alleged anticompetitive consequences in *undesignated lines of commerce* is tantamount to asking the Court to engage in judicial legislation. This the Court emphatically refuses to do.

Thus, according to the District Court, conglomerate (or other) mergers must be evaluated according to their effect on competition in a well-defined line of commerce. Impacts on aggregate economic concentration per se were ruled to be beyond the reach of the antitrust laws as they are currently written.

The government appealed the case, but it was settled by consent decree prior to reaching the Supreme Court. Under the terms of the settlement, ITT agreed to divest itself of approximately $1 billion in assets and to refrain from acquiring any domestic companies exceeding certain size limits. In other words, the ultimate outcome of the case (but not the law) appears to be much the same as it would have been if the District Court had ruled against the merger.

17–7 MERGER GUIDELINES

The most recent Merger Guidelines, issued by the Department of Justice in 1984, do not make use of the adjective *conglomerate* in describing the government's enforcement policy toward this category of mergers. Instead, both conglomerate and vertical mergers are discussed under the heading Horizontal Effect from Nonhorizontal Mergers. This heading, in conjunction with the notable absence of the word *conglomerate*, implies that the enforcement agencies have come to endorse the standard for assessing competitive harm that was so clearly enunciated by the Court in the *ITT* case. That is, the decision of whether to attack a conglomerate merger will hinge on a consideration of the likely effects of that merger on competition in a specific well-defined market. Broader, more nebulous considerations, such as the impact of the merger on aggregate concentration or political influence, will not play a role in the department's enforcement decisions.

Given this standard for assessing competitive harm, the 1984 Merger Guidelines rely on the theory of potential competition as the sole determinant of whether to attack a conglomerate (or "nonhorizontal") merger. Following a brief (and not particularly clear) discussion of the distinction between perceived and actual potential competition (the latter of which is not to be confused with actual competition), the guidelines state:

> Because of the close relationship between perceived potential competition and actual potential competition, the Department will evaluate mergers that raise either type of potential competition concern under a single structural analysis analogous to that applied to horizontal mergers.

Four structural conditions that the guidelines indicate as determinative of the decision to attack a given merger are then described. These conditions follow logically from the underlying theory of potential competition (alias limit pricing). First, since potential competition is important only in situations where actual competition is weak or lacking among the incumbent firms in a market, the guidelines state that mergers are unlikely to be challenged in markets where the Herfindahl-Hirschman index (HHI) is less than 1,800. The probability that the merger will be challenged increases as the HHI rises above this critical level, which is roughly equivalent to a four-firm concentration ratio of approximately 65 percent.

Second, since the entry of a potential competitor through a merger with a nondominant firm may often result in a translation of potential competition into actual competition, the guidelines indicate that toehold acquisitions are unlikely to be challenged. If the acquired firm (i.e., the firm that already occupies the market in which the competitive impact is being assessed) accounts for less than 5 percent of the market, the merger is unlikely to be challenged. If the incumbent firm enjoys a market share that exceeds 20 percent, however, the merger is likely to be challenged if the other determinative conditions are satisfied. Where the incumbent firm's market share falls between 5 and 20 percent, the guidelines do not explicitly state the likelihood of attack.

Third, since the loss of one potential competitor is not likely to reduce the vigor of competition in markets where significant entry barriers do not exist, the government is unlikely to challenge mergers in markets that are characterized by easy entry. As the height of entry barriers increases, the department is increasingly likely to object to the merger.

And fourth, since the loss of a potential competitor is not likely to reduce significantly the threat of entry in situations where numerous equally efficient potential competitors are present, the guidelines make allowance for the effect of other firms on the edge of the market:

> The Department is unlikely to challenge a potential competition merger if the entry advantage ascribed to the acquiring firm (or another advantage of comparable importance) is also possessed by three or more other firms. Other things being equal, the Department is increasingly likely to challenge a merger as the number of other similarly situated firms decreases below three and as the extent of the entry advantage over non-advantaged firms increases.

In summary, the 1984 Merger Guidelines are consistent with both the economic theory of potential competition and the bulk of the case history in this area of the law. The focus of the announced enforcement policy is on the impact of the merger on the intensity of competition in a specific well-defined market, and the conditions that are logically necessary for such an impact to materialize are explicitly stated.

QUESTIONS AND PROBLEMS

1. Explain how pronounced economies of scope might lead to a natural multiproduct monopoly even in the absence of economies of scale for the individual goods involved.

2. With regard to the managerial inefficiency theory of conglomerate mergers, do you think that it is more likely that the managers of the acquiring firm would be in a line of business that is related or unrelated to the acquired firm? Why?

3. The standard deviation of the sum of two random variables, x_1 and x_2, is given by

$$\sigma_{x_1+x_2} = \sqrt{\sigma_1^2 + \sigma_2^2 + 2r\sigma_1\sigma_2}$$

where σ_1 is the standard deviation of x_1, σ_2 is the standard deviation of x_2, and r is the coefficient of correlation between x_1 and x_2. Let firm 1 have a mean profit of $1 million with a standard deviation of

$200,000. Let firm 2 have a mean profit of $2 million with a standard deviation of $400,000. If the two firms merge, what is the standard deviation of the combined firm's profits expressed as a percentage of mean profits if:

a. the coefficient of correlation between these two firm's profits is −1;

b. the coefficient of correlation between these two firms' profits is 0;

c. the coefficient of correlation between these two firms' profits is +0.5?

4. Several of the theories of conglomerate mergers that we have surveyed involving lower costs entail social, as well as private, gains from the merger. Others involve private gains with no social gains. Identify these two groups, and briefly explain the rationale for your taxonomy.

5. Look back at Figure 17–1. Assume that there are only two periods—the present and the future. If the incumbent firm charges the monopoly price, P_M, assume that it will earn monopoly profit, $abcP_M$, in the present, and it will earn half of the limit price profit, $adeP_L$, in the future (because it shares the market with the new entrant but maintains its cost advantage). If the incumbent firm charges the limit price in both periods, it can earn the full limit price profit, $adeP_L$, in both periods. If the incumbent firm purchases the potential entrant firm, it can earn the full monopoly profit in both periods. How much would the incumbent firm be willing to pay for the merger?

6. With regard to the *Procter & Gamble Company* case and the *Kennecott Copper Corporation* case, how is potential competition supposed to influence market outcomes if the law does not permit potential entrants to enter?

7. With regard to the theory of potential competition, what would be the economic effects of de novo entry by a firm into an industry that was already in long-run equilibrium? What does this imply about the incentive to enter via merger?

8. Suppose Procter & Gamble is a monopolist in the sale of detergent and Clorox is a monopolist in the sale of bleach. Also, suppose that detergent and bleach are complementary goods. What impact is a merger between these firms likely to have on the prices of detergent and bleach?

9. With regard to the trend toward increasing concentration in the coal industry that was used by the FTC to justify the Kennecott–Peabody

divestiture order, suppose that the industry was experiencing decreasing demand. Using the shut-down rule from basic microeconomics, show why the relatively small firms in an industry might be expected to exit the market sooner than the large firms. What implications does this result have for observed trends in concentration ratios in declining industries.

10. From our brief survey of four conglomerate merger cases, what can you infer concerning: (a) the economic theory that is typically employed in attacking these mergers; and (b) the standard used by the courts for assessing the legality of a merger?

11. Does the Court's distinction between entry through a major acquisition versus de novo entry by internal expansion or toehold acquisition have any basis in microeconomic theory? If so, explain.

12. One of the reasons that the Supreme Court disallowed P&G's acquisition of Clorox was because it would discourage the smaller bleach producers from competing aggressively. Is there some reason why a smaller bleach producer would be more aggressive in its fight for survival with Clorox than with P&G?

13. If the P&G-Clorox merger had been permitted, what would you expect to have happened to bleach prices (increase, decrease, or remain the same)? Explain. Who would be hurt by the price change? Would anyone suffer "antitrust injury"?

14. We described the motive for takeovers under the assumption that the profits of the acquired firm would be improved by reducing costs. Is there any other way that profits could be improved? If so, how does mismanagement create the potential for improved profit?

15. On a recent trip to the grocery store, the following per gallon prices for liquid household bleach were observed:

Clorox	$1.03
Purex	.94
Private label	.79

Since all household liquid bleach is chemically identical, how can one explain the divergence in prices?

16. If the Kennecott-Peabody merger had been approved, would anyone have suffered antitrust injury?

17. Attempt to verbalize the distinction between actual potential competition and perceived potential competition. How convincing is the case for perceived potential competition?

18. In the *Falstaff* case, how would you attempt to prove that Falstaff's position as a potential entrant had a procompetitive impact on the New England beer market?

FURTHER READINGS

Blair, Roger D., and Robert F. Lanzillotti, eds. *The Conglomerate Corporation: An Antitrust Law and Economics Symposium.* Cambridge, Mass.: Oelgeschlager, Gunn & Hain, 1981.

Justice Department Merger Guidelines, Special Supplement, *Antitrust & Trade Regulation Report,* June 14, 1984.

Levy, Haim, and Marshall Sarnot. "Diversification, Portfolio Analysis, and the Uneasy Case for Conglomerate Mergers." *Journal of Finance* 25 (September 1970), pp. 795–802.

Lorie, James H., and Paul Halpern. "Conglomerates: The Rhetoric and the Evidence." *Journal of Law and Economics* 13 (April 1970), pp. 149–66.

Peterman, John L. "The Clorox Case and the Television Rate Structures." *Journal of Law and Economics* 11 (October 1968), pp. 321–422.

Steiner, Peter O. *Mergers.* Ann Arbor: University of Michigan Press, 1975.

Turner, Donald. "Conglomerate Mergers and Section 7 of the Clayton Act." *Harvard Law Review* 78 (May 1965), pp. 1313–95.

18

Reciprocity

18–1 INTRODUCTION

In modern usage, reciprocity is defined as mutual trading on a quid pro quo basis. In other words, firm A agrees to buy a commodity from firm B on the condition or understanding that B will buy something from A. For example, General Motors might agree to buy its paint supplies from Du Pont in exchange for Du Pont's agreement to buy all of its automotive needs from General Motors. The practice can be a little more complicated in situations where direct reciprocity is not possible. For example, Consolidated Foods was a large buyer of processed foods, which it subsequently sold at wholesale and retail. It could not exploit this buying power through a reciprocal arrangement because the food processors did not buy anything that Consolidated sold. Subsequently, however, it acquired Gentry, which sold dehydrated onion and garlic to food processors. This made reciprocity possible: Consolidated could demand that its suppliers buy their dehydrated onion and garlic needs from Gentry.

The competitive evil that is supposed to emerge from reciprocal buying arrangements is market foreclosure. In the GM–Du Pont example above, rival paint manufacturers are foreclosed from supplying paint to General Motors and rival automobile manufacturers are foreclosed from selling cars and trucks to Du Pont. Reciprocity, however, is not much different from the ancient practice of barter: One farmer pays another farmer for string beans with tomatoes. No doubt, this has gone on for centuries. Nevertheless, Adam Smith condemned the practice of reciprocity as one of the "sneaking arts of underling tradesmen." In this chapter, we shall examine the economics of reciprocity to see if Adam Smith's harsh judgment is warranted. We shall also examine the rather limited case law on reciprocity.

18–2 MOTIVATION FOR RECIPROCITY[1]

As one should expect, reciprocity is motivated by the quest for profit, but it cannot always be used sensibly. There are several different sets of circumstances that make reciprocity a profitable endeavor, and we shall examine a few of these. As we shall see, reciprocity is an indirect way of earning more profit, and our discussion is intended to illustrate this. We have not tried to provide an exhaustive list. Instead, we have attempted to examine some situations where indirection may be preferred to direct price cuts.

Evading rate regulation

First, reciprocity may be used to evade price regulation. For example, the railroads are subject to regulation and cannot deviate from the rates prescribed by the Interstate Commerce Commission. As a result, large shippers cannot obtain price concessions directly because of the regulation. One solution for a major customer is to get an indirect price concession from the railroad through a reciprocal buying arrangement. This was done by two traffic officials of Armour & Company.[2] Since Armour could not benefit directly from its position as a substantial buyer of rail services, these two employees decided to extract some indirect price cuts. They acquired stock in the Waugh Equipment Company, which was a small manufacturer of draft gears, and persuaded the railroads to purchase their draft gears from Waugh Equipment. When this scheme began in 1924, Waugh was the smallest producer in the industry, but by 1930, it had the largest market share.

An interesting variant of the motivation provided by regulation involves government contracts.[3] A large government contract may provide the contractor with substantial monopsony power over its input suppliers. If it exploits that power directly by getting substantial price cuts, its profits on those contracts may appear to be excessive and subject to rebate to the government. Consequently, it has an incentive to hide some of the profits. This can be accomplished through reciprocity:

---

[1] This section depends upon Peter O. Steiner, *Mergers* (Ann Arbor, Mich.: University of Michigan Press, 1975), pp. 230–39.

[2] See *In re Waugh Equipment Co.*, 15 FTC 232 (1931).

[3] See Erwin A. Blackstone, "Monposony Power, Reciprocal Buying, and Government Contracts: The General Dynamics Case," *Antitrust Bulletin* 17 (Summer 1972), pp. 445–66.

The contractor pays a relatively higher price for the inputs used on the defense contract while its suppliers must buy something from the contractor at inflated prices. In effect, the profits on the defense contract are shifted to other products.

Reducing transaction costs

A second motive for reciprocity may involve real economies in purchasing or selling. If the costs of repetitive search and contracting are substantial and long-term requirements contracts are undesirable, reciprocity could be used to reduce transaction costs. Reciprocity provides a pairing device between two firms, each of which is kept honest by its reciprocal position.

In this connection, reciprocity can also be used to prevent strategic behavior more generally. Suppose that there is some random variation in the price of an input. Both the buyer and the seller will want a contract to fix the price and thereby reduce risk if they are risk averse, but this agreement can be strengthened with reciprocity. If the price changes dramatically and the firms do not have a reciprocal relationship, one of the contracting parties will be inclined to renege on the contract. If the price changes sufficiently, a breach of contract may make sense because customers do not often sue their suppliers and vice versa. There is always recourse to the courts, but that is expensive, it takes a long time, the outcome is uncertain, and it is generally a nuisance. Reciprocity makes a breach less likely because of the parties' reciprocal positions.[4]

Exploitation of scale economies

Third, reciprocity could be used to enter an industry or achieve a production level equal to the minimum efficient scale of operation. Suppose that a firm has some monopsony (i.e., buying) power that could be exploited directly. If the monopsonist has a subsidiary that needs enhanced volume in order to become established, the parent may put some pressure upon its suppliers to help. Reciprocal sales to these suppliers could provide the basis for the minimum efficient scale of production and the stability of demand necessary for efficient operation.

Indirect means of reducing price

Fourth, reciprocity may be an alternative to open price competition. We have already seen that reciprocity can be used to evade price regula-

---

[4] See Benjamin Klein, Robert G. Crawford, and Armen A. Alchian, "Vertical Integration, Appropriable Rents, and the Competitive Contracting Process," *Journal of Law and Economics* 21 (October 1978), pp. 297–326.

tions, but it can also be important in oligopolistic industries where open price cuts invite retaliation. The oligopolists may evade a tacit agreement not to compete on price or simply mask a price cut by practicing reciprocity. If a firm is reluctant to openly reduce its price, it can hold firm on its price but agree to buy something from its customers at inflated prices. In effect, it grants a price concession, but it does so indirectly. This strategy of disguising price cuts is very important to the firm during periods of excess capacity because a price war can push prices far below average total cost. In fact, price could fall all the way to average variable cost under these circumstances.

18–3 CONDITIONS CONDUCIVE TO RECIPROCITY

The structural conditions that are most conducive to the emergence of reciprocity are intuitively plausible. First, an oligopolistic market structure makes nonprice rivalry more important than otherwise. Each firm must face a negatively sloped demand curve indicating that it has some market power. Second, the existence of excess capacity or constant marginal costs over a wide range of output is also important. This follows because the firm can use reciprocity to expand output on nonprice grounds without increasing per unit costs. Diversified firms benefit at the expense of specialized firms because they can keep production levels up and average costs down through reciprocity rather than through price cuts. In contrast, a specialized firm with excess capacity can expand production only through the offer of lower prices. Third, there must be a two-way flow of transactions (i.e., suppliers must be potential customers). There is no need for this to be a purely bilateral situation because one or both of the parties may have subsidiaries, which can be used in the reciprocal dealing. It is obvious, however, that diversification of the firm's product line helps because it broadens the opportunities for reciprocity. Finally, asymmetry among the firms involved makes reciprocity more likely because buying power then will be unequal.

18–4 EMPIRICAL RESEARCH ON RECIPROCITY

There is a glaring absence of empirical research on reciprocity. A notable exception is provided by the work of Bruce Allen,[5] which attempts to explain the incidence of industrial reciprocity. In his statistical analysis, Allen considered four possible influences on the likelihood that a firm would practice reciprocity: the average degree of concentration in the firm's markets, the average market share in the firm's markets, total

---

[5] Bruce T. Allen, "Industrial Reciprocity: A Statistical Analysis," *Journal of Law and Economics* 18 (October 1975), pp. 507–20.

purchases made from other firms, and the number of different industries in which the firm participated.

There were two reasons for thinking that concentration could have a significant impact on a firm's propensity to adopt reciprocal buying practices. First, when concentration is high, one may suppose that oligopolistic interdependence will inhibit open price competition. As a result, firms may use reciprocity as a way of making clandestine price cuts. Alternatively, the large firms in an industry may have gotten large by practicing reciprocity to the disadvantage of their smaller rivals. Allen's statistical analysis indicated that concentration was not statistically significant. In other words, concentration cannot be said to have an impact on a firm's decision to engage in reciprocity.

Market share could be an important determinate for two reasons. First, the smaller firms in an industry could practice reciprocity rather than open price competition. In this event, the goal would be to avoid open warfare with the dominant firms in the industry. Alternatively, the large firms could use reciprocity to take business away from their smaller rivals. Allen found that this variable had a negative sign and was statistically significant, which means that the smaller firms in the industry are using reciprocity to shade prices without attracting adverse attention from the larger firms.

The volume of a firm's purchases is important because the larger a firm's purchases are, the more pressure a firm can exert on its supplier/ customers. This variable was not statistically significant.

Finally, the diversification is important because greater diversification provides more opportunities for reciprocity. The wider the array of products produced, the more likely that any set of input suppliers will be in the market for one of that firm's products. Moreover, the wider the variety of products, the wider the variety of inputs purchased and the greater the opportunity for reciprocity. Allen's statistical analysis discovered a positive and statistically significant coefficient on diversification.

In summary, the data indicate that a firm is more likely to practice reciprocity the more diversified it is and the smaller its market share is. On the whole, Allen's results suggest that reciprocity enhances competition within the industry as it is presently constituted.

18–5 ECONOMIC IMPACT OF RECIPROCITY

There is substantial disagreement among economists regarding the economic impact of reciprocity. Those who are critical of this business practice contend that reciprocity introduces an alien and irrelevant factor into the decision process. Moreover, it can create a priority on the business at comparable prices. The contrary view extends that reciprocity is either innocuous or it is actually beneficial.

The critic's view[6]

When the conditions spelled out in Section 18–3 hold, the critics claim that reciprocity is apt to surface in an anticompetitive way. The circumstances under which reciprocity can have the adverse competitive effects attributed to it by the critics are best illustrated by the facts found in one of the better known reciprocity court cases, the *General Dynamics*[7] matter. This company was one of the largest firms in the defense industry. In 1957, it had purchases of some $500 million from approximately 80,000 separate suppliers. The case was instituted by the Antitrust Division when General Dynamics acquired the Liquid Carbonic Corporation, which was an established firm with excess capacity in the oligopolistic carbon dioxide industry. The cost and demand conditions facing Liquid Carbonic are shown in Figure 18–1, with the per-unit cost curve drawn as a horizontal line beyond some given volume of production (quantity Q^*) to indicate that costs remain constant as output expands over a substantial range. The demand (D) curve's downward slope indicates that the acquired firm, Liquid Carbonic, sells in an oligopolistic industry. One further assumption is necessary to complete our model here—namely, that the prevailing price for carbon dioxide exceeds marginal cost but is not at the monopoly price level (i.e., the price that would maximize the joint profits of the industry's member firms).

One of the 80,000 suppliers that had been selling to General Dynamics was Kirkhill Rubber, a company that used carbon dioxide in its operation. Kirkhill Rubber immediately became a candidate for a reciprocity arrangement after General Dynamics' acquisition of its carbon-dioxide producing subsidiary, Liquid Carbonic. The parent company, General Dynamics, clearly *could* threaten to withdraw its own business from Kirkhill Rubber if Kirkhill should refuse to buy its carbon-dioxide requirements from General Dynamics' new subsidiary, Liquid Carbonic. But would such a threat be credible? That depends on (*a*) the price at which General Dynamics wants to sell its subsidiary's carbon dioxide and (*b*) the competitive situation in the rubber and carbon-dioxide industries. If the carbon dioxide offered by Liquid Carbonic and its competitors is considered homogeneous by Kirkhill Rubber, and if the price is not being raised above the competitive level, then Kirkhill Rubber would presumably be indifferent as to whether it gets its carbon dioxide from Liquid Carbonic or one of the latter's competitors. In other words,

---

[6] The most influential argument against reciprocity is due to Stocking and Mueller who contend that reciprocity is anticompetitive. See George W. Stocking and Willard F. Mueller, "Business Reciprocity and the Size of Firms," *The Journal of Business* 30 (April 1957), pp. 73–95.

[7] *United States* v. *General Dynamics Corp.*, 258 F. Supp. 36 (1966). Not being a Supreme Court decision, this case does not have precedential value. This case does provide an excellent illustration of several important issues.

FIGURE 18–1

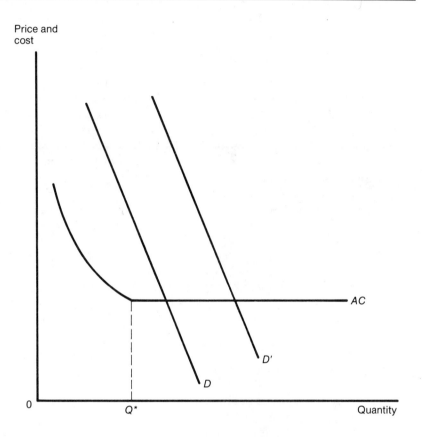

Kirkhill Rubber will then have nothing to lose by going along with the demand that it participate in General Dynamics' reciprocity plan.

But does it have anything to gain by going along with that arrangement and giving the General Dynamics' subsidiary its carbon-dioxide business at competitive prices? That depends on whether (a) it is dependent on General Dynamics as a customer for its own rubber products and (b) whether it thinks its own competitors can handle the General Dynamics' business if the firm should decide to carry out its threat to stop buying from Kirkhill Rubber. On the first point, the question is whether Kirkhill Rubber could replace the lost General Dynamics account at no economic cost to itself. Presumably, the larger the proportion of Kirkhill Rubber's total sales that are made to General Dynamics, the more difficult and costly it would be to find replacement customers for the lost business and thus the more Kirkhill Rubber would have to gain by acquiescing in the proposed reciprocity arrangement.

On the second point, Kirkhill Rubber would have to believe that its own competitors were capable of taking over its role of supplying rubber products to General Dyanmics before it would consider the latter's threat to stop buying from it a credible one. If Kirkhill Rubber was in itself a monopolist selling a product that General Dynamics had to have, then a threat by General Dynamics to take its business elsewhere unless Kirkhill agreed to its reciprocity demands would not be particularly believable. Assuming that this is not the case and assuming further that there would be at least some economic cost in replacing the lost General Dynamics account, Kirkhill would indeed have something to gain by going along with the reciprocity demands of that customer—namely, the preservation of its current profit picture.

The assumption that Kirkhill Rubber operates in an effectively competitive market in the sale of its own rubber products means that it is by definition earning only a competitive rate of return on its operation and would have to go out of business if it were compelled by a reciprocity arrangement to pay a higher price for its supplies than its competitors are required to pay or to accept a lower quality (relative to price) than those that its competitors are able to get. Thus, the assumption of effective competition in Kirkhill Rubber's market precludes the existence of any monopoly profits from which General Dynamics could extract any economic advantage for itself without impairing the former's long-run competitive viability. A practice that systematically puts one's trading partners out of business is not likely to prove profitable over the long haul.

It is not the potential injury to the initiating firm's own suppliers that is the appropriate concern of antitrust in the reciprocity area. Instead, it is the potential it might have, if any, for altering the long-run structure of the industry in which its selling subsidiary operates (i.e., the carbon-dioxide industry in our example here). Assuming that Kirkhill Rubber and the other users of the product acquiesce in General Dynamics' demand that they stop doing business with their current suppliers of the product and shift over to its subsidiary, Liquid Carbonics, what effect would this have on that subsidiary's industry?

Assuming that General Dynamics continues to be successful in finding new reciprocity partners that can be persuaded to abandon their prior suppliers of carbon dioxide and shift over to Liquid Carbonic, the latter firm will find its own individual demand curve shifting continuously to the right (e.g., to D' in Figure 18–1). Since this subsidiary had excess capacity at the time the reciprocity-induced growth began, this increase in its sales volume will raise its profits even without an increase in its unit prices above the competitive level. If the carbon dioxide industry originally had been in equilibrium in the sense that the industrywide rate of profit was not sufficient to attract new entrants, the only change we would expect here would be a reduction in the number of firms in the industry. An expansion of Liquid Carbonic's sales at the expense of its rivals would raise its own profits while those of the industry as a whole would remain the same. Provided that potential entrants appraise their profit prospects on the basis of those being earned by the least profitable firms in the industry, no new entry would be induced.

This reduction in the number of firms selling carbon dioxide presumably would make collusion more likely among Liquid Carbonic and the survivors. Charging a collusive price, however, would attract new entrants if there were no entry barriers thereby enlarging the number of firms and causing the price to be driven back to the competitive level. Thus, if reciprocity was, in fact, a practice that all firms had equal access to, then it would be true that its tendency to foreclose competitors from sales at equal (competitive) prices would be a matter of no competitive significance. But the capacity to engage in reciprocity depends on diversification, and all firms are demonstrably unequal in this latter respect.

The skeptic's view[8]

Many economists are skeptical of reciprocity's competitive importance. First, one must recognize that firms A and B may buy from one another at the lowest available prices because each is the most efficient producer. This, of course, represents a sound business practice. No coercion is necessary, and each firm is better off than it could be otherwise. Second, if one of the firms has significant buying power, reciprocity is simply an indirect way of exploiting it.

Ferguson has analyzed three different market structures in which reciprocity may occur. We shall consider these analyses in some detail as they highlight the economist's difficulty with understanding reciprocity. The first case involves many producers and suppliers of both products. Suppose firm A sells alphas and firm B sells betas. By hypothesis, there exist many competitors for both A and B. This means that neither firm has much (if any) purchasing power. The purchasing power of firm A is determined by the proportion of all sales of beta that it accounts for. It is not determined by the percentage of the alpha market that it controls, which in this case was assumed to be small. Nor is A's purchasing power determined by the percentage of its alpha sales to B. In this situation, reciprocity may occur, but its results will be innocuous. Reciprocity may simply be accidental, or it may be due to efficiency consider-

---

[8] The most notable skeptics are James Ferguson and George Stigler. See their influential articles: James M. Ferguson, "Tying Arrangements and Reciprocity: An Economic Analysis," *Law and Contemporary Problems* 30 (Summer 1965), pp. 552–80; and George Stigler, "Working Paper IV: Reciprocity," *Antitrust Law and Economic Review* 2 (Spring 1969), pp. 51–52.

ations. In either event, it is not in conflict with the independent profit maximization of firms A and B. If each firm views the other as a low-cost firm, reciprocity will be adopted voluntarily. Market foreclosure is not a problem because if firms A and B pair up, their rivals can follow a similar practice without any competitive disadvantage.

Suppose that firm A buys its beta requirements from firm B, but firm B fills its alpha needs from one of A's competitors. A simple request by A that B switch suppliers will not be a sufficient motivation for B to begin buying its alphas from A. Unless the buying pattern was determined randomly, firm A bought betas from B because B offered the best deal. Similarly, B elected not to buy from firm A because A's terms were inferior to those of at least one of its rivals. Firm B cannot be coerced: In the absence of market power, all sales are at competitive prices. Firm A's threat to stop buying from B is not credible if B offers better terms than its rivals and is of no consequence otherwise. As a result, any effort by A to impose reciprocity cannot be anything more than an effort at sales promotion.

Second, suppose we have one or a few buyers of betas, but many sellers of betas. Since there is significant concentration on the buying side, there is monopsony power, which can be exploited. If the beta suppliers are earning *competitive* returns, however, a large buyer cannot impose additional costs on them. Thus, a demand for reciprocal purchases of alphas from firm A can only be satisfied if the terms for the alphas are at least as good as those offered by firm A's rivals. In that event, it is not clear just what benefit firm A gets from the reciprocity. If firm A's terms are inferior to those of its rivals, the beta suppliers will refuse overtures at reciprocity because to acquiesce would be to drive returns below the competitive level, and they need not accept such terms.

The beta suppliers may be earning excess returns. In this event, firm A may use its purchasing power directly to obtain lower prices on its beta requirements. Reciprocal purchases of alphas could be imposed on the beta suppliers on terms that are inferior to those offered by firm A's rivals. This is made possible by the excess returns earned by the beta suppliers, but reciprocity is still an indirect means of exploiting one's buying power. It may well be that the beta supplier cannot cut its prices on the sales to firm A due to the Robinson-Patman Act. As a result, it agrees to pay a higher price for the alphas that it buys to give firm A an indirect rebate on A's purchases of betas.

Third, suppose there is concentration on both sides of the market. The beta supplier can charge a price that makes the buyer's costs of producing alpha just less than they would be without using the monopolistic supplier's product or just less than the cost to the buyer of obtaining the product from another beta supplier or by integrating backward and producing betas for its own use. Similarly, the alpha buyer cannot make the beta supplier pay more for his needs than the cost to the beta supplier of doing without the product made by the firm at the latter stage or the cost to the beta supplier of buying from other alpha sellers or of integrating forward to make the product himself. It is true that reciprocity may create a priority on business at equal prices, and competitors charging equal prices may be foreclosed from sales to some suppliers. But in the absence of market power to enforce the agreement in the presence of lower prices offered by other sellers, these agreements do not appear to lessen competition.

18-6 JUDICIAL TREATMENT OF RECIPROCITY

The judicial attitude toward reciprocity is basically hostile. We shall examine this attitude in the context of two major reciprocity cases: *Consolidated Foods* and *General Dynamics*.

In the *Consolidated Foods*[9] case, the Federal Trade Commission complained that Consolidated Foods' merger with Gentry violated Section 7 of the Clayton Act because it employed reciprocal buying arrangements. Consolidated Foods owned some food processing plants and a network of wholesale and retail food stores. In 1951, it acquired Gentry, Inc., which primarily manufactured dehydrated onion and garlic. Because Consolidated Foods was a substantial purchaser of processed foods and food processors use dehydrated onion and garlic, reciprocity was possible. In deciding this case, the Court ruled at the outset that reciprocity is "one of the congeries of anticompetitive practices at which the antitrust laws are aimed." The Court cited some language from tying cases to the effect that reciprocity resulted in "an irrelevant and alien factor" influencing the choice among competing products. Moreover, it can create "a priority on the business at equal prices." Justice Douglas went on to point out that reciprocal buying arrangements can arise from blatant coercion or from more subtle arrangements. An important customer can threaten a withdrawal of orders if the products of an affiliate cease being bought. It can condition future purchases on the receipt of orders for products of that affiliate. In Douglas's view, these practices are anticompetitive. With respect to Section 7 of the Clayton Act, Douglas said that "[r]eciprocity in trading as a result of an acquisition violates §7, if the probability of a lessening of competition is shown."

In the case at hand, Douglas noted that the dehydrated onion and garlic market was concentrated. In 1950, Gentry accounted for about 32 percent of total sales. Its principal competitor was Basic Vegetable Products, Inc., which had about 58 percent of total sales. The remaining 10 percent was divided between two other firms. The total industry output had doubled by 1958—some seven years after the merger. Gentry's

---

[9] *Federal Trade Commission v. Consolidated Foods Corp.*, 380 U.S. 592 (1965).

share had increased to 35 percent while Basic's had fallen to 55 percent. When onion and garlic were considered separately, it turned out that Gentry's share of the dehydrated onion market increased by 7 percent while its share of the dehydrated garlic market fell by 12 percent. Since the FTC had found that Basic's product was superior to Gentry's, Douglas was impressed by Gentry's ability to increase its share of onion sales and hold its losses in garlic to 12 percent. He attributed this to the success of Consolidated Foods' reciprocal buying program. Accordingly, the Supreme Court agreed with the FTC's view that the merger was illegal because reciprocity could cause a substantial lessening of competition.

In *General Dynamics*,[10] Judge Cannella ruled that reciprocity can violate Section 1 of the Sherman Act or Section 3 of the Clayton Act. Prior to its acquisition of Liquid Carbonic, General Dynamics had no way of exploiting its monopsony power. Following its acquisition of Liquid Carbonic, it began a systematic reciprocal buying program. In fact, General Dynamics linked its purchases from a present or prospective seller to that seller's purchases of carbon dioxide from Liquid Carbonic. Consequently, Liquid Carbonic's success in the carbon dioxide market resulted from General Dynamic's purchasing power as a defense contractor and not because Liquid Carbonics had a better product or a lower price. Thus, reciprocity frustrates competitive criteria in determining which firms make which sales.

The Court noted that the antitrust laws were intended to preserve free competition. Reciprocity is inconsistent with this purpose because it excludes competitors by the exercise of large-scale purchasing power. On this basis, reciprocity is objectionable.

The Court went on to distinguish the standards for proving a violation of Section 1 of the Sherman Act and those for proving a violation of Section 3 of the Clayton Act. The government argued that General Dynamics systematically interjected reciprocity into the Liquid Carbonic sales presentations. The statistics as well as the statements of the defendants indicate that these efforts were successful. Thus, the government wanted the Court to infer the existence of contracts in restraint of trade. The Court was unwilling to do this:

> The Section's reference to contracts, combinations and conspiracies is necessarily directed at bilateral arrangements. The statistics which the government mentions have been found by the Court to be credible. Nonetheless, the business secured could be the result of the mere presence of the reciprocity power. Vendors of General Dynamics to curry favor or protect present sales to the defendant, might unilaterally decide to purchase the products of Liquid Carbonic. In such instances, no actual contracts would occur and thus no agreements would be present to serve as a predicate for

---

[10] *United States* v. *General Dynamics Corporation*, 258 F. Supp. 36 (S.D.N.Y. 1966).

a Sherman 1 violation. This is true even though if a sufficient volume of trade was diverted in this fashion, a Clayton 3 violation would be established.

To prove the presence of vendor contracts on condition, particular contracts with identifiable parties must be introduced into evidence, or legitimately inferred from the conduct of such identifiable parties.

Thus, a reciprocal buying arrangement can invalidate a merger under Section 7 of the Clayton Act. Alternatively, it could constitute a violation of Section 3 of the Clayton Act or Section 1 of the Sherman Act under certain circumstances.

18–7 CONCLUDING COMMENTS

Reciprocity can arise in a variety of circumstances. The employees of a monopsonist may exploit its buying power indirectly for their own benefit as in *Waugh Equipment*. A monopsonist may use reciprocity in a coercive way by threatening to buy elsewhere unless the supplier reciprocates. Reciprocity may emerge on a voluntary basis because both parties to the agreement want the exchange. This could arise due to real economies in avoiding selling and purchasing expenses and in assuring stable supplies and prices. In some instances, reciprocity is just a sales tool—salesmen attempt to expand sales by persuasive means and just use a firm's purchases as a tool. Finally, one firm may voluntarily begin to buy from a potential customer to curry favor. Reciprocity, however, does not result unless the favor is returned.

The alleged anticompetitive effect of reciprocity stems from one party's making sales on some basis other than competitive merit, but reciprocity seldom offsets the offer of lower prices by smaller rivals. Thus, the concern is over one firm enjoying a priority on the business at equal prices. It is not clear why this is an antitrust concern. It can only seriously disadvantage a firm if there is substantial excess capacity in the industry. When this is the case, the industry should be rationalized and some capacity should leave. There is no obvious way to select whose capacity will be the one to go when all firms are equally efficient.

QUESTIONS AND PROBLEMS

1. In Allen's empirical work, two reasons were advanced for looking at concentration as a determinant of reciprocity. These reasons have conflicting public policy implications. Why?

2. As a business practice, does reciprocity have substantial anticompetitive consequences? What are they? If not, why not?

3. If reciprocity has no anticompetitive consequences as a business practice, can reciprocity considerations have any impact upon the admissibility of a merger? Explain.

4. Can the Robinson-Patman Act provide any explanation for the practice of reciprocity? Explain.

5. Why is the presence of excess capacity so important to a sensible explanation for reciprocal buying arrangements?

6. Most firms purchase on a reciprocal basis only when price, quality, and service terms are equal. If this is the case, the identity of the seller is irrelevant. Why is reciprocity a concern?

7. Can the government win a merger case by simply pointing out that the merger creates the mere possibility of reciprocal dealing without offering any proof of anticompetitive effect in any specific market? See *United States* v. *International Telephone and Telegraph*, 306 F. Supp. 766 (D. Conn. 1970).

8. A recent suit by some farmers against a feed company involved the following arrangement: The farmers agreed to buy feed for their hens, and the feed company agreed to buy the hatching eggs that farmers produced. The judge felt that this business practice involved tying because the feed company's commitment to buy the eggs was tied to the farmers' commitment to buy feed. Was the judge very clever or just confused? See *Spartan Grain & Mill Co.* v. *Ayers*, 582 F. 2d 419 (5th Cir. 1978).

9. In *FTC* v. *Consolidated Foods*, it was alleged that Consolidated used reciprocity on behalf of Gentry. This raises several interesting questions:
   a. Would reciprocity raise barriers to entry in the dehydrated onion and garlic market?
   b. Would reciprocity strengthen Gentry's dominant position?
   c. How would reciprocity affect the likelihood of entry in food processing?

10. Is reciprocity always "coercive"? Can there be a case for mutually beneficial reciprocity? If so, should that be legal?

11. A large, highly diversified firm merged with a financially strong firm that operated in an unrelated industry. The Antitrust Division challenged this conglomerate merger because of the potential for reciprocity. The conglomerate defended by pointing out that it was

organized into independent profit centers. If true, would this defense be persuasive?

12. Consolidated Foods owned a large number of wholesale and retail food outlets. If a food processor refused to buy from Gentry, Consolidated could stop buying that processor's brands. Would such a strategy cost Consolidated anything? If so, how would Consolidated weigh the costs and benefits?

FURTHER READINGS

Allen, Bruce T. "Industrial Reciprocity: A Statistical Analysis." *Journal of Law and Economics* 18 (October 1975), pp. 507–20.

Blair, Roger D. "Reciprocity: A Reconciliation of Conflicting Views." *Antitrust Law and Economics Review* 6 (1973), pp. 77–86.

————. "Reciprocity in an Uncertain Environment." *Antitrust Bulletin* 21 (Summer 1976), pp. 271–93.

Ferguson, James M. "Tying Arrangements and Reciprocity: An Economic Analysis." *Law and Contemporary Problems* 30 (Summer 1965), pp. 552–80.

Stocking, George W., and Willard F. Mueller. "Business Reciprocity and the Size of Firms." *Journal of Business* 30 (April 1957) pp. 73–95.

Name index

Subject index

This book has been set Linotron 202, in 10 and 9 point Palatino, leaded 2 points. Part numbers and titles are 16 and 20 point Palatino Bold Italic, chapter numbers are 24 point Palatino Italic, and chapter titles are 18 point Palatino Bold Italic. The size of the type page is 30 by 47 picas.